HISTORY OF VATICAN II

HISTORY OF VATICAN II

General Editor

GIUSEPPE ALBERIGO

Istituto per le Scienze Religiose, Bologna

Editorial Board

History of
Vatican II

Vol. V
The Council and the Transition
The Fourth Period and the End of the Council
September 1965 – December 1965

edited by

Giuseppe Alberigo

English version edited by

Joseph A. Komonchak

Translated by Matthew J. O'Connell

2006

ORBIS | PEETERS
Maryknoll | Leuven

Cover illustration:

Evening Silhouette of St. Peter's Basilica by Alex L. Fradkin,
reproduced by license from Getty Images (www.gettyimages.com)

Acknowledgment:

The Menil Foundation, Houston TX
The Rothko Chapel, Houston TX

Library of Congress Cataloging-in-Publication Data

A record for this book is available from the Library of Congress

CIP Royal Library Albert I, Brussels

History of Vatican II. — Vol. V
edited by G. Alberigo and J.A. Komonchak. — Leuven: Peeters, 2006

No part of this book may be used or reproduced
in any form by print, photo print, microfilm or any other means
without written permission from the publisher.

ISBN 90-429-1649-4 (PEETERS)
ISBN 1-57075-155-2 (ORBIS)
D 2005/0602/84

ORBIS BOOKS
PO Box 308
Maryknoll, NY 10545-0308

© PEETERS
Bondgenotenlaan 153
B-3000 Leuven
BELGIUM

TABLE OF CONTENTS

PREFACE

With the work accomplished in the autumn of 1965, which is reconstructed in this volume, Vatican II came to its conclusion as decided by Paul VI. As for the preceding volumes, we must note again that, despite every effort, access to the personal papers of Paul VI dealing with the Council was unfortunately possible only in chance fashion and fragmentary form. As a result, the part he played in the labors of the Council has very seldom been adequately verifiable in first-hand sources.

The international team of scholars who committed themselves to this *History of Vatican II* has remained faithful to the task of acquiring an adequate and scientifically rigorous knowledge of the dynamics at work in a collective phenomenon of quite unusual proportions. Their aim has been to track the daily progress of the work done by the assembly and its numerous assisting bodies. For this reason they have given a privileged place to the real unfolding of the assembly's experience, even amid its undeniable meanderings, rather than providing a thematic reconstruction that would have been more linear but less respectful of the concrete details of the event.

The reading of the present volume will, however, prove to be even less linear than that of the preceding volumes. Despite the effort to respect as much as possible the ongoing course of the assembly's life, within any given chapter there has been an accumulation of diverse activities that were occurring even at the very same time.[1] The reader can thus glimpse the difficulties met by all the members of Vatican II during the final weeks, as weariness began to set in.

In this spirit the contributors have used to advantage all the sources coming from all the groups at the Council without favoring any current of thought. Especially during these final months the documentation for the "minority's" views is especially rich and varied.

The broad and fruitful international scientific collaboration was carried on in an atmosphere of deep friendship and "teamwork," both during

---

[1] To allow the reader to grasp this complicated progress of events, I found it necessary to ask some sacrifices of the collaborators in this volume. I am particularly grateful to Gilles Routhier and Peter Hünermann for their willingness to allow their contributions partially to intersect or "crisscross" so that the narrative could respect the actual development of the debates.

the preparatory researches and the discussions of these[2] and during the writing of this historical reconstruction. The collaborators in this volume repeatedly compared their work at joint meetings during which they went more deeply into the critical difficulties of the fourth conciliar period. The different points of view of the collaborators were discussed, but were respected and regarded as one of the merits of the joint enterprise. The authors pursued the ambitious plan of producing a work by several hands that would not have the composite appearance that often marks works organized in this way, but would offer a continuous and organic historical reconstruction and not simply a collection of essays.

Also further pursued was the acquisition of unpublished documents on the course of the Council, these being provided by many participants, whether fathers or experts or observers. This documentation has been collected and classified at the Istituto per le Scienze Religiose in Bologna, as well as at others from Louvain-la-Neuve to Leuven to the Institut Catholique in Paris, from the Centro di Sao Paulo to that of Quebec. New inventories have also been published of various documentary archives, while Msgr. V. Carbone has completed his gigantic undertaking of editing the irreplaceable official sources on the work done at the general congregations and on the functioning of the directive bodies and the secretariat of the Council.[3]

The utilization of these new sources has made it possible to move beyond narratives of the chronicle type and to provide a hitherto impossible multidimensional knowledge of the conciliar event. By this I mean a knowledge that takes into account the many levels within the event itself: the general congregations, the commissions, the informal groups, the echo in public opinion, and the influence of this last on the Council's work. Only in this way has it been possible to follow developments within the assembly step by step, to weigh the influences that caused these

---

[2] Since the publication of volume IV of the *History*, the following have appeared: *Experience, Organizations and Bodies at Vatican II*, ed. M. T. Fattori and A. Melloni (Leuven, 1999); G. Turbanti, *Un concilio per il mondo moderno: La redazione della costituzione pastorale "Gaudium et spes" del Vaticano II* (Bologna, 2000); *Herausforderung Aggiornamento. Zur Rezeption des Zweiten Vatikanischen Konzils*, ed. A. Autiero (Altenberge, 2000); A. Melloni, *L'altra Roma: Politica e S. Sede durante il concilio Vaticano II (1959-1965)* (Bologna, 2000); and *Volti di fine concilio: Studi di storia e teologia sulla conclusione del Vaticano II*, ed. J. Doré and A. Melloni (Bologna, 2000).

[3] For reasons of age, Msgr. Carbone has surrendered the responsibility for the Archive of the Council, a responsibility which he carried out for so many decades with a devotedness that deserves our gratitude. The Archive itself, while preserving the accessibility established by Paul VI, has been joined to the Vatican Secret Archive.

changes, and to grasp the great importance of the work done during the
ten-month-long intersessions. In fact, we have come to realize that the
"invisible council" which went on during the pauses between the assembly's periods of work had an importance too often ignored or underrated.
The intersessions were something peculiar to Vatican II as compared with
the most recent councils. Even when the assembly was not in session,
the Council and its problems seemed to dominate Roman life.

In addition, our knowledge of the Council's labors has been considerably enriched, especially in regard to some crucial moments that were
hitherto known only as episodes.

* * *

During the preparation of this volume John Paul II beatified
John XXIII, approving a request that had already been made, in vain,
during Vatican II and had given rise to a steady and deeply felt popular
consensus. The final part of this *History* could not but be dedicated to
Pope Roncalli as a modest tribute to the fruitfulness of the impulse toward
renewal which he introduced into contemporary Christianity and which
is still active and has been strengthened by the Church's recognition of
his exemplary life.

Since the publication of volume IV some of the leading figures at Vatican II have died: Helder Pessoa Câmara of Brazil, archbishop of Olinda
and Recife; Jean Zoa, archbishop of Yaoundé (Cameroon); and André
Scrima (Budapest). All three followed the progress of this *History* with
a lively interest, and we take note of them here as a public expression of
our deep gratitude.

The generation that experienced Vatican II is passing away, giving way
to the next stage: the complex (and problematic) reception of the Council. It may be, and this writer fervently hopes so, that the history of the
Council will be followed by a history of its reception, a task no less
demanding and difficult.

* * *

The work continues to appear in six parallel editions: Italian, ed.
A. Melloni (Bologna: Il Mulino); English, ed. J. A. Komonchak (Mary-
knoll: Orbis Books/Leuven: Peeters); Portuguese, ed. O. Beozzo
(Petrópolis: Vozes); German, ed. K. Wittstadt (Mainz: Grünewald);
French, ed. É. Fouilloux (Paris: Cerf); and Spanish, ed. E. Vilanova

(Salamanca: Sígueme). Peeters of Louvain has skilfully coordinated all
the editions. The reception of the volumes by the press and scholarly
periodicals in the various cultural and linguistic areas has thus far been
very cordial and encouraging. A translation into Russian has begun, due
to the initiative and under the editorship of the St. Andrew Academy of
Moscow and with the help of the Banca Intesa of Milan in meeting
expenses.

    As in the case of the preceding volume, the Rothko Chapel and the
Menil Foundation of Houston, Texas, have contributed generously to the
cost of research, while the European Secretariat for Scientific Publications
(SEPS; Bologna) has contributed to the cost of translation

                                  * * *

    This fifth volume of the *History of Vatican II* brings to completion an
undertaking that began over ten years ago and has enjoyed the enthusiastic collaborations of several dozen scholars from all parts of the world.
It has provided the occasion for the sometimes difficult but always fruitful and joyous meeting of men and women from different generations,
environments, and specializations but all united in the task of providing
knowledge of the Council held in Rome from 1959 to 1965 to those who
did not have the good fortune of attending it in person.

    Having taken part in every phase of the undertaking, I shall not have
any better opportunity than this of expressing my full and heartfelt gratitude to all who, in quite different ways — from the many preparatory
studies to the composition of the thirty-six chapters that make up the five
volumes, from the patient editors and translators of the various editions
to the publishers who saw to the issuance of the volumes — have contributed to the success of a project born amid not a few uncertainties.

    In the first phase of the work, the difficulties met had to do chiefly with
locating the unpublished sources that could complement the official
sources gathered by the secretariat of the Council and organized in the
Council's Vatican Archive in Rome. Thanks to the cordial cooperation of
many groups and the resultant establishment of centers for collecting and
classifying the very numerous accessible unpublished documents, this
problem proved relatively easy to deal with. We then tackled the more
important gaps in our knowledge: those having to do with the preparation for the Council (1959-1962), the crucial work of the conciliar commissions, and the "invisible" council that was busy during the months
between the periods of the conciliar assembly's work.

The hermeneutical criteria that presided over this undertaking were discussed beginning with the very first contacts among the collaborators and have effectively controlled all the researches. Special attention has been given to providing the reader with a calm reconstruction that is faithful to the complicated and sometimes tumultuous events at the Council. These events did not leave indifferent even those reconstructing them historically. Despite all our careful attention and common commitment to objectivity, some subjective feelings may have made their way into the reconstruction; it will up to the shrewd reader to discern them.

Despite the obvious incompleteness of this initial period of research, it has been possible to reach results that are convincing and satisfying due to the dozens of specialized explorations and a good ten international meetings, from Leuven to Moscow, from Houston to São Paulo, of the scholars engaged in the project.

Giuseppe Alberigo   Bologna, January 25, 2001

My thanks go, once again, to Matthew J. O'Connell who translated all five volumes of this work, to William R. Burrows, managing editor of Orbis Books, to Joan La Flamme for her invaluable skills in copy-editing, and to Janel Renee Baker for her help in proof-reading.

Joseph A. Komonchak   Washington, D.C., February 2005

ABBREVIATIONS AND SOURCES

AAQ	Archives of the Archdiocese of Québec
AAS	*Acta Apostolicae Sedis*, Vatican City
ACO	Archives du Conseil Oecuménique des Églises, Geneva
ACUA	Archives of the Catholic University of America, Washington, D.C.
ADA	*Acta et Documenta Concilio oecumenico Vaticano II apparando: Series prima (antepraeparatoria).* Typis Polyglottis Vaticanis, 1960-1961
ADP	*Acta et Documenta Concilio oecumenico Vaticano II apparando: Series secunda (praeparatoria).* Typis Polyglottis Vaticanis, 1964-1995
AS	*Acta Synodalia Sacrosancti Concilii Vaticani II.* Typis Polyglottis Vaticanis, 1970-2000
Attese	*Il Vaticano II fra attese e celebrazione*, ed. G. Alberigo. Bologna 1995
AUND	Archives of the University of Notre Dame, South Bend, Indiana
Beitrag	*Der Beitrag der deutschsprachigen und osteuropäischen Länder zum zweiten Vatikanischen Konzil*, ed. K. Wittstadt and W. Verschooten. Leuven 1996
Belgique	*Vatican II et la Belgique*, ed. Claude Soetens. Ottignies, 1996
BPR	Biblioteca de Pesquisa Religiosa CSSR, São Paolo do Brasil
Caprile	G. Caprile, *Il Concilio Vaticano*, 5 vols. Rome, 1966-68
CCCC	Centrum Coordinationis Communicationum de Concilio
CCV	Centrum voor Conciliestudie Vaticanum II, Faculteit Godgeleerdheid. Katholieke Universiteit Leuven
CivCatt	*La Civiltà Cattolica*, Rome
CLG	Centre "Lumen Gentium" de Théologie, Université Catholique de Louvain. Louvain-La-Neuve
CNPL	Centre National de Pastoral Liturgique, Paris
COD	*Conciliorum Oecumenicorum Decreta*, ed. Istituto per le Scienze Religiose. Bologna 1973
Commentary	*Commentary on the Documents of Vatican II*, ed. H. Vorgrimler. 5 vols. New York 1968

Commissions	*Les commissions conciliaires à Vatican II*, ed. M. Lamberigts *et al.,* Leuven 1996
Council Daybook	*Council Daybook.* 3 vols. Washington, D.C. 1964-1966
CrSt	*Cristianesimo nella Storia*, Bologna
DBetti	Diary of Umberto Betti, edited in *La "Dei verbum" trent-anni dopo.* Rome 1995
DC	*Documentation Catholique*, Paris
Deuxième	*Le deuxième Concile du Vatican (1959-1965).* Rome 1989
DLebret	Diary of L. Lebret
DMC	*Discorsi Messaggi Colloqui del S. Padre Giovanni XXIII*, 6 vols. Vatican City 1960-67
DFenton	Diary of Joseph Clifford Fenton, Washington
DFlorit	Diary of E. Florit, Bologna
DOttaviani	Diary of A. Ottaviani, edited in E. Cavaterra, *Il prefetto del S. Offizio: Le opere e i giorni del card. Ottaviani.* Milan 1990
Drama	H. Fesquet, *The Drama of Vatican II: The Ecumenical Council June, 1962–December 1965.* New York 1967
DSiri	Diary of G. Siri, edited in B. Lai, *Il papa non eletto: G. Siri cardinale di S. Romana Chiesa.* Rome/Bari 1993, pp. 301-403
DTucci	Diary of R. Tucci, Rome
DUrbani	Diary of G. Urbani, Venice
EtDoc	*Études et documents*
Evento	*L'evento et le decisioni: Studi sulle dinamiche del concilio Vaticano II*, ed. M.T. Fattori and A. Melloni. Bologna 1997
Experience	*Experience, Organizations and Bodies at Vatican II.* Leuven 1999
History	*History of Vatican II.* Vols. I, II, III, and IV. Leuven/Maryknoll, 1995, 1997, 2000, 2003
Horton	Douglas Horton, *Vatican Diary*, 4 vols. Philadelphia, 1964-66
ICI	*Informations Catholiques Internationales.* Paris
Igreia	*A Igreia latino-americana às vésperas do concilio. História do Concilio Ecumênico Vaticano I*, ed. J.O. Beozzo. São Paolo 1993

Indelicato	A. Indelicato, *Difendere la dottrina o annunciare l'evangelo: Il dibattito nella Commissione centrale preparatoria del Vaticano II*. Genoa 1992
Insegnamenti	*Insegnamenti di Paolo VI*. 16 volumes. Vatican City, 1964-1978
ISR	Istituto per le Scienze Religiose di Bologna
JCongar	Journal of Y. M.-J. Congar, now published as *Mon Journal du Concile*. Paris, 2002
Jde Lubac	Journal of H. de Lubac, Vanves
JDupont	Journal of J. Dupont, Louvain-La-Neuve
JEdelby	Journal of N. Edelby, Aleppo
JLabourdette	Journal of M.M. Labourdette, Toulouse
JPrignon	Journal of A. Prignon, CLG, Louvain-la-Neuve
JS	Pope John XXIII, *Journal of a Soul*, revised edition. London, 1980
Laurentin, II	R. Laurentin, *L'enjeu du Concile: Bilan de la deuxième session 29 septembre–4 décembre 1963*. Paris, 1964
Laurentin, III	R. Laurentin, *L'enjeu du Concile: Bilan de la troisième session*. Paris, 1965
Lettere	G. Lercaro, *Lettere dal Concilio, 1962-1965*. Bologna, 1980
NChenu	M.-D. Chenu, *Notes quotidiennes au Concile*, ed. A. Melloni. Paris, 1995
OssRom	*L'Osservatore Romano*, Rome
Primauté	*Primauté et collegialité: Le dossier de Gérard Philips sur la Nota Explicativa Praevia (Lumen gentium cap. III)*, ed. J. Grootaers. Leuven 1986
Protagonisti	J. Grootaers, *I protagonisti del Vaticano II*. Cinisello Balsamo 1994
RT	S. Tromp, [Relationes secretarii commissionis conciliaris] De doctrina fidei et morum. Typescript in fourteen fascicles
Rynne, II	X. Rynne, *The Second Session*. New York 1964
Rynne, III	X. Rynne, *The Third Session*. New York 1965
Rynne, IV	X. Rynne, *The Fourth Session*. New York 1966
TJungmann	Diary of J. Jungmann, Institut für Liturgiewissenschaft, University of Innsbruck
TSemmelroth	Diary of O. Semmelroth, Frankfurt am Main

Vatican II commence	*Vatican II commence... Approches francophones*, ed. E. Fouilloux. Leuven, 1993
Vatican II in Moscow	*Vatican II in Moscow: Acts of the Moscow Colloquium, 1995*. Moscow-Leuven 1996
Vatican II Revisited	*Vatican II Revisited By Those Who Were There*, ed. A. Stacpoole. Minneapolis 1985
VCND	Vatican II Collection. Theodore M. Hesburgh Library. University of Notre Dame, Notre Dame.
Volti	*Volti di fine Concilio: Studi di storia e teologia sulla conclusione del Vaticano II*, ed. J. Doré and A. Melloni. Bologna 2000
WCC	World Council of Churches
Wenger, II	A. Wenger, *Vatican II: Chronique de la deuxième session*. Paris 1964
Wenger, III	A. Wenger, *Vatican II: Chronique de la troisième session*. Paris 1965
Wenger, IV	A. Wenger, *Vatican II: Chronique de la quatrième session*. Paris 1966
Wiltgen	R. Wiltgen, *The Rhine Flows into the Tiber: A History of Vatican II*. New York, 1967

SOURCES AND ARCHIVES

In the course of research on the history of Vatican II, access has been requested and granted to many private collections of people who participated in the Council in various ways. These papers integrate and complete the documents of the Archives of Vatican II which, under the careful direction of Msgr. Vincenzo Carbone, Pope Paul VI wished to remain distinct from the secret Vatican Archives and to be open to scholars. Systematic use of such collections has been made in numerous studies, in monographs, and in the colloquia which prepared and complete these volumes of the *History of Vatican II*. For these see J. Famerée, "Vers une histoire du Concile Vatican II, in *Revue d'Histoire Ecclésiastique* 89 (1994) 638-64; A. Greiler, "Ein internationales Forschungsprojekt zur Geschichte des Zweitens Vatikanums," in *Zeugnis und Dialog: Die katholische Kirche in der neuzeitlichen Welt und das II. Vatikanische Konzil*, ed. W. Weiss (Würzburg 1996) 571-78; G. Routhier, "Recherches et publications récentes autour de Vatican II," in *Laval Théologique et philosophique* 53 (1997) 435-54; 55 (1999) 115-49; 56 (2000) 543-83; 58 (2002) 177-203; 59 (2003) 583-606; 60 (2004) 561-77.

The authors of this volume have made use of documents (original or copied) collected in the archives of various research-centers: Istituto per le Scienze Religiose di Bologna; Biblioteca de Pesquisa Religiosa CSSR, São Paolo do Brasil; Centre "Lumen Gentium" de Théologie, Université Catholique de Louvain, Louvain-la-Neuve; Centrum voor Conciliestudie Vaticanum II, Faculteit Godgeleerdheid, Katholieke Universiteit Leuven; Vatican II Collection, Archives of the Catholic University of America, Washington, D.C.; Vatican II Collection, Theodore M. Hesburgh Library at the University of Notre Dame, Indiana. In addition, many dioceses, libraries, religious houses, and families have given access, under various restrictions, to particularly valuable documentation.

The location of all unpublished sources used in this volume can be found in *Il concilio inedito*, ed. M. Faggioli and G. Turbanti (Bologna 2001).

CHAPTER I

TOWARD THE FOURTH PERIOD

GIOVANNI TURBANTI

I. THE DIFFICULTIES OF THE INITIAL RECEPTION

During the months of the 1964–65 intersession, public opinion was able to follow developments in the Council's work only indirectly, since they were taking place unobserved within the commissions. At the end of 1964 and the beginning of 1965 the religious press took time to comment on what had occurred during the third period and to summarize the results thus far achieved. There was lively interest in the innovations that had begun to appear, and in the local Churches the tensions that had divided the Council fathers flared up again. In many regions the experience of the debates in the council hall primed an ecclesial renewal that brought with it extensive discussions and controversies.

The influential ecclesiological themes had sparked a great deal of attention in the various ecclesial milieux which had begun to reflect on the practical significance of the principle of collegiality and on the concrete developments that flowed from it. Lengthy discussions of the *Nota praevia* continued during the spring and summer, and the divisions that had been manifested in the Council were revived in the interpretations it received. At its March meeting the doctrinal commission had wondered whether or not to intervene in the debate and give an authoritative interpretation, but the idea was dropped. The Holy Office, as usual, would be the body competent to pass judgment in problems of doctrine and of the correct interpretation of the doctrinal documents issued by the Council.[1]

---

[1] It was not by chance that right after the end of the third period Cardinal Siri sent a circular letter to the clergy of the archdiocese of Genoa, reminding them that "the Council is to be found in its written and approved Acts and nowhere else. The Council becomes normative whenever careful consideration has worked through all its concerns and prudence has put a seal on all the investigations." Siri's concern was itself a sign of an agitation that in fact prescinded from the definitive outcome of the documents being discussed (see *Il Regno* 10/1 [1965], 32). Siri went on to say: "Any other impression [of the Council] is *subjective*, may be *self-interested*, and may become *misleading*. No one should behave as if what began at the Council and now continues is a merry fair, for this will do harm to the truth and to ecclesiastical discipline."

The consistory in February and Paul VI's many references to the synod of bishops and to the reform of the Curia had given rise to various discussions of possible reforms in the various offices and of the ways of exercising authority in the Church. Almost everyone expected the establishment of a collegial body to assist the Pope in his teaching office and his administration of everyday ecclesiastical problems. There was a good deal of talk about a "limited senate," but no one knew whether this would be formed within the college of cardinals or as a synod of bishops or whether this body would be representative in character and given effective authority.

During the week following the appointment of the new cardinals, a circular letter of Cardinal Cicognani to all the curial offices had referred explicitly, but quite narrowly, to the reforms of the Curia that many were awaiting. That the new appointments considerably increased the number of cardinals (now over a hundred) and that many of them were residential bishops were interpreted by many as a sign pointing in this direction. But this reshaping of the college of cardinals, based on criteria of internationalization that could appear also to follow a standard of representativeness, raised many questions about what would happen to the parallel proposal, of a synod of bishops.[2] In addition, addressing the cardinals on his name day, the Pope spoke of studies in progress for the statutes of the episcopal conferences.[3]

No less attention was paid to ecumenical matters, the concrete developments of which were clearly visible in the intense activity of the Secretariat for Christian Unity and the start of bilateral conversations with some Christian confessions. At the local level, especially in countries with a greater openness to ecumenism, this ecumenical thrust gave rise to various liturgical and spiritual dialogues with the "separated brethren," notably on the occasion of the Week of Prayer for Church Unity. In this area, again, developments at the Council and especially the approval of the decree on ecumenism aroused among the faithful widespread hopes that they could set aside at least those doctrinal divisions that had become incomprehensible to many people and initiate common ways of bearing witness to the faith. On the other hand, the decline in significance of differences that once had helped form a clear confessional identity also led to many uncertainties. The ease with which many people were now engaging in joint liturgies with the faithful of other confessions caused

[2] See, e.g., C. De Clercq, "De cardinalicia dignitate," *Apollinaris* 37/2 (1965), 101–7.
[3] Allocution to the Sacred College, June 24, 1965, in *Insegnamenti* 3:366–67.

concerns among bishops and gave rise to attacks from those who saw in such doings the danger of a facile irenicism.[4]

Sunday, March 7, 1965, was the important day on which mass began to be celebrated according to the revised rite, with many parts in the vernacular and the altar facing the congregation. On that day Paul VI himself celebrated in Italian in a Roman parish and urged the parishioners to cooperate in the implementation of the reform.[5] This liturgical renewal probably provided the main setting in which the faithful were able to gauge the extent of the reforms introduced by the Council, and it is difficult to overestimate its importance.

The new arrangements were introduced into a situation that was already quite fluid. While in general people had kept to the usual ritual rules, in various countries innovative ways of celebrating the mass and the sacraments had been introduced under the rubric of "experimentation." In some instances it was the episcopal agencies in charge of the reform that directed these initiatives in order gradually to prepare, also psychologically, for the official introduction of the new norms. In other cases, however, there was a proliferation of proposals quite diverse in content and motive; for the most part these originated spontaneously in local settings and produced important differences in usage among neighboring dioceses or parishes. Holland in particular saw liturgical experiments that went beyond the limits set by Rome; for example, the regular distribution of communion under two kinds or the distribution of communion into the hands of the faithful, the direct access of the laity to the consecrated hosts, and the substitution of a communal celebration of penance for individual confession.[6]

Reactions to the novelties introduced on March 7 depended also on this fluidity, which some people wanted to bring under control. There was hostility from those who maintained that the reform had gone too far and was subverting a sound and solidly grounded theological tradition of worship that was still nourishing the spirituality of the faithful. On the other hand, spirited criticisms were advanced by sectors that were more

---

[4] See the Dutch bishops' "Direttive episcopali sui limiti e le possibilità di communione religiosa tra cattolici e protestanti," published in *DOC* 102.

[5] "Paul VI presse les prêtres de mettre en œuvre la réforme liturgique," *ICI* 236 (March 15, 1965), 14. At the beginning of March the same periodical published an extensive interview with Cardinal Lercaro about the innovations in the new rite of the mass: "Nouvelle étape de la réforme liturgique: Le 'pourquoi' du 'comment,'" *ICI* 235 (March 1, 1965), 26–29.

[6] See "La réforme liturgique entre l'indolence et les innovations arbitraires," *ICI* 237 (April 1, 1965), 9–10, which gives information from *Hechos y Dichos* and from *Tijd*.

open to the renewal and thought that the new arrangements were an insufficient response to the new demands of a highly secularized society and
of the ecclesial communities that had to incarnate themselves in it.

The dynamics at work during the spring and summer of 1965, in the
reactions to the liturgical reform and to other aspects of the conciliar
renewal, illustrate the difficulties of the first steps in the reception of the
Council. In this perspective a more detailed analysis would be needed, one
that would look at the differences in the situation of the Church in the various countries and would take into account the fact that, precisely because
of the Council, local Churches were acquiring a more important institutional role in relation to Roman centralism. But, at least right up to March
7, Paul VI had not ceased to urge bishops and clergy to embrace the liturgical innovations with conviction and without fear.

Statements of bishops and of episcopal conferences showed that the
main concerns came initially from the reactions of conservatives.
In France, in particular, quite difficult situations were created by the early
emergence of a definite opposition to the conciliar renewal. Strongly hostile positions were taken, loudly, by various groups and associations, for
example, the Action Fatima of Father Jean Boyer, a priest already suspended from his priestly ministry, or Cité catholique, a movement widespread especially in the southwestern provinces, and the Promotion du laïcat movement, which especially attracted young people. Near Troyes,
Father Georges de Nantes founded the "Maison Saint Joseph," a fore-run-
ner of the "Contre-Réforme Catholique," and began to circulate his
Lettres à mes amis, a document strongly challenging the Council.[7]
Markedly anticonciliar "integrist" broadsheets came out every two weeks
in thousands of copies, a fact that Msgr. André Pailler, coadjutor of
Rouen, interpreted as the sign of a serious crisis, even bringing the danger of schism.[8] The publication of Michel de Saint-Pierre's novel *Les nouveaux prêtres*, as well as the challenges Fr. Yves Congar encountered
during a lecture in Nîmes at the end of January, were indicative of a profound malaise that was creeping through French Catholicism.[9]

Beginning in March, more urgent alarms were raised by bishops and
even by the Pope at symptoms of a crisis in danger of arising on the
opposite side, that is, among groups and movements that were claiming

[7] See M. Panciera, "Quando il concilio scomoda," *Il Regno* 10/3 (1963), 97–99.
[8] See "Il pericolo di scisma nel giudizio dei vescovi francesi," *Il Regno* 10/6 (1965),
267.
[9] See "Débat autour des 'Nouveaux Prêtres,'" *Signes du Temps* 7/16 (1965), 13–22.
On these incidents see also Y. Chiron, *Paul VI: Le pape écartelé* (Paris, 1993), 232–33.

greater room for openness and were ready to go much further in their challenge to ecclesiastical authority. This had quickly become the more worrying front, especially in France, the Netherlands, Belgium, and to some extent, even Italy.

The beginning of the process of reception seemed to show the possibility of more or less serious rents in the ecclesial fabric. A wide-ranging poll taken by *Informations Catholiques Internationales* in January 1965 sketched a panorama of lights and shadows in the responses of the faithful to the conciliar innovations.[10] At the end of March, the case of the Jeunesse Étudiante Chrétienne (JEC) exploded in France. In a document issued at the beginning of that month, the officers of the association came out in favor of a more determined commitment, along with other active student movements, even those of Marxist inspiration, against the government's plans for the reform of the schools. In response to an annual program conceived along these lines, the standing committee of the episcopal conference firmly intervened, posing five fundamental questions to the officers as a basis for retaining the trust of the bishops. The officers of the association were divided on the questions. The bishops asked for the resignation of those who had rejected them, but these officers intensified the crisis by opposing this request also and appealing to the membership of the association.[11]

The dangers of a situation that seemed to be escaping the control of the bishops became even more serious with the rekindling of the worker-priest question, still an open wound in the French Church. In fact, the bishops had been trying very carefully to restudy the question and had undertaken a series of conversations with some priests of the Mission de France and some theologians in order to determine how they could relaunch an apostolate among the working classes that would also take into account the positive aspects of the experiences of the 1950s.[12]

---

[10] "Du trouble dans l'Église? Surtout de l'espérance," *ICI* 231 (January 1, 1965), 5–24.

[11] "Les laïcs dans l'Église: deux affaires mettent leur rôle en question," *Signes du Temps* 7/20 (1965), 14–18; see M. Olmi, "La crisi della 'Jeunesse Étudiante Chrétienne' di Francia," *Humanitas* 20/5 (1965), 535–43.

[12] See J. Vinatier, *Les prêtres ouvriers, le cardinal Liénart et Rome: Histoire d'une crise, 1944–1967* (Paris, 1985), 207–15. Among the participants in these meetings were Bishops Ancel, Gufflet, Huyghe, Schmitt, Himmer, Van Zuylen, and Fragoso, and theologians Chenu, Le Guillou, Martelet, and Laurentin. Begun in November 1963, the meetings continued into the third period of the Council and led to a report, drawn up by Laurentin, entitled "Sens du prêtre-ouvrier dans la mission de l'Église en milieu industriel" (Lercaro papers, 480); see F. Leprieur, *Quand Rome condamne: Dominicains et prêtres-ouvriers* (Paris, 1989), 486–89.

But during 1964 a group of worker-priests who at the time had not submitted to the orders of the episcopate but had remained secretly in the factories wrote a letter to the Council fathers asking that the Council itself
discuss the problem. Some of the bishops replied privately, expressing
their sympathy for the cause, and the priests decided to publish their
action and the replies they had received.[13] The incident caused a degree
of sensation, especially in France, and no little embarrassment among the
bishops.

At the very time of the JEC crisis, a serious disagreement broke out
regarding the review *Témoignage Chrétien*. The standing committee of
the French Episcopal Conference sharply censured its editors for publishing two articles by Roger Garaudy and Jean-Yves Jolif about the
meeting on dialogue between Christians and Marxists that had been conducted at the Centre Catholique des Intellectuels Français.[14] Magnified by
the press, the incident led to some disquiet in public opinion. Besides the
dangers in the application of the liturgical reform, developments in dialogue with Marxists were probably the greatest source of concern for the
national episcopates. Rome issued increasingly urgent calls for caution
lest the establishment of the Secretariat for Nonbelievers, which had been
entrusted to the wise and competent Cardinal F. König, create false expectations, despite the explicit reference to dialogue that was fundamental to

---

[13] The initiative had arisen within a group of former worker-priests led by B. Chau-
veau. The suggestion of writing to the Council had been made at a meeting in February
1964, and the document took concrete form in the following months after numerous meetings for study and many suggestions and plans. Between July and August the letter was
sent to a select number of Council fathers. Around the middle of October the authors of
the letter decided to make it public and sent it to *Le Monde*, which gave it a great deal of
prominence. But the bishops involved quickly retreated, explaining the meaning of their
reply and distancing themselves from a move that seemed intended to go over the heads
of the French episcopate (see M. Margotti, "Une lettre de prêtres-ouvriers aux Pères du
Concile Vatican II," in *Chrétiens et ouvriers en France (1937-1970)* [Paris 2001], 168-
180).

[14] See *Témoignage Chrétien*, March 18, 1965, which carried on its front page the title
"Christians and Marxists Speak of God". This is how the review introduced the two statements: "The 17th Week of Catholic Intellectuals has just been held in Paris. Subject of
the discussions: God today. Thus atheism in all its aspects was studied…. The best attended
session was the one on dialogue between Marxists and Christians. In this issue *Témoignage
Chrétien* is continuing the discussion by opening its pages to two individuals who did not
have the chance to speak at the Salle de la Mutualité: Roger Garaudy and Jean-Yves Jolif."
See also "Les laïcs dans l'Église: deux affaires mettent leur rôle en question," which published the note of March 30 from the episcopal conference. The reply of the review was
entrusted to F. Biot, "L'Épiscopat français remet en cause le dialogue entre chrétiens and
marxistes," *Témoignage Chrétien*, April 1, 1965. See also J. M. Llanos, "La promoción
del laicado: Crisis francesa," *Razón y Fe* 171/6 (1965), 567–70.

the organization. In April, addressing the national congress of the Catholic Association of Italian Workers (ACLI), Paul VI warned the faithful against misunderstandings on this matter. To the Jesuits, who in May held their general congregation for the election of a new general, Paul VI entrusted the special task of combating atheism.

In the spring, the Pope began to issue continual calls for obedience, an indication of his growing uneasiness, signs of which he had already given by his interventions in the work of the conciliar commissions. At his Wednesday general audiences he warned from time to time against the spread of unduly innovative theological views that rudely criticized traditional teaching; he reminded his hearers of the duty of obedience to ecclesiastical authority and lamented the hostility with which doctrinal and disciplinary appeals were being met; he censured the "spirit of restlessness" and almost of "rebellion" that was abroad.[15] In August he was still denouncing an uneasiness among Catholics "regarding religious truth, the habitual teaching of the Church, and the faith which the Church authoritatively taught and normatively professed."[16]

The statements of Msgr. Pailler in June on the possible dangers of a schism within the French Church gave rise to extensive discussion in both the religious and the secular press; the discussion then spread to other countries.[17] But Rome's major concern was for the Netherlands. At the same time the French bishop was making his statements, the journal of the English Jesuits, *The Month*, published a rather disturbing analysis of the "crisis" in the Church in Holland:

> On the doctrinal points, too, the winds of change blow with gale force. The most progressive — let us say, plain wild — opinions about celibacy, married life, the liturgy and the Real Presence find place in all sorts of newspapers and periodicals and are even proposed from the pulpit.... In the Netherlands, the Church is being strongly threatened by an attack of this bitterness and emotional resentment which is directed particularly against "Rome." The disappointment about what people regard as missed opportunities threatens to pass over into a collective exasperation that misrepresents the reality. Others — the parish priest, the Bishop, the liturgy, the Roman Curia, the Pope, or finally the Church itself — are being confronted about what is seen as an unbearable situation....
> There are reasons for speaking of a very serious breakdown in communication between Rome and the Netherlands, as a result of which the authority of Rome and of the Bishops has been affected.... Lastly, there is the

---

[15] See in particular the audience on Wednesday, July 14, in *Insegnamenti* 3:983–86.
[16] See "Crisi di obbedienza," *Il Regno* 10/9 (1965), 324.
[17] See, e.g., "Konzils-Malaise in Frankreich," *Wort und Wahrheit* 20/4 (1965), 313–16.

"faith crisis." If one were to seek the root of the present crisis, one would probably find it in a blurring — a withdrawal into the background — of certain essential elements of Christianity…. If this is true then we can see at once where for us the great danger lies. It lies in a certain dogmatic relativism, together with a sham ecumenism, and the disappearance of a personal life of prayer among a large number of our Catholic people.[18]

The article concluded bitterly that "the Catholic Church in the Netherlands is undoubtedly at the present passing through its heaviest crisis since the Reformation. May the good that has been done in the past be of help in paving the way for a brighter future."[19] People were irritated and disturbed that the author of the article, Father E. Schoenmaeckers, who was in charge of the Apostolate of Prayer in the Netherlands, had not chosen to publish the article in his own country. He described the present crisis as one not only of authority and teaching but even of faith. There was no longer question simply of avant-garde experiments in the area of the liturgical renewal or of dialogue with the Protestants' people were now subjecting to debate not only ecclesiastical authority but a series of very important doctrines on the sacraments, especially on confession and the Eucharist.

The previous March the Dutch bishops had spoken out in a joint letter reminding the faithful of the importance of the sacrament of penance and emphasizing in particular the need of private confession. In some parishes the practice of holding communal penance services, for which some of the faithful claimed sacramental value, had been spreading.[20] In April a new letter set forth permanent aspects of the Eucharist. Recent statements by Jesuit P. Schoonenberg and Capuchin P. L. Smits, in which they proposed a new interpretation of the eucharistic mystery along personalist lines, had elicited protests from those who saw in the proposal the intention of denying the real presence of Christ in the Eucharist.[21] The letter of the Dutch bishops restated traditional dogma but at the same time acknowledged that in the past the explanation of the Eucharist had focused too exclusively on the theme of presence, thus obscuring other

[18] E. Schoenmaeckers, "Catholicism in the Netherlands," *The Month* (June 1965), 335–46.

[19] Ibid., 346. See also "Gli ardui tentativi del riformismo olandese," *Il Regno* 10/7 (1965), 307–8.

[20] The text of the letter "La pénitence et la rémission des péchés" was published in *DC* 47/1451 (1965), cols. 1175–79; to the letter were attached instructions addressed more directly to priests.

[21] "L'Eucharistie," *DC* 47/1451 (1965), cols. 2275–79. See also P. Kreykamp, "Débat aux Pays-Bas sur la Présence réelle," *ICI* 243 (July 1, 1965), 29–31.

important aspects of the sacrament. At the end of June an authoritative article in *L'Osservatore Romano* recalled the frequent references of Paul VI to the importance of the Eucharist and, in particular, to the dogma of the real presence.[22] That some of their faithful were taking their accusations directly to Rome may have dissuaded the Dutch bishops from taking a clearer stance themselves. In any case, even during the following months, the Dutch bishops defended their Church against attacks from inside and from outside. But this attitude only deepened Roman worries about the Dutch Church.

A. Expectations of the New Conciliar Period

In this somewhat tense atmosphere the coming period of the Council aroused various expectations. Although the public did not know in detail the ongoing work of the commissions, the various subjects on the agenda were widely echoed in the press and in turn were also affected by events in the news.

With regard to the schema on the bishops, people awaited clearer statements on the practical implementation of episcopal collegiality, on the renewal of the office of bishop, and on his pastoral role. Some once again raised the question of the participation of the faithful of a diocese in the selection of their bishop. Lay organizations, which had had many opportunities to meet and exchange ideas during the spring and summer, looked with great hope to the schema on the lay apostolate, with particular attention to the renewal of the place of the faithful in the Church and a redefinition of their relations with the hierarchy. The incidents involving the JEC had increased expectations and concerns in this area.

Men and women religious had great confidence in the progress of the schema dealing with them. During the summer the general chapters of various orders (including the major ones, like the Jesuits and Dominicans) had met in order to prepare for the renewal the Council was to bring

---

[22] G. Concetti, "Paolo VI esaltatore dell'Eucarestia," *OssRom*, June 28–29, 1965, 4. Of the various articles on the subject that appeared in theological journals, the following may be noted: P. de Haes, "Les présences du Christ-Seigneur: Différentes modes d'actualisation dans la liturgie," *Lumen Vitae* 20/2 (1965), 259–74; J. P. de Jong, "Die Eucharistie als symbolische Wirklichkeit," *Zeitschrift für katholische Theologie* 87/2 (1965), 313–17; L. Gillon, "La vera prospettiva escatologica della Eucarestia come comunione, sacrificio e culto," *Rivista di Ascetica e Mistica* 10/2 (1965), 144–51; see also N. Afanassieff, "L'Eucharistie, principal lien entre les Catholiques et les Orthodoxes," *Irénikon* 38/3 (1965), 337–39.

in their life. It was a renewal strongly desired by many religious institutes, within which there were obvious signs of crisis at the difficulty in regaining for the religious life a meaning adequate to the changed conditions of Church and society. Similar expectations were cherished regarding the schemas on the ministry and life of priests and on seminaries. At stake here, too, was a comprehensive redefinition of the figure of the priest, the need for which was being felt with growing urgency.

Other subjects that the Council was to take up in the coming period were of great interest both in the Church and in the political and social worlds; during the intersession there was a great deal of concern about these subjects. The schema on the Church in the contemporary world elicited strong interest in ecclesial circles because it was expected to introduce new modalities in its description of the relationship between the Church and temporal realities. Many articles had appeared in theological journals on the relationship between Church and world and between creation and incarnation, as well as on specific problems in anthropology.[23]

The greatest attention was paid to specific subjects such as dialogue, relations with atheism and Marxism, and peace. During the intersession many more or less original contributions were made on the subject of dialogue; these evaluated the efforts made in various quarters, especially in Italy and France, to reformulate the Church's relationship to milieux distant from it. A good deal of confusion was caused because the term *dialogue* was taken to refer to quite different realities, and people were looking to the Council to clarify the matter. The establishment by the Holy See, at the beginning of April, of the Secretariat for Nonbelievers was welcomed by many as a recognition of efforts at dialogue on the

[23] Connected with these latter problems there was also renewed interest in the relationship between faith and science; quite frequent references were made in many periodicals, even in those of a less specialized kind, to Teilhard de Chardin. See, among others, Ch. Journet, "L'effort théologique du P. Teilhard de Chardin," *Nova et Vetera* 39/4 (1964), 305–10 (also in *Studi Cattolici* 9 [1965], 7–10); C. F. Mooney, "Teilhard de Chardin and the Christological Problem," *Harvard Theological Review* 58/1 (1965), 91–126; E. Colomer, "Teilhard de Chardin diez años despues," *Razón y Fe* 172/1–2 (1965), 17–36; P. Crozon, "Interrogations sur l'œuvre de Teilhard de Chardin," *Masses Ouvrières* 21/4 (1965), 33–55. The problem of the relationship between faith and science was approached not only along traditional apologetic lines but also in the form of a dialogue between two humanisms: see Y. Congar, "Théologie et sciences humaines," *Esprit* 33/7–8 (1965), 121–37. The last issue of *Studi Cattolici* for 1964 was devoted to this dialogue and had several articles on the modern sciences; see, in particular, J. M. Albareda, "Idolatria e verità nella scienza," *Studi Cattolici* 8/12 (1964), 68–70; J. Daujat, "La chiesa incoraggia la ricerca scientifica," *Studi Cattolici* 71–73; E. Riverso, 'L'etica dell'umanesimo scientifico,"*Studi Cattolici* 73–79. J. Maritain also spoke out on the subject:"Le témoignage rendu par les sciences à l'existence de Dieu,"*Nova et Vetera* 39/4 (1964), 302–4.

local scene, but this event was rather quickly followed by the restrictive warnings of Paul VI.

As for the problem of birth control, it was known that Paul VI had appointed an extraconciliar commission to study the question. The public was greatly interested in the work of the commission, and there was still a lively expectation that the Council might say something new on the subject. That Paul VI received the commission at an audience in February was taken as a sign that a conclusion was close, but no information got out about the content of the commission's work. Discussion of the subject was fed by some statements of U.S. President Lyndon B. Johnson in favor of birth control. In July a decision of the United States Supreme Court had declared the prohibition against birth control products to be unconstitutional; the reactions of the U.S. bishops were initially cautious but gradually became stronger in rejecting any public policy in favor of birth control.

Meanwhile, international organizations had begun to look more closely at demographic problems. In July, the World Health Organization issued "Health Aspects of the Worldwide Demographic Situation." That Henri de Riedmatten, the Holy See's expert, was officially consulted during the drafting of the document showed the Catholic Church's interest in the initiative. The position he took did not seem entirely hostile to the purposes of the declaration, even in the area of birth control, although he remained firm on the moral principle governing the means to be used.[24] In September, the United Nations sponsored a large international congress in Belgrade to deal with these problems. Within the Catholic world, discussion especially of the moral and ethical aspects went on continually and elicited interventions that were often scientifically quite penetrating. New controversies arose in Great Britain after the publication of a book by Archbishop Thomas Roberts that brought together the views of authoritative representatives of English Catholicism who were in favor of birth control.[25]

Even greater were the expectations of the public on the subject of peace. The urgent appeal that Paul VI issued in Bombay for the reduction of military expenditures had not met with much interest in diplomatic

---

[24] See H. de Riedmatten, "La politica demografica dell'ONU a una svolta?" *OssRom*, December 23, 1964, 2.

[25] Thomas Roberts, ed., *Contraception and Holiness: The Catholic Predicament* (New York, 1964); on this incident see the article "USA, contrastanti opinioni di teologi. L'intervento dello Stato e la limitazione delle nascite," *Il Regno* 10/9 (1965), 344. Roberts, an English Jesuit, had been Archbishop of Bombay from 1937 to 1950, when he resigned so that a native bishop could occupy the see.

circles, apart from general pro forma statements. The international situation, with its anxious and often tragic movements of decolonization in Africa and Asia, was conditioned to a great extent by the battle between the great world powers for control of the new countries. The U.S. bombardment of the Viet Cong had begun in February and was to become increasingly intense; it provoked increasingly strong opposition. Also in crisis was the United Nations whose authority and ability seemed completely inadequate to the situation.[26] In the face of this the Holy See greatly increased its activity to restore the political authority of the international organization, evidently with the intention of playing the part of an authoritative interlocutor with it.[27]

After the international conference held in February on *Pacem in terris*, which had received a great deal of comment in the Catholic press, Paul VI's references to peace became more frequent. The Holy See seems to have been truly worried about the possibility of a nuclear escalation of the conflict in Southeast Asia. In July, rumors began to circulate of a possible visit of Paul VI to New York and the United Nations.[28] Meanwhile, Catholic organizations continued their activities for peace. The previous December Pax Romana held its seventeenth assembly, in Bombay; in February, at the same time as the conference on *Pacem in terris* in

[26] On this point in particular, see M. Villary, "La crise des Nations Unies," *Études* 91/5 (1965), 603–16.

[27] Public celebrations for the twentieth anniversary of the United Nations Charter were held in New York on June 23–27 and ended with a "Religious Convocation in Behalf of World Peace." Paul VI was invited to the celebration, but he sent a high-level delegation and a personal message of support (see *OssRom*, June 28–29, 1965). All this was prelude to the journey planned for the following October.

[28] Here is a telling passage from Congar's diary: "Father Courtois (of the Sons of Charity), whom I saw in Lyons on July 5, told me that in Rome there is a great fear that August may see a use of atomic weapons in the conflict between the United States and China in Vietnam. There is a group in the United States which thinks: 'This is the moment to put China out of action. China does not now have a really effective bomb, and Russia supports it only from afar. In a few years, it will be too late.... The future of the free world is now at stake.' — The Pope, conscious of the immensity and, as he thinks, the imminence of the danger, would like to go to New York and the podium of the United Nations in order to avert the danger. He has formally asked to be invited by the UN. On the other hand, he does not want to make this gesture unless he has some advance assurance that they will listen to him. If he goes to New York and speaks and then, eight days later, the bomb is dropped, how will things look?"

"But it is useless to wait until one is sure of being heard before speaking! It is his very words that must *act* and stop the evil! If the Pope is certain that the danger is very close, he obviously ought to act. He should be haunted by *The Deputy*" (*JCongar*, July 1965, II, 379–80). See also "Se il papa andasse all'ONU: L'incontro al vertice piu clamoroso della storia," *Il Regno* 10/7 (1965), 281; and "L'observateur du Saint-Siège confirme les projets de visite de Paul VI à l'ONU," *ICI* 20/3 (1965), 119.

New York, the general council of Pax Christi met in Paris.[29] Paul VI's call in Bombay for disarmament continued to echo in the religious press, and careful attention was paid to the problems affecting positive efforts at the building of peace, to disarmament, to poverty, and to development in the Third World.

As lively as the expectations with regard to schema XIII, on the Church in the modern world, were the ones with regard to the schemas that treated religious freedom and Judaism, issues very important in the political life of many nations and of great interest to the public. The year 1965 began with a burst of confidence regarding religious freedom because of the approval of laws concerning it in Spain. General Franco's 1964 year-end address had been quite explicit on the matter. But just a few days earlier a new Spanish law had been passed dealing with the right of association; it imposed some very serious limitations and had been met with open hostility from Spanish Catholics.

While the Spanish law was intended primarily to protect the equal rights of non-Catholic confessions, in other countries there was an opposite situation; there the episcopates called for the recognition of religious freedom in order to defend the prerogatives of the Catholic Church. Problems arose especially in the Soviet countries of eastern Europe, where religious freedom was the main subject of dispute with the civil authorities. But even in the United States there was still great sensitivity on these subjects, especially in connection with the new educational standards in legislation that President Johnson signed in April, since these seemed to threaten some rights won by Catholic schools. Serious concern was also aroused by news of plans to nationalize schools in some recently independent countries that were under communist influences (for example, Burma).

---

[29] On this last occasion Cardinal Alfrink had some important words to say that also referred to the work of the Council: "The purpose of the Church is to promote peace. This is an evangelical task. But the Church does not have simply a duty to preach peace; it must also support all efforts being made to preserve it and must therefore study all the problems having to do with war and peace, in order to find ways and means of preserving and consolidating peace.... What the world looks for from the Council's 'schema 13' is not a purely theoretical and casuistic response. What the world wants is that the Council show it the way to avoid having to live with the terror of atomic weapons, which are opposed to the dignity of the human species, even if they do not destroy it. Pope John XXIII understood this truth and that is why he asked, in his encyclical *Pacem in terris*, for all the nations to ban atomic weapons. We should not forget that the Church cannot prevent the use of these weapons, even by a solemn condemnation; it is the peoples themselves, and they alone, who have the ability and power to prevent humanity from committing suicide" (*Il Regno* 10/3 [1965], 119).

As for the statement on the Jews, some signs of the political importance of the debate appeared in February, when, under pressure from the Holy See, Italy banned the staging of R. Hochhuth's play *The Deputy*. This action had the foreseeable effect of increasing people's interest in the play, and *L'Osservatore Romano* was driven to defend the entire range of Pius XII's activity, stressing especially his activity for peace. But public opinion had believed Hochhuth's accusations and had shown that it thought the Catholic Church owed some act of reparation to the Jewish people; in particular, it wanted the withdrawal of the accusation of "deicide" that had traditionally been made against the Jews.

Meanwhile, the organization of the Secretariat for Non-Christians had begun, but its activity was directed primarily to the search for contacts with bishops in regions of non-Christian cultures. In March, Cardinal Marella, president of the new secretariat, had been in Japan as papal legate at the celebrations commemorating the discovery of descendants of the first Japanese Christians and celebrating the revival of Catholic missions.[30] At the beginning of May the Pope established within the secretariat a special section for "relations between Muslims and Christians," which was led by J. Cuoq of the Missionaries of Africa.[31] Meanwhile, the secretariat was continuing its theological study on the salvation of non-Christians.[32]

B. ACTIVITY OF THE EPISCOPAL CONFERENCES IN ANTICIPATION OF THE NEW PERIOD

As the fourth period drew near there was increasing uncertainty about the impact that the Council's innovations were already having on the life of the Church in various countries. The many schemas still on the conciliar agenda and the sensitive character of subjects still to be discussed continued to cast worrying shadows on the possible development of the Council's work. On June 12 the General Secretariat sent the fathers five

---

[30] On March 25 Marella was the guest of honor at a reception sponsored by the Japan Society for the Study of Religions, the International Institute for the Study of Japanese Religions, and the Orient Institute for Religious Research (see Caprile, IV, 558).

[31] Ibid., 557.

[32] "Synthèse des travaux du Secrétariat et des Consulteurs sur le thème du salut des non-chrétiens" (Lercaro papers, 227). See Cicognani to Marella, July 8, 1965, praising the work done on this document, which Cicognani hoped would be published (Lercaro papers, 225).

of the eleven schemas on the agenda. Once the fathers reached Rome, they would find the texts of other schemas as well, on which they would have to vote only on the *expensio modorum* or to cast a final vote.[33] Bishops and theologians were thus able to spend the summer months on a careful study of the schemas.[34]

As during the previous intersessions, the exchange of ideas on the new drafts was important and surely more extensive than is documented in the presently available sources. During these months many episcopal conferences had put the examination of the schemas on the agenda of their meetings so that when the work resumed they could present common positions. In general, the episcopal conferences stepped up their efforts to organize themselves more efficiently and to ensure effective internal communications. The exchange of views on conciliar subjects and documents led to a greater awareness of specific problems and made it possible to express common positions in civil and political society.

For many of the episcopates these were also months for important experiments in organized episcopal action in dealing with institutions in their own countries. The second plenary assembly of the Episcopal Conference of Equatorial Africa-Cameroon was held June 11–15 in order to discuss liturgical reform,[35] but it also tackled problems of economic and social development on the continent.[36] At the meeting's end the group promulgated a message "to Christians and all who are working for a better Africa"; it contained a strong emphasis on respect for human dignity, in particular against torture, and against the arms race. The message elicited a noteworthy response even from the international press. At the end of July the standing committee of the Congolese episcopate met and

---

[33] When Felici sent the schemas on June 12, he also urged the Council fathers who intended to speak on the first two schemas on the agenda (religious freedom and the Church in the modern world) to send a summary of their statements before September 9 (*AS* V/3, 332–33).

[34] Tromp to Schauf, June 27, 1965, on the state of the schemas; and Schauf to Suenens, June 27, 1965 (Schauf papers, Briefe).

[35] The Benedictine monasteries of Mont-Febe in Cameroon and La Bouenza in the Congo were asked to collaborate in the establishment of a center of liturgical research and documentation.

[36] The first assembly had been held the previous year; the conference established a series of committees whose presidents formed a central council that was to meet annually, while the assembly was to be brought together every two years. The seat of the assembly and its offices were located in Yaundé (see "Cameroun: Seconde assemblée plénière de la Conférence épiscopale d'Afrique équatoriale-Cameroun," *ICI* 243 [July 1, 1965], 9; and "La conferenza episcopale dell'Africa Centrale sul problema dell'etica politica," *Il Regno* 10/7 [1965], 312).

drew up instructions for future pastoral activity in that country.[37] In Latin America, on July 7, the bishops of Colombia at their general meeting published a collective letter on the social situation in their country and called for the changes needed so that all members of society might have their legitimate portion of material goods; they appealed to the social teaching of the Church in reminding landowners of their duties to the community.[38]

During these same months the first attempts were made to make the permanent organs of the episcopal conferences more efficient. In France the permanent council met to discuss the pastoral situation in the various regions of the country and to tackle the difficult question raised by the positions taken by the JEC.[39] In Italy, beginning in December 1964, plans were studied for revising the constitution of the Italian Episcopal Conference. The undertaking had been begun, at the request of Paul VI, by Cardinal Siri, president of the conference, who entrusted the task of drafting an outline to the secretary, Castelli. The conference was involved in developing the draft during the first months of 1965, and the final plan was then submitted for examination by the Pope and the Congregation of the Consistory. The constitution was meant to be the heritage left by Siri to the conference, but when his term as president ended in September 1965, Paul VI thought it better to signal a change by appointing, as the leadership of the conference, a governing committee composed of Urbani, G. Colombo, and Florit; he thus put an end to the initial, incubation period of the conference and laid the foundation for it to be relaunched on a different basis.

In addition, many episcopal conferences also turned their attention to the coming resumption of the Council's work. Beginning in July and appearing every two weeks, the informational bulletin of the French Episcopal Conference devoted all its issues to analyses of the new drafts by theologians who had collaborated closely in the drafting.[40]

---

[37] See "Congo Leo: I vescovi africani: superare il proselitismo per un servizio disinteressato alla communità," *Il Regno* 10/9 (1965), 346.

[38] See "Colombie: Lettre collective de l'épiscopat sur la situation sociale," *ICI* (August 1965), 8.

[39] Some resentment was caused by the fact that at the end of the working session a lengthy press conference was held to report on the problems taken up (see "La situazione della chiesa francese," *Il Regno* 10/7 [1965], 309–10).

[40] Y. Congar, "Le schéma *De ministerio et vita sacerdotali*," *EtDoc* 2 (May 14, 1965); Le Bourgeois and Ch. Moeller, "Le schéma du décret *De accommodata renovatione vitae religiosae*," *EtDoc* (May 31, 1965); Y. Congar, "Le nouveau schéma *De activitate missionali Ecclesiae*," *EtDoc* 5 (June 14, 1965); T. Camelot, "Les propositions *De institutione sacerdotali*," *EtDoc* 6 (June 22, 1965); T. Camelot, "La déclaration sur l'éducation chrétienne," *EtDoc* 7 (July 3, 1965); J. Daniélou, "La déclaration *De Ecclesiae habitudine*

The Italian Episcopal Conference put off taking up the new schemas until the beginning of the conciliar period, when all the bishops would be present in Rome. At the beginning of July, Siri informed the bishops in a circular letter that during the coming period the practice of the weekly study meetings, which had produced notable results during the two preceding periods, would be continued; they would meet every Thursday afternoon at the Domus Mariae.[41] In preparation for the meetings the secretariat of the conference gathered and sent to each member some study materials on each schema; these consisted mostly of observations or reports of Italian bishops and theologians. The first of the meetings was called for September 16, and in preparation for it several reports — by Carli, Florit, Siri, and C. Colombo — on the schema on religious freedom were sent out to the bishops or made available to them upon their arrival. Other reports — by Carli, Nuzzi, and Marafini — dealt with the schema on the Church in the modern world.[42]

Some regional conferences held their preparatory meetings during August, in particular the conferences of the Flaminia and Emiliana regions and of the Lombardy and Veneto regions.[43] At this latter meeting, held in Verona, August 17–19, some important reports were given, especially one by C. Colombo on religious freedom, in which he substantially defended the text of the schema that had been prepared during the preceding months. The text of this report was included among the materials prepared for the general meeting of the entire Italian Episcopal Conference on September 16, where it represented the position dialectically opposed to the very critical positions taken by Siri, Carli, and, to some extent, Florit.[44] Another participant in the Verona meeting was G. Gargitter, Bishop of Bolzano-Bressanone, who was to explain the chapter on

ad non christianos," *EtDoc* 8 (July 3, 1965); P. de Surgy, "La nouvelle rédaction du schéma sur l'apostolat des laïcs," *EtDoc* 9 (July 16), 1965; P. Haubtmann, "Le schéma de la constitution pastorale *De Ecclesiae in mundo huius temporis*," *EtDoc* 10 (August 25, 1965).

[41] A. Castelli to the Italian bishops, July 5, 1965 (D'Amato papers).

[42] F. Sportelli, *La Conferenza episcopale italiana (1952–1972)* (Galatina, 1995), 213–17. The reports are in the Gasbarri papers, 573.

[43] The meeting of the episcopal conference of the Flaminia and Romagnola region, held August 24–25, 1965, at the Revedin Villa (Bologna), discussed religious freedom and schema XIII. Dossetti took the notes for the minutes (see the ms in Dossetti papers, 592). For Dossetti's quite critical judgment of the *De libertate religiosa* and of schema XIII, see *DNicora Alberigo*, September 14, 1965.

[44] The documents are in the Carraro papers,1/2-3. Colombo's report appeared in the Italian Conference's bulletin no. 6 for 1965: "Considerazioni sulla Dichiarazione 'De libertate religiosa': Relazione tenuta da Sua Eccellenza Mons. Carlo Colombo, Vescovo tit. di Vittoriana, a S. Fideno (Verona), nel Convegno degli Episcopati della Regione Lombarda e delle Regione Veneta (17–19/08/1965)."

war and peace in schema XIII. He had asked Hengsbach, who had been directly involved in drafting this chapter, for some useful ideas in making his report.[45] Gargitter was regularly a valuable liaison between the Italian and German episcopates.

The German bishops also devoted their annual meeting at Fulda (the last week of August) to the study of the new drafts. They discussed, in particular, the two most important schemas: on religious freedom (with a report by Jaeger) and on the Church in the modern world (with a report by Hengsbach). They spoke also of other schemas: the lay apostolate (reporter: Hengsbach), priests (reporter: Janssen), and revelation (reporter: Schröffer).[46] The meeting was noteworthy because during it the hostility of the German episcopate toward the new draft of schema XIII took clearer form. In preparing his report Hengsbach had asked for the help of Hirschmann, his trusted theologian, but he also had consulted other experts such as O. von Nell-Breuning for the chapter on economic and social life. Döpfner, for his part, had asked K. Rahner for a detailed judgment on the schema; he then gave this to Hengsbach.

Rahner's remarks were especially critical of the approach taken in the text and of its theological basis, which he considered completely inadequate. The schema dealt with the reality of the world, he said, in solely sociological terms, without a theological interpretation of its deeper reality; it did not take enough account of the relationship between the natural and supernatural dimensions; and it did not consider how the history of salvation gives the world a special significance. But, since it was clear that the Council could no longer decide not to issue this document, on which such great expectations were focused, Rahner suggested two approaches: one was that the Council should give its general approval to the schema and then entrust it to a postconciliar commission, along with an explicit mandate; the other was that the Council should approve the schema as it stood but also state openly that the document was not sufficiently mature theologically and was intended as only a first step in the dialogue of the Church with the world.[47]

---

[45] Gargitter to Hengsbach, July 2, 1965 (Hengsbach papers, cart. 122).

[46] Döpfner to the German bishops, July 7, 1965 (Hengsbach papers, cart. 123).

[47] [K. Rahner,] "Anmerkungen zum Schema De Ecclesia in mundo huius temporis (in der Fassung vom 28.5.65)" (Hengsbach papers, 114 and 122). See J. Komonchak, "Le valutazioni sulla Gaudium et Spes: Chenu, Dossetti, Ratzinger," in *Volti di fine concilio: Studi di storia e teologia sulla conclusione del Vaticano II*, ed. J. Doré and A. Melloni (Bologna, 2000), 115–53; G. Turbanti, *Un concilio per il mondo moderno: La redazione della costituzione pastorale "Gaudium et spes" del Vaticano II* (Bologna, 2000), 617–26.

Hengsbach, one of the most influential members of the central sub-commission responsible for the schema, took Rahner's critical remarks to Fulda, where he defended the text and the work done by the commission. He acknowledged the validity of the objections to it but maintained that during the fourth period, thanks in part to the debates on the schema, it would be possible to correct and improve it in the areas Rahner had singled out. If it were not possible to effect these improvements, desired by all, a possible solution, according to Hengsbach, would be to acknowledge in the introduction the insufficiently mature character of the document and to publish it as simply a "letter" from the Council.[48]

After a rather heated discussion, Hengsbach finally succeeded in getting a "possibilist" position accepted, with a document that began by highlighting the positive aspects of the new draft and was then relatively mild in its criticisms. He also raised the possibility of calling the schema an "(Encyclical) Letter from the Council." An appendix to the document reported Rahner's remarks, in all their incisiveness, but they were kept anonymous ("General remarks of a theological expert") and did not contain the two proposals with which they had originally ended.[49]

II. PAUL VI AND THE END OF THE COUNCIL

A. SIGNS OF CONCERN

The new, and last, period of the Council was to begin on September 14, the feast of the Exaltation of the Holy Cross. The Council fathers

[48] At the meeting in Ariccia the preceding February, Wright had already suggested the idea of publishing the schema as a collective pastoral letter of the whole episcopal college (see *JCongar*, February 3, 1965, II, 312–13). Cicognani offered a similar proposal at the meeting of the Coordinating Commission (CC) on May 11, 1965: "His Excellency Morcillo observed that the description 'pastoral constitution' for the document is exaggerated because it makes too much of the content and of the way in which questions are discussed and answered in the schema. Cicognani agreed with this observation and added that a way must be found of not committing the Church in questions still being debated and having no certain solution; he therefore proposed calling the schema not a 'Constitution' but rather a 'Letter' or 'Declaration' of the Council to the world. But the proposal did not meet with agreement from many of the cardinals" (*AS* V/3, 302).

[49] "Animadversiones propositae nomine Conferentiae Episcoporum linguae Germaniae et Scandiae ad Schema Constitutionis Pastoralis 'De ecclesia in mundo huius temporis' (forma a die 28.5.65)" (Hengsbach papers, 114 and 122). There were two appendixes, both taken from Rahner's "Anmerkungen": "Adnexum I: Animadversiones in particulari Secretariatui tradendae," and "Adnexum II: Animadversiones Generales alicuius theologi periti" (see also *AS* V/3, 28–33 and 902–10).

from all parts of the world were to return to Rome "near the tomb of Peter the Apostle, bringing with them to this center of Catholic unity the expectations, desires, and anxieties of their peoples, who look with immense hope to the ecumenical meeting. By their labors they will bring the great conciliar celebration to its end." Such was the desire that Paul VI expressed in an apostolic exhortation of August 28, 1965, written in preparation for the new period of the Council.[50] The Pope placed the coming period under a twofold sign: first of all, that of the cross of Christ, the saving power of which the Council would attest to the world. The Council was to bear witness to "the rights which by his cross the Savior has won over every human heart," and the Council fathers were to proclaim

> in a loud voice the message of hope, love, and peace, which Christ alone addresses with divine authority to the generations of humanity that today are rightly proud of their conquests in knowledge and progress, their bold scientific discoveries and experiments, and their social and political accomplishments. And yet without Christ, that is, without accepting his heavenly teaching and without willingly and faithfully obeying his commandment of love, they are always subject to anxious uncertainty about questions they cannot answer and to the erosive effect of distrust, sickness, hunger, and war.[51]

None of the fathers and theologians who read these words could fail to grasp the signals they contained regarding one of the most important schemas on the agenda, the text on the Church in the modern world, which in its search for a language it could share with modern men and women and in its attempt to interpret the amazing progress of history seemed to be leaning toward a completely positive assessment of the human situation. To bring out the saving meaning of the cross, on the afternoon of September 14, after the ceremonial opening of the new period had been celebrated that morning in St. Peter's, the Pope and the Council fathers were to go in penitential procession, with the sacred relics, from the Church of Santa Croce to the Basilica of St. John Lateran, the cathedral of Rome.

The second sign was even more explicit. Throughout the entire period the Blessed Sacrament was to be exposed in the Pauline Chapel of the apostolic palace, "so that the hearts and prayers of the fathers working at the Council and of all those — priests, consecrated souls, and lay faithful — who serve in our house, may be constantly turned

---

[50] Apostolic exhortation *Quarta Sessio Concilii*, in *AAS* 57 (1965), 689–93.
[51] Ibid., 690.

toward Jesus Christ in the eucharist, the center of love and the bond of unity in the Church." The intention here was obviously to rekindle the spiritual dimension of the Council. But the publication of the encyclical *Mysterium fidei* a few days later would make it clear that the choice of eucharistic exposition was also and primarily meant as a clear signal of opposition to attempts that had surfaced among theologians to call into question some of the traditional dogmas of the Catholic Church.

Paul VI gave a further sign of the spirit that should inspire the Council's work when, on September 12, just before the opening ceremony, he went down into the catacombs of Domitilla for a celebration of atonement. In his homily he explained that he assigned a profound ecclesiological meaning to this gesture: "On the eve of the final resumption of the ecumenical Council we have come here... to drink from the sources; we have come to honor these lowly but glorious tombs and to draw admonishment and strength from them; we have come to feel, flowing through our present experience, a tradition that is not forgetful, not faithless, but always the same, always strong, always fruitful." The catacombs, he said, memorialized "a lengthy history of the concealment, unpopularity, persecution, and martyrdom" to which the Church of the first centuries was subjected; at the same time, they preserved the memory of "a personal and collective closeness to God that is very beautiful and fruitful, a peaceful and humbled profession of faith."

This sign of the catacombs was obviously meant to remind the fathers of the "Church of silence," and it did so most clearly when the Pope referred to the freedom of faith as a freedom of spirit that was brought to maturity by Christians in the time of persecutions. The early Church was thus given a mythic significance: precisely in the hostility of the surrounding world it had found its most authentic dimensions. It was a model valid in every situation: "Here Christianity developed an awareness of its inalienable commitment; here the challenge was given, not noisily, not rashly, not insultingly, to the negative forces in the surrounding world."

On the eve of the new phase of work, Paul VI's main concerns seemed to be focused, first, on the danger that the reception of the conciliar innovations would get out of control, and second, on the question of the right relationship to the modern world, one that would strictly preserve the necessary distance between the Christian faith and temporal realities. These two concerns dominated the Pope's Wednesday allocutions from the end of July to mid September, in which they were expressed with a constant insistence.

On July 28 Paul VI reminded the faithful that they should think of themselves, in accord with their proper role, as participants in the Council when it came to the reception of the truths of faith and to guarding and bearing witness to what the Council would decree. But in this context the Pope also found fault with people who "take advantage of the problems which [the Council] raises and the discussions it carries on, to stir up in themselves and others a spirit of restlessness and radical reformism, in the areas both of doctrine and of discipline, as if the Council were an opportunity to challenge dogmas and laws which the Church has written on the tablets of her fidelity to Christ the Lord."[52] Comparable criticisms, it is true, were addressed to those who were proving reluctant to accept and carry out the Council's directives, but they were not expressed with the same force.

In the following week, when he returned to the subject of the Council, the Pope dwelt only on criticism of people who were reviving "errors ancient and modern which had already been corrected and condemned by the Church and excluded from its heritage of truth," or who were advancing hypotheses that "call into question principles, laws, and traditions to which the Church is firmly bound and from which it cannot be thought she could ever depart," or who were slipping in "loathsome criticisms of the Church's history and structure and proposing radical revisions of her entire apostolic activity and presence in the world, with the result that the Church, far from acquiring those new virtues and forms sought by the conciliar *aggiornamento*, would end up assimilated to the world, the very world that was looking to the Church for rays of her light and the strength of her salt, not for a complacent acceptance of the world's disputable theories and profane habits."[53]

In these allocutions Paul VI never referred to the principle of dialogue that he himself had proposed in *Ecclesiam suam* as a program. Instead, he warned against the danger of an excessive assimilation of the Church to the modern world. On August 11 he again found fault with the spirit of radical criticism seen in people who thought and acted "as if we had to begin building the Church today, to reshape her doctrines starting not so much with the data of revelation and tradition as with the temporal realities of contemporary life." He lamented that "truths which are timeless because they are divine are being subjected to a historicism which at

[52] *Insegnamenti*, 3:998.
[53] Ibid., 1004.

times strips them of their content and their permanence."[54] The following week, while recognizing the legitimate autonomy of human activity
in its various fields, he reminded his hearers of the necessary reference
to God as revealed by Christ, when these activities had for their object
"human beings and their true interests, that is, their ultimate end," when,
in other words, "the activity becomes moral."[55] And on August 25 he
again warned against the kind of naturalism "that preumes to lead humanity to an end within earthly life and attainable by human powers, aug-
mented by the possibilities given by science," and he showed his worry
that this naturalism was spreading even among the Catholic faithful.[56]

It would be useful, of course, to learn which aspects of the Church's
situation pushed the Pope to so cautious an attitude, but that will be possible only when scholars have access to sources and documents presently
out of reach. In any case, we cannot but note a real change of tone in the
references to the modern world as compared with previous years; this
was a sign of fears that grew during those months in the uncertain and
tense climate of reactions to the introduction of the conciliar novelties
into the practice of the Church and to the first reception of conciliar ideas
in theological discussion. This was the spirit in which Paul VI prepared
to open the new period during which the center of everyone's attention
would be precisely the relationship of the Church to the modern world.

B. THE "FINAL" PERIOD:
UNCERTAINTIES AND STRATEGIES FOR THE FUTURE

The transition from the intersession to the resumption of the Council's
activity was a sensitive matter for the Pope and called into play his own
understanding of the Council. In the apostolic exhortation of August 28,
with its emphasis on the return of the fathers to Rome, Paul VI clearly
stated his perception of the coming conciliar period and how it differed
from the intersession. His relationship with the Council differed in the two
phases. Although the conciliar bodies continued to function during the
months of the intersession, and there was a constant focus on the coming meeting, it was clear that for the Pope the time when the Council was

[54] Ibid., 1008.
[55] Ibid., 1012.
[56] Ibid., 1015. Paul VI was here repeating verbatim the words of "a contemporary
scholar" whom he does not identify.

really meeting was that of the general congregations of the fathers. He told A. Wenger at an audience: "We know that [the Council] is a time of grace, a major moment in the time of the Church. It is like a striking of the hour, preceded and followed by silence."

In an article in *L'Osservatore Romano* for June 28 of that year, Giovanni Caprile took up this image in order to bring out the special attitude of listening that the Pope cultivated even during the most turbulent incidents of the preceding period, an attitude that many commentators had been unable to perceive and had mistaken for uncertainty and indecision. But the image of the hour striking and of silence also helps to understand the distinction Paul VI saw between the time of the Council and ordinary time, how they intersected, and his role in these two different times.

Several times during the weeks before the beginning of the Council, Paul VI again spoke of the Council as the "hour of God." In addition to the theological and spiritual meanings the expression might carry, it was clear that he was thinking of the Council as an extraordinary moment and therefore limited in time. His insistent references to the fact that the fourth period would be the last revealed how urgently he wished to bring the conciliar experience to an end. Contributing to the urgency were his worry about the signs of restlessness and tension during those months.

It is therefore not surprising that the acts of ecclesial government that he performed during the final period were, with increasing decisiveness, performed in a postconciliar perspective. In the ordinary kind of time that preceded and followed the Council, it was up to the Pope to implement what the Council decided. In the allocution to the Sacred College on his name day, June 24, Paul VI gave clear expression to this idea:

> The Council will, we hope, be able to come to definitive positions on the subjects of its program; these will not, however, put an end to all questions about the life of the Church. For the Council itself is opening up many new and important questions, which, when the Council is over, We will take up with all due reverence and try to consider and answer, not without the cooperation and advice of the episcopate as well as with the collaboration of religious and those faithful who have a right to do so, in the best way. Life goes on.[57]

Concerns about the postconciliar period would significantly affect developments within the final period. The experience of the *Consilium* for

---

[57] Address to the Sacred College, June 24, 1965; *Insegnamenti*, 3:365-73..

implementing the liturgical reform had shown how important and sensitive was the question of the body chosen to implement the conciliar
decrees. It was not by chance that the Secretariat for Christian Unity worried about being allowed to produce its own ecumenical directory. Bodies to implement the conciliar decrees were also planned for other areas,
from the lay apostolate to work with international organizations, and it
was clear to all that the effectiveness of the gains won at the Council
would depend also on the activity of such bodies.

During the months of the intersession Paul VI governed the Church with
an eye not only on the continuation of the Council but also on its ending and,
above all, on its reception. On his own personal authority, not shared by the
bishops, he took initiatives that would greatly affect the Church's future.
The silence that preceded and followed the Council was the time of ordinary
government, and this the Pope regarded as his job alone. In some cases these
initiatives meant the removal of subjects that of their nature came within the
Council's purview. Although some of them had already come up in the
assembly, Paul VI, on his sole authority, sometimes for reasons of timeliness, had removed them from discussion by the bishops. This happened with
regard to birth control, ecclesiastical celibacy, the reform of the Curia, the
establishment of the episcopal synod, and other sensitive subjects.[58]

Of a similar character were two other initiatives, less known but no less
important, the results of which would become evident only years later.
The first was the idea of revising the profession of faith; Paul VI had
probably begun to think more seriously of this at this time. In a letter
written in April to Colombo, U. Betti suggested that a formula reflecting
decisions already promulgated in *Lumen gentium* be added to the profession of faith that the fathers would be pronouncing on their arrival in
September. In his letter of reply Colombo told him, in secrecy, that a
general revision of the profession of faith was already being studied.[59]

---

[58] On some of these subjects Paul VI spoke to the moderators after the beginning of
the new period; according to Lercaro in a letter sent to his boys on September 19:
"On Thursday evening [September 16] the four moderators had their usual audience with
the Holy Father, who spoke to them of his coming journey to the United Nations and of
some subjects that were to be studied apart from the Council, although by commissions
made up of the presidents of the episcopal conferences: mixed marriages, the diaconate,
indulgences, forms of penance adapted to the times (abstinence and fasting), and so on.
Mainly, however, he dealt with the 'Synod of Bishops,' which is certainly one of the important fruits of the Council and can become for the Church an effective means of learning
the true state of affairs and making timely provision" (Lercaro, *Lettere*, 346).

[59] Father U. Betti wrote of this in his diary: "I wrote to Msgr. Colombo. I pointed out
the appropriateness of adding to the profession of faith which the new fathers would make
in the Council hall on the coming September 14 a formula mentioning the teaching of

As a matter of fact, the idea had an even longer history, reaching back to the preparatory period of the Council, when the theological commission was given the task of developing an ad hoc formula for the conciliar assembly. The formula drafted at that time was not used, however, for reasons never completely explained.[60]

The idea of writing a new formula that would clearly express the conciliar spirit had been revived in April 1964 by Msgr. Elchinger, who spoke of it directly to Paul VI at a private audience.[61] Some weeks later Congar repeated the suggestion and, at the request of Paul VI himself, drew up a concrete proposal.[62] A few months later the matter seemed to

---

Lumen gentium. I suggested the words that might be added: 'Likewise, I faithfully accept and embrace the teaching on the Church that has been declared and handed down at this sacred Vatican Council II.' The purpose was to obviate ambiguous or unauthorized interpretations that are already being given of the dogmatic Constitution just promulgated. The Schillebeeckx case... is symptomatic" (*DBetti*, April 20, 1965, 65). Colombo's response was not slow in coming: "Note from Msgr. Colombo in reply to my letter of the twentieth. He writes: 'Your suggestion is very interesting, and your formula seems to me a good one; for my part, I shall not fail to offer it at the right time to the person in charge. But I fear it will not be possible to introduce the formula immediately at the beginning of the fourth session; it will perhaps be more easily introduced in a possible revision of the profession of faith (I tell you privately: I think the revision is being studied). In order to underscore the importance and timeliness of the proposal, I think it very useful, even necessary, to provide documentary evidence of the divergent interpretations of the teaching, along with the theological qualification and "note"; the reason is that a modification of the profession of faith is a matter of very great importance'" (*DBetti*, April 24, 1965, 65–66). Betti's suggestion was still on the table at the end of August: "Note from Msgr. Colombo at Castelgandolfo, almost a continuation of his note of April 24. He writes: 'I presented the problem you raised about supplementing the profession of faith with a reference to Vatican II. The answer was the one I foresaw: (a) it is difficult to change a profession of faith; (b) supply a memorandum that will adequately justify the suggestion. If you can present such a memorandum before September 2–3, I can pass it on and explain it'" (*DBetti*, August 23, 1965, 67).

[60] See A. Indelicato, "La *Formula nova professionis fidei* nella preparazione del Vaticano II," *CrSt* 7 (1986), 305–40.

[61] "Msgr. Elchinger spoke of drafting a new profession of faith. The Pope, who seemed not to have thought of it, was very interested and underlined it twice in the margin" (*JCongar*, April 29, 1964, II, 77).

[62] "I spoke of my desire that the Council draw up a new profession of faith, as Lateran IV and Trent had done, but in a more biblical and kerygmatic style, suited to our age. The Holy Father agreed and told me: 'Write a text. I ask you this as a private matter.' I answered: 'I will try, and will send you a draft by way of Msgr. Colombo'" (*JCongar*, June 8, 1964, II, 116). Congar has another reference to the matter in the following October: "On arriving at St. Peter's I saw Msgr. Carlo Colombo. I asked him if he knew anything about the draft of a profession of faith that I had sent to the Holy Father; he said: Yes. The Pope had read my text carefully, and had the text of Father Tromp brought to him [the one not accepted for the Council]. He gave my text to some theologians to be studied. He liked the biblical tone but thinks that a profession of faith should speak in a more formal manner" (*JCongar*, October 3, 1964, II, 178).

have been dropped,[63] but it was obviously still on the table of the Pope, who would decide on the matter apart from the Council.

The second initiative had to do with the commission for the revision of the Code of Canon Law and the proposal to develop a *Lex fundamentalis* for the entire Catholic Church, both Eastern and Western; this law would precede the two codes and have a higher rank. When Paul VI made the idea public during the 1970s, it aroused more than a few debates and controversies among theologians and canonists. Various sources make it clear that the idea went back to the years of the Council, although the assembly of bishops was not told of it. The first proposal for a *Lex fundamentalis* was made by Cardinal Döpfner in a list of remarks on the revision of the code that he sent to Paul VI in February 1964.[64] In light of the various problems that the revision would have to face and the difficulties in resolving them, Döpfner wondered whether a reunification of the two existing codes was expedient. Seeing the difficulties such a suggestion would encounter, he proposed, instead, a "fundamental and constitutional" law, which, like the constitutional laws of a state, "would represent the supreme positive law, would define the organs and tasks of the government, and would order, at a fundamental level, the exercise of public authority and the protection of rights."[65]

[63] "I saw Cardinal Martin, who was putting on his coat to go to an audience with the Pope. I told him what I had done about a new profession of faith; it interested him, and he said he would make a note to speak about it to the Holy Father" (*JCongar*, May 11, 1965, II, 378).

[64] J. Döpfner, "Animadversiones ad Codicem Juris Canonici recognoscendum": Onclin papers/CIC I, 1, 8 [inv. C. 110]). I am grateful to P. Noël, who kindly told me of the existence of this document. On the discussions of the plan in the 1970s, see *Legge e Vangelo. Discussione su una legge fondamentale per la Chiesa* (Brescia, 1972).

[65] "Careful consideration must be given to the question whether there should be a single code or two codes, one for the Latin Church, the other for the Oriental Churches. A single Code would promote a unity in government, but would bring with it the danger that unity would be turned into uniformity. The discipline prevailing in the Latin Church is so different from the discipline in the Oriental Churches, which, in addition, differ greatly among themselves, that the idea of establishing a code for the whole Church cannot be implemented. The Oriental laws promulgated under Pius XII were not received by some Oriental Churches, because they bore too much of a Latin spirit. Legislators should learn from that experience to avoid establishing a code for the universal Church and then finding that their work was in vain. On the other hand, many norms, especially those based directly on the dogmas of the Church, are undoubtedly common to all the local Churches, and there is nothing to hinder the establishment of a fundamental or constitutional law, just as states normally establish a constitutional law that is regarded as the supreme positive law, defines the organs and tasks of the government, and orders, at a fundamental level, the exercise of the state's authority and the protection of rights. I think it very useful for the whole Church to establish such a fundamental law, because the unity of the Church would shine forth clearly, while there would be little fear of uniformity. I am convinced

In the spring of 1965 a completely informal commission was set up to study the proposal. The commission, which worked within the commission for the revision of the code, was to draw up a document that would translate into basic juridical language the principles ratified in the recently approved *Lumen gentium*. The appointed head of the commission was Father R. Bidagor, who in the preceding February had replaced Father G. Violardo as secretary of the Commission for the Revision of the Code of Canon Law. At an audience on April 2, 1965, Paul VI had told Fr. Bidagor of "his desire ... that a Fundamental Code or a constitutional Charter of the Church be drawn up, in which the theological and juridical principles that are the foundation of the Church's *unity* would be brought together in a brief and succinct form." This charter would have to set forth "the nature of the Church of Christ, its goal, its unity as instituted by God, and the factors which over the centuries have brought out the fundamental *unity* of the Church's life, which due to circumstances connected with the spread of the faith has taken a variety of forms."[66] The commission held its first meeting on April and met again several times during the following weeks.[67]

that such a law would have great value ecumenically as well, because it would make clearer the essential structure of the Church. For a constitutional law would have to include those norms by which the nature of the Church has been established *iure divino*, but also those norms that are based solely on ecclesiastical tradition. It would also evidently have to deal with the relationship between the particular Churches, an area in which articles 1–15 of the Motu Proprio *Cleri sanctitati* have already established a number of points. Here we have, in a way, a first effort at establishing a law for the universal Church" (Döpfner, "Animadversiones").

[66] "Minutes of the meeting on April 26, 1964" (Eldarov papers, II, 50). Two days after the papal audience Bidagor visited de Lubac in order to talk about the charge given him by Paul VI, who "would like to promulgate a kind of constitutional charter of the Church, containing only those essential matters that precede the Latin, Oriental, etc. (eventually, Anglican) codes" *(Jde Lubac)*.

[67] Participants in the informal meeting on April 26 included, in addition to Bidagor, Gagnebet, Stickler, Faltin, Eid, Schultze, Welykyj, Eldarov, Bertrams, and Alfaro. Alfaro's name was given to Bidagor by de Lubac as that of an expert to be consulted. In the Eldarov papers there are other documents having to do with the activity of the commission, especially a copy of the minutes of the meeting on May 17, 1965, to which is attached two versions of a "Conspectus cuiusdam Chartae Constitutionalis Ecclesiae Catholicae"; a few days later came "Principia cuiusdam Chartae Constitutionalis Ecclesiae Catholicae" and an outline of a lengthy document sent by Welykyj, entitled "Constitutio Ecclesiae" and subdivided into "Principia constitutiva" and "Principia structuralia" (Eldarov papers, II, 45–51). The connection of this group with the Commission for the Revision of the Code of Canon Law is not entirely clear. On May 6 there was a "confidential" meeting of the consultors of the latter commission, with Cardinal Ciriaci presiding, in the commission's new office in via dell'Erba, Rome. The first point on the agenda was the question of "whether one or two codes were to be drawn up, one for the Orientals and the other for

Despite the special importance of the project and the fact that it dealt directly with questions essential to the Council, this was an extraconciliar commission, and the fathers were not even informed of its existence. Paul VI clearly meant to pursue this project independently of the Council and in parallel with it, as an expression of the personal authority that he considered to be exclusively his on whatever concerned the postconciliar period and for the use of which he was already making plans during these months before the end of the Council.

It is in this same focus on the postconciliar period that we must also interpret the two very important actions of Paul VI during September 1965, actions that had a significant impact on the Council. At the beginning of September, as the bishops were preparing to leave for Rome, the Pope published the encyclical *Mysterium fidei* on eucharistic doctrine and worship. The Pontiff had already spoken out several times on this subject, emphasizing the importance of the mystery of the Eucharist and the validity of the dogma of transubstantiation; he was evidently concerned about the spread of theological opinions that were proposing new, nontraditional interpretations of it. He also wished to nourish a eucharistic devotion and piety that seemed to have fallen into second place behind an (over)emphasis on the community aspect of the celebration of the mass. Significant, from this point of view, was the apostolic letter *Investigabiles divitias Christi* (February 6, 1965), written in anticipation of the solemn commemoration of the second centenary of the apparitions at Paray-le-Monial and of the establishment of the cult of the Sacred Heart, which Paul VI regarded as closely connected with eucharistic worship.[68]

The Italian National Eucharistic Congress, held in Pisa in June 1965, gave the Pope an occasion for emphasizing these ideas.[69] Right after the congress an important article of G. Concetti in *L'Osservatore Romano* summarized the basic elements of the Pope's teaching and listed the points that would be made again in the encyclical: the mystery-dimension

---

all others, with a fundamental code of some kind prefixed to it." Three provisional subcommissions were also set up, the first of which, composed of nine members with Father D. Faltin in the chair, was to concern itself specifically with this problem. The minutes of the commission's meeting say the members of the subcommission were elected the next day, but this probably meant the confirmation of members of the group that had already begun to meet informally (see the records of the commission as published in *Communicationes* 1 [1969], 35–37).

[68] Apostolic letter *Investigabiles divitias Christi* (*AAS* 57 [1965], 298–301).

[69] Homily, June 10, 1965, on the occasion of the seventeenth Italian Eucharistic Congress (*AAS* 57 [1965], 588–92).

of the Eucharist, the real presence, transubstantiation, and eucharistic worship and its importance for the Church.[70] This article brought out the heavy emphasis laid on tradition in the definition of the teaching as well as Paul VI's firm determination to defend the tradition.

The encyclical made clear the "reasons for serious pastoral concern and anxiety" that motivated the Pope:

> We are aware that, among those who speak or write about this most sacred mystery, there are some who, with references either to Masses celebrated in private or to the dogma of transubstantiation or to devotion to the eucharist, are spreading opinions that are upsetting the faithful and filling their minds with great confusion about matters of faith. These people act as though it were permissible to consign to oblivion doctrine already defined by the Church or to interpret it in such a way as to weaken the genuine meaning of words or the acknowledged force of the ideas behind them.
> To corroborate the point with examples: it is not allowable to emphasize what is called the so-called "community" Mass to the extent of disparaging Masses celebrated in private; or to stress the sign-value of the sacrament as if symbolism, which, of course, everyone acknowledges in the eucharist, exhaustively expresses how Christ is present in this sacrament; or to discuss the mystery of transubstantiation without mentioning the marvelous changing of the whole substance of the bread into the body and of the whole substance of the wine into the blood of Christ as stated by the Council of Trent, so that only a so-called "transignification" or "transfinalization" is involved; or finally, to propose and to act on the opinion according to which Christ the Lord is no longer present in the consecrated hosts left after the celebration of the sacrifice of the Mass is ended.[71]

The whole encyclical was a rejection of the teachings indicated and of the theologians who were professing them; its style closely resembled that of documents emanating from the Holy Office, and it is likely that the document originated in circles within that congregation. It reaffirmed the mysterious character of the Eucharist, as such inaccessible to the human mind, but the teaching about which had been set down in an absolutely certain tradition of the Catholic Church. The Pope also emphasized the dogma of transubstantiation and the real presence of Christ in the consecrated host. On these bases the encyclical reaffirmed the value of the latreutic worship of the Eucharist and called for a renewed effort to spread a specific eucharistic spirituality.

[70] G. Concetti, "Paolo VI esaltatore dell'Eucaristia," *OssRom*, June 28–29, 1965, 4.

[71] *Mysterium fidei* (*AAS* 57 [1965], 735). Vatican translation reprinted in *Documents on the Liturgy 1963–1979: Conciliar, Papal, and Curial Texts*, ed. International Commission on English in the Liturgy (Collegeville, Minn., 1982), nos. 1153–55, p. 379.

The connection between the document and the Council was stated in the introductory part, which recalled that the Second Vatican Council "has made a new and most solemn profession of the faith and the worship" of the mystery of the Eucharist, which the Catholic Church had always guarded as a most precious treasure. But as the encyclical moved on, references to the conciliar liturgical renewal proved to be secondary compared with references to the Church Fathers and especially to the Council of Trent.[72] That the text was more doctrinal than liturgical was indicated by the almost complete absence of references to liturgical texts.

If read from the viewpoint of reception of the Council, the encyclical was a problematic document, because it significantly underplayed elements that seemed fundamental in the liturgical reform being promoted by the Council, in particular the primacy of communal celebration over individual worship and the significance of the Eucharist as the center of the ecclesial community.

On September 14, during the celebration that opened the new conciliar period, the Basilica of St. Peter was full of comments on the encyclical as everyone tried to grasp its real significance. The more attentive observers noted that the encyclical was a specific signal of the criteria for interpreting the conciliar documents. Apart from general appreciation that a doctrine dear to all had been reaffirmed, many also thought the encyclical represented above all a reassertion of the Pope's authority over the Council, a view confirmed, in the minds of many, by the choice of the time chosen for its promulgation, that is, just before the opening of the new conciliar period.[73]

---

[72] This fact can be ascertained by simply comparing the frequency and centrality of references to *De doctrina de ss. Missae sacrificio* and *De ss. Eucharistia* of Trent with those to *Sacrosanctum concilium* and *Lumen gentium* of Vatican II. The latter are a good deal less frequent and are all concentrated at the end of the section on sacrifice in order to assert its ecclesial value and to restate, as a consequence, the "social and public nature of every Mass," including private masses, which for that reason were recommended to priests.

[73] "I also see Msgr. Willebrands. He immediately talks about the encyclical on the Eucharist. The document obviously intends to create a climate of opinion. The entire Italian press claims that the criticisms in it are aimed at the Dutch theologians and that a schism in Holland is to be feared. The Dutch cardinals are very unhappy at these insinuations, and Cardinal Alfrink has already held a press conference on the matter. Willebrands doesn't think the encyclical contributes very much and that in five years people will no longer be talking about it. Father Lanne, for his part, thinks the encyclical 'disastrous'; in particular he finds the tone disagreeable. In addition, the Pope published it just two days before the Council, as if to assert the independence and superiority of his teaching office.... I note here that as we were leaving the ceremony, I saw Father de Lubac with H. Roux on the steps of St. Peter's. He was defending an entirely opposite point of view to Roux. The encyclical, he said, was benevolent in tone. It is restrained and expressly says

As we shall see in greater detail in the next chapter, remarks in many ways analogous can be made about the other action of Paul VI, the Motu Proprio *Apostolica sollicitudo* by which he established the Synod of Bishops on September 15, the day after the opening session. This action was quite different in kind from the encyclical; while it had a more immediately institutional value, it had important doctrinal implications, and, above all, it dealt with a matter of close interest to the Council. Although the conciliar commission for bishops had several times addressed the question of some representation of bishops alongside the pope in the government of the Church, the establishment of the synod took place without consulting the commission. In all likelihood the Motu Proprio was drafted within the Congregation for Bishops and under the direct control of the Pontiff.

In addition, the establishment of the synod in this way and in this form represented an important and in many respects decisive step at the beginning of the process of reception. In this respect Paul VI's strategy during the last phases of the Council seems clear. Real worry about possible postconciliar developments drove him to act quickly to reassert the prerogatives of his primacy and to deal with all the matters excluded from the Council's business, matters on which he intended to pass judgment personally. As a result, he powerfully affected the process of reception. Prescinding from the consensus with which the Council fathers would submit to papal authority, we must acknowledge that these actions taken independently of the Council and with a view to the postconciliar period anticipated in a striking manner the fathers' own awareness of the importance and sensitivity of the processes by which their decisions would be received.

On the other hand, during this intersession Paul VI did not always manage to achieve positive results. Among the matters that the Council had explicitly left for his decision was mixed marriages, a subject on which there had been hurried discussion in the hall at the end of third period. Although there were widespread expectations and a sense of urgency among the bishops, and despite his oft-stated intention to issue a Motu Proprio on the subject soon, a definitive text was still far off when the new period began. There had been several consultations with the episcopates and with individual bishops to whom suggestions for a text had been sent; but the suggestions ran into major difficulties, especially among the English bishops. It seems that a tenth draft had been prepared at the end

that study must continue. But it was necessary, given what is being said, even in France: things bold, if not even unacceptable" (*JCongar*, September 14, 1965, II, 388–89).

of August, but this too did not garner a consensus, much to the annoy-ance of the Pope.[74]

The incident shows that on certain matters Paul VI felt constrained by the search for an adequate consensus, and that on some sides he felt more exposed than the Council did in the face of differing views. Speaking to Congar, Willebrands remarked that "a council has means for putting down an opposition and overcoming the objections of a minority. The pope does not."[75]

Moreover, this incident of the projected Motu Proprio on mixed marriages and the Pope's difficulties in publishing it reflect something that became rather important in the course of the final period, namely, Paul VI's insecurity in making certain decisions, and the way in which, presumably or in fact, his opinions could be influenced. In many circumstances he had been the object during those months, and would be even more so in the months to come, of pressures from various sides, especially from representatives of the conciliar minority, who made skillful use of direct appeals to him. Several times Paul VI seems to have been a hostage of the minority, which, by withholding its much-desired agreement, would be able to divide the Council and weaken even the Pope's authority. But even prescinding from such interpretations, the difficult relations between the Pope and the Council fathers were obvious and were often due to a surprising lack of communication.[76]

III. THE COMMISSIONS RESUME THEIR WORK

A. THE COORDINATING COMMISSION

At the end of August Felici informed the members of the Coordinating Commission of the next meeting on September 13, just a day before the

---

[74] "Regarding the still awaited Motu Proprio on mixed marriages: the Pope wanted to publish it before Easter of this year. But he had sent the schema to some bishops and some episcopates; difficulties came in from all sides, but especially from England. The Pope is very annoyed and does not know what to do. He told Willebrands that they were working on the tenth version. What do you say? Willebrands: I'm waiting for the eleventh" (*JCongar*, August 25–27, 1965, II, 386–87).

[75] *JCongar*, August 25–27, 1965, II, 386.

[76] "I see Msgr. Elchinger. Some time ago he told me a story which I did not write down at the time and the details of which I no longer recall. It had to do with the Motu Proprio on mixed marriages and Cardinal Döpfner and also the archbishop of Berlin. From what I was told, some responses were reported to the Pope in Rome with some inaccuracy. The reaction of Munich was said to be negative, when it was not. Cardinal Döpfner later set the Pope straight directly" (*JCongar*, July 11, 1965, II, 380).

official beginning of the Council's new period. The agenda contained
the work schedule for "the fourth and final session of the Council." With
the letter of convocation Felici included a series of notes that was to be
the basis of the discussion. From the subsequent minutes we deduce that
the notes were the ones already drawn up by Felici along with the memorandum of May 11, 1965, on "the schemas to be studied during the
fourth and final period," namely, the ones that had already been studied
during the third session.[77] It would be, then, a meeting that was hardly
more than a formality, confirming what had already been discussed in
May, and the rather laconic minutes confirm that the meeting had little
importance.

In his introductory address, after conveying the Pope's greetings to the
cardinals, Cicognani briefly summarized the work done up to that point
and the work still to be done; he referred to the request of some fathers
that at the end of each general congregation there be an announcement
of the agenda for the next congregation; he expressed the desire that the
work of the new period be carried out rapidly; and he asked the board of
presidents and the moderators to prevent reports and interventions from
lengthening into repetitive addresses: "It is our fervent desire that all the
schemas, which have been drafted with such wisdom and love of the
Church, be well received, reach their definitive and complete form, and
then become a new source of spiritual life among the clergy, the religious, and the entire people of God." The remainder of the meeting consisted of a report by Felici on the state of the schemas and on his proposed calendar. The minutes do not mention any discussion; if there was
any, it must have been rather brief, because the cardinals were awaited
in St. Peter's to practice the next day's ceremony.[78] Once again, Liénart
was the only one to offer some alternative proposals, but these repeated
in substance what he had already suggested in May: to reserve the first

---

[77] The memorandum is in *AS* V/3, 296–301. Also added to the points was Felici's letter of June 12, 1965, to the Council fathers on the sending of the schemas, but this letter
did not introduce anything new regarding the schedule (the letter is in *AS* V/3, 332–33).

[78] Lercaro narrated the meeting as follows in one of his letters to the "family": "At
5 p.m., after a visit from Father Bugnini, who told me about his journey to the Netherlands
to look into some rather daring liturgical experiments, I had to attend the first preconciliar meeting of the Coordinating Commission, the secretary of state presiding; a calendar
for the work of the fourth session was decided on — or, more accurately, confirmed in
principle.... Then, at 6:30 in St. Peter's there was, not really a practice, but a kind of setting of the scene for the concelebration of all the members of the governing bodies of the
Council — board of presidents, moderators, Coordinating Committee — with the Pope"
(September 13, 1965, in *Lettere*, 341).

four weeks of the period for the debate on the four schemas still to be discussed, without interrupting these discussions with votes, which would
begin only after the fourth week.[79] Liénart's suggestions do not seem to
have found any kind of hearing in the commission, and in the end Felici's
proposal was accepted. This left only the first three weeks for discussion
of the schemas and provided that during that same period the first votes
would be taken on the other schemas.

Everything seemed to have already been determined in advance, even
regarding the conclusion of the Council, which was set for December 8.
The little volume already printed and distributed to the fathers for assisting at daily mass went only up to that date, with the notice that if further
days should be needed, provision would be made in the future. Consequently, the conjectures being circulated — for example, that the period
would be prolonged until Easter, with some interval — do not seem to
have much foundation.[80] In any case, it was known that Paul VI wanted
to end the Council as soon as possible, and the bishops probably agreed
with him on this.[81]

The course of this meeting rather clearly confirmed that the Coordinating Commission had lost much of its relevance, something only in
part justified by the fact that as the Council now neared its end, the
commission's programming role was diminishing. Many problems, even
those directly having to do with the working out of the new phase and

---

[79] A. Liénart, "Propositiones" and "Kalendarium propositum," in *AS* V/3, 349–52.

[80] See Caprile, IV, 523, who cites an item from the *NCWC News Service* for September 8, 1965.

[81] On this same September 13, at a press conference in the press office of the Council, Döpfner remarked that Paul VI's repeatedly expressed desire for a quick end to the
Council was shared by the majority of the Council fathers: "When the Council began on
October 11, 1962, no one expected it would last so long. The complexity and multiplicity
of the problems required that the work be prolonged, But everyone knows that while a
council is needed at crucial moments in history — and in the history of the Church in particular — it can never be considered an ordinary event, either in the life or the government
of the Church, either at the center or in the dioceses." The tone of these and ensuing
remarks seemed so consonant with thoughts expressed by the Pope that one might think
he was the real inspiration behind them: "The same need that the Council pass from the
phase of study to the phase of implementation suggests that it is right for the Council to
end, because a council is like a moment of pause in the life of the Church, a moment for
reflection, revision, renewal, but a moment also that ought to yield decisions and directives for entering on a new path. As long as the Council has not dealt thoroughly with the
subjects it studies, there will always be the danger of some uncertainty in the application
of the decrees passed. The now overly long absence of the bishops from their dioceses will
only slow the implementation of the decrees already approved. The spirit of the Council,
which has now permeated people and the age, will foster the working out and solution of
problems which today are not yet mature" (Caprile, IV, 523).

which should have been within the competence of the commission (for example, the modalities of voting and of the discussion of the schemas), were apparently not even raised.[82] A more substantial meeting did take place the next week (September 20), but after that the commission would not meet again until December 1, that is, in the Council's final days.

The loss of the CC's authority did not profit the moderators, whose image also seemed to have been weakened. They met for the first time only on September 16 to discuss the request, made by Bea in the name of the Secretariat for Christian Unity, that the schema on religious freedom be submitted for a preliminary vote. On this occasion, too, Felici's negative response seems to have conditioned the outcome of the meeting, which ended without a clear decision.[83] During the final period the meetings of the moderators that were entered into the official minutes seem to have been quite few.[84] According to some testimonies, the moderators were fenced in by the distrust of the Curia, which did not miss any occasions to attack their authority.[85]

On the other hand, Secretary General P. Felici had increasingly acquired a role of the first importance; Paul VI seems to have relied on him almost unquestioningly for the concrete management of the Council. His importance in the eyes of the Pope had become such that the latter intervened personally in a proceeding against Felici brought by Reuss, an Austrian, after Felici had grabbed from his hands some flyers

[82] The meeting did not bring up even the problem of what the bishops were to do in the hall after the first weeks of discussion, when all the work would be in the hands of the commissions. This question was raised by Martimort in a letter to Lercaro (A.-G. Martimort to [Lercaro], September 12, 1965, with a note composed by Martimort, Msgr. Bonet, and Msgr. Etchegaray [Lercaro papers, 800]).

[83] See the minutes in *AS* V/3, 734.

[84] The moderators took part in the meeting of September 13, along with the other governing bodies, in order to prepare and "practice" for the opening ceremony the next day. The minutes published by V. Carbone report only four meetings: September 16 and 28, October 12 and 26 (*AS* V/3, 734–42). But the moderators did participate in the important meeting with the other governing bodies on September 20 and in the meeting with the CC on December 1 (*AS* V/3, 355ff., 637ff.). Lercaro's letters from the Council also show that the moderators continued their scheduled Tuesday afternoon audiences with Paul VI; these are attested at least until the Council became involved in the discussions in the hall (see Lercaro, *Lettere*, 346, 350, 357, 369, 387, and 419).

[85] "At a meeting of the Coordinating Commission, Cicognani said that 'the moderators should not speak, as the curial people do not, although the latter would have much better things to say than were often said in the hall.'" The moderators did not accept the invitation, "but, of course, they were greatly disturbed" (*DNicora Alberigo*, July 27, 1965). This was something let slip by Cardinal Lercaro; R. La Valle heard of it and reported it informally to the Bologna group).

Reuss was distributing at the time of the vote on the communications media.[86]

In any case, on the eve of the opening of the new period a strong sense of pessimism had spread among some of the leaders of the Council. In an informal conversation with R. La Valle at the end of July, Lercaro pointed with concern to a shifting of the balance: on the one hand, the European episcopates, as a result of what had happened in their Churches, especially in Holland and in France had been weakened; on the other hand, Siri was once again taking the initiative in dealing with the Italian bishops, who had been strongly urged to take part in the Thursday afternoon meetings. La Valle remarked: "The Cardinal is afraid that there will be an Aventine of some Italian bishops at the Council and an Aventine of other Italian bishops at the Domus Mariae."[87] While the change that Paul VI wanted made at the top of the Italian Episcopal Conference

---

[86] "Msgr. Elchinger has just seen Msgr. Reuss, auxiliary bishop of Mainz. Two stories: (1) It was from Msgr. Reuss' hands that Felici violently snatched a sheaf of flyers opposing the vote on the Decree on the Means of Social Communication. Reuss then started proceedings against Felici before the administrative tribunal of the Council. He was asked to abstain from this, but he held fast. Finally, he was told that it would please the Pope if he gave up, because the tribunal would find him right and Felici wrong, He then withdrew his complaint. The Pope personally thanked him for this. (2) More recently, Reuss received a letter from Felici after an article of Reuss on birth control which appeared in translation in the *Supplément de la Vie Spirituelle*. Felici demanded (in the name of higher authority?) that he publish nothing more on the subject. Reuss answered that he had a conscience and that he would write what he thought in conscience he ought to write. He then received a letter from Cardinal Cicognani, insisting that he stop publishing on these subjects. I think Reuss once again refused to yield. At that point he saw the Pope in connection with the preceding affair. He told the Pope he wanted to speak with him on another subject and for an hour he discussed the problems of birth control with him. The result — all honor to the Pope! — was that Reuss was asked to join the commission which the Pope had established on birth control" (*JCongar*, July 11, 1965, II, 380–81).

[87] "A letter of La Valle from Bologna, informing us of a conversation he had with the Cardinal: the latter was very worried.... He is very afraid of what attitude the Italian bishops will adopt at the Council. Siri has taken the reins in his hands once again: he has sent the bishops a circular in which, for practical purposes, he calls upon them to keep coming together in the Domus Mariae every afternoon of days when the Council meets, in order to discuss the texts and what votes to cast" (*DNicora Alberigo*, July 25, 1965). Lercaro's concern sprang from the real ambiguity in the letter of Castelli that called the Italian bishops to these meetings: "I have the honor of letting you know that it will be useful for the Italian episcopate to meet right after the opening of the coming session of the ecumenical Council. Beginning therefore on September 14, the large hall in the Domus Mariae will be free for our meetings at 5:00 p.m. throughout each week. Each of their excellencies, the bishops, will, of course, be free to speak on the subjects to be discussed and voted on. The various regional conferences can commission some one of their members to report on whatever meetings may have been held during the summer" (Castelli to the Italian bishops, July 5, 1965 [D'Amato papers]).

when Siri's term expired — the presidency was to belong to a committee composed of Urbani, Florit, and G. Colombo — surely served to reassure Lercaro with regard to his darker forebodings, it did not give the lie
to his analysis of new balances of forces at the beginning of the new conciliar period.

B. The Work of the Commissions

Soon after the new period began, the conciliar commissions began to
meet again in order to assess the work done, to examine the reactions to
the schemas that had gone out in the summer, and to prepare their reports
for presentation in the hall. As early as the first two weeks of September
impressions and stands taken began to become known. People noticed
the change of climate regarding the Council as well as the difficulties
that would arise during the new period. At the end of July the *Coetus
Internationalis Patrum* had sent a letter to Paul VI, asking that there be
a minority report on the schemas on which the bishops strongly disagreed; it also presented a series of other requests to assure that the views
of the minority would be adequately considered.[88] Answering the letter,
Cicognani expressed disapproval of the form the *Coetus* had now taken,
that of a lobby within the Council, but he added that nevertheless the
requests made in the letter would be presented to the Pontiff.[89] At the
beginning of September, Siri sent in some observations on the schemas
on revelation, religious freedom, and the Church in the modern world. His
was another authoritative voice bringing pressure to bear against the positions of openness found in these schemas.[90]

1. The Doctrinal Commission

In September the situation of the schema on revelation appeared to be
substantially different from what it had been during the preceding spring.
The delicate balance reached by the subcommission had been subjected
to constant attacks, which it had found it hard to resist, especially because
the Pope himself seemed to be heeding the demands of the minority. In his
observations Siri wanted greater clarity on the subject of constitutive

---

[88] M. Lefebvre, G. de Proença Sigaud, and L. Carli to Paul VI, July 25, 1965 (Caprile,
V, 53–54).
[89] Cicognani's reply was dated August 11, 1965 (Caprile, V, 53–54).
[90] *AS* V/3, 352–54.

tradition, especially by "making the tradition and magisterium of the Church the first and supreme hermeneutical principle." It was obvious, the Cardinal added, "that a divine book must have an interpretive tool available which is adequate for the purpose, and this means a tool backed by divine authority itself."[91] Paul VI was not indifferent to these pressures and sent the observations, via Cicognani and Felici, to Ottaviani, so that the commission could take them into account as it continued to work on the schema.[92]

Florit and Betti had already become convinced in the spring that they had to defend the wording of the text decided on by the subcommission as well as the consensus behind it. Now they began to realize that the positions of the minority had gained strength and authoritative backing and that to preserve a sufficient consensus, some compromises with the minority's request were necessary. A clear signal in this direction was given at the first meeting of the Italian bishops in September. At that meeting approval was given to a common proposal, four emendations whose general purpose was to emphasize the role of the magisterium and tradition in the interpretation of some truths of faith that could not be maintained solely on the basis of scripture. As the *Coetus Internationalis* requested, the emendations also eliminated the expression *veritas salutaris* (saving truth), in order to avoid suggesting qualitative distinctions within revelation.[93]

2. The Mixed Commission for Schema XIII[94]

There was a change in atmosphere from May to September also with regard to schema XIII on the Church in the modern world. Public opinion was increasingly focusing attention on two subjects: birth control and peace. The latter was of topical interest in view of the deepening international crisis and, in particular, of the increasingly massive involvement of the United States in the war in Southeast Asia. There was also a very keen expectation of the visit Paul VI was now planning to make to the United Nations. Within the mixed commission, however, there were different concerns.

[91] Ibid., 354.

[92] Cicognani to Felici, September 15, 1965; and Felici to Ottaviani, September 23, 1965 (*AS* V/3, 352 and 376).

[93] R. Burigana, *La Bibbia nel concilio: La redazione della costituzione "Dei Verbum" del Vaticano II* (Bologna, 1998), 388–89.

[94] On this section, see the more extensive treatment in Turbanti, *Un concilio per il mondo moderno*, 615–35.

On his journey to Rome for the fourth session Congar met Elchinger
and immediately sensed that the atmosphere was not favorable to the new
draft of the schema. Congar had written to Elchinger some weeks earlier
about a possible intervention in the hall. Now, in conversing directly with
him, he found he had to deal with criticisms much more radical than he
had anticipated, criticisms that seemed "excessively severe," because
they overlooked some objective aspects of the complex subjects being
treated and also disregarded the situation in which the Council found
itself.[95] On some more important matters, however, he was forced to
admit that Elchinger was correct, at least insofar as his criticisms confirmed some of Congar's own deeper impressions of the new draft of the
schema. The new draft lacked a sufficient christological and anthropological framework, and the superficiality of some assertions smacked of
demagogy.[96]

Congar was uneasy not only because he recognized the schema's
defects but also because he was aware that the schema could be
attacked from standpoints dictated by divergent and even opposite presuppositions. The ambiguity of the situation can be seen by comparing the criticisms of the schema by Lebret and by Rahner, both of
them speaking with authority since they represented, though in different degrees, two important episcopates, the French and the German
respectively.

---

[95] "He [Elchinger] finds that this, that, and the other thing are lacking, and what he says
is often correct. But (1) I challenge him to situate these points within a consistent *whole*,
an *ensemble* of so many things; (2) many of the things he would like said go beyond the
middling genre which a document of this kind *has* to embody. I have often noticed that
an idea that is a little strong, a little subtle, is beyond the average intelligence of the bishops. At times, this has been for me a matter of astonishment and a bitter experience"
(*JCongar*, September 13, 1965, II, 386).

[96] "(1) There's no strong line or overall movement. It should have been christological
and anthropological: to give a 'human' face to biblical and Christian assertions.
(2) At times, there is an element of demagogy. It's rather ACO [Action Catholique
Ouvrière]. And some sections, on the economy, for example, say all the needed things, but
without allowing enough room for the discovery of new forms and without contributing a
deep *spirituality*. It stays too much on the level of recipes, a program, thingamajigs.
Elchinger is not wrong when he says that the schema is a casuistry that presupposes a stable situation; what was needed was to point out major directions, large needs, and such
means as one can see for meeting them. Everything, or almost everything, is said but often
rather vaguely. This is because, in my opinion, they used to excess a method of accumulation. That was Msgr. Guano's tendency: an overly large mixed commission, numerous
subcommissions, a mass of documents and a mass also of requests to be satisfied. Some
individual or very small group should have worked on a synthesis. There is a touch of
gigantism in the enterprise of schema XIII" (*JCongar*, September 13, 1965, II, 386–87).

Lebret's observations came via Liénart, who asked that they be taken into account and suggested that the French bishops as a body were in agreement on some of the corrections proposed by Lebret.[97] Although the criticisms were not meant to be categorical, they were quite representative of one type of expectation. Lebret complained, in particular, that the new draft was not conceived as "an encounter with the totality of today's world." In some ways it was still too Western a text: "it is not based enough on valid elements in various civilizations and on non-western aspirations as these can be seen in the Far East, in the Islamic world, and in Black Africa." On the other hand, as far as the West was concerned, the schema did not take enough account of valid elements in the systems of thought that characterize the modern world. The impulse to carry on a dialogue with modern men and women was therefore not enough:

> In short, insufficient account is taken of the various searches for a humanism, as this word is understood today. The same thing is true with regard to socialism, the forms of existentialism, the philosophies of value, the anti-rational reactions of the Arab world and of Africanism. Similarly, not enough attention is paid to the efforts to purify Hunduism or to the non-atheistic sector of Buddhism. As a result, there are non-Christians who will be disillusioned after the hopes raised by the first part of the introduction.[98]

Rahner's severe criticisms, accepted in part by the German episcopate, called into question the fundamental choices on which the schema had been based: the excessive emphasis given to sociology, the inadequacy of the theological perspective, the oversimplified view of the relations between the "natural" and "supernatural" dimensions of the world, the insufficient attention given to the reality of sin and to the fact that the

---

[97] L. Lebret, "Notations à la lecture du texte français du 26 juin 1965" (Haubtmann papers, 1742). See also Liénart to Haubtmann, September 1, 1965, and the latter's reply on September 9, in which he expressed some agreement with the observations (Haubtmann papers, 1789, 1790). Lebret had felt the first symptoms of illness in April and was forced to spend long periods in the hospital throughout the summer. It was there that he read the new draft of the text and formulated his observations: "My lengthy stay in the hospital has brought me so many proofs of friendship that my imprisonment weighs less heavily on me. From working too long on my thoughts about schema XIII and on a paper I promised the Holy Father, I have been feeling somewhat exhausted, a condition aggravated by the radiation that at present I am not tolerating as well" (*DLebret*, September 1, 1965). It is not clear how widely Lebret's comments circulated within the mixed commission; when he arrived in Rome at the end of September, he was disappointed that Garrone had not received them (*DLebret*, September 30, 1965).
[98] Lebret, "Notations."

entire created world has union with God as its end. The German bishops
were taking a stand against the schema in their two concrete proposals:
the schema should be left to a postconciliar commission or else should
be reduced to the status of a simple "letter" from the Council so that it
would not enjoy the Council's full authority.[99]

These were the criticisms that most worried the mixed commission,
especially since they seemed to come from opposite sides; the commission could see only reasons to fear a confrontation of the two in the hall.
Then, too, there would be the traditional hostility of those broad sectors
of the episcopate that from the beginning had seen in the schema the danger of an imprudent and untimely opening to the modern world, a weakening of traditional positions, and the Church's refusal to defend its own
truth and the authority of its tradition against hostile forces at work in the
modern world.[100]

The central subcommission of the mixed commission also had some
organizational problems as it began the new period of the Council.
Although he was hoping for a rapid recovery, Guano was still unwell and
could only take part indirectly in this sensitive phase in the drafting of
the schema. He had already had to give up writing the report that would
introduce the discussion in the hall and would be an important moment
in explaining the text to the fathers and justifying its novelties. In fact,
despite Guano's best hopes, steps had already been taken rather quickly

---

[99] The criticisms of the Germans were not isolated. During the summer, in a document
meant for Lercaro's study group in Bologna, U. Neri expressed similar criticisms just as
severe as those of Rahner (see "Osservazioni generali," Alberigo papers, VI/3).

[100] Telling, from this point of view, were the criticisms of Siri, who lamented that the
schema "deals only with certain aspects or problems of the modern world. It does not deal
with some much more serious aspects that have to do directly with the supernatural and
eternal mission of the Church; for example, the problem of sin and of its entire immoral
organization; the problem of indifferentism and relativism in the area of religion; the problem of the laicism that is dominant even among Catholics; the problem of the spiritual and
educational situation of the young; the problem of the formation of the masses; the problem of the increasing aridity and sadness in the life of souls; the terrible problem of the
priority which society gives to technology, and so on. I am really afraid that Christian
people will be scandalized when they read a conciliar document that passes over in silence
matters directly concerning the supernatural mission of the Church. I am just as afraid that
public opinion — which is not always to be condemned — will accuse the schema of
being Maritainist in inspiration. I am not referring here to that outstanding man but to his
self-styled disciples who go by the name of Maritainists. The fact that the Church does not
concern itself in a solemn way with the very serious 'sin' of the world and with its wicked-
ness and refusal to believe could lead many to think that the intention is to replace the main
concern left to us by the divine Savior" ("Animadversiones card. Siri circa schema
'De Ecclesia in mundo huius temporis'" [AS V/3, 353]).

and discretely to replace him. At the beginning of September, probably at the request of Paul VI himself, Felici had approached Glorieux and asked him for some names of possible substitutes.[101] A few days later (September 5) Felici received the answer of Paul VI, who chose Garrone to replace Guano.[102] But this institutional change was not at all clear. On September 9 Guano claimed that he was still the real president of the central subcommission and that his functions were to be assumed temporarily by Ancel. Guano remained worried about the report to be given in the hall.[103] Some days later, however, he was told that the Pope had appointed Garrone as reporter.[104]

The central subcommission did not raise the question of the presidency but simply accepted the Pope's solution.[105] With regard to the time to be allowed for discussion, Haubtmann had already suggested to Felici a prospectus that anticipated finishing the discussion in about eight days, but the decision on this matter depended on the governing bodies of the Council. It was also necessary to organize the work to be done within the central subcommission and the other subcommissions, so that the corrections suggested by the Council fathers could be quickly introduced into the text. There was thought of increasing the number of subcommissions and of redistributing members and consultors. Thus ten subcommissions were

---

[101] Glorieux answered by giving the names of members of the central subcommission and singling out Ancel (who was vice-president), Wright, and Hengsbach, who were "the only ones who have been able to participate really in the development of the schema." He also mentioned Garrone and Poma, who, among the bishops appointed in November 1964, "played an active role in the work of the intersession" (Glorieux to Felici, September 1, 1965 [AS V/3, 336–37]). On that same day Felici sent the names to Dell'Acqua (AS V/3, 337).

[102] Dell'Acqua to Felici, September 5, 1965 (AS V/3, 340).

[103] Guano to Felici, September 9, 1965: "I think it my duty also to let you know officially that I will not be able to be present for the beginning of the coming session of the Council; the reason is my illness, which now, however, seems close to its end. I know that you have met with Canon Haubtmann. Through Msgr. Glorieux, secretary of the commission, or through Canon Haubtmann I shall keep you up to date on my intentions and suggestions. The presidency of the subcommission will, of course, be assumed by Msgr. Ancel, while leaving open the question of who will introduce the schema in the hall" (AS V/3, 345–46).

[104] See Guano to Garrone, September 14, 1965: "I have learned that the Holy Father has appointed you to replace me in giving the report on schema XIII in the hall. I am very satisfied with this, even if some may be puzzled because you are ... French (although through your distant ancestors you are Italian and even, I believe, Genoese)" (Guano papers, 60).

[105] In view of the opening report, Guano sent Garrone an outline to follow and some specific points (E. Guano, "Qualche nota per la relazione introduttiva allo schema 13" [Guano papers, 30]).

planned that would imitate those already present at Ariccia. In addition to the central subcommission (enlarged by the inclusion of the presidents of the other subcommissions) there would be one subcommission for the introductory explanation, three for part one (one for the first and second chapters *De homine*, one for *De humana navitate*, one for *De munere Ecclesiae*), and five for part two (one for each chapter).[106]

3. The Secretariat for Christian Unity

During the summer the secretariat had been heavily involved in the start of a new and decisive stage of ecumenical relations with other Christian confessions, namely, the planning of official bilateral conversations. After the establishment, in February, of a joint working group consisting of Catholic representatives and representatives of the World Council of Churches and the planning of a joint commission with the Church of Constantinople, conversations had also begun at the end of August with the Lutheran World Federation.

Meanwhile, contacts with the Eastern Catholic Churches had continued with a view to forestalling the rise of other problems connected with the declaration on the Jews. In mid July Paul VI decided it would be appropriate for some representatives of the secretariat to go to the Middle East once again in order to present and explain the new text of the declaration to the patriarchs.[107] It was, once again, Willebrands and Duprey, accompanied this time by De Smedt, who undertook the journey that lasted from July 16 to July 24. They met with the various Catholic patriarchs, especially with Maximos IV Saigh. After the meeting the patriarch sent Paul VI some more concrete proposals for improving the new text. On the one hand, these proposals did not exclude the possibility of a collective guilt of all of Israel in the death of Jesus, and they emphasized that the divine promise had shifted from the Jewish people to the Church of Christ. Another correction was meant to relativize the condemnation of anti-Semitic persecution by placing it within the context of a condemnation of all racially inspired persecutions. Finally, Maximos IV asked that Romans 11:28–29 be cited in its entirety, for it spoke not only of God's special love of Israel because of the fathers, but also of Israel's

---

[106] RT (September 14–December 1965), 1–2; and P. Haubtmann,"Réunion de la s.c. mixte dit 'groupe de Zürich'" (Haubtmann papers, 1881).

[107] For a report of what Willebrands had told the meeting of the secretariat on September 13, 1965, see *JCongar*, September 15, 1965, II, 392.

enmity toward God because of the gospel.[108] On the other hand, in general, it seemed that in the form proposed, that is, with the removal of the condemnation of the accusation of deicide, Maximos IV could accept the new form of the text.[109]

At the beginning of September, Willebrands answered Felici's request for information on the state of work on the schema. Referring to the *modi* suggested by Maximos IV, Willebrands remarked that these were "in line with the *modi* already handed in at the time of the vote in the Council." But he reserved to a later plenary meeting of the secretariat the final decision on the *expensio modorum* to be presented first to Paul VI and then in the council hall.[110] As a result, the CC was unable to see it at its meeting on September 13, and Felici could only announce that the final draft would be ready in a few days.[111] The secretariat met again in plenary session on September 15. The *modi* submitted by Maximos IV were all

---

[108] It is worthwhile giving Maximos's letter at length, with the corrections he wanted in italics: "Here, then, are some emendations of the text, which it seems to us can still be made (we underline them): 'Although the Jewish authorities and their followers urged the death of Christ, nevertheless the things inflicted on him in his passion cannot be imputed, *without distinction, either* to all Jews living at that time *or* to the Jews of today. *Although the Church is the new people of God, yet* the Jews are not to be depicted as rejected by God or as accursed, as though such a depiction followed from the sacred writings. Therefore, let all take care, whether in catechesis or in sermons, not to teach anything that is not in keeping with gospel truth and the spirit of Christ. In addition, mindful of our common heritage with the Jews and impelled not by political considerations but by a devout evangelical charity, the Church deplores all hatred and persecution of Jews and all manifestations of anti-Semitism, at any time and by any person, *just as it deplores the same attacks on any other human being.*' On page 4, when the text cites St. Paul saying that the Jews are 'beloved because of the fathers,' it should add the words 'yet enemies because of the gospel.' If these last words seem overly harsh, then avoid citing St. Paul at all, because this kind of cutting up a verse of scripture so as to cite the favorable part and omit the unfavorable may be interpreted as a falsification of scripture for systematic apologetic purposes" (De Smedt papers, 1475).

[109] With regard to the sending of the *modi* first to Paul VI and only indirectly to the secretariat, see what is said to have gone on within the latter in *JCongar*, September 15, 1965, II, 392). Some other interesting remarks also are found there: "Maximos has sent new *modi*. After learning of them, the Pope sent them to the secretariat for evaluation. Willebrands explained the three *modi* of Maximos. De Smedt noted that the attitude of the Orientals changed for the better once they saw the text amended in May and once it was explained to them. They then said that there would be serious difficulties but that they were ready to defend the text, explain it, and to work together for a successful outcome. Willebrands read the letters sent to the governments of Syria and by Maximos: the letters contained a complete and loyal defense of the Council. Tappouni: once the text has been promulgated, the entire Syrian Church will follow the Council."

[110] J. Willebrands to P. Felici, September 2, 1965: "Nota sullo stato attuale del testo dello schema della dichiarazione *De Ecclesiae habitudine ad religiones non-christianas*" (*AS* V/3, 338–39).

[111] Minutes of the meeting (*AS* V/3, 348).

accepted save for the last, the one that asked that the citation from Romans 11:28 be completed by addition of the words "but enemies because of the gospel." The reason for the rejection, as was explained in the report, was that the words in scripture referred to persecutions inflicted on the first Christian communities and not to Jews of later centuries, still less to the Jewish people as such.[112]

At the end of the third period, when the schema on religious freedom was withdrawn from a vote by the Council, it was decided that this schema would be the first one discussed at the beginning of the new period of the Council. The new draft, sent to the fathers in June, was now ready for debate, which promised, once again, to be a stressful one. This new text was perhaps the one most closely studied by the episcopal conferences during the preceding months, and reactions to it were in general mixed; there were also some rather severe criticisms of it. It was known that the *Coetus Internationalis Patrum* was preparing for battle, but there was also opposition from theologians known to be close to the Pope.

On June 23 Father C. Boyer published an article in *L'Osservatore Romano* that addressed one of the most crucial points in the schema: the common good. Repeating the classical thesis-hypothesis position, he maintained that the common good must be based on the principles of justice taught by the Church, and that only a state which followed these principles and respected the rights of the true religion could satisfactorily ensure their implementation. The principle of the common good as preached by a totalitarian regime such as the Soviet Union, which trampled on the true religion and its teachings, was certainly false and to be resisted. On the other hand, the common good as professed by the Western liberal states, which on the basis of it legalized the equal dignity of all religions and the freedom to profess them, was acceptable only as a "hypothesis" and as long as it was not possible to restore the exclusive rights of the true religion.[113]

This article, which seemed to be a direct attack on the schema in its current form was disavowed in the following week. At the public audience honoring the second anniversary of his coronation, the Pope himself turned explicitly to the subject of religious freedom and defined it juridically in terms of the two formulas *nemo impediatur/nemo cogatur*

---

[112] "Schema declarationis de Ecclesiae habitudine ad religiones non-christianas – Expensio modorum" (*AS* IV/4, 709).

[113] Ch. Boyer, "Lo stato e il bene commune," *OssRom*, June 23, 1965, 2.

(let no one be hindered/let no one be compelled), which appeared to be steadfast elements in his thinking on the subject. The terms he used on that occasion, the explicit reference to the schema being debated, and the overall tone of the address seemed to be a solid endorsement of the work of the secretariat and a distancing of the Pope from the positions taken by Boyer. But in the critical observations that he sent to Paul VI at the beginning of September, Siri succinctly restated the traditional arguments put forward by Boyer and thus showed that the conservative wing of Council fathers was determined to fight the battle against the schema to the end, despite their awareness that the schema had the Pope on its side.[114]

It was up to the secretariat to draw profit from this favorable situation; it was not an accident, then, that Bea went directly to the Pope to obtain a preliminary vote on the schema right at the end of the discussion. Bea did not hesitate to remind Paul VI how appropriate it would be if at his coming visit to the United Nations he could present himself as having the backing of the Council's approval of this text.

---

[114] Siri's comments are in AS V/3, 352–54: "The schema for the Declaration on Religious Freedom leaves me greatly puzzled, especially for the following reason. It repeatedly defends, and does not just state, the 'religious freedom' of all communities. Now, not 'all' religious communities are in the truth and in the divine law, at least the natural law; on the contrary, everywhere outside the Catholic Church are to be found errors at least, and often deficiencies and deviations, some of them immoral and bloody. When it comes to the wicked use of freedom, God 'tolerates' it; he does not 'legitimize' it. We ought, it seems, to conclude, therefore, that we cannot defend 'religious freedom' where there is objective evil; we can only 'tolerate' it, and this when narrow limits imposed by the requirements of the common good are not in place. But the 'schema' appears not to take this approach, and essentially ignores the concept of 'tolerance alone' (and not of 'defense') when it comes to the application of religious freedom. In my opinion, the consequences can be serious in various areas and will especially benefit religious indifferentism."

CHAPTER II

FINISHING THE WORK BEGUN:
THE TRYING EXPERIENCE OF THE FOURTH PERIOD

GILLES ROUTHIER

Once again, and for the fourth time, the fathers converged on Rome. For the second year in a row Paul VI had settled on September 14, Feast of the Exaltation of the Holy Cross, as the date for resuming the Council.[1] What was special about this autumnal gathering was that it would be the last one, as Paul VI had already made clear in his address at the end of the third period and had since restated.[2] On September 13, Cardinal Döpfner, an authorized spokesman for the governing bodies of the Council, made it clear that the Pope's desire coincided with that of the great majority of the fathers, who had not anticipated that the Council would last more than three years. A council, he added, cannot be regarded as a habitual part of the Church's life, and it was time to move on from the phase of study to the phase of implementation of the conciliar decrees; and this new moment in the life of the Church required the bishops to be present in their dioceses.[3] There was even speculation that the final vote on schema XIII might be taken through the mail after the fathers had returned home.[4]

That the fourth period would see the Council's completion and conclusion, however, was not something that could be taken for granted. Despite the road already traveled and all that had already been achieved, a great deal of work was still in process. Eleven texts remained, four of which has been discussed a first time but still had to pass through all the

---

[1] See Paul VI, Allocution *Ex audientia,* January 4, 1965; Apostolic exhortation *Quarta sessio Concilii,* August 28, 1965 (*AS* IV/1, 14-17).

[2] See the allocution of January 4, 1965, and the audience on July 28, 1965; *Insegnamenti,* 3:997-99.

[3] Press conference at the Press Office on September 13, 1965. Döpfner's analysis was shared by Prignon: "There is an increasing desire, not only in Roman circles, but also among many of the residential bishops, to bring the Council to an end.... There is no doubt that many of these bishops have spoken of the matter to the Pope and asked him to close the Council at the end of the fourth period" ("Aperçu sur les travaux des commissions conciliaires," Prignon papers, 1145).

[4] Msgr. Charue had heard this proposal (see *JCharue,* September 13, 1965, 5).

stages of the conciliar process. Inevitably, there were questions about the fate of all these schemas, some of which dealt with difficult and complex issues and tackled new and contingent problems in novel manners. Would the Council set aside these difficult questions, or would it end with ambiguous and even mediocre texts? Was schema XIII to be anything more than "rough notes" for a future encyclical that would complete the reflection still in process? On the eve of the fourth session, then, how the Council would end was still in doubt.

People realized that the Council would not satisfy all the hopes placed in it, and that it was necessary to adjust these hopes in a realistic way and to agree on the compromises demanded by circumstances. In addition, rumors were circulating in the press; for example, that a counter-schema on religious freedom was being circulated[5] and that the text on the Jews, despite the vote taken on it, might be revised on the subject of deicide.[6] Certainly the Council seemed to have its back to the wall; some thought that all the schemas on the agenda would never be completed before Christmas unless current procedures were changed.[7]

There was some fear that the Council would not end successfully. The end of the third period had left bad memories. In addition, despite the Pope's repeated gestures in favor of the implementation of the conciliar decrees, his statements during the general audiences of the summer, when he spoke of the "crisis of authority" or the "crisis of obedience,"[8] as well as his comments on *aggiornamento* or on relations between the Church and the world, seemed to some to be warnings that made them wonder if they were heading for a period when things would be closed down. On examination, one can see the one major theme that ran through all the Pope's addresses: the importance of maintaining the unity of the Church when the conciliar decrees, which he regarded as inevitable and indispensable, began to be implemented. Nothing worried him more, he said, than the sight of disunion and disagreements where there ought to be harmony and charity.

---

[5] *JDupont*, September 15, 1965, 4.

[6] See *DButler*, September 12, 1965. Butler got his information from *Il Messagero*.

[7] E.g., Bishop Dworschak (see his Council Diary, Fourth period, September 14, 1965, 1).

[8] The diagnosis of a "crisis of obedience" was widely shared. Tromp told de Lubac: "'There is confusion; people are no longer obedient in the Church or even in the Society [of Jesus].' This is only too true. (But why have he and his like buried themselves in a stubborn opposition to any and all renewal? This is what gave a revolutionary appearance to the first acts of the Council, and from then on made disorder outside the Council so much easier.)" (*Jde Lubac*, September 10, 1965, 619).

Similarly, the publication of the encyclical *Mysterium fidei* just before the beginning of the new period disconcerted many fathers of the Council and left the non-Catholic observers even more puzzled.[9] The encyclical did not seem capable of being harmoniously integrated with the teachings of the Council. At the very moment when the decisions contained in the Constitution on the Liturgy were being implemented, it seemed that its doctrinal and theological foundations had not proven capable of inspiring a discourse outside the categories of Scholasticism. On the other hand, one sector of the press took delight in using the encyclical to attack developments in Dutch Catholicism. The Pope's words on September 12 in the Catacombs of Domitilla against persecutors of the Church were interpreted by some as a criticism of schema XIII; at least, that is how *Tass* read it.[10]

When the fathers gathered for the fourth period, then, the Council had entered into a new phase, the implementing of the conciliar decrees, in particular with regard to liturgical reform and to the Council's ecumenical program and its general attitude of openness to the world. While all these reforms were in general favorably received, a better grasp of the road to be traveled and of the obstacles on that road was now possible. The passage from reform movements to conciliar texts had already given rise to fears and opposition within the conciliar assembly; this new transition, from texts to institutions or to the life of the Church, could not fail to shake the hopes that had marked the beginning. How great the difficulties of implementing the reforms would be was illustrated by the delay in reforming the Curia. It seemed that nothing could be done except to add new bodies that would be poorly grafted on to the old ones, which remained in place. The Consistory at which new cardinals were created, too, had balanced the tendencies at work by giving a greater voice to a new generation at a time when the cardinals who had spearheaded the majority during the first two periods seemed overcome by weariness.[11]

---

[9] Reactions may be found in the reports from the Council or in the Council diaries of Blakemore, Horton, Moormann, Outler, and others. Moormann observed that the encyclical was out of place in the setting of a Council that was trying to address the contemporary world and was attempting, for this purpose, to free itself from Scholasticism and Tridentine theology. Like others, he remarked that the doctrinal foundations of the Constitution on the Sacred Liturgy were being ignored (John Moorman, *Vatican Observed: An Anglican Impression of Vatican II* [London, 1967], 157).

[10] Picked up by Wenger, 4:36 n.20.

[11] After the Consistory, Outler observed: "There is not a single really prominent immobilist on it (unless you count Archbishop Dante) and yet there is also no zealot. Twenty-one or twenty-two of them are moderate to strongly progressive ... so that now the block of curial cardinals is outgunned and outmanned; the Secretariat for Promoting Christian

Paul VI was not the only one to foresee that the contradictions which had marked the assembly during the first three periods would now agitate the local Churches. According to Prignon's assessment, many bishops "are of the opinion that the turbulent ideas stimulated by the Council are close to reaching their critical point. It is time to restore a little order in the house and to reap the fruits of the Council while preventing or at least reducing the exaggerations on both right and left. It seems to me that the majority of the western-European bishops are convinced of this. The situation in the Netherlands is a catalyst for this thinking, although we evidently must not forget the sporadic manifestations in Germany, Belgium, France, and Great Britain."[12]

Thus, as J. Grootaers wrote on the eve of the period, reservations about the reforms were not felt only at the center but also on the periphery, even in places where some groups were impatient to move beyond the possibilities opened up by the Council.[13] This somewhat paralyzed those who had been leaders of the majority during the first two periods at the very moment when the minority seemed to be profiting from the situation. The Council had evidently reached a new stage, and the contradictions coursing through Catholicism as a system were proving to be complicated and tricky to manage.

In this atmosphere the Pope's opening address for the period was much awaited. What direction would he give to the period now beginning? Would he take a minimalist position in regard to the Council's ambitious program? Would he curb hopes and rein in overly ambitious initiatives? What tone would he give this period?

Surprisingly, the Pope did not directly address any matter under study and deliberation by the Council; he did not wish to limit the fathers' freedom of opinion. While at first sight his address was inoffensive, a simple exhortation on charity, this seeming reserve did not prevent his setting the tone for the fourth period. At three key moments in the address

---

Unity is obviously favored" (A. Outler, "Vatican II — Between Acts," in Stransky papers, 11.4, p. 15).

[12] "Aperçu sur les travaux des commissions conciliaires."

[13] See J. Grootaers, "Au-delà du Concile et de l'Église," *ICI* 248 (September 15, 1965), 21. Extensive excerpts in English and French translations circulated of Grootaers' article of September 11, 1965, in *De Maand*. A survey of pastoral letters issued by bishops during the intersession is enough to show that the upheaval was being felt in many centers of Catholicism. Caprile lists the letters of Cardinals Feltin, Lefebvre, Heenan, and Gilroy, and that of Msgr. Weber (Strasbourg), as well as the note of the Portuguese episcopate. All seem marked by tensions inherent in the initial reception of the Council: haste *vs.* resistance (see Caprile, IV, 50-51).

he stated that this would be the final period of this ecumenical assembly, thereby cutting short rumors that the fathers could not finish their work during this final period. The entire first part of his address was marked by joy and thanksgiving; the tone was not at all stern or austere. Paul VI was not entering unwillingly or reluctantly into this final stage of the Council. The opening section contained in germ all the rest of the address; that attachment to the word of God, agreement in faith, and the free search for solutions were the conditions for reaching the end in harmony and charity. Then, after listing these attitudes and dispositions, he clearly identified two goals: "to establish more perfect bonds of communion with our still separated brother Christians" and "to send the world a message of friendship and salvation."

The Pope was holding to the course, then, without any reservation. Without descending directly into the fray, he set the tone for the period: free investigation, but also a care for concord and charity in studying questions, and, above all, docility to God's word, which he himself enthroned on this first day. He also gave directives at the thematic level. In particular, the third point that he developed, on love of humanity, anticipated the debates of the fourth period. This conciliar assembly, he said, would not be closed in on itself, "deaf and insensible to the needs of others, of those countless throngs of human beings." "The Church in this world is not an end in itself, but is at the service of all peoples; it must make Christ present to all, both individuals and nations, as widely as possible and as generously as possible; that is its proper mission. It is the bearer of love, the creator of true peace."

By emphatically expressing his gratitude for the work of the conciliar commissions and by his strong emphasis on peace, on the mission of the Church, and on the Church's relationship to humanity, the Pope was in a way putting his stamp of approval on some conciliar texts that would soon be the subjects of debate. "This gaze outward to the world," he said, "will be one of the activities of the period now beginning." Almost in the very words John XXIII had used at the opening of the first period, Paul VI pointed out the way the Council should take: "This Council must certainly be clear and unyielding in what has to do with fidelity to doctrine. But ... instead of issuing condemnations of anyone, this Council is to have sentiments only of kindness and peace."[14]

---

[14] See the opening address in *AS* IV/1, 125-35, esp. 131-33; English translation in *Council Daybook, Session 4*, 4-7.

The most striking elements of Paul VI's opening address, which did not
generate many newspaper headlines, were doubtless the announcements
that came at the end: the establishment of the synod of bishops (which
was warmly applauded), and the Pope's upcoming visit to the United
Nations. It was these announcements, rather than the exhortation to charity, that were emphasized by the press agencies. According to a dispatch
of the Agence France-Presse, picked up by many dailies, the announcement of the establishment of an episcopal synod naturally gave satisfaction to those at the Council who wanted greater collegiality. In addition,
by creating precedents that committed the Church to concrete action, the
two announcements reassured people of Paul VI's steadfastness. By surprising the fathers in this manner, the Pope seemed to be taking the initiative and displaying his determination; he gave the impression of a man
on the move, in contrast to the image that people had of him as a wavering man who was paralyzed when it came to action.

On that day, moreover, it was more the change in style than the address
of the Pope that struck observers, journalists, and participants: absence of
pomp and ceremony, simplification of the ceremonial, greater participation in the liturgy.[15] To the observers the liturgical reform seemed already
established.[16] The Council was definitely leaving its mark on the Church,
and Paul VI was clearly determined not to let it fade. The afternoon's penitential procession from the Basilica of the Holy Cross of Jerusalem to the
Basilica of St. John Lateran was another, more symbolic way of bringing
out the Church's need to do penance, to be converted, and to reform.

In retrospect, the opening celebration and the Pope's address seemed
completely in accord with Paul VI's actions during the intersession.

---

[15] Examples of this simplification abounded: no tiara, no chair carried in, no court
around the pontiff, a simple crucifix as pastoral staff, no kissing of his feet, simple vestments, no entrance procession, no stream of cardinals coming up to greet the Pope, Gregorian chants sung by the assembly (see *JEdelby*, 242-43; Rynne, IV, 26). Even Congar,
who had been put off by Roman pomp since the beginning of the Council, did not fail to
note the difference (see especially "Le bloc-notes du Père Congar," *ICI* 249 [1965], 2).
See also *TSemmelroth* and Dworschak's diary. The same feelings were expressed by
observers (see, e.g., Horton, *Vatican Diary*, September 14, 1965, 13; and W. B. Blakemore
in his first report of the fourth period).

[16] Many observations on this point can be found. One example is in the diary of Sanschagrin for September 14: "The Mass obeyed all the requirements of the liturgical
renewal: Gregorian chant sung alternately by choir and the crowd (something that could
not have been obtained in the past from the Sistine Chapel choir), recitation of the
antiphons of the Mass with the choir beginning them and everyone else picking them up....
'An austere liturgy!' says *L'Osservatore Romano*, 'with no polyphonic variations disturbing the purity of the common prayer.' This is a novelty in Rome."

His emphasis on charity and unity could be heard all through his weekly addresses at public audiences; the theme of docility to the Holy Spirit could be found in his exhortation of August 28, in which he summoned the fathers to the fourth period. He showed the same determination to involve the Church in concrete ways in the conciliar reforms. His two announcements gave the lie to the rumors of indecisiveness that were beginning to spread regarding him. The fourth period was launched, it seemed, under happy signs.

The reassembled Council had not only evolved in its attitudes or dispositions, but it had a different appearance as well. There were twenty-seven new cardinals. The number of lay auditors, men and women, had been increased (to twenty-three women, twenty-nine men, and, for the first time, a couple, the Alvarezes from Mexico). The presence of the auditors was to be very important, especially in the work of the commissions dealing with schema XIII. The number of non-Catholic observers increased from seventy-six to ninety-nine (101 in October); they represented twenty-eight ecclesial communities. For the first time the Ecumenical Patriarch of Constantinople was represented by a bishop, Msgr. Emilianos.

I. The Synod of Bishops

Although the synod had been desired by the fathers,[17] and Paul VI had made repeated promises about it,[18] the announcement of its establishment took the fathers by surprise.[19] They did not have much time to react,[20] for

---

[17] Recall especially the wish expressed by Maximos IV on November 6, 1963; the proposal made by Cardinal Lercaro on November 8, 1963; and the constant efforts made by M. Hermaniuk, beginning with the work of the preparatory theological commission. See also the contribution of J. Famerée in *History,* 3:121-32. In a letter of September 14, Lercaro wrote, "The solution adopted, it seems to me, reflects to a great extent one of my interventions during the second session" (*Lettere,* 343).

[18] See especially Paul VI's address to the Curia on September 21, 1964; his addresses to the Council fathers on September 29, 1963, November 21, 1964, and at the closing of the third period; and his address at the Consistory when twenty-seven new cardinals were created, on February 25, 1965.

[19] "SURPRISE!... no one expected it," said Msgr. Garrone to *La Croix,* September 17, 1; "There was a great sensation," commented Ph. Delhaye in *L'ami du clergé* 75/39 (1965), 562.

[20] In his Sunday letter Lercaro wrote that the synod of bishops is "certainly one of the great results of the Council and will be a means for the Church to have an effective knowledge of the state of affairs and to make timely provisions for them" (*Lettere,* 346).

on the following day, at the 128th general congregation (the first of this new period), Paul VI was present at the presidents' table for the publication of the Motu Proprio *Apostolica sollicitudo*, the document that established the synod of bishops he had "announced in a summary way" the day before.[21] After a presentation by Cardinal Marella, president of the Commission for Bishops, in which he recalled the circumstances leading to this decision, Msgr. Felici read the text of the Motu Proprio, which was greeted by lengthy applause.[22]

Marella's presentation, however, did not help to lift the veil on the preparation of this Motu Proprio; this remained a well-guarded secret, kept even from the members of the commission responsible for drafting the decree on bishops. Marella said that before establishing the synod the Pope had asked the advice of many bishops and listened to the counsel of experts, but until this day the available documents remain silent about this.[23]

According to Vincenzo Carbone, the idea of a Motu Proprio emerged at the end of 1964 or the beginning of 1965.[24] After carefully studying

---

[21] For the official documents see "Litterae apostolicae Motu proprio datae: Synodus episcoporum pro universa Ecclesia constituitur," *AS* IV/1, 19-24; "Epistula ad Summum Pontificem," *AS* IV/1, 25-26; "Processus verbales congregationum generalium CXXVIII," *AS* IV/1, 65-66; "Congregatio generalis CXXVIII. 15 septembris 1965," *AS* IV/1, 139; "Em.mm P. D. Pauli card. Marella. Relatio super Motu Proprio *Apostolica Sollicitudo*," *AS* IV/1, 140-42. For an English translation of the Motu Proprio, see *Council Daybook, Session 4*, 13-14.

[22] The synod, which is a permanent organ of the Church, allows the bishops of the entire world to share more clearly and more effectively in the pope's care of the whole Church. Though permanent in nature, the synod exercises its role in a temporary and occasional way. There can be three kinds of assembly: ordinary, special, and extraordinary. The synod is made up chiefly of bishops elected by the episcopal conferences, with the pope retaining the privilege of appointing 15 percent of the members. The heads of the Roman congregations participate, except in special assemblies, where this is not specified.

[23] At his reception of the moderators on September 16, Paul VI emphasized once again the studies and the different stages of discussion that led to his announcement. See *JPrignon*, September 16, 1965 (Prignon papers, 1585, 1). It does not come as a surprise to learn that W. Bertrams, who signed an article on the synod in *La Civiltà cattolica* for December 4 (417-23), was involved in the drafting of the Motu Proprio. Prignon seems to have been very well informed about the Pope's intention on the eve of the opening of the fourth period. He wrote: "On the subject of an episcopal council: the Pope continues to speak of it. But he is said to be more in favor of calling together a certain number of bishops, chosen in view of the problems to be discussed, and not according to a set timetable" (Prignon papers, 1145, 3). This is the clearest piece of information we have from before the beginning of the period. The source of this well-founded information may have been Onclin.

[24] V. Carbone, *Paolo VI e la collegialità episcopale* (Brescia: Publications of the Istituto Paolo VI, 1995), 15, 121-23; see also J. Grootaers, "Willy Onclin et sa participation à la rédaction du Décret *Christus Dominus*," in *Actes et acteurs de Vatican II*, 446ff.

the *textus emendatus* of *De episcopis et de dioecesium regimine* during the month of November 1964, Paul VI came to the conclusion that in light of some interventions during the discussion in the hall, the interpretation of no. 5, on the establishment of a synod of bishops, could be debatable. This, at least, is what he said during an audience with Cardinal Marella, whom he had summoned on December 23, 1964, not as president of the commission on bishops but as a member of the Secretariat for Non-Christians. Marella convinced the Pope that since the work of the commission was finished, it was impossible for him to correct the text, except at the express written demand of the Pope, which would justify calling the commission into session again. The two men then agreed to submit the matter to the general secretariat of the Council. The analysis given by two experts agreed with that of the Pope: the text was open to divergent interpretations.

Various solutions were available, including an intervention by the Pope to have the text changed, or a new *Nota explicativa praevia*. Because both of these solutions had shown their limitations when tried at the third session, a third way was agreed upon: a distinction would be made between establishing a synod and setting down the modalities of its establishment. While the assembly called for the institution, it left it to the Pope to determine its concrete modalities. On the basis of this distinction it was decided to opt for a Motu Proprio, the drafting of which was entrusted to the Council for Extraordinary Affairs within the Secretariat of State, under the supervision of Msgr. Samoré and the watchful eye of Paul VI, who followed every stage of the drafting process.[25] The document was ready by August 1965. It remained only to choose the date of publication; Paul VI decided on the opening of the Council.

In general, the fathers were very receptive of the announcement, even though they were not in a position to assess the development of the new institution.[26] The same was true of the non-Catholic

[25] Prignon was told by Bonet that the drafting of the Motu Proprio was done by a commission made up of Roberti, Pinna, and Felici (*JPrignon,* October 10, 1965 [Prignon papers, 1602, 6]). There is no confirmation of this statement. According to Carbone, Paul VI personally made several changes in the text submitted to him.

[26] We must, of course, distinguish between official reactions and confidences shared behind the scenes. The letter that Tisserant addressed to the Pope on September 20 (see *AS* IV/1, 69) and that was approved by the conciliar assembly cannot give the true measure of the satisfaction of the fathers. The same letter thanked the Pope for the encyclical *Mysterium fidei,* although we know that that document had not been welcomed with enthusiasm. In like manner, the applause in the hall, important though it was, did not reflect the sentiments of the Council fathers. The personal diaries of the fathers or the experts, as well

observers[27] and the press, except in the United States, where the beginning of the debate on religious freedom would eclipse all other headlines.[28]

There was a feeling that something was changing the course of the
Roman Curia's long centuries of centralization and ever-increasing
autonomy, and that "the chapter, which some thought had been closed,

as their correspondence, give better insight into their reaction, which was generally very
good, even if still somewhat cautious. "On the subject of the synod: Msgr. De Smedt says
he is not very impressed, and he seems not to attach any great importance to it. He said
at a meeting of the bishops that he was afraid it would not be of much use. But the general view of all those whom I have seen is that we do have the synod, whatever the reasons officially given for it. The thing now exists and in time it may take on a quite different character. Dossetti said this is what he thinks of it, and he ended up granting that it
was a good thing we had obtained this synod from the Holy Father" (*JPrignon,* September 16, 1965 [Prignon papers, 1585, 4]). The group of bishops representing the various episcopal conferences who met at the Domus Mariae seemed quite satisfied at their meeting
on September 17, 1965 (see the minutes in the Baudoux Archive). The most critical commentary that followed upon the Motu Proprio was the one that appeared in *Antiochena*
(J. K., "A propos du *Synodus episcoporum,*" *Antiochena* 11/3 [1965], 5-7). The author said
that the document was a step back by comparison with the conciliar texts already promulgated or about to be promulgated. He was also critical that the synod was established
by means of a papal Motu Proprio. He found that the reasons given for establishing the
synod were quite weak and that the proposed purpose was less the exercise of collegiality than the lightening of the Pope's burden of care for the universal Church. May we see
in this view a reaction of Maximos IV to the synod that Paul VI granted in response to his
request?

[27] The reports of the observers differed along confessional and geographical lines.
North American and English Protestants were enthusiastic (Blakemore, Moorman, Outler,
and Horton). John Moorman remarked: "This was seen by the observers as a very important move. Perhaps the thing that struck us most was that, for the first time, a democratic
element had found its way into the government of the Church of Rome" (*Vatican
Observed,* 156). Horton thought that "this could prove to be the cornerstone of the *aggiornamento*" (*Vatican Diary,*15). Both men thought that the institution would evolve in time
to acquire a more deliberative character. Some European reactions, however, especially
those of the Orthodox, were lukewarm. Thus Msgr. Emilianos added a qualifier to his
favorable reception: "In the eyes of the Orthodox the Patriarch is not above the synod but
within it" (*ICI* 251, 16). O. Clément (*Réforme,* October 9, 1965) admitted that the synod
was an ambiguous fulfillment of the most fruitful promises made in the Constitution on
the Church, a document that was itself ambiguous, but he added: "The important thing,
when all is said and done, is that the synod exists" (reprinted in *ICI* 251, 16). From a distance, L. Vischer gave a more nuanced opinion: "The Motu Proprio emphasizes dependence on the pope, and several of its provisions allow doubt that this will be a real synod,
a real *signum collegialitatis.* The pope alone decides that, and when, it will meet, as well
as the agenda; he decides whether the synod will simply discuss or whether it will cast
votes.... The synod is an occasion for following up on experiences at the Council and for
manifesting the collegiality of the bishops." He concluded that "in the final analysis, the
existence of the synod is more important than the provisions" ("IV. Rapports sur le 2ᵉ Concile du Vatican," *Istina* 11 [1965-66], 218).

[28] See the review of press coverage in *ICI* (October 1, 1965), 21. In the United States,
UPI and AP dispatches had room only for the interventions of Cushing and Spellman. The
debate on religious freedom was presented in a sensational way, in the language of battle.

on the conciliar life of the Catholic Church" had just been reopened.[29] Had not Paul VI himself said that it was the conciliar experience and the benefits that his closer association with the bishops had brought him that had motivated his action? The most enthusiastic were insisting that "something of the Council is thus to be made permanent."[30] They realized that the synod was to be a stable institution and that it was under the authority of the Pope, who would decide on its convocation, the questions submitted to it, and what kind of authority it would have. Above all, the majority of the participants would be elected by the bishops and would represent the bishops of the entire world. Many remarked that the word *collegiality* was not used in the Motu Proprio,[31] although Cardinal Marella did not hesitate to use it,[32] and also that the text did not make any explicit reference to *Lumen gentium*.

At the moment, however, the Pope's announcement gave both the majority and the minority cause to rejoice. Strong opposition from the minority on this subject had been expected, and the outcome had not been certain. The Pope's decision dispensed the Council from a difficult discussion that was far from desired by all.[33] By giving the impression that he had come down in favor of what the fathers wanted, Paul VI gave the

[29] Y. Congar, "Le bloc-notes du Père Congar," *ICI* 249 (1965), 2. Rouquette, in his chronicle in *Études*, likewise interpreted the synod in the light of collegiality.

[30] Garrone, in *La Croix*, September 17, 1965.

[31] This remark was frequently made. Prignon notes it in a commentary by Dossetti: "Like everyone else, of course, he [Dossetti] notes that the document makes no reference to the definition of episcopal collegiality or, to put it more accurately, to the teaching of the Constitution on the Church on this subject.... It seems that in the minds of those who drafted the document the synod is conceived as the Pope's granting of a share in his personal authority rather than as an expression of the universal responsibility which the text on the Church acknowledges bishops to possess" (*JPrignon*, September 16, 1965 [Prignon papers, 1585, 4]). In his diary for September 16, Butler refers to an article published in *L'Avvenire* for September 16 and notes that the Motu Proprio makes no reference to the *De ecclesia* and that thus Rome continues to think in preconciliar terms. The synod, he remarked, was conceived as an exercise of the Pope's personal authority over the Church in its entirety and not as an exercise of the collegial authority of the bishops (*DButler*, September 16, 1965). Somewhat similar remarks can be found in Dworschak's diary, 4 and 6.

[32] See his presentation in the hall on September 15, his signed commentary in *OssRom* for September 16, and his press conference of September 24, published in *OssRom* for September 26. Prignon also notes that Paul VI told the moderators that "he truly wanted to make the synod an expression of episcopal collegiality and that he expected a great deal from it" (*JPrignon*, September 16, 1965 [Prignon papers, 1585, 1]).

[33] Such was the judgment of *ICI* (February 15, 1965), 5. As Carbone observes, a good many *non placet*s or *placet iuxta modum*s could have been expected if the text of the schema had been put to a vote (Carbone, *Paolo VI e la collegialità episcopale,* 132); the first chapter of the *De episcopis* had not obtained a two-thirds yes vote during the third period.

majority the feeling that it had won its case; such, at least, was the perception at the time.[34] Others, however, had the impression that the Pope
had snatched from the majority an even more resounding victory. After
all, Paul VI established the synod on his own and by his own authority.
There were those who understood this very well: "A monsignor of
S. Carlo is exulting over the Motu Proprio: the Pope has trapped the
Council! He did not let something be forced on him but made the decision that pleased him."[35]

What to make of the synod remained a subject of debate. Marella's
press conference on September 24 did not bring much clarity. He clearly
minimized his use of the term *synod,* so laden with meaning. In addition,
he would not hear any suggestion that there could be a conflict between
the synod and the Curia. Paul VI's decision added a new body to the central government of the Church, but the question of reforming the Curia
remained unanswered and would condition the role the synod could have
in the future.

A careful reading of the Motu Proprio quickly shows its limitations.
In addition to the absence of references to *Lumen gentium* and to collegiality, the synod was subject to the authority of the pope for its convocation, its agenda, and the authority to be given to it (the synod could be
deliberative if the pope allowed it to be and if he ratified its decisions).
Moreover, it was the pope who would appoint its permanent general secretary, as well as the special secretaries for each assembly. Despite all
these limitations, however, Paul VI's announcement helped to produce a
calmer atmosphere at the beginning of the fourth period and to mute
somewhat the dramatic end of the third period. Contrary to the impression created by the publication of *Mysterium fidei,* the announcement was
a clear signal that he was not a prisoner of the old guard. In short, by creating the movement that he did, he gave an impulse to the period just
beginning.

Paul VI's action caused a predicament for the Commission for Bishops, since the schema *Christus Dominus,* which was to be discussed during the fourth period, already contained an article on the synod. Now the

[34] See, e.g., Lercaro's letters of September 14, 15, and 19 (*Lettere,* 342-46). Like a
number of others, he hoped at the time that this new institution would develop in a way
that would enable the pope to become familiar with the situation in the whole range of
Churches and thus provide data to balance the action of the Roman bodies, which were
too often knowledgeable only about their local traditions.
[35] *JDupont,* September 15, 6.

commission was faced with a fait accompli: the synod, announced *in concilio*, if it found support in the desires of the fathers, had not been conceived *synodaliter*. The conciliar commission that had accepted the proposals of the assembly had been kept in ignorance of the pontifical initiative.[36] The commission now had to adjust its aim; it did so gracefully at its meeting on September 24.[37]

II. Works and Days

Once the opening ceremonies were finished, the fathers moved into the heart of the proceedings: the discussions of religious freedom and of schema XIII. In his address at the close of the third period Paul VI had insisted that the declaration on religious freedom, far from being "buried," would, along with schema XIII, "crown" the Council. But no one was deceived. While these schemas, which had already undergone trial by fire, would undoubtedly be the chief accomplishments of this final period, they labored under considerable difficulties. They tackled complicated problems, some of which were new or were being approached in a new way or by a new method.

Lively opposition was expected from the minority, which had not let down its guard or relaxed the tension. On August 13, Bishop Sigaud, Archbishop Lefebvre, and Abbot Jean Prou met at Solesmes in order to decide on a strategy. Despite having been sternly rebuked by the Pope, the *Coetus Internationalis Patrum* committed a new offense in September when it sent a circular letter to all the fathers asking for their Roman addresses if they wished to receive advice on how to vote. Having circulated its *animadversiones*, the group prepared for the final battle. How strong the opposition was, how widespread the resistance, and how intense the debate would be were still unknown. Only the results of the votes during this period would give an accurate idea of how much support the *Coetus* would rally; for the moment, the worst was to be feared.

[36] At least there is nothing in the archives of Veuillot and Onclin, two important members of the commission, that allows us to maintain the opposite. My own view differs from Carbone's interpretation: while I readily admit that pope and council cannot be separated, we must distinguish the action of the pope *in concilio* or *synodaliter* from the action of the pope when he acts *motu proprio*.

[37] The commission was anxious, however, to reintroduce into the corrected no. 5 a reference to no. 23 of *Lumen gentium* (see the documentation in Veuillot papers, 1561-65).

The outcome of the discussions on key schemas such as religious freedom and schema XIII would determine whether or not the Council could
complete its agenda before Christmas.[38]

In any case, however, Paul VI's decision to make this the final period of
the Council obliged the fathers to bring their work to a close, with whatever
compromises this might require. The fear remained, however, that overly
stormy debates or overly long or complicated negotiations among the different parties might make it necessary to withdraw some schemas from the
agenda, and these two disputed schemas in particular. To speed up the
debates, Felici had sent the bishops an instruction in July 1965, requiring the
fathers who wished to say something about these two schemas to send in the
text of their statement, or at least a summary of it, to the General Secretariat
by September 9.[39] Although this measure could indeed speed up the process
and not overly polarize the debate, it was not well received by the fathers.
Some asked what kind of debate was possible if the interventions were written over a month in advance and without their being able to take account of
how ideas were developing. Some wondered whether this was not a trick to
enable the General Secretariat to eliminate anything it did not want to hear.

Another pressure weighed on the discussions: the expectations of the
world outside. People were watching the Council, and it would have to
satisfy not only the expectations of Catholics but the hopes of non-
Catholics, believers of other religions, and nonbelievers; several of the
schemas under discussion would contain appeals to men and women of
good will or would have to do with atheists or believers of other religions. In addition, the schemas being discussed, especially schema XIII,
had been the subjects both of extensive consultations of the laity, who
were now expecting results, and of unprecedented press coverage.
By now, the lay auditors were more organically involved in the work of
the conciliar commissions, and their opinions were not unimportant.[40]

[38] The close of the period had not yet been announced, but there were indications that
it would end on December 8. For example, the pamphlet on celebrations that was distributed to the fathers contained a calendar ending on December 8 (see *Missae in quarta perio-
do concilii oecumenici Vaticani II celebrandae* [Vatican City: Vatican Polyglot Press,
1965], 11). Some, however, had thought that the period might be prolonged until Easter
(see NCWC News Service, September 8, 1965).

[39] At the beginning of the period, Cardinal Tisserant, while taking care not to suggest
any restriction on the freedom to speak, asked the fathers to restrain their *cupiditas loquendi*
(lust to speak), because of the pressure to finish the Council (see *AS* IV/1, 24).

[40] During the debate on the Declaration on Religious Freedom, Msgr. Maloney made
himself the spokesman for the auditors: "All the auditors, both men and women, approve
the teaching in the schema on religious freedom. They also fervently desire its promulgation" (ibid., 322).

Nor were the fathers unaware of the pressure that the non-Catholic observers were bringing to bear on the Council. In fact, at one point there was even thought of not inviting them for the fourth period. But the question of credibility immediately arose: Was the Catholic Church really sincere or was the Council only a kind of stratagem for drawing the separated brethren into the Catholic Church? Paul VI's announcement of his intention to appear at the General Assembly of the United Nations was still another source of pressure.

A. Religious Freedom

At last, on September 15, the debate on religious freedom began in the conciliar hall, while several lectures on the subject were given to various audiences around Rome.[41] This text, the discussion of which in the third period had ended dramatically, had a long history.[42] It had gone through several printed versions, and there had been many other drafts. During the intersession it had been extensively recast on the basis of the intervention by Msgr. Carlo Colombo during the third period[43] and of the 218 suggested corrections sent in writing to the Secretariat for Christian Unity,[44] and under the watchful eye of the United States episcopate.

---

[41] John Courtney Murray lectured at the Dutch Documentation Center on the development of doctrine and showed how papal teaching since Leo XIII had gradually dealt more profoundly with religious freedom (for the text see *Council Daybook, Session* 4, 14-17). Murray had also written a number of articles on the subject before the beginning of the fourth period (see, for example, "This Matter of Religious Freedom," *America* 112 [January 9, 1965] 40-43; it was also published in Italian in *Aggiornamenti Sociali* 16 (April 1965) 303-10 and in German in *Wort und Wahrheit* 6-7 [June-July, 1965] and 8-9 [August-September, 1965]). On September 15, Martelet, too, gave a lecture on religious freedom to a group of bishops of the Pan-African Conference (see "Sur la vraie nature de la liberté religieuse" [Archives of the Diocese of Bordeaux, 1D9.96.19.301]). On September 16, Congar lectured on the subject to African bishops at their residence on the Via Traspontina.

[42] For a broad survey of the history of the text on religious freedom see S. Scatena, "Lo schema sulla libertà religiosa: momenti e passaggi dalla preparazione del concilio alla seconda intersessione," *Experience*, 347-417; see also *History*, vol. 4, chap. 7, sections 3.3.1 and 3.3.2.

[43] See also Colombo, "La libertà religiosa," *La Rivista del clero italiano* 46/6 (June 1965), 309-21. The *textus reemendatus* was composed by the same special subcommission that had been elected at Arricia in 1964; it included Bishops Shehan, Cantero, Primeau, and De Smedt (reporter), and Fr. O. Degrijse; the experts were Pavan, Hamer, Murray, White, and Congar, who lent his help at this stage.

[44] See, among other places, *AS* IV/1, 605-881.

During the summer of 1965 the fathers received a new version,[45] followed by a lengthy report,[46] which in its second part explained in detail the idea of religious freedom used in the schema. Despite the frustrations caused by the suspension of the vote at the end of the third period, the schema seemed to have benefited from the postponement.[47] Civil freedom in the area of religion was clearly distinguished from several other forms of freedom, among them moral freedom and freedom of conscience. The subject of the schema was clearly limited to external juridical and civil freedom, which prevents any human authority from forcing persons to act against their conscience in the area of religion.

The schema, which was not divided into chapters, had three parts: a statement of principle about the Church's recognition of religious freedom, which is based on the dignity of the human person and on revelation; a presentation of the doctrine of religious freedom on the basis of rational arguments; and a discussion of the matter in the light of divine revelation. The report sent out to the fathers anticipated many objections and seemed to narrow considerably the scope of the schema by clearly marking out its limits. In addition to this official report, Murray gave numerous explanations of the schema in an effort to win over the greatest possible number of the fathers.[48] Despite everything, however, no one

---

[45] It contained, in side-by-side columns, the *textus emendatus* and the *textus re-emendatus* (*AS* IV/1, 145-67). This text, the sending of which Paul VI approved on May 28, had been worked up during February 1965, before being submitted to the plenary meeting of the secretariat at the beginning of March, communicated to the doctrinal commission at the beginning of April, and approved by the Coordinating Commission at its meeting of May 7-11. After all these stages it underwent slight changes at the plenary meeting of the secretariat on May 7-11.

[46] For the report, see *AS* IV/1, 168-99. Murray and Pavan worked closely with De Smedt on the drafting of the report. Feiner also "made important contributions, in addition to taking on the *labor improbus of pars prima* (in that he was heroic!)" (Murray to De Smedt, August 27, 1965, in De Smedt papers, 1455). It was submitted for discussion and approval by the secretariat and by one of its members (Hamer) who had been absent. The first part of the report, after briefly recalling the origin of the declaration and its travels through the Council (168-70), considered the various *animadversiones* submitted to the secretariat (170-82). The second part, titled "De methodo et de principiis schematis," first studied the idea of liberty that was at issue in the schema (183-85), before talking about the method of the schema (185-86), explaining its teaching (186-89), and touching on the difficulties the teaching raised (189-192). It ended with some thoughts on the subject of rights, on the nature of the state, and on public order (192-95).

[47] This was acknowledged by Congar (see *Documents épiscopats*, June 14, 1965, 1) and by Murray. See also Rouquette, *Études*, 868.

[48] Murray's debate with de Broglie is well known. Less well known is his correspondence with Cardinal Browne. The last exchange of letters between the two came only a few days before the opening of the fourth period (Murray papers, 18:1004 [letter of Browne to Murray, September 4, 1965]). In a letter to De Smedt, dated June 25, 1965, Murray

thought that the minority would give up without a fierce battle that could result in the schema's being watered down.[49]

As before, it was Msgr. De Smedt[50] who gave the report that inaugurated a new period in the debate on religious freedom.[51] After noting that the great majority of the 218 written observations received were favorable to the text, the Bishop of Bruges went on to remind his hearers once again of the specific purpose of the declaration and of its foundation, since most of the objections sprang from a misunderstanding of the purpose of the schema; that is, they confused civic freedom in religious matters with other kinds of freedom (moral, ontological, psychological, and so on). In conclusion, he asserted that while the modern idea of religious freedom is not explicitly found in the gospel, there is no opposition but rather an accord between evangelical freedom and the religious freedom of which the schema speaks. He also observed that from the viewpoint of the Secretariat for Christian Unity there was no opposition between what was said in the schema and the doctrinal principles governing relations between Church and state.

As the debate would show, this set of remarks, as well as all the precautions set down in the long written report accompanying the schema, was not superfluous. From the very beginning of the debate the discussion would focus on the traditional character of this teaching and on its scriptural basis and, above all, would move completely away from the specific subject of the schema and into the area of moral freedom rather than that of civic freedom of religion. As was remarked, one could believe that some did not understand the question at all.[52]

1. First Morning: Setting their Sights

After all these preliminaries, the debates of the fourth period could at last begin. During the summer, both sides had polished their weapons for

---

spoke of his desire to convince Browne at least not to attack the schema. After all, Murray said, my mother was Irish (De Smedt papers, 1454).

[49] See *DDworschak,* September 14, 1965, 2.

[50] On De Smedt's role in the development of the schema on religious freedom, see M. Lamberigts, "Msgr. Émile-Josef De Smedt, Bishop of Bruges," *Experience,* 431-69 (on the fourth period, see 460-67).

[51] See "Relatio super schema Declarationis De libertate religiosa," in *AS* IV/1, 196-99. In preparing the report, De Smedt consulted Murray. See especially Murray's letters to De Smedt dated June 25, 1965, and August 27, and the corrections Murray made to the draft of De Smedt's report (De Smedt papers, 1454-56).

[52] The remark came from Dupont (*JDupont,* September 15, 1965, 5) after the interventions of Siri and Ruffini.

the debate. A statement of the Archbishop of Madrid on July 13 did not forecast any relaxation of the opposition from the Spanish bishops,[53] a group of Italian bishops, and some members of the *Coetus Internationalis Patrum*. Determined not to yield to pressure this time, the United States bishops were ready for the debate. In August, Murray had written to Cardinal Ritter, suggesting that he prepare a set of interventions that would follow a well-planned sequence and would tackle all the important doctrinal themes involved in the schema.[54] But the bishops of the United States were not the only ones who supported the schema. Their neighbors to the north, the Canadian bishops, supported it unreservedly,[55] as did a sizeable group of French bishops, despite their somewhat different conception of the foundation of religious freedom.

[53] In his New Year's message (December 30, 1964) General Franco had given his support to "a just and properly understood religious freedom." In his July statement Msgr. Morcillo González took a firm stand on the traditional position of tolerance, arguing that even evil and error must be tolerated. While he thought it "difficult to find a passage in the scriptures that had to do with full religious freedom," he acknowledged that because of "ecumenism and the socialization of international relations and for the good of the entire universal Church, it could be prudent — though not on philosophical or theological grounds — to promulgate a law of religious freedom for Spain." But, he emphasized, "for the sake of the ecumenical spirit, the separated brethren must abstain from any proselytism or any attempt to evangelize Spain, which is already a Christian country. If ecumenism is a quest of unity, then to shatter the unity of a Christian country would be to act in a despicable and senseless way" (NCWC News Service, July 13, 1965). A new law on religious freedom in Spain would be introduced on September 10, 1965.
[54] Letter of Murray to Ritter, August 13, 1965, with a handwritten addition from Primeau (Murray papers, 18, 1001). There is a variant of this addition in the Primeau Archive. The sequence was to be the following: Spellman (freedom); Cushing (freedom as a positive value); Ritter (explain that freedom and its protection are part of the common good); Shehan (development of doctrine); O'Boyle (religious freedom is not indifferentism but a true image of the Church); Primeau (religious freedom and Christian freedom within the Church); Hallinan (religious freedom and schema XIII). See *Council Daybook, Session 4*, for the speeches of Spellman (21), Hallinan (27), Shehan (34), and *American Participation in the Second Vatican Council*, ed. V.A. Yzermans (New York: Sheed and Ward, 1967) 656-64.
[55] At the beginning of September the Canadian Episcopal Conference printed and distributed a twenty-seven-page article by Murray ("Remarks on the Schema on Religious Liberty"). In addition, the opinions expressed to Léger and Roy were entirely favorable, even though they included suggestions for improvement and were more cautious in tone (see the opinions of Arès, Ryan, Lafortune, and Naud in Léger papers, 2035, 2050, 2051). For Roy, see AAQ 21 CM, vol. 13. The Baudoux team (Baudoux, De Roo, Hacault), which had been preparing for the fourth period, agreed on three interventions in support of the schema. De Roo would deal with the timeliness of the declaration; Hacault would show that the declaration was faithful to the traditions of the Church; and Baudoux would show that the declaration was nuanced and balanced. None of these interventions was to be read in the hall.

For lack of time, only eight of the twenty-one fathers listed were able to speak on the first day of debate;[56] in accordance with the rules governing precedence, all of them were cardinals. Even more important, in these eight interventions the fathers heard the voices of only five countries,[57] all of them belonging to either North America or western Europe. Despite this limited representation of the diverse worlds present at the Council, these interventions did give a first idea of the tendencies that would be expressed in the debates of the coming days. If we look at the morning of September 15 as a literary whole,[58] it can be described as an inclusion: the very strongly committed United States Cardinals Spellman (first speaker) and Cushing (next-to-last speaker) opened and closed the debate; between these two was voiced the no-less-foreseeable resistance of Cardinals Siri[59] and Ruffini, who were hoping to form an alliance with the Spanish bishops, represented by Cardinal de Arriba y Castro[60] and, beyond them, with the Spanish world.

It is possible to characterize in various ways the different literary motifs in this inclusion. One of them is that of the philosophical a prioris at work. One could say, for example, that the two interventions of the United States bishops took as their starting point the needs of the present age: "Since especially in present day…," "this is today a pastoral need of the first importance."[61] Both referred to the pastoral context (for Spellman, the credibility of the Church in the eyes of states and non-Catholics; for Cushing, the credibility of the Church in its preaching of the gospel), to the concrete world, to the life of the Church, to the life of human beings in society, and to the expectations of contemporaries.[62] The interventions of Ruffini and of Siri, in particular, were on a different level: defense of

[56] For the minutes of the 128th through 132nd general congregations, during which the schema was discussed, see AS IV/1, 145-67 and 65-71.

[57] Italy (3), United States (2), Germany, Spain, and the Netherlands.

[58] For the interventions of the 128th general congregation, see AS IV/1, 200-19.

[59] On September 5, Siri sent a letter to the Pope that gives a glimpse of his great confusion about the schema (see AS V/3, 352-53).

[60] A softening of the Spanish positions was expected as a result of events during the intersession. The Congress of Catholic Jurists, sponsored by Pax Romana in Salamanca (September 8-13, 1965), issued a six-point final communiqué that endorsed the conciliar declaration. In addition, Congar had gone to Spain during the summer (end of July-beginning of August 1965). On the other hand, J. Urresti's "Observationes et correctiones ad schema declarationis *De libertate religiosa*" (July 30, 1965) did not suggest that resistance was at an end, an impression confirmed by de Arriba y Castro's intervention.

[61] Spellman (whose address had been prepared by Murray), 200; Cushing, 215-16. Different ways of saying "today" appear five times in Cushing's intervention.

[62] The question of the credibility of the Church would reappear at regular intervals in this discussion. It would be taken up again on the third day in the discussion between Heenan and Baldassari.

the "divine order" and the "divine law" (Siri) and of the "true religion"
(Ruffini). The former approach was concrete and historical, the latter
metaphysical and ahistorical. For the one side, persons were the subjects
of rights; for the other, truth is the object of a right. These two divergent
approaches were clearly brought out by Cardinal Heenan on the third day
of the debate: "It seems absurd to say that error in itself (or truth in itself)
has rights. For rights have their place in persons alone and never in
things."[63] A different starting point led Ruffini to assert the duty of the
state to worship God and to further the true religion, and de Arriba y Castro to assert that "the Catholic Church alone has the right and duty to
preach the gospel,"[64] a position that clearly contradicted the Decree on
Ecumenism that the Council had adopted during the third period. With
such different philosophical a prioris, it was difficult to reach a common
position.

As fascinating as it may be, the literary device of inclusion with its
bipolar structure is nevertheless unable to give a real account of the events
of this first day. More significant still was the emergence between these
two "strong minorities" of a very important middle way that strengthened
the hopes of moderates. Frings, despite his very substantial criticisms,[65]
and Alfrink, in particular by some concrete suggestions, helped move the
debate forward, while clearly endorsing the principle of the declaration.
The agreement of Urbani in the name of thirty-two Italian bishops was
a good omen for what followed. Paul VI's decision to entrust Urbani
with the presidency of the Italian Episcopal Conference seemed to be
yielding the dividends the Pope had counted on, and the endorsement of
the schema by Msgr. C. Colombo was finally bearing fruit.[66] This first
Italian shift of allegiance[67] thus opened a breach in the front that might

[63] *AS* IV/1, 295.

[64] Ibid., 209.

[65] Frings supported the principle of the declaration and the direction taken in it but
nevertheless suggested important revisions: an expansion of the first part (the declaration
itself, with additions on the limits of religious freedom, the role of civil authority, the
rights of the family and of religious communities); and the elimination of the second part,
with its rational arguments used to found religious freedom. He suggested some other
changes as well: on the recognition of a particular religion and, in no. 9, on the foundation of religious freedom in the history of salvation (*AS* IV/1, 201-3).

[66] See, in addition to C. Colombo's article cited earlier, the sixteen-page report that he
gave at the meeting of bishops of the Lombardy and Veneto regions (August 17-19, 1965).
On several points there was a clear bond of kinship between Colombo's report and the
intervention of Urbani, who had probably attended that meeting.

[67] This was to be followed, on day three of the discussion, by that of Baldassari, who
spoke in the name of twenty bishops of the Emiliana and Flaminia regions (*AS* IV/1, 311).

have been expected to form among countries living under a system of concordats.

During this first morning of debate almost all the subjects involved had been raised: the discussion of physical, psychological, and moral freedom (Urbani, Spellman, Ruffini); the relationship of what was said in the schema to the doctrinal tradition of the Catholic Church (Siri, Cushing, Urbani); state recognition of a particular religion, especially in the form of a concordat (Ruffini, de Arriba y Castro, Frings, Alfrink); the acceptance of tolerance rather than of an assertion of religious freedom (Siri, de Arriba y Castro); the question of subjectivism and indifferentism (Ruffini, Siri), and so on. Most of the arguments to come in the debate could be related to this basic nucleus of themes.

2. The Schema Comes under Heavy Fire

While the discussion on the first day, like the overture to an opera, gave a good idea of the various positions and themes, no one could have imagined, in even the worst scenario, that the schema would be the object of such powerful opposition. Some, like Congar, were optimistic because they did not see any great difficulties in the text of the schema.[68] But, despite all the clarifications given in the written and oral reports, the attack on the schema that was now to begin was directed as much against a phantom as against the actual letter of the schema. The same arguments the opponents had used during the third period were to be brought up again. The most threatening specter seemed to be the development of the traditional Catholic teaching.

a. Dangerous Innovation or Traditional Teaching?

The great limitation of discussion at the Council was that there was no genuine debate in which the speakers really interacted; instead, addresses were read out that had been written before the discussion had even begun. At the same time, there were clashes, as could be seen in

---

See also the open-minded remarks of Bergonzini and his assessment of the interventions of Urbani, Siri, Ruffini, Carli, Nicodemo, and Florit. The Italian episcopate did not form a monolithic bloc on the subject of religious freedom (see M. Bergonzini, *Diario del concilio* [Modena, 1993], 173-74).

[68] In his article in *Documents épiscopats*, Congar wrote: "It seems that the schema ought to be very widely accepted since it takes its stand on the foundation of *immunitas a coactione* [immunity from coercion] and leaves room for the assertion of the objective eternal law, the duty of seeking the truth, the oneness of the true Church, and even the possibility of a confessional state."

the interventions on the first morning. Whereas Siri cast doubt on the
theological sources used and on the doctrinal agreement of the schema
with the Catholic tradition, Cushing claimed that "the schema's teaching on the right of human beings to freedom in religious matters is
solidly based on Catholic doctrine,"[69] and Urbani argued that while
pontifical documents, especially those of recent popes, did not explicitly pronounce on religious freedom, they did shed light on connected
questions: the dignity of the person and relations between persons and
states.

These crisscrossing and clashing arguments raised some particular
problems, such as the interpretation of tradition, doctrinal development,
and the use of scripture in conciliar documents. Albert Outler was not
mistaken when he wrote, before the period began, that if the Declaration on Religious Freedom were to be adopted, "it will be the most
drastic break with the tradition of *piononismo* of all the conciliar
actions."[70] But the debate showed that this would not happen without
bitter discussions.

Almost all the opponents of the schema attacked its biblical basis.[71]
Morcillo González claimed that the biblical arguments used were incomplete, selective, and tendentious. Modrego maintained that the statements
taken from revelation "neither prove nor confirm the thesis of a natural
right to full freedom in religious matters."[72] Carli asserted that the interpretation of the Bible in the schema was invalid because it contradicted
tradition, "which is no less part of revelation than scripture is."[73]
He found fault with the schema's one-sided approach to scripture, that is,
to its selection of passages that fit in with its thesis while blocking out
all the passages that denounce false religions. In addition, he said, the
texts taken from the Old Testament deal only with psychological freedom

[69] *AS* IV/1, 215.

[70] Outler, "Vatican II – Between Acts," 15.

[71] The report on the re-emendation of the schema had foreseen this attack when it said
that "a great distance, so to speak, can be seen between the teaching of scripture and the
modern concept of religious freedom in society" (*AS* IV/1, 186). Carli took advantage of
this remark to claim that the commission, faced with the choice of agreeing with the teaching of scripture or watering it down, had chosen the latter.

[72] Morcillo (*AS* IV/1, 247-48); Modrego (ibid., 255).

[73] *AS* IV/1, 264-65. On August 31, 1965, in a twelve-page document for the Italian
Episcopal Conference, Carli had given his "Osservazioni e proposte di emendamenti al
nuovo testo dello schema sulla Libertà religiosa." After listing in twelve points the positive aspects of the *textus reemendatus* (about one page), his text devoted two pages to the
debatable aspects of the schema and then explained his suggested improvements (see
Paul VI papers, A2/29).

and offer no proof of a natural right to religious freedom. Similar fault-finding can be seen in Ottaviani's intervention.[74] While other fathers (Elchinger, Baldassari) also expressed reservations about the use of scripture in the schema, they did so from a completely different perspective.

Opponents of the draft also attacked the way the Church's tradition was interpreted in terms of doctrinal development, the issue raised in contrasting ways on the first day by Siri and by Cushing and Urbani. On the second day of the debate, the Maronite Patriarch of Antioch immediately posed the problem: "One hundred years after Pius IX's condemnations of the errors of his time concerning the true concept of religious freedom,... our Council is turning its attention to the same difficult problem of freedom, but with a different outlook and in different historical circumstances."[75] At this point the discussion was not so much about the specific problem of religious freedom as about the problem of the development of doctrine, that is, whether doctrine is open to evolution because of changed mentalities and historical circumstances.

To Siri and Morcillo, who were of the view that the teaching of the popes since Leo XIII was practically ignored in the schema, we must add the names of Modrego y Casáus, who maintained that "the teaching in the schema certainly contradicts ... the explicit teaching of the Roman pontiffs up to and including John XXIII"; of Velasco, who judged that "our schema ... perverts the doctrine taught for centuries by the magisterium of the Church"; and of Tagle, who spoke in the name of forty-five Latin American fathers.[76] In addition, interventions by Gasbarri, Del Campo y de la Bárcena called for revising the schema in accordance with "the teaching of the Roman pontiffs from Pius IX to our time," and Ottaviani said that the declaration not only refused to abstain from controverted questions but also gave solutions to them, "solutions that are for the most part contrary to common teaching."[77] For this reason he asked that the declaration be corrected so that it would "be in accord with the earlier teaching of the Catholic Church." In Modrego's view, this contradiction of older teaching was shown by the fact that the declaration

---

[74] Ottaviani said that the citations were chosen in a one-sided way and that all the passages were omitted that condemned those who refused to accept the gospel (AS IV/1, 300).

[75] Ibid., 233.

[76] Siri, AS IV/1, 207-9; Morcillo, ibid., 247; Modrego, ibid., 255-56; Velasco, ibid., 252. Velasco's intervention was perhaps the most harshly argued of the debate. He directly reproached the secretariat for not having taken into account the observations of the "glorious minority." See also Tagle, ibid., 275.

[77] Gasbarri, ibid., 327; Del Campo, ibid., 317; Ottaviani, ibid., 299.

clashed with some clauses in concordats signed by the Holy See. The opposition between traditional teaching and the statements in the schema was also found in other interventions, for example, though to a lesser degree, in that of Nicodemo.[78]

By locating themselves on this ground, these bishops were naturally led to pull phantoms of the past from the cupboard. Thus Velasco, repeating ideas almost identical with those voiced by Ruffini and Siri, found that the schema encouraged pragmatism, indifferentism, religious naturalism, and subjectivism. Tagle, too, found fault with it for favoring indifferentism and liberalism. Similar accusations were repeated on the third day by Ottaviani (irenicism), Del Campo (naturalistic humanism), Pereira (indifferentism), Gasbarri (laicism, indifferentism, existentialism, irenicism, situation ethics), and De Sierra y Mendez (naturalism, indifferentism).[79] Those who perceived these dangers were given solid answers in the remarkable intervention of Jaeger,[80] who spoke for 150 fathers, and in the serene intervention of Msgr. Silva Henriquez, in whose view the schema, far from promoting indifferentism, led to responsibility.[81]

Phrasing the question in terms of the encyclicals of recent popes presupposed an earlier problematic, different from the one the declaration clearly desired to engage. The question of right, in particular, would give rise to numerous commentaries. Thus, instead of engaging the question of the rights of persons, the rights of God were invoked (Baldassari, García y Mendez) and the right of truth and of error (Velasco, Carli, Florit, Pereira). The schema was blamed for treating truth and falsehood alike — the latter can only be tolerated — and for putting the true religion and false religions on the same level (Ottaviani). The schema was too complacent toward the false religions, to which, instead, the traditional thesis of toleration must be applied (de Arriba y Castro, Tagle, Pereira, and, to a lesser degree, Lokuang).

---

[78] His reservation had to do only with no. 3, on the limits of civil authority; this statement did not seem to him to be in keeping with the teaching of the encyclicals (ibid., 243-44).

[79] Velasco, ibid., 252-54; Tagle, ibid., 275. Marafini expressed a similar fear, but much more moderately (ibid., 170-71). See also ibid. for Ottaviani (299-302), Del Campo, 314-18, Pereira (323-25, especially his notes on 324), Gasbarri (325-26), and De Sierra y Mendez (328-31). Baraniak did not accuse the schema of flirting with these errors, but rather warned "against erroneous interpretations of our text, as though it promoted indifferentism, relativism, indifferentism" (ibid., 307).

[80] Ibid., 239-42. For further remarks see Jaeger's lecture on September 16.

[81] Ibid., 226-33.

It was, however, precisely from the application of this double standard that the schema intended to extricate the Church.[82] Thus Heenan pointed out that the Church cannot appeal to the "rights of truth" when Catholic are in the majority, and on that basis suppress the freedom of non-Catholics, yet be in favor of freedom when Catholics are in the minority and the Church is not supported by the state.[83]

Some of the opponents also wanted a return to the traditional assertion of the duties of the state in regard to religion (Morcillo, Modrego, Marafini) and of the rights of the Catholic Church as the only true religion (Lokuang, Cooray, Pereira, Ottaviani). Ottaviani wanted the schema to begin with a solemn proclamation that "the Catholic Church has a true, innate, objective right to its freedom, because it has a divine origin and a divine mission."[84] Although Jaeger replied that the schema *did* contain the statement that Catholicism is the only true religion, the critics did not regard this as enough.

This approach to rights, different from that of the schema, would lead to the use of various kinds of argument. The one with the greatest impact was the one elaborated by Cardinal Florit (Florence) that there are two kinds of right involved: a natural right common to all human beings and a supernatural right possessed only by Christians and proper and peculiar to the Church.[85] This argument, also used by Ottaviani, was repeated in different forms by Del Campo y de la Bárcena,[86] Gasbarri,[87] and García y Mendez.[88]

The danger was that of returning, step by step, to the double standard attacked by Heenan; that is, claiming for the Catholic Church a freedom

---

[82] The position was mentioned whenever the opponents of the schema called for "toleration" rather than freedom for those in error. Gasbarri appealed to it explicitly when he invoked "thesis" and "hypothesis," depending on the historical and social context.

[83] *AS* IV/1, 295.

[84] Ibid., 299.

[85] Ibid., 284. This intervention repeated almost verbatim a text of Florit, written on September 6, that was circulated by the Italian Episcopal Conference on September 9. Following Urbani's lead, Florit tried to pass himself off as a mediator, but few were deceived. Dupont remarked: "Florit sets himself up as a mediator; in fact, he is a mediocre reactionary" (*JDupont*, September 17, 1965, 10).

[86] The argument in his case was slightly different because he spoke of rights belonging to different orders: "the rights of the human person" and "the rights of God" (*AS* IV/1, 315).

[87] He distinguished between genuine right and the positive law that is in force in societies and that can sometimes tolerate error (ibid., 326).

[88] He spoke of divine right, belonging to the supernatural order, in contrast to natural or human right: "The right of the Church is based on her divine mission; it is of the supernatural order, indeed it is the right of God. The right to religious freedom is based on the natural dignity of the human person; it is natural, it is man's law" (ibid., 329).

not allowed to others. Can Catholicism be grouped among other religions
and granted only the same right to freedom? (Pereira). Does the Church
not have an exclusive right to preach the gospel? (Ruffini, García y
Mendez[89]); in other words, "is the Roman Catholic religion the only true
religion and the one Church of Christ?" (Cooray, Pereira).[90] It is clear that
the schema's subject was closely tied to other conciliar documents, especially the documents on ecumenism and on non-Christian religions.

The discussion, then, took place in terms of an older problematic and
not the one that the draft had addressed. In the background could be seen
the *Syllabus* of Pius IX and the various condemnations of succeeding
popes. As in the first period, the Council had to locate itself in the line
of continuity or in the line of progress, to use De Smedt's categories.
Despite the protestations of both sides, it was obviously very difficult for
the Council to take a fresh approach to questions sabotaged by the old
problematic. It was in vain that Maloney explained that the schema did
not say that one who errs has the right to err, but said rather that such a
person had a right to act without coercion.[91]

b. Between Two Minorities:
   The Churches of Different Catholic Worlds

The dividing line in the debate on religious freedom was clearly not
the same as that between the classic minority and majority that had
emerged since the beginning of the Council's work. Some suggested that
the line here was between the United States fathers and the Spaniards;
others thought that it was between countries where Catholics were a
majority and those where they were a minority.[92] None of these distinctions is completely satisfactory. In fact, a different majority and a different minority were being built. The members of the classic majority had
somewhat different views on the subject of religious freedom. No longer
led by the leading lights of the first period, the majority was disoriented
and momentarily uncoordinated, almost paralyzed.

As for the minority, this now had at least two components: the curial
cardinals and the *Coetus Internationalis Patrum*. Although anxious not to
be confused with each other, the groups shared common interests. The
Coetus had a program and a strategy that enabled it to engage in concerted

---

[89] Ibid.
[90] Cooray, ibid., 282-83; Pereira, 323.
[91] Ibid., 321.
[92] This distinction was Edelby's (*JEdelby*, September 15, 1965, 244).

action.[93] In its opposition to the draft it could, at least for the time being, also count on the support of a good many Spanish fathers, which made the group even bolder, to the point that there was danger of its becoming counterproductive.[94]

While religious freedom seemed dangerous to Churches of the Mediterranean basin that were protected by concordats, it was assessed quite differently by Churches in countries with different historical experiences such as the Church in the the United States and Churches living in communist countries and in situations where Christians were a minority. Any majority that might emerge, then, would have to be built on a new foundation. Cardinal Conway recalled that the Irish had been deprived of the right to religious freedom for almost two centuries,[95] a sentiment strongly echoed by those who were being deprived of that freedom at the moment, especially the countries behind the Iron Curtain. Thus the entire Polish episcopate seemed to rally to the cause, with Baraniak speaking in its collective name. Cardinal Šeper argued from "particular experiences" that religious freedom was a condition for the flowering of religious life and represented a fundamental necessity for the exercise of the Church's mission.[96] The strong support given by Henriquez, although anticipated, proved equally important because it showed that South America as a whole would not follow the line set by the Spaniards, as had been the case especially during the third period.

Other points raised in the discussion of the first few days were the idea of "public order" used in the schema (Arambaru and Nicodemo[97]) and the idea of a "confessional state." On these two questions the participants outside the Mediterranean world gave the discussion a special depth. Argentinean Arambaru first called attention to the question of public order, stating that Christians can always be accused of upsetting public order. This can be the case under a communist regime as well as in settings where discrimination is denounced by the preaching of the gospel. As history shows, Christianity brings challenges, and if the idea of public order means that no one may challenge the established social order,

---

[93] See Luc Perrin, "Il Coetus Internationalis Patrum e la minoranza conciliare," in *Evento*, 173-88.

[94] Hermaniuk was doubtless not the only one to be "irritated by the Spanish and Italian attacks on freedom: these people see only the particular situation in their own countries" (reported in *JDupont*, September 16).

[95] *AS* IV/1, 297.

[96] Ibid., 292.

[97] Aramburu was the first to raise the question, and he did so in a magisterial manner (ibid., 261-63). The remarks of Nicodemi on this matter were limited to asking that the words "common good" be used instead of "public order" (ibid., 244).

then at all times, as well as in the first century, Christians can be accused of harming public order. This idea needs, therefore, to be more closely defined and limited to a legitimate and natural public peace.

The bishops from the communist countries also hammered home this point, beginning with Šeper, who was followed by Baraniak.[98] They said that the idea of public order in the text was ambiguous and could give rise to varying and even abusive interpretations. To forestall mistaken interpretations, these bishops asked that reasonable limits placed on religious freedom in the interests of public order be based on some moral and juridical norm.

If the question of the recognition of a particular religion or of a confessional state came up in intra-European debates (Frings), it was raised on an even broader scale by non-Europeans, few of whom favored a confessional state.[99] Lourdusamy was convinced that it would be better to remove from the schema the lines referring to the recognition, in certain historical circumstances, of a particular religion. In his view, this could be a real obstacle to the spread of Christianity in non-Catholic countries.[100] As for Šeper, if he did not close the door to the idea, he had strong reservations about it. The role of the state, he said, is not to arbitrate among the different religious confessions. Similar views were expressed by the Lebanese bishops, Ziadé of Beirut and Doumith of Sarba.

On still other points constructive suggestions were made by Ziadé (the right to religious freedom of the partners in a mixed marriage),[101] by Frings (the rights of families and religious communities), by Conway (confessional schools), and so on. On other points, the declaration entailed a real examination of conscience, since the Church could not ignore the

---

[98] Šeper observed that any limits placed on religious freedom must be based on rights and conformed to justice. Otherwise, mentioning limits in references to the abuse of religion for political ends opens the way to arbitrary applications (ibid., 294). On September 5, before traveling to the Council, the Yugoslavian bishops published a joint pastoral letter in which they claimed religious freedom on the basis of the dignity of the human person (see *The Tablet* [September 25, 1965], 1073). In the name of the Polish episcopate, Baraniak likewise asked for clarification of the term *coercion,* so that an exhortation to attend mass, for example, would not be considered coercion (*AS* IV/1, 307).

[99] Lokuang (Formosa) claimed that a confessional state was much preferable to a state that was agnostic or indifferent in matters religious. These two situations could not be placed on the same level (ibid., 251). The bishops from communist or Muslim countries, as well as those from India and Scandinavia, were unanimous in asking that this mention of a confessional state be removed.

[100] Ibid., 260.

[101] See ibid., 272.

fact that there once "existed, even in the Church, institutions that acted against religious freedom."[102] Religious persecution had prevented the development of Catholicism at such times.

Throughout this discussion it was clear that different contexts and different situations greatly influenced the positions taken.[103] As Cardinal Journet would say later, pastoral situations led to different assessments of the problem of religious freedom. In pluralist countries this freedom was a pastoral need (as Cushing had said[104]); it was an obvious need in totalitarian countries; it was desired in mission countries, in which Catholics were very much a minority (India, Muslim countries, the East); it seemed suspect in the Mediterranean countries of Europe. Did this mean, as some opponents said, that the application of the principle should be left to the different episcopal conferences or to the different countries?[105] Or from the fact that this freedom was useful in Catholic apologetics, could one argue that the schema should be reduced to a few principles that state the de facto situation or simply acknowledge that religious freedom is demanded by present circumstances?[106] Was the issue simply one of appropriateness or timeliness, or did it concern a universal doctrine, valid everywhere and always, as Spellman urged?[107] Could one infer a right from these varied historical situations and these varied experiences? Could socio-religious facts, as Del Campo y de la Bárcena described them, especially pluralism and the solemn proclamation of religious freedom in the constitutions of states (Conway), constitute an argument in favor of an absolute and universal juridical principle of religious freedom?[108]

Some people smelled a trap in all this, and the arguments were often only delaying tactics for rejecting the schema. Still, they sowed discord

---

[102] A. Baraniak, ibid., 306. This theme would be repeated by Cardinals Beran, Rossi, and Lefebvre.

[103] Jaeger had insisted at length on historical contexts, reminding his hearers that the society of the Middle Ages had disappeared. The subject was also taken up by Meouchi, Slipyi, and others.

[104] Morcillo, too, made reference to pluralism, but from a contrary perspective.

[105] See de Arriba y Castro and Cantero Cuadrado, ibid., 302.

[106] This was the line taken by Morcillo and Pereira; the latter's proposal, in five points, is found as an appendix to his address (ibid., 325). Several speakers, Heenan and Elchinger in particular, had shown the apologetical usefulness of religious freedom in that it removed from the Catholic Church the suspicion of opportunism or duplicity. After the vote, Gagnebet said that the fathers should have been "satisfied with saying that in the present situation freedom is necessary, without seeking to take a doctrinal position" (*JDupont*, September 21, 1965, 21).

[107] *AS* IV/1, 200.

[108] Ibid., 314.

and made the fathers face a new questions: How can a theological discourse be based on historical situations? Can doctrine be historically conditioned? Was the truth not immutable and eternal? Was theology not a
deductive science in which one started with principles and drew from
them practical applications to concrete situations? Not only was the
Council faced with new questions, but the classical methods for reflecting on problems were being tested. In any case, the Council became aware
that the catholicity of the Church and the conciliar majority, which had
gathered around the countries of Central Europe, was no longer able to
lead a Council that now embraced the entire world. Regional interests, so
to speak, became obvious in the hall.

There was a further difficulty: to whom was the schema addressed?
Was it meant solely for Catholics, or did it intend to speak to all people
of good will? Even at this stage of the discussion caution was needed
when it came to the style to be used in the declaration. Meouchi,
the Maronite Patriarch, in particular, was severely critical of the text's
form and terminology, neither of which squared with contemporary forms
of thought and language. In his view, the material should be presented in
much less objective language and according to a method more experiential and relational than theological and philosophical.[109]

Precisely because of the addressees of the text, Rupp suggested that the
Council be satisfied with a declaration inspired to a great extent by the
seven-point declaration developed by the World Council of Churches; to
this end he proposed eliminating parts II and III, thus insinuating that the
argument based on scripture proved nothing.[110] Elchinger was less radical and proposed eliminating the biblical and theological parts, which did
not suit the genre of the document, since the declaration did not claim to
be a dogmatic constitution but only a statement addressed to all of humanity.[111] If the Council really wanted to address the entire human family,[112]
it had to place its discourse on a different foundation and adopt a different tone and a different way of expressing itself. Maloney put the issue
clearly: "Our intention is to speak of something that we have in common

---

[109] Ibid., 233-35.

[110] Ibid., 319. The World Council of Churches' declaration had been approved on
July 11, 1965.

[111] *AS* IV/1, 313. This proposal was the exact opposite of Frings's, who wanted instead
to eliminate the second part, which set forth the arguments from reason.

[112] The problem of the addressees was also brought up by Florit, who supported the
idea that the declaration should be based on the dignity of the human person. He said:
"This method certainly signified that our declaration should be intelligible not to Christians alone but to all peoples" (ibid., 284).

with the whole human family, and therefore we cannot speak the language either of scripture or of anything else; to speak more clearly we have to talk in terms of the personhood given by God."[113]

Here again, however, such criticisms by individuals in favor of the schema risked playing into the hands of the opponents, who also wanted to reduce the scope of the schema as much as they could and, if possible, to dismiss it because of its inadequate argument from reason and the weakness of its proof from scripture.

c. A Shaken Confidence

The first week of the Council's activity ended without the possibility of deciding between the forces at work. As a Canadian bishop noted in his diary: "Opinions are divided"; "no conversion as yet."[114] At all levels the discussion had created more puzzlement than anything else. The confidence of the first days[115] was succeeded by a hesitation that seemed to paralyze the majority in face of a belligerent opposition. Thus this Friday became an occasion for a first assessment of profits and losses.

Certainly, the strong opposition seemed to be having an effect on the bishops themselves. "It cannot be denied that Cardinal Ottaviani gave the impression of accusing the text of trying to canonize or at least to teach very solemnly a doctrine that is still under debate in the Church. Even Msgr. De Smedt said he was impressed."[116] At this stage, then, the schema did not seem sure of success. In fact, "chance meetings with bishops and theologians in St. Peter's showed that minds were wavering. Several bishops said openly that they did not know what they ought to think and how they should cast their votes."[117] Was there going to be another impasse? While some were very optimistic about the outcome of a possible vote, others had reservations. Onclin predicted "at least 400 votes against"; this was close to Laurentin's estimate that less than 80 percent would vote in favor of the schema.[118] The tactics of the opponents seemed

---

[113] Ibid., 321.

[114] Msgr. Sanschagrin, September 16, 1965.

[115] After a meeting with De Smedt on the eve of the day when the latter was to read his report, Dupont wrote: "He is confident of the success of the schema; he does not know what *emendationes* the Coetus Internationalis is proposing" (*JDupont*, September 14, 3).

[116] *JPrignon*, September 17, 1965 (Prignon papers, 1585, 1).

[117] "In the evening a new telephone call from Medina who also had observed a hesitation among the bishops; he is uneasy and strongly insists that there be a vote of preliminary acceptance" (reported by Prignon, ibid., 4)

[118] Ibid., 1.

to be succeeding. Their multiplied interventions had given the impression that the assembly was divided and that a vote would reflect this division. There was even a rumor that as many as a thousand fathers might vote against the schema.

Even individuals in favor of the schema seemed shaken, and some other approaches began to win support: reduce the schema to a simple declaration; rework the proof from scripture; state more clearly "God's right" to be worshiped; and so on. Table talk at the Belgian College attested to a readiness, even among converts to the schema, to accommodate the opponents. "According to De Smedt, Suenens, too, was very impressed by the debates.... He supposedly said during a meeting that he was leaning toward a very short declaration that gave no arguments."[119] Furthermore, that some of the leading figures did not join the fray, as they usually did, caused some to question the quality of the schema. Léger, who had gathered signatures in favor of a vote at the end of the third period, was now silent;[120] Lercaro did not get involved;[121] and the French did not support the schema with much fervor.[122] While the opponents were conducting an intelligent and seemingly well-orchestrated

---

[119] Ibid., 5. According to Prignon, "Our bishops ... are, on the whole, in agreement on the text. They think that we should not be satisfied with a simple declaration but should introduce the justification for it; Msgr. De Smedt has convinced them on this point." "Msgr. Heuschen insists, even to Msgr. De Smedt, that the argument from scripture should be revised." "Msgr. Philips tells me he would prefer a declaration that would, in one or other form, assert the two great principles: ... God wills that he be recognized and adored ... and the other: God wants this to be done freely" (ibid., 4).

[120] On Monday, some bishops asked Sanschagrin: "Why doesn't Cardinal Léger speak out?" In fact, Léger, who unreservedly supported the principle of a declaration on religious freedom, had thought of intervening (see his "Remarques sur le schéma *De libertate religiosa*" and his "Projet de redistribution de la matière du *Schema declarationis de libertate religiosa*" [not delivered], September 1965 [Léger papers, 2031]).

[121] After a conversation with Dossetti, Prignon wrote: "He told me that he would remain passive because he was resigned, just as his cardinal [Lercaro] was.... Dossetti thinks the text on religious freedom is very poor. He too would have preferred a very short but formal, precise, and firm declaration, without the arguments developed in the text" (*JPrignon*, September 16, 1965 [Prignon papers, 1585, 3]). This agrees with a note of Dupont: "Dossetti ... thinks that the schema is hopeless from a juridical standpoint; it completely lacks any basis in positive law. Dossetti adds that he wishes that its scriptural foundations were more solid!" (*JDupont*, September 29, 1965, 51). In the fourth period Lercaro allowed the bishops of the Emilia region to speak in his stead. On religious freedom, see Baldassari's intervention.

[122] While Congar was quite happy with the text (*Document épiscopats* [June 14, 1965]), Elchinger's intervention was very critical, and that of Sauvage unremarkable even though in the French episcopate it was he who was responsible for pursuing the matter (see the file he sent to the bishops on August 31, 1965 [eight documents, including the debate between Murray, de Broglie, and Riedmatten, as well as Féret's contribution]). The French

campaign, there seemed to be no coordinated action of the majority in support of the text. Only the interventions of the United States bishops, who had become truly involved in the Council only after the end of the third period,[123] seemed to have been planned with care.

The "higher authority," whose opinion would certainly count, had not yet completely endorsed the schema, even though the Pope wanted a declaration on religious freedom. The Pope's first interview with the moderators made it possible to test his determination. According to Suenens' report of the meeting, the Pope said he had been "very impressed by the arguments of Siri, Ruffini, and the archbishop of Tarragona." He had also received letters very critical of the schema, even from bishops in favor of religious freedom,[124] and his judgment on the text was therefore nuanced:

> He was not especially for it, nor was he against it; he certainly wanted some declaration; he would like the arguments to be curtailed for fear of future abuses, especially by civil governments; he seemed to expect the moderators to make a proposal, namely, to submit the text once more to a new, more theological commission, but the moderators carefully avoided doing so in view of the urgency, the circumstances, and the fear of the false impression that the announcement of such a new reworking of the schema would give,

bishops' reservations about the schema are well known; they thought it was based too much on the juridical argument developed by Murray. The latter, who wanted the schema to be restricted to the question of civil liberty in religious matters, remained quite critical of the position of Elchinger, who wanted the schema to establish a complete theology of freedom (see Murray to De Smedt, June 25, 1965 [De Smedt papers, 1454]). de Provenchères, who had Cottier for his expert, found himself "utterly unable" to make his own an intervention prepared by Congar; he wondered whether it was possible "to set forth as the teaching of the Church [certain propositions], when these were still being debated among the schools" (de Provenchères to Congar, August 23, 1965, in Congar papers, 1264). But in the dossier of the French bishops he had written (June 23, 1965): "I am very pleased with this schema." Cottier had expressed his views on the subject in several articles during the intersession (see especially "La liberté religieuse," *Études*, 322 (April 1965) 443-59.

[123] Cardinal Cushing, for example, did not remain in Rome during the first two periods, because he did not see what he could contribute to the Council. The situation was reversed at the end of the third period, when he spoke on religious freedom in the name of the United States episcopate. The refusal to allow a vote on this schema was the stimulus needed to mobilize that episcopate, which would not yield during the fourth period.

[124] *JPrignon,* September 16, 1965 (Prignon papers, 1585, 1). Prignon reports that Suenens told him that Paul VI "had given the moderators some letters he had received that brought out the difficulties of the text. The Cardinal [Suenens] said there were two of them, one from another cardinal and one from a bishop, both of whom were regarded as strong defenders of religious freedom; the letters did not in fact point in the direction generally attributed to these individuals. But the Cardinal did not tell me their names. He said only that people would be surprised if their names ever became known…"

and for fear also that they would not be able to finish in time, and for fear of the reactions around the world.[125]

Meanwhile, the weekly meeting of the representatives of the twenty-two episcopal conferences made another voice heard. In the name of Suenens, Veuillot asked the participants whether it would not be better to take a vote on the schema immediately. The response was unanimously positive: a vote would help clarify the situation, and the secretariat would then be able to find out the real extent of the opposition. At this stage the bishops needed a vote in order to restore confidence; in addition, public opinion was calling for them to take a stand.[126]

3. To Vote or Not to Vote

a. The Vote in Suspense

On the Friday evening that ended the first week of debate, the strategy to be adopted did not seem clear. That the work of the general congregations was suspended did not mean a holiday for everyone. From this point on, two constraints would exert a very strong pressure on the work to be done: time, and the judgment of the world on the eve of Paul VI's visit to the United Nations. "In fact," Prignon wrote, "people are less optimistic today than yesterday, because of the influence of today's addresses on the minds of the fathers."[127] Everything depended on the estimates of the number of *non placet* votes or of the impact of the lack of a vote or of a split vote. In these circumstances, should one continue to call for a vote, as the secretariat had already done?

As early as September 15, Bea, promotor of the schema, speaking in the name of the secretariat, expressed the desire that at the end of the discussion the fathers proceed to a vote on the schema in the following terms: "Is the re-emended text acceptable in its substance or as the basis of a definitive declaration that is to be further improved according to the

---

[125] Ibid., 1-2.

[126] These are three motifs found in Stransky's notes and in those taken by Baudoux at the meeting (Stransky papers, 5, and Baudoux papers). The minutes of the meeting are less explicit. At no. 2 in the agenda (*De Schematibus Conciliaribus nunc in disceptatione positis, 1. Schema "De libertate religiosa"*), the minutes say: "In accordance with art. 34, the general sense of the participants is that on the coming Monday a vote should be taken on the acceptability of the text, in order that the competent commission may be informed of the opinion of the fathers. A request to this effect is to be made to their Excellencies, the Cardinal Moderators" (Baudoux papers).

[127] *JPrignon,* September 17, 1965 (Prignon papers, 1585, 2).

corrections voiced by the fathers in the discussion?"[128] Two of the moderators, Suenens and Döpfner, seemingly had no objection to the taking of a vote.[129] But things were more complex when it came to the governing bodies of the Council.

The question of a vote was studied by the moderators at their preliminary meeting with Felici (September 16), before they were received by the Pope at an audience. The words "in its substance" in the suggested vote seemed unfortunate and ambiguous. Thus "Felici was very strongly opposed to a vote expressed in this way.... After such a vote no one would know precisely the meaning of this 'substance.' The work would continue amid ambiguity.... He therefore pleaded that this vote not be taken."[130] The majority of the moderators also had difficulty with the ambiguous formulation, since with such a formula the *non placet* votes would be cast "partly by representatives of the majority, partly by representatives of the minority, even if for contradictory reasons, since it is quite clear ... that some representatives of the majority are not satisfied with the text." According to his report on the discussion, Suenens proposed "a vote, using a modified formula, but his colleagues did not go along."

The Pope, for his part, was quite reserved about a vote on the text. "He was afraid that the majority was not large enough and, as he looked forward to his visit to the United Nations, he dreaded having to appear there, trailing behind him a vote that would show perhaps 300, 400, or 500 fathers opposed to religious freedom."[131] In the end, the Pope thought that the matter should be submitted to the Council of Presidents.[132]

---

[128] *AS* V/3, 355. Bea's request probably resulted from the first meeting of the secretariat during the fourth period, on September 15, at 5:00 p.m. See Bea's letter to Suenens, September 15 (Suenens papers, 2556) and his letter to Lercaro (Lercaro papers, XXIV, 644).

[129] Such, at least, was Stransky's opinion. Prignon was more nuanced, as we shall see.

[130] *JPrignon,* September 18, 1965 (Prignon papers, 1586, 1). The published minutes of this meeting give the same information but in less detail.

[131] *JPrignon*, September 18, 1965 (Prignon papers, 1586, 1). Edelby suggested the number 400 (*JEdelby*, September 16, 1965, 245). Dupont heard talk even of 1000 *non placet* votes (September 20, 1995, 17). Hence the Pope's fears of a humiliating vote.

[132] *JPrignon*, September 18, 1965 (Prignon papers, 1586, 1). It does not seem, however, that the question was brought to the Council of Presidents. In his minutes of the meeting of the governing bodies on September 20, Carbone observed that at their meeting on September 16 the moderators concluded that it would be enough to end the discussion with a declaration from the secretariat to the effect that the schema would be corrected in accordance with the written observations of the fathers and then be brought to the floor again for a vote (see *AS* V/3, 366). He added that Bea had been informed of this solution and had said he was content with it. But Carbone also noted that on September 17 the secretariat once again insisted that a vote be taken. This claim is to some extent

Referring the question to the Council of Presidents, however, was likely to muddle rather than clarify the situation. The multiplicity of governing bodies, the fact that the Council had several heads, tangled things still further. Another factor was the lack of formal procedures for audiences of the moderators with the Pope, which tended to render all decisions fuzzy and to enable intermediaries to turn themselves into interpreters of the will of higher authority. It was difficult in these circumstances to know what precisely had been decided. "Suenens and others thought that the presidents were agreed on proposing a vote and that things could move ahead, while Agagianian gave the impression that in his opinion the decision of the presidents needed to be forwarded to the Holy Father for his definitive agreement." On Friday evening, then, the decision of the moderators not to propose a vote by the assembly seemed firm, despite the insistence of the secretariat.

The Council seemed caught in a trap. If no count were taken, how could the schema be established as a base text from which there could be no retreat? The danger would remain of a possible repudiation of the text. The two scenarios envisaged (a vote or the return of the text to the secretariat for correction) entailed sizable difficulties, and those in charge hesitated to decide. The promoters of the schema were faced with a dilemma. Not voting on the text would amount to a victory for its opponents, as at the end of the third period. This would send a very bad signal to all those who regarded the determination of the Catholic Church to commit itself to religious freedom as a test of its sincerity. A failure to vote on the text would clearly show the Church hesitating, shying away.

Not to vote would have another serious consequence. If the declaration went back to the secretariat without a general vote of approval, the minority, as it had at the end of the third period, could judge the next corrected text, when it was brought back to the assembly, to be too new to be voted on without new discussion. Such a postponement could mean the end of any declaration on religious freedom by the Council, a risk that could not be taken in this fourth and last period. Time was running out; it no longer favored the adoption of the text. It was therefore necessary to forestall any delaying tactics. A vote also seemed risky "because the size of the majority was uncertain." If the text did not receive extensive support, it would

consistent with the version given by Prignon, who is our main source here. Grootaers says that the moderators "decided not to consult the Presidents (as they had promised the Pope they would do) and not to organize a straw vote" (see J. Grootaers, "Paul VI et la Déclaration conciliare *Dignitatis humanae*," in *Paolo VI e il rapporto Chiesa-Mondo al Concilio* [Brescia: Istituto Paolo VI], 103). This matches what we find in our documentation.

end up irremediably weakened. There was fear that "the psychological impact would be disastrous if the majority were not large enough at the first vote."[133] Even within the secretariat, estimates were divided. Stransky noted: "Some are saying 500-600 [negative votes]. I have been saying 220-250. The very vocal opposition is not as numerous as people think."[134]

In this atmosphere of uncertainty the secretariat met on Friday evening, September 17. "Going into Friday evening, the people [in the secretariat] had obviously not come to a decision…. There is no doubt that they must expect difficult days ahead and long days of work. Definitive approval is not in sight for the immediate future, which seems to indicate that the session will be longer than some liked to say during this past week."[135] The members of the inter-conference, at their weekly meeting, favored a straw vote on the schema as a whole. Their desire may have expressed the mind of a large number of fathers, but they were not in a position to alter the situation, which seemed at an impasse.

b. A Vote at Any Cost

In the end, the promoters of the text decided to go forward. On Saturday, September 18, Bea wrote a letter to the Pope asking that a vote be taken on the schema and arguing for it on the basis of conciliar procedure and in political terms.[136] A vote was needed, he said, because the text had twice been corrected in accordance with the oral and written observations of the fathers, yet it had never been voted on, "whereas for the other schemas votes had always been cast." He added, moreover, that this was not a new procedure, "since in numerous cases not unlike ours votes have been cast." In a political analysis of the situation Bea said, "I do not share the forecasts of some who predict a large number of votes against the schema …. I think that even more serious would be any further delaying of a vote … even so close to the visit of Your Holiness to the United Nations." In short, another Black Week had to be avoided. Such a possibility was in Bea's mind when he met with the observers that same day. After recalling the difficulties of the preceding period, he

---

[133] *JPrignon*, September 17, 1965 (Prignon papers, 1585, 2).

[134] Stransky papers, 5.

[135] *JPrignon*, September 17, 1965 (Prignon papers, 1585, 2-3).

[136] See *AS* V/3, 357. According to Stransky's notes, Willebrands and De Smedt worked on its composition (Stransky papers, 5). Grootaers speaks of similar steps undertaken by Shehan (see "Paul VI et la Déclaration," 103).

added: "It is certain that we shall encounter difficulties in this session as well."[137] From then on the members of the secretariat worked with the idea of a straw vote in mind, even though they knew this would be difficult to obtain and even though they did not completely agree on the point even among themselves.

Meanwhile, at the Belgian College things were moving in a different direction. According to Prignon, after several meetings between Suenens and De Smedt, the Cardinal announced "that they [the moderators] had decided to have Felici say, in the name of the moderators, that the text would be sent to the secretariat for correction as desired by the fathers and would then come back to the assembly for a vote, nothing being said about a preparatory vote."[138] Faced with the decision of the moderators, De Smedt resigned himself to accept this wobbly decision and take the risk of getting the text recognized without any vote.

To those who were calling for a vote, however, this was unsatisfactory and dangerous. Unless Felici's statement were very carefully drafted, it could prove ambiguous. It had to be drafted in such a way that "the fathers and the entire world would be given the impression that this return to the secretariat for correction amounted in fact to an acceptance of the text as a basis of discussion and that there would be no question later on of being able to withdraw it by some juridical trick."[139]

For this reason the moderators' solution was challenged as soon as it became known.[140] In the evening Cardinal Martin (Rouen) went to Bea to try "to get a reversal of the decision taken" by the moderators.[141] At a meeting of the secretariat, positions became increasingly clearer, and half-measures were set aside; whatever might come, a vote had to be taken.[142] It was also decided that De Smedt "be commissioned to give a

---

[137] *DC* no. 62 (October 17, 1965), 1804.

[138] *JPrignon*, September 19, 1965 (Prignon papers, 1586, 3).

[139] Ibid.

[140] Prignon refers to numerous steps taken by Etchegaray in the name of the French bishops, "who are very uneasy, and he asked me to intervene once again with the Cardinal [Suenens] in an attempt to change the decision. Msgr. Veuillot in particular seemed very displeased" (ibid., 3-4). On the working group of the French episcopate, see Dupont papers, 1326.

[141] Prignon papers, 1585, 4.

[142] Martimort told Prignon that "all the members of the secretariat, at least at the executive level, beginning with Willebrands, intensely wanted a text, no matter what the size of the minority the vote might show (*JPrignon*, September 19 [ibid., 4]). Martimort's phrasing seems to point to De Smedt's ambivalence at this moment. At the end of Saturday Prignon wrote: "Msgr. De Smedt seems to me a little less tense, but at this hour of the day, 10:40 in the evening, I no longer know what solution he will come to. He seems

concluding report in order to pull together the conclusions reached in the debate, to show the minority the extent to which their proposed amendments had been considered, and thereby to rally a large number of vacillating minds."[143]

Beginning on Sunday, unaware that the opponents, too, were busy,[144] defenders of the schema began to take steps on several fronts to implement the decision. Within the secretariat members hastened to prepare the report that De Smedt was to give when the debate ended.[145] Meanwhile, in parallel with the work of the secretariat, others were devising another strategy should the desired vote not be granted. A committee of five (Bonet, Medina, Martimort, Etchegaray, and Prignon) held a lengthy meeting to fine tune the different scenarios. They composed two questions in case a vote were to be taken.[146] But Willebrands did not like this strategy. When reached on the telephone, he said that he did "not want to hear of two questions, because he was afraid that the first would give the impression that the secretariat was dubious about its majority."[147] The same committee also drafted the text that would be read by Felici in case the schema were to be sent back to the secretariat for correction without having been put to a

still hesitant about the final solution" (ibid.). The next day Prignon wrote: "Msgr. De Smedt ... tells me he has changed his mind and that for psychological reasons he too thinks it better to try to obtain a straw vote from the Holy Father" (*JPrignon*, September 19, 1965 [Prignon papers, 1587, 1]).

[143] *JPrignon*, September 19, 1965 (Prignon papers, 1587, 1).

[144] The opponents would present a petition from 165 fathers asking to present a counter-report before a vote was taken.

[145] Willebrands, De Smedt, Murray, and Hamer took part in this meeting (Stransky, handwritten notes in Stransky papers, 5). A first version of this final report, dated September 19, is in Prignon papers, 1338, with a handwritten note of De Smedt: "to be submitted to the meeting of the secretariat at 5.00 p.m."

[146] There are two questions, in Martimort's hand, dated September 19, in the Prignon archive (Prignon papers, 1333). The first was of a general kind and aimed at securing a large majority: "Does it please the fathers that the Council should make some declaration on religious freedom?" The second was more specific and concerned the direction to be taken in this declaration. The aim was to have the assembly approve the present schema as the base text of the declaration, with whatever significant amendments might be needed. At the bottom of the Martimort document is a notation: "Rejected by the secretariat." This picture corresponds very closely to the version of the facts that is given by Prignon in his diary (*JPrignon,* September 19, 1965 [Prignon papers, 1587, 2]). But the committee did not therefore give up on its approach. On September 20, 1965, Medina sent Suenens the typewritten text of the two questions "as an alternative plan for the meeting of the Board of Presidents" at 5:00 p.m. on September 20 (Prignon papers, 1334).

[147] *JPrignon*, September 19, 1965 (Prignon papers 1587, 2). Caprile makes reference to a formula that would have anticipated taking five votes (see Caprile, V, 46, n. 32).

vote.[148] This was an attempt to ensure that there could be no ambiguity about how to interpret this measure; that is, even if not voted on, the schema was henceforth to be regarded as the base text for subsequent discussion.

Sunday ended without the outcome being decided and without any knowledge of Paul VI's decision about a vote.[149] In preparation for the following day, Suenens accepted the text prepared by the committee in case there should be no vote. "He will try to get his colleagues to accept it. If a vote is to be taken, he himself has prepared a question" that is not very unlike the second question drafted by Prignon's committee.[150]

Despite all the steps taken at the end of the week, a vote still seemed unlikely. Work was about to resume, punctuated by the beginning of votes on the *De revelatione*,[151] and September 20 would bring the end of the debate on religious freedom in accordance with the formula decided on Sunday evening. But the weekend did allow the majority to pull itself together somewhat. The French episcopate's working group on religious freedom met on September 17.[152] In addition, Msgr. Ancel (Auxiliary Bishop of Lyons) had set about preparing an intervention that would try

---

[148] The text: "Now that the discussion of the schema for the *Declaration on Religious Freedom* is finished, and since there will be no discussion of details inasmuch as everything, both general and specific, has already been said, the moderators decree, in accordance with article 58, 1 of the regulations for celebrating the Council, that the corrections offered by the fathers are to be sent to the competent commission" (Prignon papers, 1330). This text was subsequently corrected (in writing) by De Smedt (Prignon papers, 1331), who added the sentence: "After the text has been reviewed, it will be immediately put to a vote without any new discussion of it." On September 20 a new typewritten version was then made with De Smedt's addition (Prignon papers, 1332).

[149] According to Suenens, Paul VI's position was that while the Pope feared the ill effects of a straw vote and while he still had reservations about some aspects of the present schema, "he clearly does want a declaration on religious freedom but one that is as short and as narrow as possible, this because of fear that it will be misused later on" (*JPrignon,* September 18, 1965 [Prignon papers, 1586, 4]).

[150] See *JPrignon,* September 19, 1965 (Prignon papers, 1587, 2); see also ibid., 1333. At the bottom of the page containing the two questions drafted by Martimort, there is this note: "If the other moderators are in agreement, a single question will be asked, the one composed by Cardinal Suenens that corresponds to no. II, but with the words *servata indole schematis.*" It would not be surprising if similar approaches were made to the other moderators. Within the secretariat "Moeller was commissioned to tell the Cardinal that the secretariat absolutely wanted a vote" (*JPrignon,* September 18, 1965 [Prignon papers, 1586, 4]). Further on, Prignon noted: "Tomorrow morning they will approach at least three of the moderators in order to try to settle the problem."

[151] From this point on, the work of the general congregations was continually interrupted by votes on the various schemas that still had to be handled.

[152] The minutes of this meeting are in Haubtmann papers, 695.

to reconcile positions.[153] Other cardinals, too, were asked to speak along the same line, among them Lefebvre and Journet.

c. Toward Agreement

The weekend also provided the promoters of the schema the time needed for developing an answer to the continual attacks on the document. The debate had become more and more muddled, and clarifications in the council hall would be welcome, such as those made, outside the assembly, in Murray's lectures on September 15 and Congar's the following day.[154] Cardinal Lefebvre had been asked to intervene for this purpose, so that the undecided fathers would be better able to act if a vote were to be taken.[155]

On Monday morning, September 20, Cardinal Lefebvre was the first to speak at the 131st general congregation. His address, which was the most rigorous in the entire debate, addressed the fears and "unfounded" objections that had been expressed up to that point.[156] He sought to rally to the schema those fathers who "fear that they cannot in good conscience approve of such a schema." He systematically tackled the six objections most frequently raised by opponents of the schema.[157] His answers to them, derived from the text of the declaration, were more closely and systematically argued than any previous responses to the critics. With great self-assurance and serenity, the Cardinal dismantled all the structures built up by the opposition during the previous week.

In addition, on this subject the Cardinal possessed great authority. While the addresses of the United States bishops were foreseeable when they argued that the schema was not opposed to the traditional teaching

[153] The summary of Ancel's coming intervention was submitted to the meeting and is found in Liénart papers, 903. Msgr. Garrone was also planning an intervention.

[154] Sanschagrin noted: "This afternoon I attended a lecture by Father Congar, O.P., on religious freedom. Very clear and brilliant ... on a subject that is not easy" (*JSanschagrin*, September 16).

[155] Martimort and Medina got the idea on the preceding Friday of asking Cardinal Lefebvre to speak (*JPrignon*, September 17, 1965 [Prignon papers, 1585. 1]).

[156] *AS* IV/1, 384-86. Phrases based on the noun *timor* occurred four times; the construction "dicunt ... sed e contra" was repeated twice. The Cardinal responded to the fears that would be expressed that very day by the Bishop of Sydney: "Many of us have experienced a profound uneasiness" (*AS* IV/1, 416).

[157] The objections were these: that the schema fosters subjectivism and indifferentism; that the Council is ceasing to teach that there is only one true religion; that recognition of freedom favors the spread of error; that recognition of freedom will lessen missionary fervor; that freedom places the rights of human beings over the rights of God; that the schema is contrary to the traditional teaching of the Church.

of the Church, the emphatic support of Cardinal Lefebvre impressed "uneasy" minds. His concluding statement called for agreement and unity:

> Perhaps these few remarks of mine will help us rise above some groundless objections. In ending, let me express the wish that the drafters of the schema will profit by all the observations offered in the hall and thereby remove anything that may still be ambiguous. It seems to me, then, that we can already give our *placet in genere* to this schema, while nonetheless expecting that in so serious a matter the ideas of the schema will be even more clearly expressed.

The address of Cardinal Shehan (Baltimore), a member of the commission for the revision of the text, was intended to rebut one of the principal arguments of the adversaries of the schema: that the schema was unfaithful to traditional Catholic teaching.[158] Here, again, the rebuttal was closely argued and systematic. Shehan reviewed the teaching of Leo XIII, Pius XI, Pius XII, and John XXIII, bringing into perspective the developments that had taken place over a lengthy period, and, as he advanced, correcting the mistaken statements of the opponents of the schema. The line of evidence was rigorous and very concrete. The conclusion came like ripe fruit falling: "The teaching ... found in the schema is sound and salutary and completely consonant with the body of doctrine handed down by the Church. The ardent hope is that the fathers will approve the schema almost unanimously."

Opposition to the schema thus seemed to have been effectively met on the basis of arguments. It is significant that both Lefebvre and Shehan referred to the position that Urbani had set out on the very first day of the debate.[159]

d. The Authority of Experience and of a Confessor of the Faith

To the intellectual and moral authority of Lefebvre was added the authority of a confessor of the faith. The intervention of Cardinal Beran (Prague),[160] speaking at the Council for the first time since his liberation, made a very great impression because he spoke from experience and in the light of history. It had been his experience that any restriction on freedom of conscience led to hypocrisy and corrupted the moral fiber and

---

[158] *AS* IV/1, 396-99. He also said in his introduction that the teaching of the schema is equally confirmed by scripture, but he was unable to develop this point in his intervention.

[159] See ibid., 384 and 396.

[160] Ibid., 393-94.

spirit of a people. Referring specifically to the condemnation of John Huss, he showed how the history of his native land teaches that, far from serving the progress of the Church, recourse to the secular arm to uphold the Church's rights leaves on souls a lasting wound that works against any religious progress. His conclusion was strongly worded: "Thus history, too, warns us that at this Council the principle of religious freedom and freedom of conscience must be set forth clearly and without any restriction flowing from opportunistic considerations."

The intervention of the aged Cardinal Cardijn likewise had in its favor the experience of sixty years' work among the youth of the entire world,[161] an apostolic experience that, more than the quality of his speech, made his words credible enough that he could rally bishops who were still wavering. Taking his stand in the world of the missions, he maintained that the effectiveness of apostolic and missionary activity was conditioned by the recognition of religious freedom.[162] The intervention of Cardinal Wyszynski (Warsaw),[163] although very different in its phrasing, also claimed the authority of experience. He wanted to be a voice to the Council from a different world, that of "Diamat" (dialectical materialism). That world was often misunderstood in the West and had its own interpretation of the ideas of law, the state, and freedom. As Baraniak had already done in the name of the Polish episcopate, Wyszynski openly supported the purpose of the declaration, namely, "that this kind of freedom be safeguarded," but he asked that the text of the declaration be preceded by an introduction "in which attention is called to the different ideas of law, the state, and freedom maintained by the different ideologies of our age: ideas that must be distinguished among themselves." This would forestall the confusions, the corruption of meaning, and the misinterpretations often given to texts of the magisterium in the countries of the East.

e. The Non-Aligned Decide

The sense of the conciliar assembly could also be gauged from the intervention of Cardinal Rossi (São Paulo, Brazil), who spoke in the name

---

[161] In a letter from Brussels on July 14, 1965, Cardijn had asked Congar to help him prepare a statement on the schema (Congar papers, 1285). See also the other correspondence of Congar and Cardijn on religious freedom and schema XIII (Congar papers, 1279-84).

[162] See Cardijn's address, *AS* IV/1, 406-7.

[163] *AS* IV/1, 387-90.

of eighty-two Brazilian bishops.[164] He effusively praised the schema for "its timeliness, synthetic character, and depth" and said that it met present expectations because it rested on solid foundations and used language suited to contemporaries. But he wanted a section added that would explain the pastoral consequences of the assertion of the right to religious freedom, that is, what it meant for the education of the faithful in their faith and the formation of the consciences of Christians. Apart from its relevant suggestions, this intervention was valuable because of what it revealed about the sentiment of the assembly. If important episcopates, such as those of the United States and Brazil, as well as the episcopates of Germany and Poland, were behind the schema, and if the Italian episcopate was, as it seemed divided on the matter, then the opponents were not as numerous as was thought. (On this fourth day of debate it was already possible to begin counting heads.) This rallying to the cause of religious freedom also showed that the opposition of the Spaniards was not effective outside their own country; they were unable to win over the South Americans, especially the bishops of Portuguese tradition. The contagion was limited, therefore. It was clear that the Brazilian episcopate was not going to obey the voting instructions of the *Coetus Internationalis Patrum*, of which Msgr. G. de Proença Sigaud, a Brazilian prelate, was an important representative.

f. Building a Majority

As the debate continued, a majority seemed to form and to grow, even though the supporters of religious freedom had some difficulty in reaching agreement among themselves, with some wanting to base this freedom on the gospel, others on positive law, and still others on natural law. Some gave only halfhearted support to the schema and did not go out of their way to win over other adherents. This was the case with Cardinal McCann (Cape Town),[165] who did not think it was enough to assert the obligation of every person to seek, according to his or her conscience, the truth revealed by God and proclaimed by the Church; a stronger statement was needed of the objective duty of every individual to embrace the truths of Catholic doctrine. Even with such conditions, however, his *placet* was added to the others, and it helped the people who had begun counting heads to take the temperature of the assembly.

---

[164] Ibid., 399-403.
[165] Ibid., 395-96.

Support from some others was clearer, as, for example, from Msgr. Gran, Bishop of Oslo, who also spoke from experience, living as he did in a situation of religious pluralism. In his view the declaration would give the world a pledge of the sincerity of the Catholic Church; it would meet the expectations of the contemporary world (a point he made three times), and if the Council did not move forward on it, many people would be scandalized. The Church cannot claim privileges for itself or ask of others what it cannot provide them itself; otherwise it will be accused of duplicity, and people will doubt its sincerity. In addition, "no dialogue can be carried on without this reciprocal generosity." These arguments could not fail to be convincing at the moment when Paul VI was preparing to leave for New York.[166]

g. The Opponents Run out of Ammunition

While the replies to objections had become more solid and more vigorous, the fourth day of debate also showed that the opponents had pretty well exhausted their ammunition. Two leaders of the opposition did speak once again, but without offering any new arguments. Cardinal Browne repeated the claim, twice rebutted by other speakers during this general congregation, that the schema was opposed to the teaching of preceding popes. He then simply repeated arguments already heard: that governments are able to discern the true faith and to know that the defense of the true religion is a good; that the spread of other religions in Catholic countries is a violation of public morality and an offense against the Catholic faith; that in such cases Catholic citizens have a right not to have their faith exposed to danger.

Archbishop Marcel Lefebvre followed the same line, but his address was so excessive that it disqualified itself and, compared to the interventions of Beran or Martin, carried no weight.[167] His plea was a cry of despair that did not seem to reflect the century he lived in and was in remarkable contrast with the calm confidence of the other two men. In the second part of his speech he referred eighteen times to the divine law. He also insisted that the thinking which had led to the contemporary awareness of the dignity of the person had not originated in Christian reflection but outside the Church in seventeenth-century philosophers whose thought had been solemnly condemned by the popes. Thus "this

---

[166] His intervention is in ibid., 411-13.
[167] See *AS* IV/1, 409-11; see also Caprile, IV, 38.

concept of religious freedom is not one conceived... by the Church," and it cannot be proved "either from tradition or from sacred scripture," as was evident from the arguments adduced in the schema.[168] The entire line of argument in the schema collapses, he said, if the divine law becomes the basis for the concepts used (freedom, conscience, human dignity).

To this rejection by Europeans must be added an important reservation coming from Asia. Cardinal Santos (Manila) repeated an argument already heard, namely, that while the keener awareness that the contemporary world has of the dignity of the person could be an argument for the timeliness of the declaration, it could not serve as a foundation for establishing religious freedom as a right. Santos proposed another principle as the starting point: the obligation of the human being to worship God both inwardly and outwardly. He thought that with this principle as the point of departure, a correlative right to religious freedom could be deduced. Other religions have a moral personality, he admitted; but, unlike the Catholic Church, they do not have a juridical personality that would enable them to be the subjects of a right.[169]

h. The Secretariat Challenged

Since it had exhausted its arguments and realized that it could no longer call upon a large number of speakers for a continued attack on the schema, the opposition had to change its strategy. Knowing that it could not effectively move against the schema in the conciliar assembly, it now worked to shift the struggle to more favorable ground. As early as the second day of the debate, Modrego had been angered by the fact that the re-emended schema had not taken the minority's viewpoint into account. In addition, steps were already being taken behind the scenes to strip the Secretariat for Christian Unity of its exclusive competence in promoting the schema. On Thursday, September 16, Ruffini sent the Pope a letter to this effect.[170] He proposed that, at the very least, some members of the Doctrinal Commission be allowed to work with the members of the secretariat in revising the text. In his view, the members of the secretariat who had drafted the schema were incapable of judging opinions contrary

---

[168] Archbishop Lefebvre referred to a work published by a Mason in which the writer expressed the hope that the Council would approve the declaration on religious freedom and that the World Council of Churches would issue a similar statement.

[169] *AS* IV/1, 390-92.

[170] Ibid., 356. Felici would make the contents of the letter known to Bea on September 22 (*AS* V/3, 373-76).

to their own; they were acting as judge even though they were a party in the dispute. Moreover, "the question of religious freedom cannot be considered solely in its technico-juridical aspect."

On September 18 a new assault was made, this time directed to the moderators. A petition signed by 165 fathers asked, on the basis of article 33, §7 of the Council regulations, that before any vote there be read in the assembly a "general proposal 'that would expound and defend, completely and systematically, another way of conceiving and stating this teaching.'"[171] The signers were relying not only on the Council regulations and parliamentary procedure but also on precedents and on the fact that all the reports hitherto supplied by the secretariat had aimed at defending the doctrine held by the secretariat rather than allowing the expression of a different viewpoint. An elementary principle of justice, adopted by courts in which the defense as well as the crown could state its point of view, called for greater equity here, with the result that the report would echo the opinions expressed in the hall by a number of fathers. In the eyes of the opponents, the secretariat, which had not been established for such a purpose, showed partiality and did not really represent the opinion of the Council fathers.[172] The signers avoided, of course, saying that the Council should give up making a declaration on religious freedom; their clever proposal was that the problem be posed more broadly and more clearly.

At the end of the general congregation of September 20, the question of the secretariat's competence was raised in the hall for the first time. In the second part of his intervention,[173] Msgr. Añoveros Ataún (Cadiz) maintained that this "openly doctrinal" schema was beyond the competence of the secretariat and should be submitted to a subcommission made up of jurists, theologians, and experts in public law. Since this was not a matter of drawing up a schema simply to please separated brethren, the

[171] Ibid., 360-61. Among the signers were Archbishop Lefebvre, Carli, G. de Proença Sigaud, Menéndez, Nicodemo, de Arriba y Castro, and García de Sierra y Méndez. This petition repeated more or less the request that the *Coetus Internationalis Patrum* had addressed to the Pope at the end of July, which Paul VI had not granted. This *postulatio* to the moderators is found, in a different form, in Suenens papers, 2557.

[172] "In our opinion, since the Secretariat for Unity does not adequately represent the sense and outlook of the Council as a whole but rather only a partial vision of the problem, one worthy of consideration but certainly incomplete; and this Secretariat for Unity was not established for such a purpose..." (*AS* V/3, 361).

[173] Ibid., 415. The speaker also said that the foundation of the schema, namely, the dignity of the person, did not seem fully settled, that several biblical scholars assert that the position adopted cannot be based on the scriptures, and so on.

responsibility for the document did not belong to the secretariat. At the same time, a petition was being circulated in the hall seeking the submission of a counterschema, a modification of procedure, and the establishment of a mixed commission.[174]

i. Paul VI's Decisive Steps

Publicly, at least, the question of a vote seemed taboo. Only Shehan made a vague reference to it at the end of his intervention, when he said he would like the schema put to a vote and approved by a strong majority of the fathers.[175] Others, even some less in favor of the schema, also called for a straw vote.[176] The press in the United States was becoming alarmed,[177] and the observers were beginning to be seriously worried.[178] Was the Council once again, as in the previous year, on a dead-end street?

Facing this impasse, Bea made new pleas to the moderators and the Pope. He addressed a letter to Agagianian asking the moderators to reconsider their decision not to take a vote. He also submitted a new formula and emphasized that it took into account the difficulties raised during the last few days in the discussion in the hall.[179] In addition, he intervened again with the Pope, asking him directly to authorize a vote of principle on the schema. In a short letter Bea told the Pope of the formula he had already submitted to Agagianian, "which seems to promise a good majority."[180] Paul VI's reply came during the general congregation. According

---

[174] This fact is attested by several sources, among them Dupont and Prignon in their record of the meeting on September 20.

[175] *AS* V/3, 398. Shehan had also approached Paul VI in order to obtain a vote.

[176] For example, Msgr. Schoemaker (Purwokerto) called for a straw vote, although he himself was not enchanted by the schema and preferred that a new draft be undertaken (see Suenens papers, 2558).

[177] The headline of the *Daily American* for September 21 read "Report Pope Petitioned by Conservatives," and the *New York Herald Tribune* announced "Vatican Council near Crisis over Religious Liberty Issue."

[178] See Horton, *Vatican Diary*, September 20.

[179] *AS* V/3, 363-64. Willebrands sent a copy of this letter to Felici (ibid., 364). Bea's new formula read: "Does it please the fathers that, while the revealed doctrine of a single true religion for all human beings remains untouched, there be a declaration that there exists a natural right to religious freedom, based on the dignity of the human person and to be recognized by civil law, in keeping with the doctrine expounded in the schema and to be further completed according to comments approved by the fathers?"

[180] Ibid., 365. That same day Paul VI had the following note sent to Msgr. Dell'Acqua: "See the adjoined sheet that came via Msgr. P. Felici; and see the text which it seems it would be good to present for a straw vote of the conciliar assembly (the text may perhaps be touched up by the Secretariat for Unity); and if there is nothing against it, send the sheet to Msgr. Felici, while informing the secretariat (and Cardinal Bea, to whom I showed the

to Carbone, Paul VI "wanted at least a straw vote taken on the schema on religious freedom before he left for the United Nations."[181] To this end the Pope put pressure on the General Secretariat. In a handwritten letter to Felici, the Pope urged him to consider the vote requested by the secretariat.[182] It seemed, then, that a resolution was at hand.[183]

On September 20, at 5:00 p.m., Felici, as ordered, assembled the members of the governing bodies of the Council: moderators, Council of Presidents, and Coordinating Commission.[184] At the end of a lengthy, sometimes confused discussion, in which various formulations of the question were suggested, it was decided once again to reject the idea of a vote[185] and not to accept the Pope's proposal.[186] According to various reports, the

letter yesterday)" (Carbone, "Il ruolo di Paulo VI nell'evoluzione e nella redazione della dichiarazione *Dignitatis Humanae*," in *Paolo VI e il rapporto Chiesa-mondo al Concilio* [Brescia: Instituto Paolo VI, 1991], 160; see Paul VI papers, VI A2/26h).

[181] Reported by Claude Soetens in his "Interventions du Pape Paul VI au Concile Vatican II," in *Paolo VI e i problemi ecclesiologici al Concilio* (Brescia: Istituto Paolo VI, 1989), 579.

[182] *AS* V/3, 365: "All things considered, it seems appropriate to accept the request." The letter already contains a parenthesis whose content would be taken up again later: "while reaffirming the teaching on our true religion" (see Paul VI papers, VI A2/26i). The formula suggested by Paul VI followed almost verbatim what Colombo had said in the hall, while also borrowing some points from Bea.

[183] In Liénart's papers, under the date of September 18, there is a list of "precedents," that is, occasions on which a straw vote was taken on a schema. This list was attached to Bea's letter of September 18 to Paul VI.

[184] There are at least five accounts of this meeting: two in Prignon's diary, representing Suenens' report about it (September 20, 1965, 2-4; September 21, 1965, 6-7); one by V. Carbone, who was present at the meeting as its secretary ("Il ruolo di Paolo VI," 161-62); Felici's *Rapporto*, drawn up on that same day (Paul VI papers, A2/26t); and, finally, the minutes of the meeting published in *AS* V/3, 366-69. Liénart also left some notes, dated September 21, on the meeting (Liénart papers, 908). At the same time the secretariat was also meeting. Some members also had strong reservations about the formulation of the question, which they found too long. They discussed the formula to be adopted, fearing that the simple formula might elicit as many as a thousand *non placet*s (this was Willebrands' view). They favored, therefore, a formula that would cause the opposition to vanish. For an account of this meeting, see Moeller papers, 02599.

[185] In the end, only nine fathers came out in favor of a vote: Döpfner, Shehan, Liénart, Spellman, Alfrink, Suenens, Krol, Le Cordier, and Kempf. Opposed were Tisserant, Cicognani, Frings, Caggiano, Gilroy, Lercaro (after having been in favor), Urbani (after trying to play the mediator), Agagianian, Ruffini, Siri, Wyszynski, Confalonieri, Roberti, Nabaa, and Morcillo.

[186] The text that the Pope proposed for the vote was this: "Does it please the fathers that, while firmly maintaining revealed doctrine on the one true religion for all human beings, it be declared that there is a natural right to religious freedom, a right based on the dignity of the human person and to be recognized by civil law, according to the teaching expounded in the schema and to be completed in keeping with the observations approved by the fathers." This formula, which has often been attributed to Colombo, was in fact, except for one variant, the one that Bea had suggested to Paul VI during the day. Item 1335

meeting was dominated by Tisserant, Agagianian, and Felici, with the
first two expressing strong reservations about the vote and still stronger
reservations about the formula that the Pope proposed for the vote. Their
arguments were so similar as to legitimize the thought that their interventions had been coordinated.

Agagianian spoke first and reviewed the steps taken thus far, stressing
the point that the secretariat had been content with the position taken by
the moderators, who at the end of their discussion had agreed to send the
schema back to the secretariat for correction before it returned to the assembly for a vote. An orientation for the debate had already been given, and
it should not be abandoned in any significant way. After Felici explained
Paul VI's proposal, Tisserant argued that there was a danger that the fathers
would not grasp the meaning and value of their vote. A vote might also
create an air of tension, and this would be dangerous at the moment.
It would be better, therefore, to follow the usual course taken by schemas.

The opponents of the schema then rushed into this breach in the wall.
Ruffini, the second speaker, referred explicitly to Tisserant: "Cardinal
Ruffini says he agrees with Cardinal Tisserant."[187] Of what value was a
vote? Agagianian also feared confusion; he would prefer the course
planned by the moderators (to send the text back to the secretariat without any vote), which was in keeping with the regulations; this, he said,
"substantially satisfies the wishes of the secretariat, without disturbing the
calm atmosphere of the Council." Next, Gilroy (Sydney) referred to the
"ordinary course" mentioned by Tisserant, while Caggiano (Buenos
Aires) took over the language of Agagianian and spoke again of confusion. At the end, the motion put to a vote (introduced by Tisserant)
repeated exactly the terms that Agagianian had suggested earlier in the
discussion: "whether, neglecting the line already set down by the moderators in accordance with the regulations..."[188] Felici, for his part, setting himself up as authorized interpreter of the Pope's thought, under-
mined the credibility of the question that had been submitted for

in the Prignon papers, which gives us the text, bears this note of Suenens: "Text proposed
by the Pope (Colombo) at the meeting of the Council of Presidents, September 20, 1965,
at 5:00 p.m."

[187] *AS* V/3, 367. Siri repeated an argument of Tisserant, and Confalonieri one of Agagianian's, remarking that it was odd that "after the president and the secretary of the secretariat had agreed on not taking a vote, they then had recourse to the Holy Father" (368).
Agagianian would return to the theme.

[188] See "Processus verbales," 369. Just before, Agagianian "concluded that the course
set down by the moderators in keeping with the regulations substantially satisfied the
wishes of the secretariat" (ibid., 368).

consideration and turned attention to a different formulation that dropped the idea of natural law and put greater emphasis on Catholic teaching.

Positions were becoming increasingly well defined. Among the moderators, after September 16, Agagianian blocked every move toward a vote;[189] Suenens and Döpfner supported the request of the secretariat; and Lercaro, while in favor of the schema, remained ambivalent.[190] At the Council of Presidents, Tisserant "moderated" all moves toward a vote, and Felici likewise barred the way from the very outset. The whole business was back where it had started, and this on the day before "the De Smedt text" was going to be read at the close of the discussion. Things could not remain in this state.

There remained the authority of Paul VI to take the initiative, and he, despite the repeated pressures brought to bear by the opponents of the schema, seemed more and more determined to have a vote taken.[191] For, in the final analysis, after the vote had they not left the matter to his decision? That very evening, Bea,[192] and perhaps also Shehan, addressed Paul VI once again.[193] Dell'Acqua called Cicognani, Tisserant, and Agagianian, and Felici to a meeting the following day, September 21.[194] Two

---

[189] While the report on the meeting that Suenens gave to Prignon differed slightly from that of Carbone, the two certainly agreed on the role of Agagianian. Prignon observed that after the rejection of the Pope's text, "Agagianian intervened to say that the text was to be read with the inclusion of De Smedt's sentence. Suenens interrupted to tell him that before deciding on this, it was necessary first to examine the matter and decide if there would be a vote. The Pope's text (Bea's text) had been rejected, but this did not prohibit a different way of asking the questions." Suenens also attributed the "usual course" motif to Felici (*JPrignon,* September 20, 1965 [Prignon papers, 1588, 3]).

[190] This is confirmed by several sources: Carbone, Prignon, Stransky, and others.

[191] According to Grootaers, after the decision of the governing bodies of the Council, Willebrands and Bea brought new pressure to bear on Paul VI to obtain a vote; see Grootaers, "Paul VI et la Déclaration," 103.

[192] According to Prignon, who got his information from Arrighi, Bea also had a conversation with Colombo immediately after the meeting of the "great Caliphate" (see *JPrignon,* September 28, 1965 [Prignon papers, 1594, 6]).

[193] This, at least, is what Xavier Rynne says: "Card. Spellman, one of the Coordinating Commission members, emerged from the meeting in anger, and Card. Shehan was believed to have gone to see the Pope to protest the decision" (Rynne, IV, 48). Prignon also says that that very evening Bea and Colombo worked on a text, which was probably the one in question (*JPrignon,* September 21, 1965 [Prignon papers, 1589, 3]).

[194] *AS* V/3, 369; see also Carbone, "Il ruolo di Paolo VI," 162. Stransky has a slightly different version and a different date. He notes that on Monday, September 20, at 8:30 a.m., just before the resumption of the Council's work, the Pope's secretary, Msgr. Macchi, sent an "urgent" call to Willebrands. The latter was to see Dell'Acqua before a decision was made on a vote, while the Pope himself summoned Tisserant, Agagianian, and Felici (Stransky papers, 5).

other cardinals were also to take part in this meeting. The moderators, too, were summoned to a meeting at 8:45 a.m., before the beginning of the session, in order once again to discuss the question of a vote.[195] Arrighi, for his part, worked until midnight to produce a report, requested of the secretariat by the Pope, on the composition of the schema and the contacts between the secretariat and the theological commission during its drafting.[196] There was, therefore, still hope.

But the opponents had not surrendered. That same evening, after the meeting of the Council of Presidents, Ruffini went to Dell'Acqua and gave him to understand that during the next few days another schema could be presented that would win an almost unanimous vote. Dell'Acqua had to tell him that the withdrawal of the schema could have serious consequences on the international scene, especially in view of Paul VI's coming visit to the United Nations.[197]

The next morning, at 9:00, the Pope met with the summoned cardinals. He said he was in favor of a vote, but not necessarily in the terms proposed by the secretariat. After an exchange of ideas, it was agreed that a vote should be taken on the basis of a formulation discussed the previous evening by the governing bodies of the Council.[198] Thus, less than a year after the events of Black Week, Paul VI seemed to be redeeming

[195] This meeting was canceled that very morning. At 8:15 a.m., Döpfner told this to Suenens as coming from Agagianian, who was "called to the Pope in order to settle definitively the question of the attitude to be adopted in the assembly" (*JPrignon,* September 21, 1965 [Prignon papers, 1589, 1]).

[196] This report was to be given to Dell'Acqua by 7:50 the next morning (*JPrignon,* September 21, 1965 [Prignon papers, 1589, 3]); a copy of it, dated September 21, is in Paul VI papers, VI A2/26h. It sets down the history of the schema during the Council in two pages, which are followed by a note of Willebrands in which he points out the need of a vote if the extent of the opposition to the schema is to be measured.

[197] See Dell'Acqua's notes in Paul VI papers, A2/26o.

[198] See Carbone, 162. This formula was itself inspired by the text of Paul VI's reply to Bea's request. The formula adopted can be compared with the one discussed on the previous evening (*AS* V/3, 328), at the suggestion of Felici, supported by Tisserant, which read: "Is the re-emended text — to be further improved in keeping with Catholic teaching on the one true religion and with consideration being given to the corrections proposed by the fathers during this discussion — acceptable as the substance or basis of the definitive declaration?" The formula adopted was the following (wording taken from the preceding formula is italicized): "Is *the re-emended text* on religious freedom — *to be further improved in keeping with Catholic teaching on the... true religion* and in accordance with the corrections proposed by the fathers during the discussion and approved in accordance with the regulations of the Council — *acceptable* to the fathers *as ... the basis of the definitive declaration?*" (*AS* IV/1, 434). Some of the words in the section "in accordance with the corrections ... the Council," although not verbatim from the preceding formula, convey exactly the same thought.

himself in the eyes of the majority.[199] "Faced with a majority that seemed to be suffering from inertia and a minority as combative as ever, Paul VI's leadership emerged more clearly than before."[200]

4. "The Big Day" — "A Day of Destiny" — September 21

According to the calendar given to the Coordinating Commission, the debate on religious freedom was to last for only a week (September 15-18).[201] But now the debate seemed to have bogged down, and no one could find a way of ending it. It was no longer a secret that efforts to obtain a vote on the schema had to pass through a mine field.[202] The question now in many minds was whether they would succeed in getting over the hurdle.

The opening of the 132d general congregation on September 21 did not fool the better informed. The arrival, after mass, of Tisserant and Agagianian and of Felici was a sign that important things were happening behind the scenes. Agagianian, whose turn it was to be moderator, announced there would be twenty-three speakers during the meeting. A report on schema XIII was distributed, and it was announced that this schema would be distributed the next day in the principal European languages. But everyone realized that something else was in the works. Paul VI's upcoming visit to

---

[199] Paul VI's determination seems to have been motivated by two factors: his coming visit to the United Nations and his desire to make up to the fathers who had been frustrated by his refusal to grant their request in November 1964. Carbone suggested this second motive in a conversation with C. Soetens: "Perhaps Paul VI's intervention on September 20, 1965, is also to be explained by a desire to give satisfaction to those bishops" (Soetens, "Intervention du Pape," *Paul VI au Concile Vatican II,* 579).

[200] Grootaers, "Paul VI et la Déclaration conciliaire *Dignitatis humanae,*" 102. Noting how Paul VI was exercising leadership "amid the disarray and apathy of the majority view," Grootaers concluded: "Thus, during this final period of Vatican II, the Pope would show himself as the most active element in the entire conciliar assembly" (see ibid., 104-5; and J. Grootaers, "Le crayon rouge de Paul VI," in *Les commissions conciliaires à Vatican II,* 323). For Shehan's remarks, see NCWC News Service, October 11, 1965. Rynne gives pretty much the same analysis, observing that opponents of the reform, working especially through members of the Curia, had free access to the Pope, whereas "by contrast, the majority were negligent about making their wishes known with the same regularity" (Rynne, IV, 3). Appreciation of the leadership of Paul VI in this affair was repeated by a very large number of witnesses and analysts; Rynne (ibid., 49), even compared the impact of this initiative at the procedural level with that of John XXIII's intervention during the first period, when he rescued the schema on revelation from the quagmire in which it had been bogged down by the conciliar regulations.

[201] Coordinating Commission, minutes of meeting XXI (*AS* V/3, 351).

[202] Well-informed "leaks" in *L'Avvenire* had finally made the matter known outside of limited circles.

the United Nations was increasingly on the minds of the fathers;[203] the debate on religious freedom was drawing to its end, and the final shots would probably be fired at this morning's meeting.[204]

Cardinal Dante opened the discussion by emphasizing the "very serious ambiguity" to which the schema lent itself. For, in seeking to establish religious freedom at the juridical level, it seemed to be making its own the claims of Montalambert, Lamennais, and liberalism. It even took over a demand of the French Revolution that said "no one should be harassed for his opinions, even his religious opinions, provided their manifestation does not disturb the public order established by the law."[205] Moreover, this ambiguity was increased by the fact that the ideas of "peace," the "right of citizens," and "public morality," which would justify setting limits to religious freedom, could be turned into instruments of tyranny in non-Catholic or communist countries.

Journet's intervention was meant to offer a synthesis and to rally support.[206] From the beginning of his address, the new cardinal[207] expressed his judgment that there was a "basic doctrinal unity" among the fathers and that the disagreements came "from pastoral concerns." He then claimed that these differences "could to a great extent be reduced if some themes already found in the schema were emphasized"; that is, everything was already contained in the schema and needed only to be made explicit. He repeated this thesis in his conclusion: "All these matters are contained ... in the schema for the declaration ... where they can perhaps be better highlighted. And therefore this declaration, in my view, should be given the strongest approval." This intervention, backed by the speaker's recognized authority as a theologian, was politically skillful

---

[203] The day before the Council had associated itself with the Pope's visit to the United Nations by sending a letter from Tisserant. On this day Felici read out the names of the cardinals who would accompany the Pope to New York.

[204] Douglas Horton spoke of it as "the big day," "the day of destiny" (*Vatican Diary*, 35-36).

[205] *AS* IV/1, 422.

[206] The secretariat, probably in the person of Father Hamer, had asked Journet to intervene. The Belgian episcopate was divided. Msgr. Daem was unwilling to give his signature, which would have assured that Journet's speech was supported by seventy fathers and therefore able to be read even after the close of the debate (see *JPrignon,* September 20, 1965 [Prignon papers, 1588, 5]; ibid., 1336).

[207] During this whole debate, several of the new cardinals strongly supported the schema, among them Beran, Šeper, Cardijn, and Journet, while certain influential cardinals in the majority remained silent. This showed that Paul VI's choice of cardinals had the concrete effect of strengthening a declining conciliar majority at a time when it needed new support. For Journet's address see *AS* IV/1, 424-25.

and of a kind to reassure the undecided. On the other hand, it also simplified matters and erased differences; it certainly could not win over the most stubborn adversaries. Nevertheless, the distinction Journet made between the temporal and the spiritual orders would mark the subsequent debate.

Two other interventions allowed the voices of Africa and South America to be heard.[208] Interrupted by votes on the *De revelatione*, the debate continued, but without any really new arguments being put forth. Finally, at 10:30, the moderator, after observing that there had already been sixty-two interventions on the schema,[209] asked the fathers to indicate, by a standing-sitting vote, whether they wanted to end the discussion in the hall. The proposal was supported by a very large majority. After this, things began to move very rapidly.

Msgr. De Smedt was asked to present his concluding report. In his relatively brief and shrewd remarks,[210] the Bishop of Bruges began in an accommodating manner, thanking the fathers for contributing to a truly constructive discussion, which contained several valuable points.[211]

---

[208] See the interventions of A. Kozlowiecki (Lusaka) (*AS* IV/1, 426-27) and P. Muñoz Vega (ibid., 429-31).

[209] *AS* IV/1, 431. More accurately, sixty fathers had spoken, seven of them Spanish bishops. In addition, there were over 100 written observations. At this point, twenty-two fathers had put their names down but had not yet spoken. According to Caprile, the great majority of them were in favor of the schema; the exceptions (for reasons we have already seen: a text not conformed to papal teaching, ambiguous, dubious in its foundation, dangerous, and unacceptable) would have been Mingo, de Proença Sigaud, Cuenco, Abasolo, Muñoz, and de Castro Mayer (see Caprile, IV, 44).

[210] See *AS* IV/1, 432-33. The Prignon Archive contains two rough drafts of the report. The first, dated September 19, is four pages long. All the elements of the final report were already there, but the formulation was still brusque. Instead of beginning by stressing that the discussion had been constructive, it began by emphasizing the fact that two tendencies had made their appearance when the discussion began. Next, it tackled the fact that the problem was new and had to be distinguished from the other questions raised. It ended by saying that the commission had accepted various points for improving the schema. The second rough draft (September 20) is much shorter (two pages); it inverted the order of what was said and began by recognizing the merits of the discussion. It was quite close to what De Smedt would say in the hall. In addition, the second part would be rearranged to make it less negative, and a sentence would be added not found in the first two versions.

[211] He called attention in particular to points having to do with the ideas used in the schema (give a better and more positive definition of religious freedom as a civil and social freedom from all coercion; avoid ideas connected with indifferentism or a false irenicism; emphasize more strongly the necessity of education for freedom and responsibility); with the argumentation (shorten the scriptural part); with the limits of religious freedom (clarify and explain more thoroughly the ideas of peace and order and of the common good); with the duty of the person to seek the truth and acknowledge the rights of God. At a press conference the next day, De Smedt would be even more detailed (see Agence Kipa-Concile, September 22, 1965. When Dupont questioned him about his

In the second part of the report he focused on showing that the Council had to deal with a new problem and that this required doctrinal progress equivalent to that which could be seen in the development of social teaching. Although connected with the question of the moral obligation to seek the truth and to follow it and with the question of the right of the Catholic Church to preach the gospel, the problem of the moment was a different one, and the Council ought to limit itself to a resolution of this problem alone.

In his conclusion he assured the fathers that the text would be "re-re-amended" according to their suggestions. He also asked for their collaboration so that the Council might draw to its close in harmony and unanimity,[212] as it had in dealing with other documents that had provoked lengthy efforts. His last words skillfully reasserted the challenged authority of the commission over the schema: "Our commission, which is responsible for the revision of the text, will be truly grateful for the collaboration of *all* the fathers, whatever their views."[213]

As soon as the report was finished and had been greeted with applause, Agagianian, speaking in the name of the moderators, announced that a vote would be taken.[214] Amid some confusion (because at the same time votes were being taken on the *De revelatione*), the Secretary General read out the question: "Is the re-emended text on religious freedom — to be further improved in keeping with Catholic teaching on the true religion and in accordance with the corrections proposed by the fathers during the discussion and approved in accordance with the regulations of the Council — acceptable to the fathers as the basis of the definitive declaration?"[215] This differed from the usual formulation of such questions and

intention of shortening the scriptural section, De Smedt replied: "That is not what I said; I said only that I had the impression it would have to be shortened" (*JDupont*, September 21, 2).

[212] This was the speaker's second appeal for agreement, the first having been issued at the transition between the first and second parts of the report.

[213] This was the only new idea in comparison with the text of the report that the secretariat had approved on September 29 (Prignon papers, 1339). It dissatisfied some. Pierre Lafortune, for example, and Lanne, who thought De Smedt had gone too far. It also failed to convince Hamer "that it was in the properly understood interests of the secretariat" (*JPrignon*, September 21, 1965 [Prignon papers, 1589, 1]). Dupont's judgment: "He [De Smedt] had already humbled himself in his address; it was doubtless necessary in order to obtain the result" (*JDupont*, September 23, 1965, 27).

[214] It is notable that the vote was called for in the name only of the moderators and not in that also of the Council of Presidents. In fact, from then on the governing bodies would no longer be called upon to hold joint meetings, like the one held the evening before.

[215] For the wording of the question, see above and *AS* IV/1, 434. This was Vote 293.

seemed convoluted to many, but everyone knew that it had been designed to rally the largest possible majority. Some remarked on the rather Byzantine formulation; some were surprised that the Council felt it necessary to proclaim that it must conform its teaching to Catholic doctrine;[216] others feared the consequences;[217] many were happy with it.[218]

The clause about being in accord with Catholic doctrine has been given all kinds of interpretation. It was clearly meant to reassure the still hesitant. But did it mean that the drafters were doubtful about the doctrine in the schema, thinking it would have to be corrected in the light of past papal encyclicals, as some had asserted in the course of the debate? This is highly unlikely. The lengthy history of the drafting of the question, in which each new draft added a word to the preceding text, undoubtedly helped to misshape the question. It repeated a formulation proposed by Felici during the discussion by members of the Council's governing bodies on September 20, but it depended also on the letter that Paul VI wrote to Felici on that same day as a result of Bea's entreaties.[219]

[216] Perhaps it was this that led Daniélou to say that "this formula meant that the declaration in its present text is contrary to Catholic teaching; this in turn implied that it ought to be drafted anew by a new commission" (*JRouquette*, September 21, 1965). Some would make the convoluted formulation an excuse for calling for a substantial revision of the declaration.

[217] This was the case with Philips, Heuschen, and others who feared that the minority would interpret it strictly and claim that the majority of its observations should be introduced into the schema (see *JPrignon*, September 21, 1965 [Prignon papers, 1589, 4]).

[218] See *JEdelby*, September 21, 1965, 248; G. C. Zizola, in *L'Italia*, September 22, 1965; Haubtmann papers, "Le point sur le concile" (October 13, 1965), 4.

[219] See *AS* V/3, 365-68. Bea's formulation was by far the longest and most complicated. According to Rynne (IV, 48), Murray had worked on it. It was addressed to Paul VI, on the eve, and he gave his consent to the vote the next morning, but he added in parentheses: "while reaffirming the teaching on our true religion." In Felici's version this became "in accordance with Catholic teaching on the one true religion." As a result of successive alterations the end result was the question that had its source in Bea's proposal. The words *teaching* and *true religion* are found in all the versions. De Smedt was therefore not in error when he said that "the question asked, on which the fathers are to vote, is one of the three proposed by the secretariat; it has been revised a bit, for they wanted to adapt it to the circumstances, and that is very good" (*JDupont*, September 21, 1965, 22; see also ibid., 27). The question has often been attributed to Msgr. Colombo. The diaries of Dupont and Prignon, based on the rumor circulating at the time, point in this direction, and Grootaers repeats the hypothesis ("Paul VI et la Déclaration," 103 and 105). But the documentation shows that the process was one of addition and that the formula did not depend on the influence of any one individual, though Colombo may have played a part in it and have put the final touches on it during morning Mass. Dupont writes: "The question formulated yesterday for a vote on the *De libertate* was composed by Colombo during Mass. Willebrands did not know of this ... and learned of it only when Felici read it out. It is not from De Smedt. He could not have lowered himself to the point of deliberately relying on ambiguities" (*JDupont*, September 22).

The final words of the question ("and to be approved in accordance with the regulations of the Council") appeared to be much more important. They were not in any earlier version and were probably from Paul VI. They represent an answer to the petition of the 165 fathers who appealed to the Council regulations in order to challenge the competence of the secretariat. So, the schema was to be corrected again and approved in accordance with the conciliar regulations. Everything had now been said.

The result of the vote (1997 for and 224 against, out of 2222 votes cast[220]) surpassed all expectations and was greeted by warm applause. Not only could the members of the secretariat emit a great sigh of relief, but the result also restored the confidence of the Council and opened the way for taking up the rest of its work. The count had been taken, and the minority had shown itself to be less weighty than all its noise and activity had led people to believe. As *La Liberté* (Geneva) remarked on September 26, the opponents were a much smaller group than had been suggested by the number of their interventions during the first two debates. They had been revealed to be only paper tigers.

The vote also illustrated the distance between the mind of the assembly and that of the governing bodies, which were made up of unelected members. The evening before, the latter had for the most part spoken against the vote; they clearly did not represent the assembly, which had now come out so heavily in favor of the schema. From all this we must infer that in this case Paul VI, though obliged by his role to offer as much as possible to the minority in order to safeguard the unity of the Church, grasped the mind of the assembly better than did the governing bodies of the Council, and that he analyzed the situation with greater sensitivity and insight than did many others. On the following day, Bea wrote to thank him and tell him of the deep gratitude of the members of the secretariat for his decision in favor of a vote.[221] Paul VI thus earned the visa for his mission of peace to the United Nations. In addition, he redeemed himself in the eyes of many for his refusal to intervene and call for a vote at the end of the third period.

Reactions to the vote were revealing. Several of the individuals chiefly involved remarked on the great importance of the vote. In his *Lettera dal Concilio,* Msgr. Colombo wrote: "This week will remain famous in the history of the Council as the week in which the great majority of the

---

[220] *AS* IV/1, 564.
[221] Bea to Paul VI, *AS* V/3, 370.

fathers gave their substantial approval to the schema on religious free-dom."[222] The reaction of the observers, especially those from the United States, was likewise very revealing, while the press, especially in the English-speaking world,[223] did not fail to point out the importance of the vote.[224] *The Daily American* devoted its longest editorial since the death of President Kennedy to the vote. Several newspapers in Italy, France, and the United States recounted in great detail the ups and downs that had led to the vote.

On the other hand, the press representing more conservative groups continued its campaign. There is an example in the *Bulletin du Cercle d'information civique et sociale* of Paris. Its issue of October 2 gave a minimalist interpretation of the vote, pointing out that the question asked the fathers required that the schema be "clarified *in accordance with Catholic teaching* and with the amendments proposed."[225] According to G. de Couessin, editor of the publication, a competent doctrinal com-mission would not yield to the demagogy and bourgeois liberalism of the northwestern countries or to the desire to please Protestants.

Reactions among non-Catholics were often enthusiastic. For Prince Tay-lor, president of the Council of United States Methodist Bishops, the vote had "a significance of worldwide importance." Among the Presbyterians, E. Blake said that the action would "permanently improve relations between the Reformed and Presbyterian Churches around the world and the Catholic Church." This outlook was shared by the United States Conference of Chris-tians and Jews, in whose view the effects of such a declaration would be felt "for thousands of years." According to Horton, this was "a vote with end-less consequences," while for Blakemore it was the crowning achievement of a week that had turned out to be "the climactic moment of the Council's four years... and one of the greatest weeks in the history of Catholicism."[226]

[222] *L'Italia,* September 26, 1965.

[223] The *Times* of London, September 22, 1965, hailed the vote as "a great event in the history of Catholicism and in the history of freedom."

[224] The *ICI* offered a survey of the press response in its edition of November 1, 1965, 14-15, from which I am borrowing here. For the reactions of the observers see also *ICI,* no. 251 (November 11, 1965), 16, which reports five Lutheran reactions and two from the Reformed Church. In private, Pastor Roux said that he found "the trick rather transpar-ent" (*JPrignon,* September 21, 1965 [Prignon papers, 1589, 2]). His reaction was given in a press release and reprinted in *ICI.*

[225] *Bulletin du Cercle d'information civique et sociale,* October 2, 1965, 1 (emphasis in the original).

[226] Horton, *Vatican Diary,* 39; W. B. Blakemore, "A Great Week for the Council and the Pope," Report 1 of the Fourth Session of the Second Vatican Council, 1; Outler spoke of "the most important victory" of the Council (*Methodist Observer,* 147).

Visser 't Hooft remained more reserved as he waited for the definitive adoption of the text and hoped that the schema would not be too watered down during the revision. H. Roux had reservations because the declaration relied too much on a rational foundation; he would prefer that it be based only on scripture.[227] The same tempered approval was shown by Pastor Boegner, for whom the vote had been taken on a "Jesuit" formula; he was outraged that a Council should need to declare that it would follow Catholic teaching.[228] The reactions of the observers did not differ solely for confessional reasons; they also depended on whether or not the observers belonged to Anglo-Saxon countries.

After the vote, the debate was to continue a while longer, but the attention of the fathers was no longer focused on it. And yet the remaining interventions were not without interest.[229] Msgr. Wojtyła (Cracow), speaking in the name of the Polish bishops, reminded his listeners that the declaration ought not to be limited to repeating what is found in the constitutions of states. He asked that the schema be based more on the moral law than on juridical regulations, so that whatever restriction may be placed on religious freedom will conform to the moral law. Msgr. Doumith spoke in the name of seventy fathers from the Middle East, Africa, and Asia. Not only was this another voice from Asia, but his was also the strongest position taken thus far against the confessional state, which some religions can make especially intolerant. In a short statement Msgr. Grotti then implored the bishops not to take too seriously the results of the previous day's vote but to note carefully what De Smedt said in his report and to make sure the promises contained in it were kept.

The final speaker, Msgr. Ancel, speaking in the name of a hundred French bishops and of thirty-one Indonesian bishops,[230] emphasized the

---

[227] To this end, Roux brought pressure to bear on several individuals when the time came for the revision. Horton reports on the presentation of the declaration at the weekly meeting of the observers, giving the positions of Cullmann, Scrima, Roux, and others (*Vatican Diary*, 27-29). We can see there the diversity of confessional and cultural positions. The Orthodox wanted religious freedom grounded less in natural law; the European Reformed Church observers wanted greater emphasis on the scriptural basis; the Anglo-Saxons were quite happy with the arguments used in the schema.

[228] See *JRouquette*, September 21, 1965, as well as his article "Le programme de la quatrième session du Concile," *Études* 322 (January-June 1965), 541.

[229] The interventions are in *AS* IV/2, 11-20. Only interventions backed by more than seventy fathers were heard in the hall.

[230] *AS* IV/2, 16-20, and the appendix on 608. This intervention made a deep impression on Paul VI and would win Ancel membership in the commission that would revise the text. Later, on September 24, Msgr. Lopes de Moura also proposed giving an ontological foundation for religious freedom (De Smedt papers, 1561).

ontological basis of religious freedom, namely, the obligation, inscribed in human nature, to seek the truth. This obligation grounds religious freedom because the search requires not only the psychological freedom of the individual but also the individual's freedom from any coercion. He asked, therefore, that the connection between the obligation to seek the truth and religious freedom be brought out more clearly in section 2 of the schema. Ancel's intervention was important because it was of a kind to rouse greater enthusiasm in the French episcopate, which remained dissatisfied with the schema even though it had held back its criticisms.

5. "Re-re-amending" the Text

For the third time the text went back to the commission for a revision on the basis of the oral interventions and the sixty-eight written interventions sent to the secretariat.[231] This time, at least, the text was now solidly established. As the result of the opening given by De Smedt and of numerous pressures to this effect, the question of expanding the commission had now been raised. While some form of expansion seemed to be accepted by the members of the secretariat,[232] the best way of accomplishing it still had to be found. Some were inclined to follow a tested solution, namely, the formation of a mixed commission together with the theological commission (Hamer); others had strong reservations about

---

[231] See *AS* IV/2, 59-298. I mark with an asterisk the interventions scheduled but not made by the time the debate was closed. Among those fathers who submitted written observations, we find some who had already spoken in the hall: Journet, Siri, Carli (who suggested radical changes in the text [98-107]), Tagle, Gonzi, Hervás y Benet, D'Souza, Cuenco, Welykyj, Fares, Attipetty, Muñoz Duque, Mingo, Vairo, and Doumith. Several of these interventions were very reserved about religious freedom, especially the bishops of Italy, Spain (Hervas points out that the report was a unilateral defense of the schema), and Latin America (Muñoz Duque spoke in the name of seventy Latin American fathers). We also find a number of remarks from several Belgians (Dayez, Daem, Heuschen, Himmer) who had not intervened in the hall, probably out of deference to De Smedt. Some of these remarks would become important as events unfolded. See, in particular, the suggestions of Léger (61-72), who proposed a redistribution of the first seven articles, and of Ayoub (82-84) on the confessional state in the East. The French bishops, few of whom had intervened thus far in the debate, made their point of view known (de Provenchères, Gouyon, Garrone*, Veuillot). The bishops of the United States continued their effective work in written interventions by O'Boyle, Primeau*, Krol, Boudreaux, and Whealon. The Canadian episcopate, which supported the schema, also made its viewpoint known; in addition to Léger's remarks, see those of De Roo*, Hacault, Baudoux*, Carter, and Hermaniuk*. There were also remarks from Sigaud*, Wojtyła*, and Hurley*.

[232] De Smedt himself, however, still had to be persuaded (see *JPrignon*, September 21, 1965 [Prignon papers, 1589, 9]).

this course (Philips).[233] In any case, the secretariat quickly realized that it was in its own interests to make the first move rather than have someone impose a method that might prove awkward.

In fact, the opposition had not lowered its guard. As early as September 21 it sent a petition to the Secretary General of the Council, asking that those who voiced their disagreement in the hall have a role in the revision of the text. They based this request on De Smedt's statement that he was ready to ask for the collaboration of all the fathers and on the fact that there was agreement that the schema should be revised in accordance with Catholic teaching on the true religion. They also requested that the revision be conducted under the oversight of a mixed commission composed of members of the secretariat and of the Doctrinal Commission.[234]

The secretariat had to react quickly, not only because time was short but also because an "Appunto sullo schema *De libertate religiosa*," originating in Felici's General Secretariat and dated September 22, said that the new text ought to be edited by a body not composed solely of members of the secretariat but by a mixed commission of the Doctrinal Commission and the secretariat; it also observed that it would be helpful to add to the commission some new members who were very competent in the subject.[235] This suggestion was taken seriously at the highest level. On September 27, Ottaviani sent to Paul VI the names of five members of the Doctrinal Commission who could be joined with the secretariat in the editing of the conciliar text. The chosen members were Cardinal Browne, Msgrs. Parente, Colombo, and Pelletier, and Father Anastasio.[236] All avenues seemed open, therefore, but De Smedt wanted, above all, to avoid having a mixed commission imposed on him.[237] It was doubtless

---

[233] See *JPrignon,* September 21, 1965 (Prignon papers, 1589, 9-10). Hamer also suggested that Philips join the team, but the latter decided he was not in a position to do so.

[234] There were ten signers of the petition: M. Lefebvre, G. de Proença Sigaud, E. R. Compagnone, F. Erviti, A. de Castro Mayer, J. Prou, X. Morilleau, D. Mansilla, A. Temiño, L. M. Carli, and G. Cabana (*AS* V/3, 372, and the appendix on 373). In addition, a text that the Bishop of Valparaiso circulated in the name of the *Coetus Internationalis Patrum* was harshly critical of the secretariat.

[235] Paul VI papers, A2/27a; see also *AS* V/3, 373.

[236] *AS* V/3, 380. Paul VI had received Ottaviani at an audience on Saturday, September 25. The Pope spoke to him of Felici's suggestion that the commission be expanded. Ottaviani, in addition to the names on his list, suggested three more: Cardinal Roy, Father Fernández, and Msgr. Poma. We know of another handwritten list, dated September 26, sent to Willebrands; this contained the names of Charrière, Boyer, Pavan, Ancel, and Colombo (Paul VI papers, A2/27c).

[237] That was De Smedt's position during a discussion of the subject with Willebrands and Bea (Stransky papers, 5 [September 23, 1965]). Prignon reports that at one moment De Smedt even contemplated inviting Carli to come and explain his views to the

to this end that Willebrands got in touch with Dell'Acqua and informed him of the steps the secretariat had taken to broaden the study of the amendments offered to the declaration.[238]

In addition to an expansion of the commission in charge of the revision, the opponents also wanted clear directives to be given to this commission. In particular, they wanted the amended declaration to bring out clearly the continuity of the teaching of the magisterium on this subject; that it avoid the danger that might be occasioned by the assertion of the lay character, in principle, of the state; that the problem of the true religion's objective right to recognition in civil life be rethought; and that the level of the document's authority be determined. Above all, the opposition wanted the new text to be submitted to higher authority (along with the report of the subcommission) before the new text was sent to the fathers for a new debate in the hall. Questions were also asked in high places about how to communicate these directives without giving them too solemn a form.[239]

Meanwhile, the French working group of bishops had met on September 23 in the rooms of Cardinal Lefebvre at the French Seminary in order to draw up a proposal for ordering the section on scripture.[240] The new text was sent to Msgr. Sauvage (Annecy) on September 27, but the slow response of the French group finally discouraged Dupont; weary of fighting, he used another channel to transmit the text he had composed on this question.[241] Although several others would intervene on the

commission (*JPrignon*, September 22, 1965 [Prignon papers, 1590 and 1591]). There was also talk of bringing in the bishop who was secretary of the Spanish episcopate, so that the Spanish would be represented.

[238] Letter of Willebrands to Dell'Acqua, *AS* V/3. 381-82.

[239] See "Dichiarazione De libertate religiosa" (September 25, 1965), Paul VI papers, A2/28. There were also some instructions of Paul VI on the revision of the text: to emphasize the obligation of seeking the truth; to present the traditional teaching of the ecclesiastical magisterium; to avoid basing religious freedom solely on freedom of conscience; to state the doctrine in such a way that the lay state would not think itself dispensed from its obligations to the Church; to specify the authority of the declaration (doctrinal, dogmatic, juridical, or practical?). See "Dichiarazione 'De vera religione,'" with a handwritten note of De Smedt: "instructions de Paul VI pour la révision du texte" (De Smedt papers, 1575).

[240] Present were Cardinal Lefebvre, Sauvage, Guerry, and three other bishops. Among the experts were Dupuy, Cottier, Le Guillou, Dubarle, and Dupont, the last named being assigned to draw up a new draft of the passage (*JDupont*, September 23, 1965, 32). At the same time, Benoit wrote a lengthy text entitled "Le problème de la liberté religieuse: Aperçus néo-testamentaires" (Léger papers, 2045).

[241] On September 29, after Sauvage said he wanted to consult once more with the French bishops on the drafting of a text, Dupont wrote: "I answered that this was not likely to be of any great use: they will reach their conclusion when the secretariat will have already finished its work! He answered that it can be of service for the *modi*.... For

question (among them Benoit, Rigaud, and Hamer), it would be Dupont who would work at this to the end,[242] trying to readjust nos. 9 and 10.

6. Tenacity and Exhaustion

It was only on September 27 that the work began again in earnest. A special subcommission of the Secretariat for Christian Unity was formed and given the task of studying the 200 interventions on religious freedom;[243] it was this commission that would develop the fifth version of the schema, or the *textus recognitus*. Initially, the group proceeded very rapidly because the oral and written interventions had been under study since the commission had received them and even while the debate was still going on.[244] As a result, on September 27 they had a "Plan for Reworking Based on the Addresses of the Fathers."[245] After a first discussion, the group had in hand a new text for nos. 1 and 2.[246] On September 28 it established guidelines for the revision: the text was to be regarded as accepted and, for this reason, no suggestions were to be accepted that required any important reworking. On the other hand, special attention was to be paid to suggestions that might be able to bring peace to the minds of the fathers, but without prejudice to the direction taken by the majority.[247]

---

practical purposes, then, I can expect nothing from that quarter. How ineffectual!" Dupont was to send his text to Hermaniuk on September 29 for submission to the General Secretariat through official channels. Hermaniuk, who was well acquainted with Nabaa, could be a good intermediary (see Dupont's letter to Hermaniuk, September 29, 1965 [Dupont papers, 1530 and 1537]; idem, "Notes quotidiennes," September 29, 1965, 52).

[242] *JDupont*, September 27, 40.

[243] See *AS* IV/5, 105. Its members were Hermaniuk, Cantero, Charrière, Ancel, De Smedt, Primeau, Lorscheider, Colombo, Willebrands, and Degrijse. The experts were Murray, Pavan, Congar, Benoit, Feiner, Medina, Hamer, and Becker. This list differs from the one of which Willebrands wrote to Dell'Acqua on September 27, where the names of Charrière and Benoit do not appear but Hamer does. Willebrands had asked Colombo and Ancel to be on the commission (see *AS* V/3, 386). Hermaniuk, for his part, was a resolute proponent of religious freedom because of the persecution in the Ukraine (see his "Memorandum sulla persecuzione della Chiesa cattolica in Ucraina," pro manuscripto with no indication of place or date, and his circular letter written in Rome and consigned by thirteen other fathers belonging to the Ukrainian rite, November 12, 1965 (Léger papers, 2065 and 2065a).

[244] The group met for this purpose on November 15, 16, 17, and 20. Ancel and Lorscheider were later added to the group.

[245] See Prignon papers, 1343. The document was from Heylen.

[246] Prignon papers. The handwriting is that of Ph. Delhaye.

[247] See "Suggestiones quaedam ad ordinandum laborem reemendationis textus schematis Declarationis de libertate religiosa" (De Smedt papers, 1576).

The work was distributed among several groups, all of them dependent on a central subcommission and ultimately on the secretariat. The Belgian group (Heylen and Delhaye) was particularly active,[248] Heylen having been coopted to draft the section on the limits on religious freedom and its relationship with the state and public order.[249] In addition, Ancel contributed a text that would permit the amending of the schema to underscore more clearly the ontological foundation of religious freedom.[250] De Smedt, who had made the revision of the text almost his personal business,[251] showed so much good will toward the views of the minority that he disturbed his entourage who were concerned that if the text were too radically revised it would be unacceptable to the majority, especially with regard to the religious duties of civil authorities.[252]

From September 27 to October 3 a number of versions succeeded one another, sometimes two a day. One of them was sufficiently advanced to be submitted to the secretariat for study on September 30 and October 1.[253] At an audience granted to De Smedt on September 30, Paul VI expressed contentment with the text; far from sending any negative signals, he added: "This document is of cardinal importance. It establishes the attitude of the Church for the next few centuries. The world is waiting for it."[254] This endorsement of the line taken in the text was in continuity with the positions he had previously taken. His only requirements were that the text clearly state that "the Church is the only true religion" and that people are obliged to seek the truth, and that it show that this

---

[248] On September 28 there were, once again, new texts from Delhaye and Heylen (see Prignon papers, 1345, 1246, 1347, 1348, 1349; also in Moeller papers, 02594). This document, a new version of nos. 1-5, was discussed on September 29.

[249] There is also a document from Charrière on this subject (De Smedt papers, 1577).

[250] See especially Ancel's letter to De Smedt on October 3 (De Smedt papers, 1583). On the ontological foundation of religious freedom, see also the remarks of A. Lopes de Moura (De Smedt papers, 1561).

[251] This judgment, shared by Moeller and Murray, is reported by Congar (*JCongar*, October 1, 1965; II, 416). Prignon's judgment was a bit more nuanced but along the same line. In fact, by October 1, De Smedt had rewritten a text, which he submitted to the secretariat. Willebrands responded that same day, expressing regret that De Smedt had taken too many liberties with the *textus reemendatus*, which was to be followed as closely as possible and which was already at a very advanced stage of revision (see Willebrands's letter to De Smedt, October 1, 1965 [De Smedt papers, 1578]).

[252] See especially *JPrignon*, September 28, 1865 (Prignon papers, 1594).

[253] The various versions are in the archives of De Smedt, Stransky, Murray, Moeller, and others.

[254] *JCongar*, October 1, 1965; II, 415. The same impression emerges from a conversation between De Smedt and Prignon (*JPrignon*, September 30, 1965 [Prignon papers, 1596, 5], and October 1, 1965 [1597, 1]). For the Italian original of the report on the audience, see Carbone, "Il ruolo di Paolo VI," 164.

teaching is in continuity with the teaching of his predecessors.[255] At this point Paul VI was still managing to ward off the repeated assaults made on him with regard to the schema.[256]

On October 5, after much labor, the group finally produced a first version of the *textus iterum recognitus*.[257] This came at a price: Murray had become seriously ill and had to abandon the group, and Congar was literally exhausted.[258] And Congar's troubles were not over. After a lengthy discussion he still had to revise the *textus recognitus* produced by Pavan and to touch up nos. 9 and 11, while on October 7 it was necessary to discuss where in the text a statement would be introduced saying that the assertion of religious freedom did not detract from the Church's teaching on the one true religion and the one true Church.[259] The work was going forward briskly, but almost by forced labor. There was meeting after meeting, and Murray's absence led to a shifting of the tone of the text, as the theological dimension received greater emphasis at the expense of the more strictly juridical or rational argument proposed by Murray.

On October 11 a new text was ready and was submitted to the full commission of the secretariat for study from the 11th to the 13th.[260] Even though the commission avoided excessive alterations of the text that had been discussed and put to a vote in the council hall, it did make some significant changes: nos. 1, 8, and 10 were practically rewritten, as was the

[255] Prignon says that things were more complicated than they appear in Congar's report. De Smedt, he says, returned from the audience with five points that had to be taken into account in the drafting of the schema (see *JPrignon,* October 1, 1965 [Prignon papers, 1597, 1], and October 4, 1965 [Prignon papers, 1598]).

[256] During the audience with De Smedt, Paul VI showed him a petition from 125 bishops asking that the discussion of the re-re-amended text be preceded by a report from the opponents, since the secretariat did not represent the entire Council. Paul VI did not accede to the request (see *JCongar,* October 1, 1965; II, 415).

[257] See De Smedt papers, 1584, and *AS* V/3, 463. The secretariat had held three plenary meetings.

[258] After October 4 Murray was unable to work, but fortunately he had had time to submit his text before he fell ill. Congar, for his part, wrote in his diary: "Today I can stand up — that's right: merely stand up — only with great difficulty. The meetings in St. Peter's have tired me out to an unbelievable extent. My right leg I cannot move; I have no strength at all. I am always, and every day, without energy or strength, like a tree that has been struck by lightning and is no longer alive, but is broken, except for a centimeter of bark and wood through which a minimum of sap still makes its way. Just the same, it produces apples or plums. But how hard it is to do so!" (*JCongar,* 734; II, 422).

[259] The text modified by Congar is in De Smedt papers, 1587. Congar also had to revise the draft of the introduction.

[260] There are several copies of the text. I take as my point of reference the one contained in De Smedt papers, 1588. From his hospital bed Murray had sent in his own observations.

second part of no. 2. Yet the commission was satisfied with patching up the text, for it feared that any change in the ordering of the material would provide the minority with an excuse for demanding a new discussion and thereby delaying the adoption of the text.[261]

This text was submitted for consultation to some Council fathers who represented divergent tendencies: Cardinals Browne, Journet, and Urbani. Journet found the text "excellent and capable of bringing all desirable clarity to this difficult and important subject"; Urbani judged it to be better than the preceding text because of its clarity and exhaustive character; Browne was forced, to his great regret, to say that the new text could not satisfy him.[262] So, while the changes would meet approval with a very large number, it was clear that one part of the opposition remained implacable.

Meanwhile, the opposition was working in several different settings. Fr. Charles Boyer conducted his own campaign, sending his thoughts on the schema to Paul VI on October 5.[263] An appeal to the administrative tribunal was made on October 8 by Archbishop Lefebvre, Sigaud, Carli, and Castro Mayer.[264] Before September 30 Siri approached the Pope and asked that some of his own points of view be introduced into the schema. He then sent these to the secretariat, claiming to do so "by special order of his Holiness." When Paul VI was asked whether Siri was indeed acting by his "special order," the Pope said he was not, and that he, the Pope, had simply told Siri to send his remarks to the secretariat.[265]

---

[261] The commission had thought of putting the argument from scripture at the beginning of the text, in no. 2, but this proposal was withdrawn. It was due to interventions of Willebrands and Colombo that the commission returned to this solution (*JCongar*, 738). Some have thought that this insertion was ordered by "higher authority," but no trace of such a communication has thus far been found.

[262] See the letter of Willebrands to Browne and Urbani, October 12 (*AS* V/3, 411-12), his letter to Journet (ibid., 420), as well as the three letters, dated October 13 and 14, sent to Willebrands by Journet, Urbani, and Browne (ibid., 421-23). Willebrands sent these three letters to Msgr. Dell'Acqua on October 15 (ibid., 427-48). According to a letter from Colombo to De Smedt, Urbani and Colombo had together studied the new text. In addition, Colombo would revise De Smedt's report before it was presented (see letter of Colombo to De Smedt, October 19, 1965 [De Smedt papers, 1594]).

[263] Paul VI papers, A2/33a and b. Boyer raised three main questions: Can the right to err be defended as a means of safeguarding public order? Can the state prohibit the spread of error? Can a religious freedom that permits the spread of error be understood as a legitimate development of doctrine? Boyer's answer to all three was negative.

[264] Furey papers, ACUA. On the basis of section 2 of article 37, the bishops asked for a vote of *placet, non placet*, or *placet iuxta modum* on each article of the text, so that as many amendments as possible might be introduced; this, they claimed, would make the views of the fathers more clear.

[265] *AS* V/3, 352-54.

Paul VI likewise closed the door against a petition asking that the minority make its own report. On October 17 the Pope had to resist another assault: a group of Spanish bishops sent him a letter denouncing the declaration, not for political reasons but for doctrinal reasons. According to them, the declaration represented a new orientation of the magisterium of the Catholic Church. This new teaching amounted to an unacceptable break with the past, and the teaching of the Roman pontiffs could not be abandoned or contradicted.[266] A new petition was sent to the Council fathers on October 18,[267] but on that same day Paul VI approved the text, which was then sent to the printer.[268]

On Friday, October 22, the new text of the schema was distributed to the fathers in anticipation of a vote that could come as early as Monday.[269] While the substance of the text had not been changed, many concessions had been made as a result of various pressures put on the secretariat. The title had been modified,[270] and nos. 1 and 2 had been rewritten in order to make it clearer that the subject of the declaration was limited to civil and social freedom in religious matters and in order to state more unmistakably the Church's belief that God has revealed himself and that the true religion subsists in the Catholic Church.

In addition, no. 1 stated that the doctrine of immunity in religious matters does not detract from traditional teaching of the Church about the duties of individuals and associations in regard to the one, catholic Church. A section was added to no. 2 in order to honor Ancel's claim that the right to religious freedom was founded not on a subjective disposition of the person but ontologically, on the nature of the human being. In accordance with observations from the fathers, some alterations had been made in no. 5 (formerly no. 7) on religious freedom in the family; in no. 6 (formerly no. 5) on the recognition of a particular religion, but with an insistence that juridical equality among citizens must never be

---

[266] How many signed the letter is not known. The names of de Arriba y Castro and of Larraona are found; the latter, although a curial cardinal, joined the Spanish episcopate in this cause. The text is in J. Iribarren, *Papeles y memorias* (Madrid, 1992).

[267] The letter introducing it was signed by Franciscus Brazys (see Florit papers, I/520).

[268] See the letter of Dell'Acqua to Paul VI (*AS* V/3, 445). According to the *Acta* (V/3, 428-36), this text had been ready since October 15.

[269] *AS* IV/5, 77-98. The accompanying report, to which Feiner had contributed a great deal, described the work of the commission: "Observations on the schema in general; observations on the title, on the structure or order of the parts of the schema, on the individual numbers of the text" (ibid., 105-58). The original calendar drawn up by the General Secretariat had planned the distribution of the text for October 17 (*AS* V/3, 736).

[270] The words *ad libertatem et civilem* had been added.

infringed; in no.7 (formerly no. 4) on the limits on religious freedom, in order to ground it in the objective moral order. The part on the scriptural foundations of religious freedom (nos. 9-11, formerly 8-10) had been rewritten. No. 12 stated more clearly the failures of the Church in this area down the centuries. Of course, not everyone liked all these alterations.[271] The changes were interpreted rather negatively by the English and American press. The *New York Herald Tribune* for October 26, for example, had this headline: "Council Revision Makes It a Duty of All to Be Catholic." The same interpretation was carried by the UPI agency.

The controversy over the schema resumed as soon as it was distributed. The *Coetus Internationalis Patrum* sent to a number of fathers various documents intended to show that the present text was in opposition to scripture and to the past teaching of the popes.[272] In addition, it rebuked the reporter (De Smedt) for not having kept his promises to the fathers at the time of the vote on September 21. Finally, in addition to recommending a *non placet* vote, the *Coetus* offered thirteen substantial changes in the text.

Against this background of controversy De Smedt spoke for a sixth time to present the new text and explain the main alterations.[273] He emphasized that the observations of the fathers had been taken into account[274] and that at the end of their difficult work the members of the commission had approved the schema unanimously. The reporter stressed in particular that the new text was clearer on the fact that religious freedom did not absolve anyone from the moral obligation to seek God and

[271] Dupont wrote that "the French are quite displeased by the lengthy addition to no. 1, which was made in order to satisfy the minority" (*JDupont*, October 26, 142). And, in fact, the French episcopate's working group on religious freedom came up with a number of *modi* on October 24 (see de Provenchères papers, 1265).

[272] "Doctrina romanorum pontificum collata cum doctrina contenta in schemate declarationis de libertate religiosa". In his diary for October 26 Congar wrote: "I am made aware of the completely negative reactions of the Coetus Internationalis to the De libertate. It cannot be denied that this schema gives a *different* teaching than the Syllabus did. But *who* would dare hold, unchanged, the doctrine of the Syllabus and of *Quanta cura*, a passage of which they cite?" (II, 451-52).

[273] *AS* IV/5, 99-104. The first draft of this report was dated October 17 (Prignon papers, 1353; Moeller papers, 02590; some parts are in De Smedt papers, October 18). The report was completed on October 20. On October 19 Colombo offered three amendments to the first draft (De Smedt papers, 1594). In his report, De Smedt tackled, first of all, the question of the moral duty of seeking the truth and embracing the true religion; he then clarified the idea of religious freedom, explained its foundation, linked this teaching to earlier papal documents, and explained its limits and its root in revelation; he ended with an exposition of the freedom of the Church.

[274] For a detailed explanation of the responses to proposed changes, see *AS* IV/5, 105-58.

to embrace the true religion and that the declaration was dealing with religious freedom in general and not with the rights of the Church, which, as no. 13 pointed out, were not to be neglected. He concluded with a reference to the encyclical *Ecclesiam suam* of Paul VI.

On October 26 and 27 each paragraph was put to a vote,[275] and *modi* were then presented. Each article of the declaration easily received a two-thirds majority in the voting, while the vote on each section likewise received a large majority, although the number of those who wanted further changes remained relatively high.[276]

Despite a majority of over 90 percent in favor of the declaration, some individuals were still uneasy about the fate of the text. Dworschak noted his apprehension: "We are experiencing a very uneasy feeling that something will be done by 'higher authority' to water down not only this schema on religious liberty, but also the schema concerning the pastoral office of bishops."[277] It was in this atmosphere of uncertainty that the commission began the forced labor of dealing with the very large number of *modi*.[278]

---

[275] The newspaper *Il Tempo* (October 26) asked for a postponement of the vote because, in its view, the fathers had not had time to acquaint themselves with the new text. The votes were votes number 407-12. For the general congregations on October 25 and 26, see *AS* IV/3, 76-77; for the votes, see ibid., 205.

[276] For example, the vote on nos. 1-5 as a whole was 1539 yes, 65 no, 543 yes with reservations, and 14 void; on the second section (nos. 6-8) the vote was 1715 yes, 68 no, and 373 yes with reservations. The majority was even higher for the last two sections; for nos. 9-12, 1751 yes, 60 no, and 417 yes with reservations; for nos. 13-15, 1843 yes, 47 no, and 307 yes with reservations (see *AS* IV/5, 546-47 and 552).

[277] Dworschak, *Council Diary*, October 26, 37. He added: "We are afraid that the same technique will be used in these two schemas which was used in the *De ecclesia* and on Ecumenism at the end of the third session: I am afraid that they will wait until the voting has been completed except for the ceremonial ballot during the public session and then make 'corrections' in the text or append 'interpretations' to the document, Certainly, in the case of the schema on religious liberty the secretariat has leaned over backward to insert a whole paragraph in one instance and several phrases in other places emphasizing the teaching of the Church on the true religion, which safeguards against any possible use of this declaration by our people as an excuse for indifferentism. But there is a strong feeling that the Curia crowd will not be satisfied unless the whole heart is taken out of these documents."

[278] Congar's journal entries give an idea of the atmosphere while the members of the commission were applying their remaining energies to saving a text that was still under attack. On November 4 he wrote: "I did not realize that this work could be so boring and thankless. But it has to be done." On November 5: "I would never have thought that this work could be so boring and tiring. It's frightful: there's no intellectual object one could follow; but only attention to be given to each item in a stream of unconnected remarks. Each time one has to go back to the text and weigh or calculate the arguments" (II, 461-62).

Even though October 29 had been appointed as the cut-off date for submitting *modi*, it did not bring an end to the difficulties. There was no letup in the pressures being applied. On October 30 J. Guerra sent in some observations on the *textus recognitus*, claiming that these reflected fundamental concerns of a very large number of fathers, especially those belonging to the Spanish episcopate.[279] For his part, Wyszynski, in the name of the entire Polish episcopate, insisted that limits be put on the concession that allowed states to restrict religious freedom when public order and security required it.[280] He brought the matter to the Pope, who referred him to the commission, which the Pope asked to take the Cardinal's remarks into account. Difficult negotiations then began.[281]

On November 1, Fr. Boyer, of the Unitas Center, sent the cardinal vicar of Rome two *modi*, which, if accepted, would keep a sizable group of bishops (around 200) from voting no and would thereby ensure a large majority, reaching almost unanimity, in favor of the schema. Two days later Traglia relayed this message directly to the secretariat, which in turn transmitted it to Willebrands on November 5, so that he could submit these observations for consideration by the competent commission.[282] On November 6 a new request came, this time from Msgr. A. Vuccino, who, for the sake of "his own peace of conscience," also addressed Paul VI, sending eight pages of remarks.[283] On November 8 a new attack came from de Arriba y Castro, who sent his reflections with regard to a letter, dated October 23, from a lawyer in Barcelona on the subject of religious

---

[279] De Smedt papers, 1630 and, for the *modi*, 1631. At almost the same time, some Catalan Catholics, most of them connected with Catholic Action movements, spoke in a different voice in their "Message of the Catholics of Barcelona to the Council Fathers" (October 28, 1965). The religious situation in Spain was described not as ideal but as a Catholicism in crisis (ongoing dechristianization, especially among intellectuals, the young, and workers), that was marked by the "complete lack of respect for the rights and freedoms of the human person in public and political life" and oppressive, especially regarding the language, culture, and institutions of Catalonia.

[280] See Wyszynski's letter to De Smedt (October 28, 1965) with his *modus* on the subject, and De Smedt's response (November 5) (*AS* V/3, 488 and 490-94). Wyszynski was determined to vote against the text if it were not changed to his satisfaction. He also asked that the remark he had made in the hall about the difference between Western vocabulary and Marxist vocabulary be introduced into the schema (see *JPrignon*, November 14, 1965 [Prignon papers, 1614, 1]).

[281] The negotiations on November 12 involved Wojtyła, De Smedt, Willebrands, Pavan, and Hamer (*AS* V/3, 563-64); they led to the introduction of four changes in the text, which was already at the printing house.

[282] See *AS* V/3, 485-87.

[283] See ibid., 494-503. His request was also passed on to Willebrands.

freedom.[284] Careful consideration was given to all these requests, even those that came in after the deadline, but it was like trying to square the circle.[285] The commission quite firmly resisted all these requests.[286]

On November 6 the subcommission approved the *textus denuo recognitus*. This had then to be approved by the plenary assembly of the secretariat, which was to meet for two days. After the approval of the *expensio modorum*, everything seemed finished, or so, at least, it was hoped. The new text was sent to the Holy Father before being printed.[287] The Secretariat for Christian Unity met its deadlines: distribution of the text on November 12 and proclamation on November 18. But there would be further ups and downs.

On November 12, in addition to the ongoing pressure from the Spaniards and the Poles, a new petition was addressed to Paul VI in which the declaration was attacked for putting the various religions on the same level and thereby surrendering the perennial teaching of the popes in order to satisfy non-Catholics.[288] Still more important, on November 13, when the declaration was already at the printer, Willebrands was asked to delay the printing. On November 15 Paul VI relayed to the secretariat six *modi* composed by Boyer or inspired by Ciappi; the commission was to consider these that very day.[289] As soon as the answer to these was given to Paul VI, he authorized the printing of the text but asked that the report to be given include a passage answering the objection that the teaching was not in continuity with the teaching of the magisterium.

---

[284] For this entire set of documents, see ibid., 526-30.

[285] Congar speaks of the meeting on November 6 of the three subcommissions at which an effort was made to satisfy the requests of Wsyzinski and Boyer (*JCongar*, November 6, 1965; II, 463-64).

[286] Hermaniuk confided that things had gone well, even if the commission had not been able to do everything it wanted. But he stressed the point that the commission had not let itself by moved by pressure from the *Coetus Internationalis Patrum* (see *JDupont*, November 13, 1965, 195).

[287] See *AS* V/3, 516. There was already a failure to meet the deadlines in the calendar established by the General Secretariat (*AS* V/3, 742).

[288] Among the forty-eight signers were Carli, Sigaud, Santos, and Morcillo (see *AS* V/3, 551-53). This petition was to be sent from Felici to Willebrands (ibid., 554). It led to the addition of a passage at the beginning of the report.

[289] For the *modi*, see *AS* V/3, 566-67. A rough draft of a response to these *modi* is in Prignon papers, 1356: "Msgr. De Smedt. Response to one of the *modi* from the Pope, which were handed to the Secretariat for Unity on November 15, 1965." Four of these *modi* were rejected, including one that spoke of the Church as "indulgens moribus modernis." Acceptance of this would have meant that religious freedom was being based on mere opportunism, a point on which some Spanish bishops had insisted on occasion (see Bea's letter to Dell'Acqua, November 15 [*AS* V/3, 564-65]).

On November 17 the new text and its *expensio modorum* were distributed to the fathers; De Smedt was yet again to explain it to them.[290] Judging by the new text, some observers thought that the members of the secretariat had been more sensitive to the objections of the opposition than to the judgment of the majority.[291] But this response misjudged all the efforts made by the promoters of the schema to avoid weakening it too much and to guarantee its completion.

Meanwhile, the *Coetus Internationalis Patrum* continued its campaign in favor of a *non placet* during the final vote, which was to be taken on November 19;[292] at one point Father Tucci thought that "the Pope would hesitate to promulgate the *De libertate* because of the opposition it continues to elicit."[293] The *Coetus Internationalis Patrum* is said even to have intervened once again with the Pope in an effort to get the declaration stricken from the conciliar agenda on the grounds that the text had not been sufficiently changed, especially in no. 1 on the teaching about the true religion.[294]

Despite all the amendments and toning down of the text, out of 2,216 fathers voting there were still 249 implacable bishops who voted no.[295] Moreover, since it had not been possible to promulgate the declaration at a public session on November 18, as had been intended, it continued to be subject to various pressures from stubborn opponents. Thus, after the vote had been taken, a new move was made by Ruffini, who, on November 19, rather than following the normal channels, sent directly to the Secretary of State some observations on the schema that his "love of the Church" suggested to him.[296] Msgr. Staffa did the same thing.

[290] See *AS* V/3; the text is on 703-18; the *relatio de modis* is on 718-77. For the oral report, see 718-23. This happened while Abbé Prévost's book *Rome ou le chaos*, with a preface by Ottaviani, was being presented to the public in Rome and in the presence of Michel de Saint-Pierre.

[291] See Moorman, *Vatican Observed,* 162.

[292] In his diary for November 19, de Lubac wrote: "Father Charles Boyer is worried about the possible consequences of the decree on religious freedom; a bishop told me Boyer was advising people to vote against it" (*Jde Lubac,* 669).

[293] *JDupont,* November 24, 1965, 215.

[294] See *JCongar,* November 19; II, 479.

[295] For the results of the votes, see *AS* IV/7, 95-96.

[296] See the letter from Ruffini to Cicognani (*AS* V/3, 590-92). While acknowledging that the new version of the schema was much better than those that preceded it, Ruffini still found serious problems with it, especially its recognition of the right of other religions to propagandize and its weakening of the rights of the Catholic Church, "the only true religion," rights recognized in concordats. Dell'Acqua sent this letter on to De Smedt on November 23, while emphasizing that Paul VI not see how changes could be introduced into the schema after its approval. The Pope did ask, however, that, if possible, account be taken of the objections in the report or in commentaries (De Smedt papers, 1676).

On November 26 he too addressed the Secretary of State directly. Once again, Dell'Acqua urged De Smedt to see how he could respond in his report.[297] Still another attack came from Browne, who on November 26 sent new proposals of Boyer to Cicognani.[298]

As a result, it was only at the end of the period, during the public session on December 8, that the Declaration would be promulgated. The Declaration on Religious Freedom had been introduced to the Council on November 18, 1964, as the fifth chapter of the schema on ecumenism; it then followed a very winding course that was strewn with crises and bitter confrontations. Despite all his efforts, Paul VI had not succeeded in putting together the consensus he so badly wanted, even at the price of compromises for which many reproached him. Reduced now to fifteen articles, the Declaration had, after its introduction, two parts: I. General teaching on religious freedom; II. Religious freedom in the light of revelation. Along the way, it defined the object of the religious freedom with which the schema was dealing, asserted more clearly the ontological basis of this right, clarified the concept of public order, brought out more clearly the duties of human beings in regard to truth, and went more fully into the teaching of revelation on the subject. In the eyes of some, this refining of the subject had reduced the impact of the Declaration. To the majority, however, this Declaration was a major success of Vatican II.

Exchanges of views on the apple of discord that religious freedom had become continued even after the Council was over. On December 15 Willebrands replied to Ruffini's objections, and on December 26 the latter wrote once again to Dell'Acqua on the same subject.[299] This is how the reception of the declaration began, and it would have a long future before it during which the declaration would show itself to be a Vatican II document of the first importance.

B. Schema XIII

Even though the mixed commission in charge of revising schema XIII had made substantial progress, the discussion of this document promised

---

[297] See *AS* V/3, 628-29 and 660.

[298] See ibid., 648-50 and 652; see also the letter of Siri to Paul VI, November 29 (ibid., 633-35).

[299] See *AS* V/3, 657.

to be full of dangers.[300] In fact, several individuals admitted that the schema would have profited from several more months of work. Only the most optimistic thought the text could attract 95 percent of the votes.[301]

The new version was quite different from the previous one. The appendixes had been incorporated into the text to form the second part, and the whole was now much longer.[302] After an introduction the schema began with a description of contemporary conditions. It was against this background that the four chapters of the first part were written: the vocation of the human person; the human community; the meaning of human activity in the world; and the role of the Church in the world.

The second part took up particular questions: the family and marriage; culture; social and economic activity; the political community; and war and peace. The questions tackled in this ninety-page section were so many, so complex, and so marked by contingency that it seemed it would be difficult to get a majority to approve the entire schema because several groups might well have good reasons for reservations on one or other point. In addition, because of the questions of a political kind that were treated in the schema (war and peace, atheism and Marxism, social justice, and so on), national divisions or the different social and historical situations in which the fathers were living might still play a role, even though the consultation that had preceded the most recent revision had been so extensive as to guarantee that in some measure the divergent orientations within the assembly had all been guaranteed proper representation.

That consultation had involved thirty fathers of the Doctrinal Commission and as many more from the Commission on the Lay Apostolate, along with another seven fathers who gave a better representation of third-world countries and those of the people's democracies. This broad consultation gave a new dimension to the relationship between commission and assembly. In addition, no other schema had been drafted so transparently, almost in the public square. A further unprecedented factor: a good hundred lay people had contributed to the development of the schema, whether as consultants or as members of the commissions,

---

[300] I am grateful to Giovanni Turbanti for the important suggestions he made to me during the writing of this section. I read with great interest his doctoral dissertation since published as *Un concilio per il mondo moderno: La redazione della costituzione Gaudium et spes del Vaticano II* (Bologna, 2000).

[301] See Y. Congar, "Le bloc-notes du Père Congar," *ICI* 248, 5.

[302] The text is in *AS* V/1, 435–516; it had increased from 25 to 106 articles.

to say nothing of all the lay people to whom the bishops had submitted the schema for comment.[303]

Reactions were generally enthusiastic, though with slight differences. The comment most frequently made was that the Council had achieved a tone and manner of expression suitable for speaking to the contemporary world. The response of a group of Catholic Action workers from independent backgrounds was a good example of the tone of some reactions: "We have here a text that is quite remarkable both for the range of subjects treated, these being at the heart of human concerns, and for the way in which they are treated: with simplicity of expression and a persuasive tone."[304]

The schema had also profited from extensive press coverage during the intersession, a fact that disturbed some: Glorieux wrote to Haubtmann that "Msgr. Felici was upset by the review in *Le Monde* of your recent press conference. He regretted that you had given so many details of schema XIII."[305] No other conciliar text benefitted more from media coverage or attracted more attention from the public because it was addressing the problems of the contemporary world and of Catholics.

There were difficulties, however. In this schema the Church accepted the bold task of explaining itself to the modern world and in so doing raised some problems, inasmuch as the schema supposed a revision of

---

[303] The Haubtmann Archive contains a list of fifty individuals "who have participated in the study of the documents [the French version of four chapters of the schema]" in March 1965 (Haubtmann papers, 1735). Items 1729 and 1731 contain the commentaries of these persons, who were from varied backgrounds: professors of theology, law, history, economics, and philosophy, manufacturers, engineers, trade unionists, militants in the political arena or in Catholic Action, social organizers, researchers (economics and humanism), members of the editorial teams of reviews, and so on. In addition to the more official consultations organized by the mixed commission itself, many readers of different backgrounds had been asked to study the schema as it was being prepared. Such consultations continued after the schema had been sent to the fathers.

[304] Haubtmann papers, 1722 (August 15, 1965). See also a reaction of the same type from the national secretariat of Action Catholique Ouvrière (France), which offered a real eulogy of the schema because of "its spiritual and missionary inspiration." This response, however, was more reserved about the second part of the schema, which dealt with the most serious problems, especially in the chapter on the family, in which the problem facing a good many families, often the most disadvantaged, namely, birth control, was not taken up (see Prignon papers, 1217, 14pp.).

[305] Glorieux to Haubtmann (Haubtmann papers, 1641). The interview given to *La Croix* (March 25, 1965) by Msgr. Ancel, vice-president of the central subcommission for schema XIII, likewise contained abundant information about the contents of the schema. Finally, the interviews which Daniélou gave to *La Croix* (April 8, 15, and 22), and his article "Le sujet du Schéma XIII," in *Études* for January 1965, gave detailed information on the contents.

earlier teaching. Another difficulty was that decisions had to be made about the nature of the document (message, directory, solemn declaration, or pastoral constitution? the last was the one finally chosen by the Coordinating Commission), its tone (exercise of prescriptive authority or fraternal dialogue?), its addressees (Christians or all persons of good will?), its point of reference (rational arguments or revelation?), its content (testimony of solidarity with humankind and basic reflection on the destiny of humanity or concrete, detailed study of the problems of the hour?), its method (deductive or inductive?), its style and language, and so on. All these contained pitfalls that would have discouraged even the most enterprising, and the general introductory report would have to raise them all.

The question of the addressees, which in turn controlled the question of style, had been raised in Haubtmann's report of August 1965 and in the written report that accompanied the schema. The drafters of the schema were not unaware of all these difficulties.[306] In the end, the question being asked was whether this "premature infant" (to use the expression of Charue) had been given enough time to reach maturity.

In its current state the schema began with an introductory section on the situation of the contemporary world and then was divided into two parts of almost equal length: "The Church and the Human Condition" (nos. 10–58) and "Some More Pressing Problems (nos. 59–103). The new schema was accompanied by a general report that covered the history of the draft since November 1964, gave a general overview of the text (title, addressee, style, method of argumentation, and the organization of the schema), and provided information about the changes made in the new version. The general report was followed by specific reports on each chapter of the schema.[307] The section devoted to marriage was the longest, occupying eight of the nineteen pages of the report on the second part. By comparison, the subject of culture occupied three and a half pages, economic and social life one page, the political community a page and a half, and war and peace four pages. It is at once clear where the sensitive points were to be found.

There was also such disagreement on the doctrinal perspective to be adopted that it threatened to break down the important Franco-German coalition[308] and, more broadly, the Central European coalition, which had

---

[306] See G. Philips, "L'Église dans le monde d'aujourd'hui," *Concilium* 6 (New York, 1965), 11–25.

[307] See *AS* IV/1, 517–28 and 529–52.

[308] De Lubac pretty much shared the views of the Germans. He wrote, as he listened to the interventions of König and Döpfner, that he was hearing "words that made good sense." Commenting on those of Frings and Volk, he wrote: "These observations seem

from the outset exercised a real leadership at the Council.[309] This situation had to be brought under control quickly, before the debate began in the conciliar hall, because everyone now knew that "the French are enthusiastic about the first part and find the second very inadequate; the Germans, on the other hand, are very unhappy with the first part (Father Rahner has criticized it harshly, finding it to be full of somewhat romantic idle chatter, and so on), but are satisfied with the second part. It is said that Cardinal Frings will intervene rather harshly against the first part, and that Cardinal Villot (Lyons) is to respond for the French side (Cardinal Liénart is a personal friend of Cardinal Frings and does not want to be the respondent)."[310]

In order to bring the two sides to some agreement, Elchinger suggested a meeting of the Franco-German group on September 17.[311] Prignon's report gives us the flavor of this meeting.

> Things were difficult from the start. Ratzinger attacked the text radically and violently. The French bishops answered that in the drafting of the text account had been taken of the petitions of a large range of opinion...; that the commission had accepted the petitions made to it and therefore drafted the text to satisfy them; that it was important to produce even an imperfect text, given the disappointment of world opinion if no schema were produced. Msgr. Philips obviously supported this view and told me that while

---

to me... to be accurate and important. But too many people of good will, who are incompetent and superficial, are clinging to this schema: Where will it lead?" Lastly, after reading the remarks of the Germans, he observed: "It is regrettable that no comparable work has emerged from the French episcopate, despite the zeal, sometimes unenlightened, of some." Finally, he told McGrath, "At least Dr. Josef Ratzinger, a theologian as peace-loving and benevolent as he is competent, ought to be asked to collaborate with the team drafting the schema" (*Jde Lubac*, September 22, 27, 27, and October 6 [pp. 626, 631, 634, and 644]. But de Lubac also distanced himself a good bit from the positions of Elchinger, finding his intervention on culture to be "lamentable" (ibid., October 3, 1965 [p. 642]).

[309] This coalition, the membership of which could vary somewhat, usually included Suenens, Liénart, Alfrink, Montini, Lercaro, Frings, Döpfner, and König. To this group should be added Léger, the only North American in the group, Bea, as a curial cardinal; and Maximos IV, as representative of the Easterners. This group had taken shape during the preparatory phase and had been very enterprising before the Council and during the first period. But as the Council advanced, this coalition seemed to fray.

[310] *JPrignon*, September 16, 1965 [Prignon papers, 1585, 2).

[311] Semmelroth, an expert on schema XIII, was very much in favor of this meeting, which was also supported by Volk. In Semmelroth's view the alliance of the French and Germans during the first and second periods needed to be revived. The meeting also included Belgian and Dutch participants (*TSemmelroth*, September 16 and 17, 1965). According to Semmelroth, Elchinger and Volk held another meeting of the same group on September 24. Finally, de Lubac spoke of another attempt, made by Hamman on October 6, to renew the bonds between the French and the Germans (*Jde Lubac*, October 6, 1965 [p. 644]).

he had not convinced Rahner, he had certainly made an impression on him and on many bishops, and that, in any case, no one had answered him. People knew very well that he, Philips, was himself not especially satisfied with the theology of the text and that he would have liked to compose a different draft; that the commission had decided otherwise and that it was better to produce a puny, weak, and sickly child than no child at all. He also asked the German bishops to take into consideration the disappointment of the world if the child was not brought to term; to consider also that this period of the Council would certainly be the last and that the text had been drafted with the knowledge that there would be no sixth version.[312]

Haubtmann's notes inform us of the content of the exchanges.[313] On the German side, Hengsbach seemed rather isolated. Being a member of the mixed commission, he could not disavow the schema; on the other hand, while the schema pleased him, he had some important reservations. As he saw it, the German episcopate was holding fast to two points: that from the outset the text was imperfect and did not constitute a starting point for a dialogue with the world, and that it should be presented as a letter from the Council to the world. In addition, Hengsbach thought the weakest chapter was the one on culture.

Rahner's objections had to do chiefly with the dogmatic foundations of the schema; he also thought that a theological epistemology was sorely lacking. Ratzinger focused his attention on six points: suppressing the first part; the difficulty in determining who the active subject of the text is ("The people of God!" "What people?"); the confusing of rational arguments and the Christian mystery; the secondary place given the Christian aspect, tacked on, with Christ appearing at the end; an excessive optimism regarding experience; and finally, Christ at the very root of faith.[314] Msgr. Volk agreed with Ratzinger: the Christian message must not be diluted in order to make it more accessible; there is a darkness in the world that can be dispersed only by Christ; we must therefore introduce the message of Christ to the world, start from Christ.

In face of this avalanche Haubtmann answered that the structure of the schema, its anthropological section, its introductory exposé, the material of the second part, the choice of addressees, and the style of the document had been decided in cooperation with Hirschmann, Tucci, and Moeller and on the basis of the remarks of the fathers. All the rest of

---

[312] *JPrignon,* September 17, 1965 (Prignon papers, 1585, 3); see also Daniélou papers, 115 and 116).

[313] Haubtmann papers, 1850a.

[314] In conjunction with what is said here, see Ratzinger's commentary in his *Theological Highlights of Vatican II* (New York, 1966) 147-71.

the arguments on the French side, as well as those of Philips, dealt with possibilities: "See what is really possible and indispensable; improve the schema in the direction of a consensus; do not endanger the schema." "The novel character of this text partially explains its imperfections, and because of these there was a danger of jeopardizing it" and of disappointing the world's expectations.

Two factors were clearly creating a burden for the work of the fathers: first, time was running out and did not allow for a rewriting of the schema *ab ovo;* and, second, the world had vast expectations of the schema now that public opinion had become aware of its content. Meeting within these narrow confines, the French and the Germans, if they did not smoothe away all differences, at least now had a better grasp of what was possible and knew they had to forego the ideal. The changes Rahner had proposed back in August were not immutable positions. Some continued, however, to ask for a change in the title on the grounds that many difficulties could be obviated if the document were called a letter rather than a constitution.

The German-speaking bishops met again on September 20,[315] and the French bishops and theologians on September 21.[316] The latter meeting, in particular, showed how outlooks had developed as the debates were about to begin. What was possible was limited by the same two considerations defining the present situation of the Council. The Council had only a few weeks in which to issue the schema, which excluded the idea of replacing it with another, and yet this was the text in which to try to achieve the ultimate goal of the Council's work as envisaged by John XXIII and maintained by Paul VI and the entire Council: that the Church should finally and truly make contact with the modern world and the real problems it was facing. If the world's expectations were not to be disappointed, the text would have to be notably improved.[317] As Philips liked to say: "The child is weak and feeble, but the important thing is that it exists. We must work not to smother it but to help it live."[318]

Among the other episcopates, positions were less sharply defined. The Italian episcopate, which met on September 14 at the Domus Mariae, did

---

[315] Ninety-one bishops were present at the meeting on September 20; Elchinger, Döpfner, and Frings were absent, probably because of the meeting of the governing bodies of the Council (Haubtmann papers, 1851).

[316] Dupont wrote: "They were very, very severe. Especially Martelet...: it's boy-scout theology" (*JDupont*, September 22, 26).

[317] Féret, "Observations générales sur le schéma XIII" (6 pages, with a one-page appendix).

[318] *JDupont*, September 18, 13.

not adopt a common view. While the *modi* that Siri had sent to the Pope on September 5 certainly did not represent the generally accepted views, the group, as a whole was quite reserved toward schema XIII.[319] The Dutch bishops, for their part, were satisfied with the text, even though some readers to whom they had submitted it had reservations.[320] The text was also very well received by the Canadians, both French speaking and English speaking,[321] as well as by the Belgian bishops, although there, too, there were some opponents.[322]

While the fathers had profited from the support of the observers in connection with the schema on religious freedom, that they would support schema XIII was far from certain. At the meeting at the Anima on the evening of September 21, Haubtmann heard from the Reformed and Lutheran observers criticisms similar to those he had heard from the German bishops; that is, the schema does not state clearly enough the reality of sin and does not take into account the great struggle between God and Satan that goes on in the world. As Haubtmann himself would note that evening: "There is far from unanimous agreement on this question: 'Is the kerygma to be given priority or, on the contrary, should we begin with the natural order in order to end with Christ?'"[323] The Orthodox, for

[319] Siri's *modi* were sent to Felici by Cicognani on September 15, and Felici in turn sent them on to Ottaviani and Cento on September 23 and 24 (*AS* V/3, 353–54, 376). The Italian Episcopal Conference published Florit's general observations on the schema on September 9, as well as his particular observations on no. 19 (on atheism) and on chapter I of the second part (on the family) on September 30. His remarks were on the whole very critical of the schema. On September 17, C. Boyer sent a note to Florit, telling him that he was right to say that atheism and communism were inseparable.

[320] *JPrignon*, September 17, 1965 (Prignon papers, 1585, 3). The English episcopate was to meet on September 22 to discuss schema XIII.

[321] The most recent commentaries of B. Lambert were much more favorable to the schema. The English-speaking Canadians invited Butler to give them a talk on September 26 on the subject of war and peace in schema XIII. Butler wrote: "Among other questioners, most of them more left-wing than myself" (*DButler*, September 26, 1965).

[322] Cornelis "is very dissatisfied with schema XIII, which he has just read, and especially with its second part. It does not take up the real problems, especially the question of marriage. This will prove an enormous disappointment for the world. The impression given will be that the Council was content to talk worthless nonsense about these questions, without really tackling the subject" (*JDupont*, September 20, 15). For an overview of reactions, see the exchanges on schema XIII at the interconference meeting on September 17 (Carnets Baudoux).

[323] See Haubtmann's handwritten notes and his text "To the Observers," dated September 21, 1965 (Haubtmann papers, 1821). See also *ICI* 251 (November 1, 1965), 17. Haubtmann's own answer to the question is interesting: "After deliberation and not without difficulty the Commission chose a third path: start not with what people have agreed to call the natural order, but with the most universally admitted truths, these being explained, whenever possible, in a biblical way."

their part, thought that there were not enough references to the Spirit; they wished the eschatological aspect emphasized more and the whole approach to adopt the perspective of divinization. The Reformed also were ill at ease with the text: a more extensive anthropology ought to precede the Christology; there was too much optimism in regard to the world, this last being a concept whose major aspects were not developed; and so on.[324]

Nor was there any lack of activity in the area of publications, whether official bulletins of the episcopal conferences or scholarly journals. There, too, the questions most affecting the concrete lives of Catholics seemed to be the ones most hotly debated, especially questions of marriage and the family.

In addition to all this, the gathering of the fathers in Rome set in motion a cycle of lectures. Among the most important on the subject as the debate began we must count those of Philips on September 20 at Tre Fontane; of Congar on September 24 at the Domus Mariae; of Butler on war and peace at the Irish College on September 26; of the Alvarez couple on September 28 on marriage; and of Schillebeekx on the next day on the same subject.[325] Surpassing all the others in importance, however, was the lecture which Chenu, who had practically been excluded from the drafting of the schema,[326] gave at *DO-C* on September 22.[327]

---

[324] Pastor Roux, "Questions critiques sur le fondement théologique de la Constitution L'Église dans le monde contemporain" (September 28, 1965), in Prignon papers, 1214. For a survey of the observers' views, see Horton's report on the meeting of the observers with Haubtmann on September 21 (*Vatican Diary*, 42–44).

[325] Notes taken during these lectures can be found in the Carnets Baudoux for the fourth period.

[326] Guano had asked Chenu to suggest some observations for his general report. See Chenu's reply of September 3, 1965. On September 23, Chenu did take part in the meeting of the subcommission dealing with the "signs of the times."

[327] According to Chenu's correspondence with Guano, the writing of the lecture had been completed as early as September 3. Though briefly hospitalized by a herniated disc, Chenu was "absolutely determined to give his lecture tomorrow on schema XIII, since they had excluded him from the drafting of this schema" (*JDupont*, September 21, 25). The lecture was printed in *DO-C*, no. 25 (no. 187 in the Italian edition) and partially reprinted in *Témoignage chrétien* for October 7. *L'actualité catholique* for October 15 published a different article of Chenu's, but one that contained substantially the same ideas. In it, Chenu strongly defended the status of "pastoral constitution" that had been given to the text. The most fully developed part of his lecture had to do with the Christian anthropology contained in the schema. The entire lecture solidly supported the text. It is echoed in Haubtmann's papers 45/1823 (typed or handwritten notes on sheets of different sizes) and 53/1881 (notes directly devoted to the lecture), 1854 and 1887.

Work was begun immediately on the more official level. Right at the beginning of the fourth period of the Council (Thursday, September 16) the central subcommission, known as the Zurich Group, met to decide how the work would proceed. The appointment of a new reporter to replace Msgr. Guano was then raised, even though the question had in fact already been settled; the subcommission, it seems, was unwilling to accept this decision without discussion. Guano's letter to Ancel was read; the group discussed the question asked by Guano of Garrone, who was to be the reporter on the first part;[328] and finally, the content of Guano's letter of September 9 to Felici was made known.[329]

But the main concern was to put in place an effective structure for the work still to be done: a commission for drafting; a commission for general matters (equivalent to the existing mixed central subcommission) that would concern itself with the coordination of the entire work, with the introduction and conclusion, the style, the method, the overall structure, and the harmonization of all the parts; and ten subcommissions.

At 9:30 a.m. on Sunday, September 18, the mixed commission in charge of schema XIII met for the first time.[330] Garrone, who had taken Guano's place, presented his oral report, and the members chose the subcommission to which they wanted to belong.[331] The next meeting was then set for Thursday, September 23. In the interval Philips drew up some "Directives for the Work of the Subcommissions."[332] Well before the beginning of the debate, then, the mixed commission was quite ready to enter upon a new stage in which everything would have to move along briskly because, according to the calendar, once the debate was finished,

---

[328] The first draft of this report was done on August 9, 1965. See Garrone's letter to Haubtmann (Haubtmann papers, 1783).

[329] Guano to Felici (*AS* V/3, 345–46). Guano suggested that Ancel, vice-president of the mixed central subcommission, be the one to present the schema in the hall.

[330] See A. Glorieux's letter of September 16, calling for the meeting (Prignon papers, 1213). According to Prignon, "Father Tromp wanted to keep the experts from coming, saying that this was not a real meeting for discussion" (*JPrignon,* September 16 [Prignon papers, 1585, 3]).

[331] McGrath also presented his report at the same meeting. We know of several lists of members of the subcommissions, one dated September 18 (Prignon papers, 1219 and 1220) and another dated September 22 (ibid., 1221), although these were incomplete since some members had not yet indicated their preferences; the lists differ only slightly. Here we shall accept the composition of the subcommissions according to the list of September 22.

[332] A two-page document, dated September 20, 1965 (Prignon papers, 1225). The directives were divided into ten points.

the amended text would have to be submitted to the secretariat on November 5, or by November 10 at the latest.

According to Haubtmann's plan,[333] the discussion in the hall was to be quite brief, eight or nine days at most. But the closer the date for it to begin came, the more the plan seemed too optimistic, especially since the Council was already lagging behind the planned calendar. The experience of the debate on religious freedom had made forecasts unreliable, especially now that it was known that the opposition would be unyielding. The success of the vote on religious freedom on September 21, however, gave some hope even to the most cautious. It was against this background, with all its contradictions, that the debate began.

In his report[334] Garrone set out, first, to show that the schema was in keeping with the pastoral purpose of the Council and with the desires expressed by John XXIII and Paul VI, as abundant references illustrated.[335] To these two authorities, a third could be invoked in support: the *vota* and suggestions of the Council fathers or, as other expressions had it, "the will of the Council," "the mind of the Council," or again, "the mind of the fathers."[336] A fourth authority was the makeup of the commission itself: all the fathers were represented in some way: "For this schema, the number of bishops was greatly increased so that there might be a truly universal representation." Finally, Garrone appealed directly to the authority of the Coordinating Commission.[337]

---

[333] Handwritten copy of a proposal sent to Felici on September 8, with the various translations of the schema (Haubtmann papers, 1833). Typewritten copy to Liénart, September 9 (ibid., 1790). This was the proposal that Liénart would defend at the meeting of the Coordinating Commission on October 13 (see *Processus verbales*, 349–51).

[334] *AS* V/1, 553.

[335] The report ended with a reference to *Ecclesiam suam* on the dialogue of the Church with the world; this came after a reference to John XXIII, who had opened the way for the Church by finding a language the world could accept. The six-page text refers twice to John XXIII and three times to Paul VI.

[336] These thoughts crop up everywhere in the text, especially in the opening paragraphs: "If the text seems at first glance to differ from the preceding text, the commission firmly asserts that it has intended, and has in fact done, nothing but adapt the preceding text completely to the wishes of the fathers. If the text also seems longer, know that the commission has scrupulously endeavored only to satisfy the wishes expressed by the fathers."

[337] "An almost insuperable task. but one that seems very well expressed by the Coordinating Commission when, in determining the theological value of this text, it decided on the title 'Pastoral Constitution.' This language would undoubtedly have pleased Pope John, by whose decision this Council came into being; we also think that it is fully consistent with the manner of acting and speaking of the Supreme Pontiff."

On all the points raised, then (changes in the text, its considerable length, its organization, style, and theological qualification, its addressees, and so on), the report always argued on the basis of authorities outside the commission that drafted the text and thereby placed the commission almost beyond attack. In short, this report was more an introduction of the authorities who supported the schema than a report on the schema itself. True enough, various problems were raised: the status of the text, its addressee, its style. But all of that was secondary to the main argument, which had to do with the authority or authorities that would be challenged if one opposed the schema.

The other constant in this report was the continual acknowledgment of the special difficulties of this schema: "The work was very difficult. Difficult by reason of the subject matter.... Difficult also by reason of its form." "When it came to the style ... the difficulty was not small"; "a difficult course indeed," and so on. The text was studded with such expressions, which could have given the impression that until that point the Council had not met with difficulties so radical. Garrone appealed for the fathers' understanding, "since the subject matter was dangerously complex and the diversity among the addressees had to be taken into account." The schema must be addressed to all human beings of good will, and, to do this, it had to avoid all technical, abstract, and theoretical language and be alive, dynamic, simple, and close to the gospel.

The report, particulary in its central part, which presented the first part of the schema, thus addressed in advance difficulties that had already been expressed. The strategy here was simply to show the doctrine that governed the schema: a Christian anthropology that gave full due to Christ as the one who recapitulates the history of the human race.

In accordance with conciliar procedure, the debate would begin with reflections on the schema as a whole. Beginning right after the vote on the Declaration on Religious Freedom, it was to last from Tuesday, September 21, to Friday, September 24. It would be interrupted by votes on the schemas on revelation and on the lay apostolate, and on September 22 it would be interrupted briefly in order to give the platform to four speakers who, with the support of seventy or more fathers, could still speak on religious freedom.[338]

In general, the schema was very favorably received; many stressed the considerable progress made in the revision of the text and congratulated

---

[338] See the minutes of general congregations 132–34 (*AS* V/1, 70–75).

the commission on its work.[339] But criticisms were not long in coming. A good number of them had to do with matters of form: its length (Landázuri Ricketts, Silva Henríquez, Rugambwa, Mason), its many repetitions (Döpfner, Landázuri Ricketts, Bea), its atrocious Latin translation (Bea,[340] Landázuri Ricketts, Ruffini, Siri, Baudoux), and its style, which some liked (Spellman, Bea), but which others wanted to see improved (Landázuri Ricketts).[341] Others desired greater unity in the text, the clarification of some concepts, and so on. The question of the addressees of the text was also raised,[342] along with the related question of the schema's style. In short, it was recognized that despite the great amount of work done on it, the text had not yet reached the desired degree of refinement.

As for the substance of the schema, while the fathers expected strong criticisms from the German side,[343] the opposition in fact came chiefly from Italian bishops (Ruffini, Siri, Amici, D'Avack) and, in a more balanced way, from Latin America (Sigaud, Castro Mayer, Aramburu[344])

---

[339] For example, Landázuri Ricketts, Bea, König, Döpfner, Lourdusamy, and Baudoux. Similar remarks were made by Ruffini, Morcillo, Aramburu, and Rusch, but in these cases they were simply rhetorical. The "but" that followed such introductory congratulations introduced lengthy attacks on the schema.

[340] Bea, in particular, found fault with the very mediocre Latin of the schema, especially in the first part, for which he offered no fewer than eighteen pages of corrections (AS IV/1, 579–96). Some Latin phrases seemed to him so obscure that he had to refer to the French text in order to determine what was meant. He reminded his hearers that the Latin text alone would be put to a vote and insisted that this official text must be intelligible; otherwise it would open the way to endless discussions of its meaning and to that extent would weaken its doctrinal authority (see AS IV/1, 578).

[341] Bea thought the schema had found the right tone and a suitable vocabulary (AS IV/1, 576). Spellman, too, insisted that this simple and humble way of speaking was entirely suitable (ibid., 559). Landázuri Ricketts disliked its use of rhetorical turns of phrase, which he thought were not suitable in such a document (ibid., 561–62).

[342] König, Hermaniuk, Rugambwa, Morcillo González. In addition, König took over a criticism of Ratzinger's and raised the question of the "subject" of the schema: Who is speaking in it? the Church? the people of God? the Council? we fathers?

[343] In fact, the criticisms of Jaeger and Döpfner, speaking in the name of ninety-one German-speaking fathers, and also the criticisms of König, were quite moderate; they praised the schema, acknowledged in particular the balance struck between the exposition of traditional teaching and the answer to contemporary questions (Jaeger, AS IV, 575), the depth of the doctrinal section, and the suitableness of its method (Döpfner, ibid., 28). Döpfner's most important criticisms were given in four notes (31–33). The first took over, verbatim, Rahner's main criticism, the gnoseological deficiency of the schema. The other three notes dealt with the theological weaknesses of the schema; that is, the relation between the natural and supernatural orders, the theology of sin, and eschatology. Of the German-speaking bishops only Rusch really attacked the schema, following the line taken in the written remarks he had submitted during the intersession (see AS IV/2, 1061–67).

[344] These views were, however, offset by the interventions of other Latin Americans who supported the schema: Landázuri Ricketts, Silva Henríquez.

and Spain (Morcillo). This opposition was not surprising, since these bishops had already expressed their reservations during earlier discussions and during the summer,[345] but the debate seemed to show more clearly the formation of a Mediterranean bloc, with a Latin American fringe, that corresponded to what until then had been the conciliar minority. Contrary to the more pessimistic forecasts, the conciliar majority, based on the bishops of Central Europe, seemed to be holding firm.

On concrete problems, such as those having to do with the economic order and social life, a new sphere seemed to be opening up: cultures foreign to the Western world. When Sigaud asserted that "it is not Asia and not Africa but Europe and later America that have driven scientific progress," African Cardinal Rugambwa could reply: "If I am not mistaken, problems are sometimes examined with Western eyes and with a somewhat Cartesian outlook. I do not say that this is done maliciously, but I do say that a better method might emerge if use were more often made also of the means supplied by the psychology of those peoples who have now reached the point of sharing in the government of the world."[346] Along similar lines Lourdusamy raised the point that "the description of the human condition in the contemporary world ... holds mainly for people living in regions that already enjoy the benefits of economic and technical progress and are excessively influenced by the effects of 'socialization,' 'industrialization,' and 'urbanization.' But, I ask you, what about the larger part of the human race that lives outside those regions, especially in Asia, Africa, and Latin America?"[347]

The validity of this analysis by the Indian bishop seemed verified in the hall itself, for it was in North America, where the phenomena in question had left such a deep mark on society, that this schema, with its exaltation of the values of progress and freedom, found its most enthusiastic supporters (Spellman, Jordan, Hermaniuk, Shehan, Baudoux).[348] To these

---

[345] See the observations sent in during the summer by D'Avack and Castro Mayer (*AS* IV/2, 1028–34).

[346] See Sigaud (*AS* IV/2, 49); and Rugambwa (ibid., 367).

[347] *AS* IV/2, 380–81. On October 1, Cardinal Slipyi supported the same judgment on the schema: "But it can escape no one that this world of ours, and at this very time, also lives behind a veil or, as they say, behind a 'curtain'; I mean the European and Asiatic East, North Africa, the Soviet Union, India, China, Japan, where over 300 million Christians also live and very frequently follow a different way of life. Rarely indeed do we hear applications of Christian principles being made to this exotic East" (ibid., 107).

[348] The intervention of Msgr. McVinney on the crisis of authority in the Church had nothing to do with the discussion — "an absurd speech," Butler wrote in his diary — and he was twice called to order by the moderator, who asked him to deal with the schema and nothing else; *AS* IV/2, 41-44; English text in *American Participation in the Second Vatican Council*, ed. V.A Yzermans (New York: Sheed and Ward, 1967) 255-58.

worlds another must be added, made up of the countries of the East with their requests and concerns.[349] In summary, even though the Council was at this point discussing the text in only general terms, it was already clear that when the discussion of concrete questions came, these regional sensibilities would make themselves heard. Indeed, the question of atheism had already been raised (Castro Mayer and Kominek), as well as the question of the legitimacy of a nation preparing itself for war and, to this end, requiring its children to serve (Spellman).[350]

But the dividing line between groups of fathers was not determined solely by regional or geographical imperatives. Different evaluations of the schema could also depend on basic theological options (theology of creation and redemption, Christian anthropology) and even on philosophical presuppositions. Depending on which side of this line one stood, the schema could seem either a "Magna Carta of modern paganism" or a "Magna Carta for the life of contemporary humanity."[351]

1. Philosophical Presuppositions and Theological Options

Some fathers, such as Döpfner, liked the concrete way in which the schema reflected on the questions of contemporary humanity, while Hermaniuk, for his part, regretted the Scholastic tone and overly static point of view of its reflections.[352] Others, however, regretted the abandonment of Thomist philosophy, and of metaphysics as well, in favor of a more concrete, phenomenological approach. Sigaud condemned this shift:

> The authors of the schema seem to have deliberately abandoned the principles, method, and spirit of Scholastic philosophy and to have adopted the method and principles of modern phenomenology, or so it seems.... But this desire to speak like the philosophers of today and in the language of phenomenology easily leads to the acceptance also of the principles of that school. But that school does not reach metaphysics, the abstract knowledge of beings. As a result, it does not attain to principles and to firm and immutable metaphysical truths.
> If the Church accepts such a philosophy, it will meet with very great dangers. For phenomenology, especially in the form of "existentialism," denies any knowledge of the nature of things. As a result, our ideas do not grasp objective truth, which is the position taken in nominalism. But if we accept

---

[349] See Kominek, who spoke in the name of all the Polish bishops (AS IV/2, 387).

[350] Spellman had already taken up this question in the written remarks he submitted during the intersession (see AS IV/2, 1000).

[351] De Proença Sigaud ended his intervention with the first expression, and Hermaniuk ended his with the second (AS IV/2, 50 and 53).

[352] See AS IV/2, 51 and 52.

nominalism, we throw the door wide open to Marxism. Marxism is nothing else than the radical, antihuman consequence of the denial of the objective value of our universal ideas.[353]

Aramburu was in complete agreement with Sigaud. The first task of the schema was not to study the concrete problems people have to tackle but "to explain the natural human condition, as philosophically accepted by everyone."[354] It must therefore avoid speaking of what is transitory, of concrete phenomena, and deal rather with the nature of things. König spoke along the same line, but he was less radical and had different reasons for doing so. In his view the analysis of the human condition in the contemporary world carried with it the danger of attaching so much importance to what is transitory that the constitution could rapidly become outdated and its teaching obsolete. Rather than starting with concrete realities and particular facts, then, more attention should be paid to those ultimate questions that keep on rising under new forms in every generation.[355]

Several fathers found fault not only with the schema's optimism but also with its excessive confidence in the temporal order; it did not bring out clearly enough the ambiguity of present realities (Jaeger, Bea, Renard) and the presence of evil (Renard, Rusch) in earthly things, marked as these are by original sin (Renard, Sigaud). If the reality of sin is not taken sufficiently into account (Döpfner, Siri, König), the reality of the cross of Christ (König, D'Avack) and of grace (D'Avack, Rusch) is in danger of being played down. In fact, along with the order of salvation and redemption, the supernatural order is in danger of being devalued (D'Avack). The schema could almost be accused of giving in to naturalism (D'Avack) and being satisfied with offering the people of our time purely earthly hopes (Castro Mayer) instead of shedding the light of revelation on all of reality (Amici, Döpfner, Sigaud, Siri). From this point of view, the schema risked being more a philosophical text than a clearly theological one (Rusch), of being just one more form of wisdom rather than the living gospel (Lourdusamy). The Church should answer questions of the temporal order by clearly presenting the teaching of the gospel (Siri), for if the Church refuses to offer the gospel to the world, there will be no commitment to dialogue.[356]

---

[353] Ibid., 48. He added: "If, then, the commission thinks it useful to use language smacking of phenomenology, let it also take care to present clearly the philosophical and sociological principles of Thomism, which the ecclesiastical teaching office has sanctioned by its authority."

[354] Ibid., 39.

[355] König, ibid., 26–27; see also Rugambwa, ibid., 367.

[356] This was the point made especially by Amici (ibid., 34–35).

With a large number of fathers offering the same criticisms on the crucial point of the schema's theology, the Germans found themselves with
strange bedfellows. This particular question also led on to some others,
among them that of the view taken of the modern world and the more
theological question of Christian anthropology. The German school,
whose sensibilities were closer to those of the Lutherans and undoubtedly
bore the impress of recent tragic history, called for a clear distinction
between the natural and supernatural orders. Döpfner was the one who
most clearly presented this demand of the German-speaking group, a
demand rooted in Ratzinger's sharp critique of the schema.

The viewpoint taken in the schema was different. It preferred to emphasize the continuity between creation and redemption, nature and grace, the
natural order and the supernatural order. Shehan was the most ardent
defender of this approach and even asked that the schema join the natural and supernatural still more closely. To his way of thinking the two
orders are intimately united in concrete reality. The concrete human person is the place where a harmonious synthesis is made of the natural order
with the supernatural.[357] The Christian accepts both levels without dis-
sociating them, and an authentic Christian anthropology must be able to
unite them. Jordan (Edmonton) likewise liked the fact that in the schema
social and economic progress was harmonized with the mysteries of creation and redemption.[358]

2. *Two Readings of the Contemporary World*

Both of these divergent emphases in anthropology came from the reading of the scriptures, one side putting more emphasis on the texts of John
and Paul, which they frequently cited (Jaeger, Bea, D'Avack, Sigaud),
while the others rarely referred to them. At a deeper level these different
emphases resulted from two readings of the contemporary world and its
history or from two different basic attitudes toward creation and earthly
realities. Where Jaeger found an "unrealistic optimism," Baudoux (Saint-
Boniface) saw a "healthy optimism."[359] When three European bishops
wanted to moderate the optimism of the text (Jaeger, Renard, Kominek),
two Canadian bishops (Baudoux and Jordan) said that they were satisfied
with the optimistic tone of the text. Two different historical experiences
were at work here, leading, in the one case, to a more tragic reading of

---

[357] Shehan (ibid., 368–69).
[358] Ibid., 37.
[359] Jaeger (ibid., 575); Baudoux (ibid., 374).

the world and, in the other, to a more optimistic assessment of progress and development.

Beyond these differences in sensibility could be seen a different attitude to the present age. In the contemporary world Ruffini saw primarily "a confused mass of crimes and sins that are corrupting a great part of society, especially in countries that boast of a highly refined human character"; "base morals, hostile even to the natural law, are daily becoming more widespread, as the means of corruption are continually increased."[360] This assessment went beyond even the more tragic interpretation of the world; only representatives of the classic minority — Ruffini, Siri, Sigaud, and others — were still found adopting this radical critique. For them, the world was demonized; it was a menace, and the Church was a fortress.

The two readings of the world also appealed to two different authorities: to the teaching of Pius XII, on the one hand, and to the teaching of John XXIII, on the other. Jordan pointed out that the optimism of the schema was not foreign to the sense of optimism and trust in humanity found in John XXIII.[361] While references to John XXIII were certainly more numerous (Kominek, Rugambwa), in Sigaud's view the Council could find in the twenty volumes of Pius XII's teaching a simple yet profound teaching on all the problems of the modern world.[362] Thus, depending on the direction in which minds were moving, appeal was made to different scriptural authorities and to different papal authorities. The difference was not due simply to a failure to define the word *world;* rather, as Bea brought out, the terminological obscurity reflected also imprecision on the doctrinal level.[363]

3. Conciliar Constitution or Synodal Letter?

The most important disagreement during this initial general discussion was about the schema's title and about the significance and theological qualification of the text. According to Silva Henríquez, the title was ambiguous; it could suggest that the schema had no dogmatic value even though "a number of doctrinal points are contained in our document."[364]

---

[360] Ibid., 21.

[361] Ibid., 37.

[362] Ibid., 49.

[363] Ibid., 577. See also König, who asked that the schema take as its point of departure the biblical understandings of "world," "man," and "history" (ibid., 27).

[364] Ibid., 566; see 565–66.

As for its theological note, it was enough to refer to the declaration of the Doctrinal Commission on March 6, 1964. The adjective *pastoral* could be dropped because it applied to all the conciliar documents: "Let the schema be called simply 'A Constitution on the Church of the present time.'"

But this view was not shared by Siri and Morcillo González. They challenged the very word *constitution*. Sigaud argued in syllogistic form:

> A constitution is a fundamental law in one or another area, and is known as an essential law.... But our schema cannot be described as a law ... either in its content or in view of those to whom it is addressed. It is neither a law concerning belief nor a law concerning action. The non-baptized are not subject to the Church's authority. But schema XIII is addressed to both Catholics and non-Catholics, to the baptized and the non-baptized. It cannot be a law, therefore, due to a lack of authority in the lawgiver. But if it is not a law, then much less is it a constitution.[365]

He suggested, therefore, that the schema be called a message or a letter. Kominek replied to this argument two days later. Passing over the reasoning based on the addressees, he established the legislative value of the schema by arguing from its content:

> To us, the Polish bishops, this pastoral constitution seems to deal with pastoral practice and to be equivalent to *Lumen gentium,* which sets forth the fundamental constitution of the Church and in which timeless dogmas and other obligatory beliefs of the Church are explained in light of the signs of our time and in appropriate language. To that constitution, which can be described as containing the "law of belief" *(lex credendi)* corresponds schema XIII ... as containing a "law of action" *(lex agendi)* that establishes for us a program and way of acting in the contemporary world.[366]

Morcillo González echoed Sigaud's argument based on the addressees of the schema, but he added that the theology of earthly realities had not developed sufficiently for it to have value as law for Catholics. Moreover, in recent councils, the title "constitution" had been given only to texts of a dogmatic kind. Finally, he reminded the fathers that, contrary to what the report had said, it was not the Coordinating Commission that decided that "pastoral constitution" best fitted the text. That commission — and not even a majority of it — had only approved the title suggested to it by the mixed commission. In his judgment the title was unsuitable, and he suggested that the schema be called "A Declaration of the Church on

---

[365] Ibid., 47–48.
[366] Ibid., 387.

Establishing a Dialogue with the Contemporary World" or "A Declaration of the Church to the Contemporary World."[367]

Doubtless in order not to multiply unnatural alliances, the Germans for their part bracketed their own keen desire to change the title of the schema. But, while not attacking its status as a pastoral constitution, they did work to lessen its importance. Döpfner emphasized that, even if the schema were amended and improved, it would remain weak and full of imperfections. That is why it had to be said openly and humbly that "our document is a kind of beginning of a new dialogue with the world, and this beginning is marked by quite a few difficulties";[368] it was to be hoped that the future would bring a "clearer, more abundant, and more effective teaching." Jaeger, for his part, had a complementary but more concrete suggestion; he proposed that after the Council a special commission be formed for developing a compendium that would give a summary of Catholic teaching on present-day problems and show the harmony between progress and Catholic teaching.[369] However cautiously, these interventions clearly displayed significant reservations about both the doctrinal value of the schema and its teaching.

At this stage time could be either in favor of the schema or against it: the text might be adopted simply because of the pressure of events, or out of weariness; on the other hand, the lack of time might be made a pretext for putting an end to it. Here, too, the positions were not hard and fast and did not follow the usual divisions.[370] While the attacks by Siri and Ruffini had nothing surprising about them, the criticisms of the Germans left many fathers confused. And geography alone could not explain the divisions that had arisen. Two types of mind were confronting one another: some preferred a more notional and dogmatic approach, others one more experiential or more existential.

---

[367] Ibid., 380; see 379–80. As the debate continued, this question would arise again. For example, Heenan would suggest that the schema be called simply a message; Conway preferred "A Pastoral Letter from the Council to the People of Our Time" or "A Synodal Letter from the Council to the World" (ibid., 66).

[368] Ibid., 29.

[369] Ibid., 576.

[370] The following note made by Dupont after a conversation with H. Denis and J.-M. Tillard, was quite representative of the atmosphere: Denis and Tillard "are uneasy with the rapid pace of the votes; the majority of the bishops are voting without knowing too much about the subject; anything at all could be passed, all they want is for things to move quickly. As for schema XIII, it might be asked whether it would not be better to leave final approval of it to the Synod of Bishops" (*JDupont*, September 24, 23). After a conversation with Morcillo, Philips agreed with his suggestion that the document be titled a "synodal letter" (Prignon, personal notes, September 26, 1965 (2); Prignon papers, 1592).

4. Winning the Vote to Accept the Schema

At the end of the first week of debate,[371] despite all the imperfections of the schema, the "possibilist" option seemed to be winning out. "Everyone is well aware," Prignon wrote, "that it is impossible to produce a new rehash of the schema or, more accurately, to start all over again from the beginning ... that in this case the better is the enemy of the good."[372] The Germans, despite their considerable, if restrained, criticisms[373] and despite their desire to play down as much as possible the significance of the schema, had opted for the solution that the schema had to be improved. König's conclusion pointed in that direction: "The schema has already entered upon essentially the right path, and we approve this new kind of conciliar teaching. But the schema will better achieve its purpose if its scope is even more clearly perceived, if its manner of presenting doctrine is simplified, and if the text is limited to the more serious and more fundamental principles."[374] But at the end of a meeting of Volk with experts Klostermann, Hirschmann, Ratzinger, and Rahner, Semmelroth was forced to conclude that despite the depth of the discussions he had gotten nothing useful for improving the schema. Rahner was not realistic enough and could not identify adequately what concrete results he wanted to obtain.[375]

Only the irreducible opposition remained against voting on the schema. The most pessimistic, for whom Msgr. Amici became the spokesman, did not believe that the schema could be improved in the short time left for the Council. Even if it might deeply disappoint the expectations of public opinion, the fathers must resolve to give answers drawn from the gospel, without other developments or commentaries, to concrete and urgent questions, instead of stubbornly trying to revise the schema.[376]

---

[371] Some later interventions discussed the schema in general, for example, those of Gracias and Slipyi on October 1 (see *AS* IV/2, 103–1100).

[372] *JPrignon*, September 22, 1965 (Prignon papers, 1590).

[373] By and large, although they did not violently attack the schema, the Germans did not retreat from the position they had taken in August except on one point: they did not call for naming the schema "A Letter from the Council Fathers" instead of "Pastoral Constitution." All their other criticisms were voiced: the epistemological defects and theological lacunas of the schema (distinction between the natural and supernatural orders, absence of a theology of sin, grace, and redemption), inadequate consultation with lay experts in economics, vagueness of the subject of the schema, lack of a definition of *world*, and so on).

[374] *AS* IV/2, 27.

[375] *TSemmelroth*, September 28, 1965, 128.

[376] See *AS* IV/2, 34. Amici spoke in the name of the bishops of the Flaminian and Emilian regions. His intervention was composed by U. Neri, one of Dossetti's collaborators.

When the time came to move on to a vote accepting the schema, of the twenty-six speakers eighteen seemed determined to support the schema. But on September 23, after the assembly had agreed to end the general discussion of the schema and the sitting moderator, Lercaro, called for the vote on the schema, 2,111 of the fathers voted yes, only 44 voted no, and one vote was invalid.[377] Even so, despite everything, the Council fathers gave the impression of lagging behind the views of the Catholics so far consulted. With only a few exceptions, such as Jordan and Baudoux, no one was heard to express strong support for the schema.

5. The Signs of the Times

Once the text was accepted, it was possible to move on to a discussion of its various parts. On September 23 the subcommission dealing with the signs of the times had met in order to take stock before the discussion in the Council. The largely non-European makeup of this subcommission gave it a special character, and indeed it produced a text that stood apart from all the others produced by the Council.[378] Msgr. McGrath (Santiago de Veraguas), who was to give the report on the "introductory exposition," emphasized the aptness of the method if the intention was to begin a dialogue with the world. He then noted that the subcommission had been anxious to include fathers and experts from all parts of the world, but especially from Asia, Africa, and Latin America, so that the schema would not be a purely Western text.[379]

A preliminary account of the human condition in today's world served as a kind of descriptive introduction to the schema, a scenario intended to suggest the changes that the contemporary world was undergoing and to bring out their significance. McGrath was aware of the somewhat unusual nature of this descriptive section, but he claimed that it was needed in light of the method adopted: the reading and interpretation of the signs of the times that John XXIII had proposed.

[377] The vote was taken toward the end of the general congregation, and the result was announced the next day. See AS IV/2, 390, as well as the minutes of the general congregation (AS IV/1, 75).

[378] According to the minutes, the bishops present at the meeting were McGrath, Nagae, D'Souza, Fernandes, Wright, and Câmara. The experts were Ligutti, Martelet, Medina, Galilea, Gregory, Chenu, Houtart, Caramuru, Sugranyes de Franch and de Habicht. On that same day the mixed commission for schema XIII also met to approve Hengsbach's report. The list of the members of the various subcommissions was also distributed.

[379] McGrath's report is in AS IV/2, 391–94.

On September 23 and 24 eight fathers, three of them Belgian, spoke
on this short introduction to the schema; all in all, their speeches did
not really enrich the arguments heard thus far, but simply gave further
support to remarks already heard. Thus the significant reservations of
the Italians were expressed by Marafini, and the German criticisms were
repeated, harshly this time, in the interventions of two leading lights,
Frings and Volk. It was not simply the accuracy of what the schema
said that caused the Germans and the Italians difficulty; they challenged
the very method of the schema. Although the point was not clearly
made, it was the inductive method of the schema, its empirical and
descriptive approach, that baffled these speakers. They were disconcerted at not finding a classical treatise on Christian anthropology that
would present a theological vision of the world as created by God,
fallen into sin, always searching for happiness and immortality,
redeemed by Christ, caught up in the continual struggle between good
and evil, and journeying toward its supernatural destiny. They wanted
the schema to paint this theological fresco (which is permanent and
unchangeably valid for the world, to use Volk's words) and to leave
aside circumstantial or empirical details, the things that change in this
world.[380]

In contrast, Cardinal Cardijn, a man used to a different kind of thinking due to his practice of the "see-judge-act" method, was very much at
ease with this concrete and descriptive approach. He even wanted to add
to the section.[381] Similarly, Himmer said that the schema deserved the
fathers' assent because of the high quality of its description of the
world.[382]

The other main debate had to do, once again, with the interpretation of
the word *world*. On the one hand, the "vague" and "confused" meaning
given to the concept in the schema led Frings to conclude that the schema
needed "radical revision" and not simply minor alterations or corrections.
But Charue, Bible in hand, wanted *world* in the prologue to mean the
modern world to which the Church preaches God as love and proclaims

---

[380] See the interventions of Volk and Marafini (respectively, *AS* IV/2, 406–10 and
410–14). According to Volk, the schema should tell the world what it cannot know on its
own: the theological aspect of its existence.

[381] Cardijn insisted that it was "extremely important [that the Council] consider human
beings not in a general way but as they concretely are in today's world." He suggested
that three sections be added, one on the young, another on workers, and a third on the
peoples of the Third World (see *AS* IV/2, 394).

[382] *AS* IV/2, 417–19.

salvation in Christ; he also wanted the schema to be submitted to a team of biblical scholars who would be able to make the needed corrections.[383]

Once again, it was the blows inflicted on the schema that dominated the day's discussion. Frings, for example, a habitual supporter of Church reform, had dissociated himself from the schema; the opposition was not coming solely from those labeled conservatives. Once again, Elchinger tried to take a middle position. He too recommended a restructuring of the schema and asked, in agreement with his German colleagues, that the purely descriptive developments on the world be "abridged or summarized." But this did not cause him, as it did his colleagues across the Rhine, to seek a purely theological description of the world. He proposed rather that everything having to do with relations between the Church and the contemporary world be expanded and dealt with concretely and practically so that the Church would be better able to serve today's world.[384]

All these different proposals for restructuring the schema ignored the schema's special method: the reading and interpretation of the signs of the times; for Chenu, this method was the most important aspect of the schema.[385] The point was to start, neither from the teaching of the encyclicals and councils nor from the explanation of a theological vision, but from a reading of the reality that is the world. Such a turnabout seemed hardly possible. This kind of misunderstanding about the basic direction

---

[383] Frings had two other complaints against the schema: the Church's condescending attitude toward the world, and an ambiguity with regard to the purpose of the schema. Recognizable here were J. Ratzinger's criticisms of the ambiguity in the concepts of "people of God" and "world" (according to Semmelroth, Frings's intervention was composed by Ratzinger [see *TSemmelroth*, September 24, 1965, 127]). Frings's intervention is in *AS* IV/2, 405–6, and that of Charue, ibid., 419–22. Abasalo y Lecue (India) likewise pointed out the ambiguity in the use of the word *world* (ibid., 397).

[384] This intervention by the Auxiliary Bishop of Strasbourg was fully argued and developed on the basis of what the text asserted (in no. 2) to be the purpose of the schema, namely, to explain how the Church conceives of its presence and activity in the world. Elchinger's wanted the schema, in connection with all the characteristic features of the modern world, to explain very concretely how the Church intended to meet the challenge that each feature posed for it (*AS* IV/2, 118–26). Later, on September 30, in a paper distributed by the German Press Center, Elchinger began by protesting that "schema XIII is not a French schema." On Elchinger's role as mediator between the French and the German bishops, see K. Wittstadt, "Bischof Elchinger auf dem Zweiten Vatikanischen Konzil: Eine Bischofspersönlichkeit zwischen den deutschen und der französischen Kirche," *Würzburger Diözesangeschichtsblätter* 61 (1999) 367-80.

[385] On October 2, Chenu sent a note to McGrath about the various interventions that he had heard on the first part of schema XIII (McGrath papers, 1/04, 4 pp.) On October 10, he sent some observations to Hengsbach along the same lines (Hengsbach papers, 118 and 122).

and fundamental plan of the schema did not augur well for the remaining discussion.

Once the introductory explanation had been dealt with, it was possible to move on to the first part of the text with its four chapters: the vocation of the human person, the human community, the significance of human activity in the world, and the role of the Church in the modern world. The discussion began on Friday, September 24, but the time remaining at the general congregation that day barely allowed the debate to be opened before the weekend pause. Thirty-eight fathers were scheduled to speak in this three-day debate.[386] Some of these fathers spoke on points that were judged to be off the subject.[387] Others voiced a general judgment on the schema, as if they were still discussing the schema as a whole;[388] in particular, two German bishops returned to the attack by asking that the schema be restructured and that it adopt a different method than the one followed in the general exposition. Schick, Auxiliary Bishop of Fulda, proposed that the schema be restructured and deal with the various topics more briefly, more organically, and from a biblical perspective on humanity. Although this intervention passed almost unnoticed, it elicited a lively reaction from Chenu, whose cup was now full after listening to four German bishops attacking the schema with tooth and nail.[389] On that same day the very critical intervention of Bengsch (Berlin) further unsettled matters.[390] Even though he exercised great moderation and excused the trial-and-error approach of the commission as due to the novelty of such a text

[386] There were six interventions on September 24, thirteen on Monday, September 27, and fifteen on Tuesday, September 28. One more intervention was made on made on October 1.

[387] D'Souza (Bhopal) spoke on the reform of the Church and was called to order by the moderator, Döpfner; Batanian spoke on the introduction.

[388] This was true of the intervention of Cantero Cuadrado (Saragossa), who stated that the schema contained a mishmash of clerical and naturalist elements, that it erred by its naive optimism, and that it was marked by a Western mentality. The same was the case, this time in a much more positive tone, of A. Rossi, who spoke in the name of ninety-two Brazilian bishops and said he was glad that the commission had taken into account the observations offered during the third period.

[389] See AS IV/2, 636–38; Chenu's reaction is in a letter to Haubtmann of October 1, 1965 (Haubtmann papers, 1855). In Chenu's view there was no need to alter the structure and inspiration of the schema. It was not out of opportunism that the text began with observation of the human condition and ended with Christ; rather, this approach expressed a theology that refused to deduce a Christian anthropology from Christology or to present a "social doctrine" based on authority. Its intention was to discern within humanity the capacity — an obediential potency — for receiving the word of God.

[390] AS IV/2, 653–56. Eight fathers signed this intervention.

in the history of the councils, he torpedoed the schema by greatly reducing its scope, suggesting that the Council restrict itself to the clear and succinct statement of some general principles, while leaving to the pope, the bishops (especially the synods of bishops), the theologians, priests, and the faithful the responsibility for carrying on the dialogue with the world.

In Bengsch's view the discussion had made it quite obvious that the very conception of the schema was defective. In any case, the document could only be taken as a declaration and not as a constitution.[391] A schema of this length (106 numbers), taking up so many concrete questions that called for different solutions from nation to nation, and trying to meet the wishes and expectations of so many people, could not possibly be produced in the fourth period. The commission would only botch its work under the pressure of the calendar.

As the assembly turned and focused its attention to the question of atheism, other speeches on the introductory section made little impression, whether because they were less well articulated or because they dealt with less central points.[392] Even some that were of high quality did not get much attention, for example, the speeches of Guerry, who repeated the call Paul VI had issued in Bombay, and of Garrone, who spoke on the dogma of creation.[393] During the debate light also came from the East. The speeches given on the first day of the debate by Ziadé (Maronite Archbishop of Beirut) and Meouchi (Maronite Patriarch of Antioch) raised the tone of the discussion. Both spoke of the resurrection as the heart of the Christian anthropology that the schema ought to develop.[394]

---

[391] Bengsch, who had offered an alternative schema of his own, was here taking over a suggestion of the German episcopate, which, if it could not sink the schema, wanted at least to reduce it to a very simple form. Bengsch also voiced a suggestion of Volk: to invert the order of the chapters of the first part, with chapter four becoming chapter one. See also Bengsch's written remarks in AS IV/2, 656–57.

[392] See, in particular, the intervention of Méndez Arceo (Cuernavaca), who criticized the schema's silence on psychoanalysis (AS IV/2, 625–27); his intervention created many waves and was received very favorably by the press. Under this same heading also fall the interventions of Kłepacz (Lodz), Corboy (Zambia), Corral (Ecuador), Kuharic (Zagreb), and Romero Menjibar (Spain).

[393] See, respectively, AS IV/2, 485–87 and 634–35. In this same category is the intervention of Richaud (Bordeaux), who, largely satisfied with the schema, suggested some small revisions, in particular the use of the expression "social teaching of the Church." Here, too, belonged the intervention of A. Fernández (master general of the Friars Preachers), who emphasized the universal brotherhood of human beings, which followed from the oneness of their origin and their creation by God (ibid., 498–501).

[394] Ibid., 422–31 and 437–39.

6. *Atheism and Communism*

In the end, the observations on the next section focused on no. 19 of
chapter I, which had to do with atheism. Ever since the beginning of the
Council, in fact since discussion of the message to humanity, the Council had tried by all means to avoid a confrontation with representatives
from the Eastern countries and an explicit condemnation of communism;
up to this point, it had succeeded in dodging the two issues. The text now
under discussion was the result of painstaking compromise, and it was not
surprising that it was not as clear as desired. It juxtaposed a polemical
tone with openness to dialogue; it gave a very precise description of
Marxism while avoiding the name.

Several leading personalities spoke during this debate, among them König,
president of the new Secretariat for Non-Christians; Maximos IV, who spoke
for the first time during the fourth period; Florit, one of the three vice-presidents of the Italian Episcopal Conference; and Father Pedro Arrupe, new
general of the Jesuits. It was Cardinal Šeper, whose authority was all the
greater because he had lived under an atheistic regime, who started the debate
on the subject. The fourteen interventions that followed ran the gamut of
positions. Fortunately, in his opening statement, Šeper adopted a moderate
tone and opened up perspectives that a good number of the speakers could
endorse. First of all, he made it clear that the Council could not be silent on
the subject. Too many people had atheism as their inheritance and considered it to be an authentic humanism[395] and a condition of human progress.
But how was the Council to deal with such a sensitive question? How was
it to speak correctly of atheism? The Archbishop of Zagreb excluded three
approaches: condemnation, the preaching of the word of God, and the conversion of atheists. He preferred that the Council endeavor to show how
Christians could understand atheism and accept the existence of atheists.
He ended by emphasizing the point that responsibility for the spread of atheism sometimes falls on Christians who defend the established order and are
incapable of promoting the evangelical values that are sometimes seen in
atheists, even if their divine foundation is not immediately evident.[396]

These views were largely shared by other speakers. While there was
quick agreement that the question of atheism had to be tackled, most of
the speakers followed Šeper's lead; that is, they did not want condemnations but a positive presentation of Catholic teaching and a more

---

[395] This was also Msgr. Marty's view.
[396] *AS* IV/2, 435-37.

explicit commitment of the Church to the promotion of justice.[397] Also echoing Šeper, several speakers expressed the view that atheism, or at least its spread, was largely attributable to injustices and to the oppression of some human beings by others (Msgr. Pildáin, who thought capitalism the cause of atheism; Maximos IV), but no less also to the weakness of Christian witness. Maximos stressed the point that many people had become atheists because they were scandalized by "a mediocre and self-centered Christendom" that could not "make a sustained effort at solidarity with the poor," and by "the selfishness of some Christians."[398] Citing Paul VI, he, too, pointed out the values of atheists that were "borrowed from our gospel" and needed to be "traced back to their real sources." Just beneath the surface of their statements, speakers were hinting that many atheists were not opposed to God but were only waiting for "a truer presentation of God," for "a religion more in harmony with the historical evolution of humanity,"[399] and for a more authentically Christian life. In fact, as König insisted, was not the human soul naturally Christian and would it not be enough to remedy the evil of atheism if the Church did a better job of promoting social justice and combating religious ignorance?[400]

---

[397] This was true in particular of König, who insisted that a pastoral outlook would avoid excommunicating anyone and would, instead, seek ways of coexisting with the rest of humanity, a view shared by Pildáin and by Maximos, who said that humanity would not be saved from atheism by condemning Marxism. The Patriarch added that socialism and Marxism, as modern forms of economics and sociology, called not for condemnation but for the leaven of the gospel, if the aim was to separate them from atheism.

[398] AS IV/2, 451–54. Eleven bishops had signed his statement, among them Himmer, an important leader of the the Church of the Poor Group. According to A. Wenger, Maximos's intervention owed much to Father Gauthier (Wenger, IV:149). At the very least the views proposed by Gauthier in a lecture in Rome on that very day (CCCC, September 28, 1965) were quite consistent with the intervention of Maximos IV; I note, in passing, that on September 30 the Patriarch was to take part in the presentation of the Italian translation of Gauthier's book on the Church of the Poor and the Council. Speaking of the Patriarch's intervention, de Lubac wrote in his diary: "They are using him, and he is too old to realize it. Today he allowed himself to be overly controlled by Abbé Gauthier" (Jde Lubac, September 27, 1965, 633).

[399] The cited words were formulas used by Maximos IV. König would speak along the same line, giving it as his view that many atheists were such because they did not have a correct understanding of God. Marty presented similar ideas at length (AS IV/2, 632–33). De Lubac was very disappointed by Marty's intervention, which he thought overly naive in claiming that there are no real atheists. In de Lubac's view this was an invitation to "put the Church into the hands of the communist party, whose conception of the human person and of the human order was thus supposed to be perfect and not deserving of any criticism." The two men later met on September 29 to sort things out (Jde Lubac, September 28 and 29, 634 and 636–37).

[400] See his intervention in AS IV/2, 454. He referred expressly to Cardinal Šeper.

Those concerned that atheism be understood before being condemned brought up other distinctions; distinction among different forms of atheism (König); the distinction made by John XXIII between atheistic teachings and movements and atheists themselves (Maximos IV, Marty, König[401]); and distinction between atheism springing from personal conviction and a forcibly imposed mass-atheism (Wojtyła). On the other hand, Florit thought it impossible to distinguish between dialectical materialism and its atheistic nature. In fact, he thought the schema ought to declare, clearly and unequivocally, the impossibility of this distinction, so that Catholics might not think Marxism could be made acceptable by limiting it to the economic area and by rejecting the atheistic and materialistic teaching that went with it. For Florit, the two dimensions were "necessarily" linked together.

While a number of bishops called for dialogue (König, Maximos, Marty), their position was not shared by all. The bishops from Eastern Europe, who spoke on the basis of experience, feared that the Council might prove weak in the face of this scourge of the contemporary world. The harshest outburst was undoubtedly that of Msgr. Hnilica, a Czechoslovak bishop who had been in a concentration camp and was now living in exile in Rome. He reminded his hearers that one trait of the Church's condition in today's world was precisely that, in large measure, it lived under oppression by a militant atheism that depended on a political and economic system forcibly imposed on its citizens.[402] Stating that he was speaking not out of hatred but out of love for his persecuted brothers, he reminded the Council that atheism was the most serious threat of our time; he even suggested that a special schema be devoted to the subject.

The same tone appeared in the intervention of Msgr. Rusnack (Ukrainian rite auxiliary of Toronto), who on April 13, 1955, had been arrested, along with all the religious of the country, and imprisoned in a concentration camp. He directly attacked "communism" (the word occurred ten times in his intervention), and he found it scandalous that a twentieth-century Council should fail to face this problem. In his view the question of communism was not reducible to that of atheism, and the Council could not remain silent about it.[403] While some fathers were afraid that a confrontation with communism would contribute to a deterioration of the

---

[401] This distinction is taken not from König's intervention in the hall but from an interview he gave to *Corriere della Sera* on October 24.

[402] *AS* IV/2, 629–31.

[403] Ibid., 639–42. While he liked what was said about Marxist atheism (although the statement was too brief), it was insufficient. Needed were a longer section that would go more deeply into the question of atheism and a special declaration on theoretical and

Church's situation in the Eastern countries, Rusnack thought that, on the contrary, the communists were afraid of these facts being made public and would in the end grant what worldwide public opinion was insistently demanding. With more nuance Msgr. Elko (of the Ruthenians, Pittsburgh) also wanted the Council to issue a more explicit condemnation of atheism.[404] It is not surprising that it was hard for the observers from the Orthodox Patriarchate of Moscow to listen to this debate.

It was the intervention of Father Arrupe, Jesuit Father General, that created the greatest stir in the aula, in the media (especially in the United States), and in his own order.[405] He focused his intervention on organizing the struggle against atheism and wanted to offer the Council a plan of action somewhat similar to the one developed in his Society as the result of an express call from Paul VI.[406] Unfortunately, the tone of his intervention was too aggressive, even military, as he described atheism as a scourge that was invading the Church, contaminating almost the whole of culture, and exerting an almost unqualified control over the media; this last claim, of course, stung the journalists.[407] Eager to swing into action with serried ranks and a coherent plan, he urged that all the special concerns of individual dioceses be sacrificed for the sake of "absolute obedience to the Supreme Pontiff," a proposal that left many

practical communism. Pildáin also spoke on communism, but, unlike Rusnack and in keeping with the classical teaching of the encyclicals, he wanted the Council to condemn liberal capitalism as well.

[404] At this same time a petition signed by 473 priests of the United States asked the Council to issue a clear condemnation of communism.

[405] *AS*, IV/2, 481-84; English translation in *Council Daybook, Session 4*, 61-62. Dupont speaks of a "severe echo at the Biblicum.... On this intervention the General had consulted almost no one (except for one or another Spaniard). His entourage told him straight out that he had made a mistake" (*JDupont*, September 29, 1965, 50). Rouquette confirms that the assistants had not been consulted (*JRouquette*, September 28, 1965). Arrupe's claim that press circles had been infiltrated by communism deeply shocked journalists, especially in the United States, and they did not fail to condemn the statement.

[406] When Paul VI received the general congregation of the Jesuits on May 7, 1965, he entrusted to the Society the task of fighting atheism. A plan for this was developed, and on September 23 (four days before his intervention), Arrupe was received by Paul VI. According to Rouquette, the Pope had approved the text, as had Dell'Acqua (*JRouquette*, October 11, 1965).

[407] See *Études* (November 1965), 575ff.; *ICI* (October 15, 1965), 22; *The Tablet* (October 16, 1965), 1162; *The Tablet* (October 30, 1965), 1224–25; *Der Spiegel* (October 27, 1965), 85–87; *NCWC News Service* (October 22, 1965); and *Catholic Herald* (October 29, 1965); *Council Daybook, Session 4*, 59. The reactions of Rouquette and de Lubac differed sharply. The former looked at the limitations of the intervention; the latter found it to be "rich and timely" and thought it had been misunderstood and criticized (*Jde Lubac*, September 27 and 28, 1965).

of the fathers puzzled. Did he mean to put the entire Church under the rule of the Society of Jesus? Arrupe, who had not been present during the struggles of the earlier periods, did not understand how bitter the battle over collegiality had been and how the bishops were now annoyed if anyone seemed to want to go back on that subject by asking for centralized action. In any case this rough intervention elicited a great deal of discontent among journalists, among some episcopates, the French in particular, and among many observers.[408] Coming from a Spaniard, the thought of "establishing a Christian society" left his audience dazed. Was this a call to set up a Christian state à la Franco? All these misunderstandings contributed to Arrupe's stumble at this, his entrance into the Council.

The discussion of atheism also brought up again the question of religious freedom. König suggested that the Council condemn every kind of persecution, since freedom of conscience must be an inalienable right of every human person. He even suggested that the Council ask atheistic governments to subscribe publicly to a text guaranteeing religious freedom. At the other extreme, Santos wanted every reference to religious freedom removed from this schema; he thought it was out of place because another document was dealing with that question. Not surprisingly, this was also the opinion of Msgr. Llopis Ivorra (Coria-Cáceres).

At the end of this long and feverish debate the moderator announced the end of interventions on the first part of the schema; the fathers could now move on in the discussion of schema XIII.[409] Clearly there was still a lot on the plate, especially if one wanted a more satisfactory version of no. 19, which had given rise to so many problems.[410] For the moment, the

---

[408] See *JRouquette*, September 29, 1965, on the "explosion" it caused in the American group and on the reactions of Duff, who accused the Father General of being worse than McCarthy and seeing communism everywhere, and so on. Rouquette even admitted that Arrupe gave the impression of "returning to the themes of our integrists regarding the atheistic mafia that rules the free world." Arrupe had to meet with the ten or so Jesuit journalists from *La Civiltà Cattolica* and justify himself. Rouquette had the impression of having listened to a speech for the defense that had run into a "wall of incomprehension," which was, he added, perhaps "more apparent than real," for he realized that Arrupe was a highly intelligent man and could not go back on his word in public (ibid. [October 11, 1965]). In addition, he noted that Arrupe later adjusted his aim. Arrupe also met with the French cardinals, along with Garrone and Veuillot, and explained his thinking more clearly.

[409] There would be three interventions on October 1 at the 140th general congregation, by Slipyi (on atheism), Gracias (Bombay), and Schmitt (Metz).

[410] Before the end of the debate on schema XIII, that is, on September 29, a group of fathers circulated a petition for the introduction into no. 19 of a condemnation of communism (*AS* V/3, 557–63) (see G. Turbanti, "Il problema del comunismo al concilio Vaticano II," in *Vatican II à Moscou (1959–1965)*, ed. A. Melloni [Leuven, 1997], 147–87).

only thing to do was to follow the suggestion of Marty and entrust the new version to the secretariat in charge of the dialogue with non-Christians.

7. *Disputed Questions*

On September 29, after seven days of long and difficult work, the Council entered upon a transition that promised to be even more turbulent and sensitive.[411] Hengsbach's report signaled the opening of debate on the second part of the schema,[412] which had five chapters: marriage and the family; culture; economic and social life; the life of the political community; and war. As the reporter noted, this transition would lead into the discussion of concrete questions that were likely to give rise to many disputes. He reminded the fathers that, given the variety of situations to be seen around the world, the Council should not get involved in the study of overly specific questions and therefore that even in this second part a distinction had to be made between general principles and specific applications. In particular, he pointed out the difficulty the commission had in reaching a position on the question of war and peace. While he referred to the possible controversies on the chapter on war and peace, he made no such prediction about the discussion of the chapter on marriage and the family, even though no other chapter in schema XIII gave rise to as many disputes. Twenty-six fathers would speak on the subject, a number greater than the number of speakers in the general discussion of the schema.[413] (The four chapters of the first part had elicited only thirty-eight interventions in all.) The fathers were thus forewarned that the Council was entering a turbulent period.

a. From *Casti connubii* to Vatican II

During the general debate on schema XIII, Msgr. de Proença Sigaud had pointed out that in the twenty volumes of the teaching of Pius XII the Council fathers would find instruction on all the problems of the contemporary world. Vatican II had only to repeat, more fully and more

---

[411] The course of work on the second part of the schema had been decided at the meeting of the moderators on September 28 (see the minutes, *AS* V/3, 383). The moderators required that, unlike the discussion of the first part, the discussion of the second part proceed chapter by chapter so that the discussion might be more coherent and not deal with several questions at once (see the letter of Msgr. De Vito, ibid., 384).

[412] *AS* IV/3, 13–16.

[413] It might be said that this chapter was evenly matched with the chapter on war and peace, but the three interventions on the last day of the debate (October 8) had nothing to do with chapter V.

solemnly, the teaching of the ordinary magisterium of recent popes. There was no need to think about new questions or to adopt a new language and new perspectives on the teaching of the past. Contrary to what John XXIII had urged in his opening address, it seemed that the Council need only repeat and put its seal on the teaching of the popes. Thus, in discussion of the chapter on marriage, according to de Proença Sigaud, it was impossible to advance beyond *Casti connubii*: "At the beginning of his Encyclical *Casti connubii*, Pius XI has already ... explained the nature and dignity of marriage and has done so better and more briefly!"[414] Everything had already been said; it only needed to be repeated. This was true especially in the key questions of the ends of marriage. "In its resolution of February 1, 1944," Muñoyerro reminded the fathers, "the Congregation of the Holy Office barred the opinion that the primary end of marriage is not the procreation and rearing of children."[415] The same was also true of the question of fertility.

Referring back to Ruffini's intervention, Msgr. Reuss made it clear that since the question had been entrusted to a commission, it was not to be regarded as already answered.[416] On the contrary, it must be further studied, as Suenens had asked, in an intervention that in the end had disappointed many.[417]

b. Rethinking the Church's Teaching on Marriage and Family

Although a number of fathers took their stand firmly on the positions found in *Casti connubii*, others wanted a renewal in what the Church had to say about marriage and the family. The first two interventions illustrated the difference between the two approaches.

As soon as the debate began Cardinal Browne brought up for discussion the distinction between "the primary end, that is, the end which

---

[414] *AS* IV/3, 17. He also referred to recent decrees of the Holy See. Several other fathers would likewise refer to the encyclical of Pius XI: Muñoyerro (ibid., 37–39), Majdanski (ibid., 42–44), Da Silva (ibid., 73–74), and von Streng (ibid., 90–91).

[415] Alonso Muñoyerro (ibid., 38).

[416] Reuss (ibid., 84).

[417] See his first *votum* (*AS* IV/3, 30–31). In the Prignon papers there is a draft of an intervention for Suenens, as well as the reflections of S. Moore, sent to Prignon on September 16, 1965, on this *votum* of Suenens (Suenens papers, 2764 and 2675). His second *votum*, suggesting a celebration of the renewal of marriage promises, led to a controversy in the Italian press, which interpreted it as a proposal that marriages be for a limited period and renewable. Suenens had to send the press a demand for a retraction (see *Il Messaggero*, September 30, 1965 [the telegram sent by Suenens on that same day is in Prignon papers]).

essentially determines the nature of the object of the conjugal covenant, namely, the procreation and rearing of children," and "secondary ends, or essential concomitants," namely, "mutual help and a remedy for concupiscence."[418] This statement would be repeated, as in a litany, by Ruffini and Alonso Muñoyerro. Immediately after Browne it was Léger's turn to speak. While acknowledging that the new draft of the schema was better than the preceding one, he feared that in its present form its teaching would deeply disappoint the legitimate expectations of the faithful. The main defect of the schema was that it continued to describe marriage as "an institution ordered to the procreation and rearing of children,"[419] instead of basing the description on the persons that marriage brings together into a community of life and love. According to the Archbishop of Montreal, to describe marriage as an institution in the service of procreation "is certainly both false and destructive of the dignity of love." The need was to think within another perspective, that of "an intimate community of love."

Without completely adopting Léger's radical proposal to rewrite the chapter from a different perspective, a number of fathers did regard conjugal love as the reality that ought to be the basis for thinking about marriage. The fathers taking this approach were also the ones who referred to the expectations of the faithful and the world; the defenders of a repetition of past teaching made no such references.[420] R. De Roo, in particular, who spoke in the name of thirty-three bishops and had consulted many married couples, brought out clearly the riches of conjugal love. Urtasun (Avignon) spoke at some length along the same line, arguing

---

[418] *AS* IV/3, 69.

[419] Ibid., 21. Léger offered a new text in place of the one that had been submitted for discussion (ibid., 25–29). Later, Devoto would say in his written remarks that he accepted the position of Léger (ibid., 194).

[420] Such references are found in the interventions of Léger ("I fear that the schema will disappoint the legitimate expectation of people" [ibid., 21]); R. de Roo ("Look at what the laity in particular are expecting" [ibid., 75]); and of Urtasun ("[The schema] does not answer adequately the expectations of people today" [ibid., 78]). The Canadian bishops, especially the French-speaking ones, regularly consulted their faithful throughout the course of the Council, from the preparatory period to the very end. We know of seventeen formal and extensive consultations of lay people, priests, and religious men and women before the beginning of Vatican II. These consultations continued during the Council, especially on the part of Coderre, Charbonneau, De Roo, and some others. But De Roo was perhaps the one who most clearly pointed out the organic link between the *sensus fidelium* of the entire Church and the work of the bishops in council. At the beginning of his intervention he said that he was speaking "in the name of many married lay people in the region of Canada" (ibid., 75–76).

that no other interpersonal relationship had as sacred a character as the relationship of conjugal love and that for this reason it deserved to be promoted and defended by pertinent rights.[421] However, depending on the culture, the recognition of conjugal love did not always take place in the same perspective: in one culture, love led to marriage; in another it sprang from the union.[422]

While the more personalist approach, based on interpersonal relations, thus succeeded in making itself heard, the approach in terms of primary and secondary ends was still firmly entrenched. It was matched by an entirely juridical conception of marriage in which everything seemed to hinge on the idea of contract.[423] Had not Cardinal Gasparri in his time warned against the omission of this concept?

Into this array of opposed views Msgr. Carlo Colombo, speaking in the name of thirty-two Italian bishops, entered as mediator. Speaking after Ruffini and Léger, he tried to combine the two approaches. He liked "the fully human and personalistic teaching" of the schema and endorsed its statements according to which "conjugal love is asserted to be an intrinsic end of marriage," but he regarded this end as "co-essential with procreation as an end." While he was ready to acknowledge the principle of responsible parenthood, which included the need to use only honorable ways to achieve this purpose, he also wanted the schema to contain a clear and strong rejection of all means that vitiated conjugal relations. Colombo's openness, combined with a great firmness, seemed for the moment to be the *via media* that could lead not only thirty-two Italian bishops to subscribe to the teaching of the schema but also a larger, still hesitant number to commit themselves to a revision of the Church's teaching on marriage and the family.[424]

A second characteristic emerged from this debate: some fathers wanted to anticipate everything, spell everything out, condemn everything: "Nothing is said [in the schema] about divorce"; "It is to be regretted that the many forms of vice are passed over in silence"; "The schema observes a reckless silence on this subject"; "Nothing is said about the

---

[421] Ibid., 78–80.

[422] This was the point of an amendment that the Bishop of Jakarta suggested for no. 64: "conjugal love ... which either leads to a legitimate union or emerges from and is nourished by the couple's intention to start a family" (p. 70). In some countries, the bishop said, people marry because they love one another; in others, they develop love because they are married.

[423] This was the gist of Muñoyerro's intervention (*AS* IV/3, 37–38).

[424] Ibid., 33–37.

primary end of marriage"; "Our schema is completely silent about whatever directly prevents nature from being fruitful!"[425] The schema should have taken up the questions of divorce, adultery, abortion, and sterilization. These fathers did not want the Council to limit its teaching to a few principles, but rather to enter into very concrete questions. But, as Heenan pointed out, the document was far from restricting itself to general principles."On the contrary, it descended at times to the level of specific questions: birth control, adoption, the education of children, sterilization, the indissolubility of marriage, divorce, polygamy, and others.[426]

To this desire to have everything spelled out must be added an obsession with exactness. There should be no ambiguity; the teaching in the schema, which is "sometimes vague, less specific, less clear, less prudent,"[427] should be replaced by teaching that is well defined, "clearer," and "without possible ambiguity."[428] The chapter erred "also by silence or ambiguity" and by its "excessive timidity."[429] This "lack of clarity" could be eliminated only by a return to the teaching of *Casti connubii*, which "without hesitation clearly propounds" a doctrine that is certain and precise.[430]

Among the specific questions most often raised those of birth control and responsible parenthood became the subjects of considerable debate. Here again a number of fathers seemed to think that the question had been answered in advance and that study of it was useless. The problem was addressed successively by Alonso Muñoyerro, in whose opinion the teaching of the schema resembled a resolution passed by a "congress of Anglican Protestants" (the Lambeth Conference of August, 1930); by Yoshigoro, who feared that the schema's principle would puzzle the faithful, especially in the East, where children are considered a form of wealth; by Nicodemo, who regretted that the criteria used were so subjective and so uncertain; by Goicoechea, who feared that the schema would encourage and justify propaganda in favor of birth control in Africa, Asia, and Latin America; and by a number of others. The schema was also criticized for its lack of fidelity to the orientation desired by the plenary mixed subcommission.[431]

---

[425] See, respectively, Ruffini (ibid., 17–18); Alonso Muñoyerro (ibid., 37); and Nicodemo (ibid., 49).

[426] See, respectively, Alonso Muñoyerro, ibid., 39, and Heenan, 61.

[427] Nicodemo (ibid., 48). Conway added: "These words do not clearly..." (ibid., 65).

[428] Da Silva (ibid., 74). These terms were contrasted with "formless," "vague," "obscurely," and so on.

[429] Conway (ibid., 66).

[430] Von Streng (ibid., 91).

[431] See, respectively, Alonso Muñõyerro (ibid., 39); Nicodemo (ibid., 48); Goicoechea (ibid., 96); Rossi (ibid., 62); Da Silva (ibid., 73); and Conway (ibid., 65).

Divorce and the indissolubility of marriage were taken up in passing by several fathers.[432] While Volk and Bednorz (coadjutor of Latowice) paid the greatest attention to these subjects,[433] it was the speech of Zoghby (patriarchal vicar of the Melkites in Egypt) that elicited the deepest feelings.[434] In his view, when it came to pastoral care of the family, there was a problem "even more crucial than that of birth control: the problem of the innocent spouse who in the prime of life and without any fault is left alone by the sin of the other partner."[435] In his view the question raised for the Council was this: In such a case did the Church have anything to say to these distressed faithful except "Sort things out for yourself"? Or was it reduced to practicing a subtle casuistry, close at times to acrobatics, in order to detect an impediment that could invalidate a marriage that had been regarded as valid for ten or twenty years? Had the Church not received from Christ the authority it needed in order to offer all its children the help of divine grace, according to their strength and condition? To compel an innocent partner to practice, for the rest of his or her life, a chastity that belongs to the state of perfection and is not of obligation seemed like a real punishment. In these cases why not adopt, for pastoral reasons, the discipline of the Oriental Churches separated from Rome, which, while retaining the firm conviction that marriage is indissoluble, is authorized by the principle of economy to allow an innocent partner to remarry?[436]

Such a statement could obviously not be left there. After leaving the general congregation Zoghby made a statement to the press in which he added to what he had said. He stressed the point that the teachers of the East who had laid the foundations of this doctrine had not yielded to political pressures in doing so and that the Code of Justinian (sixth century) could not have influenced Basil and John Chrysostom, since they had lived long before. He also stressed the point that this Oriental practice had been adopted at the time when these Churches were in union

---

[432] Ruffini, Conway, and von Streng.

[433] For Volk, see ibid., 50–51; for Bednorz, ibid., 88–90.

[434] After remarking that Weber was deeply moved by this intervention, Dupont wrote: "In bus 28 people also talked about this intervention; it was the only outstanding intervention of this morning" (*JDupont*, September 29, 1965, 51).

[435] *AS* IV/3, 45. According to Dupont's diary for October 27, Zoghby had given the text of his intervention to Congar to be vetted for its orthodoxy. He had first asked Dupont to translate it, but the latter showed no enthusiasm and even found its thesis to be "very shocking" (*JDupont*, 43). In the end it was O. Rousseau, convinced that the intervention was relevant, who helped Zoghby.

[436] Zoghby referred to the exegesis of the phrase in Matthew (Mt 5:32; 19:9) that is given in those Churches on the basis of patristic texts (*AS* IV/3, 46).

with Rome and that it had never been condemned in all those centuries of union.[437]

While the press was seizing on Zoghby's statements and even attributing to him the word "divorce," which he had carefully avoided,[438] a damage-control operation was going on in the corridors of the Council. On the following morning, September 30, the order of speeches was suspended,[439] and Cardinal Journet was called upon to exercise his authority as a theologian and give a firm answer to Zoghby's intervention.[440]

Journet reminded his hearers: "The teaching of the Catholic Church on the indissolubility of sacramental marriage is the very teaching of the Lord Jesus that has been revealed to us and has always been safeguarded and proclaimed by the Church."[441] After giving an exegesis of the gospel of Mark (10:2) and the First Letter to the Corinthians (7:10–11), Journet concluded that the passages which Zoghby cited from the gospel of Matthew (5:32; 19:9) could not contain a different teaching. In addition, he maintained that the practice of the separated Eastern Churches was to be explained by political motives, the Church having been given a dictate of civil law that it then justified by means of the Matthean phrase.[442] The conclusion, then, was irrevocable: "The authentic teaching of the Church on the indissolubility of sacramental marriage has always prevailed in the Catholic Church. This Church has no authority to change what is of divine law. The Church... cannot fail to obey the command of Christ."

---

[437] See *DC*, no. 62 (November 7, 1965), 1905–6.

[438] Zoghby's intervention in the hall was published in *Le Monde* for October 1, 1965. Msgr. Edelby, referring to Zoghby's statement in the hall, also spoke of "the possibility of divorce in certain cases" (*JEdelby*. September 29, 1965). In general, Edelby was quite cautious in speaking of Zoghby's intervention. He would return to it very briefly on October 2, when clarifying what Maximos IV had said, and on October 4, the day when Zoghby would speak again at the general congregation. The whole business does not seem to have caused much of a stir among the Orientals, less of a stir, in any case, than the new text of the Declaration on the Relationship of the Churches to the Non-Christian Religions, which was distributed on September 30.

[439] Slipyi would normally have been the first to speak, but the sequence of speakers was interrupted to allow Journet to intervene.

[440] Prignon learned on October 10 that the Pope himself had ordered this intervention (Prignon papers 1602, October 10, 1965, 2). During this period a number of individuals were at work trying to counter Zoghby's ideas. Dauvillier was one (see "Notes sur l'indissolubilité du mariage," October 10, in Haubtmann papers, 1879), and Wenger another (in *La Croix*, October 2, and in his *Chronique*, 4:200–46; see also his remarks on the incident in *Paolo VI e il rapporto Chiesa-Mondo al Concilio* [Brescia 1991], 39–40).

[441] *AS* IV/3, 58.

[442] Ibid., 59. Butler, an exegete, had strong reservations about Journet's interpretation of Matthew 5:32 (see *DButler*, September 30, 1965).

Even after Journet's clarification, Zoghby's intervention continued to make waves.[443] On October 2 Patriarch Maximos dissociated himself from Zoghby's statement and told the press that the latter "represented only Zoghby's own views."[444] But Zoghby had already issued a clarification to the press on September 30 and on October 4 would again speak on the same subject at a general congregation; this was very unusual.[445] He did not "retract" or "correct" himself, but he said that his intervention, which was motivated solely by pastoral concern, did not at all intend to cast doubt on the principle of the indissolubility of marriage. His intention was not to permit divorce but simply to explore the possibility of adding a further dispensation to those already recognized by the Church. For Journet's benefit he added that "the proposal... was based on the indisputable authority of the holy fathers and holy teachers of the East, who cannot, without rashness, be accused of having yielded to political and human considerations when they gave this interpretation of the Lord's words."[446] While not desiring to add anything further, he again made it known that, in his estimation, the Church had the authority to allow a new kind of dispensation, since it already had such an authority when it introduced the Petrine privilege. He concluded, therefore, unlike Journet, that "it is for the Church to exercise its judgment here."[447]

It was chiefly the Polish bishops who called attention to the subject of abortion; they highlighted the complete indifference of our contemporaries about abortion, which claims more victims than modern wars.

---

[443] Dupont reports that, according to O. Rousseau, "Zoghby is delighted with all the to-do about his intervention. This was a problem to which attention had to be drawn" (*JDupont*, October 1, 1965, 57).

[444] *DC*, col. 1906. While acknowledging that Zoghby, "like all the Council fathers, was completely free to say what he thought," Maximos added that, as far as the substance was concerned, the different practice of the Orthodox Churches can take advantage of some texts of the fathers (texts contradicted by other fathers) and that in any case there is no constant tradition that can cast doubt on the teaching about indissolubility. The evening before (October 1) the Patriarch had met with Paul VI in order to ask him a number of questions. But we have no information leading us to conclude that Paul VI asked Maximos to make such a clarification in the presence of the journalists. Edelby did not connect the two subjects, which he reports in his diary for October 1 and 2 (254).

[445] *AS* IV/3, 257–58; English translation in *Council Daybook, Session 4*, 91-92.

[446] Ibid., 47.

[447] Ibid., 48. In their written remarks other Oriental bishops tried to explore ways similar to those that Zoghby proposed in this intervention. See the remarks of Descuffi (ibid., 188–91) and Sana (ibid., 228–30). Zoghby did not stop there. For the use of the Council fathers he prepared a sizable dossier (26 pp.) on remarriage while the original spouses were still living, but drawing this time on the Western tradition from the third to the eleventh century (Léger papers, 771).

In order to move against this scourge, which had its basis in "a wide-spread religious indifference and an ethical relativism"[448] and was a sign of a decadent society, the Church needed to proclaim "the absolute inviolability of every life." Their petition, which was in complete agreement with the teaching of other episcopates in the Eastern countries, was also echoed in the West, where Nicodemo (Bari) and some other bishops also referred to it.[449]

c. Marriage: West and East by Way of Africa and Asia

As Zoghby's intervention could hardly be accepted by the Latin Church, so the idea of different experiences of marriage and family was not well received. The first to raise the point was Djajasepoetra, Archbishop of Jakarta, who said that he had difficulty "in recognizing the forms of marriage known among us in this text," a schema that started with "a conception and form of marriage that are overly Western."[450]

But the question was not simply one of geography. At a deeper level it confronted the Council with a latent philosophical problem, inasmuch as some fathers discussed marriage and the family as if these were mental constructs, while others looked upon them as historical realities. When a speaker dealt with marriage "in itself," he took the nature of things as his starting point and could then reason "according to divine law, which is indeed beyond doubt, as well as according to natural law."[451] Given this perspective, it was obviously easy to reach the clarity many desired. There was no need to attend to "subjective, varied, and uncertain criteria such as health of mind and body, educational and economic conditions, the good of one's own family and the needs of civil society, all these being criteria that vary according to circumstances and state of life."[452] As long as one remained outside of time and history, one could speak with assurance, for one started with a consideration of substances (family, marriage) and judged real experience in the light of these pure substances, eternal ideas, and timeless essences.

But this kind of thinking could hardly be sustained in face of the catholicity of the Church. Had not the drafters of the schema turned

---

[448] Majdanski, *AS* IV/3, 43. This view was fully in tune with the pastoral letters of the bishops of Yugoslavia (September 12, 1965) and of East Germany (November 7, 1965).
[449] Nicodemo, *AS* IV/3, 49.
[450] Ibid., 70. See also the written remarks of Pinto (ibid., 219).
[451] Ruffini (ibid., 18).
[452] Nicodemo (ibid., 48–49).

the Western experience of the family and marriage into the very substance of these realities? Something even more fundamental was at issue:
The modern time referred to in the title of the schema (*huius temporis*),
as well as the method by which the schema was worked out allowed a
different kind of experience to assert itself. This different experience was
necessarily in tension with the reified realities of marriage and family
that the drafters had ended up regarding as acultural and transcultural,
even as pure gospel. Was it possible to go out to this *huius temporis* with
an arsenal of statements by the Holy Office or from *Casti connubii* with
no further thought? This was the question underlying this debate.

One could not, at this stage of the debate, go back to consider the concept of *world* again. Yet deep down it was still and always at that level
that the debate was being carried on. How was the Church to be
"the Church in the modern world"? Were social changes to be considered
"signs of the times" that were calling the Church to proclaim the gospel
in a new historical situation? Or were industrialization and urbanization
to be regarded as threats to the stability of the family; was work undertaken by women simply a danger that might lead to their emancipation?[453]

Here again, the temptation was to solve the problem by passing over
it in silence. This question was raised earlier with regard to the schema
itself. Now it was raised in connection with this particular chapter:
"It would be better to say nothing about marriage in this document if in
speaking of it we avoid what might be called the supreme problem."[454]
This was also the suggestion of Cardinal Rossi, speaking in the name of
seventy Brazilian bishops. Since the study of the subject of birth control
had been entrusted to a pontifical commission, it was better to say nothing
about it except for a few vague generalities.[455]

By the end of the debate some fathers had expressly given approval to
the chapter: Colombo: "Very acceptable"; Conway: "Acceptable in its
substance"; Cardinal Rossi: "Generally acceptable." But even for these
fathers considerable reservations remained on one or another point. To the
cardinals just named must be added the less prestigious names of such

---

[453] See the intervention of Bednorz, representing the Polish episcopate (ibid., 88–89).

[454] Heenan, ibid., 61. "It would be better to omit this chapter," he added, for if the
schema did not take up particular problems, "it could only be defective."

[455] Rossi (ibid., 62–63); Orbegozo Goicoechea was of the same view. In his written
observations Shehan insisted that the chapter not be eliminated (ibid., 152), whereas
Hurley's view was that if the Council could say nothing about birth control, then let it
abstain completely from dealing with the family (ibid., 205). See also Formosa's position
(ibid., 211).

bishops as Reuss and others. Without saying so explicitly, other fathers seemed to support the schema. Many suggested improvements, but some of them so changed the direction of the chapter that one could not be sure that these fathers really accepted it. There was a general sense, however, that the discussion had lasted long enough and that it was time to move on to another subject. Those who had not spoken could still submit written remarks.[456]

8. Less Important Problems?

Judging by the length of the discussion of family and marriage, the large number of interventions, the variety of opinions, and the bitterness of the debate, the discussion of the second part of the schema promised to be long and exhausting. But once the discussion of marriage was finished, the debates on the three following chapters (culture, economic and social life, and political life) moved along quickly and without difficulty. It seemed that the question of marriage and the family — a more traditional area for the Church — was more important than these others. The bishops were undoubtedly less familiar with the other matters, although they were being given more and more room in papal teaching. In any case, on the first day of October there was an increasing urgency about finishing the work, since by now the fathers had departed from the initial plan of limiting the discussion of the entire second part of the schema to three sessions.

a. Culture

While the subject of marriage was familiar to the Church, the subject of culture seemed a more novel one. In fact, up to this point, no conciliar document or encyclical had ever dealt specifically with culture. As a result, the debate was not burdened by earlier statements of the magisterium. This may explain why the debate on the chapter "Development of Culture" did not involve any considerable controversy. After the

---

[456] Seventy fathers sent in their written remarks to the commission (ibid., 145–244). In these, essentially the same tendencies were manifested that had been expressed in the hall. A number of these fathers remained caught in the problem of primary and secondary ends, with *Casti connubii* the point of reference (Florit, Silva Henríquez, Balaguer, Carli, de Castro Mayer, Forer, Maccari (whose comments were signed by many members of the *Coetus*), Corral, Muldoon, Rusch, Samoré, Schoemaker); others argued for a more dynamic presentation of the Church's teaching on marriage and family, with an emphasis on conjugal love (Shehan, Huyghe, Sauvage). Some offered new drafts of the text (de Cambourg, De Oliveira, Léger, and others).

stormy stretches occasioned by the discussion of marriage, the Council
was now sailing in calm waters.

While the word *culture* seemed new, the reality was not. For the
Church to deal with culture meant it had to state openly its attitude to the
contemporary world and to the development of ideas that the contemporary world was fostering. It also meant that the Church had to examine
its relationship with non-Western traditions.

Although the discussion was not unrelated to the schema on the missions, only one of the speakers on the subject came from outside Europe.
Of the Europeans, there were five Frenchmen, two Italians, five
Spaniards, and two Germans. Msgr. Padin (Tremitonte), secretary general
of Catholic Action in Brazil, took the occasion to follow what earlier
speakers from "mission territories" had done in the discussion of other
chapters of the schema: he criticized the tendency to generalize what was
said about culture, to flatten territories into a single kind of culture by fail-
ing to take into account the specific historical situations and divergent
mentalities of each people and by ignoring the distinctions that needed to
be made among cultures or the ways in which these cultures complemented one another.[457] It was quite clear that, despite warnings from
Catholic organizations, the Council was in danger of canonizing a particular kind of civilization.[458]

Several speakers came from the world of the universities,[459] a fact that
helped to turn the discussion in the direction of an old debate that haunted
the Church: the relationship of the Church to science. This problem was
taken up in the interventions of Blanchet and of Veuillot, who made himself the spokesman of scientists on the schema.[460] The coadjutor archbishop of Paris feared that this chapter, which expressed only reservations
toward science and never clearly defended it, would disappoint scholars
who had voiced their expectations of the Council. Veuillot's view was
that the Church ought to praise science, express its respect for it, and
"give positive praise to its great dignity." Here again, the French and the

[457] *AS* IV/3, 140–41. When Gracias (Bombay) returned to the Council after being
delayed by the troubles between India and Pakistan, he too spoke during this general congregation, but not about cultures. He did urge the Council to take up the subject and adopt
a universal vision.

[458] International Catholic Organizations had made culture the theme of its third meeting, held in April 1965 in Vienna.

[459] P. Fernández, master general of the Dominicans; Msgr. Pellegrino, formerly professor at the University of Turin; and Msgr. Blanchet, rector of the Institut Catholique of
Paris.

[460] For Msgr. Blanchet, see *AS* IV/3, 137–40; for Msgr. Veuillot, see ibid., 255–57.

German views were in opposition. Spülbeck (Meissen), who had spoken just before Veuillot, had urged moderation of the optimism that this chapter showed about science.

But the debate also turned to the area of popular culture and drew attention to a new cultural reality: leisure. Reference would be made to leisure in the intervention of Elchinger, who spoke of mass culture and the civilization of leisure.[461] Lebrun (Autun) dealt specifically with sports and the basic values found in them.[462] Elchinger undoubtedly offered the most fully developed vision of culture, going beyond the classical meaning given to the word to a more anthropological understanding of it. He thought the schema's notion of culture too narrow. Culture needed to be viewed as "what is manifested in the way the people of a given region and at a given time express themselves, not only in religious worship and the intellectual and artistic realms, but also in their technical structures, the kinds of work they do, and the organization of their leisure."[463]

The first speech, by Schmitt (Metz), had placed the dialogue of the Church with humanity in a new perspective. The schema should not only call attention to the contribution of the Church to the world, it should also stress all that the world has brought to the Church: a livelier awareness of human dignity, the need to promote social justice, the absurdity of war, and so on.[464] Elchinger would follow the same line:

---

[461] Ibid., 118. Although he did not mention it, Elchinger's intervention very closely resembled the very critical observations made by the Centre des Intellectuels Français. Later (beginning October 12) Elchinger was to be very active as the chapter on culture was being revised by a subcommission; he wanted it to be completely revised. According to Suenens, Elchinger said that the subcommission "ought to be locked up for fifteen days in a convent near Rome, all by itself with the texts and the summary of what the fathers said in the hall, and be required to rewrite the schema" (*JPrignon* Monday, September 27, 1965 [Prignon papers, 1593]).

[462] See *AS* IV/3, 128–30. Thirty-six French bishops signed this intervention.

[463] In his notes Elchinger continued his thoughts: "As described in the schema, culture might be thought of as a 'luxury,' whereas it has become a 'mass phenomenon.' Culture develops *pari passu* with leisure" (ibid., 122); and elsewhere: "It is a mass phenomenon. At present there exists a 'culture of the masses' that is infiltrating everywhere thanks to the vast communications media. An entire civilization based on leisure is developing" (ibid., 123).

[464] *AS* IV/3, 116–17. Schmitt spoke in the name of seventy fathers. Writing in the journal *Itinéraires* for November 1965, J. Madiran expressed astonishment at the request that the Church acknowledge what it owed to the world and identify the values it had received from the world. Because he could not believe that this was really the position of Schmitt and the seventy fathers who had signed his statement, he challenged the report of the speech given in *La Croix*.

"The Church has a duty, first of all, to listen to what is going on in the culture, and this with an attitude of receptivity and openness, sympathy and trust" and "to understand and acknowledge the cultural values of today's world."[465]

A different voice was heard from J.M. Hernandez, whose intervention, relying on Vatican I, was occupied chiefly with opposition to the atheistic and anti-Christian materialistic culture that was spreading everywhere, notably in the universities and especially in Latin America. He claimed that because of Christ's divine teaching, which it propounds, the Church has more to offer the world than it could possibly receive from the world.[466] His point of departure was different: "The distinct and supernatural culture of the Church" must be broadcast and spread throughout the world so that it may reach all human beings and extend to all nations.

The speech that drew the most attention was undoubtedly that of Msgr. Pellegrino, the new archbishop of Turin, who had been professor of early Christian literature at the University of Turin.[467] This intervention, in masterful Latin, was a real plea in favor of the right, based on human dignity, to freedom within the Church in the study of truth. The deepest impression was made by his remark that violations of the right to freedom in research did not belong only to a distant past; he continued: "I think it enough to recall that a few years ago I met a religious who was living in a not strictly voluntary 'exile,' because of doctrinal views he proposed that we are happy to read today in pontifical and conciliar documents. Everyone knows that his was not the only such case."[468] Everyone understood the allusion to Congar.

The discussion of culture served as an interlude after the more acrimonious debate on marriage; the main personalities of the Council refrained from taking the podium. The fundamental oppositions remained, however, between a theology of the incarnation, which assigned genuine value to human culture, and a theology of redemption, for which the culture needed to be redeemed and science was suspect. Once again, some

---

[465] *AS* IV/3, 122 and 124. The six pages of written remarks appended to this intervention were even more important than the intervention itself. Elchinger's was undoubtedly the most solid intervention made during this debate.

[466] See ibid., 134 n.13.

[467] Appointed to the see of Turin by Paul VI despite strong pressures for less open candidates, Pellegrino had not yet been consecrated. His intervention was warmly applauded.

[468] *AS* IV/3, 136.

wondered whether this second part of the schema ought not be simply withdrawn and handed over to a postconciliar commission.[469]

b. Economic and Social Life

As soon as the debate on culture ended, on Monday, October 4, when Paul VI was preparing to deliver his address to the United Nations,[470] the fathers moved on to chapter III of the second part, the chapter on economic and social life.[471] To a certain extent this chapter continued the social teaching of the Church as inaugurated by Leo XIII but much revitalized by the encyclicals of John XXIII *(Pacem in terris* and *Mater et magistra)*, which had created a considerable stir.

To judge by the number of interventions (twenty-one), this discussion held the attention of the fathers more than the discussion of culture had. Geographically, the speakers were better distributed. The fathers heard views from the two "worlds" (the developed world and the "underdeveloped" world[472]) and from bishops who had experienced both of the main types of economy, the liberal capitalist economy and the centralized and statist socialist economy (Franić and Wyszynski). Once again, the differences of outlook were not simply between poor countries and rich countries or between East and West. Even in western Europe there was no consensus, and root differences could be discerned in the remarks made by Spaniards, Germans, Italians, and so on. Divergent approaches to the economy and the life of society thus found expression at the Council. Moreover, since the leading lights who had occupied the stage during

---

[469] See the end of the intervention of C. Morcillo González (ibid., 248–50).

[470] Paul VI flew to New York at dawn on October 4, accompanied by Cardinals Tisserant, Cicognani, Agagianian, Gilroy, Caggiano, Doi, and Rugambwa, and by Msgrs. Samoré, Dell'Acqua, and Felici (see *AS* IV/1, 69–70).

[471] The subcommission responsible for drafting this chapter had Hengsbach as its president and included Franić, Larraín, and Helder Câmara. The experts were Lio, Calvez, Ferrari-Toniolo, Rodhain (Lebret). The auditors were Vanistendael, de Rosen, and Keegan.

[472] The schema spoke of "regions in process of development." Larraín denounced this euphemism and wanted the schema to speak of underdevelopment or even of regression (*AS* IV/3, 373). Six bishops from the Third World took part in the debate, three from India and three from Latin America (Larraín Errázuriz from Chile, president of CELAM; Ruiz of Ecuador; and Parteli of Uruguay). Africa and Asia remained silent during this debate, but Fernandes (Delhi) spoke in the name both of the Indian episcopal conference and of 150 fathers who were mainly from Asia, Africa, and Latin America, along with eight from Canada, and a few from Europe. The speeches of Larraín, who referred to the right of development and the duty of justice, and of Fernandes were the ones most fully based on the realities of the Third World.

the discussion of the schema in general and the debate on the family did not take part in this debate,[473] other bishops had a chance to speak, in particular representatives of the Church of the Poor Group.[474]

The debate on the third chapter of the second part once again brought to light the weaknesses of the schema that had already been pointed out: an overly Western perspective;[475] excessive optimism in regard to development and economic progress;[476] a deficient analysis of the socio-economic scene;[477] inadequate reference to natural law or to undiluted doctrine;[478] and so on. The discussion of this chapter provided the Germans with another opportunity to decry the schema's weaknesses: excessive optimism, lack of rigorous analysis, and so on. The strongest criticism was doubtless that of Höffner, who spoke in the name of eighty German-speaking bishops. Right at the beginning of his statement he emphasized that the schema added nothing new to the three recent encyclicals on socio-economic matters; in fact, it fell far short of the mature, clear, and decisive thought of those encyclicals. It was content with pompous formulas and pious exhortations, its course was marked by simplifications, and it took refuge in moralism.

---

[473] Only five cardinals intervened. Apart from Siri and Wyszynski, there were no eminent figures. The other sixteen interventions came from bishops of the second rank or from religious. In fact, the Council seemed to be moving along in a minor key. The number of cardinal presidents was reduced from twelve to five and that of the moderators from four to two.

[474] Himmer and Coderre, members of this group, spoke one after the other. De Arriba y Castro said: "The Church of Christ is the Church of the poor" (*AS* IV/3, 263).

[475] Bueno y Monreal (Seville) thought that the schema seemed captive to the mindset of the individualistic and capitalist liberalism of the Western world (*AS* IV/3, 265).

[476] See Franić (ibid., 288).

[477] This reproach came as much from those in favor of the schema as from those who wanted it withdrawn. Coderre (ibid., 292–93) regretted that the schema referred to socio-economic conditions that were in the process of disappearing but neglected new, emerging conditions; Höffner and Hengsbach (ibid., 269–77; and ibid., 288–89) asked for the contribution of experts in the political and economic sciences in order to produce a discourse more reflective of concrete realities and socio-economic data. Cardijn (ibid., 364–67) thought that the schema addressed workers in language that was too theoretical and unrealistic; it overlooked some very important distinctions, especially the difference between ownership of consumer goods and ownership of the means of production. According to Franić (ibid., 285–88), many questions were not developed sufficiently; in the view of Añoveros Ataún, the schema remained too abstract and too general (ibid., 377); and in the view of De Vito, the schema had not found a language suited for addressing the millions of people living in wretched conditions (ibid., 384–85).

[478] Franić deplored the weakness of the recourse to natural law as the root and foundation of truth and right; the paucity of references to the essence and nature of things (metaphysics); and the abandonment of the Scholastic method (ibid., 287). Siri wanted the schema to be content to reaffirm immutable principles and not to descend to the level of overly technical debates on contingent realities (ibid., 262). While a similar remark was made by García de Sierra y Méndez (ibid., 294–95), others wanted practical solutions.

More constructive but no less scathing was the very surprising critique of Hengsbach, president of the subcommission responsible for the text. Giving many examples, he attacked the vagueness of many statements that, in his judgment, were beyond the competence of the Council and should be left for others to think about freely. The fifty written remarks that he added to his oral intervention made up a clear, systematic, and devastating critique. In fact, of course, relations between bosses and workers in Germany had their own special character, and Hengsbach, who came from the Ruhr, preferred that the text not settle questions having to do with entrepreneurs' freedom of initiative.

Although the majority of the speakers were concerned with the problem of workers or with questions raised by industrialization, the subject of agriculture also found a place in the debate. The three bishops who tackled it (De Vito, Castellano, and Parteli) all maintained that the subject was neglected in the schema. Parteli raised the question *ex professo*; on the basis of twenty years' experience with the UN's Food and Agriculture Organization, he stressed the contribution of that organization to the elimination of problems of hunger through the expansion of agricultural production. He suggested that the Council explicitly support the establishment of truly human conditions in rural areas in order to check migration to the cities and the lessening of agricultural production. Franić took advantage of the discussion on this chapter to return to the proposal that the part of the schema that seemed to represent mature thought be published in the form of a letter or a message and that the rest be assigned to a possible synod of bishops.

The discussion of this chapter did not become a pretext for bringing up the condemnation of communism. References to communism were few and these were not found where they might have been expected. They were made, first, by the Spanish bishops, who were overly represented in this debate and who defended a quasi-corporative conception of the economy.[479] There was an allusion to communism in the speeches of Himmer and Ruiz. Wyszynski was content to repeat the classical teaching that the question of the workers was not solved either by capitalism or by communism, since both were based on an individualist philosophy that lacked

[479] See the intervention of de Arriba y Castro (ibid., 8), who said that communism had never been, could not be, and never would be a solution, because it denied the value of the human person. The reference to communism in the intervention of Bueno y Monreal was of a different kind: he simply observed that the Church was often accused, especially by Marxists, of lagging behind in the area of economic and social questions. This suggested to him that the schema ought to speak not of the past but of the present. He also very sharply attacked the capitalist mentality (ibid., 265).

respect for the human person. The solution was to be found in a sound doctrine about the human person, one that has redeemed humanity as its focus.[480] The only other bishop from a socialist country who spoke was Franić; he favored the participation of workers in businesses[481] but stressed the point that the conciliar document should explicitly reject class struggle as a remedy for social ills.

This debate, then, revealed a very broad consensus, inasmuch as all the speakers agreed that the Church should promote justice and development. The largest agreement was about the need to establish a postconciliar body that would be part of the Curia and would have as its duty the spread of the Church's social teaching.[482] This body would, according to Fernandes, be a means of carrying on the dialogue with the world and, in the view of Thangalathil, of promoting economic cooperation among countries, defending the rights of peasants, and establishing a right to emigrate.[483] The suggestion for such a body, which was set forth in a very detailed way by Swanstrom (auxiliary of New York) and by Father Gerald Mahon (superior general of the Mill Hill Missionaries),[484] was destined to have the greatest effect later.

c. The Life of the Political Community

On October 5 the fathers moved on to a new chapter, added during the intersession. The discussion seemed now to have found its own rhythm, and the nearer the end of the discussion came, the brisker the debate became, to the point that surprisingly few interventions were made on

---

[480] Ibid., 361.

[481] On this question Franić was disappointed that the text fell short of what had already been said in *Mater et magistra*. Siri, in contrast, was against saying anything about the participation of workers in businesses.

[482] This proposal was endorsed by speakers representing varying schools of thought: de Arriba y Castro, Swanstrom, Thangalathil, Mahon, Fernandes, and Echeverria Ruiz (Ecuador). It would also be endorsed by Cardinal McCann during the discussion of the chapter on war and peace (*AS* IV/3, 400–401).

[483] The Indian bishop saw in the establishment of a right to emigrate the solution to the problem caused by demographic explosions (this last was discussed outside the Council, especially in connection with birth control) (see ibid., 279).

[484] Swanstrom distinguished two levels: organizations created by the episcopal conferences and dedicated to development, and an organization of the Holy See (ibid., 267–69). Mahon, for his part, assigned four purposes to his new body: to mobilize all the energies of the Church in the struggle against poverty; to support the activities of missionaries in behalf of development; to support the charitable works of bishops in many countries; and to remind the world of its responsibility for development (ibid., 368–69).

the life of the political community.[485] Only four bishops — who registered at the last minute — desired to speak: two Spaniards (Beitia Aldazábal and Del Campo y de la Bárcena), who were always very much involved in the discussion of the questions taken up in the second part of schema XIII; one Pole (Baraniak); and one South African (Hurley). Here again, national sensitivities found expression. Beitia defended the legitimacy of concordats,[486] and Baraniak discussed the limits of obedience to, and collaboration with, an atheistic and totalitarian regime that fights against religion.[487] With his own particular setting undoubtedly in mind, Hurley urged an *aggiornamento* in relations between the Church and political society and called for a greater freedom for the Church, which in turn should not first of all be claiming her own rights but rather defending human rights, even if this leads to conflict with political authorities.[488]

d. War and Peace

On October 4 and 5 the Council seemed in a state of dormancy, being distracted by an event outside the hall: the visit of Paul VI to the United Nations. The discussion on the second part of schema XIII did continue, but in a mechanical way and without eliciting much feeling; the presidents' table was half empty. Address followed address as though by routine. No spark kindled the debate, and the chapter on the the political community passed through the hall like a letter through the mail. There was no enthusiasm for it, and the fathers were strained and weary. They could be seen leaving their seats sooner, going to the bar, strolling in the corridors. Very quickly, however, the passion that had marked some exchanges would awaken the assembly from its torpor. The debate on the chapter on war and peace, which had been discussed amid controversy

---

[485] The subcommission in charge of this chapter had László as its president.

[486] As the Spanish bishops had done during the discussion of religious freedom, Beitia asked that the schema restrict itself to a recall of perennial principles, while leaving it to the bishops to apply these principles to particular situations. In his opinion it was legitimate that the Church be recognized as possessing a public status "by right" (not by privilege), because the state has an obligation to serve the kingdom of God (*AS* IV/3, 387–92).

[487] Ibid., 392–94. Baraniak thought the schema inadequate in its presentation of what constitutes the common good.

[488] Ibid., 395–95. This view was the very opposite of Beitia's. Hurley also distinguished clearly between political authority and political society. He also voiced his satisfaction that the schema had avoided the expression *perfect society*. On October 1 Ddungu, speaking in the name of seventy fathers, had raised the question of racial discrimination in his remarks on the first part of the schema (ibid., 110–11).

during the third period and had been almost entirely rewritten, would revive tensions.[489]

While the discussion on economic and social life and the very brief discussion on political life led into the discussion of peace,[490] it was undoubtedly the remarkable address of Paul VI to the United Nations that was the real introduction to the final chapter of schema XIII.[491] As the assembly awaited Paul VI's return from New York, the debate began, somewhat chaotically. The first two speakers registered, Liénart and Lercaro, withdrew their names.[492] Two interventions were given, however, by Alfrink and McCann. The former took up several questions: the distinction to be made between the possession of weapons and their use; the balance of terror, which could produce positive results despite its harrowing and shaky character; the fallacious distinction between small and large wars; and conscientious objection.[493]

No sooner had the debate begun, however, when the moderator interrupted it at 12:10 p.m. because the arrival of Paul VI from New York was

[489] See the remarks on this subject in Hengsbach's report. He admitted that the commission had remained uncertain on the subject and had been satisfied with setting down an indisputable principle: every act of total war (that is, involving the complete destruction of cities or regions and the death of their inhabitants) is, in itself and objectively, a criminal act. On October 24 Himmer called upon the Council to proscribe the possession of atomic weapons; his call was signed by various personalities (Prignon papers, 1315).

[490] Thangalathil made an explicit connection between peace and the scandalous imbalance between rich and poor (AS IV/3, 278). The connection was even more explicit in the speech of Larraín, for whom underdevelopment not only represented a threat to peace but "is already a breaking of the peace," if one really claimed that "progress is the new name of peace" (ibid., 273).

[491] For the address see AS IV/1, 28–36; also in AAS 57 (1965), 877–85.

[492] Lercaro's written intervention adopted a perspective entirely different from that of the Pope's at the United Nations. For his method, the Cardinal of Bologna drew support from contemporary humanity's desire for peace and from the observed fact of the inordinate growth in the destructive capacity of atomic weapons. This "sign of the times," actualized in the intensification of the United States' intervention in Vietnam, came as a call to a better understanding of the gospel message of peace. The gospel calls for an open and radical attitude, without strategic circumlocutions or political calculations, in the struggle not only against war but also against the production and stockpiling of weapons. In this chapter the Church had an obligation to proclaim unequivocally, by its words and its actions, that peace is a primary theme of the gospel, one that historical events have led the Church to grasp with a clarity hitherto unknown. Lercaro thus took a much more radical position than that of the majority at the Council and that of Paul VI. What John XXIII had said about any "just" war being a thing of the past found in Lercaro's address a faithful and undaunted echo, without any ambiguity or human prudence. For the text see AS, IV/3, 761-64; for the Italian text, see Per la forza dello Spirito: Discorsi conciliari del card. Giacomo Lercaro, Bologna: Dehoniane, 1984), 253-61.

[493] AS IV/3, 397–99. Alfrink was chaplain general of the Dutch armies and international president of Pax Christi.

expected. The journalists and members of the diplomatic corps had time to take their places in the tribunes before Paul VI arrived at the doors of the basilica a few minutes before 1 o'clock, he was greeted there by the Council of Presidents and the moderators and then walked up the nave amid very warm applause from the Council fathers. Once the Pope had been seated at the presidents' table, Liénart conveyed to him the assembly's best wishes and suggested that the Pope's address to the United Nations be included in the Acts of the Council. The Pope then addressed the Council fathers, who spontaneously stood up to listen to him.[494]

The Pope had twice sought the agreement of the fathers for the step he took and had taken Council fathers from all nations with him to New York; he was now determined to end his journey here in the assembly. His authority had been weakened for a moment during the third period, but he managed to overcome his handicap and reassert himself. Despite the occasional criticism,[495] the frail figure of the "pilgrim for peace," which throughout his visit was uninterruptedly aired by many television networks around the world, had an overwhelming emotional impact on viewers. Thanks to the inspired intervention of Paul VI, the conciliar debate on peace, which might otherwise have bogged down in technical discussions, had at last found its right path. The debate gained depth, and the Council acquired new momentum.[496]

The debate began in earnest the next day, October 6, and lasted into the next day. Twenty fathers asked to speak, and, once again, the leading lights made their appearance: Liénart, Léger, Butler, Garrone, Ottaviani, Carli, and so on. Quite surprisingly, only one bishop from the United States spoke during the debate, and he limited himself to the problem of demographic expansion while avoiding the heated questions of disarmament and the legitimacy of the war.[497]

Three major questions dominated the exchanges in the hall: whether to abandon the classical theory of just and unjust wars, nuclear deterrence, and conscientious objection. The tone of the debate was set by the first intervention, by Liénart, but even more so by the second, by Léger.[498]

[494] See ibid., 402; for the Pope's address, see *AS* IV/1, 36–38.

[495] See the very critical article about Paul VI in *Time* (September 24, 1965).

[496] A number of fathers would refer to Paul VI's action for peace; among them were Liénart, Martin, Ottaviani, Duval, Kłepacz, Cantero, and Boillon.

[497] The speaker was Marling (Jefferson City). All the other major figures of the United States episcopate remained silent. Hannan had registered to speak but gave up his right to do so as the debate was ending. He wanted the text to pay tribute to those who perform their military service, lest the Council approve only the action of conscientious objectors.

[498] See *AS* IV/3, 509–12.

The classical theory of just and unjust wars had to be put aside because of the new means of war; the theory had become inapplicable in practice. Henceforth, the question had to be put in different terms; the question of the morality of war was now outdated. The fathers were concerned much more with the legitimacy of using atomic weapons than with the classical theory of just war. "War must be completely outlawed," said Ottaviani at the beginning of his intervention, and he elicited exceptional applause from the assembly.[499] Most of the speakers made this view their own.[500] Only Carli stood firmly by the classical theses on just and unjust wars.[501]

The second question, the legitimacy of possessing modern weapons in order to deter an enemy, also gave rise to well-argued interventions, especially by the English fathers. Dom Butler rejected the distinction between the possession and the use of weapons of deterrence; Wheeler and Grant asked for the removal from the text of the statement that it is not illegitimate to possess weapons of deterrence.[502] Without contradicting them, their colleague Beck had a more nuanced view on the question.[503] As he made clear, this question had as a corollary the establishment of an international authority that could limit national sovereignty and mediate in conflicts. The proposal that a supra-national authority be established was also the subject of the intervention of Ancel, who had already made the same suggestion during the third period.[504] The proposal was endorsed by many of the French bishops; sixteen fathers had signed Ancel's intervention, while Cardinal Martin and Gouyon and Boillon

---

[499] Ibid., 642–44.

[500] This was the case with Cardinals Duval and Martin and with Gouyon, Rusch, and Boillon. Boillon referred to Léger's address and, on the basis of his experience during the Second World War, he rejected as obsolete the distinctions between conventional and nonconventional weapons, small conflicts and large ones, and so on (ibid., 732–34).

[501] Ibid., 657–60. The Bishop of Segni attacked the text as obscure, illogical, and incomplete. His remarks matched his written observations on schema XIII, which he submitted on September 23, 1965, and in which he insisted that the text contained a mass of material, the theological value of which varied widely because sure doctrine was mingled with debated and debatable doctrines, and statements of scripture were linked with journalistic descriptions. It was not possible to rule on the theological qualification of such a disparate whole.

[502] See ibid., 617–20. Wheeler wanted the schema to adopt the position taken in *Pacem in terris*, which did not rule out the possibility that possession of weapons of deterrence could be legitimate.

[503] According to Beck, steps had to be taken to render illegitimate the possession of weapons of deterrence, but in the meantime the Church had to be able to offer a "morality of deterrence" (ibid., 660–62).

[504] See *AS* IV/3, 720–23.

gave it their support in their speeches. The idea is also found in Otta-viani's intervention.

Conscientious objection was the subject of more lively discussion. While many fathers wanted a stronger statement on the subject (Léger, Butler, Wheeler, Grant, Beck[505]), Carli and the Spanish bishops were quite reserved toward what was said in the schema. According to Carli, the question was simply not ripe and should be left to free discussion by theologians. For their part Castán Lacoma and Cantero Cuadrado preferred to leave the question to the judgment of the civil authorities, because conscientious objection can at times run counter to the needs of the social order.[506] This was not the only question on which these two Spanish bishops separated themselves from others. Both made ref-erence to civil wars, with Cantero Cuadrado saying he was surprised to see the schema (no. 101) describing as "minor wars" the revolu-tionary and subversive wars that could degenerate into civil wars. On this subject they were joined by Ottaviani, who was sorry that the schema used such a vague concept of war. It should have included every armed or guerilla revolution, especially those begun by commu-nists in the guise of wars of liberation, which, in fact, aimed at impos-ing an ideology.

As had been the case during the discussion of socio-economic life, a suggestion to establish a central body, a secretariat for coordinating the actions taken by the worldwide Church on behalf of peace, met with wide agreement. The suggestion was repeated by Wheeler, Grant, Rusch, and Brezanoczy, who spoke in the name of the Hungarian bishops.

Finally, the questions of hunger, development, and overpopulation, which had been raised during the discussion of the other chapters of the second part, were raised here again in a rather cacophonous way. Duval's speech was the one that most organically connected the problems of hunger and distorted development with the question of war.[507] Simons,

---

[505] Roberts had prepared an intervention that strongly supported conscientious objec-tion, but because he had not submitted it in time to the General Secretariat, he was unable to speak in the hall.

[506] For Castán Lacoma, see *AS* IV/3, 621–24; for Msgr. Cantero Cuadrado, see ibid., 650–52. Apart from this point, Cantero found that the question of the moral and juridical merits of war, especially in regard to the balance of terror, was realistically posed in the schema. In his view, given the present situation, this was the only practical way of ensur-ing security and removing the danger of war. Lokuang, who surrendered his right to speak as the debate was ending, wanted the schema to speak clearly about legitimate defense and to omit what was said about conscientious objection.

[507] Ibid., 604–7.

Marling, Grant, Gaviola, and Rupp took up the questions of overpopulation and hunger, but much less convincingly.[508]

October 8 brought the end, at last, to the debate on schema XIII, which had lasted since September 21. Begun amid controversy and a great deal of tension, the debate ended amid calm, doubtless because of a general feeling of exhaustion. There was a sense that the fathers wanted an end to the work and that the Council, which was becoming a voting rather than a deliberative assembly, was quite readily accepting everything put before it.

Garrone's final report brought out the lessons taught by the discussion.[509] After thanking the fathers for their contributions to the clarification of a text that had presented many difficulties, he explained the main lines to be followed in the revision of the schema; he did not, however, raise any question at all of the direction to be taken, as had at one point been desired.[510]

The end of the Council was now in sight. Schema XIII, which provided the main course for the fourth period, had survived the debate on it, even though the Germans and Spaniards would still have preferred to see it replaced by some kind of message from the Council.[511] As the work of the general congregations drew to its end, the work of the commissions was only beginning. Their task now was to amend the schema before returning it to the assembly; this was no small task, even though as early as September 30 the central subcommission for schema XIII had given each of its subcommissions directions for their coming work.[512] All the

---

[508] Simons's intervention was doubtless the one that left his audience most puzzled. He saw birth control as the only means of combatting overpopulation, while also saying that he had doubts about its morality. It might be justified by applying the principle: "If the law is doubtful, one is free. A doubtful law cannot be enforced." He had previously suggested that the question be studied in light of the fact that laws are made for men and not men for laws. Gaviola took a diametrically opposed position, urging the Council not to let it be thought that overpopulation was a certain fact, and to take a clear position on birth control and the use of contraceptives.

[509] He called to mind the various problems raised during the discussion: the name of the schema, its style, the ambiguity in the use of some terms *(world, Church),* and so on (see his "Conclusio disceptationis" [*AS* IV/3, 735–38]).

[510] Haubtmann and Garrone had considered raising such questions, but the moderators did not accept their proposal (see Haubtmann papers, 1905; Philips papers, 2593; and Prignon papers, 1600).

[511] Even men involved in the working up of the schema (Semmelroth, for example) still hoped that the schema would be entrusted to a postconciliar commission (see *TSemmelroth,* October 7, 1965, 131).

[512] See Haubtmann papers, 1887 and 1886 (in French). At the same time, a summary was made of the remarks that Döpfner had sent to the drafting team in the name of the German bishops (Haubtmann papers, 1852; for Döpfner's German original, dated September 22, see ibid., 1842). Finally, on October 7, the presidents and secretaries of each

subcommissions were to finish their work in eight days.[513] Philips's
instructions for the work were very strict: no changes in the order of sections; abridge as far as possible; and prescind from the distinction
between the natural and supernatural orders or, in other words, speak simply of creation.[514] Given such a tight calendar, the various subcommissions met twice a day. Everything was done at high speed, and the revision of the chapters advanced rapidly and without great difficulty.[515]

III. THE SCHEMA ON THE PASTORAL OFFICE OF BISHOPS AND THE GOVERNMENT OF DIOCESES

Discussed during the third period, this text had been judged to be of a
lesser quality than *Lumen gentium* and had barely received a vote of
acceptance; in fact, many of its paragraphs had not been approved by a
two-thirds vote. With the strong support of Onclin, the commission had
quietly worked to improve it along the lines desired by the majority. But,
here again, a stubborn opposition could be expected. After all, in a sense
this decree had for its purpose to apply the principles of the Constitution
on the Church. These principles were in danger of remaining simply declarations if they were not applied.

Although the question of the synod of bishops had been settled by
the Pope, other sensitive questions remained: the "sacred power"
bestowed by consecration and giving the bishops all the authority
needed for their mission, except in matters which the pope reserved to
himself; episcopal conferences as a way of exercising collegiality; and
the relation between nuncios and the episcopal conferences. An amendment supported by several hundred fathers wanted to exclude the last
of these. In fact, as Jan Grootaers had discovered in the summer of
1965, a number of nuntiatures had undertaken to "chaperon" the local
Churches or even to control them altogether in the areas of doctrine,

---

of the subcommissions met to mark out the work that had to be done in the very short time
allotted.

[513] On October 14 a calendar was drawn up showing when the work had to be completed in order for the Council to end on December 8 (see Prignon papers, 1218).

[514] On October 5 the assignment of fathers and experts to the ten subcommissions was
made, and on October 7 the general norms for the work of the subcommissions were settled (see Prignon papers, 1222 and 1229b).

[515] For a description of the work done by the commission on the various chapters, see
Chapter V herein.

ecumenism, and pastoral practice.[516] Moreover, a normative statute
that the Congregation of the Consistory drew up for the episcopal conferences during the intersession tended to subject the undertakings and
decisions of the conferences to the control of the nuncios, something
that did not agree with the direction taken in the decree under discussion. Evidently, the theology of the local Church and collegiality was
in danger of being nipped in the bud without its more "practical"
complement as developed in this decree on the pastoral office of the
bishops.

When the commission on bishops began work again, on September 24,
the discussion quickly turned to whether to keep or omit the *votum*
addressed to the Pope asking for a truly representative synod of episcopal conferences. "Everyone is aware that with the synod now established
the text must be altered. Not a few bishops have readily resigned themselves to, or even desired, the elimination of the *votum* for reasons readily guessed. But others think that it is absolutely necessary to retain the
votum because the synod as established by the Pope does not satisfy...
the desire of the majority."[517] The commission quickly agreed to retain
the section, on the grounds that a conciliar text had more authority and
permanence than a Motu Proprio and that to eliminate the *votum* would
amount to taking from the Pope his base of support in the Council.[518]
The whole point was to put things in such a way that, despite all opposition, the idea of collegiality might emerge clearly.

On Thursday, September 16, the revised text was given to the fathers
along with the *expensio modorum* on the schema, which had been much
improved; on Tuesday, September 28, at the 137th general congregation,
the report on it was distributed, as well as a separate sheet containing the
modus on the episcopal synod.[519] On the next day Veuillot read the report
on the *modi* for the introduction and chapter I, and the assembly then
proceeded to vote. The schema won extensive support, with the number
of no votes not surpassing fifty-four (this was on no. 10).[520] From then
until October 1, votes were to be taken article by article.

[516] J. Grootaers, "L'enjeu de la quatrième session," *De Maand* (Brussels) 8/7: 2. He noted
similar moves in Germany, Belgium, the Netherlands, the United States, and Argentina.

[517] *JPrignon*, September 24, 1965 (Prignon papers, 1591).

[518] *JPrignon*, September 24, 1965, 5 (Prignon papers, 1591); see also Veuillot papers,
1565.

[519] At the general congregation on September 28, the fathers were given a modification in the schema (see *AS* IV/1, 78 and 618; see also Veuillot's report on no. 5 in *AS*
IV/3, 12).

[520] See *AS* IV/1, 79 and 80.

But as the fathers began to vote, new difficulties arose. The moderators received a list of fourteen *modi* to be added to the text. At the suggestion of Samoré and urged on by Carli and Siri,[521] the Pope had sent a considerable list of corrections, one of which wanted it said that the bishops were members of the college insofar as they had received jurisdiction.[522] There was a great commotion. Were changes once again to be made in a text on which the Council had already voted? Onclin and Felici agreed on proceeding to a vote. While the votes were being taken on September 30 (votes 335–39) and October 1 (votes 340–43), the commission met in haste. Onclin was assigned to draw up the report, which was passed on to Marella, who at first was troubled that he had nothing to send "on high."[523]

In the evening the commission met again. This time the atmosphere was less tense, and despite the wishes of Marella, the commission remained firm in its rejection of most of the *modi*. Finally, thanks to the persevering work of Onclin, the commission rejected all the corrections having to do with the substance of the decree and allowed only changes in form. The commission also refused to have the Council take a separate vote on the *modi*. On October 1 there was a meeting of a small committee assigned to draw up the final report to the Holy Father.[524] As a

[521] So we are told by Prignon (*JPrignon,* September 30, 1965 [Prignon papers, 1596, 3]). Congar attributes the *modi* to Carli (*JCongar,* October 1, 1965,II, 415).

[522] For the list of *modi,* numbered 1–14, sent on two sheets titled "Osservazioni sullo schema De pastorali episcoporum munere" and dated September 27, see *AS* V/3, 388–90. There is a complete file on this episode in the Onclin archive at Leuven. In the paragraph that states that by reason of their episcopal consecration bishops are made pastors, judges, and so on, one *modus* wanted mention to be made also (in addition to consecration) of canonical mission and hierarchical communion. Another had to do with episcopal conferences; it should be said that their decisions, which were really only wishes, would have no real force until they had been ratified by the Holy See. According to Onclin, the whole set of *modi* had for its purpose to gain the insertion of this last statement, which Carli defended fiercely. According to a handwritten note of Onclin, Carli was the only father who did not rally to the commission's position on this last *modus*. On the entire matter see J. Grootaers, "Willy Onclin et sa participation à la rédaction du décret *Christus Dominus,*" in *Actes et acteurs de Vatican II* (Leuven: Peeters, 1998), 443–50.

[523] The development of this debate can be followed by means of the scraps of information scattered throughout the archives of Veuillot, Onclin, and Himmer, and the notes in Prignon's diary for September 30, 1965.

[524] It is known that Onclin, Veuillot, and Himmer attended this meeting. The participants were tempted to ask Paul VI to drop even the points that had been accepted; so insignificant were the changes that they were likely to elicit more ridicule than anything else. Veuillot indeed was ready to go to Dell'Acqua and beg him to ask the Pope not to intervene (*JPrignon,* October 1, 1965 [Prignon papers, 1597, 2]). For the commission's response to the *modi,* see *AS* V/3: "Observationes factae de Schemate De pastorali episcoporum munere in Ecclesia et responsa proposita." For Marella's letter to Paul VI, see

result of the report, the Pope declared himself satisfied and did not insist on anything further.[525]

Clearly, it was in the commissions and not in the hall that the real game was being played out, and the climate there was poisoning the course of the Council. Another example is an effort being made to introduce a change in the *De divina revelatione;* Staffa went to the Pope in an effort to have the competent commission make a change. In Staffa's case it was in regard to the obligation of following the principles of St. Thomas in teaching theology. It was becoming clear that putting pressure on the Pope was the way to obtain any goal, and opponents of the various schemas were doing precisely that. Concerned for the unity of the Church, the Pope wanted unanimity at any price, even if the agreements he obtained were often only lip service. His concessions also had the draw-back of raising the stakes: if people made him yield once, they were not embarrassed to increase the pressure. Finally, different intermediaries were not ashamed to claim to speak in the name of higher authority, thereby contributing to a muddling of communications between the Pope and the commissions.

On October 6 a vote was taken on the set of amendments and on the schema on bishops. Everything went off without a hitch: of 2,181 votes cast, the text received 2,167 in favor. Thanks to a leak in *Le Monde* on October 5, the fathers had been forewarned about the Pope's intervention. But at the time no correction had been received, although the commission had, on its own, accepted three minor changes in the text, two of these having to do with religious. The schema was promulgated at the public session on October 28. But this did not mark the end, since a number of points in the schema would be discussed again in connection with the reform of canon law.

Vatican II had succeeded, not without difficulty, in providing the Catholic Church with a conciliar text on bishops; it seemed thereby to balance the unfinished teaching of Vatican I on the primacy of the Bishop of Rome. On the other hand, chapter I, on the role of the bishops in relation to the universal Church, did not manage to give a concrete insight into the application of the principles set down in chapter III of *Lumen gentium*, which dealt with the episcopate. While the new schema did assert once again that collegial authority can be exercised outside a council (no. 5), it did not elaborate

---

AS V/3, 387–88. Marella's summary differed a little from Onclin's report in that it suggested that more of the *modi* had been accepted.

[525] See Colombo's answer to Marella on October 3, in *AS* V/3, 393–94.

either the means of this exercise or the norms defining it. No. 6 did reaffirm the concern of the bishops for the entire Church, but it did not suggest any way of making this concern effective. True enough, there was the arrangement for a synod of bishops, but the fathers already knew how no. 5 seemed to have been weakened in comparison with the original draft. It did indeed include the seeds of renewal, but nothing had yet been done about them.

So too, the sections on the congregations of the Roman Curia (nos. 9–10) seemed to fall short of expectations voiced during the debates, The reform had yet to come, but the text itself was timid in the directives it gave (choice of members from different countries; admission of some diocesan bishops among the members of the congregations; greater attention to the voice of the laity; renewal of the curial bodies and their working methods). In short, wishes for reforms were uttered, but there were no specific and obligatory instructions.

More important, perhaps, the decree *Christus Dominus* helped to increase the standing of the diocesan Church and gave rise to reflection — still not finished — on the nature and status of the local Churches as presence and full manifestation of the Church of Christ (no. 11). Continuing what was said in *Lumen gentium* (no. 23), this article contained in germ all future developments in relations between the local Churches and the Church as a whole. This chapter on diocesan bishops made clear the aspects of episcopacy: priority of the ministry of proclaiming the gospel (nos. 12–14), a point that made it possible to advance beyond the perspectives of Trent; the central place of the presider at the Eucharist and the sacraments (no. 15); pastoral governance of the people of God, which makes room for the local Church to develop its synodal character (no.16). The whole of chapter III (devoted to the collaborators of the diocesan bishop) went on to emphasize this synodal character of diocesan life; the bishop never acts in isolation but in reliance on his collaborators: auxiliary bishops (no. 26); diocesan curia and councils (no. 27); diocesan clergy, especially parish priests (nos. 28–32); and men and women religious (nos. 33–35).

Finally, the last part of the decree (chapter IV) was concerned with the cooperation of the bishops for the common good of many Churches. It is of interest that in the chapter on relations among the Churches the decree is much more explicit than it had been in Chapter I, where it dealt with relations between the bishops and the universal Church. In chapter IV the decree wanted the revival of synods and of provincial and plenary councils (no. 36); it tackled the question of ecclesiastical boundaries (dioceses, provinces, regions) and interdiocesan relations (nos. 36–42).

Nowhere does the decree suggest that there could be groups of the faithful, formed on a personal and not a territorial basis, that would be the equivalent of a diocese.

While discussions in the Council, especially during the final three periods, had contributed extensively to the improvement of the schema, it fell short of the expectations of many, not only in what it said about the synod but also in regard to the reform of the Curia and relations between the local Church and the whole Church. The schema remained captive to a universalist perspective, with the bishop being located first in the universal Church (chapter I) before being located in his diocese (chapter II). During the period of the reception of Vatican II, many ways of implementing the decree were reported and, in particular, many questions were submitted to the commission for the reform of canon law. There again, the reception of Vatican II would show that the final negotiations on the decree had not successfully overcome all the tensions that had surfaced in the discussions.

During this veritable obstacle course the question of collegiality, and how it fit in with the legitimate exercise of papal primacy, was raised not only at the theoretical level in the schema on bishops and the government of dioceses, especially in connection with the establishment of a synod of bishops, but also in more concrete ways. Should the pope act on his own or with the bishops? This was the question raised by the announcement on September 15 of the establishment of a synod of bishops. After that, the repeated sending of *modi* from the Pope to the various competent commissions kept raising the question anew. Was it appropriate that by way of last-minute interventions the Pope should change texts voted on by the assembly? Everyone would have been glad if the question had been raised in so simple a way.

In his opening address Paul VI had said that he wished to avoid overly specific questions in order that he might leave the Council complete freedom. Had he later forgotten the line of conduct that he had set down for himself at the beginning of the work of the fourth period? It is difficult to answer yes or no. Certainly he was assailed by petitions and requests and was subjected to very strong pressures. Those who voted against collegiality were the very ones who, when they could not prevail in the hall, took the debate to another court: the Pope. Paul VI was, in the first place, the victim of the failure of the Council fathers themselves to assimilate the doctrine of collegiality; instead, they ended up turning him into a judge over the Council. He was also a victim of his own temperament and of his scrupulous awareness of his role. His intellectual habits led him to study all possible views before deciding, and he even did his best to grasp contrary arguments and the positions of his opponents. By often sending *modi* to the competent commissions he tried to assure himself that all points of view were heard and all objections examined and weighed.

The Pope's subtle mind and intellectual honesty led him to seek explanations, and his keen concern for unity and consensus led him to try to satisfy as much as possible those who raised objections and were opposed to the majority. As a result, he opened himself to tremendous pressures from not very scrupulous people, some of them in his close entourage, and, in many instances, he saw his image tarnished in the eyes of public opinion and even in the eyes of many bishops. He was thus led, for better or for worse, to bend the reformist current that was seeking expression while he did not succeed in rallying those who were unwilling to listen to anything. At all times, however, he remained honest, a point that Häring emphasized. Although he submitted *modi* and sometimes agreed that requests for amendments be sent to the commissions, he never tried to impose his viewpoint on the Council and agreed to yield to the arguments of the commissions. To sum up, the fourth period raised, in a concrete way, the issues of a collegial government of the Catholic Church and how the activity of the primate was to fit into such a collegial framework.

The other question that emerged from all these debates was that of the concept of tradition. While this question was being vigorously discussed in the commission that put *Dei Verbum* through a fine sieve, in the debate on religious freedom and on the Church in the modern world, many of the fathers showed by their attitude and practice how they conceived of tradition. Tradition was cumulative and repetitive. All that was needed was simply to repeat, in a fuller and more solemn manner, what the Roman pontiffs had said on the subject of freedom in religious matters; to repeat the hierarchy's classical presentation of the ends of marriage, a presentation endorsed by a declaration of the Holy Office and regarded almost as irreformable; to repeat, without variation, the declarations of Pius XI and Pius XII on procreation; and so on. The Council's task was not to discern the signs of the times; it should be a machine for making even more definitive the teachings submitted to the fathers for study. In short, the fourth period eloquently raised the question of "interpretive tradition" in the Church. Throughout these conciliar debates the entire question of doctrinal development was likewise being raised. Could a Council give a new direction to pontifical teachings of the previous century? This was a question on which views obviously differed.

Despite the resistances, procrastinations, and displays of impatience, Albert Outler could regard the months of September, October, and November, 1965, as a "Reformation Day" for the Catholic Church, which many Protestants had looked upon as "unreformed and irreformable." True enough, for this admirer of Paul VI, whom he regarded as a brilliant tactician, it was a "Reformation Roman-style," but even so, something important had changed.[526]

---

[526] See A. C. Outler, *Methodist Observer at Vatican II* (Westminster, Md.: Newman, 1967), esp. chap. 10: "Reformation Day Updated," 139–45, and chap. 14: "Reformation Roman-Style," 161–71.

Chapter III

COMPLETING THE CONCILIAR AGENDA

Mauro Velati

After the exciting start of the week, when Paul VI made his journey to the United Nations, the Council returned to its usual routine on Wednesday morning, October 6: "This morning we were back to normal," wrote Douglas Horton, an American observer.[1] The Council's agenda awaited its completion in an atmosphere marked by a mixture of frenzy and weariness. The general congregations were studying chapter V of the schema on the Church and the modern world, and there was a series of important interventions on the subject of war and peace. At the same time, the voting on the schema on the pastoral office of bishops was ending, while another schema — on the renewal of religious life — was entering the last phase of its journey with Compagnone's final report and the fathers' vote on the *expensio modorum*.

During these days a number of texts would come up for a vote whose fate had at times been quite uncertain during the preceding periods. The schema on the ministry and life of priests was rebounding from a solemn defeat in the previous session and would have to be discussed once again in the hall. The schema on the laity had still to negotiate the phase of examination of proposed amendments. For four other schemas (religious, priestly training, Christian education, and relations with non-Christian religions) all that was needed was a final vote, but many doubts persisted about whether they should be promulgated. There is no need to recall here the controversies that had always accompanied the schema on the non-Christian religions. The other three schemas, which had been reduced to sets of simple propositions in the so-called Döpfner Plan but had then gradually been given a fuller form, had been approved by the fathers during the previous session, but the definitive step represented by the vote on the *expensio modorum* would be the occasion of new controversies. The assembly was divided: the conciliar minority tended to support the approval of the three schemas, which met the demands of a broad, moderate group. At the last moment, however, some third-world bishops

---

[1] Horton, *Vatican Diary 1965*, 82.

pressed for changes on some important points. The European bishops who served as spokesmen for the reform-minded majority, while aware of the weaknesses of these schemas, were hesitant about asking for exemptions from the regulations so as not to prolong the discussion. They were afraid of establishing a dangerous precedent when it came to the approval of the schemas that were dear to the hearts of the majority, especially those on bishops and on religious freedom. In varying measure this mechanism did come into play in the history of the three schemas on which we shall dwell at the beginning of this chapter.

I. The Renewal of Religious Life

It was the fifth draft (counting from the preparatory period) of the schema on the renewal of religious life that was presented to the fathers. Like the other "minor" schemas, it had suffered a reduction to a set of propositions as decreed by the Coordinating Commission in the spring of 1963, but after the debate over it in general congregations during the third period it had regained the status of an independent schema. That the subject was important to the bishops was shown by the stream of *modi* sent to the competent commission; the various commentaries on the decree are unanimous in stressing that 14,000 *modi* were sent in by the fathers, even if, in substance, they could be reduced to approximately 500 observations.[2]

During the first months of 1965 the commission had worked on this huge mass of observations and produced a new text.[3] The schema was handed out to the fathers in the hall on September 16 and, as usual, contained the new text and the preceding draft in parallel columns so that the notable differences could be clearly seen. At the same time the text of the *expensio modorum* was also distributed, with the justification for the various choices made by the commission. On September 30 the text of Compagnone's report was distributed, which confirmed the spirit in which the commission had done its work of revision.

---

[2] See E. Fogliasso, *Il decreto "Perfectae caritatis": Sul rinnovamento della vita religiosa in rispondenza alle odierne esigenze* (Turin, 1967), 56–59; A. Le Bourgeois, "Historique du décret," in *L'adaptation et la rénovation de la vie religieuse: Décret "Perfectae Caritatis,"* ed. J. M. R. Tillard and Y. Congar (Paris, 1967), 67–71; F. Wulf, "Introduction," *Decree on the Appropriate Renewal of Religious Life,* in *Commentary,* 2:301–32; J. Schmiedl, *Das Konzil und die Orden: Krise und Erneuerung des gottgeweihten Lebens* (Vallendar-Schönstatt, 1999).

[3] See *History*, 4:584-90.

The fathers, however, had many reasons for dissatisfaction. The schema had indeed undergone an almost complete revision, but on some points it had not been able to accede to the desires of the bishops, which were often contrary to one another. During these days Huyghe, a Belgian bishop and a member of the Commission for Religious, told Moeller of his dissatisfaction with section 14 on obedience, which was still seen too much in terms of passivity. But this issue had elicited divergent views in the amendments. On the one side, 399 fathers had asked for a formulation of the concept of obedience that was based on a double requirement: a sense of maturity on the part of the religious, and a respect for the human person on the part of the superior. On the other side, 405 bishops emphasized "the authentic concept of religious obedience," which does not require an effort of persuasion by the superior.[4] The text made an effort, in its formulation, to mediate between these differing demands.

Even more problematic was the question of admitting teaching brothers to the priesthood, a subject dealt with in no.10. Although the question had been discussed during the preparatory period of the Council,[5] it had not appeared in the various drafts of the text that the conciliar commission produced. Nor had it been raised in the debate in the hall during the third period, except for a brief reference in the speech of Bishop Carroll, who himself urged caution in coming to a decision on the subject. Nor were there any important references to it in the *modi*: the request of 134 fathers for a new text on lay institutes and on teaching brothers made no reference to the question of their ordination as priests.[6]

But pressures were being brought to bear in that direction. Some representatives of the Marists, especially among the Italians, had organized a campaign in support of the request and were urging the Council fathers

---

[4] *AS* IV/3, 557–59. The question is taken up in J. M. Tillard, "L'obéissance," in Tillard and Congar, *L'adaptation et la rénovation de la vie religieuse*. See also F. Giardini, "L'obbedienza dei presbiteri (Dottrina del Concilio Vaticano II)," *Rivista di Ascetica e Mistica* 35 (1966), 447–74.

[5] Between December 1960 and April 1961 a group of the commission's consultors had studied the question of giving lay brothers access to the priesthood. The text of their report was discussed on April 21, 1961, but the subject did not appear in the preparatory schema (see Archives of the Congregation for Religious, 607, 767–69, and 402–3). To this extent, the statement made by Sauvage, at that time assistant to the superior general of the Brothers of the Christian Schools, was not entirely accurate; he claimed that the question was first discussed in the spring of 1965. He made a thorough analysis of the history and content of no. 10 of the schema (M. Sauvage, F.S.C., "La vie religieuse laïque [Commentaire des numéros 10 et 15]," in Tillard and Congar, *L'adaptation et la rénovation*, 301–74).

[6] *AS* IV/3, 579.

to send notes expressing their approval to the secretariat of the Commission for Religious before the end of January 1965.[7] According to Delhaye, some Latin American bishops turned instead to the Pope and asked him to intervene with the commission;[8] their motive was probably their worry about the widespread lack of priests in their own dioceses. As other witnesses attest, the Pope did intervene, but anonymously.[9]

The question was debated within the commission during February 1965,[10] and opposition to the decisions taken was still keen in September. The Brothers of the Christian Schools and, in particular, Sauvage, challenged the insertion because it seemed to alter the strictly lay charism of the congregation.[11] In his report Compagnone explained why the commission had decided to devote a special section to lay religious institutes. On the one hand, it was necessary to reevaluate the experience of lay institutes, since these were always in danger of being marginalized; on the other, the commission wanted to raise the possibility that some members of these institutes, if their general chapters agreed, might be ordained priests because of need, especially in countries where priests were scarce. This second reason was also presented as the result of conciliar debate, even though the subject had never come up explicitly either in the hall or in the *expensio modorum*.

On the eve of the vote, then, the many reasons for uncertainty that had marked these points during the history of the schema still remained. Discussions among the Belgian bishops and experts during these days showed how positions were lining up. Huyghe was strongly tempted to ask for a new discussion of the schema, even though he knew this was

---

[7] See P. D. Anfosso, "Nota de auspicando accessu ad sacerdotium fratrum maristarum a scholis laicorum ad excellentissimos et reverendissimos patres commissionis de religiosis et alios patres in concilio oecumenico Vaticano II reverenter oblata" (January 10, 1965) (Lercaro papers, XXXI, 1064). To the petition was attached a short note to be filled in and forwarded to the Commission for Religious.

[8] See Sauvage, "La vie religieuse laique," 342.

[9] The authorship of the insertion was explicitly stated by the commission's preparatory text of February 1965 (see *History,* 4:589) and was confirmed by leaks that Moeller collected in September of the same year (*JPrignon,* September 20, 1965 [Prignon papers, 1596, 5]). Moeller also told Prignon that the Pope, when consulted, asked that his intervention be kept secret. Msgr. Perantoni, one of those who opposed the Marist initiative, wrote to the Pope asking for clarification but never received an answer.

[10] See *History*, 4:589-90. See also G. Lefeuvre, "L'accès au sacerdoce de religieux appartenant à des instituts exclusivement laïcs: Note sur le §2 du no. 10 du décret *Perfectae caritatis,*" *Esprit et vie* 86 (1976), 657–64.

[11] See Prignon papers, 1596. In Moeller's letters there are also some remarks that go back to Sauvage, as well as the draft of a reformulation of no. 10 of the schema of September 1965 (Moeller papers, 2388–2402).

against the regulations. But Moeller persuaded him that such an initiative was unsuitable, first because it would create a dangerous precedent for other schemas still to be discussed during the session,[12] and second, because a further discussion might risk compromising some of the gains made in the schema on religious. We must recall here the special circumstances in which the Commission for Religious had done its work during the preceding months; the many absences of Cardinal Antoniutti, the president, and the resulting assumption of leadership by German Bishop Leiprecht had made it possible to transform the schema much beyond the lines laid down by Antoniutti. But in many respects the situation was still unpredictable, since it was not clear what weight a possible pronouncement by the bishops would have.[13]

At this point the most realistic course seemed to be to structure the vote differently, that is, to isolate the second part of no. 10, which contained the proposal about teaching brothers. The structure of the voting as proposed by the commission provided for a global vote on the sections that had already received more than two-thirds of the votes in the previous session (nos. 18–24) and then a separate vote on each of the sections that had not received a minimal number of votes (nos. 1–17 and 25).[14] From a conversation among Prignon, Bonet, and Etchegaray in the hall on October 1 came a decision to compose a letter asking for this parceling out of the votes on the *De religiosis*; the composers would try to get a number of bishops and cardinals to sign it.[15] This initiative was probably not followed up, and it is not clear whether it had any connection with the petition addressed to the moderators during these same days by A. Lorscheider. The Brazilian bishop pointed out that in the new draft of the schema there were three completely new sections (nos. 9–11) and that these could not be voted on except after a prior examination of them by the assembly, at least in the form of *iuxta modum* votes.[16] This meant the

---

[12] *JPrignon,* September 29, 1965 (Prignon papers, 1595, 2–3).

[13] Prignon recalled the fears of Huyghe: "Msgr. Huyghe also fears an insistence on this subject [a new discussion of the schema] because of the danger that some points in the schema might be challenged and that Cardinal Antoniutti might take advantage of it to eliminate the improvements that the commission had managed to obtain" (Prignon papers, 1596, 6).

[14] *AS* IV/3, 581–97.

[15] *JPrignon,* October 1, 1965 (Prignon papers, 1597, 6). The letter would contain a similar request for the schema on Christian education.

[16] Letter of Lorscheider to the moderators on October 13, 1965 (*AS* V/3, 394–95). The date does not seem probable inasmuch as the definitive vote on the schema was taken on October 6. It is likely that the letter was really written in the early days of October.

revival of the idea of a vote *iuxta modum* on the schema; it had the draw-
back, however, of being contrary to the regulations.

In the third point among the observations attached to his letter,
Lorscheider raised another matter that had caused not a few difficulties
in the revising of the schema, namely, the question of secular institutes,
with which no. 11 of the new schema dealt. The commission had
undoubtedly made full use of its freedom in revising this part of the
schema. In order not to remain burdened by the traditional hard and fast
distinction between the active life and the contemplative life, it had chosen to propose a typology of the diverse forms of religious life that better reflected the variety of real life. As a result, the schema contained
five central sections devoted respectively to institutes of contemplative
life (no. 7), those of the active life (no. 8), monasticism (no. 9), the forms
of lay religious life (no. 10), and finally, secular institutes (no. 11). While
the last three were an addition to the original schema, on several occasions the leaders of the commission emphasized the extent to which their
choice was supported by the requests of the fathers. In Secretary
Rousseau's response to Lorscheider's letter, he gave as an example the
already mentioned request of 134 fathers for a new text on lay religious
life.[17] In like manner a group of forty fathers had asked for a fuller, separate treatment of the secular institutes.[18]

Although Lorscheider's letter had no effect, when Compagnone read
his report, he felt obliged to dwell on the question of the secular institutes,
explaining more fully the text distributed to the fathers. The subject was
obviously controversial. In the eyes of bishops more solicitous to bring
out the specific nature of religious life, the secular institutes seemed to
be a foreign body. An amendment signed by three fathers asked that the
very words "secular institutes" be removed from the text, since "the
members of secular institutes are to be counted among the laity and not
among religious." Others, of a more conciliatory outlook, said the contradiction could be removed by changing the title of the schema, avoiding the expression "religious life," and appealing instead to the evangelical counsels, which were evidently a bond of union between the
experience of the secular institutes and that of religious.[19]

---

[17] J. Rousseau, "Responsa ad observationes Exc.mi D.ni Aloisii Lorscheider Episcopi
Angelopolitani super schema decreti *De accommodata renovatione vitae religiosae*," in
AS V/3, 396–97; for instructions on the *modi* see *AS* IV/3, 579.

[18] *AS* IV/3, 580.

[19] Ibid.

Compagnone explained the choices made by the commission. Since it was impossible to change a title already voted on by the fathers, the commission had preferred to make separate room for a treatment of the secular institutes; here it explained their special nature, the works of their members, and their spirituality, without pronouncing on their canonical status. As we shall see, this solution did not fully satisfy the wishes of the principal secular institutes and would have required further corrections.

On the first day of voting in the hall, the commission was called to meet once again in order to discuss some changes. According to rumors picked up by Moeller (one of the commission's experts), these were some changes requested by the Pope.[20] But the official documentation, studied by J. Schmiedl, contains no trace of a papal intervention, but only of a proposal by Carlo Colombo.[21] Did this deal with the papal interventions regarding secular institutes of which we shall speak a little later? The meeting was very short (only thirty-five minutes), and its outcome seems to have been negative. In any case, the observations that were discussed were rejected.[22] In the history of the schema, then, this episode had no consequences.

On October 6 voting began in the hall after the reading of Compagnone's report. The schema was presented in the form originally determined by the commission: sections 1–17 and 25 were voted on individually, while a single, comprehensive vote was taken on the second part, that is, sections 18–24. The votes on the individual sections showed almost unanimous agreement, except for no. 10, which saw a higher number of no votes (57) than the average. In any case the percentage of no votes was quite low. The vote on the schema as a whole on October 11 showed the approval of the fathers, with a trifling number of negative votes (only 13 out of a total of 2,142).

---

[20] For Moeller's testimony, see *JPrignon,* October 5, 1965 (Prignon papers, 1599, 2). It seems that the letter accompanying the papal *modi* stated specifically that the commission retained its freedom of choice and discussion. Antoniutti himself was probably opposed to the *modi* offered.

[21] J. Schmiedl, "Erneuerung im Widerstreit: das Ringen der *Commissio de religiosis* und der *Commissio de Concilii laboribus coordinandis* um das Dekret zur zeitgemässen Erneuerung des Ordenslebens," in *Commissions,* 311. For the very succinct minutes of the meeting, see *Acta commissionis conciliaris "De Religiosis," IX conventus commissionis 1965 durante Quarta et ultima Sessione Concilii,* 83. I thank Schmiedl for providing me with a copy of the minutes. The text of Colombo's observations is not in any archives, although they were registered with the secretariat of the commission (no. 592/65).

[22] The minutes of the meeting say only: "All things considered, the commission does not think that these observations are to be accepted at the present stage in the course of the conciliar schema that is to be voted on tomorrow" (*Acta commissionis conciliaris "De Religiosis,"* 83).

The results of this vote, and of the votes on other texts during the succeeding days, seemed to show almost unanimous agreement among the
bishops, but it is necessary to consider the general atmosphere in the
assembly during those days. Prignon notes on October 8: "For the last
three or four days the debate has become rather dreary. One senses that
the bishops are incredibly weary. Many of them can be seen walking the
corridors as early as ten o'clock." Again, he dwells on "the growing apathy of the great majority of the assembly, which clearly wants to finish
and is no longer excited except on some exceptional questions."[23] The testimonies of the observers also describe a general climate of weariness in
which the fathers would vote yes on everything simply in order to finish.[24]

II. A New Spirit in Ancient Institutions:
The Training of Priests

The last week of conciliar debate began on Monday morning, October 11, the third anniversary of the memorable ceremony that had opened
the Council, a coincidence that did not escape attentive observers, even
if only as an occasion for measuring the distance traveled.[25] The agenda
was a heavy one, and a good three documents would be definitively
approved during these few days. While the debate on the schema on the
missions was going on, Carraro, a member of the Commission for Seminaries and Studies, gave a report on the schema on priestly formation.
As Guyot later remarked, this was a schema "that caused the fewest difficulties within the conciliar assembly, and the one that was least spoken
of outside it."[26]

The history of this schema, however, did show some peculiar features. When it came before the footlights of the Council hall for a very
short period (November 12–17, 1964), it had been profoundly

---

[23] *JPrignon,* October 8, 1965 (Prignon papers, 1601, 1–2).

[24] D. Horton wrote on October 7: "One has the impression that the fathers in their
eagerness to bring the Council to an end are now ready to cut the debates short and vote
approval of anything that is not absolutely intolerable" (Horton, *Vatican Diary 1965,* 87).
See also K. E. Skydsgaard, "Report on the Fourth Session of the Second Vatican Council, n. 5" (November 19, 1965), in ACO 7.24.

[25] Horton asked himself whether John XXIII, for all his foresight, could have imagined
the results of these three years (Horton, *Vatican Diary 1965,* 93). Congar, on the other
hand, heavily involved as he was in commission work, said nothing about the anniversary.

[26] L. J. Guyot, "Le décret sur la formation sacerdotale: présentation d'ensemble,"
Seminarium 2 (1966), 313.

transformed when compared to the initial draft in the preparatory period, thanks essentially to the many interventions and written corrections sent in by the fathers in successive stages beginning with the first intersession.[27] Early drafts of the schema had been burdened with myriad juridical or overly specific questions; thanks, however, to the work of some members of the commission, such as D. Hurley, Archbishop of Durban (South Africa) and Jesuit Father Dezza, it incorporated many of the desires widely voiced in the debate on priestly training then going on.[28] Shored up by the opening statement that the episcopal conferences were to be responsible for developing a plan containing concrete directives for the renewal, the schema had been approved during the third period by a crushing majority (2,076 yes votes, 41 no votes).

During the third intersession the schema had been revised in light of the corrections sent in by the fathers. The definitive version was distributed to the fathers, along with the text of the *expensio modorum*, on September 23, 1965. But some points in this revised text were challenged before the final vote. At the end of September a letter from Msgr. Darmajuwana reached the board of presidents; in it, this president of the Indonesian episcopal conferences, supported by all his bishops, challenged the work of the commission on two specific points in the schema.

The first was the passage on the importance of major seminaries: "Major seminaries are necessary for priestly formation." This statement was not found in the 1964 text and, according to Darmajuwana, had been introduced by the commission on its own initiative, without any specific request having been made by the fathers, who, in fact, had in some cases called into question the uniqueness of seminaries as means of priestly

---

[27] See A. Mayer and G. Baldanza, "Genesi storica del decreto *Optatam totius*," in *Il decreto sulla formazione sacerdotale,* ed. A. Mayer and G. Baldanza (Turin, 1967), 13–28. For a presentation of the entire decree, see G. Martil, *Los seminarios en el Concilio vaticano II: Historia y comentario* (Salamanca, 1966); D. E. Hurley and J. Cunnane, *Vatican II on Priests and Seminaries* (Dublin-Chicago, 1967); J. Frisque, "Le décret *Optatam Totius:* Introduction historique," in *Les prêtres: Décrets "Presbyterorum Ordinis" et "Optatam Totius." Textes latins et traductions françaises,* ed. J. Frisque and Y. Congar (Paris, 1968), 187–89. For the third period and the intersession, see *History*, 4:356-64 and 590-97.

[28] For a description of the debate at the time, see A. Mayer and G. Baldanza, "Il rinnovamento degli studi filosofici e teologici nei seminari, Rassegna bibliografica," *La Scuola Cattolica* 2 (1966), 83–146. For the contribution of D. E. Hurley, Archbishop of Durban, see P. Denis, "Archbishop Hurley's Contribution to the Second Vatican Council," in *Experience,* 233–60. Hurley's vision is well described in his article "Pastoral Emphasis in Seminary Studies," *The Furrow* (January 13, 1962).

formation. Indeed, the report on the *expensio modorum* showed the existence of a minority view that wanted to move beyond the seminary: an
amendment signed by fifty-two bishops raised the possibility of the Council's not only reforming the seminaries but also conceiving a new organization for priestly formation that would be more adapted to the times.
This would be a historic choice on the level with the one made by Trent.[29]
In addition to the Indonesian bishops, there were some among the South
American bishops, Larraín in particular, who wanted to move beyond the
seminary system.[30]

The second point was even more controversial; it dealt with no. 10, on
ecclesiastical celibacy. At the beginning of the year Darmajuwana had
already intervened to ask for a reform of the law of celibacy; he now
challenged the commission regarding an expression that seemed to imply
that a negative answer had been given to the debate.[31] The question was
a very sensitive one, as would be shown by the sudden end of the debate
when Paul VI intervened on October 11.

The letter from the Indonesians was discussed during the plenary meeting of the Commission for Seminaries and Studies on October 1. According to the sparse information we have, the tendency of Msgr. Daem seems
to have been to find a way to bring out the real sentiments of the bishops on controverted points. To this end, a suggestion that the schedule of
votes be revised gained strength. A conversation of South American theologian Medina with Prignon brought Suenens in, and he in turn got
Döpfner and Silva Henríquez involved.[32] It is probable that a further intervention of Silva Henríquez, which is documented in the *Acta Synodalia*,
had its origin in these conversations.

The address of the Chilean prelate was closely argued and carefully
constructed. First of all, he stressed the lack of conciliar regulations for
the norms to be followed in the study of the corrections. But the actual
practice of the commissions yielded some general norms, which the

---

[29] See *AS* IV/4, 47. The commission had rejected the suggestion on the grounds that
the majority thought the seminary was still a valuable institution.

[30] Prignon learned from Etchegaray that Larraín and another South American bishop
had difficulties with the statement about major seminaries. They seemed to agree fully
with Darmajuwana's analysis (see *JPrignon*, September 27, 1965 [Prignon papers, 1593,
2]).

[31] The words in italics are the ones that had been introduced into the text: "Students
who, in accordance with the *holy and firmly established laws* of their own rite, follow the
venerable tradition of priestly celibacy." See the letter of J. Darmajuwana to the Council
of Presidents, September 28, 1965 (*AS* V/3, 382–83).

[32] *JPrignon*, October 5, 1965 (Prignon papers, 1599, 3).

bishop's exposition summarized for the purpose of showing that these were not completely respected in the work of the commission responsible for the schema on priestly formation. Without citing specific instances, Silva Henríquez repeated Darmajuwana's remarks about the introduction of changes without any prior request from the bishops. He dwelt chiefly, however, on the commission's proposed plan for voting on the text, which did not allow the bishops to pass a specific judgment on the parts of the schema that had undergone the more important changes, because the vote was to be cast on each section as a whole. Silva Henríquez proposed a schedule of votes on the separate new parts, while leaving the parts of the text that were already familiar to a single comprehensive vote.[33]

But in a note of October 6 Felici rejected Silva Henríquez's requests; he challenged, among other points, the speaker's remarks on the conciliar regulations, and he urged that a formal request be made of the Council of Presidents. The Secretary General made no mention of the letter sent in during the previous week by the Indonesian bishops. In fact, however, probably because of Döpfner's intervention, the request was considered by the authorities of the competent commission; on October 7 they sent Felici a revised schedule of votes on the schema. In this new draft, which was distributed to the fathers on the following day, the questions to be answered numbered fifteen, thereby giving room for a specific examination of all the controverted points.[34] Thus the substance of Silva Henríquez's request had been accepted. But during a short period in the conversations with Suenens the suggestion was made to obtain from the General Secretariat something quite exceptional: permission for a vote that would include *iuxta modum* votes, at least in dealing with some limited points. Such a procedure would probably provide an adequate solution to the problem raised by the Indonesian bishops.

On October 7 the question of an *iuxta modum* vote, not only for the schema on priestly training but also for the schema on education, was discussed at a short meeting of the moderators (Lercaro, Suenens, and Döpfner) with Felici and Tisserant. Suenens found himself alone in supporting the suggestion. Felici minimized the importance of the problem,

---

[33] See R. Silva Henríquez, "Animadversiones circa expensionem modorum Schematis Decreti 'De Institutione sacerdotali,'" in *AS* V/3, 401–40. The plan for reformulating the questions allowed for eighteen votes instead of the seven proposed by the commission.

[34] Letter of A. Mayer to Felici, October 7, 1965, in *AS* V/3, 404 (the text of the questions is in an appendix on 405–6).

even while acknowledging that the arguments in the letter from the Indonesians had some validity. Lercaro and Döpfner were not enthusiastic about the prospect. Tisserant, for his part, decisively rejected the possibility of straining the regulations, and he advised the bishops to appeal to the administrative tribunal.[35] Efforts of the Belgian group to start a movement among the bishops in favor of improving the schema ran into the spirit of apathy that was spreading through the assembly. On the next day, at the meeting of the representatives of the episcopal conferences, it was already clear that there was no room for joint action, and the attempt to have a different kind of vote on this schema was therefore abandoned.[36]

All of the needs and requests that lay behind these initiatives were brought out clearly during these same days by a one-page anonymous document intended for the Council fathers.[37] It cited five weak points in the schema that required a radical revision. Two already had been cited in Darmajuwana's letter: the assertion of the necessity of seminaries, and the section on celibacy, a practice judged to be lacking in universality. But there were other unpersuasive aspects in the schema. The phrase in the introduction that stated the scope of the decree's application (*especially* the diocesan clergy but in a broad sense the entire clergy) set up a harmful opposition between the two clergies. The section on ecclesiastical vocations (no. 2) sounded like "vocational proselytism" or at least could be interpreted as such. Finally, the section on minor seminaries (no. 3)

[35] *JPrignon*, October 8, 1965 (Prignon papers, 1601, 1–2). Prignon noted Suenens's impression that Lercaro was "increasingly exhausted." Nothing is said of the meeting in Lercaro's letters from the Council.

[36] The minutes of the meeting make no reference to the question about the schema on priestly formation but deal solely with the schema on education ("Quarta coadunatio delegatorum ex nonnullis conferentiis episcopalibus. 'Domus Mariae' die 8 octobris 1965," in Etchegaray papers). According to Etchegaray, the movement supporting the suggestion of an *iuxta modum* vote on the first schema (on the training of priests) died because there was not enough time to prepare the corrections and because there was little support from the bishops for an appeal to the administrative tribunal (*JPrignon*, October 10, 1965 [Prignon papers, 1602, 3]). Both Prignon's notes and the minutes of the meeting agree in their analysis of the situation in the assembly, which was marked by ever-growing indifference and apathy: "There can be seen… a certain weariness in the fathers, who no longer listen to the interventions of the speakers and who vote in a passive manner; in short, they care little about how the Council is proceeding" ("Quarta coadunatio delegatorum," 1).

[37] "Animadversiones circa schema Decreti 'De Institutione sacerdotali,'" October 8, 1965, in Tucci papers, 25.II/45. Is this text perhaps to be identified with a note from South American theologian Medina, which Prignon delivered to Daem as a member of the competent commission (see *JPrignon*, October 5, 1965 [Prignon papers, 1599, 3])? There is no certain evidence for saying so, especially since the document seems to be from a later date.

appeared overly rigid, even in comparison with the previous draft of the schema.

On these points an anonymous document called upon the fathers to vote no, with the intention of assembling a sufficient number of no votes (750) to cause the removal of the section and a return to the previous text, which on these five points was preferred because of its generality and the softer tone of its assertions. The requests made in the document summed up quite well the attitude toward the schema of many bishops of the Third World and probably of some Europeans as well, perhaps reflecting an area of discontent within the commission itself. Unlike what happened in other cases, the five contested points were not matched by five amendments rejected in the *expensio modorum*. Rather, they brought to light a problematic aspect of the schema, namely, the many points on which the revisions by the commission went far beyond the requests made by the fathers, thanks to additions and insertions that substantially changed the text discussed in the hall during the third session.

On October 11 Carraro's report on the schema went back over some problems that had been discussed and summarized the criteria followed by the commission in correcting the text. The questions raised by Darmajuwana's letter and the document of October 8 did come up, but Carraro felt compelled mainly to offer a final self-defense on the question of the role that the philosophy of St. Thomas was to have. In fact, the report on the *expensio modorum* had already devoted a real "preliminary note" to the amendments made in no. 15, which dealt with the philosophical training of future priests.

This point had been the object of special attention by the fathers and two groups had formed. On the one side, there were those who maintained the need to state clearly the fundamental role of St. Thomas in seminary formation, which was in accordance with numerous statements in the recent teaching of the popes. The leaders of this group were Staffa, Browne, and Ruffini. On the other hand, many bishops did not want Thomist philosophy imposed as the "official" system for seminary training; they therefore favored a simple and unobtrusive reference to Thomism in the schema. The path chosen by the commission in face of these open disagreements was to keep the text presented in the hall in 1964. This spoke of St. Thomas only as teacher and guide in delving into the mysteries of salvation, while locating him in the broader framework of the sources of the culture of future priests.[38]

---

[38] "Each of the dogmatic treatises is to be so structured that first of all the biblical motifs are set forth; then the students are to be shown what the fathers contributed to the

At the end of September, during the plenary meeting of the commission, Staffa had been at the center of a heated discussion on the subject of Thomism, although this was geared to the discussion of an amendment to the other schema within the commission's competence: the schema on Christian education. The schema on the seminaries had reached the final stage of its drafting, and it was not possible to introduce new changes. But on October 6 there was again circulated in the hall the text of an amendment that had won a great deal of support but had been rejected by the commission. It asked that a more substantial reference to the central place of Thomist philosophy be introduced into the schemas on priestly training and on Christian education.[39] Carraro thus found himself obliged to confirm once again the choices made by the commission: "The views of the fathers as expressed in the discussions and in the *modi* appeared to be quite divergent, when not directly opposed; combining them in textual formulations proved to be difficult. On the other hand, the text enjoyed a prior approval. We did what we could and what we thought our duty according to our consciences and the conciliar regulations. Do we deserve to be reproached for this?"[40]

The votes on the various sections of the schema, ending on October 13, would show that the disagreements had lost their intensity; on all the controverted the number of no votes proved to be very small, thus yielding a picture, once again, of almost unanimous approval of the schema.[41]

---

faithful transmission and explanation of each of the truths of revelation, as well as the further history of dogma (including its relationship with the general history of the Church); then, in order to shed as much light as possible on the mysteries of salvation, the students must learn to penetrate more deeply into these mysteries with the help of speculation, with St. Thomas as their teacher, and to grasp their interconnection" (*AS* IV/4, 23; see *History*, 4:362-63).

[39] Here is the text of the *modus*: "I, the undersigned Council father, ask that, in accordance with over a hundred documents of the Roman pontiffs, the schemas on priestly training and on Christian education be completed by stating that the teaching of St. Thomas, at least in its principles, is to be religiously maintained not only in sacred theology but also in the teaching of philosophy in all Catholic schools." The twenty-two signatures included those of curial cardinals such as Staffa, Ottaviani, Marella, and Browne, and that of A. Fernández, general of the Dominicans (*AS* IV/4, 829).

[40] *AS* IV/4, 133.

[41] No. 4 on major seminaries received 88 no votes as compared with 2,038 yes votes; no. 15, which contained the reference to St. Thomas, received only 58 no votes as compared with 2,127 yes votes. The section that received the most negative votes (95) was no. 3 on minor seminaries; this was due to the opposition of some who were displeased by the commission's revalidation of this tool (see Mayer and Baldanza, "Genesi storica," 46–47).

III. The Church and the Problem of Education

On October 13 the schema on Christian education reached the hall for a vote. This schema also had had a difficult and tortuous history; unlike the schema on priestly training, however, it did not appear to have won overall approval from the fathers, at least not for the basic lines of its approach. The initial text of the preparatory period had focused entirely on the question of Catholic schools and had been marked by a tone of condemnation and disapproval of the state's claim to a monopoly in the field of education. But a turnabout came during the third period.

A. The Schema during the Third Period

On the eve of the schema's very brief appearance in the hall during the third session, the commission approved a change of title that in reality reflected the choice of a new approach to the problem: the title changed from "On Catholic Schools" to "On Christian Education." The new text (the seventh version of the schema) was three pages long and no longer had the form of seventeen propositions; it was distributed in the hall on November 19, 1964, accompanied by a report by Daem.[42]

The schema was now divided into eleven short sections prefaced by an introduction (containing the proposal that a postconciliar commission be established) and followed by a conclusion. The sections dealt with the purposes of Christian education (no. 1); the collaboration of the Church with the work of education (no. 2); the means that the Church uses in this task (communications media, associations, no. 3); the Catholic vision of what a school should be, along with a sharp rejection of a state monopoly of schools (nos. 4–6); Catholic schools (nos. 7–8); Catholic universities (nos. 9–10); and finally, the necessary coordination of Catholic institutions. The debate began in the hall on November 17 after Daem's report, which, to justify the commission's change of perspective in the schema, dwelt at length on the new challenges posed for the Church by the contemporary world in the field of education.[43]

---

[42] See *AS* III/8, 215–18; for the text of the schema, see ibid., 218–22 (Daem's report). For the history of the schema, see J. Pohlschneider, "Introduction," *The Decree on Christian Education,* in *Commentary,* 4:1–14; Ph. Delhaye, *DTC Tables,* cols. 4326–27; P. Dezza, "Declaratio conciliaris de educatione christiana," *PerMor* 55 (1966), 198–204; and V. Sinistrero, *Il Vaticano II e l'educazione* (Turin, 1970), 27–84.

[43] For a summary of the debate, see Caprile, IV, 448–64.

The line taken by the United States bishops was immediately made clear in the speeches of Spellman, Ritter, and Cody on the first day of the debate; their judgment was positive, but, given the complexity of the problems that took different forms in various parts of the world, they thought it necessary to focus on the fundamental need of a postconciliar commission and on endowing the episcopal conferences with all the discretionary authority they needed in applying the schema. With such an approach, the Council would not fail to take a stand on a subject of great importance, while at the same time it would be possible to move beyond statements of principle and study more closely the forms taken by the problems.

Far more critical were the speeches of two French bishops, Elchinger and Gouyon, likewise on the first day of discussion. Elchinger chided the schema for being alien to the "spirit of the Council" that had been manifested in the schemas on the laity, ecumenism, and religious freedom; he also asked for a radical revision of the schema's content, especially in what it said about the concept of Christian education. Gouyon, too, dwelt on this last subject: true Christian education cannot be reduced to an intellectual acceptance of doctrines but must become an education in all the dimensions of faith. To this end a radical revision of the schema was necessary.

These interventions on the first day were echoed in subsequent addresses, which in general were quite critical of the schema, although sometimes for opposite reasons. South American Bishop Enriquez Jiménez criticized the conservative tone of the schema and its failure to stay abreast of the advances made at the Council; he also warned of the danger that Catholic schools might be transformed into closed circles, isolated from the world.[44] Similar reflections were found in the interventions of McGrath and Méndez Arceo, although these were not read in the hall because of the interruption of the debate for the sake of the vote on November 19.[45] Polish Bishop Bejze, auxiliary of Lodz, focused his intervention on the need to work up a true and proper schema on education, preferably by having recourse to the advice of pedagogues and students

---

[44] Jiménez's intervention included the proposal of six propositions signed by 132 South American bishops (AS III/8, 375–79); for the other interventions of this day, see ibid., 365–89.

[45] For the written interventions on the schema, see ibid., 489–517. To be mentioned especially is the intervention of Brazilian Bishop Padin, who was supported by H. Câmara and four other Brazilian bishops; his was a radical critique of the schema ("a most miserable text"), with which he contrasted the content of Daem's report (ibid., 528).

of the subject, the purpose being to show that the Church is truly open to scientific advances. From a different perspective, Vietnamese Bishop Hoa Nguyen-van-Hien reproached the schema for neglecting the situation of Catholic schools in mission settings, where the presence of non-Christian students necessitated a comprehensive reformulation of the concept of Christian education; there was no hint of this in the schema.

The schema was also criticized for its timidity in face of the state's intrusion into the work of education and, in general, for the scant attention paid to the problems of Catholic schools. Along these same lines there was an important intervention by Rivera Damas, a young Salvadoran bishop, who asked that the subject of Catholic schools be treated with greater vigor and clarity. Rivera spoke in the name of forty other fathers and judged the text to be "faint-hearted and timid" in asserting the right of the Church (and therefore of parents) to give a Christian education to their own children. The schema should rather have emphasized the importance of schools in the defense of the faith and in the building of a Christian society.

Two Nigerian bishops intervened in support of the importance of Catholic schools. Msgr. Okoye wanted the schema to expand the section on the rights of the family.[46] This could be the basis both for the right of Catholic institutions to exist and for the duty of the state to give them financial help. Olu Nwaezeapu, in his turn, cited the case of Nigeria, where almost all Catholic children attended a confessional school. The presence of these institutions was an indispensable defense against dechristianization; the African bishop also cited the fact that in Nigeria five of the six native bishops had been educated in Catholic schools.

The interventions of Malone (auxiliary of Youngstown) and Pohlschneider (Aachen) were well constructed. The former dwelt primarily on the need to introduce into the schema the distinction between the state and civil society. Only then could the question of Catholic schools and the claims of the Church be presented in a rational way, without succumbing to various forms of maximalism or to overly simplistic positions. In that setting, among other results, the acceptance of the freedom of education could become a first test of religious freedom.[47] Speaking in the name of seventy fathers, Pohlschneider linked the subject of

[46] This point was also stressed in the intervention of North American Bishop H. Donohoe; it was not read in the hall for lack of time.

[47] Malone's intervention was signed by eighty other fathers from various countries, but in particular from Britain and North America.

education with the pastoral purpose of the Council and found it definitely lacking. Its title did not reflect its content, because that would suggest a comprehensive discourse on Christian education. The German bishop proposed that the schema be given solid theological and biblical foundations; on the question of relations with the state he favored an effort at mediation aimed at finding agreement between the institutions for the sake of the common good. He dwelt also on the question of teachers, on whom the level of the Catholic schools depends.[48]

Other addresses dwelt on the second part of the schema, which had to do with Catholic universities. The interventions of Léger, Jaeger, and Van Waeyenbergh, auxiliary of Malines-Brussels, agreed on the need to introduce a reference to the freedom of scientific investigation in the field of the sacred sciences.[49] Léger, in particular, issued a heartfelt call for a change in the attitude of ecclesiastical authorities, a shift from suspicion of theologians to encouragement and trust. He observed that the experience of the Council had shown how fruitful a free and trustful approach to theological and exegetical research had proved to be in the fields of liturgy, exegesis, and ecumenism. On November 19, however, in a disagreement with this address and especially with an earlier intervention of the Canadian cardinal (on November 14, on the schema on priestly training), A. Fernández, master general of the Dominicans, delivered a lengthy discourse, interrupted by the moderator of the day, in defense of Thomist thought against every attempt to relativize it. This discourse was a prelude to the final battle on the role of Thomist philosophy that would take place in the commission that dealt with amendments to the education schema.

On this same day, November 19, 1964, a preliminary vote was taken to decide whether to maintain the schema as the basis of future work; the dissatisfaction of the bishops became obvious in 419 negative votes (out of 1,879 votes cast), but these negative votes were not enough to defeat the schema. As a result, four other votes were taken on the separate parts of the schema; the fathers could now suggest corrections.

B. The Revision of the Schema

During the months of the intersession the commission worked on the 671 *modi* submitted by the fathers; the result was a new and much fuller

---

[48] For the text of the interventions made in the hall on November 19, see *AS* III/8, 398–422; for Daem's concluding remarks, see ibid., 425–27.

[49] Jaeger's intervention, unlike the other two, was not read in the hall.

text, which was approved in the spring of 1965. On September 22, 1965, the commission met again in order to approve the report on the *expensio modorum*; this report was a tricky matter because it had to contain the commission's justifications for the changes made in the text. At the beginning of this meeting some further small changes in the text were discussed and approved.[50]

Daem's plan for the report was enlarged and adapted.[51] After a quick summary of the votes taken in the hall on the schema and of the main stages in the commission's work of revision, the reporter explained the criteria followed in the study of the corrections. He then had to justify the considerable expansion of the schema, which suggested that this was a completely new schema rather than a revision of the earlier text. These were the reasons given by Daem: (1) the expansion had been requested by many fathers; (2) the treatment of a subject of such importance required a larger text; (3) the text had to serve as a reasonable basis for the future work both of an eventual postconciliar commission and of the episcopal conferences; (4) the work of revision had necessitated the combination of two phases that had been quite distinct in the case of other schemas: the correction of the text on the basis of interventions in the hall, and the *expensio modorum* in the true and proper sense; and (5) the expanded text did not differ in its content from the preceding draft.

The reporter then discussed the merits of the schema's content, outlining the principal choices made by the commission in order to give a basis for the more comprehensive treatment of the subject of education and to respond to the persistent criticisms emanating from some episcopal circles. One important point had required a substantial addition made after the discussion in the commission: the way in which the text dealt with the educational tasks of the Church and of the state. It seemed necessary to make it clear that on this point the commission had faced a variety of views difficult to combine: on the one hand, there were those

---

[50] See "Quaedam quaesita peculiaria subicienda Commissioni," September 22, 1965, 2 pp. (Carraro papers, 41). Here are two examples of the additions: In no. 3, on the Christian family, an explicit reference to the sacrament of matrimony was introduced. In no. 1, in which the subject was the education of the young, this phrase was introduced: "taking into account the advances made in the sciences of psychology, pedagogy, and teaching." And here is an example of the contrary: the rejection of an amendment that wanted to change the words "intellectual faculties" (to be cultivated in the Christian education of the young) to "faculties of mind and heart."

[51] See "Relationis de expensione Modorum circa schema *De educatione christiana* prima lineamenta," September 22, 1965, 4 pp. (Carraro papers, 41); cf. the final text of Daem's report (*AS* IV/4, 280–87).

whose perspective was of a pluralist society in which the laity could take responsibility in the area of education; on the other, there were those who favored a radical interpretation of the principle of subsidiarity and who regarded the schema as overly indulgent toward the educational systems of the state. The commission chose a middle way and tried to combine reminders of the dangers of a state monopoly of education with references (which were in fact quite few) to education in the state schools.[52]

This subject obviously brought into play the varying political and social conditions in the countries from which the bishops came. While the Latin American episcopates were facing a situation marked by a widespread lack of instruction, with the resultant need of encouraging the intervention of the state in the area of education, the concerns of the Italian and Spanish bishops were quite different.

On the question of the role of Thomist philosophy in the university curriculum, a very hot debate took place within the commission during these days. At the commission's final two meetings, on September 30 and October 1, Staffa, vice-president of the commission, vigorously maintained the need to urge Thomism as the official philosophy of the Church; he enjoyed the support of the 623 signers of the earlier cited amendment that had circulated among the bishops beginning at the end of January.[53] Daem, reporter on the schema, was sharply opposed, and in this impasse it was decided to have recourse to the Pope. It is not clear whether it was Felici or, more likely, Dell'Acqua or Cicognani who received the Pope's opinion on the evening of September 30; Paul VI had decided not to commit himself on this subject, and the commission was free to decide without any instructions from higher authorities.

On the following day the discussion continued in increasingly heated tones. A preliminary vote was taken on whether the schema should or should not speak of St. Thomas. Seven negative votes showed that Staffa's orientation would not have an easy time of it in the commission. The discussion grew more heated: Staffa and Daem proposed amendments quite different in kind; unfortunately we do not know what these were. After a lengthy diatribe Staffa invoked the authority of Cardinal Mercier in a final attempt to win the favor of the French-speaking bishops. Daem, on the other hand, won the support of Msgr. Blanchet, rector

---

[52] On this subject a substantial addition was made that went beyond the initial outline (see *AS* IV/4, 283–84).

[53] Prignon described the meeting in his notes (*JPrignon,* October 1, 1965 [Prignon papers, 1597, 4–5]). Camelot told Congar about the "very painful session" (*JCongar,* October 1, 1965; II, 415).

of the Institut Catholique of Paris and a member of the commission, who spoke out strongly against the idea of limiting freedom of research in the areas of theology and philosophy. Staffa then tried to make do with inserting a reference to "Christian philosophy," but resistance to this was no less strong; in fact, during the *expensio* the commission had already rejected the use of the term "Christian philosophy."[54] At the end a third amendment, suggested by Jesuit Father Dezza, repeated the content of Daem's proposal but had the advantage of simplicity and clarity. This became the definitive text that was approved by a large majority of the commission. This was probably the last change made in the text of the schema and was carefully noted in Daem's report in the hall.[55]

To blunt the edge of the many criticisms that were obviously already in the air, the commission's report ended with a final section that emphasized once more the status of the report as final, as well as the fact that the commission's work was completed. In order not to compromise the approval of the document, great emphasis was laid on the schema as in a certain sense a basic document that would require the further work of a postconciliar commission and of the episcopal conferences. The former would have as its task "to deal with a subject of such great importance in such a way that first and foremost it would deal separately and carefully with the questions raised as time goes on and, to this end, would use the help of experts, including lay persons, from all parts of the world"; the latter would see to adaptations to differing local situations.[56]

C. THE FINAL VOTES ON THE SCHEMA

Now that the competent commission had finished its work, the fate of the schema was in the hands of the conciliar assembly. On October 6 the amended text was distributed, along with the "Answers to individual *modi*

---

[54] "It is better to avoid the expression 'Christian philosophy'" (the commission's reply to modus no. 4 on no. 9 of the schema [*AS* IV/4, 276]).

[55] The reference to St. Thomas was introduced in a more general statement on the relation between reason and faith: "a deeper insight is gained into how faith and reason work together toward a single truth, following the method of the Doctors of the Church and especially of St. Thomas Aquinas" (ibid., 241). For the notation in Daem's report, see ibid., 284.

[56] It was explained once again that the subject of the declaration was Christian education "especially in schools"; this was an implicit admission of the compromise character of a text produced for a specific purpose but addressing some much broader subjects (ibid., 285)

offered by the fathers." Everyone knew that a vast array of criticisms existed. The testimonies of observers agree that among the progressive bishops there was deep dissatisfaction with the schema because of its antiquated way of posing the questions. But similar signals came from the opposite quarter. That very day, October 6, the already discussed amendment regarding Thomist teaching reappeared in the hall; the solution adopted by the commission had evidently not satisfied Staffa, who continued his opposition.[57]

Also dated October 6 is a letter to Lercaro from Michel Duclercq, founder and former national assistant director of the *Équipes enseignantes de France*, along with a document very critical of the schema. In this document, which expressed very well the opinions and hopes of those who wanted a discourse on education in the context of modern pluralist society, Duclercq rejected out of hand "a declaration that is from the outset already badly outdated" and that "can only elicit reservations and distrust throughout the entire non-Christian world and cannot but be a deep disappointment to a good many Catholics, especially those who attend or teach in public schools." After a careful analysis of the various sections of the text, Duclercq ended by questioning the real need of a document of this kind, given the developments under way in the area of education. Could not the general considerations in the chapter on culture in the document on the Church in the modern world be sufficient?[58]

In these early days of October the signs of uneasiness were transformed into a mass of initiatives without any common bond. Within the French episcopate Veuillot, who was probably responsible for circulating Duclercq's document among the French bishops, had adopted a very critical view of the schema, driven thereto by factors inherent in the situation in his own country. In France, Catholic schools had traditionally been excluded from the state's educational system, but beginning at the end of the 1950s these schools had acquired the possibility of being financed by the state.[59] Against this background some statements in the schema about

---

[57] The text of the *modus* with the handwritten notation "Picked up by Father Caprile in the Council's mimeograph center on the morning of October 6, 1965," is in Tucci papers, 24.II/40

[58] M. Duclercq, "Réflexions sur le nouveau projet de: 'Déclaration sur l'éducation chrétienne,'" attached to the author's letter to Lercaro of October 6, 1965 (Lercaro papers, XX, 367). The document was probably widely circulated; it appears also in Moeller papers, 2659.

[59] For this and other information on the situation of Catholic schools and on the positions taken by the magisterium, see P. L. Weihnacht, "Educational System, Education,

state educational systems would be greatly embarrassing. Veuillot seemed to be asking for a new discussion of the text.

Etchegaray, however, concerned about the possibility of setting a dangerous precedent, asked Prignon to get Suenens to intervene. In fact, from the outset the approach among the Belgians and among the representatives of the episcopal conferences had been to push for an improvement of the schema through a partial readmission of amendments without a complete rejection of the schema.[60] There was a great deal of uncertainty when the matter was discussed at the meeting of the representatives of the episcopal conferences on October 1. A few days later it was decided, with the support of Primeau, to gather signatures among the fathers to request a reopening of the collection of *modi* on the schema, since the text had not yet been distributed in the hall and there was time to wait. Daem, reporter on the schema, was involved from the outset, but, although aware of the limitations of the text, he observed that very few bishops would be inclined to follow Veuillot's radically critical line.

On October 7 the question came up at the already mentioned informal meeting of the moderators (Lercaro, Döpfner, and Suenens) with Felici and Tisserant. The impulse for the meeting was the letter of the Indonesians on the schema on priestly training, but the possibility of reopening the study of the amendments on the educational schema was at issue as well. Suenens vigorously defended the need for *iuxta modum* votes, at least on some disputed points, but he found little agreement either from Felici or from Lercaro and Döpfner.

On the same day, when the situation was discussed at the meeting of the representatives of the episcopal conferences, further difficulties appeared about coordinating a joint action. The call for a rediscussion of the schema on priestly training did not succeed. Both the Brazilian bishops and Veuillot took the radical position of rejecting the schema, although for different reasons. But the possibility of success along this line was very slight. The Brazilian bishops had sent Daem a list of corrections aimed at the rejection.[61] But such a scenario would have had

---

and Instruction," in *The Church in the Modern Age*, trans. A. Biggs, vol. 10 in *History of the Church,* ed. H. Jedin, K. Repgen, and J. Dolan (New York, 1981), 378–409.

[60] See Latreille's letter to Suenens, September 29, 1965, 3 pp. (Suenens papers, 2532), with its criticisms of the schema for overinsistence on the rights of parents in education. For other, anonymous notes, see Suenens papers, 2523 and 2529.

[61] From what the sources tell us, the corrections submitted by the Brazilians had to do not only with the question of the rights of the state but also with the general matter of problems of education, which in their view were insufficiently treated in the schema. Daem regarded the criticisms of the Brazilians as unfair, since many of them had been taken into

harmful consequences; according to the terms of the regulations, it would
then have been necessary to fall back on the preceding text. Veuillot's
position seems not to have been shared by many French bishops; Gouyon
and Cazaux, members of the competent commission, distanced themselves from it in a conversation with Daem.

At this point it was clear that only negotiations could lead to real
improvement of the schema. Prignon and Etchegaray set to work at this
in a packed set of meetings from October 8 to October 10. It was decided,
following the suggestion of Tisserant, to send the administrative tribunal
a request for an *iuxta modum* vote on some controverted points in the
schema; this suggestion had already emerged at the meeting of the representatives of the episcopal conferences.[62] A massive influx of *modi*
(they expected at least 300 submitters) would make it possible to balance
the content of the schema. Daem, the reporter, agreed to support the initiative but without directly involving himself in it. French bishop Sauvage
had already drawn up some of these possible amendments; they dealt
essentially with the general situation of education in the modern world
and with the question of the state's rights in the area of education. The
issue now was to find authoritative support in the circle of cardinals.[63]

On October 11, two days before the vote in the hall, the situation was
still confused. Other proposals were added to those of the French and
Brazilian bishops. English Cardinal Heenan asked Felici that in view of
the changes that had been made in it, the schema be discussed once
again.[64] The episcopal conferences of India and East Africa likewise intervened to ask that the debate be reopened,[65] and the same line was taken
in the petition addressed to the moderators by G. Mahon in the name of

---

account in the revision of the schema (*JPrignon,* October 10, 1965 [Prignon papers, 1602,
4]).

[62] "Many fathers were ready to ask, through juridical channels, that the text be
improved not by new discussions, which would lengthen the period of the Council, but by
the submission of written *modi*" ("Quarta coadunatio delegatorum," 2).

[63] Prignon's notes tell us of two informal meetings during these crucial days. The first,
which brought together Prignon, Etchegaray, Bonet, and Martimort, produced the draft of
the letter to the administrative tribunal and the outline of an overall strategy for these days.
The second meeting included Etchegaray, Medina, Sauvage, and two other bishops, who
prepared the *modi* on the points listed above; Etchegaray accepted the responsibility for
looking for cardinals to sign the letter to the administrative tribunal (Prignon papers, 1602,
3–5).

[64] Letter of Heenan to Felici, October 10, 1965 (*AS* V/3, 407).

[65] According to the bishops of East Africa (Kenya, Uganda, Tanzania, and Zambia) the
schema contained statements "insulting to those who attend state or public schools" ("Petitio ad Moderatores Concilii," October 12, 1965 [*AS* VI/4, 545–46]). For the petition of
thirty Indian bishops, dated October 11, 1965, see *AS* VI/4, 544–45.

sixteen bishops of the Society of St. Joseph of Mill Hill.[66] At their afternoon meeting on October 12, however, the moderators rejected Mahon's
request on the grounds that the regulations prescribed that in this phase
of the study of the schema there could only be a vote without further
debate.[67]

All this seems to confirm the existence of very widespread dissatisfaction with the schema. The letter to the administrative tribunal had
acquired the signatures of two cardinals and ten bishops and was handed
in on the evening of that same day.[68] But the situation was a very sensitive one: Daem, the reporter, questioned the validity of the line thus taken
and told Prignon that he feared seeing the teaching in the schema, which
had a long and solid tradition behind it, being lost because of one point
(the limitation of the state's rights in the area of education).

October 13 brought the time to vote; as a result, to use Prignon's
words, the "affair" of the schema on education seems to have been
"buried." Before the session began, the moderators discussed the matter.
Döpfner took a hard line: the petition was to be rejected lest a precedent
be created, just as the schema on revelation was about to be put to a
vote.[69] The administrative tribunal was to study the petition only during
the following weeks and would reach this negative verdict: the bishops'
petition "is beyond the competence of the commission" and, in addition,
is contrary to specific norms in the conciliar regulations.[70] All things considered, the vote in the hall showed only limited opposition either on particular points or in the general judgment on the schema. Felici noted with
satisfaction that even the signers of the letter voted yes.

[66] Mahon's request was probably the attempt of the "Americans" to which Prignon
refers (Prignon papers, 1603, 2).
[67] See AS V/3, 739. Felici's decision won the approval of Lercaro and Suenens. But
there are some inconsistencies in the minutes of the meeting. Felici said: "Anyone who
does not want the text that has already been discussed and voted on can express his opinion in the presentation of modi." But it is evident that there was no room for such an
option in the vote to be taken the next day.
[68] The cardinals were Silva Henríquez (Santiago de Chile) and Roy (Quebec). The
bishops were de Provenchères, H. Câmara, J. Zoa, M. McGrath, J. Blomjous, G. A. Beck,
A. Fernández, M. Baudoux, D. Herlihy, and N. Verhoeven. For the text of the letter (October 11, 1965), see AS VI/4, 558–59.
[69] JPrignon, November 13, 1965 (Prignon papers, 1604, 2). But Prignon was critical
of the German's cardinal's reasoning: "Döpfner is mistaken on this point because the two
texts are not by any means in the same juridical situation and do not follow the same procedure."
[70] See the note that Felici added when he sent the text of the petition to the Pope
("Appunto," October 15, 1965 [AS VI/4. 559–60]). His letter anticipated the uncertainties
shown in the verdict of the tribunal and probably symbolizes the key role that, here again,

The only open sign of dissatisfaction was the statement of protest that was signed by a group of Latin American bishops and distributed to the fathers under the title "Arguments for Revising the Schema on Christian Education."[71] The document listed a series of reasons explaining the position of the signers and then urged the bishops to vote against the schema. The main objection to the schema was essentially that it uncritically identified the concepts of education and school, in keeping with a typically Western kind of thinking. The phenomenon of education, with which the schema was dealing, should have been considered in its totality, that is, as an experience that is not just for the young but runs throughout life, is not reducible to static and abstract models, and above all, is not identifiable with instruction pure and simple.

In addition, according to the signers, the matter of the rights of parents in choosing schools was formulated in overly abstract terms; in fact, in many circumstances (the reference to the Third World was clear) the exercise of this right is simply impossible. As for the role of the Church in education, there should have been a clearer separation of its evangelizing mission from a specifically educational and scholastic mission, because only the former is properly of the essence of the apostolic mandate. Next, on the controverted subject of the rights of the state in the area of education, the compilers of the document pointed out the inadequacy of the schema, which did not consider, for example, the relationship between the wishes of the parents and the demands of the common good. They then repeated a remark already made in Duclercq's dossier on the failure to recognize the part played by Catholic teachers in the state's system of schools. These brief references to the document make rather clear the depth of the opposition to the schema, even though it had no significant impact when the vote was taken.

Essentially, the only positive result of the intense work of the French and Brazilian bishops during the days before the vote was the reformulation of the questions to be asked of the fathers. The original six questions had become thirteen when they were distributed in the hall on October 12.[72] The focus on some debated sections of the schema would allow

---

Felici played in this event. See the letter of Felici to P. Macchi, October 15, 1965 (*AS* VI/4, 558).

[71] For the undated two-page text, see Tucci papers, 25.11/24. The document was signed by eight bishops from various countries: J. Blomjous (Tanzania), H. Câmara and C. Padin (Brazil), J. Dammert (Peru), J. Podestà, A. Quarracino, and R. Staverman (Argentina), and L. E. Henríquez (Venezuela).

[72] This new formulation of the questions meant that every section of the schema was voted on separately, thus allowing for more specific evaluations (see *AS* IV/4, 278–80).

the opponents within the assembly to unpack their grievances more easily. Yet all this did not produce any appreciable effects when the vote was taken on the mornings of October 13 and 14. Admittedly, the schema received a higher number of no votes than did the other schemas voted on during these days, but all things considered, the percentages were low (183 negative votes out of 1,996 votes cast on the approval of the schema as a whole); this was far less than the quorum needed to force a revision of the schema (that is, two thirds of the valid votes cast). The desire not to prolong the conciliar period by a further onerous debate and the general atmosphere of "Everyone home!"[73] were probably the dominant reasons for this outcome.

But we must not forget, on the one hand, the reluctance of many bishops to change the traditional Catholic position on Catholic schools (a position that stemmed in large measure from Pius XI's encyclical *Divini illius magistri*) and, on the other, the position taken by various representatives of the European episcopate who, while convinced of the weakness of some points in the schema, were more concerned not to jeopardize the approval of more important documents (on revelation and on the office of bishops) for which the acquisition of a conciliar majority was still questionable and uncertain. In confirmation of all this, Prignon's notes tell us of the determination of some bishops to appeal to the Pope against the approval of the schema on education. Prignon, a collaborator of Suenens, writes: "We think that this might become a dangerous precedent in connection with the schemas on revelation, on religious freedom, and on the Jews, and would, among other considerations, be to act against all that we have hitherto maintained; for this reason, we have advised the bishops not to take this step."[74]

IV. THE DECREE ON THE RELATIONSHIP OF THE CHURCH TO NON-CHRISTIAN RELIGIONS

The complex redactional history of the decree on the Relationship of the Church to Non-Christian Religions came to its end at the plenary meeting of the Secretariat for Christian Unity on September 15, 1965.[75]

---

[73] "Let's-get-home-soon" (see Horton, *Vatican Diary 1965*, 89).

[74] *JPrignon*, October 13, 1965 (Prignon papers, 1604, 2).

[75] See Chapter I above. For a picture of events during the third period, see G. Miccoli, "Two Sensitive Issues: Religious Freedom and the Jews," *History*, 4: chap. 2. For the history of the schema, see J. Oesterreicher, "Declaration on the Relationship of the Church to Non-Christian Religions," in *Commentary*, 3:1–138; *Les relations de l'Église avec les religions non chrétiennes* (Paris, 1966), which includes G. M. Cottier, "L'historique de la

The distribution of the final text and the *expensio modorum* in the hall at the end of September began the final and decisive phase, that of approval by the assembly. The main coalitions against the decree that had emerged at the time of the first draft of the document were still strong: on the one hand, the traditionalist bishops, who opposed any and every opening toward the world of the non-Christian religions and of Judaism in particular; on the other, the Arab world, which through its chanceries but also to a large extent through the Oriental bishops had nourished fierce opposition to the decree, which was interpreted as taking a pro-Israel stance.

To these two groups was added a small group of bishops who had not accepted the changes made in the section on the Jews, where the words *deicide* and the verb *condemn* had been removed. Even among the experts of the secretariat the news of Willebrands's journey to the Middle East in order to reach agreement with Melkite patriarch Maximos IV on some changes in the text had elicited reactions that were not entirely positive.[76]

The most important statement of the traditionalist bishops' position was the document of the *Coetus Internationalis Patrum* that was distributed in the hall on October 11, only three days before the final vote. It contained an implacable condemnation of the declaration and was accompanied by an exhortation to the bishops to vote no both on most of the sections of the decree and on the text as a whole. But the document ("Suggestions on the Votes Soon to Be Taken on the Schema: 'On the Relation of the Church to Non-Christian Religions'")[77] was above all a hostile disavowal of the work of the secretariat and, in general, of the entire activity of those in charge of the conciliar assembly. It even called into question the vote taken during the third period. Since the fathers had received the schema only two days before voting on it, why had a procedure not been chosen analogous to that decided on for the schema on religious freedom, that is, the postponement to the final session of every binding decision? The secretariat was accused of a lack of objectivity in

déclaration," 37–78; T. Federici, *Il concilio e i non cristiani* (Rome, 1966); M. L. Rossi, "La genesi della *Nostra aetate*," in *Il Mediterraneo nel Novecento: Religioni e stati,* ed. A. Riccardi (Cinisello Balsamo, 1994), 259–81.

[76] C. Moeller, for example, was very pessimistic about the future of the schema and disappointed by changes made during the final stage of the drafting (see *JPrignon,* September 16, 1965 [Prignon papers, 1585, 4], and September 30, 1964 [Prignon papers, 1596, 8]). On the final phase in the revision of the schema, see *History,* IV:546-59.

[77] The text is in the Carraro papers, 39, and is preceded by an accompanying letter signed by G. de Proença Sigaud, M. Lefebvre, and L. M. Carli.

its examination of the episcopal amendments which it had rejected for unpersuasive, sometimes "laughable" reasons.[78]

Under these conditions, and given that the regulations prevented any further interventions to correct the text, the authors urged a negative vote on many of the questions. It was not the section on the Jews that caused the greatest difficulties. No. 4 of the schema had been subdivided into four short parts for purposes of voting, thereby carefully isolating the most controverted passages. Of these four parts only one was decisively rejected by the members of the *Coetus Internationalis Patrum*: the one dealing with the acquittal of the Jews on the charge of deicide.[79] Opposition to the remaining parts of this section was less strong: the addition of a few meager changes would lead to a positive vote by the fathers of the *Coetus*.[80] On the final number (no. 5) on universal brotherhood, the authors of the document found fault with the text for some omissions and urged the bishops to abstain from voting.

It was the first part of the text (nos. 1–3) that elicited the sharpest opposition. After careful analysis of the introduction to the schema, radical opposition arose to the very presupposition of the schema, namely, the idea of a dialogue with the non-Christian religions. These opponents maliciously pointed out the lack of a clear statement of the purposes of the schema: "Of what kind of 'relationship' was it speaking?" If dialogue is understood as "a peaceful conversation such as goes on between civil individuals," then it was possible to accept the effort made in the schema, although it ran the risk of degenerating into something "puerile." If, on the other hand, dialogue was understood in an explicitly religious sense, the content of the schema became utterly unacceptable. Citing the Acts of the Apostles and the Letters of St. Paul, the document reasserted

---

[78] "Suggestiones circa suffragationes mox faciendas de Schemate: 'De Ecclesiae habitudine ad religiones non christianas'" (*JPrignon,* October 13, 1965 [Prignon papers, 1604, 2]).

[79] The text read: "Although the Church is the new people of God, Jews are not to be thought of as rejected by God nor as accursed, as though such charges flowed from the sacred scriptures." The challenge here was to the imposition by the secretariat of an "opinion" on the nonexistence of a collective responsibility of the Jewish people. As the word *deicide* had been "prudently" removed, so every reference to the condemnation of the idea of a curse on the Jewish people was removed.

[80] One request, for example, was to cite the complete text of Romans 11:28 in the first part of no. 4; in the second part of this number it would be enough to explain that the word *Jews* had an ethnic and not a religious meaning; finally, the Coetus asked for the addition of the phrase "on account of race or religion" in the final part of this number in the sentence saying that every form of anti-Semitism was to be "deplored."

the duty of proclaiming "the truth of Christ," which was the constant
subject of the Church's teaching and from which it was impossible to
turn away.

Thus the general drift of the schema was found unconvincing, invalidated as it was by an overly intellectual approach and by a "comparativist
ideology," the watchwords of which were the search for an "area of
agreement" or "common denominator." These analyses by the *Coetus
Internationalis Patrum* represented a clear rejection of the teaching of
John XXIII and Paul VI, who had both spoken of dialogue and search for
common ground. From these basic principles of the *Coetus* followed
directly its rejection of nos. 2 and 3, devoted respectively to the Asiatic
religions and to Islam. Was it not "unworthy, not to say scandalous,"
they asked, that the Council should claim the existence of elements common to the idea of the Most Blessed Trinity and some aspects of Hindu
mythology? As for Islam, the authors of the document reproached the
secretariat for not having responded in a serious way to the amendments
proposed by the fathers, especially those having to do with natural morality and the conflicts that had arisen down the centuries between Christians
and Muslims.[81]

Given the limits clearly displayed by the schema, the overall judgment
of the fathers of the Coetus was negative, and they urged the bishops to
vote no on the final question as well, the question on the schema as a
whole. The conclusion of their document made clear that the principal
reason for their opposition was the minimizing of the differences between
Christianity and the other religions. By doing so, the text both "delays the
conversion of peoples" and "quenches or weakens zeal for missionary
vocations." We see here a comprehensive criticism that went well beyond
the question of the Jews and was connected with a conservative vision of
the entire ecclesiastical magisterium.

More clearly anti-Semitic, on the other hand, were the attacks still
being made during these days in numerous pamphlets distributed in the
hall. One of the most typical was the document, signed by twenty-eight
traditionalist associations, that circulated among the fathers during

---

[81] The reference was to *modus* no. 51, which brought together the requests of about fifty
fathers who asked for the removal or at least the reformulation of statements about the similarities between Christianity and Islam in the area of morality. As a matter of fact, the
modus was partially accepted by the secretariat with a change that did not, however, satisfy the fathers of the *Coetus Internationalis Patrum*. On the other hand, the secretariat did
reject *modus* no. 52, which asked for an explicit reference to the resistance of the Christian world "in protecting the faith" against Muslim invasions of Europe (see *AS* IV/4, 704).

the days just before the vote and that served as an important summary of the prejudices and calumnies used in anti-Semitic propaganda. In it, bishops prepared to vote in favor of the declaration were described as heretics, and the Council was said to lack any authority to change the anti-Semitic attitude of the Church's magisterium.[82]

Opposition continued from the Arab side, but the acceptance of some amendments proposed by Maximos IV had cleared away many obstacles. The secretariat, for its part, had begun a real offensive through diplomatic mediation that, as we shall see, would bear fruit. After a series of delays due to the scant collaboration of Maronite Bishop Khoury, the plan to set up a press service devoted to the Arab world was implemented in September with the appointment of Father Cuoq, who was already an official of the commission for Islam within the Secretariat for Non-Christians.[83] The first move was to prepare a new Arabic translation of the schema, which Willebrands and Duprey then delivered personally to all the Roman embassies of the Arab world. The only negative reaction came from the representatives of Iraq. During these same days Willebrands received a Palestinian delegation, and learned from it that the watchword in the embassies of the Arab world was "There is no question of going to war against the Holy See."[84] The Arab bishops likewise attested to less hostile reactions among the ambassadors. On October 6 the Arabic text of an eight-page presentation of the declaration was widely circulated (there were 700 copies); even Patriarch Maximos IV now judged it very positively.[85] The document was sent by diplomatic packet to all the apostolic nuntiatures and delegations in Arab countries.

On the ecclesial side the secretariat was again very active. The support of Maximos IV was, of course, very important. During these days the Melkite Patriarch proposed that all the patriarchs of the Middle East

---

[82] According to Oesterreicher, the authorship of the document was uncertain; when questioned, one representative of the associations involved denied having approved of the undertaking (Oesterreicher, in *Commentary,* 3:101ff.); for the text of the document, see Moeller papers, 2546.

[83] We derive this information from a note signed by Bea and dated October 7, 1965 ("Note sur l'évolution des réactions arabes" [*AS* V/3, 440–43]).

[84] *AS* V/3, 441.

[85] "This afternoon there was distributed among us a fine Arabic translation of the declaration on the non-Christian religions, together with an excellent commentary; the whole thing was the work of Father Habib Bacha and Father Duprey. These documents will, we hope, help to forestall the 'convulsions' of last year" (*JEdelby,* October 7, 1965, 309). Father Habib Bacha was a Melkite cleric.

adopt a common stand by signing a press release in favor of the declaration. The opposition of the Maronite Patriarch prevented this plan from
being carried out, and the document would be published only as a position adopted by the Melkite synod. In Jordan, a bishop who had an excellent reputation in government newspaper circles gave assurances that
nothing would be published against the Council and the declaration.
Information was also communicated to the Arabic-speaking non-Catholic
observers present in Rome at a special meeting held by Willebrands.
In short, the efforts made by the secretariat effected a noteworthy
improvement in the overall atmosphere surrounding the declaration; in
addition, as Bea himself noted, the new climate created by the Pope's
journey to the United Nations and by his address there played a part in
this change. "It seems that the situation is advantageous and that there
is nothing to fear if the amended text is accepted. The atmosphere created by the Pope's journey and by his address allow us to think that there
will be no hostile reaction."[86]

As we have seen, a third source of opposition, certainly a minor one
but difficult to overcome, consisted of some bishops opposed to the
changes that had been made in the text; they were supported by some
Jewish groups. On October 10 Lercaro, who would be chairing the session of October 14 devoted to the votes on the declaration, received a
telegram, sent from Rome, from Joseph Lichten, a member of the Jewish association of B'nai B'rith. In the name of the Conference of Presidents of Major American Jewish Organizations, Lichten expressed "the
consternation" of the Jewish community in the United States at the
changes made in the declaration. He was referring to the removal of "deicide" and "condemns" in no. 4 of the schema. Among the Council
fathers, Leven, an American bishop, came out explicitly for the rejection
of a part of no. 4 of the schema (question no. 6); he seems also to have
circulated an explanation.[87]

René Laurentin wrote a very critical article in *Le Figaro* and followed
it up by circulating among the fathers a document that certainly gave the
clearest and most complete explanation of the "irreducible problem of
conscience" that many bishops who had supported the schema from the
outset would find themselves facing as the vote drew near. After giving
a summary reconstruction of the history of the schema designed to bring
out the central place held by the condemnation of the teaching about the

---

[86] Bea, "Note sur l'évolution," 442.
[87] See Oesterreicher, in *Commentary*, 3:129.

Jews as a "deicidal people," Laurentin analyzed the main changes introduced during the final phase of the revision. The most questionable point
was undoubtedly the suppression of a clear condemnation of the teaching
about the deicidal people (the object of vote no. 6), which had already
been present in the 1963 version of the declaration.[88] In the eyes of the
French theologian this was the decisive point and the source of the conflict of conscience that the schema was causing bishops. For this reason
the central part of his document was devoted specifically to an analysis
of the factors to be weighed in casting a vote.

Laurentin was attempting to provide information as objectively as possible, but his personal evaluation of the schema came through clearly and
moved in the direction of a negative vote. Slight emphasis on the possibility of accepting some small improvements in details (by a positive vote
on questions 6 and 7) was overwhelmed by many arguments against the
removal of the condemnation of the teaching on deicide, arguments set
forth with passion and vigor. Laurentin also relied on the Qur'an (Sura
IV, v. 156) in order to show the innocence of the Jewish people and to
attack at its root the entire movement of opposition in the Islamic countries. At the same time, he conjured up the dangers of a resurgence of anti-
Jewish persecutions and of a failure on the Church's part of its responsibility to oppose them.[89]

He also noted, as many others did at the time, that if the condemnation had not been present in the preceding versions of the schema, the
point would not have been so intensely discussed; the heart of the problem of conscience was the retreat from a text already approved by the

[88] The French theologian then dwelt on two other points. The first part of no. 4 (the
object of vote no. 5), which dealt with the responsibility of the Judaism of Jesus' time,
omitted some important arguments: the scriptural texts that spoke explicitly of the "ignorance" of those Jews who put Christ to death; the equal responsibility of the Roman authorities in the same event; and the statement of the Council of Trent on the true cause of the
death of Christ, namely, the sins of humanity. Still, in no. 4 (object of vote no. 7), the text
weakened the condemnation of all persecutions of Jews by omitting the explicit word
"condemns." Laurentin notes here that the text of the *expensio modorum* distributed by
the Secretariat gave no reason for this omission (see R. Laurentin, "Le vote No. 6 sur
l'exclusion de déicide dans le schéma sur les religions non-chrétiennes," October 14, 1965,
in Tucci papers, 26.II/104, 6). The date of the document found in the Tucci archive was
inserted by hand and does not agree with the date (October 11) in a copy of the document
found in the Moeller archive. It is legitimate, therefore, to think that the note was written
several days before the vote.

[89] "But, on the contrary, let us suppose — and history bids us be pessimistic on this
point — that a new persecution, a new genocide comes about; then the Council and the
Church will be accused of having left alive in the shadows the idea of deicide, which is
the passion-inspiring root of anti-Semitism" (ibid.).

majority of the fathers.[90] Laurentin also rejected as artificial and unconvincing the reasons given by the secretariat to justify the suppression.
What, then, were the consequences of the choice the Secretariat had
made? The maintenance of the status quo and therefore the legitimation
of an entire tradition of thought that regards the accusation of deicide
leveled against the Jews of Jesus' time to be the teaching of the Church.
Laurentin even named the epigones of that tradition, first among them
Luigi M. Carli, Bishop of Segni.

In addition to the theological and doctrinal point of view thus set out,
the French theologian went on to urge consideration of a series of "acces-
sory" problems that could weigh heavily in the voting. From a technical
point of view, was it possible to vote against some parts of the schema
without destroying the document's internal coherence? For Laurentin,
this was indeed possible in the case of vote no. 6, because the return to
the preceding version would not disturb the internal coherence of the
argumentation.

The case of vote no. 7 was more complicated: a negative vote would
necessitate the rewriting of the entire section. Another decisive question
was psychological and had to do with reverence. Everyone knew now
that the change in the text was due to an intervention by the Pope: "The
fear of displeasing the Pope seems to be one of the decisive factors and
undoubtedly '*the* most important factor' affecting the vote." But Laurentin pointed out that the Pope had not given precise instructions to the
assembly, and he appealed to the importance of the individual conscience
in making a choice. He then challenged the supposition that the Pope
expected the assembly simply to agree with his opinion; if the Pope had
not wanted a pronouncement from the bishops, he could have reserved the
question to himself, as he did in other well-known cases.

A yes vote undoubtedly represented the convenient solution for the
Council once it decided to agree with the desires of the secretariat, but
Laurentin reminded the fathers of the many bitter pills the leaders of

---

[90] "From the viewpoint of the history of the text: if the present text were the first, if
the desire to exclude deicide had not been one of the considerations that inspired the document, if this exclusion had not been clearly formulated, first in this unqualified form in
1963 and then in the form of a practical order imposed on Christians (text of 1964), if this
point had not always been the focus of discussion, if the entire first text of 1963 and the
statements of many fathers, including Cardinal Bea, had not said that the exclusion of deicide was a matter of justice and of truth, if the Church did not find itself to some extent
committed on this point and put on the carpet before the world — then the creation of a
problem of conscience could have been avoided here. But it cannot be avoided" (ibid., 7).

the secretariat had had to swallow during the history of the schema. Finally, so-called extraconciliar problems needed to be taken into consideration, that is, the old diplomatic question that had accompanied the schema throughout its history. In this connection Laurentin had an easy time showing that there were contrasting demands in favor of and against a negative vote: on the one, the defeat would improve relations with the Jewish world; on the other, the approval of the section would calm the opposition from the Arab world. There was, therefore, nothing to do but suffer the consequences of making a decision with the realization that it was impossible to satisfy everyone.

Despite the abundance of arguments and remarks in favor of a negative vote on question no. 6, Laurentin concluded not with advice on voting but with a heartfelt appeal to the conscientious judgment of the individual fathers. The conflict of conscience "is unavoidable," said Laurentin in an appended note:

> Fundamental reasons urge a *non placet*, at least on question 6; but everything is so arranged that such a decision brings many risks with it, such, for example, as dissension among the fathers, tensions between the Pope and the Council, and perhaps the withdrawal of the text. You will be pulled between conscience and opportunism.

In a last effort at a solution the French theologian suggested two conditions for obtaining a positive vote from the fathers dissatisfied with the removal of the condemnation of deicide: the publication in the official text, in some form, of some sentences from the report of the secretariat on the *expensio modorum* that explained the reason why the reference had been eliminated; and the addition to note 13 of the text of some scriptural references on the ignorance of the Jewish people regarding the condemnation and death of Jesus.[91]

On the eve of the vote further appeals reached the Pope asking him to stop work on the amended text. Cardinal Shehan was concerned by the negative reactions, especially in the United States, to the amendments introduced into no. 4 of the declaration; he therefore offered the Pope a

---

[91] The reasons given by the secretariat for the removal of the sentence were "a) the word 'deicide' is repugnant in any context whatsoever; b) the word 'deicide' can lead to erroneous interpretations." The cited considerations and the proposal were contained in a *Nota annexa,* the date of which was not given but was probably the day of the vote and therefore later than the preceding document. It is to be noted, in any case, that Laurentin himself had earlier said he was puzzled by these reasons (Laurentin, "Le vote No. 6," 7–8).

new version of the text. This would avoid the rise of erroneous interpretations that might discover in the text a kind of relativizing of persecution against Jews within the broad context of the multiple manifestations of racial hatred. Shehan proposed substituting the verb *reprobat* for *deplorat*; in this way a single term would be used in the same sentence for condemning anti-Jewish persecutions and every other kind of persecution.[92]

Cardinal Journet also wrote to Paul VI to let him know the reaction of his friend Jacques Maritain. Here are the sorrowful words of the French philosopher as reported by Journet: "I felt truly wounded when I saw that the words *et damnat* were eliminated after *deplorat*. If the Council accepts this omission, it is taking a big step backward by comparison with the condemnations of racism and anti-Semitism issued by Pius XI."[93] These two appeals were passed on to Bea by Cicognani, Secretary of State, on the very day of the voting, but the president of the secretariat could only send word back that it was impossible to introduce any changes at this stage.[94]

Despite these final protests, the result of the voting, which ended on the morning of October 15, was positive, even though it also revealed a continuing underground of opposition among the fathers. The first three questions (dealing with sections 1–3 of the declaration) received, respectively, 110, 184, and 189 negative votes, coming for the most part from conservative groups. The four questions on Judaism had a similar outcome, with the remarkable exception of no. 6, which received the most negative votes (245). The number of negative votes for the final section of the text dropped sharply (58), in keeping with the instructions of the *Coetus Internationalis Patrum*, which had left the bishops free to vote as they wished.

It is clear that on the question dealing with no. 6 the opposing group had gained in numbers. It can be hypothesized that some bishops, dissatisfied with the changes made by the secretariat in the final phase, had voted against. But how then to explain that an almost equal number of *non placet* votes (243) were cast in response to the final question on the

---

[92] According to Shehan, the text should be changed as follows (additions to the amended text are in italics): "In addition, *just as* the Church rejects all persecutions of any human beings whatsoever, *so too*, mindful of the patrimony she shares with Judaism and constrained not by political considerations but by religious and evangelical love, she *rejects* hatred, persecutions, and other manifestations of anti-Semitism against the Jews by any and all persons and at any and every time" (*AS* V/3, 426).

[93] French text of letter of Journet to Paul VI, October 13, 1965 (*AS* V/3, 427).

[94] Letter of Bea to Cicognani, October 22, 1965 (*AS* V/3, 470).

schema as a whole? Besides the voters mobilized by the *Coetus Internationalis Patrum*, from which bishops did the other negative votes come? Some Arab bishops probably were dissatisfied with the last changes. Some African bishops had challenged the declaration for not saying anything about traditional African religions and expressed their resolute opposition.[95] On the other hand, it was unthinkable that the American bishops, who had been the greatest supporters of the schema, could now have jeopardized its approval. As for the French bishops, it seems that they intended to write to the Pope to let him know that their yes votes did not imply they had forgotten the defects of the schema; this was to support a proposal by Laurentin that was contained in his *Note annexe*.[96]

V. THE SEVENTH PUBLIC SESSION (OCTOBER 28)

A. WARNING SIGNS

October 15, with its final vote on the decree on the Church's relationship to non-Christian religions, brought an end to a period of intense activity that had seen four documents approved by the Council in the short space of about ten days. The fathers now awaited the final vote on these and on the decree on bishops and their promulgation at a public session scheduled for October 28. For some of the texts, however, difficulties would remain even during the brief time before that date.

For *Nostra aetate*, however, the date of promulgation had not yet been decided. When Lercaro announced the agenda of the upcoming public session to the hall on October 14, he did not include this document. Rumors collected by Prignon during the days of voting said that Paul VI had set as a condition for the promulgation of this document that it could not have more than 300 votes cast against it! The outcome of the voting

---

[95] Cottier, "L'historique de la déclaration," 78.

[96] On the day before the vote Laurentin told Prignon of his intention, and the latter showed himself in agreement. In Belgian circles, however, there was not much enthusiasm for the activism of the French theologian; Prignon himself had previously asked Laurentin to adopt a less hostile attitude to the declaration (*JPrignon,* October 14, 1965 [Prignon papers, 1605, 3]). In the Tucci archive there is a draft of a letter from Laurentin to the Pope dated October 16, 1965; it seems to be the same as the planned letter of the French bishops. It contains two requests to the Pope: the immediate promulgation of the declaration, and the addition to the text of the requests we have already seen. Attached is a sheet in Latin that repeats literally Laurentin's final proposal.

had satisfied this demand; therefore, on the days after the voting the Secretariat for Christian Unity decided to take steps to accelerate the course of the document and to include it in the agenda for the meeting on October 28.

On October 16 Bea wrote directly to Paul VI and asked that the document be solemnly promulgated. The moment seemed favorable in view of the climate of "calm, that is, the balance achieved between the opposing sides" that had marked the most recent events. Bea stressed, among other things, the danger that a delay could cause increased restlessness and give the idea of a residual lack of decisiveness on the part of the Council.[97] The letter was accompanied by copies of two telegrams sent respectively by Pastor W. A. Visser 't Hooft, secretary general of the World Council of Churches, and by Morris Abraham, President of the American Jewish Committee, both containing a very positive response to the outcome of the vote on October 15.[98] The Pope was asked to reply, and as early as the following day he let Felici know of his desire that Bea's request be accepted and that the declaration be put on the agenda of the public session on October 28.[99]

Bea's worries had not been unfounded, however, because the coalition opposing the declaration was still very much alive. This was shown a few days later by the "umpteenth" appeal for a change to the text, this time from Alberto Gori, Latin Patriarch of Jerusalem. The Patriarch wrote to the Pope complaining about the ambiguous use of a citation from Paul (Rom 11:28) in no. 4 of the declaration. The text paraphrased the content of the passage from St. Paul and referred to the biblical text in a note. But this procedure, according to Gori, explained Paul's teaching in an incomplete and quite unclear way. On the one hand, it left in obscurity the first part of the verse, which described the Jews as "enemies"; on the other hand, this manner of citing the Bible freely only intensified

---

[97] "In fact, if we wait, the edginess felt on both sides (the Arabs and the Jews) would increase. The impression would be given of a delay due to indecisiveness, and the document would be exposed to possible new pressures and other drawbacks. In contrast, the quick promulgation would provide the Council with the tranquility needed to continue its study and approval of various important documents still being discussed" (*AS* V/3, 438–39).

[98] For a comprehensive picture of reactions to the approval of the declaration, see Caprile, V, 290–95. In Jewish circles some disappointment was felt due to the last-minute changes, but in general reactions were positive. In the Middle East the only voice raised in condemnation was that of Greek Orthodox Patriarch Theodosius VI, who described the approval of the declaration as "an attack on the foundations of Christianity in its entirety."

[99] Letter of Dell'Acqua to Felici, October 17, 1965 (*AS* V/3, 437–38).

the accusation, coming from many quarters of the East (especially from the Orthodox), of a lack of fidelity to the teaching of scripture on the subject.[100]

Gori's point had already been made in the *expensio modorum*, and Bea had the easy task of bringing this up in his reply; he also excluded categorically the possibility of changing a text already approved by the conciliar assembly.[101] At this point in the process only an intervention by the Pope could make the secretariat's decision the subject of renewed discussion. At the beginning of November (that is, after the official promulgation of the declaration), Dell'Acqua suggested to Willebrands a solution that might satisfy Gori's wishes: putting in the note the entire text of the verses from the letter to the Romans. Willebrands justified the secretariat's rejection of Dell'Acqua's suggestion on the grounds that it would have given rise to numerous controversies both because in no other conciliar document were texts of scripture quoted and because the citation was likely to reignite the oppositions and discussions of the previous years.[102] Paul VI's left to the secretariat the responsibility for the decision, recommending only that Gori be again given "some explanation that will calm him down."[103]

In this final, somewhat impassioned phase the Pope received a series of appeals and maneuvers dealing with the other texts. A few days after the final vote on the document on priestly training Ruffini wrote to Paul VI complaining about the paucity of references made in the schema

---

[100] The declaration said: "Nevertheless, because of their fathers the Jews continue to be most dear to God, whose gifts and calls are irrevocable." But the verses in Romans 11:28–29 read as follows: "As regards the gospel they are enemies of God for your sake; but as regards election they are beloved, for the sake of their ancestors; for the gifts and the calling of God are irrevocable" (NRSV). As is clear, the order of the sentences is reversed, while the first part of the citation is for practical purposes omitted. In his reply to Gori, Bea observed that, on the one hand, a similar procedure was used in many conciliar documents (he referred to a citation on the same theme in *LG*, 1), and that on the other, the omission of a part of the text did not mean that the declaration as a whole forgot about the content of that part. The text of Gori's letter is not given in *AS*; in reconstructing his remarks we have therefore taken the indirect path through Bea's reply to Gori on October 30, 1965 (*AS* V/3, 473–74).

[101] Letter of Bea to Gori, October 30, 1965 (*AS* V/3, 473–74). Note that Bea's reply came after the promulgation of the conciliar declaration.

[102] Letter of Willebrands to Dell'Acqua, November 3, 1965 (*AS* V/3, 478–79). The letter refers to a conversation that took place on that same day.

[103] Letter of Dell'Acqua to Willebrands, November 4, 1965 (ibid., 482–83). Willebrands, in turn, let Felici know of this decision (letter of November 4, 1965 [ibid., 483–84]), while in a new letter to Patriarch Gori, Bea repeated the arguments give by Willebrands to Dell'Acqua (November 6, 1965 [ibid., 489–90]).

to past encyclicals. On the question of the role of St. Thomas in the teaching of philosophy, the Cardinal found fault with the failure of the document to refer to the Apostolic Constitution *Deus scientiarum Dominus* of Pius XI,[104] while reference should also have been made to *Humani generis* of Pius XII in order to clarify the relationship between sacred scripture and the magisterium of the Church in the teaching of dogmatic theology. Ruffini's remarks were a substantial challenge to the approach taken in the schema but offered no concrete proposal for improving it and had no effect on the history of the schema. They served to vent the feelings of some in the minority groups at the defeat of their requests.[105]

The only case in which pressure on the Pope had any success concerned the document on religious, more specifically the very controversial section on secular institutes. As the vote on that schema drew closer, an appeal, signed by some officials of secular institutes and probably organized by Armando Oberti, a collaborator of G. Lazzati in the Institute Milites Christi Regis, was sent to the fathers with the hope of still having a chance to influence the content of the schema. The appeal offered some specific changes in the text, despite the fact that the voting procedure did not at this point allow for *placet iuxta modum* votes.[106] The effort was unsuccessful, but those involved managed to involve the Pope by means of an intervention *in extremis*. There was much talk during those days of an intervention by officials of Opus Dei, but the decisive factor seems to have been an initiative of Oberti himself.

On the evening of September 21, during a conversation with Father Philippe, vice-secretary of the commission on religious, the possibility emerged of introducing into the text — through an intervention by the

---

[104] The controversy over the role of St. Thomas was not to be easily calmed, as is clear from two articles published in *L'Osservatore Romano* at this time (see C. Boyer, "Lo statuto del tomismo," *OssRom*, October 27, 1965; and B. Matteucci, "Il Concilio e San Tommaso d'Aquino," *OssRom*, December 2, 1965). Both articles referred to the address of Paul VI to the International Thomistic Congress in September 1965 in order to confirm not the exclusivity of Thomism but the "preference" to be accorded to it; this, of course, is in tacit disagreement with the drafters of the conciliar document.

[105] The obviously disconsolate Cardinal ended his letter thus: "Most Holy Father, I am deeply embittered to see the disregard of the teachings of the magisterium as conveyed especially in papal encyclicals. If the popes of the past are not heard, it is to be feared that the same will be true in the future." In the same letter Ruffini showed himself also worried about the development of the text on revelation (see the letter of Ruffini to Paul VI, October 17, 1965 [*AS* V/3, 447–48]).

[106] The text of the appeal is in Carraro papers, 31, with the accompanying letter of Oberti and Carraro, dated September 30, 1965.

Pope — a clarification on the nature of secular institutes. A letter of Lazzati to Carlo Colombo during the early days of October already contained the proposal that would find its way into the definitive text. It took the form of a short clause that distinguished unequivocally between secular institutes and religious institutes: "Secular institutes, *although they are not religious institutes*, do *nevertheless* involve a true and complete profession of the evangelical counsels in the world, a profession that is recognized by the Church."[107] This did not exactly match the original request from officials of the secular institutes, who desired a change in the title of the schema and a shift of the section on secular institutes to an independent place at the end of the schema. But at least the difference in nature between religious congregations and secular institutes was made clear.

It is not clear whether this was the same proposal that had been discussed at the meeting on October 4. In any case, Lazzati's request reached the Pope by way of Colombo and was immediately accepted. On October 26 a letter of Dell'Acqua containing the request for a change in no. 11 of the decree reached Antoniutti, president of the commission in charge, by way of Felici.[108] Antoniutti used his authority to make the insertion without convening the commission, and in the hall, on the morning of October 27, Felici justified the change in the text as making good an oversight on the part of the commission: "The president of the commission asked that in no. 11 the text read as the commission had intended it to read. These words were omitted by an oversight."[109] The intervention inevitably elicited reactions among the fathers; J. Beyer has a very good description of the surprise and grumbling that were caused when Felici dictated the changed text to the fathers in view of the vote to be taken on the morrow.[110]

---

[107] The words in italics are those added by the amendment. Lazzati wrote: "It seems to me, too, that this very slight change could help save the distinction that seems necessary to safeguard the true meaning of the different religious and secular institutes." The text of Lazzati's letter is in G. Lazzati, *Il Regno di Dio è in mezzo a voi*, II (Milan, 1977), 239. On Oberti's initiative see A. Oberti, "A cinquant'anni dalla Provida mater," *Vita consecrata* 33 (1997), 38–41. I thank Professor Oberti for his valuable information.

[108] Letter of Dell'Acqua to Felici, October 26, 1965 (*AS* V/3, 472). This letter was attached to the letter that Felici sent to Antoniutti on that same day (ibid., 471).

[109] Ibid., 546.

[110] J. Beyer, "Les instituts séculiers (Commentaire du numéro 11)," in Tillard and Congar, *L'adaptation et la rénovation*, 375. See *AS* V/3, 395. But the insertion on the secular institutes was not the only change made in the text of the decree before its promulgation. Also changed was the *incipit*, which in its original form was identical to that of the document on divine revelation (*Sacrosancta synodus*) but now became *Perfectae caritatis*.

Paul VI's intervention met the demands of the secular institutes and undoubtedly corrected a paradoxical situation. The acceptance of corrections regarding the role and distinctive features of the secular institutes within a text on religious life risked denying the lay character of the institutes by forcibly assimilating them to so many forms of religious life. Apart from the content of the change, the episode was important for the way in which it came about. It showed the necessity of "concealing the crown" (hiding the interventions of the Pope in the Council's business) that was clearly manifested during these days of October and that greatly worried the progressive bishops and, in particular, the Belgian circle around Suenens. The continual interventions of the Pope in the texts being discussed, sometimes masked in very varied ways in order not to reveal their true origin, risked demeaning the atmosphere of the Council by disregarding all the procedural regulations.[111]

B. THE PUBLIC SESSION OF OCTOBER 28 AND THE PROMULGATION OF THE DOCUMENTS

The solemn public session began with the final votes on the schemas. The results, which were made known only after the end of the liturgical celebration, confirmed the pattern of the preliminary votes cast during the preceding weeks. The schemas on the pastoral office of bishops, the renewal of religious life, and priestly training received almost unanimous approval (2, 4, and 3 negative votes respectively), while residual opposition found expression in the vote on Christian education (35 negative votes) and, above all, in the vote on the attitude to be taken toward the non-Christian religions (88 negative votes).

The morning continued with the celebration of mass; notable was the simplicity, in many respects, of the ceremony, this being the direct result

---

In addition, the Constitution on the Church was more correctly referred to as *Lumen gentium* rather than a generic *De ecclesia*. The changes had no influence on the content of the schema; they originated in two suggestions made by Lorscheider in an attachment to the already cited letter in the early days of October. It should be noted, among other things, that Rousseau, secretary of the commission, had already objected to these changes: "Now is not the time to change the text" (Rousseau, "Responsa," 397).

[111] Prignon describes the explanation given in the hall as "regrettable." According to Onclin, Opus Dei also intervened (see *JPrignon*, October 31, 1965 [Prignon papers, 1613, 1]). For some earlier thoughts on papal interventions and on their secrecy, see ibid., October 4, 1965 (Prignon papers, 1598, 4–5).

of the liturgical updating promoted by the Council itself.[112] The celebration focused on prayer for peace; twenty-four bishops from various countries around the world surrounded the Pope at the altar in one of those symbolic gestures so valued by Montini. After his address at the United Nations and against the background of the conciliar discussion of *Gaudium et spes*, the Pope gathered around him prelates from the various countries in which the Church was being persecuted or which were being ravaged by wars; this represented, in a concise form, a Church that was in solidarity with the anxieties and difficulties of humanity and that yearned for peace.[113]

The homily took as its starting the point the feast of Sts. Simon and Jude and made explicit reference to the anniversary of the election of the Pope's predecessor, John XXIII. It was devoted entirely to the theme of the Church carrying out its mission in the world through a dynamic process of renewal and growth. According to Paul VI, the promulgation of the four documents about to be promulgated pointed specifically to this renewal of ecclesial structures. They were the sign of a "living Church" that derived its own "striving for perfection" from the love of Christ.[114] Echoing expressions typical of the teaching of John XXIII, Montini emphasized the vitality of an ancient institution able to renew itself in dialogue with the world and contemporary cultures without losing its irreplaceable connection with its tradition.

The Pope also referred specifically, of course, to the promulgation of the declaration on the Church's relationship with non-Christian religions and to its ties to "the followers of the other religions, especially those to whom we are united by our relationship with Abraham, the Jews in particular, who are not an object of reproach or mistrust, but rather of respect, love, and hope."

The discourse was short, relatively unstructured, and quite unlike the programmatic addresses of preceding sessions; this probably explains

---

[112] Edelby wrote in his diary: "A very beautiful ceremony. No gestatorial chair, no fan (*flabellum*), no guards. The Pope entered on foot in a procession, preceded by the cardinals" (*JEdelby*, 323). J. Lawrence, an observer from the Church of England, recorded similar impressions in his diary (J. Lawrence, "Osservatore Romano," October 28, 1965, in Council of Foreign Relations (CFR) Papers, RC Files 44/3 [Lambeth Palace, London]).

[113] The concelebrants were Cardinals Wyszynski, Gracias, Slipyi, Beran, and Seper; archbishops Capozi, van Miltenburg, de Almeida Batista, Nguyén-van Binh, Amissah, Djajasepoetra, E. Butler, Kinam Ro, and Malula; and bishops Kurteff, de Alba y Hernandez, Kovàcs, Bonomini, Lamont, Dominguez y Rodriguez, Reilly, Olu Chukwuka Nwaezeapu, and Vaivods (see Caprile, V, 313).

[114] For the text of the homily, see *AS* IV/5, 560–63; English translation in *Council Daybook, Session 4*, 164-66.

why it made little impact on the conciliar assembly, which was now looking forward to the conclusion of its work. According to observer Horton,
it was a "very general homily on the building up of the Church."[115]
On the other hand, the very context of the address suggested that the Pope
had a specific intention. In earlier solemn sessions the Pope's participation had come at the end of the celebration and had touched explicitly on
the content of the Council's work. Here, however, his address was delivered in the midst of the celebration, between the reading of the gospel and
the profession of faith; this was also contrary to the sequence indicated
in the written program distributed to the bishops and the observers.[116]

The definitive promulgation of these four decrees marked an important
stage in the shaping of the conciliar magisterium, even amid a widespread
feeling that the task had been carried out hastily, without leaving sufficient time for issues to mature and for the various positions to be properly evaluated. *Perfectae caritatis*, the decree on religious life, was unanimously seen as a decisive passage to a view of religious life as a *sequela
Christi* [following of Christ]. The timid reforms sketched out in this
area during the pontificate of Pius XII (the logic of these was to adapt
without changing the basic theological and juridical principles) were now
left behind in favor of a different overall approach that looked at religious life in a biblical and christological perspective. In addition to giving concrete directives for the renewal of the orders, the schema provided
a guiding norm: fidelity to the intuitions of the founder, together with discernment of the needs of the time. On the other hand, many questions
were left unresolved that certainly could not be tackled during the short
time available in this final period of revisions. Dossetti pointed out, for
example, the question of exemption, which in his view was decisive for
the life of local Churches.[117]

---

[115] Horton, *Vatican Diary 1965*, 128. Other observers, such as L. Vischer and W. Blakemore, said nothing at all about the Pope's address in their reports.

[116] Among others, W. Dietzfelbinger, an Evangelical observer, noted this change and
therefore interpreted the Pope's address as a simple homily rather than a general address
on the state of the Council's work. He also saw in the papal address the influence of a
French theology of the Church (see W. Dietzfelbinger, "55. Bericht über das Zweite
Vatikanische Konzil," October 30, 1965, in Schlink papers, 6).

[117] Dossetti's opinion of the schema and of chapter VI of *LG* was very critical. He also
raised the problem of a "noteworthy lack of interest in this problem on the part of the
Council." The lack of enthusiasm on the part of the large religious orders, and even, in
many instances, their restraining action in defense of their special interests, did not help
the schema, in which no sure guidelines for the renewal of religious life can be seen (see
G. Dossetti, "Per una valutazione globale del magistero del Vaticano II," in *Il Vaticano
II: Frammenti di una riflessione* [Bologna, 1996], 73–79).

The Decree *Optatam totius* on the training of priests emerged from a less agitated history and seems to have absorbed, in a less traumatic way, some of the demands for reforms and some of the ideas circulating in the discussions at the time. As A. Greiler has pointed out, the text seems to have been the fruit of the efforts of some members of the commission (in particular, Mayer, its secretary) to mediate between the traditional vision of seminary training and a movement of radical renewal that in some cases wanted to get rid completely of the seminary as instituted by Trent.[118] Hurley's attempt to move beyond the idea of theological training that involved separate blocks of material and to replace it with a harmonious integration of the theological, pastoral, and spiritual aspects of a priest's formation was not completely successful, as the author himself admitted. Yet at the time of promulgation the prevailing judgment on the schema was a positive one, the main reason being what was said at the beginning about the responsibility of each episcopal conference for drafting a plan of studies that would be suited to its time and place.[119]

Gravissimum educationis, on Christian education, can be seen as the most problematic of the so-called pastoral schemas. Its hybrid character, evident until the final stage of the drafting, flowed from two opposing concerns within the episcopate: on the one hand, the defense of Catholic schools; on the other, the contribution of the Church to the problem of education. As we noted, the schema had been in danger of being scuttled at the last moment, on the very eve of the final vote on it. The positive final vote can therefore be understood, as V. Sinistrero observed, only as the result of a series of contingent considerations: the prospect of the work being continued by a postconciliar commission; the negative

---

[118] A. Greiler, "Erneuerung das Seminäre, Erneuerung der Kirche: Ein Überblick zur Textgeschichte von "Optatam totius," in *Experience*, 344. According to Dezza, the decree was marked by"a sense of balance"(P. Dezza,"Il decreto conciliare sulla formazione sacerdotale,"*CivCatt* 2273 [1966], 13–28). On the other hand, Alberigo's judgment on the schema was critical: the schema did not reflect an adequate grasp of the crisis of identity in which the priest was caught up (see G. Alberigo,"Concilio Vaticano II," in G. Alberigo, *Storia dei concili ecumenici* [Brescia, 1990], 442).

[119] See Denis, "Archbishop Hurley's Contribution to the Second Vatican Council," 257. Dossetti, too, even while criticizing the lack of impact of the reforms mentioned in the schema and the emphasis placed on the role of major seminaries, regarded as extremely important the principle that the episcopal conferences were given responsibility: "If this decentralization is really carried out, many of the drawbacks of the decree itself will become unimportant" (Dossetti, "Per una valutazione," 80). The judgment of O. Cullmann, an observer, was likewise positive on the whole; his statement is cited in R. Aubert, "I testi conciliari," in *Storia della Chiesa 25/1: La Chiesa del Vaticano II (1958–1978)* (Cinisello Balsamo, 1994), 364–65.

impact of a possible silence of the Council on the problems of education; and finally, the presence in the schema of an exhortation to Catholics
to study more thoroughly the problems of education.[120] In addition to
the severe judgments passed on the declaration,[121] the schema was marked
— as even Father Dezza, one of the principal drafters, admitted — by a
generality that was closely connected to the complexity of the problems
with which it dealt.[122]

Finally, *Nostra aetate,* the declaration on relations with the non-
Christian religions, marked the outcome of one of John XXIII's original
insights. Reformed Pastor Richard-Molard called it "one of the finest
pages in Christian theology."[123] The schema had been born as a stance
against anti-Semitism and as the Church's reflection on its own Jewish
roots. From this point of view the final version had certainly lost some
important emphases that had surfaced in the course of the successive
drafts;[124] but it had also been enriched by broadening its perspective to
include the major religions of the world. Cicognani's decision to expand
it was essentially a tactical move meant to retain control of the difficult
diplomatic situation, but it proved to be providential in redefining the
identity of the schema as a first adoption by the ecclesiastical magisterium of a position on the subject of interreligious dialogue. The second
aspect of the identity of the schema (the real meaning of which the bishops had little, if any, comprehension of at the time) would emerge when
its richness was revealed during the phase of reception.[125] It was not by

[120] Sinistrero, *Il Vaticano II e l'educazione,* 81–82. For a brief analysis of the schema
that brings out its dependence on traditional teaching about Catholic education, see Weihnacht, "Educational System, Education and Instructing," 321–23. The opinion of J. Daem,
the reporter on the schema, is given in his article "Éducation, enseignement, école: autour
de la Déclaration conciliaire," *Seminarium* 18 (1966), 394–402.

[121] Aubert regarded it as a document that was "on the whole rather trite" (Aubert,
"I testi conciliari," 378).

[122] P. Dezza, "L'educazione cristiana nella dichiarazione conciliare," *CivCatt* 2774
(1966), 110–25.

[123] Richard-Molard, in *Réforme,* October 23, 1965, cited in R. Rouquette, *La fin d'une
chrétienté: Chroniques* II (Paris, 1968), 628.

[124] I am referring to the loss not only of the condemnation of the accusation of deicide,
but also, for example, of the pastoral exhortations contained in the first version of the text,
drafted within the Secretariat for Christian Unity during the preparatory phase (see
M. Velati, "La proposta ecumenica del segretario per l'unità dei cristiani," in *Verso il
Concilio,* 332–37).

[125] For a general survey of the period of reception, see the report of M. Borrmans,
"Présence de la *Nostra aetate* du Concile à nos jours," delivered at the Klingenthal meeting, March 11–14, 1999; *Vatican II au but? Espoirs, craintes, déceptions, perspectives* (in
press); and P. Rossano, "Il Concilio Vaticano II e il suo insegnamento circa il dialogo

accident that the document, thus viewed, met determined opposition from traditionalist bishops.

Together with the documents on ecumenism and religious freedom this document completed the work of the Secretariat for Christian Unity. This body had come into existence as a simple bureau supplying non-Catholics with information about the Council, but by putting on the agenda subjects most central to the *aggiornamento* desired by John XXIII, it had acquired a decisive influence on the Council's work.

VI. The Vicissitudes of the Schema on Priests

Among the schemas affected by the Döpfner Plan, the one that reached the fourth session as the least clearly defined was undoubtedly the schema on the ministry and life of priests. During the preceding session the revised text had met with a brusque rejection, and the commission was forced to revise it substantially in accordance with the indications given in the short debate in November 1964.[126] The new text (the sixth version!) was sent to the Council fathers in June 1965 with the prospect of a new discussion during the fourth session of the Council. Initial reactions were not encouraging: the complexity of the set of problems being faced called for further reflection, while some respondents saw the text as lacking an organic doctrinal vision of the priesthood.

A. The Question of Celibacy

While the bishops and experts were asking themselves about the need for deeper theological reflection, the public debate was dominated by the question of celibacy. For some time a series of public statements, exaggerated by the press, had been revealing that a number of people were

---

interreligioso specialmente alla luce della Dichiarazione *Nostra aetate*," *Seminarium* 38 (1987), 12–20.

[126] For the events of the third session, see *History* 4:345-56. For the overall history of the decree, see J. Lécuyer, "History of the Decree," in *Commentary*, 4:183–209); J. Frisque, *Le décret Presbyterorum Ordinis: Histoire et commentaire* (Paris, 1967), 123–33; R. Wasselynk, *Les Prêtres: élaboration du Décret de Vatican II* (Paris, 1968); M. Caprioli, *Il Decreto Conciliare "Presbyterorum Ordinis": Storia, analisi, dottrina*, 2 vols. (Rome, 1989–90); and R. Spiazzi, "Genesi del decreto *Presbyterorum Ordinis*," in *Il decreto sul ministero e la vita sacerdotale* (Turin, 1966).

opposed to the continuance of the law of celibacy; these amounted to what Robert Clément, rector of the College of Jamhour in Beirut, called "an assault on celibacy."[127] The most impressive of these statements was the appeal signed by 825 priests of the International Committee Pro Ecclesia.[128] Writing with great moderation, Clément addressed himself to Cardinal Lercaro and other Council fathers in August of 1965, in a note containing the proposal that the Oriental discipline with its noncelibate presbyterate be extended to the Latin Church.[129]

The subject also arose in the written views of the fathers that had been submitted during the intersession, with the usual opposing positions taken: while the president of the Indonesian episcopal conference spoke against celibacy being obligatory for priests, de Castro Mayer, a representative of the *Coetus Internationalis Patrum*, fiercely defended the Latin practice.[130] Finally, during the early days of October, a priest of the diocese of Strasbourg circulated among the Italian bishops a short work against celibacy; Msgr. Weber reacted by decisively disavowing the action.[131] But the Italian Church was not unfamiliar with such efforts; we need think only of the appeals signed by Italian priests and lay people, especially in Rome. During these months Dutch Catholicism experienced a heated debate on the subject.[132]

In October 1965, as the beginning of the debate drew near, then, it was possible to predict an explosive discussion, and Paul VI grew increasingly concerned. At the beginning of October, Lercaro received instructions to contact the bishops who intended to take up the question at the general congregations and to dissuade them from doing so. On October 6 he met with Brazilian Bishop Pietro Koop, titular bishop of the Diocese of Lina and author of an intervention that would not be read in the Council but would appear in the pages of *Le Monde*, on the need to establish a noncelibate clergy as a "supplement." Only the decision of Paul VI to cut off the debate on celibacy and reserve the question to himself spared

[127] Letter of R. Clément to Lercaro, August 22, 1965 (Lercaro papers, 290): "Faced with the recent assault on celibacy, I am convinced that the best way of defending it is to define its exact role."

[128] For the text (with no indication of date or place), see Urbani papers, A29.11.

[129] R. Clément, "Note à quelques Pères Conciliaires à propos du schema *De ministerio et vita prebsyterorum*," attached to the letter of Clément to Lercaro, August 22, 1965.

[130] See, respectively, *AS* V/3, 142–42, and *AS* IV/5, 295–99.

[131] See the letter of Weber to Castelli, October 17, 1965 (Carraro papers, 22).

[132] Alfrink spoke of it to the press on September 15, defending the value of a frank and honest debate; Ancel also dwelt on the subject (Caprile, V, 228). Caprile also cites two appeals of Italian priests and lay people in favor of a reform of the law of celibacy.

Lercaro the embarrassing task of convincing Melkite Patriarch Maximos IV not to give a planned intervention in favor of a married clergy.[133]

Paul VI's decision was made known on the morning of October 11 in the form of a letter to Tisserant that was read at the general congregation. In very clear language the Pope made known his desire to avoid a public discussion of celibacy and, at the same time, his intention to safeguard this "ancient, sacred, and providential law."[134] He then urged concerned bishops to send their observations to the Council of Presidents.

The Pope's decision caught even moderators Lercaro and Suenens by surprise. For lack of documentation directly traceable to the Pope it is not easy to reconstruct the origins of his decision. According to Fesquet, an audience granted by Paul VI to de Barros Camara, who supported the continuation of celibacy, was a decisive factor. But nothing is said of this audience in the pages of *L'Osservatore Romano*, and the Brazilian cardinal had not been conspicuous in the discussion of the subject. It is certain, however, that the Brazilian episcopate was indeed at the center of the uneasiness.

At their meeting on October 8, at the urging of the South Americans, the representatives of the episcopal conferences likewise dwelt at length on the subject. While there was agreement that a free debate at a general congregation would have negative results because of the way the press would blow it up, the problem was a real one and was already being debated in some local Churches. For this reason the Brazilians were pressing to find a suitable sphere for discussion, one that would combine the needed freedom with due discretion. It was therefore decided at the meeting to get the Pope involved. The minutes read: "We ask that the Supreme Pontiff be informed about the matter."[135] At the same time, a conversation between H. Câmara and Suenens led to the suggestion that the presidents of the episcopal conferences be asked to study the question.[136]

The same meeting revealed that views differed: the insistence of the Brazilian bishops elicited only tepid responses from the European episcopates. The hesitation of Suenens and many others was also based on a

---

[133] See *Lettere*, 366–67. On October 7 the Melkite Patriarch had already shown Congar his intervention; this focused on the superiority of the Oriental discipline, which combines a celibate clergy and a noncelibate clergy. The French Dominican did not tell the Patriarch of his doubts that such an intervention was opportune, but he did tell them later to Ancel (see *JCongar*, October 7, 1965; II, 425).

[134] The undated text of the letter to Tisserant is in *AS* IV/1, 40. Tisserant's reply is ibid., 41.

[135] "Quarta coadunatio delegatorum," 2.

[136] *JPrignon*, October 10, 1965 (Prignon papers, 1602, 5).

strong desire for a speedy end to the Council, which could be hindered
if so important a question were raised during these decisive days. As a
result, the desire of the Brazilians to raise the question at the Council did
not find wide support among the fathers.

This scenario probably explains the predominantly positive reactions
to Paul VI's decision. During the days that followed, it was Larraín,
speaking in the name of the Latin American episcopate, who brought out
the full agreement among the principal parties in the episode. Similarly,
a group of Brazilian bishops intervened to state that "among the bishops
who live in Brazil and work for the proclamation of the gospel there, not
one wants to do away with priestly celibacy."[137] Further positive reactions
came from the Argentinean bishops and from Döpfner, one of the moderators. The reactions of the observers were likewise marked by understanding. Vischer wrote: "In many respects I understand this decision.
The Council receives so much publicity that the discussion of celibacy
would be given a disproportionate amount of attention."[138] Vischer then
remarked that only a small minority of the episcopate regarded the Pope's
intervention as a denial of the freedom of the Council.[139]

In general, these evaluations presupposed an interpretation of the
Pope's intervention, not as the end of any debate, but as a simple transfer of the subject from the general congregation to a more suitable venue,
since, among other things, the problem did not seem to affect all the episcopates to the same degree. Anglican observer J. Lawrence heard rumors
about a possible resumption of the subject, in more limited venues, during the pauses anticipated during the following weeks.[140] Prignon was

---

[137] In this statement the bishops, Cardinal Agnelo Rossi among them, also distanced
themselves from the initiative of Koop, who spoke "only in his own name" (see *AS* VI/4,
624–25).

[138] See Lukas Vischer, "Concerning the Fourth Session of the Second Vatican Council No. 4" (October 22, 1965), 6; ACO.

[139] Schlink took a different view; he noted in one of his reports a degree of "disobe-
dience" of the Pope's instructions on the part of three cardinals (Bea, Döpfner, and
Ruffini), who touched on the subject of celibacy during the debate on the following days;
see E. Schlink, "54. Bericht über das Zweite Vatikanische Konzil," October 18, 1965, in
Schlink papers, 10–12. Congar, too, emphasized the legitimacy of Paul VI's intervention:
"According to canon law, the Council can debate only what the pope submits to it.
The pope can therefore withdraw this or that question from the agenda" (*JCongar*, Octo-
ber 11, 1965; II, 430).

[140] Lawrence, "Osservatore romano (part II)", October 11, 1965. As Horton thought
about the meaning of the applause that accompanied the public reading of the Pope's letter, he wondered whether it was for his decision to end the debate or for his suggestion
that the fathers submit their remarks on the subject (Horton, *Vatican Diary 1965*, 95–96).

less optimistic and considered the Pope's invitation to send in remarks on the subject to be a mere "rhetorical flourish."[141] In fact, the communication of Paul VI's decision was not followed by any other explanatory intervention, and the question was left pending until after the end of the Council. The *Acta Synodalia* contain only a small bit of evidence that Felici twice sent the Pope material dealing with the question.[142]

The Pope's intervention did not prevent an abundance of statements and interventions on the subject of celibacy. In the days immediately following a document circulated among the bishops that was signed by eighty-one lay people from different continents, together with a file of historical and theological material that had been put together by some scholars of the French-speaking world.[143]

It is perhaps appropriate to attempt here a kind of synthesis of the petitions and statements contained in the various documents cited. The interventions came from quite varied sources (bishops, priests, laity) and, of course, tackled the problem from various perspectives. While not utterly denying the value of celibacy, the various writers proposed greater or lesser limits on the obligation in order to open the way to the establishment of a noncelibate clergy in the West. In the view of Koop, it was chiefly pastoral reasons (the scarcity of clergy and the risk of losing all influence over the peoples of the Third World) that justified opening the

---

[141] "The letter was striking for the tone it used and, above all, for the fact that the Pope took a definitive position and said so plainly. He did add, however, that if the fathers had remarks to make to him on the subject, they should send them in writing, and he would study them in the presence of God. But that seems to have been rather a rhetorical flourish" (*JPrignon*, October 12, 1965 [Prignon papers, 1603, 2]).

[142] See letter of Felici to Cicognani, October 16, 1965 (*AS* V/3, 437); and idem, November 3, 1965 (*AS* V/3, 477). Maximos IV, on his own initiative, sent the Pope his intervention on a married priesthood (see above, note 133). Unfortunately, the editors of the *Acta Synodalia* did not think it appropriate to publish the material attached to these letters, thus depriving us of a comprehensive view of the principal utterances that reached the Pope on the subject of celibacy.

[143] "De presbyterorum coelibatu libellus patribus in sacrosancta et universali synodo vaticana secunda congregatis, humiliter oblatus," no date. The text is in both Latin and French, and it is signed by eighty-one people belonging to the world of culture, university docents in a wide variety of disciplines, and officers of Catholic associations (for example, A. M. Roeloffzen, secretary of the World Federation of Feminine Catholic Youth and also an auditor at the Council, and L. Baas, president of Dutch Catholic Action). Among the few Italians we may mention the name of the philosopher Armando Rigobello. The file contained four essays by S. Lyonnet ("L'Église et le travail des clercs selon L. Thomassin" and "À propose du schéma 'De ministerio et vita presbyterorum' no. 14; De consiliis evangelicis in vita presbyteri, pp. 35–38"); R. Clément ("Optime meriti presbyteri coniugati — Schéma sur les prêtres"), and J. P. Audet, "La sacralisation du service pastoral et les origines du 'célibat ecclésiastique'"); the file is in Lercaro papers, XVIII, 300.

clergy to married lay men for at least five years; these men would be "supplementary" and part time.[144]

The analyses given by Clément and the Melkite Patriarch started from different premises, but the two men were united in the conviction that the Oriental tradition had an exemplary value. While Clément did not undervalue the pastoral reasons, he emphasized the ecumenical aspect: in relation to both the Orthodox and the Protestant worlds, a change of attitude here would promote dialogue. To this end, a reinterpretation of some of the presuppositions of the teaching on the priesthood was needed. The internal aspects of the very idea of vocation had to be distinguished; it may be understood as a call to a way of life that is bound up with the choice of celibacy, but if it is understood by reference to a form of ministry, celibacy is of lesser importance. In the same way, according to Clément, the concept of chastity needed to be reformulated by distinguishing within it a form of perpetual continence (typical of celibates) and a temporary continence for married priests. As for the concrete form of a noncelibate priesthood, Clément simply referred to the practices of the Oriental Churches.

The intervention of Maximos IV saw in the schema a misunderstanding of the age-old tradition of the Oriental noncelibate priesthood, and this in the interests of exalting Latin practice. The restriction to a purely Western viewpoint weakened the text. The Melkite Patriarch reversed the perspective and proposed (in a still somewhat veiled manner) taking the Oriental model as a guide in a possible future evolution of Latin law: "At the moment and in the countries in which Church shall judge it opportune, this tradition can be invoked to support a historical change that may perhaps be made necessary by the changing circumstances of times, places, and persons."

But Maximos was more explicit, to the point of harshness, in the letter he sent to Paul VI along with the text of his intervention: "Most Holy Father, this problem exists and is becoming daily more difficult. It calls for a solution. There is no use in concealing the fact or making the subject taboo. Your Holiness is well aware that repressed truths become toxic."[145] Maximos's proposal was that a postconciliar study commission

---

[144] Koop's intervention in a French translation is in H. Fesquet, *Drama of Vatican II* (New York, 1967), 692–94. The Latin original is in Lercaro papers, XVIII, 294, 2 pp., as is the text of a provisional draft (ibid., XVIII, 297).

[145] Letter of Maximos IV to Paul VI, October 13, 1965 (*AS* VI/4, 550–52), with the attached text "Super n. 14 Schematis Decreti 'De Ministerio et Vita Presbyterorum': Sacerdoce, célibat et mariage dans l'Église Orientale" (September 19, 1965 [*AS* VI/4, 551–54]). An Italian translation of the patriarch's letter and intervention is in Caprile, V, 224–28.

be established to deal with the question. The Patriarch's intervention was marked by his customary straightforwardness, but the theological or pastoral reasons given were not far removed from previous interventions, based as they were on the fundamental distinction between the monastic vocation and the priestly vocation. Celibacy could not be regarded as an essential element of the latter.

Other writings dealing with the question showed a more radical tone. The booklet on priestly celibacy likewise asked for the establishment of a postconciliar commission to deal with the matter. But the request here was based on a series of reflections on celibacy in contemporary society. Apart from the practical problem of the poverty of priests, the very condition of today's world urged the removal of priestly celibacy. The new types of humanism now abroad made the witness of a married priest more convincing; in contrast, a priest risked being crushed by the weight of the choice of celibacy in a situation in which mentalities and morality had greatly changed. The document appealed precisely to the pastoral goals of the Council in asking for an intervention that would establish the possibility of allowing a priest freely to choose celibacy or the married state. The expectation here was obviously that celibacy would not be chosen due to the rapid transformations of society. The thesis was very similar to that of Audet, who saw the process of sacralization of the Church's ministries as the remote origin of the imposition of priestly celibacy and raised the question of whether it was appropriate to retain this sacral custom in a secularized world.[146]

B. The Conciliar Debate: Nostalgia for the Past *vs.* a Sense of Crisis

After October 11, with the question of celibacy provisionally set aside, the assembly prepared to discuss the schema. I have already mentioned the rather negative impression that the new version of the schema had made on the fathers. For this reason, at the beginning of the new period many efforts were made to effect a radical revision of it. The first to make a move were the French bishops, with the energetic collaboration of Marty, the reporter on the schema. At the end of September 1965 an informal working group began its activity; the group

---

[146] Audet, "La sacralisation du service pastoral," 6–7.

consisted of some French bishops, with some Argentinian and Canadian colleagues, and a small group of experts from the French-speaking world.[147]

Although this group remained active for only a few days, from it came some themes that would be important as the schema underwent revision. The call for a theology of the priesthood that was more complete and centered on Pauline teaching in Romans 16:15; the theme of the presence of the Spirit in the life of the priest; the missionary dimensions of priestly life: these were identified as the lines along which the schema should be revised. The meeting of the representatives of the episcopal conferences in the Domus Mariae at the beginning of October accepted these demands and transformed them into a program on which there was wide agreement. It was decided there to act along four lines that to a large extent followed closely the work of the French study group: a theological definition of the priesthood along the lines of Pauline theology; emphasis on the missionary aspect; a clear explanation of the reasons for celibacy; and finally, charging the episcopal conferences with the task of setting down the conditions for the exercise of priesthood.[148]

The moderators, too, were busily working. Prignon was commissioned by Suenens to compose "a thorough doctrinal intervention on the subject of priesthood," while during the early days of October, Dossetti worked on a draft of what would become Lercaro's written intervention during the debate. The Bolognese theologian offered some original thoughts on the distinctly religious dimension of the priestly role, which would exclude any claims to social relevance and strongly emphasize the values of charity and poverty in the exercise of ministry.[149]

The debate in the hall began on October 14. The bishops had received the texts both of the schema and of Marty's report, which explained the work done in the commission. His awareness of widespread dissatisfaction compelled Marty to draw up a new report, which was distributed in the hall a few days before the debate. This was much more than a chronicle of the editorial work done and, in fact, presented some lines along which the debate might move.

---

[147] Present at the first meeting of the informal group on September 23, 1965, were Bishops Marty, Atton, Bannwarth, Mazerat, Gand, Gufflet, Allex, Théas, Guyot, Polge, Vilnet, Bazelaire, and Brunon, while the experts were Colson, Frisque, Salin, Camelot, and Congar (*JCongar*, September 23, 1965; II, 404–5).

[148] Minutes of the meeting of October 1, 1965, are in Etchegaray papers.

[149] See "De ministerio et vita presbyterorum," undated, 5 pp., in Lercaro papers, XVIII, 291. The text is anonymous but easily can be shown to be from Dossetti.

First and foremost, Marty established some fixed points. The purpose of the document was still to describe the pastoral mission of priests; consequently, as far as doctrine was concerned, it did not intend to go beyond what had been determined in *Lumen gentium*. By the same token, however, the schema did not supply concrete instructions; it would be up to the episcopal conferences to provide for the multiplicity of concrete situations. Marty, therefore, pointed out some subjects of a possible debate to which he urged the bishops to contribute through their own thinking: the apostolic aspect of ministry as having its origin in a personal union with Christ; the universality of the apostolic mission, which is carried on even beyond the borders of the Church; the dimension of ecclesial communion, in the light of which a doctrine of the evangelical counsels becomes intelligible. As can be seen, Marty was repeating some of the points emphasized both in the work of the French study group and at the meeting of the representatives of the episcopal conferences.

The debate proper began on the morning of October 14. In the course of three days, fifty-five fathers (twenty-two of them cardinals) spoke; to these can be added another twelve interventions in the name of at least seventy fathers that were made when the debate continued on October 25 and 26. Many other interventions (184) were not presented orally but were submitted in writing to the secretariat.

As expected, the debate reflected the diverse situations in which Catholicism found itself in various geographical and cultural settings; as a result, in addition to concerns connected with the schema, the debate also yielded a general picture of the problems and difficulties priests faced in today's world. Thus the intervention of Costa Rican Bishop Arrieta Villalobos, delivered in the name of over seventy Latin American fathers, emphasized the painful problem of the poverty of priests; he proposed a radical redistribution of clergy among the various geographical spheres.[150] African Cardinal Rugambwa, on the other hand, stressed the need to adapt pastoral solutions to different situation in order to keep the Church from being turned into a kind of museum.[151]

This desire to escape from an excessively Western vision of problems, widespread among the bishops of the Third World, was also very much shared by an authoritative representative of the Oriental Churches, Cardinal Meouchi, who regretted the schema's lack of a global vision of Catholicism that would include in a substantive way the great Oriental

[150] *AS* IV/5, 159–63.
[151] Ibid., 14–15.

tradition.[152] Also with an eye on the East, Franić reminded the assembly of the special situation of priests working in communist countries where, along with all other sectors of the Church, they experienced the suffering of persecution. Franić suggested incorporating into the schema a reference honoring the memory of the victims of persecution.[153]

Others spoke, in contrast, of the problems typical of the clergy in the developed and secularized world of Europe and North America. Alfrink and Suenens provided, in exemplary fashion, worried analyses of the marginalization and irrelevance of the priest in today's society, now that the security given by the regime of Christendom no longer exists.[154]

What emerged from the discussion were aspects of a very complicated situation that could be described generally as a "crisis" in the situation of the priest but that was not very adequately represented in the schema. The question now was how to remedy the situation: What model of priesthood should the schema propose that would lead to a satisfactory renewal? On this point the debate revealed a series of disagreements deriving from the different mental approaches of the Council fathers, with the basis of the division being no longer merely geographical. Various commentators have seen two major theologico-pastoral orientations at work in the debate.[155]

On the one hand, we discern a primarily cultic and liturgical vision of the priest, which ought to be reasserted as an answer to the spread of the "heresy of action," that is, the draining away of the properly priestly role in numerous practical and secular activities. Presupposing an emphasis on a separation of the priest from the world, this line of thought was represented in the intervention of Ruffini, who proposed a change in the very title of the schema by inverting its two parts: "life" before "ministry," thereby showing a careful choice of priorities.[156] A similar emphasis is found in the interventions of Spanish Cardinal de Arriba y Castro, who, among other things, regarded this schema as "the most important of the entire Council," and of French Cardinal Richaud. The latter explicitly challenged the thesis of the reformers by saying that the essence of priesthood cannot be conceived solely in terms of service to humanity, because

---

[152] *AS* IV/4, 685–86.

[153] Ibid., 801–3.

[154] Ibid., 779–82 and 785–91, respectively.

[155] See J. Herranz, "Il decreto *Presbyterorum ordinis*: Riflessioni storico-teologiche sul contributo di Mons. Alvaro del Portillo," *Annales theologici* 9 (1995), 223; J. Frisque, *"Le décret Presbyterorum Ordinis,"* 132.

[156] *AS* IV/4, 686–88.

this would be equivalent to reducing the priest to a kind of lay man with a few added powers. On the contrary, the primordial function of a priest is "the external and internal worship of God."[157]

Rivaling this vision was a different, "missionary" conception of the priestly role focused on the removal of barriers and on the presence of the priest in the midst of human beings as one of them. The call for this view emerged in dominant fashion on the morning of October 15 when three consecutive interventions emphasized the need of a dialogue between priests and the people of today with a view to evangelizing them. On the basis of his own situation in a missionary Church, Japanese Cardinal Tatsuo Doi clearly asserted his view that a priest cannot be satisfied with caring for the baptized but must devote himself primarily to the preaching of the gospel, a point on which the schema seemed inadequate.[158] Doi was immediately followed by Alfrink, who censured a vision of priests living in their sacristies, far removed from the real needs of present-day humanity. Finally, Suenens challenged the excessively abstract character of the schema, which did not take into account the main problem of today's priests: the crisis of identity that seemed to deny any room for priestly activity whether in a dechristianized world or even in the Church. In Suenens's vision it was the priest's relationship with Christ that recapitulated, in a way, the various demands connected with the priestly mission and was the primary source of his missionary and evangelizing obligation. We should mention that various other interventions supported the same views, beginning with the already cited address of Rugambwa.[159]

As may be noted, the source of these opposed calls reflected, at least broadly, the division between minority and majority within the conciliar assembly. But we may not exaggerate the opposition between these several visions, because both were sometimes present in the same interventions and efforts were made to synthesize them. Léger, for example, tried in his intervention to restate the problem by appealing to the key concept of pastoral charity and to the gospel image of the good shepherd; when thus viewed, there was no opposition between interior and exterior activity, between cultic and missionary functions.[160] A similar effort at a synthesis had been worked up in the

[157] Ibid., 688–90 and 731–33, respectively.

[158] Ibid., 778.

[159] Also to be mentioned are the interventions of Léger and of De Roo (in the name of over seventy fathers).

[160] *AS* IV/4, 728–31.

preceding days by Dossetti; in his view the dichotomy between presence in the world and separation from it could be overcome only by reviving the category of "prophetic presence." Dossetti's remarks were the basis of an intervention by Lercaro that would not be read in the hall but would be sent to the secretariat of the commission. It offered a dense argument to identify a new model of priesthood, one that would be "increasingly more specifically religious," "increasingly more Christian," and would be based on the gospel demands for poverty and charity.[161]

The possibility of revising the doctrinal part of the schema was, however, very limited given what Marty had said in explaining the schema: it was the intention of the commission to remain within the lines set down in *Lumen gentium*. As a result, apart from some specific points dealing chiefly with the relationship between the theology of priesthood and the doctrine of the "evangelical counsels," the debate was to stay at a more concrete level by taking up a series of questions having to do with the role of the priest in the life of the Church.

A subject which came immediately to the fore was the relationship of priests with bishops. Even before the beginning of the Council, the episcopal *vota* had shown the problem of a widespread uneasiness about the concrete structuring of hierarchical relations. From this there flowed an equally widespread desire of bishops throughout the world for the restoration of so-called "episcopal monarchy," that is, the bishop's complete control of the priests and religious in his diocese. The debate on the schema renewed this desire, which found expression in very different ways.

While many bishops touched on the subject of the obedience owed by a priest to his superiors, views differed greatly. While for some (Renard, Polish bishop Barela, and Ruffini[162]) the schema was too weak in its urging of obedience to superiors, for others it lacked courage in renewing this relationship. According to Suenens and Charbonneau, it was necessary to

---

[161] Among other points Lercaro suggested that the present draft of the schema absolutely not be considered definitive, given the lack of time that prevented a radical revision of the text. It should be combined later with the major doctrinal lines followed in the other conciliar schemas, while also holding firmly to certain basic requirements such as the strictly religious character of priestly service, the exercise of charity on a universal scale (the "concern for all the Churches" of which *Lumen gentium* speaks in no. 23), and the mystery of the poor in the Church (see *AS* IV/5, 214–17, and, for the Italian, *Per la forza dello Spirito*, 171-79.

[162] *AS* IV/4, 813–15 (Renard); and *AS* IV/5, 61–64 (Barela).

avoid a kind of passive obedience that showed little sense of responsibility for the good of the Church.[163] American cardinal Shehan expressly rejected any form of "episcopalism."[164] According to others, the need was to develop concrete forms of collegiality at the diocesan level. In this context the idea of establishing a kind of "episcopal senate" came up again, an idea already foreshadowed in the schema.[165]

The debate echoed questions that had been topical during recent discussions of the role of the priest in society, chief among them the dispute over worker-priests. The schema in fact contained a reference to the question of priests engaging in manual work, a point on which, of course, the fathers had different views. Spanish Bishop Argaya Goicoechea agreed that such work was licit but warned against the dangers of a complete absorption in material matters (another reference to the heresy of activism).[166] Some Italian bishops, on the other hand, were against the idea; in a joint written intervention they proposed a return to the preceding text, which contained a general reference to the presence of the priest "in factories" *(in officinis)*.[167]

No less burning an issue was the question of celibacy, which Paul VI's authoritative intervention had excluded but which came up unexpectedly in some interventions. Meouchi and Döpfner censored themselves by not reading a part of their interventions,[168] but other influential cardinals such as Ruffini and Bea took up the question, although with very different

[163] *AS* IV/5, 167–69 (Charbonneau). His intervention had won the agreement of about 130 fathers from various places (Africa, Canada, France, and Latin America).

[164] Ibid., 25–29.

[165] The subject of collegiality at the diocesan level was mentioned here but had not yet been given any significant attention in the Council. Unlike the idea of episcopal collegiality, it had been ignored even in specialist literature (see T. C. Barberena, "Collegiality at the Diocesan Level: The Western Presbyterate," in *Pastoral Reform in Church Government, Concilium* 8 [New York, 1965], 19–32, which gives some bibliographical information).

[166] *AS* IV/4, 740–44.

[167] "We do not think it fitting to make room in a solemn conciliar document for an experiment, the outcome of which is unknown (in the recent past the results of such an experiment were such as to lead to its prohibition) and which takes in a very tiny part of the Church." The short document was addressed to "Your Holiness" and was signed by Bonomini, Cannonero, Monaco, Proni, Bignamini, Santin, Chiocca, Bonacini, and Aglialoro (*AS* IV/5, 538–39).

[168] Döpfner did not read in the hall the section of his address in which he brought out the contradiction between the schema's statement that celibacy is essentially a gift "which the Father gives to some" and the demand that celibacy be obligatory for Western priests. His intervention was signed by sixty-five German and Scandinavian bishops (*AS* IV/5, 764–67).

approaches. Ruffini praised the schema for its clear reassertion of the law of celibacy.[169] Bea, however, reproached it for forgetting the Oriental discipline of a married clergy; he thus made his own the contents of the letter of Maximos IV.[170] It was clearly ecumenical considerations that impelled Bea to this intervention, designed to correct the overly Western approach of the schema. Bea's intervention produced a curt reaction from Cardinal Bacci, who sent the secretariat a short, polemical piece aimed at an anonymous "father of the Council," author of an "erroneous and dangerous" address. Bacci reproached Bea not only for placing a celibate and a married clergy on the same level, but for having disobeyed the Pope's instruction not to take up the subject at a general congregation.[171]

As usual, the debate in the Council also became the occasion for stating a series of needs, problems, and suggestions on many aspects of the concrete life of the clergy. Everyone saw the need for the schema to set down the lines for a future application of its contents in different ecclesial contexts. With this in mind, Guyot's written intervention, which had been worked up by the French study group, pushed toward decentralization by proposing the addition to the schema of a norm similar to the one introduced into the schema on priestly training, that is, a statement on the responsibility of the episcopal conferences.[172] Others, however, proposed the compilation of a single, practical directory.

This concern with the more practical aspects of the question was reflected in the myriad interventions that took up individual questions of daily life. The discussion moved from the age-old debate about ecclesiastical garb to the intervention of American Bishop Leven, devoted entirely to the person of the assistant pastor.[173] The question of community life for the clergy was raised once again; some bishops were strongly in favor of this, but the schema only "recommended" it. Spanish Bishop García Lahiguera proposed the institution of a feast of Christ the Supreme

[169] See *AS* IV/4, 686–88. Other members of the *Coetus Internationalis Patrum* sent in a written intervention in defense of the law of celibacy (Carli and de Castro Mayer [*AS* IV/5, 255–58 and 295–99, respectively]).

[170] *AS* IV/5, 34–36. To the text of his intervention Bea attached a lengthy document containing suggestions for improving the schema.

[171] Bacci also indulged in sarcasm with reference to the ecumenical anxieties of the head of the secretariat: "It is an error to hope that by 'flattering' the Oriental Orthodox clergy, one can win their return 'to the one flock under the one Shepherd,' as Christ says" (*AS* IV/5, 209).

[172] *AS* IV/4, 744–46.

[173] *AS* IV/5, 52–55.

and Eternal Priest.[174] Msgr. Segedi from Yugoslavia stressed, among other things, the care of sick priests and the necessity of a sermon at funerals.[175]

After a series of further interventions, each signed by over seventy fathers in keeping with the regulations, the debate ended on October 26. The final intervention was by one of the newest prelates at the Council, Msgr. Pellegrino; the chronicler in *Le Monde* described his address as "a praise of intelligence." The new Archbishop of Turin encouraged priests to engage in intellectual activity, and his intervention won the agreement of a body made up of cardinals and bishops, including Bea, Lercaro, and C. Colombo, but also Siri, Ruffini, and Confalonieri.[176]

Taken as a whole, this final conciliar debate did not elicit any expressions of great enthusiasm. According to Rouquette, it was "a discussion that showed no depth and dragged on and on."[177] In fact, the repetition of the arguments on both sides often hindered clear-eyed analysis of the condition of priests at the time. All in all, the tendency was for scattered remarks in which very diverse needs and concerns came out, sometimes closely connected with the individual father's place of origin and limited in scope.

On that same day the non-Catholic observers met at the secretariat. Congar presented the schema on priests and sparked a stimulating debate ("a marvelous debate," according to Lawrence). Although it had only an indirect influence on the development of the schema, it showed an interesting confluence of concerns and sensibilities. Danish theologian K. E. Skydsgaard began the discussion with an address that drew the rapt attention of all for its customary theological and spiritual depth. At several points the schema urged priests to follow the way of holiness by sketching a kind of ideal portrait that risked being impossible in practice. The Lutheran theologian asked: "Isn't it a bit much? If I were a young priest — or even a priest of my age — I think I would completely give up the attempt. I would become despondent." Could not this call to holiness of life be expressed in humbler, less legalistic language, and put more emphasis on human weakness in order to exalt the grace of God? This intervention won the approval of Congar and Willebrands.[178]

---

[174] Ibid., 179–83. The intervention of the Spanish bishop was signed by 194 fathers.

[175] Ibid., 173–75. This again was a joint intervention, signed by over seventy fathers.

[176] Ibid., 200. The intervention had 158 signers (see Fesquet, *Drama of Vatican II*, 731–32).

[177] Rouquette, *La fin d'une chrétienté*, 628. Aubert called it a "dull" debate and cited a similar appraisal by X. Rynne ("I testi conciliari," 332).

[178] For an account of the meeting, see Horton, *Vatican Diary 1965*, 120–24. The complete text of the address is in K. E. Skydsgaard, "Report on the Fourth Session of the

On the other hand, the successive interventions of Nissiotis and Verghese drew a broad contrast between the Orthodox and the Catholic conceptions of priesthood. The emphasis placed by Nissiotis on the derivation of the priestly role from the community was matched by Congar's emphasis on the relationship between priest and bishop that is established by ordination. But there did not appear to be any irreconcilable differences in the fundamental theological idea of priesthood, and F. Thijssen, one of the theologians of the secretariat, asked whether these conceptions could not somehow be combined.

The concrete situation of priests and the pastoral dimensions of their ministry also became the subject of comparison. The intervention of Lawrence, an Anglican, described a situation in his own Church that was very like the one that came to light in the hall. The "crisis" of the clergy was a sign of the need to rediscover, in today's real world, the motivations for pastoral work. Other Protestant observers found the subject of little interest and the terms of the debate rather foreign, although Reid, a Calvinist, observed that Congar in his address used the expression "prophet, priest, and king," which, he said, would have pleased Calvin greatly.[179] H. Faber, delegate of the International Association for Religious Freedom, stressed the need to study the problem from a sociological and not solely a theological point of view; the present time, he noted, was characterized by the rapid transformation of the forms of leadership. It is difficult to say what influence this debate had on the subsequent revision of the text, even if, it might be presumed, some observers handed in written contributions.[180]

On October 27, Thomas Falls, a pastor in Philadelphia, spoke at the Council. The gesture had a symbolic value, considering the troubled history of the schema that had caused many fathers to remark that the Council was more or less forgetting priests. It was not possible, of course, to

---

Second Vatican Council n. 5, Enclosure II," 3 pp., in ACO, 7.24. Dietzfelbinger called Skydsgaard's address the most important of the entire debate ("55. Bericht," 1-2).

[179] See Horton, *Vatican Diary 1965*, 123. Horton himself was rather skeptical with regard to the discussion on the relationship between priest and bishop, because he saw in it a claim to measure quantitatively the divine grace granted to the ministers of the Church. L. Vischer, who said nothing about this meeting in his reports, spoke up only briefly to say that the schema dealt too simplistically with the problem of the historical origin of ministries in the Church (ibid., 122–23).

[180] Skydsgaard's intervention was passed on to the secretariat. Lawrence was asked to write down his address, but he did not do so. Finally, during the meeting G. Baum promised Vischer that he would send on to the commission Vischer's remarks about the superficiality of the historical section of the schema (origin of the figures of bishop, priest, and deacon).

expect from this intervention a contribution that would resolve the problems raised in the schema. Falls repeated many of the points made during the debate; he raised the problem of economic support for priests, and at the end he stressed the need to describe the traits of priestly spirituality as compared with the spirituality of the laity and of religious. His appraisal of the schema was positive, although he did point out some deficiencies. All in all, the general vision of the priest that emerged was very like the one defended by the bishops and theologians of the minority, both in the commission and during the general debate: a focus on the spiritual and liturgical dimension, but also a strong reminder of the missionary aspect and of solidarity with the people of our day.[181]

With this intervention the debate on the schema came to a definitive end and discussion was once again left to the commission and a new phase in the revision of the text.

C. The Work of the Commission

The debate in the hall had yielded a great many suggestions for the revision of the schema. Some of them were decidedly critical; some proposed a complete reworking of the schema with the material restructured. The general view of the schema, however, was positive, and the final straw vote confirmed it. Asked whether the schema was a good basis for a further revision, 1,507 of the 1,521 fathers present voted yes.

In his final report on October 16 Marty had set down some broad directives for this revision; these included some suggestions that had emerged earlier, both at the meetings in the Domus Mariae and in the debate in the hall (missionary aspect, responsibility of the episcopal conferences for applying the decree). At the end of the first part of the debate the commission met for an initial examination of the observations made, summarized in a document compiled by the secretariat. During the meeting Marty emphasized the request of many fathers for a less hortatory and simpler style in the schema and seemed also to be echoing what Skydsgaard had asked for at the meeting of the observers. In addition to the plan for revision presented by the reporter himself, there were plans from Döpfner and Suenens, but after a short discussion Marty's was adopted with some changes. On a few specific points there were also requests

---

[181] For the intervention of T. Falls, see *AS* IV/5, 548–50.

from above: the Pope asked that account be taken of the corrections proposed by Maximos IV on the subject of married priesthood. Congar cited, in addition, a letter of Dell'Acqua in which he asked that the text on the evangelical counsels be reworked by bringing out the specific character of priesthood when compared with religious life.[182]

The work was divided among six subcommissions, each with a small number of members and experts; the various parts of the schema were to be reworked in the space of a few days, since the plenary commission was to meet soon.[183] The subcommissions did their work from October 20 to October 26, in less than ideal conditions. Congar was charged with revising some sections but complained of the insufficiency of available material; the composite document prepared by the secretariat extrapolated the various proposed corrections but did not provide the complete texts of the interventions of the bishops. The work of the third subcommission had to be completely redone because of the lack of experience of some experts (Tillmann, in particular), who rewrote the sections completely, without taking into account the straw vote that bound the work of revision to the text discussed in the hall.[184] Everything was being done in haste. In addition, the work was being done while the debate was still going on; interventions were made on October 25 and 26, and the texts of the suggestions made in these addresses were therefore added when the work was done.[185]

The work of the subcommissions continued on the mornings of October 27, 28, and 29, while in the afternoons the commission met for plenary sessions. Minutes are lacking, and Congar's diary provides the sole, though partial, account of the meetings.[186] The French theologian singled

---

[182] For a detailed account of the meeting on October 20 at the Congregation of the Council in the presence of a limited group of members and experts (Marty, Nagae, Vilnet, Del Portillo, Herranz, Lécuyer, Martelet, Frisque, Oclin, Denis, Congar, Tillmann, and Wulf), see *JCongar*, October 20, 1965; II, 442–44. Congar noted the predominance of French speakers present.

[183] Secretary Del Portillo, some private notes on the history of the schema, in Del Portillo papers, in the Archivio Generale Postulazione, XL cart. 1, p. 12. According to Congar's diary there were five subcommissions: (1) introduction and nos. 1, 6, 7, 8, and 19 (Congar and Martelet); (2) nos. 2, 3, 4 (Nagae, Martelet); (3) nos. 11, 12, 13, 5 (Denis, Vilnet, Tillmann, and Frisque); (4) nos. 14, 15, 17 (Lécuyer and Wulf); and (5) nos. 16, 18 (Onclin). See *JCongar*, October 20, 1965; II, 442–44.

[184] *JCongar*, October 25, 1965; II, 451.

[185] See the document that brought together the proposals made in this second phase of the debate: "Emendationes in Schema Decreti De Ministerio et vita presbyterorum a nonnullis Episcopis ex Argentina, Gallia etc., sociatis curis, propositae," 21 pp., in AGP, XXXVII, cart. 1.

[186] *JCongar*, October 27–29, 1965; II, 454–58.

out the efficiency and accuracy of the work of Msgr. Conway, who presided at the meetings, and of Lécuyer, the secretary. The discussion was lively but also scattered over particular points, since the mass of suggestions developed in recent days was enormous; in addition, there recurred the tendency of the members to support this or that particular proposal: "Everyone's clinging to his own little idea." Congar also remarked on the difficulty the bishops had in grasping the theological problems in depth; this was shown by the unexpected ease with which the members approved the introduction of the Pauline vision of priesthood in Romans 15:16, the innovative character of which they clearly had had difficulty in grasping.

At the final meeting the commission focused its attention on two points. A lengthy debate arose over the need to retain the word "legitimately" in referring to the authority to which a priest owed obedience. According to some, the adverb risked being offensive when applied to papal authority; according to others, it was simply useless. The final vote decided to omit it from the text. The brief reference to worker-priests likewise caused widespread puzzlement. A conciliar document seemed the wrong place for a question that was, first of all, limited to a few special situations, and second, was by its nature merely temporary (inasmuch as a recent agreement between the French episcopate and Rome authorized an experiment for three years[187]) and that, above all, risked encouraging an unauthorized lack of control in pastoral experiments by priests. It was decided finally to keep the text but to tone it down.

From the plenary meeting, after a final work of stylistic revision, there emerged the new text of the schema that was sent to Felici on November 3, together with a proposed schedule of votes in the hall.[188] This new text reflected the contents of the debate in the hall; a simple glance revealed that most of the sections had been radically revised, although without change in their place in the overall plan. The only sections that still looked, even in their size, as they had in the preceding version were those dealing with the problem of the distribution of clergy (no. 10), the care taken for priestly vocations (no. 11), and the problems of social security for priests (no. 21). As for the rest, a radical revision of contents can

---

[187] The authorization for a small group of worker-priests was given for a limited, three-year period under the supervision of the Episcopal Committee for the Mission to Workers, of which Msgr. Veuillot was president. For the text of the communiqué printed after the meeting of the episcopal conference on October 23, 1965, along with a interview given by Veuillot, see *DC* 62, cols. 1990–94.

[188] Letter of Del Portillo to Felici, November 3, 1965 (*AS* V/3, 475).

be observed, as well as a quantitative increase in the material and, in some cases, a change in the very structure of the paragraphs.

One important new thing in the introduction was the inclusion among the addressees of the decree of religious priests engaged in the care of souls; on the other hand, there was no trace of the often-made request about the responsibility of the episcopal conferences in making concrete applications of the norms. The first chapter, on the nature of priesthood (revised by Congar), was extensively altered through the acceptance of many of the suggestions made in the hall. The former paragraph 1 was lengthened and broken into two parts.

In the first part (on the nature of the presbyterate) the reference to the role of the Holy Spirit in priestly ordination was restored (it had been present in an earlier version of the text but had been overlooked in the text presented in the hall). Many of the fathers had noticed the omission and had asked that it be included.[189] Also emphasized was the christological character of the teaching on priesthood, this through a reference to the now well-known passage in Romans 15:16. Lastly, the addition of a wholly new final sentence made it possible to underscore the unity of the priestly mission that lay behind any distinction between liturgical/sacramental activity and the evangelization of the world. The second part dealt with the condition of the priest in the world and used one of the formulations suggested by the Argentinean and French bishops regarding the presence of the priest in the midst of humanity as shepherd and proclaimer of the word.

The second chapter, on priestly ministry, was likewise subdivided, this time into three parts (I. Functions of Priests; II. Priests' Relations with Others; III. Distribution of Priests, and Priestly Vocations). The first two had been thoroughly revised, while the third was the only part of the schema that remained practically untouched. In the first part (revised by the subcommission composed of Nagae and Martelet) the new text explicitly made preaching the principal task of priests, while also underlining the missionary aspect, in continuity with the pattern followed in *Lumen gentium,* where, applied to bishops, it spelled out the three functions of preaching, celebration of the Eucharist, and government of the Church.

Interpreting the thought of many fathers who had taken part in the debate in the hall, the commission then introduced a very explicit section

---

[189] See the interventions of Guyot, Léger, Suenens, Meouchi, and D'Avack (*AS* IV/4, 804–5). On this point see G. Rambaldi, "Natura e missione del presbiterato nel decreto *Presbyterorum ordinis,* n. 2: Genesi e contenuto del testo," *Gregorianum* 50 (1969), 239–60.

on the need to adapt sermons to the concrete conditions of the lives of the faithful. As for the other functions of priests (minister of the Eucharist and governor of the people of God, nos. 5 and 6), the most important changes were the introduction of a reference to penance, borrowed from Giovanni Colombo's intervention in the hall,[190] and of a passage on the role of a priest in forming a community vitalized by the spirit of the Church's catholicity and universality. This took over some suggestions of Bea and Doi, and, though in a different form, those contained in Lercaro's written intervention.

The second part of the second chapter, on the priest's relations with other members of the church (bishops [no. 7], other priests [no. 8], laity [no. 9]), had been revised by Congar. In general, the paragraphs were not greatly affected but kept the structure they had had in the preceding text; only on some particular points were important additions or corrections made. A question debated at length had been that of the "presbyteral senate," that is, a body that would assist the bishop in the governance of the diocese. Given the contrasting visions of this body, the commission decided to keep the proposal as originally inspired and formulated. It accepted the word "senate" suggested by Spanish Bishop Fernández Conde, but did not give a detailed description of this body's tasks and status; these would have to be decided by the Commission for the Revision of the Code of Canon Law. For this reason, the commission rejected the request of Ruffini and other bishops that the consultative character of this presbyteral senate be specifically stated.

Then there was the much-discussed question of associations of priests, which some regarded as an important help in the priestly mission, and others saw as a disruptive element in carrying out the work of priests in their dioceses. On this point the commission rejected the proposal of Msgr. Jubany, supported by 391 fathers, that such associations be under the authority of the bishops or the episcopal conferences. The most important addition was a statement on the fundamental unity of priestly work, despite a variety of activities or external tasks (from pastoral ministry to

---

[190] The changes in the text were flagged and justified by the commission in a report attached to the schema given to the fathers ("Relationes de singulis numeris" [*AS* IV/6, 389–405]). In this report the interventions of the bishops are identified by numbers that can be understood only by way of the indexes published by Carbone in *AS*, "Appendix altera," 173–79. Carbone (173) names his sources, which were three documents of the commission: "Animadversiones in Schema Decreti 'De ministero et vita presbyterorum' oretenus vel in scriptis factae" (October 19, 1965, 44 pp.; the original form is in AGP, XXXVII, cart. 1); "Emendationes a nonnullis episcopis ex Argentina et Gallia propositae" (nos. 364–409); and "Animadversiones card. Julii Döpfner" (nos. 410–93).

a commitment to manual labor). In this statement the echo of various interventions on the work done by priests, whether manual or intellectual, could be heard.

The new version of no. 9, on relations between priests and laity, accepted a suggestion of Rossi and forty-three other Brazilian bishops: a citation (not a literal one) from *Lumen gentium* was introduced on the necessary freedom of the laity in developing initiatives and taking responsibility within the Church. Similarly, at the end of the section the relations of the priest with non-Catholics and more generally with non-Christians was stated in a simpler and more orderly way by referring to the decree *Unitatis Redintegratio* and by adopting Alfrink's suggestion that the order followed in the preceding text be reversed and mention of non-Catholics come before mention of non-Christians.

The third chapter of the schema (on the life of priests) had undergone an obvious transformation, especially in the part on the spiritual life. This chapter, too, was subdivided into three main parts (I. The Call of Priests to Perfection; II. Special Spiritual Demands in the Life of Priests; III. Aids for the Life of Priests). There were so many rewritings and additions to the first part (revised by Vilnet's subcommission) that few traces remained of the preceding text. Following the suggestions of such fathers as Léger, Döpfner, Bea, and Rossi, the commission connected its words on holiness not so much with the personal efforts of the individual priest as with the ministry itself and its sacramental nature. Along the same lines, the text of November 1964 was restored in no. 12, with suitable modifications.

An attempt was made to reduce the excessively hortatory tone of the text discussed in the hall without being too radical; for example, the commission did not accept the proposal of the Indonesian bishops to remove the final paragraph of no. 12, which was purely and simply an exhortation to holiness. In no. 13 some suggestions were introduced that came from the interventions of Léger, Rossi himself, and de Provenchères; the result was a new and lengthy insertion on the importance of listening to the word. No. 14, on the unity of the priest's life, was inspired by the interventions of Léger, Baudoux, Charue, and Cardinal Roy to speak of the foundation of this unity, namely, the priest's relationship with Christ, the Good Shepherd.

The structure that the second part of this chapter (revised by Lécuyer and Wulf) had had in the preceding version was radically altered. The text presented in the hall had been the object of criticism by many fathers, among them Döpfner, Suenens, Roy, Charue, and a group of thirty-two

Italian bishops. The decisive intervention, however, was by the Pope himself, who, through Dell'Acqua, suggested that the commission make the needed distinction between the spirituality of priests and the spirituality of religious, which is based on the evangelical counsels. For this reason the former no. 14 ("The Evangelical Counsels in the Life of Priests") was replaced by three distinct sections (nos. 15–17) in the new text; these were independent of one another and organized the material in a somewhat different way.

The first number touched on the subject of humility and obedience in the life of priests. This text was almost completely new and tied the subject of obedience directly to what had been said about pastoral charity in the preceding numbers. The second new number dealt with ecclesiastical celibacy and, while preserving a good deal of the preceding text, made some important additions. The demand, emerging from the debate, that greater attention be paid to the Oriental married clergy, was satisfied by the addition of a passage from an anonymous father "whose remarks were passed on to this conciliar commission, with a recommendation by the Secretariat of State, by order of the Supreme Pontiff." We may see behind the anonymity the intervention of Maximos IV, which had not been read in the hall. Another important addition was an insertion at the end on celibacy as a gift to the Church; this, however, seems to have been the doing of the commission itself rather than a suggestion from the fathers.[191]

The third and last number (no. 17) resulted from the combination of a part of the former no. 14, devoted to the subject of poverty, with the former number 17 ("The Right Use of Possessions"), as proposed, once again, in the interventions of Léger and Döpfner. It took the form of a general discourse on the relationship of the priest to earthly goods. The first part of this number repeated verbatim the intervention of Döpfner, which thus became a new introduction to the section. For the remainder of the section the two preceding texts were simply reworked with some additions and changes of detail.

The third part of the third chapter was revised by various experts within the commission. No. 18 ("Helps in Promoting the Spiritual Life") was almost completely changed by Lécuyer, who here again gave greater

---

[191] In the "Relationes de singulis numeris" that accompanied the new version of the schema the commission offered an outline of the way in which no. 16 was structured; starting with the remark that celibacy does not belong to the essence of priesthood and moving on through the theological and pastoral reasons justifying its suitability, the section went on to assert the necessity of not changing the practice of the Western Church and ended by describing celibacy as a "gift" to the Church.

room to the role of the Holy Spirit in the spiritual life. No. 19 ("Study and Pastoral Knowledge"), revised by Vilnet, arose from a retrieval of the old no. 5 and underwent a substantial reduction in length for reasons of clarity. Nos. 20 and 21, which had been entrusted to W. Onclin, a canonist, marked the end of this part. The first of the two numbers ("A Just Remuneration for Priests") had given rise to many interventions on a widely perceived problem and now profited by some suggestions made in the hall; to give but one example, the commission accepted the principle set down by Melkite Bishop Nabaa that stated the obligation to guarantee priests an "average" lifestyle, that is, one that enables them to live "neither in luxury nor in distress." On the other hand, the commission rejected the suggestion of some that the standards governing the support of priests be set by the episcopal conferences.

The schema ended with a "Conclusion and Exhortation" (no. 22). This arose from a reworking by Congar of the old text, to which was prefixed a new part on the situation of the clergy in today's world. This satisfied the request of many bishops (Suenens, first of all, but also Meouchi, Döpfner, Charue, Alfrink, and Rugambwa) that the schema not ignore the difficulties and challenges that the rapid social transformations of the twentieth century raised for the Church and its pastors.

D. The Intervention of the Pope and the Presentation of the Corrections

The new text with the commission's corrections was distributed in the hall on November 9 for the anticipated vote. Meanwhile, however, an intervention of Paul VI, transmitted as always through the Secretariat of State, threatened to block the schema's advance. The further observations of the Pope reached the commission by way of Felici and were accompanied by other observations on the *De apostolatu laicorum* and the *De missionibus*.[192] A quick examination by the leaders of the commission showed that the Pope's observations had little relevance, and for this reason the secretary, Del Portillo, asked permission of Felici to take these observations into account only in the following phase of the work — the *expensio modorum* — in order not to block the printing of the schema.[193]

---

[192] The papal note, dated November 6, 1965, was attached to a letter from Dell'Acqua to Felici, November 6, 1965 (*AS* V/3, 504; the note is on 507–8).

[193] Letter of Del Portillo to Felici, November 8, 1965 (*AS* V/3, 531). For Felici's agreement, see Felici to Del Portillo, November 11, 1965 (ibid., 537–38).

What were Paul VI's concerns with the schema? It must be noted, first of all, that his remarks were on the text earlier distributed to the fathers in the hall, except, probably, for the section of celibacy, the new version of which had been sent to him at the end of October.[194] In other words, he was commenting on an outdated text; the later work of the commission had already incorporated the observations emerging from the debate in the hall. The Pope's document had nine points, of which at least four consisted simply of the addition of single words meant to clarify or nuance some concepts expressed in the schema. The new text had already accepted the requirements that underlay the Pope's corrections, although without using the formulations he proposed. Two other corrections took the form of general observations on some points of the schema, but without a precise indication of how the text was to be changed. For example, the Pope suggested that at its beginning the schema stress that the main function of the priest has to do with God first and only then with the faithful. Similarly, the Pope wanted a greater emphasis on the importance of mental prayer, particular devotions, in the spirituality of priests.

The remaining three points in the papal document were general observations accompanied by concrete proposals that represented the Pope's belated participation in the debate. First of all, Paul VI wanted a clearer expression of the relationship between pastoral charity and Christian perfection, which was described too weakly in the schema. But in this case, too, the commission's revision of the text had rendered the remarks obsolete. Second, the Pope wanted the schema to give a clearer basis for the need for ongoing priestly formation after ordination. According to Paul VI, this ongoing formation was required by "the complexity of present-day life in society" and by the speed of social and cultural changes. For this reason the proposal to establish suitable institutes of pastoral studies could have "an important role in the success of Vatican II, comparable to that of the establishment of seminaries by the Council of Trent." In fact, this was a proposal partially contained in the text of October 1965; the new text of November had taken this over and made it more specific, so that the Pope's intervention seemed authoritative encouragement of a path already taken.

In fact, the only really new proposal contained in the Pope's note had to do with the section on celibacy: "It seems opportune to propose that, in order to give clerical celibacy the character and value of a fully free act done with a view to priestly ordination, *an explicit public vow* be

---

[194] See the letter of Felici to P. Macchi, October 30, 1965 (*AS* VI/4, 587).

taken before major orders: an explicit vow that could be temporary for
the subdiaconate and perpetual for the diaconate (or the presbyterate).
In addition, it might be proposed that every priest renew this vow annually on Holy Thursday before celebrating or participating in the holy mass
that commemorates the institution of the priesthood and the Eucharist."
This papal suggestion could have been the most awkward for the leaders
of the commission,[195] but once it became clear that the Pope's intervention was not authoritative, they included it among the great many corrections by bishops that had been collected in the hall. In addition, such
an inclusion was inevitably destined for failure, inasmuch as "such an
addition would add something substantial to a text already approved by
the Council."[196]

Paul VI's intervention thus proved to be, for practical purposes, without influence on the course of the schema that reached the hall for votes
on November 12 and 13, 1965. The meeting on November 12 began with
the celebration of the liturgy according to the rite of the Ruthenian
Catholic Church. The liturgy memorialized St. Josaphat, a missionary
and martyr in the Ukraine in the seventeenth century (the choice of
St. Josaphat as a patron of Christian unity caused great puzzlement among
the observers[197]). After some interventions of episcopal conferences on
the subject of indulgences, the morning passed wearily from an intervention of Felici in which he clarified that lectures given by progressive
theologians outside the Council had no official status,[198] to the reading of
the text of the schema on the ministry and life of priests. A report by
Marty led into the votes on the schema, as he emphasized the key points

---

[195] Del Portillo wrote to Felici: "I really think it can be said that the text of the schema,
as now corrected, already satisfies almost all the attached observations. It is a fact, however, that the requirement of an explicit vow of chastity does not come up in the text of
no. 16 of the schema, which refers to celibacy" (AS V/3, 531).

[196] In the booklet containing the *expensio modorum,* the text of the papal note was
cited (without naming its author) in order to justify the amendment in question (see
AS IV/7, 217).

[197] Horton, half seriously and half in jest, offered a bold parallel: this was like regarding Luther as a patron of unity because he had a real desire for unity in the Church (see
Horton, *Vatican Diary 1965,* 143).

[198] According to Congar, Felici's intervention was the result of requests from higher
up and had particularly in mind lectures of Schillebeeckx on the subjects of transubstantiation and marriage (see *JCongar*, November 19, 1965; II, 480). Felici's speech inevitably
evoked protests from a group of Brazilian bishops who saw themselves exposed to "deri-
sion" from the general congregation (AS VI/4, 624–25), as well as a protest to the moderators, again by South American bishops, against attributing any official character to lectures organized by the *Coetus Internationalis Patrum* ("Petitio plurium Patrum,"
December 13, 1965 [AS VI/4, 610–11]).

of this phase of revision: the description of the priest as minister of Christ, with a ministry embracing both the cultic and the apostolic dimensions (according to the teaching of St. Paul); the new connection of the subject of holiness with the ministry rather than with the doctrine on the evangelical counsels; and the improved organization of the material due to some shifts in the placement of the parts.[199]

After the reading of the text the voting began and continued into the following day, according to a schedule determined by the commission. The individual numbers of the decree were voted on: the votes could be *placet* or *non placet*. Meanwhile corrections were collected (with the addition, therefore, of a vote *placet iuxta modum*) on the larger sections of the text: Introduction, Chapter I, chapter II, and chapter III, now divided into three articles. Thus a total of six votes were taken that allowed a *placet iuxta modum* vote. The result was an insignificant number of negative votes (between 2 and 16) but a large number of *placet iuxta modum* votes (from a minimum of 95 for chapter II, art. I, to 568 for chapter II, and 630 for chapter III, art. II).[200]

The meeting on Saturday, November 13, ended a little early in order to allow the fathers and observers to set off for Florence, where the celebrations for the seventh centenary of the death of Dante Alighieri were to be held.[201] The next week began a new phase of work for the commission, to which Felici gave a deadline of November 24 for the revision of the text in the light of the *modi* received.[202] These numbered 5,671 in number, distributed unequally over the various numbers of the schema; it became immediately clear which were the critical points of the text on which the views of the assembly were still divided. Over half of them, for example, concentrated on three numbers of the schema: no. 16, on ecclesiastical celibacy (1,331 proposals); no. 18, on helps for the spiritual life of priests (972); and no. 8, on cooperation among priests (762).[203]

---

[199] See *AS* VI/4, 341–44.

[200] We derive these numbers from the document that sums up the work of the commission (AGP, XL, 1, p. 12). For the other chapters the numbers of *placet iuxta modum* votes were, respectively, 361 for the introduction and chapter I, and 544 for chapter III, art. III, with the number of voters shifting between 2,058 and 2,154.

[201] See Caprile, V, 381–82.

[202] See the letter of Felici to Ciriaci, November 13, 1965 (*AS* V/3, 542).

[203] See the report of Del Portillo in Del Portillo papers, 13. The individual numbers of the schema are listed, and alongside each the number of amendments; here we see that there were also 187 *modi* having to do with the title, and 43 on the structure of the schema. The total number does not agree with the "almost 9,700" *modi* mentioned by Congar (*JCongar*, November 21, 1965; II, 482), but the source (Del Portillo) of the number we have given is sure.

The commission collected and subdivided the amendments, which were then given to a special subcommission for examination and for possible changes in the text of the schema.[204]

During these days the commission received three requests, as always by way of the Secretariat of State, for further changes in the schema. According to the regulations, there was no room for further corrections to be made in the text, apart from the moment when *modi* were requested; but these requests proved to be in large measure belated channels for needs that had been forgotten or neglected rather than interventions on particular points in the revision of the text. By way of Father Philippe, secretary of the Congregation for Religious, Father Ignace Gillet, abbot general of the Trappists, sent the Pope a long letter in which he complained of possible dangers that the approval of the schema on priests might entail for monasteries of the contemplative clerical orders.[205] At almost the same time a similar request reached the commission from curial circles; Titular Bishop Msgr. Gino Paro, of the Pontifical Ecclesiastical Academy, sent Cicognani an appeal from Jesuit M. Flick in favor of "priests who are officials of the Curia," whom he thought had been unjustly passed over in the fervent debate over "worker-priests" and "teaching priests."[206]

Quite different in its content was the letter of French Bishop Renard, who turned directly to Paul VI and pointed out two serious deficiencies in the schema. Calling to mind some recent pronouncements of the magisterium and in particular the Pope's own encyclical *Ecclesiam suam*,

---

[204] Del Portillo's report does not tell who the members of this subcommission were, but there were surely six of them: Marty, Onclin, Lécuyer, Del Portillo, Herranz, and Congar (*JCongar*, November 17, 1965; II, 477).

[205] According to Gillet, the schema, which was built on ministry as its central theme, passed over in silence the presence in the Church of a numerous throng (1,899 in the Trappists alone) of consecrated priests far removed from the active ministry and devoted to contemplation. After pointing out this lacuna in the text, Gillet admitted that he had no confidence in the possibility of improving the text through a presentation of amendments, since the subject would interest only a limited sector of the conciliar assembly (see the letter of Dell'Acqua to Felici, November 13, 1965, with the attached letter of P. Philippe to Dell'Acqua, November 12, and the letter of I. Gillet to Philippe, November 10 [*AS* V/3, 543–46]).

[206] The tone was obviously polemical, but the letter ended with an appeal for support of priests working in the Curia: "A reference to them would be a source of consolation and an incentive for those priests, who are not few, who pass a good part of their lives, or even their entire lives, at their desks, expediting procedures in aid of the work of the Holy Father, the bishops, religious institutes, and so on." See the letter of Dell'Acqua to Felici, November 17, 1965, with the enclosed letter of G. Paro to Cicognani, November 15, 1965 (*AS* V/3, 570–71).

the French prelate noted the absence from the schema both of a specific reference to the responsibility of bishops in the sanctification of their priests and of any mention of the laws of the Church as an obligatory point of reference for priests. Both petitions repeated some amendments offered on the preceding days but then rejected by the commission.[207] Renard's request, then, had no effect; it was a belated reassertion of the Thomistic theology of the priesthood that had been left behind in the development of the schema.

During the commission's plenary meetings on November 19 and 22, 1965, the work of the special subcommission was approved, and the amended text could now return to the hall for the final phase of revision connected with the *expensio modorum*. On December 2, in an atmosphere now affected by the imminent end of the Council, Marty gave his final report as he presented the amended text. It was clear at once that the changes made in the text were quite limited, and the report simply explained the choices made by the commission on some of the points most debated.

Looking at the schema as a whole, Marty dwelt on the theological qualification of the schema, its title, and its structure. A group of forty-seven fathers had asked that the term *Constitution* be used, thereby giving it the same importance as the major schemas; the commission retained the description *Decree* because of the schema's pastoral character and because from a doctrinal point of view it relied, in this final version, ever more directly on *Lumen gentium*. A group of 139 fathers proposed that the words "especially diocesan [priests]" be added to the title, but it was clear that the emphasis placed on ministry already made the schema of interest to all priests, even religious. The commission had also rejected the request of a group of forty-three bishops to change the arrangement of the sections.[208]

Speaking of the first chapter Marty mentioned the rejection of some requests from the bishops. To those who wanted the treatment to be based on the priesthood of Christ (to be spoken of in no. 2), the reporter replied by pointing once again to the way in which the presentation of doctrine in *Lumen gentium* completed the schema. But among the amendments

---

[207] See the *expensio modorum* in *AS* IV/6, 205–6, where the reference to the "Leges Ecclesiae" is rejected as being superfluous in the context. For Renard's request, see the letter of Dell'Acqua to Felici, November 13, 1965, with the attached note of A. Renard to the Holy Father, "Animadversiones De ministerio et vita presbyterorum," no date, *AS* V/3, 547–48).

[208] For Marty's report, see *AS* IV/7, 106–9; for the general *modi,* see ibid., 114–15.

there had been expressions of dissatisfaction with the doctrine on priesthood in the schema. As we observed above, this teaching had bracketed
the Scholastic definition of priesthood, which focused on the act of
eucharistic consecration. According to some rumors collected by Congar, this difficulty had been raised by, among others, Cardinal Browne,
a Dominican, who was thinking of intervening directly with the Pope.[209]
In response to these criticisms Marty could only explain the dependence
of the schema on the teaching contained in *Lumen gentium,* which had
chosen to see priesthood as a lesser degree of the episcopate and therefore necessarily connected with the doctrine of the three *munera* or functions. It was clear, therefore, that the commission's concern in dealing
with the first, doctrinal part of the schema was to avoid any regression,
that is, the surreptitious reintroduction of positions contrary to the teaching in *Lumen gentium.*[210]

Coming to the second chapter, Marty simply mentioned some of the
changes that had been proposed in the text and had been accepted by the
commission: a fuller reference to the sacraments in no. 5; an insertion on
the pastoral care of religious in no. 6; and finally, a completely new section on the duties of the laity to priests, which had been requested as a
balance to the extended treatment in no. 9 of the duties of priests to the
laity. In contrast, Marty said nothing of the *modi* dealing with no. 8 ("Fraternal Union and Cooperation among Priests"); there had been a sizable
number of such *modi,* dealing essentially with two controverted questions: the acceptance of worker-priests, and associations of priests.

On the first question, 386 bishops signed an amendment asking for the
removal of the reference to worker-priests. This was countered by other
modi in favor of justifying and further encouraging such experiments.
A group of seventy-two bishops asked for the removal of the phrase "with
the approval of authority" and the entrusting to the bishop of all decisions
having to do with atypical pastoral experiments; another sixty-nine asked
for an addition explaining the possibility of fully exercising the priestly
ministry even in exceptional living conditions.[211] In response to these
requests the commission, of course, reminded the fathers that the text

---

[209] *JCongar*, November 22, 1965; II, 483.

[210] But even in this first part many suggestions of the bishops had been accepted. Probably the most coherent addition in chapter I was a sentence on the eschatological dimension of the priestly task; this had been requested by a group of four fathers who bemoaned
the total absence from the schema of any reference to this dimension (see *modi* 38 and 42
[*AS* IV/7, 124–25]).

[211] See *modus* no. 106 (ibid., 163–64).

approved at a general congregation could not be mutilated. For this reason the section would be retained, but with a different formulation that,
in a way, increased the number of precautions by confirming the need for
a kind of "extraordinary" approval by the authorities.[212]

On the question of associations of priests the decisive intervention was
amendment no. 130, presented by two bishops who probably came from
eastern Europe.[213] According to their analysis, the formulation in the text
could provide justification for the existence of the patriotic associations
that had come into existence in socialist countries and that competed with
the action of the bishops. For this reason it seemed necessary to specify
in the text the obligation of receiving some kind of approval from ecclesiastical authority; their suggestion was accepted.[214]

When Marty's report came to the third chapter, it dwelt mainly on the
problem of the sanctification of priests and on ecclesiastical celibacy. In
response to the persistent accusation of having neglected interior, subjective holiness in favor of the objective holiness deriving from ministry, the
reporter announced some changes in the text: the removal of a citation
from Lev 21:8 that connected the holiness of priests directly with the holiness of God; and the addition of some sentences that spoke of the need for
interior holiness in no.12. Marty also reminded the hall of the reaction
elicited by no. 16 on ecclesiastical celibacy; there had been an avalanche
of amendments that had obliged the commission to engage in a patient and
laborious work of mediating between two sides. In short, the *expensio
modorum* marked the final act of the vigorous, even if underground, debate
that had been formally ended by the Pope's intervention on October 11,
but which had continued in different terms and under different conditions.

At this point the subject of debate was not whether or not the law of
ecclesiastical celibacy was to be maintained, but rather what the position

[212] Here is how the sentence read in the corrected text (additions in this final phase are
in italics): "All priests are sent to cooperate in the same work. This is true whether the
ministry they exercise be parochial or supra-parochial; whether their task be research
or teaching; or even if they engage in manual labor and share the lot of the workers,
where that appears to be of advantage and has the approval of the *competent* authority;
or finally if they carry out other apostolic works *or works directed toward the apostolate*"
(ibid., 132).

[213] A group of 124 fathers had already asked that this activity be regulated at the level
of episcopal conferences and that an explicit reference to this effect be introduced into the
text of the schema. The commission, however, had not accepted this *modus* on the grounds
that this type of associationism could have international dimensions and thus be outside
the scope of the conferences' action (see *modus* no. 132 [ibid., 169]).

[214] To the sentence on associations of priests was added the phrase "their statutes having been approved by ecclesiastical authority" (see ibid., 168).

of the schema was to be in regard to future developments. From this perspective, a variety of positions were taken. A group of 123 fathers
who wanted the schema to adopt a kind of neutrality in regard to a possible future debate asked that, in the reference to the law in effect in the
Latin Church, the words "ratifies and confirms" be replaced by a more
neutral "does not change."[215] But the commission regarded this request
as a substantial change in the text approved by the assembly and therefore rejected it.[216]

On the other hand, the commission also decided not to yield to the
more radical requests of those who maintained the superiority of celibacy;
these requests had as their most active representatives some members of
the *Coetus Internationalis Patrum*. Thus the commission rejected the petition of a group of seventy-one fathers for the removal of the sentences
on the noncelibate priesthood of the Oriental Church on the grounds that
the sentences seemed to weaken what was then said about the "suitability" of celibacy to the priestly state.[217] At the same time, the commission
did not accept the suggestion of Paul VI about introducing a public vow
of chastity prior to priestly ordination.

There was, however, a series of more constructive amendments that led
the commission to reformulate some parts of this section in a very structured way. The central part, for example, which dealt with the reasons
why celibacy was "suitable," was changed on the basis of two *modi* presented by a large group of bishops.[218] The result was an overall restructuring of the section; the order in which the arguments for the "suitability" of celibacy were explained was reversed (first, union with Christ;

---

[215] The request was motivated by the lack of any debate on the subject: "In a word:
the Council does not change the existing law and, regardless of what may happen in the
future due to changed circumstances or to worsening pastoral needs, the Council leaves
the entire matter to the attention and study of the Supreme Pontiff. For, in accordance with
the very prudent decision of the Supreme Pontiff this question has not been discussed in
the Council hall. We ought therefore to avoid having the Council again ratify and confirm
a matter on which there has been no discussion among the fathers" (ibid., 214).

[216] In his report Marty also stressed the argument from the universality of the decree,
which therefore ought to take into account the different realities found in the Catholic
Church (ibid., 109).

[217] *Modus* no. 15 on no. 16 of the schema (ibid., 207).

[218] The first, which was signed by 332 fathers, had to do with the addition of a short
insertion that treated celibacy as an essential aspect of a priest's consecration to Christ;
the request was accepted, but in different terms in order to avoid an identification of the
consecration deriving from celibacy with the only real "consecration" deriving from ordination (see ibid., 208). On the basis of this idea of celibacy as founded not only on its
nature as a sign and witness to the divine reality but also on the depth of a priest's union
with Christ, the commission also reformulated the distinction made in the old text between

then, its role as a sign) and conformed to the order followed in the other schemas (especially *Lumen gentium*) as Marty pointed out in his report.[219] The first part, on the married priesthood, was preserved against attacks, but it too was revised in an effort to reestablish an ever better balance in speaking of the two different traditions. The insertion of a reference to the encyclical *Ad catholici sacerdotii* of Pius XI gave proof of the esteem of the entire Church for the tradition of a married priesthood,[220] while emphasis was also placed on the necessity that the married state should precede priestly ordination.[221] There were no substantial changes made in the remainder of the schema.

When Marty had finished giving his report, the voting on the *expensio modorum* began. The votes followed the schedule for votes in November, the schema being subdivided into six parts. It became immediately clear how pleased the bishops were with the schema. Negative votes ranged from 5 for the introduction and chapter I to 38 on chapter II (the question of worker-priests, raised in chapter II, was clearly still leaving its mark). But in the final vote on the text as a whole there were only 11 negative votes. The decree was finally promulgated during the public session on December 7 by an almost unanimous vote (only 4 negative votes out of 2,394 cast).

The approval of the decree satisfied the expectations and criticisms of those who had seen little consideration being given to problems of the clergy during the preceding periods of the Council.[222] A great deal of

---

theological and pastoral reasons supporting the value assigned to celibacy. Another amendment, signed by 289 fathers, pointed out that the theological reasons given in *Lumen gentium* and in the decree on the renewal of religious life as the foundation of the value of celibacy were the same ones that in the present schema were presented as simply reasons of a pastoral kind.

[219] *Modus* no. 21 also cited a parallel correction (supported by 679 fathers) made in *Lumen gentium*. There the idea had been rejected that the sole theological reason in support of celibacy was its value as a sign of and witness to the supernatural life, whereas the other arguments were to be restricted to the practical and pastoral area (see ibid., 211–12). For *modus* no. 17b, see ibid., 209–10; for Marty's report, ibid. 109. On all the vicissitudes of this number, see A. Del Portillo, "Coelibatus sacerdotalis in decreto conciliari *Presbyterorum ordinis*," *Seminarium* 19 (1967), 711–28.

[220] The new version of the text said expressly that "this sacred synod does not intend to change in any way the different tradition that is legitimately in force in the Oriental Churches." Behind this sentence lies *modus* no. 15f, which came from 5 fathers (ibid., 208–9).

[221] The request for this statement came from one bishop: *modus*, no. 15g, ibid., 208.

[222] For a substantially positive appraisal both of the work of the commission and of the leanings of the bishops (an appraisal that probably reflects a certain enthusiasm on the part of the French bishops), see Fesquet, *Drama of Vatican II*, 790–92. According to Alfonso Bonetti of Bologna, an Italian parish priest who had been invited to the Council as an auditor, there was a widespread call among priests for a Vatican III devoted to priests,

progress had been made in comparison with the formulations in the preparatory schemas and the early versions of the *De sacerdotibus*. From a view of the clergy that was linked to the resolution of some concrete problems (the "discipline of the clergy" referred to in the very name of the commission), the authors had, under the pressure of petitions from the bishops, been led to rethink the theology of the priesthood in the light of pastoral and missionary concerns.[223] On the other hand, it was noted in several quarters that the final schema was incomplete because it had not been able to profit by an antecedent, organized reflection on the theology of the presbyterate. As can be seen from the vicissitudes of the commission's work, the lines of renewal that had been developed within French theology (Congar, Colson, and others) had found their way into the schema, but without effecting a complete synthesis; part of this was due to the schema's dependence on the theology of *Lumen gentium*. As a result, later critics could say that the schema had only partially transcended the traditional Scholastic theology of the presbyterate[224] and that it lacked a radical rethinking of the theology of the local Church.[225]

VII. The Laity: A Role in the Church?

The revised text of the schema on the lay apostolate had been sent to the fathers in June 1965, and voting on it was scheduled to begin on September 23. The commission responsible for it held a plenary meeting on September 20 devoted to procedural questions.[226] A new subcommission was created for the purpose of working on the amendments from the bishops; a new chapter (the sixth) had been introduced into the new text,

---

after the two councils devoted respectively to the pope and the bishops (see G. Svidercoschi, *Inchiesta sul concilio* [Rome, 1985], 102).

[223] This shift is also emphasized in Frisque, *Le décret*, 127–28.

[224] In C. Duquoc's view this schema presented a theology of the priesthood that was in the final analysis still tied to Trent and stood side by side with a radical rethinking of priestly functions along missionary lines (see C. Duquoc, "La riforma dei chierici," in *Il Vaticano II e la chiesa*, ed. G. Alberigo and J. P. Jossua [Brescia, 1985], 399–414).

[225] See Dossetti, "Per una valutazione," 57–60.

[226] The agenda was given in the letter convoking the meeting (Glorieux papers, XLII 746). For an overall view of the history of the schema, see A. Glorieux, "Histoire du décret," in *L'apostolat des laïcs,* ed. Y. Congar (Paris, 1970), 91–139; F. Klostermann, "Introduction and Commentary on the Decree on the Apostolate of the Laity," *Commentary*, 3:273–404. On the third period, see *History* 4: chap. 4. On the work of the commission, see M. T. Fattori, "La commissione *De fidelium apostolatu* del Concilio Vaticano II e lo schema sull'apostolato dei laici (maggio 1963–maggio 1964)," in *Experience*, 299–328.

and the already existing five subcommissions presumably did not have the capacity to take on further work.[227]

At the same plenary meeting the members discussed the text of the statement with which Hengsbach, the reporter, was to present the text in the hall. There were no substantial objections to it, but a short discussion did arise regarding the reference to the collaboration of the laity in drafting the schema. The first draft of Hengsbach's report contained a very explicit mention — which Msgr. Castellano thought too "strong" — of the approval of the schema by the lay persons involved. Thanks to a suggestion of Ménager and especially to the interventions of two lay auditors, de Habicht and Sugranyes, a different formulation was worked out that combined references to the new "emphasis" taken in the schema and to the collaboration of the laity in the work of the commission.[228]

A third point discussed was the program for the taking of votes; this, as we have already seen in other cases, was very important, because it allowed the bishops to express their disagreement with particular points of the schema. On this subject the only intervention that gave rise to some debate was Castellano's request that the central part of the schema (chapter IV, nos. 15–19) be submitted to a double vote. The chapter had been radically revised through the insertion of a new section (no. 17); this probably gave rise to the demand for a more detailed examination by the bishops. A vote showed the commission to be divided on the point, and its president, Cardinal Cento, settled the question in favor of splitting the vote into two parts.[229]

In the following days, as the time of voting on the schema drew near, attempts were made to win a postponement to allow the fathers to make

[227] The members appointed to subcommission VI were bishops Larraín, Da Silva, and Bednorz (later replaced, at his request, by Kominek); Moeller, a theologian; and experts Dutch Bishop Ramselaar, Prignon, and Worlock. See *Acta commissionis conciliaris "De fidelium apostolatu,"* 181 (Glorieux papers, L, 811). See also the document "Pro memoria sulla necessità di una 6a Sottocommissione *De apostolatu laicorum,*" 1 p., September 10, 1965 (Glorieux papers, XLII, 743).

[228] We do not have the first version of Hengsbach's statement and therefore must rely solely on the already cited minutes of the meeting. The text of the sentence being discussed reads as follows in the definitive version: "If new emphasis is placed on some points — for example, on the theological foundations, spirituality, the unity and distinction of goals, training, and avoiding the impression of an excessively paternalistic tone — this was done in accordance with the *vota* of the fathers, while attention was also paid to the observations of the lay persons who have worked with us and whom we have consulted" (*Declaratio in ordine ad praeparandas suffragationes* [AS IV/2, 304]).

[229] For the short debate, see *Acta commissionis conciliaris "De fidelium apostolatu,"* 182. Also introduced was an added vote on the introduction. For the final schedule of sixteen votes and their results, see ibid., 183–84.

a more careful analysis of a text that had been extensively revised.
A group of four fathers, among them K. Wojtyła of Poland, asked the
moderators for a change in procedure: the novelties introduced into each
chapter should be explained in detail by the commission, and the fathers
should then be given a few days' time to prepare amendments.[230] A group
of thirty-two fathers from South America made an even more radical
request; given the many novelties in the text, they asked that the debate
in the hall be reopened for two or three days.[231]

Rather than signaling organized opposition to the schema, these
episodes represented yet more attempts to slow the frenetic pace of these
final weeks of the Council's work and to give the assembly a role to play
in decision-making. In addition, the document on the laity was coming
up for a vote at a time when all attention was focused on the vote on the
document on religious freedom (September 21) and on the ensuing start
of debate on the schema on the Church in the modern world (September
23). Amid this widespread lack of attention Felici was in a good position,
while introducing the vote, to remind the hall that the schema had been
distributed over two months before, so one could hardly speak of a lack
of time for analysis. The most that could be done was to allow a few
more days for the presentation of amendments.[232]

The voting began on September 23 and ended two days later. Votes on
the individual articles alternated with votes on the chapters, the latter
allowing the proposal of amendments. There were few negative votes on
the individual parts of the schema; no votes ranged from 3 to 19 and
were cast especially on no. 4 (spirituality of the laity) and nos. 26–27
(the establishment of pastoral councils and cooperation with non-
Catholics). The chapter that elicited the largest number of amendments
was chapter III, on the various fields of the apostolate (311 *placet iuxta
modum* votes). On the following days the subcommission began to study
the proposed amendments on the basis of some common instructions
issued by the leaders of the commission.[233]

---

[230] This was a short petition signed by A. Fernándes, K. Wojtyła, L. Satoshi Nagae, and
M. McGrath ("Petitio quorundam patrum quoad schema de apostolatu laicorum" [*AS* V/3,
374]).

[231] Ibid., 375.

[232] For the text of Felici's statement, see ibid., 374.

[233] Secretary Glorieux assembled the secretaries of the subcommissions on October 27
for an examination of these regulations (see "Ratio agendorum in examinandis 'modis'
schematic 'De apostolatu laicorum,'" September 20, 1965, 2 pp. [Glorieux papers, XLII,
748]). The regulations in question were simply a selection from the instructions in the
conciliar regulations that applied to the work of all the commissions. The document also

During October the work done by the subcommissions was discussed and approved at a plenary meeting, as was the report Hengsbach was to deliver in the Council hall.[234] The text did not appear to have undergone any major changes. The basic decisions of the commission had been approved by the votes of the Council fathers and were now solidly in place. The rejection of contrary amendments made clear the commission's determination not to turn back. Requests for a change in title were rejected. The call for shortening the text because the same subject matter was present in many other conciliar documents was rejected in order to maintain the character of the decree as a synthesis of the main elements belonging to teaching on the laity and to their pastoral care. Some seeming contradictions — or, better, some divergent emphases on parts of the decree — were justified by Hengsbach by the need to safeguard the wide variety of conditions and experiences existing in the Church.

It is impossible to give a detailed picture of the variations introduced by the *modi*, but it can be noted that some parts of the decree caught the attention of the bishops and obliged the commission to revise the text in a more than simply formal way. This was true of no. 4 on the spirituality of the laity, one of the sections that had undergone major changes. In addition to adding a reference to the paschal mystery and to persecutions suffered "for justice's sake" (requested by a group of thirty-eight fathers), it was decided at the plenary meeting to introduce a section (the work, it seems, of Castellano and Streiff) on the special character that the spirituality of lay people can acquire in various life settings (marriage, celibacy, and so on) or in lay associations (such as the third orders) connected with a particular spirituality. This request came from forty-nine fathers.[235]

Similarly, the *modi* on no. 20, on Catholic Action, saw a revival of the debate in the hall. On the one hand were supporters of the central place of this association and of the idea of a hierarchical "mandate"; on the other the enemies of exclusivism, who wanted the section omitted.[236]

---

assigned the end of October as the end of the work on the *modi* (including their approval at a plenary meeting). For the composition of the various subcommissions, see "Subcommissiones pro elaboratione 'Modorum,' 1965," undated (ibid.).

[234] For the text of the first draft of the report, the draft discussed at the plenary meeting, see "Relatio generalis De expensione modorum ad Schema 'De apostolatu laicorum,'" (Glorieux papers, XLV, 777).

[235] For the new text, see *AS* IV/6, 19–20 and 42; see also *Acta commissionis conciliaris "De fidelium apostolatu,"* 188 and 196.

[236] Some maintained the need to include an explicit reference to a mandate; others wanted Catholic Action "to be more clearly recommended"; still others suggested citing Pius XI, who described this association as "the apple of his eye." In contrast, forty-eight

The commission reasserted its choice of a middle way between the divergent tendencies and retained the original text: "The *modi* proposed by many fathers have not been accepted, because the text follows a middle way, as it were, while the *modi* are one-sided."[237]

An important variation, however, was the addition to no. 9 of a section on the role of women, inserted at the suggestion of two bishops. The text they proposed was reworked by Hirschmann; a further, simplified version of it, offered by Rosemary Goldie, a lay auditor, was approved at the plenary meeting.[238] No less important, despite its brevity, was the sentence added to no. 2 (participation of the laity in the mission of the Church), an interpolation (later on regarded as one of the most important elements in the schema) that identified the Christian vocation with vocation to the apostolate.[239]

With the new version sent to the printer, as well as the report on the *expensio modorum*, the history of the text seemed close to completion. But on November 7 Glorieux, the secretary of the commission, was summoned by Felici to receive an urgent letter from Dell'Acqua; this letter accompanied some amendments of the schema requested by the Pope. The commission thus found itself in the awkward position of having to revise the text after its redaction had been completed and it was being printed. Why so late an intervention by Paul VI? The arguments used by Felici in rejecting the requests of the bishops for a delay in the voting could have been applied here with even greater validity, since the schema had been sent to the Pope for his approval in June 1965. The incident can probably be explained by the composite character of Paul VI's observations.[240]

The Pope had certainly written down some amendments to the text during the summer. These were the "Observations made at Castelgandolfo," which occupied the first part of the Pope's set of remarks; they

bishops disparaged the identification of the lay apostolate with Catholic Action and asked for a clarification. Some even asked for the removal of the entire section. For all the requests of the fathers, see *AS* IV/6, 95–100. From other sources we learn that one of the *modi* opposed to the exclusive role assigned to Catholic Action came from Suenens and was composed by B. Häring (*JPrignon*, September 29, 1965 [Prignon papers, 1595, 6]).

[237] *Acta commissionis conciliaris "De fidelium apostolatu,"* 192.

[238] Ibid., 196–97: "Since in our days women are taking an increasingly active share in the whole life of society, it is very important that their participation in the various fields of the Church's apostolate should likewise develop"; see also *AS* IV/6, 61.

[239] This was due to *modus* no. 5 on no. 2 of the schema; it was proposed by a single bishops and accepted without change by the commission. For some brief thoughts on the importance of the addition, see the interview with R. Goldie in Svidercoschi, *Inchiesta sul concilio*, 139.

[240] On the general attitude of Paul VI toward the work of the commissions and on his numerous interventions, see Jan Grootaers, "Le crayon rouge de Paul VI," 316–52.

had not been sent to the commission at once. These were twelve requests for changes; they were of different kinds and were based on different arguments, but the majority of them expressed a concern to have the schema emphasize the legitimate role of authority in the Church. There was a recurrent fear of possible abuses due to the ambiguities in the text of the decree, as the Pope worriedly referred to "undertakings that are more original than constructive" in the field of the lay apostolate.

The Pope asked that the phrase *ius et officium* be inverted to *officium et ius*, evidently to stress the point that every pastoral charge is based on duty (no. 1); for the omission of a short sentence to emphasize the duty of bishops to judge the authenticity of charisms (no. 2); for greater emphasis on the "spiritual duties of the young" in the section devoted to them (no. 7); for the need for small groups to maintain communion with their pastors (no. 9); for an explicit reference to communion with the hierarchy as a guarantee of the fruitfulness of the apostolate (no. 10); the substitution of the weaker term *facultas* for *ius* in the section regulating the foundation of new associations by the laity (no. 11); and, finally, the removal of the expression "implicitly or explicitly," thereby rendering more flexible the need to obtain the consent of the hierarchy when describing any lay undertaking as catholic (no. 12).

Different in their tenor were the amendments having to do with the duty of the laity to carry out "social reforms" inspired by the social teaching of the Church (no. 8);[241] the insertion of a short clause to emphasize the religious finality of the work of the laity in the temporal order (no. 3); the addition of the adjective "legitimate" to the acknowledged autonomy of the laity in the temporal order (no. 4); the reference to the order of charity as the foundation of the apostolate in parishes (no. 5);[242] and the reference to the "rights" of the family rather than simply to its "legitimate autonomy" (no. 6).

But Paul VI focused his attention above all on no. 7, which probably brought together all his worries about the Catholicism that was in process of transformation during the sensitive transition accompanying the end of

---

[241] This amendment was to be rejected by the commission because the subject was raised in no. 7, and it did not seem suitable to raise it again in no. 13. For the text of the papal amendments, see *AS* V/3, 505–7. The minutes of the commission's meeting are in *Acta commissionis conciliaris "De fidelium apostolatu,"* 198–200.

[242] Paul VI wrote: "In general, I have emphasized the suitability of underscoring the necessity of an order of charity, which is determined by the hierarchic discipline of the Church, this also in the following paragraph (page 32, lines 7–24), in order not to show too much favor to undertakings that are more original than constructive" (*AS* V/3, 505).

the Council. "It seems necessary," the Pope wrote, "to add something about the spiritual duties of the young: the duty of obedience to legitimate authorities, especially in the Church (obedience, love, fidelity...); the duty of respect for and trust in their elders; the duty of an attitude of good will toward good traditions."

The Pope's proposals did not reach the commission before the vote in the hall, even though they had been formulated for some time; the last papal audience at Castelgandolfo was held, in fact, on September 8. Of the first twelve amendments proposed at least three dealt with points in the schema that the commission had already modified (in nos. 1, 2, and 9).

In addition, there was some connection between the Pope's action and the presentation of bishops' *modi*, since at least ten of the papal amendments repeated almost literally some of the *modi* presented. But it is not easy to decide in which direction the relationship ran. It is likely that the Pope's notes came into the hands of some trusted bishops and through them entered the *expensio modorum* anonymously. This would explain the late interventions of Paul VI: only at a second stage, when he was disappointed by the results of the commission's work, did he decide to intervene in person.

Congar offered a different explanation when he learned from Ménager of the papal intervention; Congar interpreted it as the result of pressures brought to bear by bishops dissatisfied with the *expensio modorum*. Congar wrote: "As a result, the poor Pope is beginning again what he did not succeed in doing at the end of third session ... on a less sensitive matter.[243] This hypothesis is not easy to reconcile with the date of the Pope's note; it is certain that at the time of the vote in the hall and during the work on the *expensio modorum*, the Pope was not residing in Castelgandolfo. In a later reconstruction of the events, Glorieux regarded the observations set down in the first part of the Pope's note as a text not written by the Pope but "received" by him during the summer.[244] According to this hypothesis we can understand why the same observations appeared in the amendments of the bishops.

It was obvious, however, that the second part of the papal note was closely connected with more recent events at the Council and that its author was Paul VI.[245] This part refers to only the three amendments that

[243] *JCongar*, November 8, 1965; II, 467.

[244] Glorieux spoke of "observations submitted to the Sovereign Pontiff during the summer" (see Glorieux, "Histoire du décret," 135).

[245] The papal note contains but a single date (November 6, 1965), but it is clear that the text was made up of two parts written at different times. This is the only way to explain the presence among the amendments of some requests already satisfied in the *expensio*

were seen as more urgent (no. 7, again, but also nos. 10 and 12). The Pope wrote: "These are also observations that won a sizable number of *modi* from the fathers, thus barely concealing a degree of dissatisfaction with the work of the commission." He expected, therefore, a further intervention by the commission that would do justice, first of all, to the three observations cited, and second, to amendments nos. 5 and 8, which in the *expensio modorum* had received "an improvement that was excessively weak ... given the importance of the subjects being treated." In this case it was certainly plausible that the Pope's behavior was due to pressures from some bishops, although, of course, it is not easy to determine the precise sources.

The commission, which met hurriedly on November 8 after being convoked by telephone, found itself faced with a sensitive task. It must be noted, to begin with, that the discussion did not manifest any scruples connected with obedience to the Pope. On the contrary, the amendments were debated and weighed solely in light of the overall structure of the schema, its internal balances, and a comprehensive vision of its content. In the end, for different reasons, the majority of the observations contained in the two documents were rejected, apart, of course, from the three already explained in the *expensio*.

No. 3 was rejected because the substance of the sentence added by the Pope was already found clearly in other points of the same section. No. 4 was rejected because the addition of the adjective "legitimate" would have required further explanations in the text. No. 5 gave rise to a lively debate. In the view of Ménager, every community, at whatever level in the makeup of the Church, not only the parish, was a field for manifesting the "order of charity." For Streiff and Larraín, the term *parish* covered very different realities, as was clearly shown in South America. The amendment was rejected, then, because it could be interpreted in very different senses.[246] No. 6 was likewise rejected with an appeal to the debate in the hall. Nos. 8 and 10 met the same fate, while in the case of no. 11 (substitution of *facultas* for *ius*) the original term was defended by recourse to a citation of a decree of the Sacred Congregation of the Council from which the term *ius* was taken. Essentially, the only two papal amendments that the commission accepted were nos. 7 and 12. These

modorum (month of October), with which Paul VI shows, in the second part, that he is quite familiar.

[246] "The commission therefore decides that the addition is not to be allowed, because it would not be clearly understood and because, in addition, the proper balance of the text would be disturbed" (*Acta commissionis conciliaris "De fidelium apostolatu,"* 198).

supplied the text of the "variations" that were to be voted on along with the definitive version of the schema.[247]

On November 9, with the backing of Felici, to whom a copy of the minutes of the meeting and of the variations had been sent, the votes were taken, according to the regulations, on the *expensio modorum* of the schema on the lay apostolate. After mass, which was celebrated according to the Byzantine-Melkite rite, and after the announcement of the results of the voting on the *De revelatione*, Hengsbach read his general report on the work of the commission. He first explained the chief amendments made in the text, as well as the lines along which the commission did its work of revision. He then stressed the need of reading the schema in the light of the *Lumen gentium* and of the pastoral constitution on the Church in the modern world (not yet definitively approved). He made no reference to the intervention of the Pope, but the communication of the variations on a separate page made clear that there had been a last-minute intervention.[248]

The outcome of the voting immediately showed very widespread agreement; the largest number of negative votes on the six chapters was 16, while in the final vote on the schema as a whole there were only 2 no votes. Except for some alterations of a stylistic kind (which were also carefully noted in the minutes of the commission) and a last-minute change in the first of the *variationes*, the text that emerged was to receive its final approval during the solemn session on November 18, 1965.[249] In a symbolic act during that session Paul VI himself gave a copy of the document to three male and three female auditors, charging them with its application.

Thus this document, too, came to the end of a troubled history that had begun with a personal decision of John XXIII, who, at Dell'Acqua's suggestion, had established the appropriate preparatory commission. The decree was a complete novelty, being the first document of a council

---

[247] The document given to the fathers contained three *variationes*: the insertion of the words "inspired by obedience and love of the Church" and of others on respect for tradition in no. 12, which dealt with youth; and the removal of "*implicite vel explicite*" in no. 24 of the schema (see *AS* IV/6, 129–30; see also *Acta commissionis conciliaris "De fidelium apostolatu,"* 203).

[248] Horton referred to the *variationes* without connecting them with a papal intervention; instead, he emphasized their lack of impact on the schema as a whole. His attention was focused, rather, on the "important interpolation" on the role of women in the Church (Horton, *Vatican Diary 1965*, 132).

[249] In this final vote there were still two bishops who voted against the schema, in contrast to 2340 Yes votes (*Acta commissionis conciliaris "De fidelium apostolatu,"* 203).

that dealt specifically with the laity. It appropriated many of the impulses that thinking about the laity had produced in the decades before the council, and it represented a move beyond the traditional idea of participation by the laity in the hierarchical apostolate of the Church. In the years immediately following its promulgation, people became aware not only of the great potentialities of the text but also of its limitations (to give but two examples: the lack of a theological definition of a lay person, and a less than complete agreement with the perspective adopted in chapter IV of *Lumen gentium*). If within a few years of its approval it was already possible for some to speak of it as outdated, this was precisely because the dynamics called into play by the document had brought out both the merits and the limits of a schema that opened up wide vistas for the activity of the laity in the Church but also remained bound to some theological and pastoral models of an age now past.[250]

---

[250] The work containing the essay of Glorieux on the history of the schema also contained some interesting appraisals of the situation of the laity a few years after the approval of the decree. These showed clearly a sense of the limits of the decree especially as seen in the light of the historical situation of the Churches. Aubert cites the opinion of R. Rémond, an eminent lay man who was rather critical of the schema, and points rather to the greater potentialities of the chapters on the laity in *LG* (Aubert, "I testi conciliari," 367–68). For a judgment on the commission's work, see Fattori, "La commissione *De fidelium apostolatu*."

CHAPTER IV

THE CHURCH UNDER THE WORD OF GOD

CHRISTOPHE THEOBALD

The events surrounding the final revision of the schema on divine revelation bring us back to the beginning of the fourth period and require us
to review again, but from a different angle, the two months separating the
resumption of the Council's work on September 14, 1965, and the solemn
session on November 18, at which both the dogmatic constitution *Dei
Verbum* and the Decree on the Apostolate of the Laity were promulgated.
Back in the fall of 1964 these two documents had been debated, one after
the other, and they would remain "neighbors" until the final vote.

The reader will recall that the amended text of the future dogmatic constitution had already been distributed on November 20, 1964; the new text
was printed in a parallel column beside the previous text and was accompanied by the reports of Florit (on chapters I and II) and of van Dodewaard (on chapters III to VI).[1] At the same time, it was announced that
a vote would be taken only during the following period.[2] On September
17, 1965, the fathers received the schedule of the votes that were to be
taken at the beginning of the following week (September 20–22).[3] We will
recall that this simple procedure, entirely in accord with the regulations
of the Council, was not accepted without difficulty; until the beginning
of the fourth period uncertainty reigned about the form that subsequent
work was to take, a juridical uncertainty to begin with, but sustained especially by the increasingly determined actions of the minority.

When, on November 20, 1964, Felici had urged the fathers to send
their observations on the text to the secretariat of the Council, he had let
it be understood that the text would be submitted for debate once again.
In fact, however, the different drafts of the calendar for the fourth period
showed that beginning on December 23, 1964, the question of a new discussion was not really raised,[4] but this left unsettled the problem of

---

[1] *AS* IV/1, 336–81.
[2] See *History,* 4:231.
[3] *AS* IV/1, 282.
[4] See the report that Felici sent to Paul VI on December 23 and submitted to the Coordinating Commission (*AS* V/3, 94–96 and 120–22). Yet at that time Cardinal Urbani,

the status of the observations submitted on a schema that had not yet been put to a vote. The study of these observations by Tromp, the memoranda issuing from the *Coetus Internationalis Patrum* and from the Biblical Institute, the steps taken by the minority in dealing with the governing bodies of the Council and with Paul VI, and what became known of the Pope's personal views — all this mass of opinions showed that the fundamental positions taken on the *De revelatione* and formulated as early as 1962 had hardly budged and continued to inspire opposing strategies.[5] Within the subcommission responsible for the schema, a group still led by the Florence-Louvain team (Florit and Charue/Betti and Philips), it was decided on the eve of the opening of the period that the commission should abstain from any response to the *Coetus Internationalis Patrum* and should avoid a new report on the observations submitted to the secretariat up to the previous January, although Florit did not like withdrawing the report that his theologian, U. Betti, had already prepared during the summer.[6]

The votes were taken, then, on September 20 and 21, while the assembly continued the debate on religious freedom that had started at the beginning of the fourth period. On Tuesday, September 21, right after the much-awaited vote on chapter II of the *De revelatione*, Felici interrupted the ongoing discussion for the straw vote on religious freedom: "Are the fathers satisfied with the re-amended text on religious freedom as the basis of a definitive declaration, although this needs to be improved in accordance with Catholic teaching on the true religion and with the observations made during the discussion?"[7] The formulation of the question remained a matter of controversy until the last minute. Prignon commented: "The impression was given that the question had been formulated with a view to eliciting a very large majority, this with a view to the Pope's journey to New York." With 1997 yes votes out of 2,222 cast,

---

reporting on the text *De revelatione*, was still counting it among the schemas that would be discussed before being voted on (ibid., 125). The same thought was conveyed in the schedule prepared by Felici for the meeting of the commission on May 11, 1965 (ibid., 296–301 and 333–33) and for the meeting on September 13 (ibid., 347–48).

[5] See *History* 4:514-18; and R. Burigana, *La Bibbia nel concilio: La redazione della costituzione "Dei Verbum" del Vaticano II* (Bologna, 1998), 365–89.

[6] See *DBetti*, September 11–13, 1965, in *La "Dei Verbum" trent'anni dopo: Miscellanea in onore di Padre Umberto Betti, o.f.m.* (Rome: Editrice Lateranense, 1995), 356, and in *JPrignon*, September 18, 1965 (Prignon papers, 1586): "It seems that Cardinal Florit is suffering because his talk was withdrawn, and is returning to the attack; he would certainly like to speak."

[7] *AS* IV/1, 434.

the result was clearly positive, even though there were still 224 fathers opposed: "This will be one of the great days of the Council, a sort of a fools' day."[8]

The debate on schema XIII then began, even while the voting continued on the final chapters of the *De revelatione*. Once this vote had been completed on the next day (September 22), a series of votes began on the decree on the laity; these ran from Thursday, September 23, to Monday, September 27, parallel with the debate on the future pastoral constitution. The preliminary report of Hengsbach on the decree on the laity reminded the audience of the connections among this text, chapter V of *Lumen gentium*, which provided its doctrinal basis, and schema XIII, which had been developed by a mixed commission that drew on the Commission for the Lay Apostolate and the Doctrinal Commission.[9] There were 1,374 *modi* submitted; since a number of these covered the same points, 659 remained to be studied. It would take a good part of October to go through them and decide on their fate; the work on each of the six chapters was done by one of the six subcommissions and was completed at eight meetings of the entire commission.

As for the vote on the *De revelatione*, the result showed that the text of November 20, 1964, had succeeded in winning a very large majority.[10] Should the conclusion be drawn "that the bishops are tired and will vote trustingly for all the texts set before them, except on some hotly debated points of which they have been made more keenly aware and to which their attention has especially been drawn"?[11] In fact, the majority

---

[8] *JPrignon*, September 21, 1965 (Prignon papers, 1589, 1, 3).

[9] *AS* IV/2, 303–5.

[10] The vote on the individual numbers allowed only for a yes or a no, but the summary vote on each of the six chapters allowed for *modi* to be offered. Chapter I: 2,079 votes cast, 1,822 yes, 3 no, and 248 *placet iuxta modum* (6 void votes); chapter II: 2,246 votes cast, 1,874 yes, 9 no, and 354 *placet iuxta modum* (9 void votes); chapter III; 2,109 votes cast, 1,777 yes, 6 no, and 324 *placet iuxta modum* (2 void votes); chapter IV: 2,233 votes cast, 2,183 yes, 47 *placet iuxta modum* (3 void votes); chapter V: 2,170 votes cast, 1,850 yes, 4 no, and 313 *placet iuxta modum* (3 void votes); chapter VI: 2,132 votes cast, 1,915 yes, 1 no, and 212 *placet iuxta modum* (4 void votes). A considerable variation can be seen in the number of votes cast, ranging from 2,253 (vote on nos. 9 and 10: scripture/tradition/magisterium, on September 21, the day on which the straw vote was taken on religious freedom) to 2,012 (votes on nos. 23 and 24: role of the theologians and the relation between scripture and theology, on Wednesday, September 22). Normally, the number of voters dropped in the middle of a session or after an important event such as the straw vote on religious freedom (2,222 voters); thus the vote that followed (on nos. 12 and 13 of the *De revelatione*: the interpretation of the scriptures and the divine condescension) dropped to 2,064 votes cast.

[11] Remark of Prignon, September 21 (Prignon papers, 1589).

thought that the present schema marked "a considerable advance over
the very early text," even if, according to Jauffrès, "it could be left to
some specialists to offer *modi*."[12] In some cases the number of "specialists" amounted to about 15 percent of the voters.[13] Were these *modi* simply the requests of specialists that aimed at improving the text, without
weakening the large consensus already won,[14] or were the *modi* a sign that
the doctrinal conflict which appeared in 1962 was still troubling a part of
the assembly that was especially aware of the serious issues at stake in
the future constitution?

To grasp the situation clearly, we must first analyze the schema that
was voted on and do so in the climate prevailing at the beginning of the
fourth period. The written reports that accompanied the schema allow us
to grasp the exact tenor of the consensus reached, as well as the meaning
and scope of the opposition shown in the negative votes.[15] On this basis
it will be possible to look first at the treatment of the 1,498 *modi* by the
commission, which began its work as early as September 22. We shall see
that this treatment throws a new light on the doctrinal conflict and on the
way in which the authorities in charge of the Council reached their goal.

I. An Irreducible Doctrinal Conflict

A. The Text Presented for the Vote

To begin with, the votes cast on September 20, 21, and 22, 1965, confirmed two points especially highlighted by the reports that accompanied
the text of November 20, 1964:[16] the doctrinal line taken in the schema

---

[12] See, e.g., Auguste Jauffrès (last Bishop of Tarantaise and not a member of any commission) in *Carnets conciliaires de Mgr Auguste Jauffrès* (Aubenas-sur-Ardèche: Maison
Sainte-Marthe, 1992), 249f.

[13] Chapter I: 248 *modi* (11.92%); chapter II: 354 *modi* (15.76%); chapter III: 324 *modi*
(15.36%); chapter IV: 47 *modi* (2.1%); chapter V: 313 *modi* (14.42%); chapter VI:
212 *modi* (9.94%). This added up to 1,498 amendments that had to be studied.

[14] See Jauffrès, September 22, in *Carnets conciliaires*, 253.

[15] The no votes clearly reveal three areas of profound disagreement on the schema; the
no votes ranged by and large from 0 (chapter IV) to 21 (nos. 23 and 24; 28 for nos. 12
and 13), but they rose suddenly where there was question of the relationship among tradition, scripture, and the magisterium (no. 8: 49 no votes; nos. 9 and 10, 34), the inspiration of scripture No. 11: 56 no votes), and the historicity of the gospels (no. 19: 61 no
votes).

[16] The complex set of reports had several levels: (1) reports that followed the text of
each chapter: at the beginning, a general report with some general remarks on the main
lines of the text and a conclusion on the procedure adopted by the commission, followed

and the strategy of the subcommission in safeguarding this hard-won line, namely, drawing a clear line between what was really asserted and what should remain open.

As for *the line taken in the text*, we should bear in mind, above all, the remark of the reporter on the status of the introduction (no. 1), which had now acquired its almost definitive form. The two citations, one locating the doctrinal work of the Council in the line of the Johannine kerygma (1 Jn 1:2–3), the other pointing to its universal aim, namely, the implementation of the three theological virtues (St. Augustine, *The Instruction of Beginners* IV, 8), were justified by the fact that "this Constitution is, in a way, *the first of all the Constitutions of this Council*, so that its introduction serves, in a sense, as an introduction to all of them."[17] The request that more emphasis be placed on the ecclesial aspect of revelation was rejected, since this was already honored in the Constitution on the Church. It is clear from the report, then, that as early as 1964 the Doctrinal Commission was well aware of the connection between the two major conciliar texts, an awareness now shared by the entire Council.

We may recall next the division of the text into two parts, the work of two distinct subcommissions, the first being responsible for the first two chapters on revelation and its transmission, the second for the following four chapters on scripture (its inspiration and interpretation, the Old Testament, the New Testament, its presence in the life of the Church). In October 1964 van Dodewaard had summed up the connection between the two parts: after dealing with the relations between scripture and tradition, attention was focused on scripture *in itself*, "which, given the orientation of the Council, must be approached not only in a doctrinal perspective but also, and above all, in a pastoral perspective." It was on the basis of St. Jerome's saying, "Ignorance of the scriptures is ignorance of Christ," that the frequent reading of the scriptures was urged on *all* Christians (no. 25). This presupposes that the pastoral emphasis in the four chapters of the second part is based on solid doctrine and that the function of churchmen, especially "the teachers of exegesis," is well defined in relation both to doctrinal judgments (no. 12), on the one hand, and to the ministers of the word (no. 23), on the other.[18]

---

by reports on each number of chapter I; a preliminary remark on the procedure adopted, followed by reports on each number of chapter II; then the reports on each number of chapters III to VI; (2) two summarizing reports, that of Florit on chapters I and II, and that of van Dodewaard on chapters III to VI.

[17] *AS* IV/1, 341, report on no. 1, emphasis added; see also the report of Florit on September 30, 1964 (*AS* III/3, 131f.).

[18] *AS* III/3, 268f.

The "organic" character of the text made clear here is expressly mentioned in the general report that accompanied the schema offered for a vote in September 1965.[19] This trait was to be henceforth a fundamental norm in dealing with any improvements the commission might accept; the principle embodied in this norm was clearly stated: "a solid and well-tested teaching drawn from sacred scripture and ancient tradition." This teaching was rooted in a "christocentric and personalist conception of revelation"[20] that was reflected in the manner of its transmission (the nature, content, and era of tradition was here, for the first time, an express subject of a document of the supreme magisterium[21]). That conception also had its completion, and its real point of departure, in a pastoral theology of scripture that would make explicit the status at once historical and theological of the scriptures, the whole of this project being unobtrusively accomplished by a repositioning of the roles of the magisterium, exegetes, and theologians in dealing with scripture; its completion would also consist of an interpretation of scripture that was at once doctrinal and pastoral.

It was surprising, however, that the report made almost no mention of the principal conflict concerning the pivotal paragraph of the constitution, namely, that on relations between scripture and tradition (no. 9). The report mentioned it only insofar as it rejected as a bloc all the amendments "which in any way whatsoever seek to change the long-sought balance within the text."[22] This way of safeguarding what had been won, based on the conciliar principle of "leaving to the further studies of the theologians any points still the subject of debate or not absolutely necessary," was itself confirmed by the vote in September 1965.

In addition to validating this overall orientation and the doctrinal strategy of the commission, the votes ratified a number of amendments designed to improve and unify what was already gained. The report listed the most important of these amendments.[23]

With regard to revelation itself (chapter I), the main points to be noted are a clearer distinction and interrelation of "supernatural revelation" (a term avoided in the schema itself) and "revelation written into the

---

[19] *AS* IV/1, 340.
[20] Ibid., 340 and 380.
[21] Ibid., 380.
[22] Ibid., 352.
[23] Ibid., 378–80.

order of creation" (nos. 3 and 6); a new emphasis (characteristic of other conciliar texts and in line with the introduction[24]) on the universality of the divine saving will; and, finally, an emphasis on the "personalist nature of faith."[25] Following St. Irenaeus, the chapter on the transmission of revelation (chapter II) distinguishes divine and apostolic tradition more clearly from ecclesiastical tradition;[26] the former, being definitive and sufficient,[27] is not *in itself* susceptible of any progress; progress is located exclusively on the side of the interior understanding human beings can acquire of it in the course of history. The Church's understanding of the Bible and its recognition of the canon of the scriptures are the clearest example of this growing insight (no. 8).

The counterpart of these points is the distinction, newly introduced into the text in no. 9, between the bearers of the apostolic tradition (the constitutive ministry of the apostles) and those who preserve, explain, and spread it (the ministry of the bishops).[28] The text touched here on questions already taken up in chapter III of the Constitution on the Church. This is most visible in no. 10, which conforms to the general definition of the authoritative magisterium that was set forth in *Lumen gentium,* 25,[29] but lays a greater emphasis on the transcendence of revelation in relation to its authoritative interpretation.[30]

---

[24] See, e.g., *Lumen gentium,* 2, 9, 16, and 17 (*Lumen gentium* had already been promulgated).

[25] *AS* IV/1, 379; see also ibid., 345, report on no. 5 (B): "Many have asked for a more biblical and therefore more personalist *description* of faith that would correspond better to the description already given of revelation."

[26] Ibid., 353 (C) and 379.

[27] Ibid., 353 (B).

[28] The twofold distinction between divine and apostolic tradition and post-apostolic tradition, on the one hand, and between the constitutive ministry of the apostles and the teaching role of the bishops, on the other, can be seen especially in the intervention of Léger on October 1, 1964 (*AS* III/3, 182–85). It came from the Montreal group (see G. Routhier, "L'itinéraire d'un Père conciliaire: Le Cardinal Léger," *CrSt* 19 [1998], 89–147, esp. 128–41) but was held by other speakers as well as, for example, van Dodewaard, reporter on chapters III-VI (*AS* III/3, 229). An analysis of the report accompanying the text of November 20, 1965 (chapter II) makes it clear that Léger's request had been accepted. Whether ambiguities remain in the formulas of the text is for a final evaluation to decide.

[29] *AS* IV/1, 354, report on no. 10 (A) and (B). See also *Lumen gentium,* 19–20. A detailed analysis discovers some important differences between the position taken in *Dei Verbum,* no. 9, and that in *Lumen gentium,* 19–20: while the Constitution on the Church uses the concept of "the death of the apostles," the Constitution on Revelation refuses to introduce the concept of "the closure of revelation with the death of the apostles," because "the formula is not without its difficulties, and this for several reasons" (ibid., 345, report on no. 4).

[30] Ibid., 354, report on no. 4.

The report on chapters III-VI instanced a certain number of improvements that contributed chiefly to unifying the teaching in the two parts of the text. The principal correction in chapter III had to do with the effect of inspiration and the truth of the scriptures (no. 11), a sensitive point, as we shall see, and one that was achieved only with difficulty during the revision of November 1964,[31] namely, that the statement saying the scriptures teach "*saving* truth" is justified in light of the concept of revelation given in the first chapter, according to which "the word implies *facts* which in the scriptures are connected with the history of salvation."[32]

In the important theological paragraph on the "condescension of divine wisdom" in the scriptures (no. 13), the proviso "the truthfulness and holiness of God being always safeguarded" was omitted, and a citation from St. John Chrysostom was introduced to make it clearer — again in line with the concept of self-revelation — that at issue here was an "unchanging norm governing the divine action in dealing with humanity, a norm verified in the sacred scriptures, in the Church, and in the incarnation, in which the divine is linked to the human."[33]

In chapter IV, on the Old Testament, as in the first chapter, the revisers gave stronger expression to what was said about the universality of God's will to save (no. 14), and they corrected a theology that spoke of the end of the Old Testament (which would also have contradicted the teaching in *Nostra aetate*) by further emphasizing the positive contribution of the Old Testament (nos. 15 and 16).[34]

Chapter V, on the New Testament, now began with the kerygma of Paul as summed up in Romans 1:16: "The power of God for the salvation of all who believe" (no. 17); this matched the kerygmatic conception of revelation and faith in the first chapter. On another sensitive point, the polemical remark against the theory (perhaps associated with Bultmann) of the creativity of the primitive community was removed (no. 19). As for the final chapter, on the sacred scriptures in the life of the Church, it is noteworthy, above all, that the emphasis on the normative role of the scriptures, which are able "to guide and pass judgment on all the preaching of the Church and even on the Christian religion itself," had disappeared.

---

[31] See *History*, 4:231.

[32] *AS* IV/1, 358f. (F).

[33] Ibid., 360 (A).

[34] Ibid., 365 (M), (L), and (P); see also ibid., 359, the report on no. 12 (K), which emphasized the unity of the two Testaments as a principle for interpreting the scriptures.

Among these voted improvements the particularly sensitive problems were the relationship among tradition, scripture, and the magisterium (nos. 8–10), the effect of inspiration on the truth of the scriptures (no. 11), and the question of the historicity of the gospels (no. 19). The higher number of no votes on these three points showed the persistence of some opposition to the text. This opposition must be situated within the framework of the amendments already rejected by the commission in 1964 and the reasons given for those rejections. Most of these amendments had to do in fact with the central thrust of the documents. At stake was the meaning of the formula in the introduction, which located the teaching of the schema "in the steps of Vatican Council I." What place was to be given to the recent magisterium in comparison with "sacred scripture and ancient tradition,"[35] which in fact determined the direction taken in the text? This underlying question is no longer even mentioned in the report.

The difference between the biblical and patristic approach, on the one hand, and the perspective adopted by the recent magisterium, on the other, did in fact appear surreptitiously when the commission refused to modify the central passage on the "intrinsic connection between events and words in revelation" (no. 2), arguing that the text was speaking of revelation "in its initial coming into existence or as an economy,"[36] whereas a number of the amendments reflected a verbal and doctrinal conception of revelation such as can be found in the texts of Vatican I.[37] A number of fathers were uneasy with the sacramental language of the text and with the analogy between the events or deeds of the Bible and the Christian sacraments;[38] it was a difficulty they felt again at the end of the text (no. 21) with the analogy between the word of God and the Eucharist.[39]

Around this key point one could bring together other amendments embodying a resistance to the "economic" and "kerygmatic" approach taken in the schema; for example, those that protested the relegation of the treatment of the "natural knowledge of God" to the end of the first chapter;[40] those that, on the contrary, wanted to reintroduce at this point

---

[35] *AS* IV/1, 340.

[36] Ibid., 342 (C).

[37] See the report of Florit on September 30, 1964, in *AS* III/3, 132: "This God reveals himself not only through words but also through deeds that he accomplished in the history of salvation."

[38] *AS* IV/1, 342 (B and C).

[39] Ibid., 375, report on no. 21 (C).

[40] Ibid., 341, report on no. 2 (A).

the supernatural orientation of the historical human being;[41] those that proposed dealing with the apologetical aspect of signs in the section on faith;[42] and, finally, those that wanted to introduce such doctrines as the Trinity[43] or redemption[44] into the description of the economy of revelation, as though Christ should be thought of as a revealer (of doctrines) whereas he himself *is* revelation ("mediator and fullness of the whole of revelation").[45] The basic difficulty appeared, finally, in the drafting of the section on the act of faith; here the report tried to justify the maintenance of both languages, the biblical or personalist approach and the scholastic or doctrinal perspective: "Faith implies by its nature the acceptance of a teaching; on the other hand, this acceptance is essentially an act of surrender to God."[46]

Other amendments rejected in November 1964 were likewise located in the same doctrinal and apologetic framework that had been established by Vatican I and had been gradually given greater detail in the Modernist period. We may point especially to some remarks on inspiration that aimed to reduce the role of the authors[47] or to reintroduce the Scholastic concept of instrument (chapter III);[48] perhaps also the proposal to speak explicitly of the law and the decalogue (chapter IV);[49] or, again, the problem of the historicity of the gospels (chapter V).[50] The disputed question of the greater objective breadth of tradition as compared with the scriptures (the nerve center of the Roman doctrinal system) appeared only at the end of the report,[51] and then in a restrained way when the commission was, on the one hand, defending the subject of chapter VI, which was the *scriptures* in the life of the Church (and not the word of God in general or tradition),[52] and, on the other, allowing that the regulatory function of scripture should be expressed in a less absolute way[53] and that its

---

[41] Ibid., 346, report on no. 6 (A).
[42] Ibid., 346, report on no. 5 (C).
[43] Ibid., 342, report on no. 2 (B).
[44] Ibid., 344, report on no. 4 (D).
[45] Ibid., 342, report on no. 2 (D).
[46] Ibid., 345, report on no. 5 (B).
[47] Ibid., 358 (D).
[48] Ibid., 360, report on no. 11.
[49] Ibid., 364.
[50] Ibid., 369f., report on no. 19 (D).
[51] For the first time in no. 17 of the report, in which the commission introduced the proviso stating that "*not everything* is reported in the New Testament" (ibid., 369 [E]).
[52] Ibid., 375 (A).
[53] Ibid., 375, reports on no. 21 (E).

relations with tradition should be spoken of "without prejudging disputed questions."[54]

The three contentious questions mentioned above clearly had their place in the anti-Modernist doctrinal system, the main elements of which we have just recalled, and, more exactly, in the area of the *mediations* of revelation, which are taken up in chapters II to VI. The fact that in September 1965 a higher number of no votes were cast on these three points was evidence that a small minority accepted neither the explanations given by the commission regarding the "saving truth" of the scriptures nor the relative silence now with regard to the historicity of the gospels and to the greater extension of tradition in comparison with the scriptures.

How are we to assess this discretion and, above all, the absence of arguments in the report on chapter II, which was *formally* justified by a "mandate by which the commission *remains* bound"?[55] The main argument, namely, "the balance attained" that must not now be affected, "leaving debated points to the further studies of the theologians,"[56] carried no weight in the eyes of a minority for whom the disputed question was not just one *theological question* among others, one that could be left open, but an essential element of *Catholic teaching*, as can be seen from the plea of Franić, reporter for the minority, in September 1964.[57] This observation, which was fully in line with the doctrinal system of Vatican I, explains the gradual escalation in the means used by the minority to win its case, both during the intersession and beginning again in September 1965.[58]

From a material point of view, the subcommission wanted to escape the impasse by developing, for the first time in history, the concept of tradition in its full breadth, "not only in its verbal aspect but also, in line with chapter I, as something real and living, inscribed in the life of the Church and at work in it."[59] This, however, succeeded only in outlining the problem. The *votum* of the Biblical Institute (January 1965), which was more aware of the real difficulty, at once challenged the use of

---

[54] Ibid., 376, report on no. 24 (N).

[55] Ibid., 352, a preliminary remark (with a reference back to *AS* III/3, 82).

[56] *AS* III/3, 133; *AS* IV/1, 380.

[57] *AS* III/3, 124–29, esp. 128.

[58] The *animadversiones* emanating from the *Coetus Internationalis Patrum* and composed by Carli specifically challenged the formal appeal to a "mandate," which the reporter for the majority made.

[59] *AS* III/3, 82; *AS* IV/1, 380.

the language of doctrine in describing the economy or the history of salvation.[60] But the Institute found itself for this reason and for others,[61] in opposition (though not very actively) to the memorandum of Carli.[62]

In any case, this opposition and, more exactly, the difficulty in moving beyond the confusion between the doctrinal perspective of Vatican I and the at once economic and kerygmatic approach to the event of revelation, both past and always current, overshadowed attention to the ecumenical aspect, which was maintained especially by Léger and the Montreal theologians. They were concerned to distinguish more clearly between revelation or apostolic tradition and its reception or interpretation by the Church and, in particular, by the magisterium.

But the usual boundaries between the currents in the Council became blurred here; in fact, it is difficult not to be astonished at the strange complicity, *on this precise point*, between the orientation of Léger and the memorandum of Carli, who likewise (but along the lines of chapter IV of the *Dei Filius* of Vatican I and the celebrated saying of Vincent of Lérins) attacked the confusion of apostolic tradition with the understanding of it by the aid of the Holy Spirit and under the guidance of the sacred magisterium.[63] But while Léger introduced the distinction in order to bring out more clearly the transcendence of the word of God, Carli did so in order to assert that the Church already possesses the fullness of objective truth.[64] Other similarities might be pointed out, for example, the rejection both by Carli and by the exegetes of the Biblical Institute of the polemical formula "The magisterium is not above the word but serves it."

Such, then, were the tensions, visible or not so visible, revealed by the schema and the accompanying reports; given to the fathers in November 1964, these had by the time of the vote in September 1965 been takenover by the movements of thought just described: longstanding oppositions, indeed, now inflamed by the barrier of "textual balance" that the commission imposed on the conciliar assembly. The very great majority of

[60] See the criticism of the formula that assigned to "actions" the ability to "manifest and confirm *doctrine*" (no. 2), and the rejection of a shift from talk of the "truth" that is Christ (no. 2) to talk of acceptance of a "truth" understood as "doctrine" in the Scholastic sense of the term (no. 5). These are among the *Modi qui proponuntur pro schemate "De divina"* (in Florit papers, 245, 1 and 3).

[61] For example, the criticism of the adjective "sacred" attached to "tradition" (ibid., 4).

[62] See *History*, 4:516-18.

[63] See *Animadversiones in schema de 'Divina revelatione"* (Florit papers, 244, 2f.).

[64] See ibid., 2.

the votes set a seal of approval on this strategy, on the central line of the document, and on the improvements made in order to achieve a greater unification of the text. But the negative votes confirmed the existence of a doctrinal conflict whose global background began to disappear from the consciousness of those involved, thus leaving in the foreground the three chief areas of disagreement. These would now be the subject of debate in the Doctrinal Commission and give rise to new strategies.

B. AMENDMENT OF THE TEXT BY THE SMALL ADVISORY COMMISSION

On the very evening of the last vote a small technical commission, working at St. Martha's, began the task of studying the 1,498 *modi*. The commission members were Charue, vice-president of the Doctrinal Commission; two reporters, Florit and van Dodewaard; and two secretaries, Philips and Tromp. At the request of Florit, the group added Betti "as a secretary" and also, at the urging of Tromp, Heuschen.[65] During eight two-hour meetings between September 22 and September 30, the commission analyzed all the amendments offered by the fathers and drew up its proposals.[66] Tromp remarked in his reports that the high number of *placet iuxta modum* votes did not reflect the real number of the *modi*, because many of them overlapped. There remained in fact 208 *modi* in all to be examined by the entire commission; sixty of them (28.8 percent) were for chapter II.[67]

To judge by the experience of the Belgian members of the team, the atmosphere in which the work was done was excellent and trusting,[68] but

---

[65] See *RT 8*, 4ff.; *JPrignon,* September 21, 1965 (Prignon papers, 1589, 8f.) Only Tromp's report mentions the presence of van Dodewaard. Betti, who could not be invited as an expert, played a by no means negligible role in the sequence of events.

[66] The group took up chapter I on September 22–23, Chapter II on September 23–25, chapters III and IV on September 27, chapter V on September 28, and chapter VI on September 30 (the first meeting of the Doctrinal Commission had taken place on September 29) (see U. Betti, "Cronistoria della costituzione dogmatica *Dei Verbum*," in *La costituzione dogmatica sulla divina Revelazione* [Turin, 1966], 40f.). Tromp spoke only of seven meetings, passing over in silence the very last meeting, on chapter VI (*RT 8*, 4).

[67] *RT 8*, 4.

[68] See *JPrignon,* September 21, 1965 (Prignon papers, 1589 8f.) and September 25, (Prignon papers, 1591, 3): "In the small technical commission that prepared the *expensio modorum* for the commission on revelation, Florit was quite conciliatory; Betti showed himself relentless in defending the text against all proposed improvements; Tromp showed an increasing trust in Msgr. Heuschen, to the point where he now left him all the secretarial work that he himself should have done. Msgr. Heuschen returned to the college each day with all the proposals for improvement, classified them, and so on. He himself prepared the proposals for the technical commission, and Father Tromp endorsed almost blindly everything that Msgr. Heuschen prepared and the commission decided."

it concealed radical difficulties that showed themselves as soon as external influences, some coming from very high up, began to be felt even
within the little commission. Tromp's report says nothing about them; we
must therefore turn to the diaries of other theologians of the group in
order to gauge what was at stake.

A first external intervention was connected with Betti, who had been
invited by the Pope's theologian, Colombo ("expressing the wish of the
highest authority"), to the meeting of the Italian Episcopal Conference on
September 15, "in order that he might propose to them two *modi* capable of emphasizing the role both of the magisterium in the safeguarding
and progress of tradition and of tradition itself in the act of communicating to us the *knowledge* of revelation in its entirety."[69] He had then formulated a first addition to the second part of no. 8, which on the basis of
St. Irenaeus stated that the perception of things as well as of transmitted
words is increased "above all by the preaching of those who through
episcopal succession have received the sure charism of truth," and a second addition to no. 9, which drew the conclusion from what was said of
the relations between scripture and tradition that "the whole of Catholic
doctrine cannot be *proved* from scripture alone."[70]

We are not surprised, therefore, to see Betti admitting his "concern to
draw the attention of the commission to these two additions, which he
himself had suggested to the Italian episcopate on September 16 and
which were supported by a substantial number of fathers."[71] The first
modus, which was backed by 175 fathers, was accepted by the small commission; the other amendment, defended by 111 fathers, gave rise to a
debate in which a second external intervention played an important role.

But before speaking of this event, let us note that this *modus* was only
one of three that had to do, not with the problem of the material extension of the scriptures and tradition, but with the question of *our knowledge* of gospel revelation. For 154 fathers asked that in no. 8, after the
mention of the canon of scripture, it be said that tradition "also makes
known to us as the word of God truths that cannot be recognized from
scripture alone"; eight others suggested the same idea but in a longer
formula (*modus* 36). The Betti amendment had the same purport but was
to be inserted in no. 9 (*modus* 40 D). Finally, three fathers asked that no.
10, which said that the magisterium "draws from the one deposit of faith,

[69] *DBetti*, September 9–13, 1965, 356.
[70] Ibid., September 16, 1965, 356f.
[71] Ibid., September 23–25, 1965, 358.

namely, the word of God, everything that it proposes for belief as being revealed by God," be completed by adding at this point: "but Catholic doctrine in its totality cannot be *proved* from sacred scripture alone" (*modus* 56). This concentration of 276 requests on three paragraphs (nos. 8, 9, and 10), plus the fact that Betti succeeded in gaining priority for his own (attached to no. 9: *modus* 40 D),[72] were of capital importance for the continuation of the debate.

It was at this point that a second external intervention, mediated this time by Tromp, changed the course of the debate. On the evening of September 24 the secretary of the Doctrinal Commission exploded "a small bomb" when he announced to the members of the working group that on the following Wednesday the meeting would begin with the reading to the commission of "a letter from very high up, which... proposed two, three small changes on the subject of tradition."[73] We know now that on September 23 Ottaviani had received, by order of the Pope and with Felici as intermediary, the letter that Siri had sent the Pope at the very beginning of the month.[74]

On the following day, September 24, Ottaviani must also have received, by the same hierarchical route, the personal suggestion of the Pope that the commission speak more clearly and more explicitly of "the constitutive nature of tradition as a source of revelation."[75] But whereas Siri's memorandum understood the idea of "constitutive tradition" as identifying tradition with the magisterium ("it is evident that a divine book must, above all, have at its disposal a means of interpretation suited to it, that is, a means supported by the same divine authority"[76]), the Pope in his note understood it rather as the Council of Trent did, that is, as oral tradition: "According to the citation from St. Augustine that was added to his letter, there are many points which the universal Church holds and which for this reason are well and truly believed to be precepts coming from the apostles even though we do not find them written down."[77]

---

[72] Therefore to *modus* 36 and *modus* 56 was added a reference to the response to *modus* 40 D; see *Modi a Patribus conciliaribus propositi a Commissione doctrinali examinandi prooemium et caput II* (Florit papers, D 247, 6 and 9).

[73] *JPrignon,* September 25, 1965 (Prignon papers, 1591, 5f.).

[74] Letter of Siri to the Pope, September 5, 1965, with three appended documents (one on the schema on revelation), communicated by the Secretary of State to the Secretary of the Council on September 15, and by the latter in turn to Ottaviani, president of the Doctrinal Commission, on September 23 (*AS* V/3, 352–54 and 376).

[75] *AS* V/3, 377.

[76] Ibid., 354.

[77] Ibid., 377.

It is understandable, then, that, according to Philips, Tromp spoke of the "letter coming from very high up." "It was not clear whether there was question of tradition in general as contrasted with scripture or of the difference between constitutive tradition (the apostles) and the tradition preserved by the magisterium."[78] If we may trust the information in Prignon's diary, Philips had an astonishingly accurate premonition of something that escaped him at the moment: the ambiguity of *two* letters, sent in the name of the same "higher authority" and giving two clearly different meanings to the concept of "constitutive tradition."

According to the information in the diaries we see also that Tromp, who did not know the content of the famous "letter," announced its coming as a support for his own strategy at the very moment when the three *modi* relating to nos. 8, 9, and 10 were being discussed. Tromp took advantage of the debate to restore credit to a small number of *modi* asking that the schema speak of a "properly constitutive tradition" in the sense of one that has a greater *material* extension than do the scriptures.[79] At this point Tromp referred to "the letter from Felici" (which of the two letters?) "in which it is said that the Pope thinks along the same line."[80] The situation produced by this off-the-cuff intervention was quite important because it brought to light the different strategies of the three principal theologians of this Romano-Florentine and Belgian axis.

Betti, "an unrelenting defender of the text,"[81] gave first a juridical argument based on common sense: possessing the authority and the means, the Pope will always be able to make his thought known *with complete clarity*; but realism requires that we recognize for the moment

---

[78] *JPrignon*, September 25, 1965 (Prignon papers, 1591, 6). The same hesitation about the views of the Pope emerges from Prignon's report after the meeting of the moderators with the Pope on September 28:"I then asked Cardinal Suenens whether the Pope had spoken of the *De revelatione*. 'Yes,' he said, 'but very little. He did however say that there were some inaccuracies in the chapter on tradition: that not enough of a distinction was made between apostolic tradition and other traditions, and that not enough emphasis was placed on the importance of apostolic tradition.' That, at least, is what the cardinal said to me. It does not match completely the content of the letter to the commission, of which Father Tromp spoke" (*JPrignon*, September 28, 1965 (Prignon papers, 1594, 3f.).

[79] The reference is to two *modi* seeking to have the schema affirm the *material* insufficiency of the scriptures, a deficiency made up for by tradition: *modus* 21, "Truths revealed orally by the apostles but not preserved in the written books have come down to us by Tradition"; and *modus* 42, backed by three fathers who asked for an addition stating that there are "two sources – in the true and proper sense of this term – of revelation and faith."

[80] *DBetti*, September 23–25, 1965, 358.

[81] See *JPrignon*, September 25, 1965 (Prignon papers, 1591, 3).

that "we cannot go further than the proposal of the 111 fathers."[82] Philips or, rather "Charue, Philips, and Heuschen *foresaw* an answer during the meeting and introduced into the passages discussed in the letter [of which no one had direct knowledge!] changes that are acceptable and do not close the door to dialogue with the Protestants and that, in addition... are true and worded in such a way as to avoid any breakdown."[83] In this account by Prignon, we see the harmonious mingling of basic conviction,[84] a strategic anticipation bordering on self-censure, and the craftiness that is characteristic of Philips's work. The point of his efforts and those of Heuschen was, then, to introduce a variant into the formula of the 111 fathers (behind which no one seems to have suspected Betti as author), namely, "that where we are asked from on high for an explicit assertion that not everything is in scripture, the text should say: not everything can be found or proved directly from scripture. The word 'directly' saves the entire schema."[85]

Tromp accepted this slight modification, while Betti "passionately" resisted it.[86] The latter's diary reveals his motive: he foresaw the twofold interpretation made possible by the new formulation. It could be that the introduction of "directly" would change nothing, provided one meant by it that one needs the help of tradition because not everything can be provided directly from scripture. "But the little addition might also change everything if the intention is to say that every truth can be proved indirectly from scripture, simply because scripture shows the existence of an infallible magisterium and the indefectibility of the Church, so that the magisterium could define a truth without any reference to scripture and this truth would nonetheless be divinely revealed, simply because scripture bears witness to the infallibility of the magisterium that defends it and to the indefectibility of the Church that professes it." Moreover, Betti concluded that Tromp evidently understood the "directly" as favoring the second hypothesis,[87] which is along the line of Siri's letter.

Florit's theologian regretted, then, that Tromp had succeeded "with the consent of the *commissio parva*, although this was given very hastily at the

---

[82] *DBetti*, September 23–25, 1965, 358, emphases added.

[83] *JPrignon,* September 25, 1965 (Prignon papers, 1591, 6), comment in brackets added.

[84] Ibid.: "Msgr. Philips told me several times that he agrees with the substance of what is being requested and that it expresses his views quite well, but that the behavior involved is obviously very disturbing and frightening."

[85] Ibid.

[86] Ibid.

[87] *DBetti*, September 23–25, 1965, 358f.

moment when the commission was going to leave St. Martha's Home on the evening of September 24."[88] Philips, however, interpreted the new formula as a victory for the Belgian group.[89] But he did not stop there. Desirous of completely avoiding any talk of the letter from on high (in order to keep from falling back into all the difficulties of the past year and "revealing the crown"), he succeeded on Monday, September 27, in convincing Tromp to "persuade Cardinal Ottaviani not to speak of this letter unless it is absolutely necessary."[90] As we now know, Ottaviani then wrote to the Pope that same day, telling him of the new formula (with Tromp's interpretation added in a note[91]) and assuring him that "in this way the constitutive role of tradition would be expressed" and that "the language used would make it clear that the deposit of faith is not contained in scripture alone." According to Tromp, other *modi* would risk giving rise to endless controversies; this remark appeared again in the response to *modus* 40 D.[92] Ottaviani also asked the Pope for instructions in case the formula did not satisfy him.[93] Was this, then, a victory for the Belgian strategy? The answer was not clear because it depended on an ambiguity that was sure to come to light.

[88] Ibid. See also G. Caprile, S.J., "Trois amendements au schéma sur la Révélation," *CivCatt* February 5, 1966, translated in *DC,* no. 1463 (1966), 625–42, and reprinted in Vatican II, *La Révélation divine* II, Unam Sanctam 70b (Paris: du Cerf, 1968), 667–87; the article was composed on the basis of Paul VI's dossier, which the Pope himself gave to the editor of *CivCatt*. This dossier (Paul VI papers, B3/1–47) is a little less complete than the dossier from which it was an extract, namely, Paul VI papers, A/1–56. Contrary to what emerges from the diaries here cited, Caprile in his article seems to say that the small advisory commission initially adopted the proposal of three fathers to introduce the formula that "not every Catholic doctrine can be proven from sacred scripture alone" into no. 10 (*modus* 56) before finally agreeing instead to place the almost identical addition of the 111 fathers in no. 9 (*modus* 40 D) (Caprile, in *La Révélation divine,* 671).

[89] *JPrignon,* September 25, 1965 (Prignon papers, 1591, 6).

[90] Ibid., September 27, 1965 (Prignon papers, 1593, 1).

[91] *AS* V/3, 379f.; according to Ottaviani, a note would explain that the word "directly" was used "instead of 'indirectly,' because the sacred magisterium of the Church is taught in sacred scripture." The response to *modus* 40 D said, in fact, "All [truths] can be proved indirectly from scripture because in sacred scripture itself the sacred magisterium of the Church is taught." The response to *modus* 40 D said: "All [truths] can be proved indirectly from scripture inasmuch as scripture clearly teaches the existence of a magisterium and the indefectibility of the Church" (Florit papers, D 247, 7).

[92] Ibid., "It is proposed that the addition in question be accepted; all agree on it and it will avoid more subtle questions."

[93] *AS* V/3, 379f.; see also *JPrignon,* September 28, 1965 (Prignon papers, 1594, 5). Prignon's report (quoted above in note 80) of the meeting of the moderators with the Pope on that same Monday (September 29) is confused. Perhaps the Pope had not yet received Ottaviani's note, which was dated the day before. What Suenens said of the Pope's position can be interpreted either in light of the interventions of Léger or according to the demands of Carli.

Meanwhile, Philips and Heuschen ended their examination of the *modi* to be presented to the commission on chapters I and II.[94] On Monday, September 27, the study of chapter III was begun in the presence of Grillmeier, the reporter on that text.[95] The only stumbling block to be surmounted was the question of the truth of the scriptures. Tromp made a radical attack on the subject of *"saving* truth." "He was determined to get rid of the word *salutaris*, because unless one said purely and simply that scripture contains nothing but truth, and this truth without reservation, one logically ends by making God a liar." According to Heuschen's report, there was no way to make Tromp listen to reason. Despite all the examples given him, whether of the material or the historical order, he resisted to the end. Fortunately, the group was able to retain the word *salutaris*, but Tromp demanded that it be said in a note that *salutaris* was not to be taken in an exclusive sense.[96]

During those days Prignon also voiced some fears regarding the third disputed question: "the amendments on the subject of the historicity of the gospels and especially of the infancy gospels."[97] But the next day this obstacle was hurdled more easily than had been anticipated because "Father Tromp was quite easy-going," according to the rector of the Belgian College.[98]

When we reread today these scraps of memoirs on the preliminary work of the "small commission," we are struck, first, by the disappearance of the overall content of the future Constitution from the consciousness of the main participants. The technical character of the work to be done required, in fact, that the members classify problems and identify the points of disagreement between majority and minority as though these were so many "obstacles" to be overcome. Doctrinal strategy thus became the focus of attention, although it did not cause either side to lose

---

[94] *JPrignon,* September 26, 1965 (Prignon papers, 1592, 3).

[95] Ibid., September 27, 1965 (Prignon papers, 1593, 1). Betti mentions the invitation extended to the reporters on the second half of the future constitution: A. Grillmeier for chapter III; A. Kerrigan for chapter IV; B. Rigaux for chapter V; and O. Semmelroth (A. Grillmeier) for chapter VI (Betti, "Cronistoria," 40). It is not known whether others besides Grillmeier present at the meeting on Monday, September 27, when chapters III and IV were discussed, and at the meetings of September 28 and 30.

[96] *JPrignon*, September 27, 1965 (Prignon papers, 1593, 1f.).

[97] Ibid., 2. See also what Prignon says about Daniélou's campaign among the bishops (*JPrignon,* September 25, 1965 [Prignon papers, 1591, 3]).

[98] Ibid., September 29, 1965 (1595), 1 and 4. No other decision of the *commissio parva* is reported in the diaries of the theologians. Chapters V (taken up on September 28) and VI (reread on Thursday, September 30) seem, therefore, not to have caused any special difficulty.

sight of its convictions; a number of participants, located at different points in the drafting process, were now looking for compromise formulas that were acceptable to the minority but did not imperil the gains made.

But these attempts brought to light, even more, the lack of clarity in dealing with the issues at stake in the main disagreement, namely, the relationships among scripture, tradition, and the magisterium. Thus, a man as well-informed as Gérard Philips did not seem to see that the introduction of the word *directly* into the statement that "not all Catholic teaching can be *directly* found in, or proved by, scripture," could be given two completely different interpretations, both of them covered by the same ambiguous concept of "constitutive tradition." One of them preserved intact the transcendence of the word of God, even while asserting the necessity of tradition on the level of *knowledge*, that is, in order to achieve an integral grasp of the deposit. The other supported the meaning given by those who could rely on the note added to the *modus* to let them find in scripture itself the idea of a *second source*, that of a magisterium that is teacher of Catholic doctrine in its totality (Carli and Siri).

The reaction of Philips and Heuschen is explained partly by the trauma inflicted by the *Nota praevia* of autumn 1964 and the political concern not to "reveal the crown," while at the same time combining ecumenical openness *and* a tolerant attitude toward the minority. Their action was certainly premature, and somewhat naive, because it was provoked by a papal letter whose content was not known by any of the people involved; this tactic of anticipating the movements of the opposition, a tactic adopted without the knowledge of Suenens,[99] was also a reflection both of the Belgian College's estimate of the general climate and of the activities of the minority. Prignon wrote:

> We are afraid that the minority will exert pressure in order to gain an excessive influence on the thinking of the Pope, this despite the drop-off in the number of the minority's agents. Now it is clear, and indeed evident to me after all the contacts I have had with many individuals here in Rome, that at least certain members of the minority are practicing a kind of blackmail on the Pope. He does not seem to be aware of it. I realize fully, and I have other testimonies to the fact, that the most influential members of the minority are not at all grateful to the Holy Father for anticipating their positions and endeavoring to push these to the point of displeasing the majority. Not only are they not grateful to him, but they speak openly of his weakness,

---

[99] *JPrignon,* September 25, 1965 (Prignon papers, 1591, 8): "Msgr. Philips expressly asked me not to say anything to Cardinal Suenens before Wednesday. For if the Cardinal reacted too strongly, he could place us all in a very difficult situation."

and they do not hide their intention of taking advantage of it in the future. I know that these are serious charges, but I am reporting what I have heard.[100]

What was really the truth about these pressures on the Pope? And how are we to understand the sending of two such different letters, that of Siri and that of the Pope himself, to the president of the Doctrinal Commission? Was the second letter written to correct the effect of the first? But, then, why was the first letter sent to the president of the commission?[101] Was this a sign of a lack of clarity on the fundamental issue?[102] Did it show a "political" desire of the Pope to win over the members of the majority? Or was it even an expression of his personal position? Perhaps all three motives came into play. And why did the second letter never reach the little commission? Did Ottaviani think he had responded appropriately when he informed the Pope on September 27 of the new formula offered by Philips (amendment 40 D), or was the holding back of the letter inspired by a still different tactic? We shall have to come back to this question.

Finally, Betti himself also played a role in the tactic of anticipating the moves of the adversary, but he acted covertly. He was made a member of the technical commission by the Cardinal of Florence[103] and was the real author of the compromise that he had already explained to the Italian Episcopal Conference and that he defended with greater precision and more perspicacity than did Philips. The "third party,"[104] which was in

---

[100] Ibid., 7. On September 24 Congar had already noted in his diary: "Father Smulders tells me that Schauf hopes for some sort of *Nota praevia* or some *modi* from the Pope for the chapter on tradition in the *De revelatione*. Someone must go to see Cardinal Florit" (*JCongar*, September 24, 1965; II, 407).

[101] We may recall here the similar case of Siri's letter on the text on religious freedom. Here is what Msgr. Prignon reported on this point (*JPrignon*, September 30, 1965 [Prignon papers, 1956]): "With regard to religious freedom I forgot to note down that two or three days ago Cardinal Siri approached the Pope; I do not know whether he did so in person or by letter. He asked that some of his viewpoints be introduced into the text; he then sent a letter to the secretariat listing his positions and saying that he did so 'by special order of His Holiness' (*de mandato speciali Sanctissimi*). The secretariat, for its part, contacted the Pope and asked whether there was indeed a special order. The Pope supposedly said there was none and that he had simply told Siri to send his text to the secretariat."

[102] This lack of clarity can be seen in what Prignon reported about the meeting of the moderators with the Pope on Tuesday (*JPrignon*, September 28, 1965, Prignon papers 1594.

[103] It is to be noted that Florit decided not to attend the technical meeting once the work on chapter II was completed (Florit papers, 1593 [September 27, 1965]). Did he take part in the final meetings of the commission?

[104] De Lubac used this expression in his report on the second meeting of the Doctrinal Commission (*Jde Lubac*, October 1, 1965).

process of being formed, was thus immediately divided due to a lack of clarity on the problem of tradition but also due to a more or less visible disagreement on strategy among the principal participants such as Colombo, Florit, and the leader of the Belgian team.

Only Tromp, who had exploded the "little bomb," seemed to pursue a course that was completely in conformity with his own theology, which could not be accused of lacking clarity. As the adversary of all others and the intermediary of Philips's precautionary activities, he became the object of the somewhat condescending humor of the rector of the Belgian College: "In general, everything is moving along well; it is tiresome work, and every once in a while Father Tromp wakes up. He is now very pleasant, but whenever a point is raised that challenges his theology, then he becomes terribly boring."[105]

C. The Impasses in the Doctrinal Commission

At 4:30 p.m. on Wednesday, September 29, in the usual place, the first of six plenary meetings of the Doctrinal Commission on the *modi* for *De revelatione* took place. While attendance was generally quite good, the participation of the bishops and the experts fell off at the two final meetings (Saturday, October 9, and Monday, October 11), which tackled chapters V and VI; these chapters were less controversial than the preceding four, and some may have considered them to be of less importance. The pace of the discussion was quite rapid, thanks to the immense amount of preparatory work done by the technical commission.[106] With a few exceptions, to which we shall return, the plenary assembly ratified the briefly argued proposals of the small commission; for the majority of the members of the commission, these represented a first commentary on the

---

[105] *JPrignon,* September 27, 1965 (Prignon papers, 1593, 1).

[106] A note of Congar, dated September 24, describes the work of some experts involved in the final correction of the texts: "I do not go to St. Peter's. The work is too boring and tiring. For us, the poor experts, it is even very appalling; I talked about this yesterday with Father Gagnebet. The prospect of putting 900 pages of Latin on index cards, of rediscussing all of it, of rewriting texts that will be modified, of reviewing the whole once again ... this prospect, this enormous machinery, are exhausting and crushing. I cannot go on with it. All the non-conciliar experts spend the morning meeting gossiping and seeing people. They have the strength for that. And they elicit or compose papers that fall down on us like rain and add still further to the weight of the papers under which we are suffocating! Oh, that it would end! I cannot go on with it" (*JCongar,* September 24, 1965; II, 405–6).

future constitution.[107] But the areas of disagreement in the schema already identified could not but reappear and at times drag out the debates, which, beginning at the second meeting (Friday, October 1), became increasingly dramatic; as Prignon put it, the commission was entering "upon the week that is decisive for the rest of the work and for the general direction of the Council."[108]

1. Safeguarding the "Economic" Approach to Revelation

Chapter I, which was reread during the first meeting, posed no special problems.[109] The authority of Vatican I, which was mentioned in the Prologue, was now flanked by the authority of Trent (*modus* 2). Several amendments were rejected that touched on the controversial relationship between the teaching of the recent magisterium and the biblical and patristic approach followed in the text. Some of these *modi* tried, once again, to reintroduce elements of doctrine into the "economic" description of revelation (*modi* 8, 10, 20); others came back again to the sacramental terminology of the text (*modi* 7 and 13). The ultimate point of reference for these amendments offered by the minority was the formal definition of revelation as objective speech (*modus generalis* 4)[110] and of faith in the narrow sense of *fides informis* (*modus* 31) as used by Vatican I. While Philips managed to avoid having people count heads on the question of revelation[111] (the response to *modus* 4 incorporated the objective definition of Vatican I into a vision of revelation as "active," that is, one which emphasized "God himself as self-revealing, the totality of the economy of salvation"[112]), he could not prevent the debate on faith (*modus* 31), in which, however, he won his case against Tromp.[113]

---

[107] This was true of the forty-five *modi* partially or wholly accepted and for the 163 *modi* rejected.

[108] *JPrignon,* October 1, 1965 (Prignon papers, 1597, 1).

[109] *Modi a Patribus conciliaribus propositi a Commissione doctrinali examinandi prooemium et caput I* (Florit papers, D 246). The results of the study of the *modi* are in *AS* IV/5, 681–91.

[110] During the work of the small commission Tromp had already raised lengthy difficulties regarding the idea of revelation, because to his mind revelation could consist solely of words (see *JPrignon,* September 27, 1965 [Prignon papers, 1595, 1]).

[111] See ibid., September 29, 1965 (Prignon papers, 1598, 1f.).

[112] *Modi a Patribus conciliaribus propositi a Commissione doctrinali examinandi prooemium et caput I; AS* IV/5, 682.

[113] See *RT 8,* 5ff., *Nodi* I (Florit papers, D 246, 6f.), and *AS* IV/5, 687f. The response amounted to what had already been said about a more biblical and personalist description of faith in the report of November 20, 1964 (B).

Two lengthier discussions had to do with the beginning and goal of the economy of salvation. The expression in *modus* 18 — "God manifested himself from the very beginning to the first parents, by personally addressing them" — was introduced by the Germans,[114] but was not accepted because, according to the members of the Biblical Institute, it favored both an anthropomorphic understanding of revelation and a historicist interpretation of the existence of Adam.[115] At Betti's suggestion, the commission considered the request as sufficiently honored by the words "in addition" that connected the two kinds of divine manifestation; it was satisfied simply to strengthen the idea of *self*-manifestation in describing revelation in the proper sense of the term.[116]

As for the goal of the economy of salvation, the phrase "*new (novum* instead of *novissimum)* and definitive covenant" (*modus* 27) was introduced after some debate, and, in order to prevent any confusion with "public revelation," the words "final revelation" were changed to "glorious manifestation *(manifestatio* or *epiphaneia)*" (*modus* 29).

The members of the commission rejected two requests of Franić and Parente that something be added to no. 4 on the motives of credibility and something to no. 6 on the "preambles of faith." This led to a first rumbling of thunder in the hitherto relatively calm heaven of the commission. Beginning with the next meeting (October 1), the rumbling became a storm, as we are told by Philips, who put himself in Parente's bad graces; Parente rebuked Philips for having torpedoed his two proposed amendments, and he added: "You will see the consequences."[117] But before the storm broke, the assembly also adopted, at the suggestion of Volk (drafter of the Secretariat for Christian Unity's preparatory schema "On the Word of God"), a new opening formula, a real speech-act that admirably applied the "kerygmatic" content of the future constitution to the relationship

---

[114] Prignon thought that *modus* 18 had been composed by K. Rahner (*JPrignon*, September 29, 1965 [Prignon papers, 1595, 2]), which is quite unlikely, given that Rahner laid more emphasis on the presence of grace even in the perception of the witness God bears to himself in created things (see the report on no. 3 of the schema dated July 3, 1964: "It is asserted that creation itself bears witness to God, but this leaves unresolved the question of whether God is in fact intervening with his grace even in the perception of this testimony").

[115] See *JPrignon*, September 29, 1965 (Prignon papers, 1595, 2); *TSemmelroth* (September 29, 1965).

[116] See *DBetti*, September 29, 1965, 359f. By using the present tense for all the "divine actions," except for God's self-manifestation to the first parents, the definitive text departs from the linear pattern of "creation – self-manifestation." In addition, the idea of "nature" disappeared from the final version.

[117] See *RT 8*, 5f.; *JPrignon*, October 1, 1965 (Prignon papers, 1597, 3).

that the Council itself said it had with the word of God: "Reverently listening to the word of God and proclaiming it with confidence.[118]

2. Should the Schema Speak More Clearly about the Constitutive Nature of Tradition?

The commission next took up chapter II.[119] According to Tromp, nos.
7 and 8 on "the apostles and their successors as heralds of the gospel"
and on "sacred tradition" raised only a few difficulties. Some twenty
minutes proved to be enough time to review the analysis of the thiry-
seven amendments.[120] In addition to some proposals regarded as unnecessary (for example, *modi* 2, 4, 11), useless (for example, *modus* 21), or
less clear (*modus* 10),[121] amendments were rejected that would have
expressed the close bond between this chapter on "the transmission of
divine revelation" and chapter III of *Lumen gentium* on "the hierarchical constitution of the Church and of the episcopate in particular."

The commission several times referred to the already promulgated
Constitution on the Church (on the role of the Spirit, *modus* 15, the
apostolicity of the Church, the role of the apostles, and apostolic

---

[118] *RT 8*, 6; *DBetti,* October 1, 1965, 360.
[119] *Modi a Patribus conciliaribus propositi a Commissione doctrinali examinandi,
caput II* (Florit papers, D 247); *AS* IV/5, 691–705.
[120] *RT 8*, 6.
[121] A detailed analysis of the proposals of the small commission reveals the great speci-
ficity of the criteria followed and the arguments advanced: stylistic criteria aimed at conciseness (what was not absolutely necessary or was useless was rejected), simplicity (e.g.,
modi 25, 32), clarity (as a reason for rejecting – *modus* 10 – or accepting – *modus* 25),
and avoiding ponderousness (*modi* 17, 18); the criterion of logical connection between
statements (e.g., *modi,* 3, 16); the criterion of accuracy in the citation of conciliar texts
(*modi* 3, 16) and of care in the citations of scripture (e.g., *modus* 6, accepted, and *modi* 19
and 37, rejected); and the refusal to consider once again questions already decided, accompanied now by referral back to arguments of earlier reports (*modi* 18, 21, 32, 37). Some
modi proposed the transfer of an affirmation from no. 8 (on tradition) to no. 10 (relationship of tradition and scripture to the Church as a whole and to the magisterium) or, conversely, the anticipation in no. 8 of what would be said in nos. 9 and 10 on the magisterium.
Such transfers were rejected as found in *modi* 23 and 29 (transferral of what Irenaeus says
about the "charism of truth" to no. 10), but a transfer was approved of what was said
about the role of the magisterium in the advance of tradition (*modus* 29 on no. 8). *Modus*
36 (no. 8) and 56 (no. 10) harked back to *modus* (no. 9), which laid out the difficulties
that would soon arise. The problem with the transfer of statements was that it involved not
only a matter of exposition but also had to do with the internal relationships among tradition, the scriptures, and the magisterium. Other *modi,* finally, touched on two fundamental matters: the hierarchical constitution of the Church (see *Lumen gentium* III) and the very
concept of tradition.

succession, *modi* 8, 14, and 20), even while emphasizing the specific character of chapter II, which intended to deal exclusively with the "transmission of revelation" (*modi* 8 and 14). The connection between public revelation and the Church was likewise touched on in some *modi* expressing fear that the reference to "apostolic men," who were in fact introduced as New Testament authors, could diminish the role of the apostles (*modi* 8, 12, and 13). Even more than in dealing with chapter I, the commission's response made clear the difference between the analytic and Scholastic language of the *modi* coming from the minority and the "global" and "nonexclusive" character of such formulas as "apostles and apostolic men" (*modi* 8 and 12) and "apostolic preaching" or "apostolic function" (*modi* 7, 8, 14, and 21); the text intended frequently to remain at the level of a description of fact (*modi* 4, 9).

Other amendments dealt directly with the concept of tradition. Thus the commission clarified the intrinsic connection between the act of transmitting and that which is transmitted (*modus* 30). It made more explicit its global statement that the canon of the scriptures became known through tradition (*modus* 29). Only one point interrupted this swift review: *modus* 29, composed by Betti and supported by 175 fathers, had to do with the role of the magisterium in the safeguarding and progress of tradition. At the urging of Congar, who was not at the meeting but had sent to Betti and Garonne a note on the controverted interpretation on the Irenaean phrase *charisma veritatis certum*,[122] the reference to it was removed, as was also the word *potissimum*, which would have given the magisterium an exaggerated place.[123]

When, about 4:30 p.m., the commission moved on to the study of the five amendments proposed for no. 9 (the reciprocal relationship between tradition and scripture), the atmosphere was already quite tense. Charles Moeller, who had not been au courant with the work of the technical commission, had just put his finger on the sore spot in *modus* 40 D (supported by 111 fathers), along with the commentary of the small commission on the term *directly*. He alerted Heuschen (!), Butler, and some other bishops, asking them not to let the *modus* pass. Rahner had also become alarmed and circulated among the fathers a page stressing the

---

[122] Congar's note is in Florit papers, F 302; see also *DBetti*, October 1, 1965, 360; and *JCongar*, October 1, 1965; II, 416.

[123] See *Modi* II (Florit papers, D 47, 4f.); *AS* IV/5, 696f.; see also *JPrignon*, October 1, 1965 (Prignon papers, 1597, 2).

danger of this amendment.[124] Another sheet from the Biblical Institute made the same point.[125]

> About thirty *modi* were reviewed very quickly… but the members were in haste to come to the essential point. Parente could not contain himself any longer and raised the question, but then there was a break, and during the break Father Rahner was indoctrinating Cardinal Léger and the German bishops, etc., McGrath, etc. Medina did the same thing; in a word, everyone sensed that the fight was about to break out.[126]

The meeting is difficult to reconstruct because of the excitement of the moment, which accentuated the diversity of the viewpoints in the reports available to us, but the result of the second meeting of the plenary commission is clear: the fight demolished the nascent third party and, above all, Philips's strategy of conciliation, which failed that evening in great part because the minority did not want conciliation. "Parente and friends wanted too much and lost everything."[127]

Philips spoke at least twice, first of all at the very beginning of the discussion,[128] when he suggested that the amendment of the 111 fathers (40 D) should be dealt with rather in connection with no. 10. This amounted to giving a privileged status to *modus* 56, which added, at the very point where there was question of "the magisterium that serves the word of God," an even paradoxical *(autem)* formula on Catholic teaching that "cannot be entirely *proved* from sacred scripture alone." But this formula made its point without the directness of *modus* 40 D and its compromising note. Had Philips been already influenced by the determined opposition of Moeller[129] and Rahner?

Parente categorically rejected this solution; on the subject of no. 9, he added that so serious a question could not be dealt with simply in passing. Father de Lubac wrote in his diary: "The little party defending the

---

[124] K. Rahner, "Animadversiones ad n. 40, pag. 7 fasciculi 'modorum' capitis II schematis De divina revelatione, sub lit. 'D' et 'Ad D' (pag. 16, lin. 13 schematis)," in Prignon papers, 1195.

[125] (Biblical Institute), "Animadversiones ad ea quae Subcommissio doctrinalis respondit circa modos a Patribus propositis relate ad cap. II Schematis De divina revelatione," in Prignon papers, 1193.

[126] *JPrignon,* October 1, 1965 (Prignon papers, 1597, 2).

[127] *JCongar,* October 1, 1965; II, 416.

[128] This emerges from the report of Tromp (*RT 8,* 6), whereas Betti (*DBetti,* October 1, 1965, 361; and de Lubac (*Jde Lubac,* October 1, 1965), mention only that Philips spoke during the course of the discussion.

[129] See the story of the meeting of Philips and Moeller in the car taking them to the commission (*JPrignon,* October 1, 1965 [Prignon papers, 1597, 1]).

'two sources' had Father Charles Boyer come as an expert; [after the break] Cardinal Ottaviani [therefore] gave the floor to Father Boyer, who read an entire dissertation."[130] But when Boyer drew the conclusion that Catholic teaching is not "sufficiently" contained in scripture (a formula that could be interpreted as referring to an insufficient *knowledge* through scripture), Parente corrected him by calling, instead of *sufficiently*, for *not totally*, which reestablished the quantitative meaning, that is, what tradition adds to scripture. Others, such as Ottaviani, Fernández, and Gagnebet supported him. Tromp, who also spoke in his capacity as secretary, introduced a *formal argument*, claiming that in the mixed commission the majority of the fathers supported an additive tradition but passed over it in silence for reasons of expediency; now, however, the opportuneness of introducing additive tradition was clearly established as a result of Paul VI's address on December 4, 1963, in which, speaking of revelation, he asked "for the elimination of certain doubts."[131]

A number of bishops responded on the same formal level with the observations that the addition would be contrary to the vote of the fathers (Henriquez[132]), that it would undermine the agreement with the Secretariat for Christian Unity and with Bea (Charue), and that it would have a disastrous psychological effect on the Council (Schröffer, Doumith, and McGrath).[133] Few members of the majority tackled the problem in depth. When questioned by Schröffer, Rahner, who had distributed his "Animadversiones" before the meeting, said he was formally opposed to the change in the text. His reason was that by suggesting the thesis of the material insufficiency of scripture and by introducing an "obscurity" into

---

[130] *Jde Lubac*, October 1.

[131] *RT 8*, 7. According to de Lubac, immediately after the break Ottaviani advanced another formal argument (which Tromp did not report): "Cardinal Ottaviani gave a short address, a kind of sales talk; he claimed that there had never been a real mixed commission established to recast the schema on the 'two sources'; John XXIII, he said, simply added some members to the theological commission; the latter thus still had full authority to decide what it wanted, and was not bound by the decision of a supposed mixed commission that never existed, and so on. At least four bishops gave the lie to this address, first among them Christopher Butler, then Schröffer, Henriquez, and McGrath. The last named said that he was restoring the true version of what had happened 'for my own peace of conscience'" (*Jde Lubac*, October 1).

[132] Betti remarked the atmosphere was quite agitated, especially because the constantly repeated *non licet, non licet* of Henriquez (*DBetti*, October 1, 1965, 361).

[133] See *RT 8*, 7; and *JPrignon*, October 1, 1965 (Prignon papers, 1597, 2). De Lubac reported that "at the moment when Ottaviani sensed that the struggle was a losing one, the cardinal cried out, as though calling for help: "Parente! Gagnebet!" (*Jde Lubac*, October 1, 1965).

the text, the amendment went beyond the competence of the commission; if it was "obvious that all Catholic teaching cannot be found explicitly and formally in the scriptures," the text as it stood was already teaching "the formal insufficiency admitted by all."[134] Léger expressed the same view at the end of the meeting.

Congar, who had given Garrone his page of thoughts on *modus* 29 *(charisma veritatis certum)*, said he agreed with the addition of *modus* 40 D, inasmuch as "these words express a fact that, as such, is certain."[135] Yet he would later regret the excessively unpolished formulation of the *modus* and, in particular, the words "from scripture," which risked being understood as meaning a "*material* insufficiency" of scripture.[136] His position was echoed to some extent in the intervention of Butler, who noted the difference between "is not contained *in* sacred scripture" and "cannot be proved *from* the scriptures."[137]

Are we to take Butler's statement as support for Betti's "formula of agreement"? Twice, in fact, Florit defended *modus* 40 D but *without* the addition of "directly," and on the second occasion was supported by an intervention of Betti;[138] he was unsuccessful. That a degree of confusion had been reached can be seen from the fact that the diaries at our disposal had trouble in correctly situating the intervention of that key individual, Colombo. de Lubac assimilated Colombo's position to that of Florit:

---

[134] Tromp recorded only this last statement (*RT 8*, 7), while Semmelroth (*TSemmelroth*, October 1, 1965) and Prignon (*JPrignon*, October 1, 1965 [Prignon papers, 1597, 2]) emphasized, above all else, how serious a matter Rahner thought the acceptance of the correction proposed by the *commissio parva* to be. According to de Lubac, Rahner spoke "in a confused and violent manner" (*Jde Lubac*, October 1, 1965).

[135] *JCongar*, October 1, 1965; II, 416; Congar agreed with Rahner on this point, but, being less mindful than Rahner and Betti of the possible interpretations of the word *directly*, he had a different appreciation of the value of the formula proposed by Philips.

[136] Congar would take a more explicit position on *modus* 40 D on the eve of the very last meeting (October 18) of the Doctrinal Commission; he did so in a note sent to several fathers and experts, "De habitudine inter Traditionem (apostolicam) et S. Scripturam" (in Florit papers, F 303).

[137] *RT 8*, 7. Semmelroth, who was not present for the second part of the meeting, seemed to take the same view in his diary, without, however, seeing the ambiguity of the word *directly*: "Father Rahner and some others were very agitated [by the *modus*] and sought to prevent its acceptance. When they succeeded, I too was glad. On the other hand, I think the *modus* to be innocuous, since it must be admitted that not everything can be proved *directly* from the scriptures, even if one maintains that the whole of revelation is contained in the scriptures. *To be contained and to think provable are not one and the same*" (*TSemmelroth*, October 1, 1965, emphasis added).

[138] *RT 8*, 6, and 7; *DBetti*, October 1, 1965, 361; *Jde Lubac*, October 1, 1965; Prignon (*JPrignon*, October 1, 1965 [Prignon papers, 1597]), on the other hand, makes no distinction between Philips's formula (containing "directly") and Betti's (without "directly").

"Some were murmuring that the Pope might have suggested this compromise";[139] Prignon saw in the intervention a support for Philips's formulas;[140] and Tromp interpreted it as an assertion of the "additive tradition" defended by the minority.[141] Philips then spoke a second time to end the debate. Although he tried to show that this correction was not as serious as Rahner or others thought ("it is not substantial nor does it contradict the text, but simply explains it"[142]), "he was obliged to admit that it was preferable not to alter the text in any way whatever, since that would immediately be interpreted as calling into question the agreement reached, and this in turn would create division in the Council."[143]

In the vote that followed, fifteen of those voting said they did not want any change in the text. The "third party" attempt at conciliation was thus unsuccessful, due both to the attitude of the minority and to the formal arguments made by the majority. Prignon was quite accurate when he noted that "Parente's intervention tipped the debate, and this was indeed the fundamental question the fathers had in mind; they evidently feared now that the correction proposed by Msgr. Philips would take them much further than they intended."[144] But the rector of the Belgian College did not say that in the final analysis the ambiguity that the word "directly" introduced in *modus* 40 D and which was increased by the explanation given of it, played a large part in the failure of the "formula of agreement" initially suggested by the people from Florence.

But at this point it must be added that the question Philips proposed for a vote, and the result of the vote, only added to the confusion. Thus Tromp noted that Ottaviani voted in favor of the present state of the text because he wanted to introduce an addition in no. 10. (Tromp added that some others were perhaps thinking along the same line.)[145] Prignon, on the other hand, gave a quite different interpretation of the result: as the question was proposed, there should have been a second vote: would those opposed to a change in the present text have accepted the addition of an "explanatory note"? "It is quite certain that there were *more than*

[139] *Jde Lubac*, October 1, 1965.

[140] *JPrignon*, October 1, 1965 (Prignon papers, 1597, 2). Philips had met with Colombo the evening before, bringing him up to date on the significance of his action and his formula and asking him to say "a few words at the meeting in support of this explanation" (ibid., 1596 [September 30], 4).

[141] *RT 8*, 6 and 7.

[142] This is how Tromp reports Philips's conclusion *(RT 8, 7)*.

[143] *JPrignon*, October 1, 1965 (Prignon papers, 1597, 2).

[144] Ibid.

[145] *RT 8, 7*

fifteen who wanted no change in the text, but would some of those who voted no perhaps have accepted, not a change, but an explanatory note?"[146].

This second vote did not take place, however, because the Cardinal President immediately ended the meeting. Did he do so in order to leave the future open and to reopen the debate at the next "crossroads," when the subject would be *modus* 56? (That is actually what would happen on October 4.) Or was the reason rather that Philips's proposal had not been very clear? This is the view that emerges from the diaries: while Tromp and Prignon reported that Philips's suggestion was to "keep the text as it was, with a note on constitutive tradition,"[147] de Lubac, Rahner, and Congar understood it to mean rather "that the explanation given in Florit's formula should be introduced into the report; this would make it possible not to change the text of the schema itself."[148] On the following day, Rahner added, when speaking with Congar, that "this would satisfy those who wanted a kind of *nota praevia*."[149]

Hardly had the meeting ended when the four main partners in the conversation, namely, Ottaviani and the members of the "third party" in the affair, Florit, Colombo, and Philips, were already trying to offer other formulas.[150] In fact, matters could not remain where they were, and during the weekend everybody set to work. They knew they would face the same problem when they came to *modus* 56.[151] At the beginning of the third meeting, at 4:30 p.m. on Monday, October 4, the commission completed its rereading of no. 9[152] and then decided, rather quickly,[153] on the first

---

[146] *JPrignon,* October 1, 1965 (Prignon papers, 1597, 2f.).

[147] *RT 8,* 7; *JPrignon,* October 1, 1965 (Prignon papers, 1597, 2f.).

[148] *Jde Lubac,* October 1, 1965.

[149] *JCongar,* October 2, 1965; II, 417.

[150] *JPrignon,* October 1, 1965 (Prignon papers, 1597, 3). Here is another highly significant fact: While the Doctrinal Commission was holding its turbulent meeting, a first meeting, co-chaired by Cardinal Martin and Pastor Boegner, was taking place at Saint-Louis des Français on the ecumenical translation of the Bible for french-speaking countries, the translation to be done by an editorial committee of sixty well-known biblical scholars, half of them Catholics and half of them Protestants. This project anticipated to some extent what would be set down in no. 22 of chapter VI of *De revelatione* (see the moving report of this meeting in Jauffrès, *Carnets conciliaires,* 264f.).

[151] *JPrignon,* October 4, 1965 (Prignon papers, 1598, 2).

[152] No. 9 brought with it only five *modi*: of these the commission had already fully discussed *modus* 40, as well as *modus* 42, which defended the theory of the two sources. Neither was accepted.

[153] Léger, however, asked, but without insisting on it, that the commission return to no. 8 (*modus* 29: "Unus postulat...," in *Modi* II [Florit papers, D 247, 4]) and that his expert, A. Naud, be allowed to speak: the latter, intending unequivocally to avoid an ambiguous

modi offered on no. 10.[154] Around 5:00 p.m. the debate on the relationship of scripture to tradition began again. The commission was at almost
the same point at which it had been on the preceding Friday; but this
time Colombo spoke out plainly and offered his own amendment: the
three formulas being debated, those of Philips, Colombo, and Parente,
represented, for the first time, *two* attempts at an agreement and the position of the minority.

Philips began the discussion and asked that, as the reporter, he be
heard to the end. His exposition, with its scholarly balance, attempted
to answer everyone. He said that his formula — "The sacred scriptures
transmit the whole *(complexum)* of the Christian mystery, without therefore giving formal expression to all revealed truths" — said nothing
about the controverted question of the material content of scripture and
tradition. Therefore, it would not change the substance of the text and
would respect what was already taught there about "constitutive tradition." Admittedly, the addition was not necessary; nor did it cause any
danger in the one direction or the other, since the formula was simply
negative. It said only that all truths were in the scriptures, but *not formally*; Rahner, Congar, and others would agree with this. At the same
time, it was useful because it could ease the fears of everyone and satisfy the request of Paul VI as expressed in his address on December 4,
1963.[155]

Speaking for himself, for Heuschen,[156] and for Butler, Colombo suggested a different formula to be added to no. 9, where the question of the
relations between scripture and tradition was directly tackled: "The result
is that the Church does not derive her certainty about divine revelation
from sacred scripture alone," a formula changed during the debate by

---

formulation that might suggest the idea of a *growth in apostolic tradition*, as distinct from
a growth in *teaching*, proposed that what was said of the actualization of scripture be trans-
ferred to no. 10 on the magisterium, whose function this actualization is (see G. Routhier,
"L'itinéraire d'un Père conciliaire: Le Cardinal Léger," *CrSt* 19 [1998], 140f). Here we
see, once again, the strange convergence between Léger's proposal and some requests of
the minority (brought together in the same *modus* 29).

[154] Of *modi* 43–55 some, of lesser importance, were rejected in the name of stylistic
criteria and others (43, 49, 52, and 55) because they had already been taken up in connection with *Lumen gentium*, chapter III, especially no. 25. In connection with no. 23, the
commissio parva defended the words "pie audit" because they reflected the insistence of
the "separated brethren" and the "kerygmatic" context of the schema.

[155] The text of Philips's proposal is in Prignon papers, 1182.

[156] According to Prignon, Philips developed his formula together with Heuschen
(*JPrignon,* October 4, 1965 [Prignon papers, 1598, 2]). Why was Heuschen a backer of
Colombo as well?

Poma to "certitude about revealed truths."[157] Finally, just before the vote was taken, Parente asked to include in no. 9 the words: "Although clearly distinct from one another, sacred scripture and tradition make up a single deposit."[158]

In the discussion that followed Heuschen observed that the two formulas of Philips and Colombo had the same purpose and that Philips's would contribute a valuable positive element. But most of the speakers of both the majority and the minority expressed reservations, beginning with Rahner, Gagnebet, and Congar. When queried by König, the German theologian did not seem to oppose Colombo's proposition but distanced himself from that of Philips, challenging the latter's statement that "*everything* is contained *in a non-formal way* in scripture," on the grounds that scripture cannot bear witness to its own canonicity. Gagnebet preferred silence to accepting a formula that does not intend to say anything.[159] Congar, too, thought "that Philips's text... does not intend to say anything; it states something so obvious (Denzinger is not part of scripture!) that the minority would never be satisfied with it. To the extent that the formula says anything, it favors rather the thesis of the material sufficiency of scripture; that is surely traditional."[160] He leaned, therefore, toward Colombo's proposal.

Among the bishops many opposed this second "Philips amendment." Some regarded the term *formaliter* to be overly scholastic (McGrath and Doumith);[161] others, among them Poma and Butler, preferred Colombo's formula. This was a moment of success for Florit and Betti, who could not fail to see the "hidden complicity" between the Colombo amendment and that of the 111 fathers, that is, *modus* 40 D, which did not contain the ambiguous word "directly."[162]

When Philips spoke again in defense of his formula, the question of procedure became unavoidable: Was a new passage to be composed by a small commission, as Charue proposed, or was there to be an end to the

---

[157] See *RT 8*, 8, and *DBetti*, October 4, 1965, 362. This statement is almost identical with the definitive formula.

[158] As formulated, Parente's proposition seems to belong to no. 9 (but Tromp's report is not very clear, and Colombo's report connects it with no. 10).

[159] *RT 8*, 8.

[160] *JCongar*, October 4, 1965; II, 420.

[161] "Cardinal Browne raised a difficulty: 'Where do the scriptures contain the whole of the Christian mystery? I have not seen it anywhere,' he said.... What he had in mind was a list of theses" (*JCongar*, October 4, 1965; II, 420–21).

[162] *DBetti*, October 4, 1965, 362.

process because it contradicted what had been determined by the Council (Henriquez), or were there, once again, to be two successive votes, one on the *necessity* of an addition and then, if this necessity existed, a choice of one of the two formulas (König)? It was this third solution that won out. A vote was then taken on the question of whether an addition needed to be made at line 37 of no. 10; 13 of the 24 voters said yes, 11 said no.

What a reversal from the day before, when a majority of 15 out of 25 voters had opted to maintain the text! Was Tromp correct, then, when he remarked in his report on the preceding Friday that Ottaviani, and perhaps others, were for keeping no. 9 as it was because they wanted to leave open the possibility of an addition to no. 10 that would support the thesis of an additive tradition? Or since that last meeting had the efforts at conciliation won greater support among the fathers of the commission than did the fifteen votes in favor of keeping the text unchanged (so Prignon thought in his report)?

The ensuing debate on procedure ended, in any case, with Ottaviani, supported by Butler of the "third party," agreeing that a formula should now be chosen. Philips then proposed that a separate vote should be taken on each of three formulas (his, Colombo's, and Parente's) and that the first one to win a majority should be adopted. A vote was immediately taken, despite Heuschen's request for a pause that would have made consultation possible. Philips's formula passed with a majority of 14 votes against 10.[163] Here was a second surprising turn after the discussion that had just taken place. But the success of this amendment was to be short lived.

When compared with what was happening on that same day outside the Council but in connection with it, the debate in the Doctrinal Commission on relations among scripture, tradition, and magisterium appeared quite restricted or even narrow. Since early afternoon Paul VI had been in New York to address the United Nations. At 8:00 p.m. all of Rome was seated before the little screen to listen to his address. The date was well-chosen for this solemn homage to the international organization, which included a vigorous denunciation of war and the arms race and a vibrant call for fraternal cooperation among all the peoples of the earth. It was the feast of St. Francis of Assisi, patron of Italy. The Council mass had

---

[163] *RT 8*, 9 (Tromp added a vote *iuxta modum* that proposed *summum* in place of *complexum*). After a well-deserved pause, five minutes sufficed for rereading the four remaining *modi* on no. 10: the response to *modi* 57 and 58 offered commentaries on the relations among tradition, scripture, and magisterium, while *modus* 60, which was accepted in part, introduced into this net of relationships the unifying action of the Holy Spirit.

been celebrated that morning for the Pope and his mission of peace; the gospel had then been enthroned by the superior general of the Capuchins. The connection between the Pope's apostolic journey, these actions at the Council, the straw vote on religious freedom, and the debates in the hall on schema XIII was deeply symbolic, for it suggested to public opinion a new and more evangelical way of being present within the history of the human race.

But this global event, which some described in their diaries as "significant,"[164] left no trace in the pages of Prignon who, that same evening, reviewed at length what had gone on during the last ten days:

> I should add that there is something mysterious about this business. In fact, no one, on our side at least, has seen the letter of the Pope of which Tromp spoke. He never showed it to Msgr. Philips, and no one knows what is in it; no one knows for sure. I raised this question explicitly with Msgr. Philips in order to clarify matters: "Was there or was there not a letter from the Pope and from the Secretariat of State?" He told me he did not doubt the existence of the letter from the Pope, because he regarded it as unthinkable that Ottaviani and Tromp invented it out of whole cloth.... Since Colombo was not au courant, he wondered whether Father Tromp had not exaggerated the matter in an attempt to obtain the result he wanted and to reintroduce surreptitiously the assertion of two sources.... Msgr. Philips told me that he found himself in a Cornelian situation. Not knowing whether Tromp was exaggerating and whether a coup was planned.... and, on the other hand, fearing new interventions of the Pope that could give rise to a new "black week" and a new *Nota praevia*, bringing in its train all the inconveniences and difficulties we experienced last year, he thought it his duty, as a lesser evil, to propose a *modus* in answer to the one called for by the Coetus Internationalis Patrum, a *modus* written in such a way that it yielded nothing essential but would give obvious satisfaction to the minority. Obvious, because in fact the *modus* voted on this evening leaves untouched the question of the two sources and cannot satisfy the minority. It is true that at the end of the meeting Gagnebet, Schauf, Balić, and Tromp did not hide their dissatisfaction. It could be asked, and in fact I asked Msgr. Philips, why, after the fathers had voted against the addition of a text in no. 9, he himself proposed that an addition be made to no. 10 along the lines I have just described. Msgr. Philips answered that this was the only way of avoiding more serious consequences.[165]

Philips's tactical argument was this: being persuaded that in one way or another the implacable adversaries of the text would go to the Pope to obtain a decisive intervention from him, "he [Philips] won the passage

---

[164] See, e.g., Jauffrès, *Carnets conciliaires*, 266–69.
[165] *JPrignon,* October 4, 1965 (Prignon papers, 1598, 3f.).

of an innocuous *modus* that could, if need be, serve as an excuse" — for the Pope? — "to refuse the demands of the minority."[166] Prignon added that "this move was very unpleasant because Philips was perfectly aware that he risked losing the trust of the majority of the group that had always supported him. These people, not being au courant with the affair, would ask what was going on and why this insistence, this even though Philips was not yielding on anything essential. 'But,' he told me, 'there are times in life when one must make a personal sacrifice for the greater good.'"[167] An admission, this, that was utterly to be respected, but also marked, perhaps, by a touch of naiveté.

Minds had not been set at rest by the Monday meeting.[168] At the beginning of the fourth meeting of the Doctrinal Commission, on Wednesday, October 5, Parente asked to speak and reopened the debate once again, remarking that for him it was a question of conscience and faith, since Philips's addition favored the idea of the sufficiency of the scriptures.[169] When Ottaviani suggested that the fathers express their views on the question, he was met with complete silence. Then König, Charue, Butler, and Henriquez spoke up to say that the commission had to remain at the point it had reached. To go back on a decision would require a unanimous vote of the commission; the question at issue was not a matter of faith.

But the wind shifted one last time when McGrath,[170] Henriquez, and Spanedda made the point, with the *Ordo concilii* in hand, that since a two-thirds majority was required for adding to a text, the vote of October 4 in favor of the "Philips amendment" was not valid. Charue then proposed returning to the previous text; Parente and Ottaviani supported

---

[166] Ibid., 4.

[167] Ibid. See Rahner's remark to Congar: "Philips has been overly diplomatic; he pointed out that in the report the subcommission for the *expensio modorum* had accepted *modus* 40 D" (*JCongar*, October 2, 1965; II, 417).

[168] As early as Tuesday challenges based on the regulations were heard. Because the text had not received a two-thirds vote, it could not be regarded as accepted, inasmuch as the regulations called for a two-thirds majority on doctrinal questions. In addition, Gagnebet of the Holy Office wanted to revive the question on the grounds that what had been accepted was ridiculous and could not satisfy the minority. A number of fathers were then alerted by Moeller, some of them indicating that they were fed up and wearied. In addition it was learned the next day that Ottaviani was alerting the group made up of Ruffini, Siri, and others (see *JPrignon*, October 5, 1965 [Prignon papers, 1599, 2], and October 6, 1965 [Prignon papers, 1600, 1f.).

[169] Ibid., October 6 (Prignon papers 1600, 2); *TSemmelroth*, October 6; and *DBetti*, October 6, 1965, 363.

[170] McGrath said first that the question was not one of faith but of timeliness, and he again brought up the matter of a two-thirds majority (see *RT 8*, 10; *JCongar*, October 6, 1965; II, 423).

this proposal. The vote that immediately followed was 18 in favor of the former text, 5 against, with 1 abstention. Congar commented: "Thus, for a second time, the opposition tried to win more and lost everything."[171]

It was, in fact, the logic of all or nothing that won the day. That was what most of the bishops of the majority had wanted ever since the meeting on October 1; it was what Gagnebet, now joined by Parente and Ottaviani, had wanted since Monday, October 4. The scattered character of the 276 amendments "in favor of agreement" on three different numbers of the text was in good measure responsible for the successive revivals of a debate, the outcome of which could be foreseen. On that evening, then, Philips's strategy suffered a definitive shipwreck but left most of the theologians of the majority in great anxiety about the future of the text.[172] Betti seemed hopeful that his own "memorandum" in favor of the amendment of the 111 fathers, sent to Florit on October 4, might end on top.[173] Ottaviani, for his part, would write to Paul VI on October 11, suggesting a *Nota praevia* as a solution.[174]

3. Do the Scriptures Teach "Saving Truth"?

Once this episode came to an end, the commission took up the rereading of chapter III on the inspiration and interpretation of sacred scripture. Work on it had begun on Monday, October 4, at the end of the third meeting. *Modi* 1–7 and 10–11, attached to no. 11 ("The Inspiration and Truth of Sacred Scripture"), had not raised any special difficulty,[175] but some

---

[171] *JCongar*, October 6, 1965; II, 424.

[172] *JPrignon*, October 6, 1965 (Prignon papers, 1600, 3f.); *JCongar*, October 6, 1965; II, 424; *TSemmelroth*, October 6; and *Jde Lubac*, October 6.

[173] *DBetti*, October 4, 1965, 362f.; on October 8 Florit informed Betti that he had sent the *Promemoria* on to Colombo for communication to the Pope (ibid., October 8, 1965, 364).

[174] On Sunday, October 10, before the end of the debate in the commission, the Pope wrote to Ottaviani asking for the amended text. It was in his answer of October 11 that Ottaviani complained of serious defects in the amended schema, telling Paul VI of his view that an intervention was needed analogous with that of the *Nota praevia* for the *De Ecclesia*. In this same letter he thanked the Pope for having safeguarded celibacy (*AS* V/3, 408–10).

[175] There were questions of style (*modi* 2 and 5), citation (*modi* 3, 4, and 11), the shifting of one or other statement (*modus* 7), and so on, all of them decided according to the usual criteria. Two *modi*, however, dealt with matters of substance: the first and general *modus* represented the mind of those who argued for maintaining the completely historical character of the scriptures as a protection of the text against improper interpretations, and of those who wanted inspiration to be described in conjunction with the evolution of religious knowledge. *Modus* 6 proposed retaining an instrumentalist conception of inspiration (see *Modi a Patribus conciliaribus propositi a Commissione doctrinali examinandi, caput III,* in Florit papers, D 248, 1–3; *AS* IV/5, 706–10).

time had to be spent on *modi* 8 and 9. The expression *veritas salutaris* (saving truth), which had been introduced during the revision of the text in November 1964, gave rise to a new debate. Philips and Tromp then explained the agreement reached in the small commission in reply to *modus* 8, that a note was to introduce a series of references to St. Augustine as well as to the encyclicals *Providentissimus* and *Divino afflante Spiritu* on the Bible and was to state explicitly that the formula "scripture teaches ... saving truth" "was to be understood in a positive and not an exclusive sense."[176]

Like the difficulties in preceding chapters, the difficulty here was between the analytic language of Neo-Scholasticism and the positive and nonexclusive language of the scriptures,[177] or even between a material or quantitative conception of the truth of the scriptures and a formal or qualitative specification of that truth, a point made by König and others (van Dodewaard, Pelletier, and Benoit).[178] König and Charue added that from this point of view the formula represented real progress. Browne and Ottaviani, joined by Garofalo, thought that, on the contrary, the formula introduced serious confusion; their chief fear was that it was based on an illegitimate parallel between the object of the Church's infallibility and the object of scriptural inerrancy. This was an argument advanced by some fathers in November 1964.[179] Finally, Florit proposed adopting the formulation suggested by seventy-three fathers, namely, that the scriptures contain "everything that God wanted to communicate through them," a formula already quite close to that which would be adopted after the Pope's intervention. The debate then ended with the decision to keep the text as it was. "I am very happy with this," Congar commented in his diary. "It is progress in the direction I have long been advocating."[180]

The commission continued its rereading of chapter III on the afternoon of October 6. Most of the responses prepared by the small commission on no. 12 ("The Interpretation of the Scriptures") passed without difficulty. The group had to dwell, however, on *modi* 24 and 25. Parente, Garofalo, and others wanted to restrict the recourse to literary

[176] See *RT 8,* 9, and Philips's note, added to his *relatio super modos* (*JPrignon,* October 7, 1965 [Prignon papers, 1175, 2bis]).

[177] See the references to the biblical expressions "the Word of truth" and "Gospel of your salvation" (Eph 1:13; 2 Cor 4:2; etc.) in the response to *modus* 8.

[178] In addition, Butler secured the introduction of a reference also to St. Thomas, and Heuschen managed to effect the withdrawal, from the response, of the reference to 1 John 3:8 and 10 as a basis for the expression "saving truth."

[179] See *RT 8,* 9; *AS* IV/1, 358f., report on no. 11 (F).

[180] *JCongar,* October 4, 1965; II, 421.

genres and to the "conventions followed in human relations at that period" (the New Testament period), while others, such as Butler and Benoit, held firmly to the existing text. Agreement was finally reached on a positive formulation:"Rightly to understand what the sacred author wanted to affirm in his work, due attention must be paid both to the customary and characteristic patterns of perception, speech... and to the conventions that the people of his time followed in their relations with one another."[181] All gave approval to amendment 27 which, at the beginning of the paragraph on the ecclesial interpretation of the scriptures (still in no. 27), introduced the Spirit as the one whose work it is to establish a close connection between the redaction, the reading, and the interpretation of the biblical text.

Finally, a further debate on amendments 30 and 33 made it possible, through an exchange among Betti, Benoit, McGrath, and Philips, to state clearly that the Church in its entirety, that is, its apostolic (and patristic) tradition, and not the magisterium alone (as *modus* 33 would have it), is the final judge in the interpretation of the scriptures.[182] In any case, this was already the teaching of Vatican I, as König reminded the commission.[183] Among the four *modi* for no. 13, only the first (*modus* 35) deserved attention; at the request of Colombo and relying on the authority of Vatican I,[184] the proviso "the truth and holiness of God being always safeguarded" was reintroduced into the remarks on the "condescension of God" in the scriptures.[185]

After a recess the examination of the *modi* for chapter IV was begun and required only about twenty minutes. The connection between no. 14 on "the history of salvation in the books of the Old Testament" and no. 3 of the first chapter, on preparation for the gospel, was made clearer.[186] In no. 15 on "the importance of the Old Testament for Christians" greater emphasis was placed on the messianic character of the kingdom, for which the entire ancient economy was a preparation (*modus* 8), and the tension was maintained between the imperfections of the Old Testament

---

[181] *RT 8*, 10, *Modi* II (Florit papers, D 248, 4); *AS* IV/5, 711.

[182] *RT 8*, 11, *Modi* II (Florit papers, D 248, 5); *AS* IV/5, 712f.

[183] See Denziger-Hünermann, *Enchiridion*, H 3007.

[184] As Tromp remarks in *RT 8*, 11.

[185] Ibid.; *AS* IV/5, 712f. The small commission had not accepted this *modus* (*Modi* II, in Florit papers, D 248, 5).

[186] *Modus* 1 (Florit papers, D 249, 1), which came from the Biblical Institute (in *Modi qui proponuntur pro schemate "De divina revelatione,"* in Florit papers, D 245, 9), was partially accepted. The verbs *intendens* and *praeparans* were brought from no. 3 to express the *universality* of the salvation willed and prepared by God.

books and the divine pedagogy, but without going into details (*modus* 11). Finally, the complex nature of the theology of fulfillment in the New Testament books was highlighted by more abundant citations (*modus* 17) and by a slight change of the end of paragraph 16 on "the unity of the two Testaments" (*modus* 18).[187]

4. Should the Historical Character of the Gospels Be Asserted?

After this interlude chapter V gave rise once again to some fundamental disagreements. The commission passed quickly over no. 17 on the excellence of the New Testament and no. 18 on the apostolic origin of the gospels, stopping only for a few moments on the naming of the New Testament prophets in the citation from Ephesians 3:4–6 (the naming was challenged by some: *modus* 6),[188] and on the question of the apostolic origin of the gospels"(*modus* 15). Some fathers feared either a denial of inspiration in regard to the facts told by the evangelists or a claim that *all* the facts were reported in the gospels. Was this a new allusion to the debate on the relationship of tradition and scripture (Parente)? This would surprise no one, since the teaching in chapter V had its basis in the teaching given in nos. 8–9 of chapter II, which obviously had to do also with the question of the historical foundation of the Church.[189] Rahner defended the text, and it remained unchanged.

Although it was already 7:00 p.m. and the meeting had already had its full share of incidents and feelings, the group did not hesitate to tackle, once again, no. 19 on the historical character of the gospels. *Modus* 16, the first of the four *modi*, raised problems both of form and of substance. First of all, the formula "the Church held and holds," used twice elsewhere in nos. 18 and 19, was discussed. Some fathers, Colombo for example, wanted it changed to "the Church believed and believes" in order to avoid basing the historicity of the gospels on a simple act of trust in what historians have reported, while others, such as Garofalo, suggested simply removing from the response to the *modus* the remark that gave the formulation a lesser theological qualification. Finally, Tromp,

---

[187] *Modi* 17 and 18 also came from the Biblical Institute (see *Modi qui proponuntur* [Florit papers, D 245, 10f.] and *Modi IV* [Florit papers, D 249, 2f.]).

[188] *Modi … caput V*, Florit papers, D 250, 1; and *RT 8*, 11f.

[189] See *modus* 2, which challenged the expression *praecellenti modo*, even though it simply repeated the words *speciali modo* used in no. 8 of the inspiration of the scriptures; *modus* 3, which wanted to introduce a remark on the foundation of the Church; *modus* 17, which likewise raised the problem of the foundation of the Church, and which, as the response noted, had already been taken up in no. 19 of *Lumen gentium*.

Salaverri, and Rahner succeeded in obtaining the clarification found in the report, namely, that the formula chosen rightly combines faith *and* reason in the acceptance of the historicity of the gospels.[190]

As for the historicity itself (the substantive question), some fathers regretted the disappearance of this concept,[191] but experts such as Philips and Rahner showed, once again, the ambiguity of the term in contemporary theological language. The text therefore remained as it was. But the question would arise again in connection with *modi* 17–19, which would be discussed on Saturday; that they would meet on a Saturday was by way of exception, the reporter added, with the agreement of almost everyone, except for the many who had already left!

On the morning of October 9, then, the commission tackled once again the question of the historical character of the gospels, but, according to Tromp, it wasted a good deal of time in ineffectual discussions. The complete citation of the beginning of Acts (1:1–2) had already been introduced into the text: "These four gospels faithfully transmit what Jesus, the Son of God, really taught and did during his life among men, *until the day when he was taken up to heaven*" (*modus* 16b). The purpose was to avoid taking a position on the resurrection as a *historical fact* (*modus* 19). But once again, late in considering decisions already taken, Parente now renewed the debate by seeking to introduce more specific statements, especially on the subject of the words of the Risen Lord (*modus* 17).[192] This way of surreptitiously introducing a purely verbal conception of revelation was immediately thwarted by a phalanx of defenders (Charue, Garrone, Heuschen, Philips, Betti, Butler, Rahner, and Benoit). The text was therefore left as it was.

The attack was then launched a second time by Spanedda (Sardinia), especially in connection with *modus* 18 but also in connection with *modus* 16c, already rejected at the previous meeting. The speaker called to mind the Instruction *Sancta mater ecclesia* of the Biblical Commission, cited in a note to the text). Cardinal-President Browne had Castellino, one of the consultors, speak. But Rahner and Rigaux immediately replied that the commission had deliberately been silent on this question; some of the bishops came to their aid: Charue, Heuschen, McGrath, Garrone, and Butler, with the last-named emphasizing the difference between the

---

[190] See *Modi V* (Florit papers, D 250, 2f.); *RT 8*, 12; and *AS* IV/5, 722f.

[191] They were the same 175 fathers who asked that the preamble of the constitution make reference to Trent and that chapter II include a reference to the *charisma veritatis* of the bishops.

[192] See *Modi V* (Florit papers, D 250, 1); *RT 8*, 13.

classical conception of history and the concept of the history of salvation, which was familiar to Protestants. The minority — Browne, Parente, and Garofalo — attacked once again, but when, after three-quarters of an hour of debate, König urged that a vote be taken, the majority once again prevailed, 13 to 7, and the text remained as it was.[193]

The response to *modus* 18a had in fact made it clear that the formulation "the sacred writers ... always transmit to us the honest truth *(vera et sincera)* about Jesus" states both the objective and the subjective aspects of the relationship of the evangelists to what actually occurred.[194] The five *modi* for no. 20 on "the other New Testament writings" caused no problems.

5. *Is Reading the Bible for Everyone?*

Finally, at the end of the morning, the commission moved on to examine chapter VI on sacred scripture in the life of the Church.[195] The debates that took place during this final stage repeated what had already happened in the rereadings of the preceding chapters; the clash and the strategies did not vary noticeably. The first and second *modi* set the tone. Some asked, unsuccessfully, that the text speak more explicitly of tradition, to the point even of changing the title of the chapter, whose "formal object, however, is the scriptures" (response to the first *modus*). Others opposed the parallel made between the bread of the word and the bread of Christ's body,[196] but they were unconvincing. In contrast, the acceptance of amendment 5, which came from the Biblical Institute,[197] made it possible to emphasize a little more the regulatory function of the scriptures, which had been perceptibly weakened in the preceding version.

After a brief discussion of the different versions and translations of the scriptures (no. 22),[198] no. 23 provided the fathers with a new occasion for

---

[193] See *RT 8,* 13f.; *JPrignon,* October 10, 1965 (Prignon papers, 1602, 1); *Jde Lubac,* October 9, 1965.

[194] See *Modi V* (Florit papers, D 250, 3f.). The response also explained the meaning of the term "form of preaching *(praeconium)*" as the most fundamental characteristic of the "gospel" genre; it connected this explanation with *modus* 3 on the Prologue, which had introduced the term "announcement" *(praeconium/kerygma)* in stating the purpose of the constitution.

[195] *Modi ... VI* (Florit papers, D 251). For the result of the study of the *modi,* see *AS* IV/5, 728–38.

[196] See *modus* 2; and *RT 8,* 14.

[197] See *Modi qui proponuntur...* (Florit papers, 245, 11f.) and *Modi VI* (Florit papers, D 251): "It is therefore necessary that all ecclesiastical preaching ... be fed and guided *(regatur)* by sacred scripture."

[198] *RT 8,* 14.

returning to the question of the material sufficiency of the scriptures. Here the correction introduced by the small commission (*modus* 18) — "The Church ... endeavors to acquire an ever deeper understanding of the sacred scriptures *and of the whole of divine revelation*" — was rejected by König and judged dishonest by Rahner,[199] whereas Colombo defended it and proposed in addition that the text keep the mention of the Fathers of the East and the West (as in the same *modus*). A number of bishops were in favor of this last proposal, even while rejecting the first addition, which would introduce anew the problem of the two sources. This was the point reached when the meeting ended at 12:30 p.m.

On Monday afternoon, October 11, the last of the six meetings of the plenary commission was held. Among the remaining amendments (19–21) offered for no. 23, only the question of the relationship of the exegetes and teachers of the sacred sciences with the magisterium led to a debate. In the end, the formula "under the guidance of the sacred magisterium" was rejected, and the old formula, which spoke of "vigilance," was retained, the point being to stress the ability of the biblical scholars and theologians to take initiatives.[200] When the group came to no. 24, on relations between scripture and theology, the fathers returned, almost as though obsessed, to the problem of tradition. Only Schröffer and Rahner noted that this was not the question dealt with in the section; the other leaders, from Ottaviani, Garofalo, and Tromp by way of Colombo to Charue, Butler, Heuschen, and Philips, accepted, to the astonishment of both sides, the correction "together with tradition"; this avoided the formula "in the light of tradition," which would have favored the thesis of an explanatory tradition.

Finally, in no. 25, the commission came to the change in the Church's outlook since the Council of Trent with regard to the reading of the Bible by *all* Christians. Here again, Philips found himself on the side of Tromp and Browne in defending the reservation introduced by the small commission.[201] But after the interventions of König (who reminded the group of the position taken by Benedict XV in *Spiritus paraclitus*) and of

[199] Thils made the point that the formulation offered by the small commission altered the proposal in *modus* 18, which *did not add* a mention of "the whole of revelation" to the scriptures, but *replaced* "scriptures" with "revelation."

[200] The responses to the *modi* 19, 20, and 21 all follow the same line (see *Modi VI* [Florit papers, D 251, 4]; and *RT 8*, 15).

[201] Among *modi* 25 to 31 only no. 26 on the reading of scripture had some importance. The reservation introduced by the small commission was formulated thus: "Although it cannot be said that the reading of scripture is necessary for each and all" (Florit papers, D 251, 5).

Charue, McGrath, and Schröffer, and Butler, the vote was 14 to 5 in favor of keeping the text in its old form, that is, the exhortation was addressed to *all*.[202]

After discussing the place of the Epilogue, which was thought of more as the ending of chapter VI, it was agreed to do away with any real Epilogue and to link no. 26 with no. 25. Florit then read his report on the Prologue and chapters I and II,[203] and van Dodewaard read his on chapters III-VI. The reports were accepted without comment, although Heuschen won consent to their being sent to the fathers of the commission for possible written observations.[204] With the work of rereading now completed, the sixth meeting came to an end; on the next day the corrected schema was sent to Paul VI, along with a letter from Ottaviani that said a summary of the principal changes, to be drawn up by Philips, and the two reports of Florit and van Dodewaard, would also be sent to him.

The prefect of the Holy Office added that the minority on the commission was unsuccessful in obtaining a clearer and more explicit statement of the "constitutive" role of tradition; in addition, he suggested to the Pope, even at this early point, the procedure to be followed in order that a possible addition to the text might not seem to be imposed from outside but to be a proposal of the commission.[205]

The final phase in the drafting of the text had thus begun. Understandably, the members of the majority and most of the experts were afraid that an intervention from on high could upset the fragile balance they had just achieved and defended.[206] The drafters had not touched the main thrust of the text, but they had made its structure more organic by some minor changes that created more links among its different parts, and they had even been able to identify further the perspective proper to *Dei Verbum* as compared with that of *Lumen gentium*. Many of the responses to the *modi* even served as a first commentary on the text.

---

[202] See *RT 8*, 15f. The final version of the response to *modus* 26 (which pointed out the contradiction between the reservation and the citation from St. Jerome) referred to the biblical encyclicals of Benedict XV and Pius XII and assured the fathers that the text was prudent enough to allay "the fear of any astonishment (*miratio*)" (*AS* IV/5, 734).

[203] He read "almost without conviction," Betti commented; *DBetti*, October 11, 1965, 364.

[204] *RT 8*, 16.

[205] Letter of Ottaviani to Paul VI, October 12, in *AS* V/3, 410f.; see also *JPrignon*, October 12, 1965 (Prignon papers, 1603, 1).

[206] See *JPrignon*, October 12, 1965 (Prignon papers, 1603, 1 and 4f.); *TSemmelroth*, October 13, 1965; *JCongar*, October 14, 1965; II, 434.

Some fears persisted, however. Did not the constitution, and especially the way in which it took history seriously, render doubtful the picture that Neo-Scholasticism had painted of the founding of the Church, thereby weakening its present hierarchical structure and its doctrinal system? And it was impossible not to see that the debates in the commission brought no further clarity on the principal points of disagreement between majority and minority: the economic approach to revelation; a more balanced articulation of tradition, scripture, and magisterium; a conception of inspiration that took into account the advances made in exegesis; a new relationship to history; and so on. On the evening of October 11, with regard to these fundamental questions relations between majority and minority were just as they had been a year before; the only difference was the gradual loss of the illusion that a strategy such as that of Philips could reconcile the two sides.

The question must be asked whether those chiefly responsible for the text were even able as yet to say just where the disagreement existed. De Lubac seemed to suspect this when he wrote, after the final meeting of the commission:

> Some partisans of the "two sources" are seeking again to introduce some formulas along that line; it seems to me that they do not understand the question, and that many of those who reject their proposals do not understand it any better. One of the disadvantages of the procedure followed in this council is that when the discussion of a schema is to begin, there is never a broad exposition of the subject by a competent and impartial man, either at a general congregation or in a commission.[207]

While Paul VI was receiving some fathers of the Doctrinal Commission (Parente, Charue, Döpfner, Florit, König, among others) and consulting with others, Congar attempted to make his own contribution to the question. On the evening of October 14 Congar went to the Belgian College to get information on the *De revelatione*. He had already discussed it that same day with Rahner, who himself had alerted König; Congar now learned that Heuschen, after having seen Charue, "believed it unavoidable that the Pope would propose a *modus*: doubtless in language of Parente's kind."[208] On the following day Congar wrote to Colombo; just as he was posting his letter, he met Moeller, who tried to dissuade him:

---

[207] *Jde Lubac*, October 11, 1965.
[208] *JCongar*, October 14, 1965; II, 435–36.

He told me he found my suggestion to be very dangerous. I was not at the
meeting at which *modus* 40 D was discussed…. If I had been there I would
have seen that the minority gave this text a sense which I would be the first
to reject. That is where the great danger lies. Moeller therefore insisted on
the rejection of all *modi* and the retention of the text as it stood. He personally thinks it uncertain that the Pope has decided to change anything in
the text. That is not what Msgr. Heuschen told me. I had written my letter
in accordance with what Msgr. Heuschen told me was certain. However,
I did add to my letter a postscript to this effect: the best thing would be to
change nothing.[209]

We find here the same hesitation noted earlier: Father Congar seemed
not to perceive the ambiguity present in *modus* 40 D with its addition of
"directly." The same impression is given by his report of his meeting, on
Friday, October 15, with Florit. The Dominican made his own the argument of Moeller, who stressed the danger of a maximalist interpretation
of the *modus*. He agreed with his interlocutor but without clearly grasping the ambiguity of the *modus* (this is all the more surprising since Florit
defended the *modus* without the addition of "directly"):

> I saw Cardinal Florit on the question of the *De revelatione*. He told me he
> was for the acceptance of *modus* 40 D, which did not affect the balance of
> the teaching; he did not understand why the commission rejected it. I said:
> out of fear of what the others (Parente, etc.) might put into it and draw out
> of it. But Florit thought — and I think — that the best thing would be for the
> Pope to urge the commission to reconsider that vote.[210]

On the following day, after a long stretch of insomnia, Congar wrote
to Florit, Colombo, and Charue:

> It is clear that the majority of the fathers would not accept a formula con-
> veying the meaning of *latius patet*; they have decided, for the sake of peace,
> to avoid any such formula. It is therefore from the viewpoint of our knowl-
> edge that we must assert the need of tradition. If we look closely at the text
> of the Council of Trent, we see that this is what it says. It must be said that
> we can know revelation or the gospel in its fullness and purity only if we
> consult tradition at the same time as we read the scriptures. I repeat: the best
> thing would be to change nothing in the present text. But if something has
> to be said or added, it is, it seems to me, along that line that we must look.[211]

Thus, while stating his preference (in which he agrees with Moeller and
Rahner), Congar in fact supported the tactic of Florit and Betti.

---

[209] *JCongar*, October 15; II, 436–37.
[210] *JCongar*, October 15, 1965; II, 437.
[211] *DBetti*, October 16, 1965, 366.

When he learned on Saturday, October 16, that the Doctrinal Commission would meet on Monday, October 18, and knowing that he could not attend, he wrote two notes addressed to Garrone, Charue, Heuschen, Colombo, Florit, Butler, and Ancel, and also to Philips, Rahner, and Betti. In the first he says he agrees with the addition of *modus* 40 D to the extent that the words state a fact, although he regrets the unpolished formulation of the *modus* and especially the words "from scripture," which risk being understood as signifying the "material insufficiency" of the scriptures.[212] His note explains clearly the distinction between the *material* insufficiency (the thesis of the minority) and the *formal* insufficiency of the scriptures, the latter being simply a fact, because "the faithful and the magisterium really need tradition *and* scripture in order to *know*, use, teach, and express the pure gospel revelation in its integrity." Without directly criticizing the word "directly" in *modus* 40 D (a point to which he remained less attentive than Betti and Rahner), he added that it was not permitted to reverse the traditional statement — "This is contained in tradition; that is why the Church believes and teaches it" — and turn it into — "The Church believes and teaches this; it is therefore contained in tradition." Congar's second note cites some support for the expression "saving truth" in the works of St. Thomas.[213]

II. The Intervention of Higher Authority

A. The Atmosphere in the Council

Meanwhile, the assembly continued to debate the schemas: schema XIII (until October 8), the decree on the mission (until October 12), and the decree on priests (until Saturday, October 16). During the same period there was an endless series of votes on texts already finished, and the fathers were becoming increasingly tired. As Prignon noted as early as September 25: "The most disturbing thing is the growing weariness of the fathers. I was struck yesterday morning, Friday, by the number of fathers who were circulating in the corridors an hour after the meeting opened. A real question is what is to be done with the bishops once the

---

[212] Congar, "De habitudine inter Traditionem (apostolicam) et S. Scripturam; see *JCongar*, October 18; II, 441.

[213] Y. Congar, "De convenientia locutionis 'veritas salutaris,'" in Florit papers, F 304.

debates in the assembly have ended. Some solution is absolutely necessary."[214] The representatives of the majority were finding it increasingly difficult to get the bishops to say anything against the texts presented; they were ready, without any response, to vote on the schemas submitted to them.[215] The assembly obviously wanted things to end and could no longer work up any enthusiasm except on some exceptional questions. According to Prignon, even the debate on the chapter on politics in schema XIII was dodged; only four or five speakers were listed.[216]

In light of this the governing bodies of the Council decided that once the debates were finished the fathers could leave for the week of October 17–24 and then again during what the Romans call the "vacation of the dead," that is, Saturday, October 30 to Monday, November 8.[217] In addition, they would receive, by way of the episcopal conferences, some questions on penitential discipline, indulgences, and other matters on which they could make note of their views during their "free time."[218]

While a search was on for useful occupations for the great majority of bishops, a small minority of fathers and experts was being crushed by the amount of work that had to be done in a short time. To this was added uncertainty about connections between the Pope and the minority, a question that had weighed on minds ever since the *Nota praevia* of the fall of 1964. Everyone knew, of course, that the Pope was governor of the Council and that as such he could intervene in decisions without this being regarded an anomalous action; his position was also symbolized, during

---

[214] *JPrignon,* September 25, 1965 (Prignon papers, 1591, 1 and 4).

[215] Ibid., October 4, 1965 (Prignon papers, 1598), 2.

[216] Ibid., October 5, 1965 (Prignon papers, 1599, 4f.), and October 8, 1965 (1601, 1f.): "For the past three or four days the debate in the assembly has become dismal. We feel that the bishops are incredibly wearied. Many walk the corridors as early as 10:00. Today, even while Garrone was giving his final report after the end of the debate on schema XIII, the noise from conversations in the side-aisles of St. Peter's was drowning out the voice of the speaker. It is time for the debates in the assembly to end, because the situation is really deteriorating." Jauffrès, a good representative of the great majority of fathers who had no special responsibility at the Council, wrote in his diary for Wednesday, October 13: "People stay at their seats, a bit under moral restraint, only because of the votes, ten of so, which follow upon one another at intervals so brief that they do not allow time to go to the bar and return" (*Carnets conciliaires,* 280).

[217] This announcement was made officially on Friday, October 1.

[218] See *JPrignon,* September 28, 1965 (Prignon papers, 1594, 1f.) and October 5, 1965 (Prignon papers, 1599, 1 and 5). Regarding the first document, on the discipline of penance, Prignon observed: "To tell the truth, the document is so weak that there is not enough to fill the eight days of vacation. Besides, the bishops have already met on the subject, and I think that by now almost everything has already been said" (*JPrignon,* October 10, 1965 [Prignon papers, 1602, 6]).

the final period of the Council, by the elevated chair behind the table of the Council of Presidents, a chair permanently reserved for him. The thing, however, that was difficult for the majority of the fathers and experts who were members of the commissions was the lack of transparency in some interventions. This had already been the case in the preceding May in connection with the debate on the Jews; the same thing happened on September 29 when, after the vote on the *De episcopis* had begun, some new *modi* or suggestions from the Pope had been sent to the moderators;[219] other additions were introduced into the schema on religious,[220] while the minority tried to get a remark on the authority of St. Thomas placed in the schema on education.[221]

The crisis intensified during the Pope's journey to New York. On the morning of Tuesday, October 5, Prignon brought Suenens up to date "on the state of tension gripping the bishops and experts who are members of the commissions, and on the deterioration of the situation due to the secret interventions of the Holy Father and on the uncertainty in their minds about the real authority of the *modi* presented to all the commissions in his name." Two days earlier Döpfner had spoken, quite angrily, about these interventions to Colombo, who was to warn the Pope before the latter's departure.[222]

Add to all this that among the questions to be tackled in the episcopal conferences was that of ecclesiastical celibacy, at the urging especially of the Brazilian bishops. Hardly a week after the Pope's return, on the same October 11 on which the Doctrinal Commission's work on the *De revelatione* came to an end, a letter from the Pope was read in the hall forbidding public discussion of questions having to do with priestly celibacy.[223]

This was the general background of the fear expressed by a number of bishops and experts that "higher authority" would intervene after the completion of work on *Dei Verbum*. Would the letter finally arrive that the "third party" so breathlessly awaited?

---

[219] See *JPrignon,* September 30, 1965 (Prignon papers, 1596, 1–4): "This new intervention of the Pope has created a painful impression, especially because it has come when the voting had already begun. It became quickly known who had suggested the insertion of these *modi* to the Pope, an insertion undoubtedly urged by Carli and Siri. As the news spread gradually through the corridors, the atmosphere began again to be somewhat like that of Black Week in the third session."

[220] See ibid., 5.

[221] See ibid., 6; ibid., October 1, 1965 (Prignon papers, 1597, 4f.); and ibid., October 4, 1965 (Prignon papers, 1598, 1).

[222] See ibid., October 5, 1965 (Prignon papers, 1599, 1f.).

[223] *AS* V/3, 408.

B. Cardinal Cicognani's Letter

On the day after the final meeting of the Doctrinal Commission, Paul VI received, by way of Ottaviani and the secretariat of the Council, some information on the present state of the *De revelatione*. He then met with the moderators and other individuals representative of the minority and the majority.

At the request of the president of the commission, Philips sent him a summary of the main changes made on important points in the text,[224] slipping in with it "a loose sheet containing a bit of commentary on *veritas salutaris*."[225] In addition, the Pope already had on his desk a report from Cardinal Dante, composed on October 7, on the two key points: the relationship of scripture to tradition and the truth of the scriptures.[226] This report, the joint work of a number of fathers who had been bewildered by the meeting on October 6, proposed for no. 9 a formula of agreement that was quite close to the second "Philips amendment"[227] (it is found, with others, in Cicognani's letter to the commission) and for no. 11 the removal of the word "*salutaris*." The commentary that accompanied this second proposal emphasized the seriousness of the decision taken by the *commissio parva* and confirmed by the plenary commission.[228]

Finally, Felici told Paul VI that his amendment regarding tradition, which had been accompanied by a citation from St. Augustine, had not been made known to the commission; he also explained to the Pope the juridical situation of a text that, while coming under the competence of the mixed commission established by John XXIII, had been revised by the Doctrinal Commission alone, *with the tacit consent of the Secretariat for Chritian Unity*.[229]

After having, it seems, seen Parente on October 11,[230] Paul VI summoned Charue, vice- president of the Doctrinal Commission and the man in charge of the *De revelatione*, in order to ask his advice and to tell him

---

[224] *JPrignon,* October 12, 1965 (Prignon papers, 1603, 1, 3, and 5f.).

[225] Ibid., 1185 and 1183.

[226] Paul VI papers, B3/10 and B3/14 (this text is printed in *AS* V/3, 448–54, as an appendix of a letter sent by Dell'Acqua to Ottaviani on October 18).

[227] Paul VI papers, B3/10, 2f. (*AS* V/3, 449f.).

[228] The document claimed that the formula "saving truth" was deliberately introduced in order to restrict inerrancy to supernatural truths concerning faith and morals; that it would give free rein to all the daring innovations of the exegetes; and so on. The text also contained harsh judgments on the attitude and work of the small commission.

[229] See Paul VI papers, B/3, 15, 16, and 17 (this written note was dated October 13).

[230] *JPrignon,* October 12, 1965 (Prignon papers, 1604, 8).

of his own worries on the two points of tradition and the phrase "saving truth."[231] Prignon reports on the meeting:

> On the first point Msgr. Charue told him that, before God, he truly did not see any reason for worry, that the difficult question remained unanswered, and so on. The Pope then said, twice, that it was a great consolation to him to know that Msgr. Charue thought as he did.... On the second point, the Pope feared the term *veritas salutaris* because he interpreted it as meaning that some things in the scriptures were not inspired. This is clearly mistaken, and one wonders how the text could have been taken in this sense since nothing in it even suggested it. Again, Msgr. Charue protested strongly against this interpretation; he did not hide from the Pope that he himself considered the introduction of *veritas salutaris* a real step forward.[232]

Was the Pope convinced by these reassuring words? Or had he already decided to change the text[233] because he lacked real confidence in the direction taken by the Belgian team?[234] In any case, the Belgian bishop won his point with regard to procedure: Paul VI became well aware that he had to intervene *before the vote within the commission* if he was to avoid what had happened the year before in connection with ecumenism.[235]

---

[231] See *JCharue*, October 12, 1965. At the beginning, the Pope spoke of the fact that his amendment had not been made known to the commission, and he asked about the involvement of the Secretariat for Unity in the drafting of the text.

[232] *JPrignon*, October 13, 1965 (Prignon papers, 1604); there is another version, ibid., October 12, 1965 (Prignon papers, 1603).

[233] On Tuesday, Charue told Philips that on the subject of *"veritas salutaris,"* "the Holy Father did not give the impression of accepting his views," and that "on the question of tradition he had the impression that the Pope had already made up his mind" (*JPrignon*, October 12, 1965 (Prignon papers, 1603, 5). In a conversation with Prignon on the following morning Charue said "that the Pope was not so resolved as he appeared to be yesterday with the moderators. And that perhaps there was still room for hope" (ibid., October 13, 1965 [Prignon papers, 1604, 1]).

[234] This was Philips's interpretation: "He interpreted this quasi-rejection of Msgr. Charue this morning as proof that he [Philips] could hardly any longer hope to influence the mind of the Holy Father" (*JPrignon*, October 12, 1965 [Prignon papers, 1503, 5]). Two days later, on October 14, Charue wrote to the Pope, suggesting that he receive Philips (Paul VI papers, B3/23); this did not happen. Prignon also mentions another characteristic of the conversation between Paul VI and Charue: "During the audience with Msgr. Willebrands (Monday, the 18th), the Pope had (said) that he had seen Msgr. Charue and that Msgr. Charue had declared himself quite at peace on the subject of the orthodoxy of the *De revelatione*, but that Msgr. Charue did not carry on his shoulders, as he himself did, the weight of the entire Church. Also that on the other hand he had been a little surprised when (to use the language of Msgr. Willebrands) Msgr. Charue seemed like a man shrugging his shoulders when the Pope had mentioned this responsibility, the power of the keys" (*JPrignon*, October 18, 1965 [Prignon papers, 1609, 1f.]).

[235] See ibid., October 14, 1965 (Prignon papers, 1605, 1), and October 16, 1965 (Prignon papers, 1606, 1), emphasis added.

At the Pope's weekly meeting with the moderators, the question was raised again:

> The Pope told them that he was not satisfied with the text, that it was inadequate on the subjects of tradition and the *veritas salutaris*. The "three Synoptics" tried to make him understand that it was better not to dissolve the agreement if he did not want to cause serious difficulties in the Council, and that the *veritas salutaris* was a good thing. But they had the impression that they were dealing with a man whose mind was made up. The Pope said that he had his own conscience and that his conscience did not allow him to accept the text.[236]

Perhaps on the advice of Charue,[237] that same evening the Pope again received Florit[238] and, later on, Döpfner.[239] Florit explained Betti's *Promemoria* to the Pope. After summarizing the essential elements of the problem of tradition, in a second part Betti proposed the following solution:

> The reasoned request of a considerable number of fathers bids us very carefully reconsider the necessity or at least the opportuneness of saying explicitly that everything in Catholic teaching cannot be proved from scripture alone. In the final analysis, the need is to make it clearer (while leaving aside the question of numerical amount) that tradition gives us a *more explicit and complete expression of divine revelation and that in some cases it can even be decisive for an accurate knowledge and understanding of that revelation.*

Of the five considerations that followed, the first and fourth were the most important: "A statement of this kind is in complete harmony with the text, adding to it *a useful complement*, yet not affecting its substance." Furthermore, the formula suggested by the 111 fathers (without the word "directly," as a note explains)

> has the advantage of being in the line of the Council of Trent, according to the interpretation of the latter that is accepted by all and confirmed by the constant practice of the Church. While it is not absolutely certain that in dealing with certain truths the Council of Trent intended to oppose *tradition alone* to the Protestant doctrine of *scripture alone*, it is beyond question that the Council did ratify the Catholic principle of *scripture and tradition* against that Protestant principle. While asserting the insufficiency of sacred

---

[236] Ibid., October 12, 1965 (Prignon papers, 1603, 8).

[237] *JPrignon*, October 13, 1965 (Prignon papers, 1604, 1). We may suppose that the Pope intended on his own to call the Cardinal of Florence, given the latter's responsibility for the drafting of the schema.

[238] See *DFlorit*, October 12.

[239] *DBetti*, October 16, 1965, 365f.

scripture at the gnoseological level, the schema would leave open the question of the insufficiency of sacred scripture at the properly constitutive level; in other words, it would explicitly state that Catholic teaching in its totality cannot be demonstrated from scripture alone and that it is therefore necessary to have recourse to tradition as well. But it would not exclude the possibility that one or another Catholic doctrine is contained only in tradition.[240]

A note from the hand of Paul VI, written probably after his conversation with Florit, contains, in this order, first the formula already proposed by Florit during the debate, which would replace the "saving truth" of the scriptures with "everything that God has willed to communicate to us in them"; then an addition that would complete the statement that the evangelists "always" tell us "the honest truth about Jesus" by adding "that is, what is conformed to the historical faith"; and, finally, the amendment of the 111 fathers on the relations between scripture and tradition.[241]

It is probable that the conversation with Florit was decisive, because it gave the Pope the doctrinal assurances that he needed.[242] The same conclusion emerges from the fact that on October 14 Paul VI sent a note to Colombo that this time repeated the three points made on the handwritten sheet in the order in which they occurred in the schema.[243] In addition, Colombo had told the Pope on Wednesday, October 13, of the outcome of a conversation with Bea, who said he was in agreement with the idea of an addition but immediately made known his preference for the Colombo amendment and asked that some other expression be used in place of "saving truth."[244]

According to the official version of events as given in Caprile's article, "On October 14 the Pope decided, therefore, that the commission

---

[240] U. Betti, *Promemoria sulla dottrina reguardante la sacra Tradizione esposta nel Cap. II dello Schema di Costituzione dommatica "De Divina Revelatione,"* in Florit papers, D 255; Paul VI papers, B3/8; and VI A3/4 (emphases added).

[241] Paul VI papers, B3/12.

[242] The *Promemoria* was very skillful inasmuch as it clearly stated that tradition provides a more explicit *showing* of revelation but left open the question of the insufficiency of tradition at the properly constitutive level. R. Burigana rightly calls attention to the ambiguity of Florit's silence about his conversation with the Pope when dealing with Charue (*La Bibbia nel concilio*, 420); this had the effect of further dividing the "third party."

[243] Paul VI papers, B3/13 and 14; and A3/22 and 3/6–9. According to the handwritten notes Paul VI also sent Dante's file to Colombo (see Paul VI papers, B3/14 and A3/6–9).

[244] Paul VI papers, B3/18 and 14, and A3/23B. This letter, then, was a response to the anxiety Paul VI had voiced the evening before in his conversation with Charue, about the position taken by the Secretariat for Christian Unity.

should be sent a note, already prepared on the 12th, containing the suggestions made by the first of the two cardinals of whom I have just spoken,"[245] that is, Florit. As a matter of fact, we possess a first list of eight
formulations of the relations between scripture and tradition,[246] a list
revised and completed on October 14,[247] after the Pope had received a letter from "the second cardinal," who was none other than Döpfner.

On October 14, then, a threshold was crossed. The Pope received several letters, from Döpfner, Journet, and Charue.[248] Repeating to some
extent Léger's position, Journet distinguished two senses of the word *tradition:* "the distinction between the illuminations of revelation and inspiration, on the one hand, and of assistance on the other."[249] But it was
Döpfner's letter, it seems, that did away with the Pope's last hesitations.
Using Rahner's language, the first part of the letter defended the statement that scripture teaches "saving truth" (or "the truths of salvation")
without error; the statement is not only orthodox but reflects the shift in
the problem since the Modernist period: "When it is said that sacred
scripture sets forth *saving* truths without error, this does not at all mean
the introduction of a material distinction between 'saving' truths and 'secular' statements in sacred scripture, as if the former contained truth while
the latter might be false; instead, a formal point of view is being indicated, according to which every affirmation in scripture that is true in
this manner is taught by God in sacred scripture and is for that reason
true."

The second part of the letter summed up, point by point, what is said
in the constitution about relations between tradition and scripture:

---

[245] Caprile, "Trois amendements au schéma sur la Révélation," 676.

[246] The first list contained formulas Florit (a), Philips 1 (b), Colombo (c) Philips 2 (d),
anonymous 1 (e: it is the Dante formula), anonymous 2 (f), Dhanis (g), and, in last place
(!), Parente (h). The Dhanis formula was already mentioned in the letter of Colombo to
Paul VI (Paul VI papers, A3/23b and B3/18).

[247] The second list, drawn up on October 12 or 13, was almost the definitive list:
the names had disappeared; the Colombo formula (c) was preceded by the Poma formula
(the introduction of this formula supposes that the Pope had learned the details of the meeting on October 4); formulas anonymous 2 (f), Dhanis (g), and Parente (h) had disappeared;
in contrast, the formula had later been added which was found in Döpfner's letter. These
various formulas were organized as follows (without naming the authors): 1. (Florit),
2. (Philips 1), 3. (Poma and Colombo), 4. (Philips 2 and Dante), then, without a number,
the *proposal* to add the Döpfner formula.

[248] These letters are in the Paul VI archive. On October 18 Dell'Acqua sent copies of
several of them to Ottaviani: the letters of Ruffini (dated October 17), Dante, Döpfner, and
Journet (*AS* V/3, 446–61). Why these letters, and why in this order?

[249] Paul VI papers, A3/25, and *AS* V/3, 458. We may note, in addition, that Journet
omits the *salutaris* and says nothing about the historical character of the gospels.

it teaches clearly the necessity of both tradition and the magisterium in the profession of the Catholic faith; the priority of the tradition that brings us scripture; and the impossibility of knowing the extent of the canon and of inspiration without tradition. "Here there is made clear the nature and existence of a tradition that is constitutive and not merely explanatory of the deposit of the faith." The only question on which the text does not speak and settle the matter is the further *material* insufficiency of the scriptures, this being a question on which theologians disagree. The Cardinal of Munich then called attention to the ecumenical importance of this silence and to the agreement of the present text with the teaching of Trent and Vatican I (this agreement being the view of the vast majority of the Council fathers). No one on the commission claimed that what the schema says is false; only a small minority wanted to say *more*.

All this having been said, Döpfner added at the end of his letter:

> If it be judged that something more needs to be said in order to set minds at peace, it may be added that it is doubtless impossible to derive all of Catholic truth from the scriptures without the help of tradition and the magisterium. This solution would make it possible to reject the Protestant doctrine of *sola scriptura*, without however touching on questions still debated among Catholics and into which the Council does not wish to enter; it would leave the way open to further studies by not excluding any opinion and without imposing in addition any burden not needed for the defense of Catholic truth and the importance of tradition.[250]

It is quite significant that Caprile's official version of the events relied only on this final remark in saying that Döpfner's position agreed with that of Florit.[251] Not only Paul VI but, it seems, Florit as well were rather closed to Döpfner's fundamental arguments in favor of the schema in its present state.

When Congar undertook his own series of consultations on October 14, writing to Colombo and conversing with Florit (October 15), before speaking to Florit, Charue, and, once again, Colombo (October 16) and before preparing his two notes (October 18), everything had already been decided. On Friday morning, October 15, some experts learned that there would indeed be an intervention by the Pope;[252] not until Sunday, however, do we find the first traces of a letter. On that day Paul VI received

---

[250] Paul VI papers, A3/26a and b; and *AS* V/3, 454–57.

[251] Caprile, "Trois amendements au schéma sur la Révélation," 675f.

[252] A note, dated October 15 (Paul VI papers, A3/27a), makes it clear that Felici had received a message by telephone, bidding him announce to Ottaviani the coming of some observations of the Holy Father on the schema *De revelatione*, in order that the latter might

two more letters. One was from Ruffini, who was worried about the
absence of a clear statement on tradition as a true source independent of
scripture. The other was from Frings, who took it on himself to voice a
certain uneasiness caused by papal interventions and certain fears that
these actions, "regarded as a form of moral coercion on the commission
and the Council," would seriously detract from the prestige of the Church
and the Council, especially in the Anglo-Saxon countries and in the
United States, where people were especially sensitive to any violation of
the regulations.[253]

. The Pope replied that same day:

> We want to let you know immediately of our firm intention to urge the con-
> ciliar commission *De doctrina fidei et morum* to consider the opportune-
> ness of improving some points in the schema on revelation, for we think that
> it is our duty to seek a doctrinal security that will allow us to join our
> approval to that of the Council fathers. We think, too, that our intervention
> in the conciliar commission is fully in accord with the regulations, for it is
> our duty not only to ratify or reject the text in question,[254] but also, like
> every other Council father, to work for the improvement of the text by
> timely suggestions. The same truth emerges also, and above all, from the fact
> that our remarks were made known to the commission by the General Sec-
> retary of the Ecumenical Council on September 24 last. It seems that this is
> the clearest and most deferential way of making known to the commission
> everything that is useful in the work assigned to it. Allow us, therefore, to
> note that no attack has been made on the authority of the Council, as you
> suspect, but rather that a needed contribution has been made to the exercise
> of its functions. As for respect for the freedom of the Council and for its
> established regulations, nothing can please us more than to see recalled these
> principles which are no less dear to Anglo-Saxons than to Romans.
> The Council has respected them in the most rigorous way.[255]

This letter, written in Italian, translated into Latin, and sent in beautiful handwriting (as if destined to be posted at the Council) represents the
official interpretation of the procedure activated that same day; it clearly
states the twofold role *(cum Petro et sub Petro)* that Paul VI intended to
play and the meaning he gave to his intervention, the purpose of which
was to *improve the text* (a formula already used by Betti). The Pope's

---

call an emergency meeting of the commission; see also *TSemmelroth*, October 15, and
JPrignon, October 16, 1965 [Prignon papers, 1606, 1]).

[253] Paul VI papers, A3/37a and B3/27a.

[254] This was what Frings seemed to infer when he asked the Pope to state *clearly*
whether he thought he could not approve the schema, instead of intervening in the commission's work.

[255] Paul VI papers, A3/37b and c, and B3/27b and c (Italian and Latin versions).

involvement in the name of his office also determined the course of his two conversations with Willebrands, probably on that same day, with Suenens on the following day, and, it seems, also with König.[256]

In any case, it was on October 17 that the much-awaited letter to the commission was readied. The decision to offer the commission seven formulas to choose from had been made several days earlier. As for the other points to be submitted to the commission, in regard to *saving truth*, the Pope had before him four proposals[257]: that of the text that had been voted on, that of the commission, that of Dhanis, and that of Bea. In fact, on that very day, the Pope received an expert evaluation of six pages from Bea,[258] who had reread the entire biblical teaching of the Popes since Leo XIII and concluded that it would be better to keep the simple formula: the scriptures "teach the truth faithfully and without error"; he also rejected Dhanis' distinction between what the author says as a sacred writer and what he says as a merely human writer.

The Pope sided with Bea as we can see from a note in his own hand.[259] The page that summarized the four proposals in regard to *saving truth* also contained a remark on the third point in dispute, that is, the historical truth of the gospels: Bea proposed that the formula "the evangelists tell us the honest truth about Jesus" be replaced by one saying that they tell us "what is true *or worthy of historical faith*." Here again, the Pope sided with him.

The handwritten note mentioned a moment ago was in fact the first draft of the letter sent to the commission. Two other versions, typewritten, are to be found in the Paul VI Archive: a summary in four points that sum up the arguments of the letter,[260] and the letter in Italian, with, at the

---

[256] *JPrignon,* October 18, 1965 (Prignon papers, 1607, 4): "The Pope told him [Suenens] that he was fully aware that [his intervention] could trigger a new Black Week, but that he had thought the matter over carefully before God; he judged that it was his duty to act, and that for the supreme good of the Church he had to run the risk of facing a new Black Week. The Cardinal told me that the Pope had spoken and given his definitive advice, that he could not further discuss the problem of faith with him. Nevertheless, he said that he would see Bea again before making his final decision." Suenens also suggested that the Pope consult Scrima, an Orthodox; since the latter had not yet returned from Istanbul, Bea had not been able to speak with him about the *De revelatione* (Paul VI papers, B3/30). For König, see *JCongar,* October 14, 1965; II, 434; and *JPrignon,* October 16, 1965 (Prignon papers, 1606, 1).

[257] These were summarized on a single page (Paul VI papers, A3/35b, and B3/28) which may have been Colombo's work.

[258] Ibid., A3/33.

[259] Ibid., A3/35c and B3/28.

[260] Paul VI papers, A3/35a and B3/28: I. The appropriateness of completing no. 9 by one of the seven formulas; II. The omission of "saving truth," accompanied by four arguments (not to hinder, however, the progress of studies on biblical inerrancy; the formula,

top of it, a request that it be sent quickly to Ottaviani as president of the Doctrinal Commission.[261]

On that same day Paul VI saw to it that the president of the Secretariat for Christian Unity was invited to the final meeting of the Doctrinal Commission.[262] It was Dell'Acqua, a close adviser to the Pope, who informed him that Bea said that he agreed with the appropriateness of an improvement of the schema on revelation; that, in regard to the text on tradition, he was willing to accept any of the four formulas, while preferring the third; that the formula of Döpfner should be added to the list; and that Congar preferred the second formula, that is, the one proposed by the technical commission (the first "Philips amendment").[263]

Ottaviani soon received two files. From Dell'Acqua came a file containing the letters of four cardinals, Ruffini, Dante, Döpfner, and Journet, along with a "private note" from the Pope, conveying the information given by Bea, but not revealing Bea's preference.[264] From Cicognani, Secretary of State, came the official letter addressed directly to the president of the Doctrinal Commission with an appendix containing the series of formulas to be used in completing no. 9 of the schema.[265] While expressing his gratitude and respect for the work done, the Pope decided that the commission should be called together again for a new study of the schema on revelation. The first part of the letter explained, first and foremost, the purpose of this step and its authoritativeness: "The attached observations have no intention of changing substantially either the work of the commission or the schema,[266] but are meant rather to improve it on some points of great doctrinal importance.[267] As a result, the Pope, as

as it stands, is not yet part of the doctrinal patrimony; to avoid the danger of false interpretation; to leave the commission in a position to formulate a clearer text); III. Change of the formula on the historical truth of the gospels; IV. The invitation to Bea, president of the Secretariat for Christian Unity, as a definitive evidence of his approval.

[261] Ibid., A3/36 and B3/35.

[262] See a note dated October 17, in ibid., A3/32 and B3/30. Had the Pope met personally with Bea on October 18? That is what Suenens said after his own audience on that date. Was this final visit on October 18 the reason the meeting of the commission, which was perhaps planned for that day (and without the experts), was postponed (*JCongar*, October 16, 1965; II, 439–40; and *TSemmelroth*, October 18, 1965)?

[263] See a second note, also dated October 17, in Paul VI papers, A3/28 and B3/26. It supposes that Bea was aware of Congar's note.

[264] *AS* V/34, 462.

[265] Ibid., 459–61.

[266] This was the main argument of the reporters.

[267] This was the main argument of Betti in his *Promemoria*.

Vicar of Christ, will be able, with full certainty, in the presence of the universal Church and before his own conscience, and on so serious a subject, to ask for the approval of the Council fathers, which is needed for the promulgation of the Constitution."

The second part of the letter dealt with the three controverted points, treating each of them differently. This last was even the essential point to keep in mind, once the genesis of the text has been reconstructed. On the question of tradition, the Pope asked the commission to consider, willingly yet freely, whether it was not appropriate to improve and complete the text by the addition of one of the formulas proposed or an equivalent one, whichever seems most acceptable to authoritative representatives of the majority. In practice, then, Paul VI was asking that the commission complete the text and complete it at a particular point (no. 9), while enjoying full freedom in the choice of the formula. It must be noted, however, that of the ten formulas considered at one moment or another, only seven were set forth here. Parente's formula had been eliminated, surely because of its leaning toward the minority and that of Dhanis and the anonymous formula 2 were eliminated, probably because of their overly complicated language. It was the "third party" that won out, because the decision of higher authority on where the addition was to be made allowed attention to be focused for the first time solely on the formula to be chosen.

The Pope's attitude on the second disputed point was quite different:

> The commission is urged to reconsider and seriously study whether it is better to remove from the text the expression *veritas salutaris*, which is used there in speaking of the inerrancy of the sacred scriptures. The Holy Father is more puzzled here than he was on the preceding point, for several reasons: because there is question here of a doctrine not yet common in the Church's theological teaching on the Bible; because the formula does not seem to have been adequately discussed in the hall; and because in the judgment of competent and authoritative individuals the formula is open to erroneous interpretations. It seems too soon for the Council to take a stand on such a sensitive problem. At this time the fathers are not in a position to see clearly its scope and the abusive interpretation that may be given it. At the same time, its omission does not prevent study of the question.

On this point, then, the commission's freedom was much more limited. At first sight the minority seemed to have carried the day, but since no fundamental argument was given and since the intention that the question be further studied was made clear, the passage leaned more in the direction of the majority.

On the third point the letter asked the commission to replace the statement "the evangelists tell us the honest truth about Jesus" with another saying that they tell "things that are true *or worthy of historical faith.*" "The first formula does not in fact seem to guarantee the real historicity of the gospels; and it is quite evident that the Holy Father cannot approve a formula that opens the way to doubts about the historicity of these most holy books." On this last point, then, the commission had no room for maneuvering, and it was the minority with which Paul VI was siding.

The letter from the Secretary of State ended with a request that Bea be present at this meeting, because he was a member of the mixed commission that John XXIII had established in order that the drafting of this memorable schema might take a new direction, and one acceptable to all.

C. The Debate in the Doctrinal Commission on October 19

The full commission met right in the middle of the "conciliar vacation" and after the meeting of the mixed commission on schema XIII. That morning Ottaviani and Browne, the two reporters on the schema, met with Florit and Charue and the two secretaries, Tromp and Philips, in order to decide on procedure. Philips was to present the different points.[268] But at the meeting did not go quite as planned.[269]

After the reading of the letter in the presence of the president of the Secretariat for Christian Unity and of its secretary, Willebrands, Ottaviani immediately yielded the platform to Bea so that he might give his view of the relationship between scripture and tradition. The Cardinal reviewed the seven formulas, which were on a page distributed to everyone. His judgment was that the first two were "obscure" (chiefly because of the word "directly" in the second);[270] he preferred the third, which had

---

[268] *JPrignon,* October 19, 1965 (Prignon papers, 1608, 1).

[269] See *RT 8,* 17–19; *JPrignon,* October 19, 1965 (Prignon papers, 1608, 1–3); *DBetti,* October 19, 1965, 366f.; *Jde Lubac,* October 19; *TSemmelroth,* October 19; *JCongar,* October 22, 1965; II, 444–46.

[270] Here is what Prignon said about the beginning of the meeting: "After the reading of the letter, Bea spoke instead of Philips. To our amazement, with a quite revealing slip of the tongue he ended by saying that it must be admitted, despite the difficulty it causes with the observers, that tradition, too, is a 'source'; then he corrected himself and said 'means of transmission' of revelation. And that, all things considered, formula no. 3 seemed to be the best. He was very careful to say that he was speaking in his own name and not in the name of the secretariat" (*JPrignon,* October 19, 1965 [Prignon papers, 1608, 1]). In consequence of an article of Daniélou that had appeared in *La Croix* two days before the final vote, Bea made it clear once again, in a letter to Wenger, that "when he intervened, *for a special reason,* at a meeting of the Doctrinal Commission, he had said explicitly that he was giving only his personal point of view and not speaking in the name of the secretariat" (Wenger, IV, 351f., emphasis added).

been offered at the meeting on October 4 by Colombo, Heuschen, Butler, and, in a slightly amended form, by Poma. After ten minutes for consideration, a vote was taken: the third (Colombo/Poma) and first (Florit) formulas came out on top.[271] In the second balloting the third formula received 19 out of 27 votes; it thus had the needed majority and was adopted: "It follows that the Church does not derive from scripture alone its certainty on all things revealed."[272]

When it came to the suppression of the words "*veritas salutaris*," Bea, to the surprise of all, repeated the arguments he had already developed in his report to the Pope: "The expression is not traditional; it is wrongly attributed to St. Augustine or St. Thomas;[273] it risks opening a door which we may no longer be able to close; in any case, it was not discussed at a general congregation."[274] The first balloting yielded 17 votes for suppression, 7 in favor of the formula, and 4 void ballots. An indesive debate on procedure followed: Ottaviani, supported by canonist Bertrams, who cited an article of canon law, thought the void ballots should not be counted, but Dom Butler's opinion was that the cited article did not apply here, since according to an article in the conciliar regulations, an outcome, in order to be valid, required a two-thirds vote *of those present*, and this had not been obtained. The president yielded, and a second vote was taken: 17 for suppression, 7 for the status quo, and 4 abstentions; one of these last ballots mentioned "out of respect for the Sovereign Pontiff," which led Ottaviani to remark that abstention was not a sign of respect for the Pope. The third balloting did not notably change the situation: 17 for suppression, 8 for the formula, and 3 abstentions.

It seems that this impasse gave Philips an opportunity to speak, something he had not done up to this point. Thanks to the support of Butler and Volk, he managed to explain his alternative formula (drawn from *modus* 8, offered by 78 bishops), which the fathers took down at his dictation: "It is necessary to assert that the books of scripture teach firmly, faithfully, and without error *the truth which for our salvation God willed should be recorded in the sacred writings*." Bea remarked that though he did not have time to reflect on it, the formula seemed acceptable to him.

---

[271] In the first balloting votes were given to all seven formulas; the first received 6 votes and the third 16.

[272] In the *expensio modorum* of October 29, this addition (*modus* 40 D) was not accompanied by any commentary (*AS* IV/5, 700); it was, however, explained in Florit's report (ibid., 740f.).

[273] An argument on which Congar disagreed.

[274] *Jde Lubac*, October 19, 1965.

A vote taken immediately showed 19 in favor of the new formula of Philips and 9 against. A two-thirds majority had been reached and the amendment was accepted. At that point Father Anastasius del Santo Rosario asked to speak. He stated that in so serious a matter no risk of an irregularity should be taken; therefore, let the question of procedure be taken to the administrative tribunal. After the meeting, however, Charue persuade Ottaviani to go directly to the Pope and not to the tribunal.[275]

On the third point it was noted that the expression "historical faith" (*fides historica*) was unfortunate and even dangerous, for it could seem to say that the Bultmannians were right.[276] Philips then suggested that in its place it be said at the beginning of no. 19: "the four gospels, *whose historicity (the Church) unhesitatingly asserts*"; this was accepted by 26 votes to 2.[277]

An appraisal of the results of this memorable meeting, which ended at 7:45 p.m., raises some questions, especially about the unexpected part played by Bea. On receiving the article in which Caprile gave the official version of the facts, René Laurentin, an expert and a journalist, responded to him on March 5, 1966:

> As one who witnessed the event, I would like to call to your attention to a very small point that may escape historians. The fact that the questions raised by the papal *modi* had been discussed a great many times and that they came up almost every day before the final revival of them; the atmosphere created at the beginning of the meeting; the presence of Cardinal Bea, which no one expected and which was never clearly explained: all these created a climate of fear, the like of which I had never seen in the commission. This explains the silence of the fathers on the first *modus*. It also explains the fact that of the seven formulas suggested the fathers chose one which they had rejected by a considerable majority on the preceding days; they had done so because of the words *non sola Scriptura*, which even Msgr. Parente had thought untimely due to the appearance it gave of "attacking the Protestants." The general impression was that Cardinal Bea had come with a mandate from the Pope to have the *modi* accepted. It was beginning with the second and most serious *modus* that the more courageous fathers

---

[275] See *JPrignon,* October 19, 1965 (Prignon papers, 1608, 2); October 20, 1965 (Prignon papers, 1609, 1); October 21, 1965 (Prignon papers, 1610, 1). See also the expert opinion asked of Onclin, who concluded in favor of Butler's interpretation (Prignon papers, 1189). On Thursday, October 21, the commission learned that the question had been settled (Paul VI papers, A3/48).

[276] *Jde Lubac,* October 19, 1965; *JPrignon,* October 19, 1965 (Prignon papers, 1608, 2); and *JCongar,* October 22, 1965; II, 444–46.

[277] See also the response to *modus* 16 in the report of October 29 (*AS* IV/5, 723): while retaining the observation on the ambiguity of the word *historicum*, the response cleared the word *historicitas* of the same ambiguity.

recovered and began to express themselves. I think that when there was question of *modi* from him, the Pope did not always take into account the atmosphere created by a set of imponderable factors.[278]

It is understandable that Philips and the Belgian team were wounded by what they felt to be an "abuse of authority" in the way Bea acted.[279] Charue, in particular, had reason to complain that at a papal audience the Pope seemed to rebuke him for not having kept the Secretariat for Christian Unity informed; Charue had reminded the Pope that Bea had been sent the text containing "saving truth" and that he had returned it saying that he agreed with the text.[280] How then could Bea so strongly oppose the formula at this meeting? Other members of the Secretariat for Christian Unity, such as Willebrands and De Smedt, were likewise embarrassed.[281] The Cardinal's attitude remains puzzling; it seems likely, though, that his opposition to *"veritas salutaris"* was really his own personal position.[282]

But apart from these personal and even psychological questions, the course of the meeting was surprising in terms of what the Pope's letter anticipated. While the decision on the first point was left to the relatively free choice of the commission, the commission showed itself to be quite hesitant. On the second point, the freedom of the fathers was restricted, and yet the fathers expressed strong resistance, perhaps because of the unexpected attitude of Bea. The third point, which was imposed on the commission but formulated rather incompetently, gave rise to the idea of a compromise that then won extensive agreement.

As far as substance is concerned, an appraisal of this final phase depends on a reading of the text as a whole. On the relations between scripture and tradition, the general sense was that "the requested addition changed nothing in the text of the chapter."[283] Betti, who had already

---

[278] Paul VI papers, A3/57.

[279] *JPrignon,* October 19, 1965 (Prignon papers, 1608, 3).

[280] *JPrignon,* October 21, 1965 (Prignon papers, 1610, 1).

[281] Ibid., October 20, 1965 (Prignon papers, 1609, 1f.).

[282] See ibid., 1: "In the car as we were returning from the mixed commission on schema XIII, Tromp said that that morning, or the evening before, Bea had told him that he had fought all his life against the *veritas salutaris* and that he was quite happy that the formula had not become part of the text." See also Congar: "Msgr. Ancel told me he had it from Msgr. Colombo that this fear (that the formula might be misunderstood and that some might abuse it to limit inspiration, and therefore inerrancy, to religious truths) came from Cardinal Bea, who had imbued the Pope with it" (*JCongar,* October 22, 1965; II, 446).

[283] *Jde Lubac,* October 19, 1965. A few days later de Lubac wrote: "Msgr. Maziers asked for my opinion. I answered that I found this *modus* an excellent one; it adds nothing to the text but summarizes its thought very well. I added that it even seemed to me not strong enough (after all, what dogmas are there on which scripture alone, without the

noted the closeness of the Colombo/Poma formula to that of the 111 fathers, observed simply that they could have reached harbor much sooner "without inconveniencing the Pope."[284] But was he happy that the addition contained the words "*sola scriptura*"?[285] From an ecumenical point of view, the seven formulas were not completely equivalent.

As for the new draft of the passage on inerrancy — "the truth which for our salvation God willed to be deposited in the sacred writings" — one cannot fail to be surprised at the equivalence between it and the passage that had been removed. How could Bea declare it "admissible" without seeing that it invalidated an important part of his argument?[286] The only possible justification for changing the text is the one given by Philips in the official commentary, published in the *expensio modorum*, in which it is said that the text was changed only "to avoid abusive interpretations on the subject of the extent of inspiration."[287]

At the end of the meeting two secret reports were sent to the Pope on October 20. One had been composed by Philips at Ottaviani's request;[288] the other, somewhat fuller on the second point was sent by Colombo.[289] On the following day the Pope gave his final approval for the printing of the text — but after some hesitation, it seems.[290]

---

traditional interpretation of it, can give us unqualified certitude?). The good bishop was quite surprised. This showed me that many people misinterpret the doctrine on revelation as much as they do that on collegiality. Thus they see the rejection of the dualism of 'two sources' as an assertion of *scriptura sola*! At that point, the stubborn little minority has it easy" (ibid., October 25).

[284] *DBetti*, October 19, 1965, 367.

[285] "It is unfortunate that this formula contains the phrase *sola scriptura*. Moeller can't get over it, and won't get over it for a long time, that it was Bea himself who recommended the formula containing *sola*" (*JPrignon,* October 19, 1965 [Prignon papers, 1608, 2]).

[286] This emerges from the "Note on the Meaning of *salutis nostrae causa* in the Constitution *De revelatione,*" which Prignon wrote for Charue and, on November 28, sent to Ottaviani to be passed on to the Pope (Prignon papers, 1580). Prignon recalls "the exclamations of Msgr. Colombo and Father Anastasio that this new formula meant the same as *veritas salutaris,*" and the "statement of a father as he left the hall: 'We drove it out the door, but they brought it back in through the window.'"

[287] *AS* IV/5, 708.

[288] *AS* III/3, 464–68 (with the *Notulae* of Philips and *modus* 8 of chapter III for the *expensio modorum*); see also Paul VI papers, A3/43–44 and B3/31.

[289] Paul VI papers, A3/41–42 and B3/31.

[290] This point emerges from a card sent to the Pope by Colombo, supplementing the reassuring telephone reply of Florit (see *DFlorit*, October 21, 1965) to the question of Paul VI whether the new formula on inspiration was "adequate" from a doctrinal viewpoint (Paul VI papers, A3/48). That the new formula did in fact cause some problems can also be seen from the Italian version of *Dei Verbum*, which appeared in *OssRom* for November 23 and which translated *nostrae salutis causa* as "Author of our salvation" instead of "for the sake of our salvation" (Latin *causa* = ablative case). The next day Felici alerted

D. The Report of October 29 and the Final Votes

With the first recess ended, the work of the assembly began again on Monday, October 25.[291] Jauffrès wrote: "This morning most of the bishops were at their seats; many (the Italians in particular) were returning from their dioceses after the eight-day respite we just had. After the Council Mass, during which we heard the *schola* of Regensburg, there was about an hour of intense attention as we listened first to the quite lengthy and always spiritual views of Secretary General Felici on the organization of all the coming sessions."[292] Here is what Felici announced: that the votes on religious freedom would be taken on the next two days; the seventh public session would be held on Thursday, October 28, at which three decrees (bishops, religious life, seminaries) and two declarations (education, non-Christian religions) would be promulgated; and, above all, that a public session would be held on November 18 at which it was anticipated that *Dei Verbum* would be promulgated.[293]

On Tuesday morning the fathers were given the schema on revelation, as well as the responses to the *modi* and the reports of Florit and van Dodewaard.[294] The Council of Presidents announced that the votes on the *De revelatione* would take place on Friday, October 29, and that the Pope had formally asked the bishops not to take another holiday before the end of that voting.

After the mass, celebrated according to the Armenian rite, this final meeting before the All Souls recess was devoted entirely to votes on the dogmatic constitution, in suspense since the first session. In his report on chapters I and II Florit[295] remarked, first of all, that the text had been notably improved and given a better form. While he simply summarized the most important changes in the Prologue and in the chapter on revelation, he devoted two sizable commentaries to the paragraphs on

---

the Pope, who asked him to get the commission to correct the translation (see Ottaviani's letter of November 29 in *AS* V/3, 635).

[291] On that day, Philips, exhausted and ill, had to stop his work; he would be forced to leave the Council before its end. Prignon wrote: "All day long I have continually received messages from all corners with good wishes and prayers for Philips. Msgr. Colombo has even offered, if need arises, to bring him to a cardiological clinic well known to him. And this evening, at the audience given to the moderators, the Cardinal brought the Holy Father up to date; the latter loaded the Cardinal down with good things for Msgr. Philips" (*JPrignon,* October 26, 1965 [Prignon papers, 1612, 2f.]).

[292] Jauffrès, *Carnets conciliaires,* 297.

[293] *AS* V/3, 742f.

[294] *AS* IV/5, 681–746.

[295] The drafter of this report was Betti, who left his mark on it (*DBetti,* October 20, 1965).

tradition and on the relation between scripture and tradition. The first answered those who feared that the idea of a development of tradition threatened the transcendence of the word of God; the text did not allow for any *objective* progress, since nothing substantially new can be added to tradition; what grows is "the *understanding* of both the things and the words transmitted." The reporter added some thoughts on "the internal development of a living reality" in order to make the history of dogmas understandable.

The second commentary was devoted to the "papal *modus*" on scripture and tradition. The report understood this *modus* first, (a) in the context of no. 9, as an explanation of what preceded it (integral transmission) and as a justification for what followed it (equal feelings of devotion and reverence toward both scripture and tradition). It then added (b) that in this way the text asserts, with full certainty, a Catholic teaching confirmed by the unvarying practice of the Church. Finally, the report gave (c) an interpretation: "It is made clear, then, that tradition is not a quantitative completion of scripture nor is scripture the codification of revelation in its entirety; the addition thus does not change the substance of the text but improves its expression."[296] The Cardinal concluded: "Keep before your eyes this document that is minimal in size but is at the same time of truly fundamental doctrinal importance. It states the connection, often direct, between all the questions treated by the Council. It places us at the very heart of the mystery of the Church and at the center also of the ecumenical problem."[297]

After this first report the fathers were asked to vote on chapters I and II in succession; they listened to songs by a Slavic chorale as they did so. Then came the report of van Dodewaard, who simply listed the most important changes in the second part of the text; he ended by citing the first words of the Prologue: "Hearing the Word of God with reverence and proclaiming it with confidence." The votes on each of chapters III to VI followed, interrupted by songs from the chorale and by explanations from the Secretary General. The results of the voting[298] came close to the "unanimous consensus" desired by the reporters.[299]

---

[296] *AS* IV/5, 740f.

[297] Ibid., 741; see also *DFlorit*, October 29, 1965.

[298] Chapter I: 23 no votes and 2 void ballots out of 2,194 votes cast; chapter II: 55 no votes and 7 void ballots out of 2,185 votes cast; chapter III: 31 no votes and 4 void ballots out of 2,189 votes cast; chapter IV: 8 no votes and 2 void ballots out of 2,188 votes cast; chapter V: 19 no votes and 5 void ballots out of 2,139 votes cast; chapter VI: 14 no votes and 6 void ballots out of 2,146 votes cast. For the schema as a whole: 27 no votes and 7 void ballots out of 2,115 votes cast.

[299] *AS* IV/5, 741.

At the end of the general congregation the secretary announced that the fathers would reassemble on November 9 and that on that day they would vote on the *expensio modorum* of the decree on the lay apostolate. During the earlier vacation the Commission on the Lay Apostolate had been able to put the final touches on the decree; on October 20, at its final meeting, it adopted the report of Hengsbach. The text had already been printed when on Saturday, November 6, Felici set up an appointment with the secretary of the commission on the next day, in the sacristy of St. Peter's; Dell'Acqua handed the secretary a letter containing some "papal *modi*."

The document contained two parts: observations sent to the Sovereign Pontiff during the summer and remarks on the *expensio modorum* with some new suggestions to be studied by the commission. A plenary meeting of the commission could not be held until Monday morning, that is, the day before the planned vote. Twelve corrections were desired in nos. 12 (the young), 19 (the many forms of organized apostolate), and 24 (relations with the hierarchy). Of these only three additions were made to no. 12, and the words "implicitly or explicitly," referring to the consent of the hierarchy to the use of the name "Catholic," were eliminated.[300] These very minor changes were printed on that same day and added to the notebook of *modi* to be voted on.[301]

On November 9, at the time of the final resumption of work, the reporter gave a short overview of the text with emphasis on the style and the new tone of the document. New emphases had been put on the theological foundations, spirituality, the unity of and the distinctions among the goals of the lay apostolate, and the formation for it. Any impression of a paternalistic tone was avoided. All this was in keeping with the wishes of the fathers, while consideration was also given to the remarks and advice of the lay collaborators.[302] The result of the votes on each chapter was highly positive;[303] on the following

[300] "4:30 p.m., plenary meeting at the Secretariat. As I was leaving I saw Msgr. Ménager. He told me that after the schema *De apostolatu laicorum* had been printed, they received some *modi* from the Pope. The commission rejected some of them...; the others would be handed out with the schema but on a separate sheet. These *modi*, Msgr. Ménager tells me, come from bishops who went crying to the Pope and complaining that sufficient attention had not been paid to their observations. Thus the Pope is starting again what ended so badly for him at the end of the third session... but in a less sensitive area" (*JCongar*, November 8, 1965; II, 467).

[301] *AS* IV/6, 12–130.

[302] Ibid., 138.

[303] Chapter I: 10 no votes out of 2,127 votes cast; chapter II: 16 no votes and 1 void ballot out of 2,116 votes cast; chapter III: 12 no votes out of 2,087 votes cast; chapter IV:

day the text as a whole was submitted to a vote and adopted almost unanimously.[304]

Between November 10 and November 17 the assembly continued to vote: first on the Decree on the Missionary Activity of the Church, then on the Decree on the Ministry and Life of Priests; work was also resumed on the future Pastoral Constitution on the Church in the Modern World in the form of an endless series of votes. At the same time, three general congregations were devoted to a debate on indulgences. Before we come to the eighth public session, at which the dogmatic constitution *Dei Verbum* and the decree *Apostolicam actuositatem* on the lay apostolate were promulgated, it is appropriate to offer a short summary of this final phase of doctrinal work.

III. The Significance of the Doctrinal Compromise and Its Initial Reception

A. The Text of *Dei Verbum*, the Dogmatic Constitution on Divine Revelation

The Prologue of the constitution relates the two dimensions of the text to one another: its kerygmatic aim and its strictly doctrinal perspective. The *kerygmatic* aim is summed up in an act of proclamation[305] undertaken by the successors of the apostles: "the sacred Council" (no. 1), the "living teaching office of the Church," places itself under the word of God (no. 10). It listens first to the word and then proclaims it: "It wants the whole world to hear the summons to salvation, so that through hearing it may believe, through belief it may hope, through hope it may come to love" (no. 1). Is it possible to state better the universal efficacy of the discourse that establishes communication between those who speak it and those who hear it, a communication that is accessible to the entire world and that contains nothing less than a "life" — "eternal life" or "salvation" — whose ultimate depths are trinitarian?

---

14 no votes and one void ballot out of 2,076 votes cast; chapter V: 8 no votes out of 2,097 votes cast; chapter VI: 6 no votes and 3 void ballots out of 2,109 votes cast.

[304] Vote on the schema as a whole: 2 no votes and 5 void ballots out of 2,208 votes cast.

[305] See nos. 1, 8, and 9.

And since the word is always an already interpreted word (nos. 10 and 12) — and a word authentically interpreted by Christ's Church in keeping with his promise[306] — the living teaching office of Vatican Council II cannot but situate itself "in the steps of the Councils of Trent and Vatican I" (1). The term "steps" is to be taken literally, to the extent that the Constitution of 1965 preserves in its very texture traces of Trent's decree *Sacrosancta* (1546) on the reception of the sacred books and of the traditions of the apostles, while it also cites the dogmatic constitution *Dei Filius* (1870) on the Catholic faith. Here we have the doctrinal dimension of the text. The complexity of *Dei Verbum* is due precisely to the linking of these two perspectives, the kerygmatic and the doctrinal, to the reciprocal interweaving of the content of the faith and the status of those who set it forth. It is for this reason that the two pivotal chapters — chapter II on the transmission of revelation and chapter III on the inspiration of sacred scripture and its interpretation — caused so many problems to the very end.

Chapter III reflects the historical character of biblical exegesis, which since the coming of modernity in the West has been characterized by the historico-critical approach. It would, of course, be naive to think that this method is neutral or free of doctrinal presuppositions. For this reason, while not losing sight of the kerygmatic perspective in the interpretation of the scriptures, *Dei Verbum* makes its own here the teaching of the three biblical encyclicals of Leo XIII, Benedict XV, and Pius XII. In no. 11 the unique place of scripture as an inspired book is set forth, as is the consequence of inspiration, namely, inerrancy. The passionate debates that took place until the last moment were the sign of a fundamental difficulty: the Council was not successful in apprehending the distinction, proposed by Rahner, for example, between the formal criterion of the truth of *all* the scriptures from the viewpoint of salvation and their cultural relativity from a material point of view.

In no. 12 the text singles out the two poles of the act of interpretation: the roots of the text's meaning in history when the text is looked at in light of its form (for example, literary genre) and respect for the Bible as a unified whole (analogy of faith). Finally, no. 13 states the principle governing the theological interpretation of the scriptures, namely, the principle of "divine condescension," which brings the reader back from the Bible to chapter I of *Dei Verbum* on revelation, although the eventual (re)introduction of the formula "without prejudice to God's truth and holiness"

---

[306] See *Lumen gentium*, 25.

shows a kind of retreat from the radical character of the quite traditional statement made here. In any case, the whole of this chapter of *Dei Verbum* already acknowledges what will be further developed in chapter VI, that is, that the Bible, being a historical book, needs the collaboration of others besides bishops and theologians.

In chapter IV and V on the Old and New Testaments the text moves from the form of biblical books to their content. A second key concept, that of economy, appears here (no. 15), but it was also basic in chapter I on the economy of revelation (no. 2). What was said in nos. 3 and 4 on the preparation for the gospels and on Christ as in his person the fullness of revelation has its scriptural basis in chapters IV and V. Nos. 14 and 15 deal respectively with the history of salvation in the books of the Old Testament (this text touches on what is said about Judaism in *Nostra aetate*) and with the importance of the Old Testament for Christians (a distinction already meaningful in itself). At the point of transition between the two chapters (in no. 16) there is an explanation of the second principle governing the interpretation of the Christian scriptures: "God, the inspirer and author of the books of both Testaments, in his wisdom has brought it about that the New should be hidden in the Old and that the Old should be made manifest in the New" — a principle drawn from Augustine.

No. 17 then gives the key to the kerygmatic theology of the constitution: "The Word of God, which is the power of God for salvation to everyone who has faith (cf. Rom. 1:16), is set forth and displays its power in a most wonderful way in the writings of the New Testament."[307] Nos. 17 and 18, on the excellence of the New Testament and on the apostolic origin of the scriptures (no. 18 introduces a new concept, challenged in the debates, that of the *vir apostolicus*), moved on from biblical history to the establishment of apostolic tradition, which was described in chapter II. In contrast, nos. 19 and 20 speak once again of history (the history of the writing of the gospels) and the passage to genuine doctrine (without leaving aside the kerygmatic dimension) in the other New Testament writings. In no.19, on the historical character of the gospels, we find ourselves in one of the major areas of violent agitation during the final period of the Council.

Chapter VI, finally, locates scripture in the life of the Church. Apart from technical observations on the different versions and translations, in

---

[307] See no. 8, which uses "special way" in describing the "power" that is the result of inspiration.

particular ecumenical translations (no. 22), the text deals, one last time, with relations among the active members of the Church. *All* Christians are emphatically urged to read the scriptures, for "ignorance of the scriptures is ignorance of Christ" (St. Jerome); this is the main pastoral aim of the text. In the final analysis the work of exegetes (no. 23) and theologians (no. 24) is determined by that goal, that is, the *ministry of the word*, which is also the ultimate purpose of the vigilance of the magisterium (nos. 10, 20, and 21). According to the pithy saying in the encyclical *Providentissimus*, "The study of sacred scripture should be the soul of theology,"[308] which has in the scriptures its foundation and a perpetual power of renewal.[309] But the most important statement in this "ecclesiological" chapter is the parallel, strongly challenged by some, between the table of the word and the table of the body of Christ, especially in the liturgy.[310] This is the final manifestation in the constitution of the sacramental conception of revelation that is at the center of the first chapter.

But before coming to this point, we must first go back to chapter II on the transmission of the divine revelation. For the scriptures as they exist (or ought to exist today) in the life of the Church (chapter VI), as they are "more thoroughly understood and constantly actualized in the Church" (no. 8, §3), as they were defined as canonical (ibid.), and as they were written — these scriptures already presuppose apostolic tradition (no. 8, §1), a tradition carried on in the Church (no. 8, §2). It is even part of their kerygmatic identity that they must become (or else risk turning into a dead letter) "the living voice of the Gospel [that] rings out in the Church — and through her in the world" (no. 8, §3 and the Prologue), a voice that requires preachers who make it ring out.

The strength of chapter II is it does not isolate the three referents — tradition, scripture, and the authority of the apostles and their successors, "who have received, along with their right of succession in the episcopate, the sure charism of truth" (no. 8, §2) —; it deals with them together: "It is clear, therefore, that in the supremely wise arrangement of God,[311] sacred Tradition, sacred Scripture and the Magisterium of the

---

[308] See C. Theobald, "L'Écriture, âme de la théologie, ou le christianisme comme religion de l'interprétation," in R. Lafontaine et al., *L'Écriture âme de la théologie* (Brussels: Institut d'Études Théologiques, 1990), 109–32.

[309] This central assertion is close to what the Decree on Ecumenism says about "renewal" and "reform" in the formulation of doctrine; see *Unitatis redintegratio*, 6 and 11.

[310] An unobtrusive allusion to the Constitution on the Sacred Liturgy.

[311] The same expression is used in connection with the relationship between the Old Testament and the New (no. 16).

Church are so connected and associated that one of them cannot stand
without the others. Working together, each in its own way under the
action of the one Holy Spirit, they all contribute effectively to the salvation of souls" (no. 10).[312]

Thus, after lengthy discussion (Léger and others), the authors finally
succeeded in distinguishing between, on the one side, apostolic tradition
and the scriptures, sustained by the *promptings* of the Holy Spirit and
inspiration, and, on the other, "the Tradition that comes from the apostles [and] makes progress in the Church, with the *help* of the Holy Spirit."
It was difficult — and perhaps too difficult at the time — to hold fast
simultaneously to the transcendence of the word of God, the "once for
all" of what went on between Jesus and the Twelve (no. 7), and the constant dialogue between God and the spouse of his beloved Son. Nos. 7–9
are set within the framework of the decree *Sacrosancta* of Trent, which
is cited at the beginning and at the end and on which these numbers in
Dei Verbum comment. No. 10 summarizes it all, while emphasizing the
relation between Church and pastors.

While the Council of Trent, with Irenaeus, had favored the term *gospel,*
Vatican I preferred, though in an entirely different context, the term *revelation*.[313] Vatican II combines the two concepts at the beginning of chapter II, which is strongly influenced by Trent, but by doing so refers the
reader back to chapter II: "Christ the Lord, in whom the entire *revelation* of the most high God is summed up (cf. 2 Cor. 1:20; 3:16 – 4:6),
commanded the apostles to preach the *Gospel*, which had been promised
beforehand by the prophets, and which he fulfilled in his own person and
promulgated with his own lips. In preaching the Gospel they were to
communicate the gifts of God to all men. This Gospel was to be the
source of all saving truth and moral discipline" (no. 7).

Finally, it is in chapter I that the fundamental decisions of the document are taken. Moreover, as we have just seen, they are taken in the
light of a kerygmatic reading of the scriptures, a reading marked by the
ancient tradition and the insights of Trent but understood in a perspective
that is completely foreign to the theory of the two sources. In the final
analysis, everything hinges on the pivotal concept — or rather, experience
— of the *self-revelation* or *self-communication* of God (no. 2). This term

---

[312] The writers of the constitution did not forget to point out, once again, its ultimate
purpose.

[313] See C. Theobald, "La Constitution dogmatique *Dei Filius* du Concile Vatican I,"
in *La Parole du salut. Histoire des dogmes IV*, ed. B. Sesboüé and C. Theobald (Paris:
Desclée, 1996), 259–313.

is shared by the two Vatican Councils[314] but has now provided the exper-imental structure, thanks to an economic and sacramental reading of the New Testament event:

> This economy of revelation is realized by deeds and words, which are intrin-sically bound up with each other. Thus, the works performed by God in the history of salvation show forth and bear out the doctrines and realities sig-nified by the words, while the words proclaim the works, and bring to light the mystery they contain. The most intimate truth which this revelation gives us about God and the salvation of man shines forth in Christ, who is him-self both the mediator and the sum total of Revelation (no. 2).

It is not surprising that the writers had then to revise the concept of faith[315] and give it a truly communicational structure without weakening its intellectual structure (no. 5). In no. 6 the teaching of Vatican I on the relationship between revelation and the natural approach to God is reor-ganized and by that very fact reinterpreted.[316]

As the *votum* of the Biblical Institute of January 1965 was aware, it was undoubtedly the difficulty of achieving this passage fully that gave rise to the acrimonious debates on chapters II and III of *Dei Verbum*. In fact, an assessment of the long history of the drafting of the constitution can-not be satisfied with an analysis of its organic theological structure. It must at the same time take into account the conflicts and their more or less satisfactory resolutions, as well as the specific place of the text in the whole of the Council's work.

B. The Significance of the Final Phase of the Drafting and of the Abiding Doctrinal Conflict

The reflections that follow are more risky and have been more influ-enced by the thirty-five years that have passed since the text was pro-mulgated. During the final doctrinal conflict Paul VI, like the reporter Florit and his theologian, insisted that the additions introduced on Octo-ber 19 improved the text. Other members of the majority downplayed these interventions, observing that "they added nothing substantial." In his letter of October 14 to Paul VI, Döpfner advanced the key argu-ment — but one concerning form and not substance — when he accepted an addition "in order to calm minds." We are thus not very far here from

---

[314] See the constitution *Dei Filius*, chapter II.
[315] See ibid.
[316] Ibid., chapters I, II, and IV.

the idea of a doctrinal compromise, which always supposes an area of
shadows that has not been illumined and that can obviously degenerate
into an area of upheaval in which strong feelings can flare up. It is necessary here to understand the complaint of the minority, who could not
distinguish as clearly and peacefully as did the majority between what was
de fide and what was left to free discussion by the theologians. It is possible to point out at least four areas in which the text seems to involve a
doctrinal compromise.

The first and most important point undoubtedly has to do with the relationship between revelation understood as a kerygmatic or pastoral event
(the proclamation of the gospel) and revelation in the form of a doctrinal
explication of the Christian faith from the standpoint of the diverse truths
or elements in the "deposit." This was the specific point at which the tension between two different languages showed itself throughout the
debates: on the one side, the biblical and patristic approach to revelation,
and on the other, the perspective adopted by the recent magisterium.
There was not necessarily opposition between the two, but the relationship between them was not thought through.[317]

We find the same problem in chapter II when the writers try to avoid
the perspective of a "material extension" of scripture and tradition. Even
if an effort was made to leave the question open, it remains on the horizon of the constitution and enters the text, at least negatively, where the
formula chosen remains an alien body, despite Betti's explanation. Betti,
along with Philips and Congar, shifted the problem from the content of
revelation to the certain and complete knowledge of it, a knowledge that
is provided by tradition. This leaves intact the question of the status of
the content of faith in relation to the event. In the relation between tradition and scripture is there really a problem of the knowledge of doctrine? Is not doctrine rather *one* way of determining conditions required,
in varying contexts, in order that within the bosom of tradition itself the
kerygmatic or pastoral event may take place, and this in all its dimensions? That is surely the intended meaning of Rahner's language when
he speaks of the "formal aspect" of scripture and dogma, and it is surely
what John XXIII had in mind when he spoke of the "*pastoral form* of
doctrine or of the teaching office."

---

[317] One might think of the difference in terms of a change of paradigm, as I have proposed in *La Parole du salut*, esp. "L'encyclique *Humani generis* (1950) ou la fin d'une
époque de dogmatisation fondamentale" (451–70) and "Le Concile de Vatican II e la
'forme pastorale' de la doctrine" (471–510).

A second point, related to the first, has to do with the difficulty of precisely determining the normative role of the scriptures. The vagueness of the formulas in chapter VI has been noted: in the next-to-last version the earlier statement that the scriptures are capable of "guiding and *passing judgment on* all preaching in the Church and even on *the Christian religion itself*" had disappeared; it was partially restored at the end: "It follows that all the preaching of the Church ... should be nourished and ruled by sacred Scripture" (no. 21). The ecumenical stakes in this question are important to the extent that Lutheranism does not at all deny the hermeneutical function of tradition,[318] while it also gives scripture, as an institution symbolizing the *extra nos* of the word of God, a critical function that makes possible an *Ecclesia semper reformanda*, something that is also suggested in the Decree on Ecumenism.[319]

The third area of conflict skirted with the help of a "compromise" was history, a reality that is certainly present in the constitution, especially in chapter III, which deals with literary genres and other forms of expression, and in chapter V, in which allusions are made to the history of the composition of the gospels. But how difficult it is to tackle the substantive question emerged in the short debate on the resurrection and in Daniélou's attempt to introduce a note on the infancy gospels. Hidden behind these seemingly purely exegetical questions is the problem of modernity and of the "secularization" of the vision of the world; the problem can also be seen on the horizon in the debates on the autonomy of history in the first part of *Gaudium et spes*. Karl Rahner laid great emphasis on the contemporary transformation of the "modernist problematic," which consists in distinguishing materially in the scriptures between the field of the "profane," this being historically relative and possibly a source of errors, and "religious" affirmations, these being definitive and revelatory. On the other hand, the new concept of "saving truth" does not point to a "sacred" area that is guarded against or exempted from the fluctuations of history but signifies rather an "interpretive key" to the whole of the scriptures, as Döpfner explained one last time in his letter of October 14. In my opinion, neither the higher authorities of the Council nor a considerable part of the assembly grasped this argument, which presupposed a real conversion of mentalities. Paul VI

---

[318] See especially the text of the Fourth Faith and Constitution Conference, held in Montreal, July 12–26, 1963, on the subject of scripture and tradition (text in *DC*, no. 60 [1963], 1205–1315).

[319] See *Unitatis redintegratio*, 4 and 6.

preferred the elimination of the "saving truth" formula, but in the end he reluctantly accepted the formula chosen at the last minute, which was objectively equivalent to its predecessor.

Fourth, a sizable number of the *modi* offered for chapter II touched on the historical foundation of the Church. The commission rejected them while referring several times to chapter III of *Lumen gentium*. This procedure, while perfectly legitimate in itself, presupposed that the question about the apostolicity of the Church, the functions of the apostles, and apostolic succession, as well as about the plurality of ecclesiologies (Eph 4:11–13), the role of the Spirit, and so on, were resolved in that text; this was not necessarily the case. The overall image that Neo-Scholasticism had formed of the foundation of the Church was a kind of ahistorical and even ideological retrojection of the present-day hierarchical structure and doctrinal architecture of the Church into an immemorial past; this had suddenly become uncertain. Strictly speaking, we cannot speak here of a doctrinal compromise, because the shared ground of *Dei Verbum* and *Lumen gentium* had never been discussed, either in the commission or in the Council hall. But the tacit elimination of a problem is also a way of leaving areas of shadow in a text and of making an appointment with the future.

C. *Dei Verbum* and the Other Conciliar Documents

In the fall of 1964 the Doctrinal Commission was vividly aware that the *De revelatione* was "in a way the first of all the Constitutions of this Council, so that its prologue introduces all of them to some degree." Admittedly, the final doctrinal debates in the fall of 1965 and the need to cross some "thresholds" in order to reach consensus led some to forget this overall background. But at the time of the final vote on the schema, on October 29, Florit returned to it, almost furtively, when he said at the conclusion of his report that this constitution "tells us the link between all the questions taken up by this Council. It locates us at the heart of the mystery of the Church and at the center of the ecumenical problem."

Without indulging in "conciliar fiction," we cannot fail to observe that the *De revelatione* with its unusually intense debates was present throughout all four periods. It takes up the very *principle* of the Christian faith, a principle that in a way, remained in suspense until almost the last moment. What would have happened if *Dei Verbum* had been completed before *Lumen gentium*? This is indeed a speculative question, but one that can make us more sensitive to a fact concerning reception, namely, that in practice the Constitution on the Church has taken first place among all the conciliar texts.[320]

Perhaps this priority was promoted by Paul VI himself and by the way in which he spoke, at the beginning of the second period, about the principal goals of the Council:

> Venerable brothers, if we set before our eyes the supreme idea that Christ is our founder, our invisible but real head, and that we receive everything from him, so that with him we form the "whole Christ" of whom St. Augustine speaks and by whom the theology of the Church is permeated, then we can better understand the principal goals of this Council. For brevity's sake and for an easier grasp of these, we shall speak of them under four headings: the Church's self-knowledge or, if you prefer, self-consciousness, the renewal of the Church, the restoration of unity among all Christians, and the dialogue of the Church with contemporary humanity.[321]

Against this background it became significant that at the moment when *Dei Verbum* was promulgated on November 18, 1965, Paul VI did not hark back to what was at stake in this constitution but rather looked at the postconciliar period from the viewpoint of institutions. Everything suggested that the page had already been turned.

Yet the two reports that we have been citing placed *Dei Verbum* at the head of the entire work of the Council. The reception of this document, therefore, must respect its "organic structure"; it cannot be satisfied with harking back to the points of disagreement that remain present behind the compromises achieved, with the idea of possibly eliminating them. No, the reception deals also, or ought to, with the whole of the Council's work in order to weigh, from a historical viewpoint, the relative importance of the texts, and of the Constitution on Revelation in particular.

In the reception it would be necessary to answer, first of all, the question of the *authority* proper to each of the two *dogmatic* constitutions, while bearing in mind that with regard to *Dei Verbum* the question received a first answer in a notification that the Secretary General of the Council sent out on November 15, 1965, three days before the promulgation of the document:

---

[320] Editions that present the conciliar texts in the order of constitutions, decrees, and declarations, often place *Lumen gentium* first, followed by *Dei Verbum*, *Sacrosanctum concilium*, and *Gaudium et spes*.

[321] *AS* II/1, 189.

The question has been raised of the *theological note* to be given to the doctrine expounded in the dogmatic Constitution on Revelation and submitted to a vote. To this question the Doctrinal Commission has given an answer in its declaration of March 6, 1964: "In accordance with the practice of the councils and with the pastoral purpose of the present council, the latter defines as having to be held by the Church only those points of faith and morals which it shall have explicitly declared to be such. As for all the remaining teaching set forth by the sacred Council: since there is question here of the teaching of the supreme magisterium of the Church, each and every Christian ought to receive and embrace it in light of the thinking of the sacred Council itself as made known either by the subject matter or by the way in which it speaks, that is, in light of the rules of theological interpretation."[322]

The reference to "the pastoral purpose of the present council" might be taken as speaking against the dogmatic value of the two constitutions. But the final words, which are not found in the note of November 15, 1964, with regard to *Lumen gentium*, but are found in the note of November 15, 1965, with regard to *Dei Verbum*, give two criteria that allow us to conclude that these texts intend "to give infallible expression to the teaching of Christ" (*Lumen gentium,* 25, §2). As far as the "subject matter" is concerned, it is not possible to deny the continuity with the Council of Trent and Vatican I and, in particular, with the Contitutions on the Catholic Faith and the Constitution on the Church (I) of the 1870 assembly. As for "the way in which it speaks," we must refer to the Prologue of *Dei Verbum*, which refers explicitly to Trent and Vatican I, and to the prologues of chapters I and III of *Lumen gentium*, which rely on the very authority of the 1870 assembly. Why name *Dei Verbum* and *Lumen gentium dogmatic* constitutions if these texts have a lesser dogmatic value than that of the texts they claim to reinterpret?

Reception must next decide on the relationship between these two principal constitutions, while being especially sensitive not only to the fact that the "christocentrism" of the two documents hides two different theologies but also to the blurred boundaries between them, evident in the response to the *modi* of September and October 1965.

Furthermore, Florit's final report located *Dei Verbum* "at the center of the ecumenical problem." This emerges clearly from the history of the drafting of the text and from the subject matter. But this rather programmatic statement raises formidable problems concerning the precise relationship between *Dei Verbum* and *Unitatis redintegratio*: What connection is to be made, for example, between the last-minute addition to

---

[322] *AS*, IV/6, 419.

chapter II of *Dei Verbum* and the principle of the "hierarchy of truths," which is set forth, as a method, no. 11 of the Decree on Ecumenism?

It is true, as the reporter said in his final words, that *Dei Verbum* "expresses the link between all the questions treated by this Council": Chapter VI, on scripture in the life of the Church, is expressly related to the liturgy, even though the constitution *Sacrosanctum concilium* is not cited; the future pastoral constitution and the problem of atheism are mentioned in the report made during the month of September on the *modi* proposed for no. 6 on the natural knowledge of God;[323] the relationship with Judaism is touched on in no. 14 on the history of salvation in the Old Testament books; and we can surely see the attempts to bring home the universality of God's "self-revelation from the beginning" (no. 3) — a theme dear to Rahner — in connection with the Declaration on the Relationship of the Church to the Non-Christian Religions.

D. Enabling Theology to Become Fully Evangelical

"A great document that provides theology with the *means* to become fully evangelical." This wise judgment of Father Congar, written on the very day of the ceremony of promulgation,[324] could be found flowing from the pen of other experts. Father de Lubac, with his Dominican colleague, had been on the preparatory theological commission and during the last period had observed, with an increasing sense of alienation, the direction that, as he saw it, one part of the Church and of the Council was taking. He did not spend the time that others did in drafting and polishing conciliar documents. He did, however, begin quite early to comment on the constitution in lectures, even before it was promulgated.

With great clarity he observed that the essentials of the constitution were controlled by the first chapter, and he remarked that, paradoxically, no member of the minority thought it useful to require in 1964 a special report on this first chapter or even to extend Franić's report to cover the first two chapters.[325] One might be tempted, he said, together with many Catholic exegetes of the conciliar period, to regard *Dei Verbum* as "the

[323] Perhaps the theology of faith in no. 5 is to be completed by that in no. 10 of the Declaration on Religious Freedom, which was adopted on November 19, 1965, shortly after the promulgation of *Dei Verbum*.

[324] *JCongar*, November 18, 1965; II, 478.

[325] See the tripartite conclusion of "Commentaire du Préamble et du chapitre I," in Vatican II, *La Révélation divine*, 1:273–302, quotation at 279.

manifesto of Vatican Council II on the Bible," but "it is not an exaggeration to say that the essential progress sanctioned by *Dei Verbum* is, first and foremost, that of fundamental theology — which is also theology of the Bible; this is not to play down the importance of the constitution's teaching on biblical interpretation but rather to see this as one of the fruits of its teaching on revelation itself."[326]

Without describing here the numerous and important consequences of the decisive choice made by the Council,[327] let us record the connection that de Lubac, at the end of his observations, established between the constitution and the gesture of "enthroning the gospel," a beautiful symbol set before the eyes of all each morning of the Council:

> When Paul VI was present, he did not leave to anyone else the responsibility for doing this. This ceremony has not always been fully understood. Many have seen in it simply the homage which the Church of Vatican II desired to pay to the Bible. While this view is not entirely erroneous, it is very incomplete (as is, at times, the interpretation of the constitution itself, as we saw earlier). It does not grasp the true meaning of the rite. After having been carried in procession, the book of the gospels was not placed on a lectern but really installed on a throne. This was because it represented Christ himself.[328]

It is not sure that at the time the fathers made this connection between the daily gesture and the text, and still less that they perceived its meaning for theology and for a "reform" of the Church, which is called upon to make its own the very form of the gospels. It was the fate of *Dei Verbum* at the Council that it reached port belatedly, that it was accepted by a wearied assembly, and that it was superseded by texts of "the home stretch" that made a greater impression on public opinion, such as the Decree on Religious Freedom, adopted soon after, and the Constitution on the Church in the Modern World. Remarks of Jauffrès were probably typical of those of many others:

> What a long road we have travelled since the famous session three years ago at which the cardinals and the assembly seemed split over this schema, which was then called, or at least its first chapter was, "The Two Sources of Revelation." To arrive at today's definitive text, a serious effort by both sides, moved by the breath of the Holy Spirit, at reciprocal understanding, study, and reflection was needed.[329]

---

[326] Ibid., 282f.
[327] Ibid., 290.
[328] Ibid., 301f.
[329] Jauffrès, October 29, 1965, in *Carnets conciliaires*, 305.

Nothing here about substance but simply astonishment that unity was restored. This is just what Paul VI wanted to achieve.

Among the Protestant observers reactions were more reserved. There were, of course, enthusiastic responses, such as that expressed by Roger Schutz and Max Thurian: "Revelation is seen throughout this magnificent text as the living word which the living God addresses to a living Church made up of living members.... This entire document on revelation is controlled by the fundamental gospel themes of word, life, and communion."[330] But critical responses were not lacking, especially in pointing out "the rather unclear relation between scripture and tradition."[331] K. E. Skydsgaard, for example, spotted the two currents of thought at the Council, but he was surprised that Jean Daniélou, "one of the progressive theologians," did not, in an article that appeared two days before the final vote, deplore the fact that the pontifical addition further emphasized tradition. Even if the document avoided giving a clear solution to the question debated in Catholicism, "in my opinion," said the professor, "the document is clear enough to allow me to say that this question remains a clear line of division between the Roman Catholic Church and the Churches born of the Reformation."[332]

Skydsgaard also observed that the majority of the bishops had a quite fundamentalist view of the Bible. But while he thought that the exegetes would never be satisfied with chapter III,[333] a man like E. Schlink expressed his admiration that the Catholic Church was the first of the Churches to say, in the area of critical hermeneutics, that the plurality of genres and forms of expression have a properly dogmatic function. His response to chapter I was positive with regard to its concentration on Christ, but critical of the "semi-moralistic conception" of faith. On chapter II he saw as positive the abandonment of the Roman thesis on the magisterium as a proximate rule but criticized the retention of tradition as under Roman approval.

In chapter IV, on the Old Testament, Schlink regretted that nothing was said about the dialectic of the law and faith. He praised chapter V

---

[330] Roger Schutz and Max Thurian, *La parole vivante au Concile* (Taizé, 1966), 219f. See also idem, "La Révélation selon le chap. Ier de la Constitution," in Vatican II, *La Révélation divine*, 1:463–74.

[331] E. Schlink, "51. Bericht über das II. Vatikanische Konzil" (An den Vorsitzenden des Rates der Evangelischen Kirche in Deutschland, Präses Kurt Scharf), October 25, 1965, in Schlink papers, 1659, 6.

[332] Skydsgaard, "Report on the Fourth Session of the Second Vatican Council n. 5" (November 19, 1965), 3f.

[333] Ibid., 4.

for the freedom it showed in dealing with history, and chapter VI for saying "that scripture is the permanent basis of theology." In conclusion, he
voiced his conviction, shared by Congar, that the constitution would permit Roman theology to be given a biblical structure, but he immediately
added, "One would go overboard, in my opinion, if one hoped that the
constitution will produce essential transformations of certain central elements in the faith-consciousness of Roman Catholicism."[334]

Let one final witness speak: Archimandrite André Scrima, whom, on
Suenens's advice, Paul VI wished to consult before his final intervention
on October 18. Speaking for Oriental Orthodoxy, Scrima stressed, above
all else, the connection between revelation and liturgy: "One might have
desired a stronger doctrinal emphasis on the interweaving of the economy
and the liturgy. Indeed, the constitution does speak of this in its final
chapter (on the place of scripture in the life of the People of God). We are
thinking, however, of a deeper aspect: its basis in mystery, if I we may
so put it."[335]

Scrima expressed views on chapters I and II in particular. "The importance of the first chapter is not due solely to the fact that it has reordered
the principles of understanding which operated hitherto in a scattered
way, and done so in a manner more in keeping with their real theological finality, but also to the fact that it has sketched out an implicit methodology, so to speak, for reflection on the transmission of revelation."[336]
In reference to chapter II the Archimandrite called to mind the principal
advance made by the Council:

> While incorporating the undeniable, positive contribution that comes from
> questioning the past, chapter II has found the way back into the inner unity
> of the reality, the formal breakup of which led in recent times to the debate
> going on today: it rediscovered the relationship, constitutive of the revealed
> mystery, between the revelation's "localization in time" and its "contem-
> porary actualization." Thus, the Constitution does something more impor-
> tant than give a detailed discussion of an abstract problem; in this chapter
> (with, admittedly, a somewhat unequal force and clarity) it points out the
> concrete content hidden in the formula "transmission of revelation." With-
> out being excessively schematic, one might, I think, identify the three main
> facets as follows: the univocity of the scripture-tradition relationship; the
> organic unity of tradition in the sense both of *traditum* and of the *actus*

---

[334] Report of E. Schlink (Micksey's summary of reports 30 and 31), in Schlink papers.
[335] André Scrima, "Révélation et Tradition dans la Constitution dogmatique *Dei Verbum* selon un point de vue orthodoxe," cited in Schutz and Thurian, "La Révélation selon
le chap. Ier de la Constitution," 527.
[336] Ibid., 527f.

tradendi (in other words, the interior unity of its ontological content and its noetic specification); finally, the convergence, liturgical in kind, of those realities in the process of tradition which signify and actualize the very reality of the divine economy as a whole.[337]

Scrima's only criticism, cautiously made, had to do with the theology of the magisterium: "On this point the constitution seems, in a way, to stop at the outer edge of the problem."[338] And concerning the famous papal *modus* for chapter II, he remarks only (and in a note) that though the constitution is clear on the role of the Spirit in apostolic tradition and in traditions received from the apostles, it is less so when dealing with relations between scripture and tradition: "The *modus* of Pope Paul VI should be located in that context."[339]

E. A MAGISTERIUM ABOVE ALL PASTORAL

In ending this evaluation of the final phase of doctrinal elaboration, I must note that the proximity of the constitution *Dei Verbum* and the decree *Apostolicam actuositatem* at the solemn promulgation of November 19 was not, perhaps, without its deeper meaning. We must not, of course, overestimate the significance of the proximity, which was, after all, due to the accidents of conciliar programming. In any case, on one celebratory morning the Council restored not only the relationship between the word of God and an ecclesial experience of the first importance but also, and above all, John XXIII's idea, expressed in his opening speech, *Gaudet mater ecclesia*, of a pastoral magisterium that keeps in mind the intrinsic unity of doctrine and practice.

The text of the Decree on the Apostolate of the Laity contains an introduction and six chapters. Chapter I is closely linked to other conciliar documents to which reference is made in the Introduction. This chapter, "The Vocation of Lay People to the Apostolate," immediately identifies Christian vocation with vocation to the apostolate (no. 2). The theological foundation for this identification is given through the reference to the three sacraments of Christian initiation, the three theological virtues (the Prologue to *Dei Verbum* gives the trinitarian dimension of these virtues), and the theory of the charisms (nos. 3 and 4, with a reference to meditation on the word of God).

---

[337] Ibid., 528f.
[338] Ibid., 534.
[339] Ibid., 536 n.14.

In chapter II ("Objectives") we can see traces of chapter II of *Lumen gentium* as well as of the future pastoral constitution, especially in the distinction between the apostolate, which aims to evangelize and sanctify others (no. 6) and the Christian renewal of the temporal order (no. 7). Above all, we must observe that beginning in the Introduction, the text, perhaps for the first time, uses the same vocabulary for the apostolate as for mission, although the former term may, with *Lumen gentium* (nos. 19 and 20), be reserved for the apostles and for the activities of evangelization and sanctification, and the latter term for the laity, whose task it is "to seek the kingdom of God through their management of things temporal, which they order as God wishes" (*Lumen gentium*, 31).

The idea of the "participation of the laity in the apostolate of the hierarchy" is thus replaced by the idea of "collaboration" (see no. 20) and the unity of the two dimensions of world-transformation and proclamation (a unity of deeds and words, see *Dei Verbum*) is affirmed in a number that singles out charitable activity as the seal on the Christian apostolate (no. 8).

In chapter III the text goes further into some historical and locally diversified areas of the apostolate. "The various fields of the apostolate" are reviewed: ecclesial communities (no. 10), the family (no. 11), the young (no. 12),[340] the social environment (no. 13), and the national and international levels (no. 14). To a greater extent than chapter III, Chapter IV is subject to cultural and even national differences, for its subject is "the different forms of the apostolate"; the text maintains a balance between the individual aspect (nos. 16 and 17) and the numerous forms of organized apostolate (nos. 18 and 19). It is in this setting that the document deals with Catholic Action (no. 20), giving three characteristics more specific to this form of the apostolate. The final two chapters, V and VI, set down a number of general regulations, chiefly of a juridical kind, and then give some directives for a "formation for the apostolate."

IV. NOVEMBER 18: PAUL VI LOOKS AHEAD TO THE POSTCONCILIAR PERIOD

In his diary for November 18, at 12:40 p.m., Msgr. Jauffrès wrote:

> I left the solemn public assembly at which the Dogmatic Constitution on Revelation and the Decree on the Apostolate of the Laity were officially

---

[340] Some additions were made in no. 12 at the last minute, for example: "animated by a sense of obedience and love towards the pastors of the Church."

promulgated. It was one of the great days, but was celebrated with ordinary ceremonial, reduced to a minimum by Paul VI. There were cardinals in priestly robes, processing ahead of the Pope and his concelebrants; there were bishops in cope and mitre; the basilica was brightly lit, and there was a throng of guests and others present who had managed to get a ticket. The Pope celebrated with representatives of the superiors general, the experts, and parish priests; it was a low mass but did have hymns with verses sung alternately by the choir and the vast throng of fathers and those in attendance. I observed, to my delight, that Father de Lubac was among the concelebrants. This was a just reward for the troubles he had at one time with the Holy Office.[341]

After the celebration of mass the vote was taken: *Dei Verbum* received 2,344 yes votes out of 2,350 cast; *Apostolicam actuositatem* received 2,340 yes votes out of 2,342 cast (only two fathers voted no).[342] After each of the two votes the Pope spoke the usual formula of promulgation; he gave three men and three women from among the auditors the promulgated text of the decree in order that they might pass it on *(tradere)* to all of the laity. After all this he delivered his address, which focused essentially on two points.

A. Institutional Reforms for the Postconciliar Period

After a short introduction recalling the entirely exceptional dimensions of this Council, the Pope looked at the institutional face of the postconciliar period. "The end of the ecumenical Council is really the beginning of many things!" Three postconciliar commissions had already been established: one for the liturgy, one for the revision of the code of canon law, and one for the application of the Decree on the Means of Social Communication. The establishment of the episcopal synod had already been announced in a Motu Proprio on the preceding September 15, before being also included in the Decree on the Bishops' Pastoral Office in the Church; Paul VI now announced it would hold its first meeting in 1967. In addition to the three secretariats already in existence — for unity, for relations with the non-Christian religions, and for nonbelievers — still other services would have to be created for the renewal of the Church.

Between this first set of institutions, directly called for by the implementation of the Council, and a second, the Roman Curia, there was the

---

[341] Jauffrès, November 18, 1965, in *Carnets conciliaires*, 325f.
[342] *AS* IV/6, 687f.

institutional implementation of the ecclesiology of communion, as this appeared in *Lumen gentium* (though the terminology was not used here nor was that text cited). Paul VI made some observations on this:

> It is far from our intention to establish a new and artificial centralization; on the contrary, our wish is to involve the episcopate in the work of applying the laws anticipated by the Council, and we also intend to profit as far as possible from its collaboration, in order better to respond to the demands of our apostolic office, which is the universal governance of the Church. The effective role which the episcopal conferences were recently acknowledged as having, will play an important role in the organic development of canon law. And as we have readily desired and favored their creation, so too we hope that in the different countries and regions they will promote the growth of the Church and do it honor.[343]

Next came the much awaited announcement of the reform of the Roman Curia; this was preceded, however, by the standard defense of "this active and faithful instrument for the exercise of the apostolic office." Studies had already begun in accordance with no. 9 of *Christus Dominus*. The Pope added:

> We must say to you that there is no evidence of serious needs calling for changes in structures. On the other hand, in addition to the replacement of incumbents, a number of changes are needed, as are some simplifications and improvements. The main point is that the fundamental principles of this organization will be more clearly formulated and established. The expected transformation will seem slow and partial, and it must be so if we want to give persons and traditions the respect they deserve, but the transformation will come.[344]

This announcement was followed by the second part of the address, which was devoted to moral and spiritual reform. This section was especially important because it offered a theoretical view of an official or kerygmatic reception of the Council:[345]

> The celebration of the Council seems to us to have given rise to three different spiritual experiences. The first was that of enthusiasm, and it was normal for this to be so: surprise, joy, hope, and a kind of messianic dream welcomed the announcement of the Council's convocation.... Then came the second phase: that of the actual unfolding of the Council; this was characterized by questioning.... In this final period of the Council, its serious and

---

[343] Ibid., 691.

[344] Ibid., 692.

[345] "'Kerygmatic reception' describes all the efforts of pastors in making known the decisions of the Council and effectively implementing them" (G. Routhier, *La réception d'un Concile* [Paris: Cerf, 1993], 87).

encouraging utterances will tell us what the Church's manner of life should be. We come thus to third phase: the phase of resolutions and of the acceptance and execution of the conciliar decrees.[346]

The address laid a heavy emphasis on the contrast between the second and third phases, which were separated by the "voice of the Council":

> In some areas of public opinion, *everything was discussed and regarded as a subject of discussion*; everything seemed difficult and complex; nothing escaped attempts at criticism and the impatient search for innovations. We saw the rise of feelings of restlessness, movements of opinion, fearful attitudes, bold moves, arbitrary positions. Here and there doubts crept in even about the fundamental norms governing truth and authority, until the point at which the voice of the Council began to be heard.

As for the third phase, which was now beginning: "This is the moment in which each individual ought now to prepare himself. *Discussion has ended, and understanding begins.* Now that the soil has been ploughed, it must be cultivated in a methodical and orderly way."[347]

There was thus a very clear determination to have done with the time for debates (this being regarded as provisional) and to begin the time for *orderly* application. There is no thought here of a continuing conciliarity or synodality. And to complete this programmatic description of history, Paul VI redefined the term *aggiornamento,* which John XXIII had coined: "When he [John XXIII] used this programmatic word, he certainly did not give it the meaning which some try to give it, a meaning which would allow the 'relativization' (in accordance with the mentality of the world) of everything having to do with the Church: dogma, laws, structures, traditions…. Henceforth *aggiornamento* will mean for us an enlightened grasp of the spirit of the Council and a faithful implementation of the directives it has laid out in such a felicitous and holy way."[348]

B. Starting the Process for the Canonization of Pius XII and John XXIII

It was in this setting that Paul VI announced his decision to begin the canonical processes for the beatification of his two predecessors, Pius XII and John XXIII. Whatever may have been the prehistory of this

---

[346] *AS* IV/6, 692f.
[347] Ibid., 693.
[348] Ibid., 6983f.

announcement as far as good Pope John was concerned,[349] the Pope's address managed to tie together here at least three purposes. A beatification by acclamation, which some desired, was avoided, and the matter was entrusted to the usual channels of Roman procedure. Since each of these popes was the symbol of a period in the life of the Church, Pius XII and John XXIII were henceforth associated as links in the Roman continuity; as a result, "their authentic and very dear persons will be set before us and the centuries to come solely to be venerated for their true holiness, that is, for the glory of God and the building up of his Church." Finally, the two popes were placed in the service of the postconciliar period and of the *aggiornamento* as revised by Paul VI; this became a synthesis of John XXIII and Pius XII, or, to cite *Dei Verbum*, a reminder not to forget that this document really followed in the steps of Trent and Vatican I. "Thus, posterity will be able to profit by the integral spiritual patrimony that they left as their heritage."[350]

Father Congar, who had been unable to take part in the eighth public session of the Council, wrote in his diary:

> I rose early and set myself to typing out the *modi* for nos. 1–3 [of the Decree on Missionary Activity] and my responses to them. I worked non-stop until 4.00 p.m., interrupted only by lunch with Chenu and Peuchmaurd. It was a very long task and very exacting, one that had to be done carefully. Therefore I did not go (and, in any case, would not have gone) to the public session at which the *De apostolatu laicorum* and the *De divina revelatione* were to be proclaimed, this last being a great document that provides theology with *the means* of becoming fully evangelical. The Pope gave an address in which he did not say anything about these documents but spoke, rather at length, of the postconciliar period. He added the announcement of a Jubilee and the beginning of the beatification process of Pius XII and John XXIII. This announcement saddens me. Why this glorification of popes by their successors? Will we never abandon these old Roman habits? At the moment of proclaiming the *aggiornamento*, they perform actions not in accord with it.[351]

---

[349] See A. Melloni, "La causa Roncalli: Origini di un processo canonico," *CrSt* 18 (1997), 607–36.

[350] *AS* IV/6, 694.

[351] *JCongar*, November 18, 1965; II, 478.

Chapter V

THE FINAL WEEKS OF THE COUNCIL

Peter Hünermann

I. A Hectic Pace and Setting a Course for after the Council

A. The Assembly Ready to Leave, Pope and Curia in High Gear

The final weeks of the Council, from the end of October to December 8, have a quite different appearance depending on the perspective from which one looks at the Council. During these weeks the assembly took three rather lengthy vacations: from October 17 to 24, from October 30 to November 8, and from November 19 to 29. The reason for these interruptions was that the great debates on the texts had ended. While by at least a two-thirds majority the fathers had accepted all the texts proposed to them, they had also submitted a large number of desired changes. The commissions now had to deal with these requests, which reached into the hundreds for individual documents, and the work was both difficult and, because of the pressure of time, hectic. In the remaining general congregations the reporters gave evaluations of the requested changes and described the criteria and reasons why they had been accepted or rejected. After this, the texts were once again submitted for a vote, section by section, after which the only thing the fathers could do was once again submit requested changes in writing. Thereupon a concluding vote was taken, and the texts were submitted to the Pope, who then sent them back to the Council for a final, solemn vote.

Many non-European bishops used the vacation periods to travel in Europe. In addition, a fairly large number of Council fathers traveled to Florence on November 13–14 for the Dante Jubilee. At the same time, the fathers began their farewell visits. After announcing the close of the Council in the Letter *Laeto animo* to Cardinal Tisserant (November 9), Paul VI began to give audiences to groups of fathers. In this series of farewell visits one stood out: the reception of the Latin American bishops on the occasion of the tenth anniversary of CELAM. The Pope delivered an important address, challenging the Latin American bishops to work out a common pastoral plan for the whole of Latin America in the postconciliar period, a plan that would be geared to the great social and economic problems of that continent and, in particular, to the problem of poverty.

On December 1 the president of Italy held a farewell reception at the Quirinal in honor of the Council fathers. Finally, on December 6, the mayor of Rome gave each of them a silver keepsake medal. For the majority of the fathers, then, the final weeks were to some extent a holiday. At the beginning of this final phase of the Council the General Secretary feared that the number of fathers present for the votes would shrink; he therefore tried to bring some relaxation to the rather monotonous periods of voting through performances of church music.

The secretary's fear became understandable when one took note of the calendar of general congregations and public sessions in November and December 1965. On November 9 and 10 seven votes in all were taken on the schema on the lay apostolate. In the final vote on the schema as a whole, the text received 2,201 yes votes, 2 no votes, and there were 5 void ballots. On November 12 and 13 fifteen votes were taken on the schema on the ministry and life of priests. From November 15 to 17 thirty-three votes were taken on the improved schema XIII. On November 18, during the eighth public session the solemn final votes on the Dogmatic Constitution on Divine Revelation (2,344 yes votes, 6 no votes) and on the Decree on the Lay Apostolate (2,340 yes votes, 2 no votes) were taken; the texts were accepted and promulgated. On November 19, five votes were taken on the schema on religious freedom. On November 30, after the recess, ten votes were taken on the decree on the missionary activity of the Church, and on December 2, six votes on the schema on the ministry and life of priests. On December 4 there were another twelve votes on schema XIII, and on December 6 there was a vote on accepting this schema as a whole. At the public session on December 7 there was the solemn vote on and promulgation of the following documents: the Decree on Religious Freedom (2,308 yes votes, 70 no votes, 8 void ballots), the Decree on the Missionary Activity of the Church (2,394 yes votes, 5 no votes), the Decree on the Ministry and Life of Priests (2,390 yes votes, 4 no votes), and the Pastoral Constitution on the Church in the Modern World (2,309 yes votes, 75 no votes, 7 void ballots).

These final weeks provided the Pope and his curial collaborators many opportunities to set the course for the postconciliar work that was looming on the horizon. After the adoption of the schema on the liturgy Paul VI had established a commission for the implementation of the Constitution on the Sacred Liturgy. On November 10 he received the participants in the congress, convoked by the Consilium, for translators of the liturgical books. He established as the Consilium's basic principle that the Church celebrates the sacred mysteries and administers the sacraments in one and the same voice, even if that voice speaks in a variety of languages.[1] He also stressed that work on the liturgy, whether by individuals or by institutions, was subject to the control of the hierarchy. Liturgical texts were to be approved by the competent authority and confirmed by the Holy See. After that confirmation they were to be left unchanged.

On November 18, after the promulgation of several conciliar documents during a public session of the Council, the Pope gave a somewhat lengthy address on measures for the postconciliar period.[2] After mentioning the three already established conciliar commissions (for the liturgy, for the revision of the Code of Canon Law, and for the communications media), he announced that further commissions were to be established. The synod of bishops was to be summoned to its first meeting in 1967, and, speaking in general terms, Paul VI explained that the bishops were to take part in it so that "we may be able better to carry out our task in the governance of the universal Church."[3]

The Pope went on to speak of the importance of episcopal conferences and then bestowed high praise on the Curia. People were wrong when they decried that body as an unsuitable instrument. Like everything human it could, of course, be improved. In fact, consideration had already been given to the reform of the Roman Curia, and there had been consultations on the subject. While there was no need to "change the very structure" of that body,[4] the Pope did foresee setting limits to the terms of curial officials. He announced that in the near future norms would be issued for "the first of all the sacred Roman congregations, namely, the Holy Office."[5] He expressly confirmed the continued existence of the three secretariats: for Christian unity, for dialogue with the non-Christian religions, and for dialogue with unbelievers.

The Pope devoted almost half of this address to attitudes toward the Council. Initially, the Council had been greeted with enthusiasm; this was replaced by sobriety at the sight of the vast amount of work to be done. Meanwhile, some first doubts began to be voiced in the realm of public opinion. People began, "impatiently," to look for novelties. Now

---

[1] *AAS* 57 (1965), 968.
[2] *AAS* 57 (1965), 978-84. The address can also be found in Rynne, *The Fourth Session*, 303–9.
[3] Ibid., 980.
[4] Ibid., 981.
[5] Ibid., 983.

that the Council had come to its end and with its documents had fulfilled the task set for it by John XXIII, the need was to "affirm the solidity of the Church's teaching and structure and to implement the Council in a way that is faithful to the norms it set." The Pope expressly rejected every kind of relativism and the worldly attitude that some connected with the Council.

When, after these reflections, the Pope announced that the canonization process was to be initiated for both Pius XII and John XXIII, the gesture seemed both symbolic and programmatic. The new departure that John XXIII had brought about in the Church was evidently to be confined once more within the tight forms of the Church of Pius's time. Finally, the Pope announced the building of a church in Rome that would be dedicated to the memory of the Council under the title of the Blessed Virgin Mary, Mother of the Church; this too was a symbolic gesture. This same title had been rejected by a majority of the Council fathers in connection with the discussion of chapter 8 in *Lumen gentium* on the Church.[6] At the end the Pope spoke of his intention to proclaim a Jubilee in order that "in sermons the message of truth and love issued by the Council" might be brought home to Christ's faithful.[7]

Especially important was Paul VI's address on November 20 to the cardinals and consultors of the papal commission for the revision of canon law.[8] It is striking, to begin with, that Paul VI does not refer to any of the already promulgated conciliar documents and cites only texts of Pius XII. The Pope's very basic remarks paint a completely hierarchical picture of the Church. In the intention of its founders it is "a social... and perfect body".[9] The jurisdictional authority that Christ has given to the hierarchy has for its purpose that through the laws set down by the hierarchy humanity may win a share in the truth and grace of Christ. The Pope pointed out that some constitutive elements of the Church exist by divine law: it is a society of unequals, for divine law has decreed the primacy of the Bishop of Rome, along with the episcopate, the presbyterate, and the diaconate. The laity should likewise be mentioned here, but they have no ability to govern. Patriarchs, metropolitans, parish priests, and religious men and women exist by human law.

---

[6] See *History*, 3:332, 4:52-62 and 445-48.
[7] *AAS* 57 (1965), 984.
[8] Ibid., 985-89.
[9] The Pope referred here to Pius XII, *Mystici corporis* (*AAS* 35 [1943], 226).

The competence of the hierarchy was then described, as was the duty, in conscience, of the hierarchy's subjects to obey the laws. The prescriptions of the law make known with certainty the will of Christ, to whom we are subject as to the supreme Lord.[10] In light of these principles the Pope castigated some misconceptions, among them an inappropriate understanding of freedom, since obedience does not restrict freedom but perfects it. We must not agree with those who depreciate canon law by saying that the letter kills and it is the Spirit who gives life. The distinction between a Church of law and a Church of love was rejected. Much less could one agree with those who believe that in the Church there is no hierarchy but only a "ministry" and, above all, a ministry of the word, so that nothing existed between Christ and the community of believers.[11] Finally, the Pope rejected the view that the Church possesses only a *ius sacramentale*, that is, that the hierarchy is necessary only insofar as it is needed for the administration of the sacraments; this meant a denial of positive law.

A series of basic principles were set down that were to govern the revision of Church law. (1) Anything belonging to divine and constitutive law cannot be changed in any way. (2) Traditions are to be faithfully retained insofar as possible, for this is a characteristic of institutions that have lasted for a long time. (3) But since it is also proper to Church law that it connects the life of the Church and of its members with one another and with civil society, it follows that needed changes must be made. Consequently, the hitherto existing order is to be preserved in most cases, but renewal is needed in some areas. Finally, the Pope addressed the question of whether it does not make sense to draw up a basic, common code that contains the constitutive law of the Church and thus can provide a common foundation for the code of the Latin Church and the code of the Oriental Churches. This address clearly was one of the most important moments for setting a course that would be decisive for the destiny of the Council and its reception in the Church.

On November 21 a small commission, led by Msgr. Willebrands of the Secretariat for Christian Unity, flew to Istanbul to meet with a group appointed by Athenagoras I, Patriarch of Constantinople, and to arrange for the lifting of the mutual condemnations. These negotiations led ultimately to the solemn exchange of fraternal kisses by the Pope and the delegate of the Patriarch and between the Patriarch and the leader of the Roman delegation on December 7.

---

[10] *AAS* 57 (1965), 986.
[11] Ibid., 987.

On November 23, Cardinal Lercaro, president of the Commission for the Implementation of the Liturgical Constitution, together with the presidents of the Congregation for Rites and the Congregation for Religious, published an instruction addressed to the members of the religious orders and congregations and containing regulations for the use of the vernacular in the Divine Office, in the prayer of the Breviary, in conventual masses and community masses. In these diverse regulations, with their constant emphases on limitations, we can sense, on the one hand, how strong the pressure was in convents to celebrate the liturgy in a new and intelligible way, and on the other, the effort to "save" Latin as a liturgical language. Orders and congregations that had "indigenous" members could make more ambitious use of these permissions than would other orders and congregations.[12]

On November 26 the Pope gave a lengthy audience to journalists. On November 29 the announcement was made of the establishment of a papal commission for the revision of the Vulgate, the Latin text of the Bible. Its chairman was Cardinal Bea, president of the Secretariat for Christian Unity.

December 4 saw the beginning of a series of true and proper concluding ceremonies. During the general congregation on the morning of that day General Secretary Felici read a message from the observers and guests of the Secretariat for Christian Unity to the Council fathers. They thanked the fathers for their exceptional warmth and for the countless proofs of their esteem, love, and friendship; the dialogue everyone talks about had not remained an empty promise.[13] The observers expressed their firm conviction that the communion already established among the Churches "would surely grow." This message was greeted with great applause. On the evening of that same day a liturgy of the Word was celebrated at St. Paul's, and the observers and guests were specially invited.

At the final general congregation on December 6 the Pope gave each of the Council fathers a farewell gift of a golden ring, a certificate attesting to his participation in the Council, and a silver medal of the city of Rome.

At the public session on December 7 the remaining documents, on religious freedom, the missionary activity of the Church, the ministry and life of priests, and the Church in the modern world, were promulgated. This grandiose final solemnity, with its lifting of the reciprocal condemnations issued by Rome and Constantinople, marked the internal conclusion of the

---

[12] See *AAS* 57 (1965), 1010–13.
[13] *AS* IV/1, 56.

Council. The papal mass in St. Peter's Square on December 8 represented a conclusion intended for the worldwide public.

In these concluding solemnities, too, important courses were being set for the future, for example, the declaration by Rome and Constantinople. It is also worth noting that on December 7 the Pope also issued new regulations for the Holy Office and gave it a new name: Sacred Congregation for the Doctrine of the Faith.

B. THE DECISIVE WORK OF THE COMMISSIONS IN THE FINAL LABORS OF THE COUNCIL

1. The Working Method of the Commissions

To evaluate the significance of the commissions' labors during the final phase of the Council, we must take a look at their methods. Once a conciliar text had been accepted by at least a two-thirds majority, the competent commission had to decide which proposed changes to accept. The resulting text was then submitted once again to detailed votes in the Council. In these votes it was still possible to submit written requests for changes, but these were not publicly discussed. The text then went back to the commission, which made decisions about the proposed changes and revised the text accordingly. The text was then put to a vote, first section by section, and then as a whole. In these votes the text could only be accepted or rejected. The resulting text was then sent to the Pope; if he approved it, he presented it to the Council fathers for a solemn vote and then promulgated the conciliar document.

The final work of the commissions was done in two stages. Even while discussion was continuing in the Council hall, the contributions of the fathers were being passed on to the subcommissions charged with working on the individual chapters of the documents in question. The subcommissions organized the contributions, deliberated on whether to accept or reject them, formulated the reasons for these decisions, and gave the results of their work to the commissions. On the basis of the preliminary work of the subcommissions each commission then decided on a definitive acceptance or rejection of suggested changes and, if need be, modified the reasons given. The final redaction was the task of the secretary of the commission or of the corresponding editorial commission. The resultant text was not again checked by the commission or the subcommissions.

It is obvious that strict rules could not be followed in this work. Since texts that had gained a two-thirds majority were already approved in principle, the rule was that only on the basis of evident "usefulness" should any improvement be made. At the same time, however, the acceptance of changes should aim at the broadest possible agreement. The treatment of suggestions that called for transpositions or a new organization of chapters or long passages caused difficulty. Unity of style and terminology and the flow of the argument had to be kept in mind. Father Tromp, the secretary of the central subcommission in charge of the revision of schema XIII, produced a meticulous diary-like account of this activity with precise notation of hours and minutes; the account is a treasure trove of information on the difficulties and confusions that arose during this work.

The experts, who carried the chief burden of the labor, were often not present during the discussions in the hall, since they were weighed down with numerous other pieces of work and, in some cases, were involved in several subcommissions. How were they to turn the misgivings and requests for changes in the hall into a continuous text? Long-winded reflections had to be summarized, and interventions arising out of widely differing experiential contexts had to be harmonized.

Another important difficulty was the enormous variety of subjects addressed. The central subcommission that received the various texts of schema XIII found itself in the predicament of having to decide, in a very short time, on a host of very complex theological, social, ethical, and political questions. This represented an important difference from the situation at the First Vatican Council whose concentration on a few clearly outlined questions was a considerable help for the work in the commissions. At Vatican II the wealth of subjects, their complexity, and the open-endedness of many questions meant that the work of the commissions during this final phase acquired a new character: the commissions had to take the intellectual lead, in the hope that a large majority of the Council fathers would ratify what was presented to them.

The work had to be done within a very short time and frequently required lengthy night sessions of the editorial commissions. Further difficulties also arose. Tromp's report makes it clear that the presidents or members of the various subcommissions working on Schema XIII objected to the way in which the central subcommission was doing its work. Amendments were being discussed that did not come from requests of the fathers; the careful work of the subcommissions was not sufficiently appreciated; spontaneous impressions arising from discussion were being given priority over solid theological ideas.[14] The editorial groups were likewise criticized. In his diary for November 7, 1965, Congar remarked:

> I tremble a bit when I think of the editorial revision of schema XIII, which is being completed at the moment. The revisers worked through Monday night into Tuesday. They had to do so if they were to deliver the text to Felici on the tenth, as promised. The commission is a small, rather closed group: Haubtmann, Garrone, Tucci, and, to a small extent, Ancel and Hirschmann. Daniélou got himself onto it. They did not turn to me. I am afraid that they have paid too little attention to the work of the subcommissions.[15]

One of the most important tasks of the editors (Garrone, Haubtmann, and Tucci) was to give the document an effective style and line of thought. Garrone, who became the reporter responsible for the schema after Guano's illness, remained in close contact with Pope Paul VI, who had a tremendous personal interest in the success of schema XIII. It is very likely that in his conversations with Paul VI, Garrone secured the backing of the Pope for the larger changes introduced into the text. Congar remarked in his diary for November 7: "Msgr. Garrone returned around 8:10 from having seen the Holy Father for a full hour on the subject of schema XIII. I ask: Is the Holy Father optimistic? Answer: He wants to be, wants to have solid reasons to be so." A day later Congar wrote: "Garrone seeks cover from the Pope for the editorial changes he has introduced into a text that was approved by the mixed commission [central subcommission]; the final version of the text will not be submitted to that commission."[16] In Congar's view, the editors had obviously taken certain liberties.

Even sharper was the criticism from Bishop Carli when because of an oversight on the part of Msgr. Glorieux, a petition concerning atheistic communism was not even considered. Carli objected to the method being followed:

> It turns the commission, that is, no more than 30 individuals, into a final arbiter of the acceptance or rejection of amendments submitted by the fathers, and this without giving reasons, as in our case. The Council fathers, who together with the Holy Father are the true judges, are in practice asked whether they are pleased or displeased by those amendments that the commission has chosen to introduce, even when, for example, they have been suggested by only a single Council father! But the fathers are never asked

[14] See *RT*, September 14–December 1965, 68–74.
[15] *JCongar*, November 8, 1965; II, 467–68.
[16] Ibid., 465 and 468.

what they think of the numerous amendments (even if proposed, for example, by 450 fathers!) that do not please the commission and are therefore not
even brought to the fathers' attention. The Council, it seems, is being carried out by the commissions more than by the fathers.[17]

This assessment by Bishop Carli was a polemical exaggeration, but it
had a nucleus of truth. Another incident during the final votes and the
establishment of the definitive text shows clearly what those responsible
for redacting the text thought of themselves and of their competency.
When, on December 6, the text of *Gaudium et spes* was divided up for
definitive votes, it contained a correction that was probably the work of
Msgr. Haubtmann, the editor-in-chief. He replaced the expression "social
teaching of the Church," of which he thought little, with "teaching on
society." General Secretary Felici made no reference to this change in the
hall, but twenty-two bishops, mainly Brazilians, discovered the change
and protested to Cardinal Cicognani.[18] Behind the change in wording
there lurked, of course, a critical view of the past "social teaching" of the
Church.

The real controversy arose when the official versions were published;
on December 7 it was the text as edited by Haubtmann that was approved
in the final vote. Afterward Haubtmann defended himself by claiming
that the acceptance of the phrase "social teaching" had been due to an
oversight of the commission. He appealed to the basic agreement of
Msgrs. Guano and Garrone that by means of the other formulation they
could avoid intervening in discussions of the nature of Catholic social
teaching.[19]

2. *Important Figures in the Commissions*

The description of the commissions and their work as an independent
factor in the unfolding of the Council would be incomplete without a
glance at the individuals who worked together there, particularly those
who exerted most influence.

The first to be named is Paul VI himself. Not only did he follow the
work of the commissions very closely, especially in this final phase, but

---

[17] See *AS* V/4, 556.

[18] See S. Scatena, "La filologia delle decisioni conciliare: dal voto in congregazione
generale alla *Editio typica*," in *Volti di fine concilio*, ed. J. Doré and A. Melloni (Bologna,
2001), 84–97.

[19] See communication of Haubtmann to Glorieux, January 11, 1965 (Haubtmann
papers, 2227); and M. D. Chenu, *La dottrina sociale della chiesa: Origine e sviluppo
(1891–1971)* (Brescia, 1977).

he also influenced the work of the commissions in several different ways. First of all, he set boundaries. By determining the time for the completion of the Council's work, as well as by approving procedures for voting and for the method of work, he put the commissions in a strong position. Secondly, and perhaps more important, one may wonder whether some documents would have seen the light of day without the keen involvement of Paul VI on their behalf, an interest the Pope made public as well as manifesting it in his contacts with the commissions.

Two examples: During the third period Paul VI personally defended the schema on the missions, but the Council fathers did not accept the proposed schema as the basis for further work. We may ask whether the new draft of the entire schema, its fundamental theological revision, and its swift discussion during the fourth period would have been successful without the backing of Paul VI and his determination to have a mature decree on the missions. In this case the Pope made his own the desires of the bishops from mission countries and gave force to their request.

The influence of Paul VI showed even more clearly in making the pastoral constitution *Gaudium et spes* a reality. He saw this as one of the most important concerns of the Second Vatican Council. The enormous difficulties faced in the production of this schema — difficulties due to the new methodology, to the complexity of the problems, and to the difficulty in formulating the Church's answers to them — meant that right up to the definitive vote it was questionable whether the document would be approved by the Council fathers. The close contact that Paul VI kept with Msgr. Garrone, especially in the final editorial phase of the commission's work, sustained and supported this work to an important degree.

Above and beyond general support Paul VI repeatedly intervened in the work of the commissions by calling for insertions, changes, and additions in the texts he had reviewed; for example, the question of birth control, which was addressed in schema XIII. The letter that Paul VI had the Secretary of State compose on this question was in fact a strict instruction. In this action Paul VI was evidently placing himself above the procedure that regulated events in the Council. He claimed the right to intervene directly as the one ultimately responsible for orthodoxy. His intervention was occasioned by information from conservative experts on the commission who reached the Pope through a letter sent to him through Ottaviani, who with Browne shared the presidency of the central subcommission.

Paul VI reacted in the way just described because he obviously thought that in this question the binding doctrinal tradition of the Church was at stake. Precisely because he was so interested in the completion of the pastoral constitution, he saw himself under pressure to act. His reaction is all the more striking because he himself had earlier established a commission for further study of this very question, while the texts produced by the commission basically reflected the seeming relative openness of the question. But in the commission's text, which left the question open, Paul VI saw a danger to the preservation of the previous teaching of the Church, which strictly rejected birth control.

Reactions in the commission were interesting. Bishops belonging to the majority, such as Léger, claimed that the amendments that Paul VI had sent in the form of an instruction should be handled just like the suggested amendments of bishops or groups of bishops. This meant that the commission had to decide on these amendments in the name of the Council and could, following its own norms, take them into the text, incorporate them in modified form, or even reject them. The majority on the commission, which shared Léger's view, relied on the fact that Paul VI himself had established the commission for a closer study of these questions but had now removed them from free discussion by the Council. As a result, a simple implementation of the Pope's instruction and a corresponding reorganization of the text would mean putting into the mouth of the Council a statement that it certainly did not want to make and even could not make. In line with this argument, which carried the day in the commission, Paul VI's emendations were modified and inserted into the text at places different from those he anticipated. The original overall character of the text was retained, though in slightly weakened form. Representatives of the Curia, such as Ottaviani and members of the conciliar minority on the commission, who at the same time regarded themselves as the "sounder part" *(sanior pars)*, openly regretted the commission's decision. In the end, Paul VI tolerated the commission's decision, although in an emergency meeting with his closest curial collaborators in this situation, he appealed with great emphasis to his own conscience.

If one reflects theologically on the various ways in which Paul VI influenced the work of the commissions, several basic lines emerge. The commissions, which regarded themselves as essential instruments of the Council's work, clearly displayed their respect for the Pope's primatial authority; through their policy of keeping him informed, they made it possible for him to use his authority to secure the success of the Council and to surmount the many problems facing that body. In addition, they never challenged that the Pope had a special role and on important questions could submit amendments of the commissions' work without being bound by the regulations of the Council.

But the commissions also claimed that as responsible subjects in doing the work of the Council, they were competent, when dealing with questions that had not yet been decided to be matters of faith, to treat the Pope's suggested amendments as they did those of other bishops, that is, with respect for the majority of the Council fathers. It is significant that here an explicit distinction was made between an objective judgment on the definibility of a teaching of faith and the Pope's judgment of conscience. On the one hand, then, the commissions claimed a certain independence of the assembly as a whole and a certain competence of their own; on the other hand, in their relations with Paul VI they showed themselves to be authorities that had a duty to the Council and to the ideas of the Council and could implement the basic principles governing the Council's work, even in opposition to the primate, without questioning his authority.

As for the persons who worked in the commissions and the kind of influence they exercised there, four groups must be distinguished: the bishops; the functionaries or officials of the commissions, such as secretaries, reporters, and editorial secretaries; the experts or theological advisers; and the auditors, lay or religious, belonging to some commissions.

The bishops were the real members of the commissions. They had the right to speak, make contributions, and decide. On the central subcommission for schema XIII, however, due to circumstances, there were some bishops who had only a consultative vote, among them K. Wojtyła of Cracow. On all the commissions there was a small group of curial bishops, who also provided the presidents of the commissions. In their theological orientation most of them belonged to the conciliar minority. They differed widely among themselves in expertise, in the understanding of their role as leaders, and in the contributions they made. Cardinal Agagianian, for example, president of the Commission for Missions, gave the impression that the task was too much for him. In contrast, Ottaviani, because of his experience as head of the Holy Office, was familiar with all the critical questions of theology and social ethics and had the abilities required to run the Doctrinal Commission.

The term *moderator* or *president of a commission* perhaps suggests a mistaken image. The actual structuring of the discussion and the organization of the work were entrusted to theologians who, in addition to their education and their theological expertise, had the required communication skills. For the most part they served as reporters, that is, the speakers who in the hall presented the amendments and the work accomplished in the commissions and supported it with arguments. Within the commissions they did the major part of the work and had decisive roles in forming opinions. How much depended on their skill could be seen when, for example, Philips, reporter for the central subcommission that was developing the pastoral constitution *Gaudium et spes*, suddenly had to drop out due to illness and return to Belgium. Although the presidents of the commissions, or their deputies could make their weight felt in the discussions, for the most part they restricted themselves largely to the regulation of formalities.

Along with the members of the Curia, some other bishops formed a group with its own distinctive image. These bishops were among those who in the episcopal conferences stood out from their fellows for their independence, their theological judgment, their initiatives, and so on. As a rule, they were an elite among the bishops; that is why they were chosen. But they differed widely in the degree of their involvement in the work of the commissions. As a matter of fact, it was most often a smaller group of bishops who regularly attended all meetings and thus were the real workers. At various points in his journal Congar let his real thoughts about the bishops emerge. During the Council vacation for All Saints and All Souls, only four or five out of forty bishops showed up for work; the remainder preferred the vacation.[20]

The experts, most of them internationally known theologians, had in many respects the most self-sacrificing place in the commissions. In addition to their activities in a commission or commissions, the more distinguished among them were often overburdened with the task of drawing up positions on this or that passage in the drafts proposed for discussion in the hall. Once the discussions came to an end, they had to classify the submitted amendments and suggest changes and had to deal, in the various subcommissions, with this or that passage of the text and its revision. At the same time, however, they had no voting rights, even in the subcommissions. When "their texts" were dealt with in the relevant commission, they joined in the discussions and might possibly be asked by the president of the appropriate subcommission to give their views on particular questions. In his diary for November 6 Congar had an entry that vividly describes this selfless labor:

> Father Bernard Lambert, who is working with Haubtmann on the editorial revision of schema XIII (especially chapter III of the first part, for which Smulders had come up with an unsatisfactory version and in an unsatisfactory order) has made the same saddened observation as I myself have. We are exhausted with preparing interventions for the bishops; the latter have

---

[20] See *JCongar*, October 26 and 30, 1965; II, 453 and 459.

agreed to present them, but in the end they do not give them; as a result, we have no basis in the commission for introducing this or that idea. We can introduce it only if at least one father requests it. We work therefore through one father, we spend time composing a text for him.... It is discouraging at times, How much work has been for naught! I am thinking also of the two texts on the Church in the World, the one composed at Rome in 1963, and the one produced at Malines in September of the same year. And so many others! I could have written three books in the time I have given to those works that fell into the abyss of nothingness.[21]

A great many of the experts toiled to the limits of their abilities and beyond. Despite their frustrations and renunciations it must be said that without them there could not have been either the drafts or the revisions of the drafts after discussion of them in the hall.

The work of the experts involved two tasks. First, through an enormous investment of energies and theological expertise they did a job of theological education and persuasion of the bishops in order to put them in a position where they could deal reasonably well with fundamental questions of modern Church life. Second, the experts dedicated themselves to composing and amending the texts in order at once to give them the required objective rigor and to make them acceptable to the majority of the fathers.

It is obvious that this kind of selfless theological work could be accomplished only by the experts on the commissions, because these theologians were celibate clerics or religious and for this reason, being without familial obligations, had available the long periods of time needed for such painstaking work. The body of theologians that we have today would require considerably different working methods, to say nothing of the quite different subjects that these later theologians, men and women, would bring to the table.

The fact that the Second Vatican Council was fundamentally a council of clerics, or more specifically a council of bishops and theologians, themselves also clerics and religious, is clearly shown also in the way in which lay people took part in one or another commission. The few lay people who sat on the central subcommission for schema XIII were invited as auditors to all its meetings. They had the right to speak, but only at the request of one of the episcopal members of the commission. They were asked for statements on questions in which the bishops of the commission thought them to be especially competent, such as marriage

---

[21] *JCongar*, November 1, 1965; II, 460.

and family or the economic order. Tromp's notes do not give the impression that these statements changed the approach of the bishops to the discussion. Typically, the lay auditors were not presumed to have any competence in theology. As regards the numerous problems of the modern world that were treated in schema XIII, it seems strange that neither in the subcommissions nor in the work of the central subcommission was any attempt made to consult scientific institutions or to conduct broader hearings.

As for the officials or functionaries of the commissions, the important role of the reporters who structured the discussions within the commission has already been described; they largely influenced the content of the commission's work and then presented the results of the commission's work to the full assembly. Also to be mentioned are the secretaries, who were in many cases religious; with great devotion and accuracy they took the minutes of the meetings and recorded the results of the discussion. Finally, there were the members of the editorial commissions. The success of a commission's work depended to a very great extent on their theological expertise, their ability to enter into each problem and their articulateness, flexibility, and creativity. Very frequently the amendments on which the commission had to decide were stated only in terms of their purpose, so that the editors could introduce them in this or that form into the text but also at the same time introduce nuances and inflect in one or other direction the tone of what was being said.

In his diary Congar was very critical of the editorial commissions, but he too acknowledged the contributions of this group. On November 8, 1965, he wrote: "I realize that in the revision by the subcommissions the text lost its character of an address to human beings and became dogmatic. Many repetitions were introduced, and the order became more theological and less concrete. The editorial revision aimed at restoring the character that was desired in the text."[22]

In short, the commissions during the final phase of the Council had great importance. The work of drafting such a large mass of material on so many different subjects could not have been done by an assembly of 2,000 persons; it required the work of groups. Given the necessarily broad autonomy and freedom of the commissions in their work, it was a blessing that the different groups and tendencies at the Council were to some extent represented on the commissions. The result, admittedly, was

---

[22] Ibid., November 8, 1965; II, 468.

compromise in crafting many formulas, but the texts produced by the commissions reflected to an unusual degree the ideas of the Council fathers.

II. THE DISCUSSION OF INDULGENCES: AN UNPLEASANT EPISODE

While the intense final labors of the commissions allowed the remaining plenary sessions to be fewer in number, the votes piled up in wearying numbers. The Council of Presidents and the General Secretary did their best to prevent the fathers from absenting themselves from the sessions. In this setting a thorough and noteworthy debate was held on the problem of indulgences on November 9–11, 1965. These discussions were important theologically because they showed how juridical ecclesiology and Counter-Reformation practice lasted, like the end of a glacier, in a significantly changed theological situation.

It was from the practice of indulgences that the Reformation caught fire. The Council of Trent did indeed reject some excesses in the practice of indulgences, but it made no change in the concept of indulgences. The pontificates of the nineteenth and twentieth centuries brought with them a multiplication of indulgences; the range of possible accumulations of indulgences was vastly extended. Was this practice to continue after the ecumenical opening created by the Council? In addition, Bernhard Poschmann and, following up on his studies, Karl Rahner, had subjected Catholic teaching on indulgences, and the practice of them, to a critical theological examination.[23] The subject was an explosive one.

How did this discussion of indulgences arise in the hall, and what were its results? Some fathers, in the *vota* they submitted for the future council, had expressed a wish for a reorganization of the whole subject of indulgences. These *vota* were occasioned chiefly by the greatly extended number of plenary indulgences under Pius XII, as well as by the multiplication of other indulgences. As a result, on July 24, 1963, Paul VI gave Cardinal Cento, the Grand Penitentiary, the task of forming a commission for the reform of the system of indulgences. The commission, comprising members and consultors of the Apostolic Penitentiary and

---

[23] See Bernhard Poschmann, *Der Ablass im Lichte der Bussgeschichte* (Berlin, 1948); Karl Rahner, "A Brief Theological Study of Indulgence" and "On the Official Teaching of the Church Today on the Subject of Indulgences," in *Theological Investigations* 10 (New York, 1973), 150–65 and 166–98.

some Roman theologians, was confirmed on January 14, 1964, and composed a schema on the change in the area of indulgences.[24] This schema was summarized in a first report.

Paul VI then had Cardinal Journet examine the work of the commission.[25] Journet was enthusiastic about it. The Pope decided that the bishops should be consulted on this touchy matter. The commission revised its original report and called the improved text a position paper.[26] It was delivered to the presidents of the episcopal conferences on October 15, 1965. At the 155th general congregation, October 29, the General Secretary announced that the Holy Father had agreed to the reading at the Council of the responses given by the presidents of the episcopal conferences to the position paper on indulgences. Then and later, on November 5, it was emphasized that this position paper on indulgences was not a conciliar document and that the statements made in it were to remain outside the course of the Council.

The text presented to the fathers had two parts. The first set forth the theological principles involved and added a historical sketch of the development of indulgences. The second part contained practical decisions for the structuring of indulgences. The starting point for the theological explanation was the distinction St. Thomas had formulated with clarity: on the one hand, there is the guilt human beings contract due to sin as an offense against God; on the other, there is the temporal punishment they incur because of the disorder introduced into creation by sin and because of the ongoing effects of sin. Every sin introduces confusion into creation and has its negative effects. Guilt in God's sight, if the sin is not forgiven, leads to eternal damnation. The disorder in creation resulting from sin leads to temporal punishments, such as illnesses and other tribulations. These continue after death in limited created punishments. Theologians speak here of a "pain of sense."

According to the position paper, it is Church dogma that through the remission of sin in the sacrament of penance the temporal punishment due to sin is not simply taken away at the same time. Also described as defined dogma is the teaching that human beings can, through works of penance, cancel out the temporal punishments due to sin. Referring to the Pauline doctrine of the mystical body and to the penitential practice

[24] The experts consulted were Msgr. Rossi, Father Berti, O.S.M., Father Raes, S.J., and Father Mruk, S.J. (see Wenger, IV, 416).

[25] Journet wrote his response to the work of the commission in an essay titled "Théologie des Indulgences," *DC* no. 1481 (1966), 1867–95; see ibid., no. 1466 (1966), 354–55.

[26] *Positio de sacrarum indulgentiarum recognitione* (Vatican Polyglot Press, 1965).

of the early Church, the paper said that through the grace of God persons can make satisfaction not only for their own temporal punishments but also for those of others. Finally, on the basis of the doctrine of the communion of saints, which is contained in scripture and was confirmed by the Council of Trent, the paper teaches the possibility of making up for the temporal punishments owed by those already dead.

This first set of doctrinal principles was followed by a concise section on the doctrine of the treasury of merits that were gained by Christ and the saints and are entrusted to the Church. For justification of this teaching the paper refers to the Bull *Unigenitus Dei filius* of Clement VI (1343) and to two bulls of Leo X, *Cum postquam* (1518) and *Exsurge Domine* (1520), both of which had to do with the controversy with Luther.

The third doctrinal statement had to do with the authority of the Church to dispose of the treasury of the merits of Christ and the saints. Sacred scripture does not explicitly teach that the Church has the authority to dispose of this treasury of graces and distribute them to the faithful. But according to scripture Christ did give the Church a comprehensive authority in regard to sins generally. From this a theological conclusion was drawn: If the Church has authority to forgive the guilt of sin, it also has the authority to reduce the temporal punishments and to do this by drawing on this treasury of graces. The existence of such an authority is confirmed by tradition, which led to the institutionalizing of this reduction.

To these key theological statements was appended a survey of the history of indulgences. A straight-line development was sketched from the early Church's penitential practice and the penances that had to be performed (with corresponding possibilities of mitigation) down to the practice of indulgences in the Counter-Reformation and modern times. As for the late medieval practice, along with its corruptions, the paper remarks laconically that the good works required for the gaining of indulgences were often reduced to almsgiving; as a result, abuses could easily arise. The preachers of indulgences did not always keep to the authentic teaching of the Church, with the result that the abuses which made their way in gave the Reformers occasion for accusing the Church of selling indulgences.

In its conclusion the paper said that in recent centuries it had not been necessary to change or renew any aspect of the granting of indulgences. On the other hand, some renewal of the discipline and practice, in better accord with the theological principles of the Council of Trent, seems opportune today in order to bring home the dignity of indulgences and to promote the piety and devotion of the faithful. This first, doctrinal part

of the position paper ends with a definition of an indulgence; it covers
the elements of the canonical description of indulgences in the Code of
Canon Law, canon 911. The paper adds that the remission of the temporal punishment due to sin by indulgences is effective not in virtue of the
sacrament of penance or *ex opere operantis*, but in virtue of the treasury
of graces entrusted to the Church and, therefore, *ex opere operato*.

Conditions for gaining an indulgence are these: on the part of the one
who grants the indulgence: legitimate authority and a just cause; on the
part of the recipient: baptism, the intention to gain an indulgence, the
performance of the prescribed work, and the state of grace. The reduction in temporal punishment is indeed not necessary for eternal salvation,
but, according to the teaching of the Council of Trent, it is most useful
to the faithful. For they will gain not only a reduction of the temporal punishment due to sin, but will also, in winning an indulgence, be led to confess the substance of the faith, recognize the seriousness of sin, and
acknowledge the justice of God and redemption by Christ, as well as the
merits of Christ and the saints, the authority of the Pope, and the reality
of purgatory. Finally, an indulgence requires the practice of the virtues
and of piety toward the deceased.

This theology of indulgences displays a characteristic style that is
purely Counter-Reformational; it is typical that its points of reference in
the magisterium were the bulls on indulgences of Clement VI and Leo X,
as well as the explanations of the Council of Trent. The theology is then
confirmed by the practical norms that are set forth in the second part and
again commented on and explained in the third part.

As far as practice is concerned, the most important change was the
limiting of the possibility of obtaining a plenary indulgence to once a
day. As far as the "times" in temporally limited indulgences were concerned, the paper said that the measure of temporal punishment due to sin
that is paid off by the penitential act of the believer is doubled by drawing on the treasury of the Church.[27]

When the various views of the episcopal conferences were presented
in the Council hall, it quickly became clear that a series of episcopal conferences had fundamental reservations regarding the position paper.

---

[27] "Through a partial indulgence that is connected with a prayer or pious work, ecclesiastical authority grants to the Christian faithful, out of the treasury of the Church, a
remission of temporal punishment before God that is as much again as the person already
gains by the same prayer or pious work" (*Positio de sacrarum indulgentiarum recognitione*, no. 39).

The statement of Patriarch Maximos IV Saigh was especially lively. He challenged the theological basis of the theory and practice of indulgences as this had developed since the thirteenth century because there was no recognizable continuity with the previous practice of the early Church. In that early period there had been public penance, and the Church had authority to dispense from the penances imposed. From the thirteenth century on, however, the direct issue was the remission of temporal punishments due to sin, and that is an entirely different matter.

This thirteenth-century transformation was also an important argument in the critical analysis of Cardinals König and Döpfner, who, speaking in the name of the Austrian and German episcopal conferences, took a negative position. Their statement, in its essentials, had been drawn up by Otto Semmelroth, who had been commissioned to the task after having given the German episcopal conference a lecture on the subject.[28] Karl Rahner had organized Semmelroth's text a little differently and added some remarks.[29]

The English episcopal conference likewise rejected the paper. Its written statement was accompanied by a reflection by Charles Davies. Other episcopal conferences, such as the Swiss and the French, agreed with the position paper; others called for a more thorough theological statement to be drawn up after the Council, although they agreed with the text now before them. Döpfner's address led many of the Council fathers to have the text of the German episcopal conference made available to them.

Disturbed by these events, Felici, General Secretary of the Council, announced on the following day, November 13, that the episcopal conferences were to submit their views in writing to the Penitentiary. Because of the many votes on conciliar texts that still had to be taken, the discussion could not be continued. Semmelroth wrote of this in his diary:

> Now they have quashed the continuation of the indulgence question. And did it in a really despicable way; this was very clearly the doing of the Curia and was charged to it. Felici announced that due to the many votes it was decided not to allow any more discussion of it. The views of the episcopal conferences are to be submitted in writing. In addition he was told that there is no question of a theological discussion of the question but only of new regulations governing practice. This was an unambiguous insult to Cardinal Döpfner and was noted by many as very disagreeable. In any case, enough has been said on the subject that it can no longer be ignored.[30]

---

[28] See *TSemmelroth*, October 25 and 27, 1965.
[29] Ibid., November 8. 1965.
[30] Ibid., November 13, 1965.

But on this last point Semmelroth was mistaken.

In the commission's final, summarizing report on the question the following episcopal conferences were listed as not having approved the draft: Austria and Germany, Belgium, England and Wales, Holland, Scandinavia, Haiti, Brazil, Chile, Congo, Dahomey, Rwanda, Burundi, Japan, and Laos; nor had Patriarch Maximos IV approved. But a distinction must be made between the episcopal conferences of Austria and Germany, Belgium, Holland, and Scandinavia, and the other conferences. The former had made known fundamental reservations and had spoken of a "preconciliar" magisterium. The other episcopal conferences had urged a fairly large reduction in the number of indulgences or had even asked for their abolition, as had the conferences of Dahomey, Japan, and Laos, and Patriarch Maximos IV.

The position paper supplied the basis for the Apostolic Constitution that Paul VI issued in 1967;[31] its theological guidelines and practical canonical regulations are still in force today.

It is understandable that the observers at the Council, especially the evangelical Christians, reacted with great consternation. At the meeting of the non-Catholic observers on November 9 Professor Schlink made a very cutting statement. The reports of the Council observers that were published after the Council likewise gave an important place to the position taken on indulgences.

It makes sense to record here the most important complaints voiced in the discussion. Since the statement of the German episcopal conference was the most detailed, we shall follow its main lines. The statement begins with a complaint that the material has been oversimplified and that no account has been taken of the theological development in recent years. The language used is almost exclusively juridical, even though the matters dealt with cannot be fully expressed in juridical categories. Finally, the statement complains of the inappropriate use of scripture and points out that positions controverted among Catholic theologians are excluded in the present text.

In particular, the statement refers to the break that occurred in the Middle Ages, when something new made its appearance in the Latin Church. The essence or nature of the temporal punishment that people bring on themselves through sin was not thought through adequately. The idea of the treasury of the Church is not appropriately described. Remission by an act of jurisdiction or by commendation of others is criticized as arbitrary. In addition, the statement criticizes the fact that the disposition of

---

[31] Apostolic Constitution *Indulgentiarum doctrina*, in *AAS* 59 (1967), 5–24.

the person gaining an indulgence is inadequately considered and that satisfaction made for another is understood individualistically.

The German bishops suggested the following description of indulgences: "In indulgences the Church appeals to its treasure, that is, the merits of Christ and the merits of the Blessed Virgin Mary and the saints in Christ, and gives the penitent effective help in wiping out the debt of temporal punishment before God, in the measure which the Holy Spirit grants, as he wills, to each person and according to the dispositions and cooperation of each person (Denz. 1259)."[32] Regarding what was said of a plenary indulgence, the bishops pointed out that it is extremely difficult to determine the theological nature of such an indulgence. The matter had been simple in the penitential practice of the early Church; the question there was of penitential practices that the Church imposed on the penitent. They suggested, therefore, that the term *plenary indulgence* be replaced by *indulgentia maior*, "greater indulgence." This was to be connected with the penitential practices of individual penitents; among these must be included, in particular, sacramental penance or an act of perfect contrition and the reception of holy communion.

The bishops considered at length the way in which the Church is active in the gaining of indulgences. They rejected the idea of a treasury of the Church that the Church itself possesses, because it leads to many misunderstandings. They likewise rejected the teaching that the granting of indulgences is a jurisdictional act. What is involved, rather, is an intercession in which the Church is identified with all its members, its sons and daughters. The bishops spoke of an "authoritative prayer of the Church."

Noteworthy about this critical and thoughtful exposition of the German episcopal conference is that when it described the disorders caused by the sinful behavior of human beings in history, not a word was said about the concrete experiences of the post-war period, the demands for reparation flowing from the sacrifice of the Jews, and the compensation called for by other peoples. Nor was anything said about the historical guilt of the Church. In fact, even in connection with individuals, the disorders arising in creation were not thought through concretely but were simply mentioned very summarily. The bishops did not adopt the original perspective of Thomas, who considered the effects of sin on the created world and the resultant claims for reparation or reconciliation.[33]

---

[32] The reference was to the Council of Trent, *Decree on Justification*, chap. 7.

[33] The passages from the statement of the Austrian and German episcopal conferences are cited from Lercaro papers, XXXI, 1073. The concluding statement is in ibid., 1072.

The conclusion of the statement of the Austrian and German bishops was not at all ambiguous: "The revised approach to indulgences in the form given in the position paper should not be published; the difficulties cited (under No. A II) are against publication, and serious bad consequences for recently improved ecumenical relations are to be feared. The subject of indulgences, at one time the immediate cause of the division of the western Church, needs to be handled with the utmost caution, in order that our separated brethren may not again take offense, but rather may be able to see in indulgences a help given us by the merciful Lord." There was no compliance with this and similar *vota* until the announcement of the indulgence for the Jubilee Year, 2000.

III. FINAL WORK ON *GAUDIUM ET SPES*

A. THE STARTING POINT OF THE COMMISSION'S WORK

At the 132nd general congregation, on September 21, 1965, Msgr. Garrone presented the heavily revised text of schema XIII. The debates on it dragged on until the 145th general congregation on October 8. At the end Garrone spoke again in order to tie together the discussion, the suggested changes, and the criticisms. His first remark was the most significant: the schema had rightly been subjected to harsh criticism. The drafters had been fully aware of the incompleteness of their work; but the subject matters were exceptionally difficult, and this was the first that a council was trying to enter into dialogue with the world in a completely new way.[34] But even the laborious final phase of work on this text — work that pushed the members of the commission and the participating experts to the limits of their abilities — basically changed nothing in the length of the text or even in the limitations that the schema was acknowledged as having. *Gaudium et spes* was a splendid new departure by the Church gathered in council. It was at the same time only the beginning of a dialogue and therefore fundamentally incomplete, although it entered new territory and opened up perspectives on the future.

---

[34] See *AS* IV/3, 735. See also R. Tucci, "Introduction historique et doctrinale," in *L'Église dans le monde de ce temps*, ed. Yves M.-J. Congar and M. Peuchmaurd (Paris, 1967), 2:104f.

Paul VI shared this view of the pastoral constitution. In his homily on December 7, after the solemn approval of the conciliar text, he spoke of the new way in which the Council had addressed humanity and the burning questions of society, but without defining any dogmatic statements. The Council was able only to lay down some fundamental lines, and Christians were called upon to give a radical assent to them, but at the same time also to work hard to deepen and implement these ideas.[35]

When Paul VI first took office, he had focused attention on the orientation of the Church to dialogue with the world. In his first encyclical, *Ecclesiam suam*, he had described the purpose and dimensions of this dialogue. In his concluding sermon on December 7 the way in which he linked the liturgy of the Church with dialogue and service to humanity showed that in his mind *Gaudium et spes* was the most meaningful result of the Council. Given this setting, we can understand why Paul VI so closely followed, encouraged, and influenced the work on the pastoral constitution, especially in its final phase.

The following five points describe in detail the starting point of the final work at the end of the public debate in the Council hall on October 8.

(1) The debate had led to an approval of the present schema in principle, although a large number of suggested changes and of criticisms had been made. This approval had already begun to emerge in August and early September. The Italian bishops of Lombardy and the region of Venetia had met in August; in his report, Msgr. L. Sartori came to the conclusion that the present schema, now to be discussed, could be approved, at least in its first part, because of its wealth of ideas.[36] On the other hand, the German bishops, relying on statements of Karl Rahner and a critical article of Josef Ratzinger,[37] had strong reservations about the text; their skepticism was deepened by Oswald von Nell-Breuning's critical analysis of the economic and social sections of the text.[38]

---

[35] See *AS* IV/7, 660.

[36] See Tucci, "Introduction historique et doctrinal," 100.

[37] Karl Rahner, "Über den Dialog in der pluralistischen Gesellschaft," *Stimmen der Zeit* 176 (August 1965), 321–30. Josef Ratzinger, "Angesichts der Welt von heute: Überlegungen zur Konfrontation mit der Kirche in Schema XIII," *Wort und Wahrheit* 20 (August-September 1965), 49–54.

[38] "Taken as a whole the chapter [on economic and social life] gives the impression of being made up of parts with very different origins, with the result that it has not succeeded in organizing the material in a meaningful way or in avoiding repetitions.... The description of the contemporary economy consists solely in features which the economy has in common with other areas; there is not even an allusion to aspects that characterize today's economy *as such*, especially the flexible monetary system with its dynamics and its structural and conjunctural importance (economic growth, inflation and deflation). As a

The shift of the German bishops to a more positive attitude was due to, among others, Msgr. Elchinger of Strasbourg, who, in a discussion group of German bishops led by him and Bishop Volk, was able to convince them of the position of the French episcopate. According to Congar's detailed description of the decisive meeting on September 17, Bishop Hengsbach summarized as follows the results for the coming discussions and votes: "1. Do not speak in a way that would ruin the credit of the schema, but acknowledge it as a possible basis. 2. Agree among yourselves on amendments, both during the discussion and in regard to *modi*. 3. Recognize that this is an incomplete text, a beginning of dialogue with the world and not a body of definitive and conclusive teaching." At the end Congar wrote: "The Germans will doubtless be less critical than they were in danger of being."[39]

In the French-speaking world the positive assessment of the present schema was supported by publications such as that of J. Daniélou[40] and, above all, by a statement of Action Catholique Ouvrière at the beginning of September 1965.[41] These affirmative voices, found also in the Latin American, African, and Asian episcopates, carried the day despite sharp public criticism by conservative groups, in, for example, the newspaper *Il Borghese* and other publications which spoke of a new alliance with the communists and the myths of the United Nations.[42]

(2) The discussion and the comments of Garrone had shown that the decision regarding the addressees was not disputed, but serious objections were raised to the title, "pastoral constitution". Some wanted to belittle the importance of the document by asking that it not be a constitution but placed in some other literary genre. The title "constitution", moreover, had until now been reserved for solemn dogmatic documents. A *pastoral* constitution seemed to many of the Council fathers to be inconsistent with the distinction hitherto made between dogmatic assertions and their pastoral applications.

---

result, crucial economic and ethical problems are hardly addressed. Perhaps nothing else is even possible in a document that is issued by an assembly of non-professionals and addressed to the world, that is, mainly to non-professionals. But then it seems questionable whether such a document should contain anything more than the relevant truths of the catechism" (Medina papers, II, 4).

[39] *JCongar*, September 17; II, 396.

[40] "Mépris du monde et valeurs terrestres d'après le Concile Vatican II," *Revue d'Ascétique et de mystique* 41/3 (1965), 421–28.

[41] See *Témoignage chrétien*, September 30, 1965, 13.

[42] See the issues of August 27, 1965, 855, and September 9, 1965, 64–65 and 87.

(3) No serious objections were raised to the Preface and the introductory description of the human situation in the contemporary world. Garrone nevertheless assured the fathers that the commission wanted the words *world* and *Church* to be more carefully defined and then to use them with the same meaning throughout the document. Behind this assurance and the objections which the use of the two words could raise there lay hidden theological problems that would be expressed both in ecumenical discussion[43] and by theologians bent on giving priority to the Johannine and Pauline view of the world.

(4) In regard to the first part of schema XIII Garrone emphasized the many objections that found fault with the text as overly philosophical, following a line dictated by "natural realities," paying too little heed to the sinful state of humanity, and being too optimistic. Not enough attention was given to the tragic aspect of human life, the struggle against evil, and the clash over what is good.

The close connection between the objections against the title and the criticism of the concept of world and Church in the introductory chapter was obvious. In the background was the question whether the social teaching of the Church should continue to be guided by natural law or whether an effort should be made to offer a theological interpretation of the historical situation into which the Church and its praxis would then be fitted. The disagreement over the concept of the world had in view precisely the problem just mentioned, since worldly structures could be discussed either in a philosophical perspective based on the concept of human nature or in light of Pauline and Johannine theology, which takes into consideration the world as enslaved to sin.

If the emphasis is placed on a philosophical, natural law reflection on human beings and their situation in the world, the Church will be seen as the "Mother and Teacher" *(mater et magistra)* appointed by God to set forth correct teaching on the actual conditions of humanity.[44] If the Church is understood within the history of salvation and is considered in its actual historical form, then it will be viewed as the community of

---

[43] The observers had met numerous times to discuss the problems of schema XIII (see Tucci, "Introduction historique et doctrinal," 106 n.102).

[44] Under the heading "Social Doctrine," in *Lexikon für Theologie und Kirche*, IX, 917 (1964), F. Klüber wrote: "Catholic social doctrine comprises all the norms derived from natural law and revelation that have to do with the ordering of society. But the contents of Catholic social doctrine are predominantly and in an essential measure derived from natural law, so that the system of Catholic social teaching can be proved *from social philosophy alone and without reference to revelation.*"

believers who bear witness to their redemption and their hope, who are in many ways entangled in their actual situation, and who fail in many respects.[45] The latter approach was foreign to the traditional theology of the schools and therefore to a large sector of the Council fathers.

It was from this problem that the controversy over the title of schema XIII derived its importance. If one took the view that the Church as a supernatural institution, especially graced by God, faces the world "from outside," as it were, and presents this world with its teaching and judgments, then the expression *pastoral constitution* is an absurdity. It can only mean that on the basis of dogmatic principles pastoral applications are presented. But if the Church as a reality in the history of salvation is by its nature part of the historical situation at any given moment and must prove its worth therein, then the expression *pastoral constitution* acquires an entirely new meaning. Then the term becomes a theological qualifier of the Church, which must be open to the concrete challenges of the day, to the needs and afflictions of people, to new departures in the culture, whether wise or detrimental, and so on, and thereby prove its worth. The term *pastoral* then acquires the full range of meaning that it already had in the original announcements of John XXIII.

These focal points in the discussion show that in this final phase the issue was still the fundamental direction and distinctive character of this schema, but also that questions essential for a renewal of theology and a new vision of the Church were under debate.

The response that the ten subcommissions and the central mixed commission had striven for was also visible in the statement of Garrone. He emphasized that the entire text, and chapter I in particular, should have a prophetic character. A section on the mystery of Jesus Christ was to be included. At the same time he insisted that the Church had accepted a series of natural truths as a foundation of faith and that this aspect must likewise be taken into consideration. Thus in the summary statement of Garrone there was already an element of "both/and."

(5) An important problem that Garrone mentioned separately in his concluding address was that of atheism. The strongest criticisms came from a rather small group of bishops who were less interested in the phenomenon of modern atheism and the widespread indifference of society

---

[45] One of the most important pioneers in this way of thinking was Marie-Dominique Chenu, O.P. See his publications *Pour une théologie du travail* (Paris, 1955) and *L'Évangile dans le temps* (Paris, 1964). In the postconciliar period he wrote *Peuple de Dieu dans le monde* (Paris, 1966) and *La doctrine sociale de l'Église comme idéologie* (Brescia, 1977; Paris, 1979).

to the faith than in the strongest possible, politically effective condemnation of communism; they made no distinction between the atheism and the social aspects of actually existing socialism and the communistic or socialistic movements in the Free World. Garrone made the point that, while atheism is the greatest danger for humanity and for the gospel in the present age, it is also a highly complex reality; but, he added, the text would again be carefully examined and revised.

It was striking that the Council fathers' criticisms of the second part consistently focused on the lack of connection between the first and second parts of schema XIII; it was not clear how the reflections on the human person and on human society with its natural and supernatural dignity grounded the decisions set down in the second part. If we take into account the criticisms of experts in the area being discussed,[46] it becomes clear from the behavior of the fathers that a dialogue with economists, political scientists, sociologists, and so on, had hardly begun.

Among the factors that conditioned the work of the commission was an important conciliar event: the journey of Paul VI to the United Nations on October 4, 1965.

B. PAUL VI AT THE UNITED NATIONS — A CONCILIAR EVENT

Paul VI's journey to New York and his address to the United Nations were in many respects a conciliar event. When the Pope returned on October 5 the fathers greeted him with great enthusiasm and decided to include his address to the United Nations in the acts of the Council; in that address the Pope provided models and a direction for the discussion of the final chapter of schema XIII.

By his public appearance in New York, Paul VI also made clear to all the position of the Church, with its world-embracing mandate, in relation to the United Nations, which likewise has a worldwide mission. At the United Nations an important step was taken in the *aggiornamento* of the Church, which John XXIII had set as the task of the Council. At the same time, Paul VI made visible what John XXIII had sketched out in his encyclical *Pacem in terris*.

The journeys of Paul VI were undoubtedly parts of a program and were closely linked among themselves historically. When he went to the

---

[46] Schillebeeckx had gathered a group of them, and we referred above to Nell-Breuning's statement (Medina papers, II, 4).

Holy Land and Jerusalem in 1964 in order to attest to the return of the
Church to its roots, he met with Patriarch Athenagoras of Constan-
tinople and the Greek Orthodox Patriarch and the Catholicos of the
Armenians. He also had a brief conversation with Sargent Shriver, a
confidant of President Johnson, about how the president would view a
visit of the Pope to the United Nations. Following upon Paul VI's journey to India in October of 1964, Rome began a correspondence with
U Thant, Secretary General of the United Nations. During his visit to
India the Pope had placed heavy emphasis on meeting with the poor.
He made a strong plea for disarmament and pleaded for the establishment of an international fund for aid to the starving and the poor everywhere in the world; the fund would be supplied by monies saved
through disarmament. As early as January 20, 1965, U Thant spoke in
a letter to Rome of the interest the United Nations had in a visit by the
Pope.[47]

At the Rome airport, as he departed early in the morning of October 4,
Paul VI introduced his companions: there were five cardinals representing the five continents, but also Cardinal Agagianian, who would represent in a special way relations with the Oriental Christians. Paul VI also
announced the main theme of his journey: the world's need for peace.

The first place visited, after a lengthy, wildly cheered ride through
New York City, was St. Patrick's Cathedral, where the Pope was greeted
by Cardinal Spellman and the Catholics of New York, a community
primarily of Irish descent. Next came a talk with President Johnson at
the Waldorf-Astoria Hotel. Around 3.00 p.m. local time, Secreaty General U Thant received the Pope in the "Glass Palace" of the United
Nations where the Pope delivered one of the great addresses of his pontificate.

After thanking the Secretary General, Amintore Fanfani, the president
of the assembly, and the assembly itself, the Pope presented himself as
representative of a "minuscule and quasi-symbolic temporal sovereignty"[48] and, at the same time, as bearer of a message to the whole of
humankind, a message that had been preached for twenty centuries. On
the basis of historical experience and as "an expert in humanity," the
Pope uttered a solemn moral recognition and confirmation of the United
Nations as an institution. He was conscious that at this hour he was speaking for the many dead who had fallen in the terrible wars of the past and

---

[47] See *Insegnamenti* 3:544.
[48] *AAS* 57 (1965), 877.

for the living who had survived those wars and, in their hearts, were waiting for peace no less than were the younger generations. He was conscious of being spokesman for the poor and disinherited, who longed for justice, dignity, freedom, prosperity, and progress. "The building you have constructed must never fall in ruins: it must be improved and adapted to the demands which world history will present."[49]

The Pope then spoke of the service that the United Nations was providing for humanity, a service meant to lead to "an ordered and stable system of international life." From this vision Paul VI derived the task of the United Nations: to build peace. He repeatedly used the phrase "Go forward!" And in this context he referred explicitly to the message of John XXIII: Peace on earth.

The basis of this urgently necessary work was the rights and duties of human beings; among these was respect for life, even in face of the great problem of the excess of births over deaths. "Your task is to see to it that there is sufficient food on the table of humanity and not to promote artificial birth control, which would be irrational, in order to limit the number of guests at the banquet of life." The Pope then cited Isaiah 2:4: "They shall beat their swords into plowshares, and their spears into pruning hooks." In order to reach economic and social goals the instruments of death must be turned into instruments of life.

By way of conclusion the Pope spoke of the spiritual principles that alone make possible the construction of such a building. "In short, the building which is modern civilization must be constructed on spiritual principles, which are the only ones capable not only of supporting it but also of enlightening and animating it. And we are convinced, as you know, that these indispensable principles of higher wisdom can have their basis only on faith in God."[50]

After this moving address, televised throughout the world, the Pope celebrated an evening mass in Yankee Stadium in the presence of 90,000 of the faithful. At his opening greeting and at his departure exuberant applause burst forth. Before the night flight back to Rome, the Pope visited the World Trade Center, where Michelangelo's *Pietà* was on display. The day was a major and important festival: the children of the city had the day off from school.

On the following day the Pope, whose face bore the marks of jet lag, made it his first act to go to the Council hall and give a report to those

[49] Ibid., 879.
[50] Ibid., 885.

present. The Council fathers spontaneously decided to include the Pope's address to the United Nations among the acts of the Council, for they felt that an *aggiornamento* of the Church had occurred there and that an authentic dialogue had begun.

C. GENERAL TRENDS IN THE AMENDING OF THE SCHEMA

When the discussion of schema XIII ended, how was the work of amending it organized and what distinctive image did the text acquire? Since the voting on the examined *modi* was to begin as early as mid-November, the work was done under immense pressure. While the discussion was still continuing, the *modi* and suggested changes were already being catalogued and sent to the subcommissions.[51] The work followed a path from the subcommissions to the central subcommission[52] and on to the editorial committee, which worked under the supervision of Msgr. Garrone.

The mass of changes that had to be examined was enormous; the 160 speeches that had been read during the discussion of these interventions, together with the proposals submitted in writing, filled

[51] See Tucci, "Introduction historique et doctrinal," 107. The bishop members and experts for the subcommissions were (1) subcommission on the current situation: Bishops Fernandes, Fernández-Conde, McGrath, Nagae, and Zoa, and experts Anastasius a S. Rosario, Medina, de Lubac, Sugranyes de Franch, and Vasquez; (2) subcommission on the human person: Bishops Doumith, Granados, Ménager, Parente, Poma, and Wright, and experts Benoit, Congar, Daniélou, Gagnebet, Kloppenburg, Nicolau, K. Rahner, and Semmelroth; (3) subcommission on human activity: Bishops Bednorz, González Moralejo, Garrone, and Volk, and experts Lattanzi, Thils, Balić, Lambert, Molinari, and Smulders; (4) subcommission on the task of the Church: Bishops Ancel, Pelletier, Spanedda, and Wojtyła, experts Vodopivec, Grillmeier, Ochagavia, Salaverri, Bellosillo, and Guillemin; (5) subcommission on marriage: Bishops Colombo, Dearden, Heuschen, Morris, Petit, van Dodewaard, and experts Géraud, Lambruschini, Prignon, Delhaye, Heylen, Schillebeeckx, Van Leeuwen, Minoli, Adjakpley, and Work; (6) subcommission on culture: Bishops Charue, Valloppilly, and Yü Pin, and experts Möhler, Butler, Klostermann, Ramselaar, Dondeyne, Rigaux, Tucci, Swieziawski, and Folliet; (7) subcommission for economic and social questions: Bishops de Araújo Sales, Franić, Granier Gutiérrez, Hengsbach, Larraín, Pessóa Câmara, and experts Ferrari-Toniolo, Pavan, Rodhain, Worlock, Laurentin, Calvez, and Lio; (8) subcommission on political life: Bishops Henriquez, László, and Quadri, and experts Guglielmi, Leetham, Ruiz-Giménez, and Veronese; (9) subcommission on peace: Cardinal Šeper, Bishops Kominek, Necsey, and Schröffer, and experts Fernández, Schauf, Alting von Gesau, Sigmond, de Riedmatten, Dubarle, Labourdette, de Habicht, and Norris.

[52] The central subcommision consisted of Cardinal Browne, Bishops Charue, Garrone, Hengsbach, Ménager, and the presidents of the other subcommissions; the experts on it were Glorieux, Haubtmann, Philips. Moeller, Häring, Hirschmann, Tromp, Tucci, R. Goldie, and M.L. Tobin.

400 closely printed pages. The regulations governing the revision were described earlier. In connection with the question of atheism it was decided to consult the Secretariat for Nonbelievers and its president, Cardinal König. Those bishops with an advisory voice who had been named the year before were allowed to take part in the meetings of the mixed commission. Tromp's diary-like report showed that of these non-voting bishops K. Wojtyła, A. Fernandes, González Moralejo, and Quadri attended almost all the meetings during the period from September 14 to December 1965.

Philips, as general reporter, established a schedule: thirteen meetings were to be held by October 30; possible meetings were allowed for November 2–4. November 10 was the deadline for the delivery of the text. Philips assumed that the Council would end on about December 10. In fact, the mixed commission held sixteen fairly lengthy meetings from October 19 to October 30.

For reasons of haste and of the different states of the work in the different subcommissions (the later ones could not begin until the early ones had finished), it was impossible at the beginning of the work to present the mixed commission with the full text of the version that was to be revised by the subcommissions. The groups were moving in every direction, and it was difficult for the mixed commission to keep a vision of the whole. It was not surprising that Philips, organizer of the work and chief reporter, was completely exhausted and had to give up his work on October 25. Two weeks later, on November 7, he flew back to Belgium a sick man.

When the first meeting was held on October 19, six subcommissions had already finished revising their sections of the schema. In order to give an impression of the working methods of the subcommissions, the mixed commission, and the related editorial commission, we may go back to an arbitrarily chosen passage in the introduction of *Gaudium et spes*. In the description of the psychological, moral, and religious changes that mark the modern world and its society (no. 7) the responsible subcommission suggested the following text on the basis of the *modi*: "The change *in mentalities and structures frequently* calls into question *received and traditional values*; this is true above all of younger people *who in their distress not infrequently become rebellious, while their parents are often no longer up to their tasks.*"[53] At the October 20 meeting

---

[53] The italicized words were added on the basis of the discussion in the hall.

of the mixed commission several members focused on the idea of "rebellious youth"; Cardinal Browne favored the term "insubordinate." In defense of the text the reporter referred to the impatience that is characteristic of today's young people. Bishop Poma urged that the text speak more positively.[54]

What did the editorial commission make of the passage? The text presented to the fathers on November 13 read as follows: "The change in mentalities and structures frequently calls into question traditional values, chiefly among younger people, who in their restlessness not infrequently become impatient or even rebellious, while their parents are often no longer up to their tasks."[55] Here an important slogan — the impatience of today's young people — was added, though no formal vote had been taken on it; the other idea of "rebellious youth" was thereby interpreted, and the whole statement was recast as a more harmonious and more easily understandable text. "Insubordination," another slogan, was not accepted. From this relatively unimportant example we can see the freedom and the importance of the editorial commission.

If we survey the work of the mixed commission, as minutely recorded by Tromp,[56] it becomes clear that the majority of critical remarks on the text presented by the subcommissions focused on individual turns of phrase. Rarely were there clashes over deeper matters.

Quantitatively, over 30 percent of the entire text was reformulated. These changes ranged from short additions to reformulations of entire sections. At the same time, the text was tightened up in a number of places. The following three general characteristics of the changes made can be discerned: First, the groups worked for more precise descriptions of key concepts. Thus, in the Introduction the concept of "world" was given a more detailed phenomenological and theological description. The same effort at precision was made for the concept "signs of the times." Only through the investigation and interpretation of these concepts was it possible to answer the basic questions people had about the meaning of the present and the future life and the relationship between the two (no. 4). The same held for the definition of "common good," which was given in a modern form, that is, with reference to the fundamental human

[54] See *RT* (14 September – Dec. 1965), 24.

[55] *AS* IV/6, 427.

[56] See *RT* (14 September – Dec. 1965) 24: "Around 4:35 p.m. Philips, the reporter, said that some wanted to discuss the title, but he thought that such a discussion would be fruitful only after the revision of the entire schema. Around 4:38, no. 7 on the psychological, moral, and religious changes was read and explained."

rights to education, adequate information, and freedom of conscience and religion (no. 26).

Second, to this work on concepts was joined a more accurate description of the problems raised by the present situation. For example, there was a clearer statement of the difficulties faced by developing countries and resulting from contemporary global changes. At the same time, the striving of those countries for participation in the new ways of life was explained (no. 6). The break away from tradition by many young people was described in greater detail, as was the ethical individualism that shapes modern ways of life (nos. 6 and 30). Even in this phase of the work, certain limits were not overcome. The description of the modern world of work betrays the fact that there was no close collaboration with experts in that area, even though on this text some of the lay people were heard in the subcommissions (no. 33).

Third, on the whole the revision of the text led to more forceful theological reflections on the various problems. The kinds of sinful behavior that appear in the various areas of life were more clearly named. It is noteworthy, however, that sin was discussed only in relation to secular relationships and not in relation to the Church. The admission of an ecclesial history of sin is made only sporadically and then with great restraint. As a result, broad sections of the schema as a whole seem like a moral exhortation. The mystery of Christ is indeed the subject of discussion throughout the various sections and according to the perspective proper to each, but it is often hard to see how this mystery of Christ is at work in the Church, what concrete historical effects it has in the Church, or how, given the ecclesial history of sin, collective calls to conversion and to reform emerge.

Nevertheless, the revision of the text did succeed in grounding human equality, social justice, and the corresponding basic human rights not only philosophically but also theologically, by reference to the concept of the human person as image of God and to redemption.[57] In such passages the Council had moved beyond the previous way of grounding the social teaching of the Church through appeal to the natural law.

Having described the general tendencies at work in the revision, we may turn in detail to four particular problems that particularly engaged the Council, and public opinion: atheism; war and peace, and the community of nations; property; and birth control. Explosive problems of a

---

[57] See no. 29.

political (including ecclesio-political) kind, they had awakened broad public interest and entailed choices to be made in Church policy.

D. THE PROBLEM OF ATHEISM AND ITS CONDEMNATION

The discussion of atheism in the Council hall had been conducted at a high level. Maximos IV had emphasized the complex character of modern atheism and urged the Council to come to grips with its causes. König had named the various historical reasons for atheism and referred to the different forms of the denial of God and the possible answers to them. Florit had spoken of the close relationship between atheism and economic or social ideologies. Arrupe, general of the Jesuits, had investigated the phenomenon of atheism in modern society and called for concerted action by the Church. Bishops Hnilica and Rusnack, like Cardinal Slipyi, had painted an unvarnished picture of the persecution of religion and of Christians in the communist countries. Wojtyła had carefully distinguished between atheism as a personal choice and atheism as a system and a political ideology. Bishop Marty, prelate of the Mission de France, had made a similar distinction from a Western point of view. During the discussion it was urged that the Secretariat for Non-Believers, under Cardinal König, should be called upon. This discussion in the hall had evoked considerable echo in the press, for example, in Russian publications.[58]

For the revision of the text a special subcommission was appointed under the leadership of König and Šeper. Three other bishops from the communist power bloc were added: Aufderdeck (Erfurt), Hnilica (a Czech Jesuit residing in Rome), and Kominek (Wroclaw). Also on the commission were theologians de Lubac, Daniélou, Miano, and Girardi.

The text drafted by this commission covered nos. 19–21. In no. 19 a description was given of the various forms of atheism. The list included the deliberate denial of God as well as agnosticism; it spoke of the methodically dubious scientific grounds given for the rejection of an

---

[58] How sensitive the question of a formal condemnation of atheism by the Council was can be seen from the record kept by Willebrands, who by order of the Vatican visited the Patriarch of Moscow and invited the Russian Orthodox Church to send observers. The greatest concern of the Orthodox authorities was whether the Council might condemn communism. Eventually, but only at the last minute, Archbishop Nikodim, representing the Patriarch of Moscow, arrived to participate in the closing ceremonies of the Council. Clearly, the people in Moscow were determined to wait for the definitive votes on the pastoral constitution. On the reactions of the Russian press, see Wenger, IV, 168f.

absolute truth, and of the various forms taken by an atheism springing from an ethical protest against suffering or based on the effects of religion on human life. In this context reference was made to the fact that Christians share the guilt for the rise of atheism insofar as atheism has sometimes been a critical reaction against religion, especially against the Christian religion.

A distinction was made between these kinds of atheism and a typically modern "systematic" atheism seen as arising essentially from the fact that human beings regard themselves as their own completely autonomous goal. Such an anthropology can also become the dominant ideology of states. The description of the relationship of the Church to atheism (in no. 21) several times stresses the point that faith in God in no way detracts from the dignity of the human person.

The cure given for atheism is not only teaching but also and above all the living witness of Christians and of the Church as a whole. Atheists can be led to Christianity only through honest and prudent dialogue. It is noteworthy that the commission spoke as little of epistemological questions and of questions that arise out of modern language about God in a world shaped by science, as it did of the possible consequences for the preaching and theology of the Church.

When the text was presented on November 15, 1965, Garrone explained its structure: "This manner of proceeding seemed to the commission to be fully in keeping with both the pastoral goal of the Council and the express will of Pope John XXIII and Pope Paul VI. This was a decision made after the commission several times dealt with this question, especially before the discussion in the hall, and, above all, after the interventions of the Council fathers."[59] This passage, which is not found in the bishop's written explanation, indicates that the revision by the König-Šeper commission was approved by Paul VI. In any case, the text presented was to give rise, once again, to an important debate.

E. The Social Responsibilities of Ownership

An intense debate went on in the mixed commission over the handling of no. 73: that earthly goods are meant to be for the benefit of all. The question of the theological understanding of private ownership, including the ownership of the means of production, was politically

---

[59] Cited from Wenger, IV, 162f.

explosive. The question affected the nationalization of property, the expropriation of farms, the formation of cooperatives and collectives, and the establishment of nationally owned businesses. The question of land reform was extremely controversial at that time, especially in Latin America. Associated with this question of private ownership was the disagreement about the overall judgment on competing forms of the economy: the communist planned economy, with its extensive program of nationalization, versus the market economy of capitalism. The subcommission offered a text that weakened or even omitted a whole series of sentences from the draft that had been discussed in the hall. Nothing was said any longer about the "purpose" or "destination" of earthly goods for the benefit of all; a key idea in the teaching of Thomas Aquinas about earthly goods was thereby surrendered. John XXIII had likewise used this idea in his encyclicals. Also deleted were the following statements: human beings "should never regard the earthly things he possesses as his own but only as owned in common." The concluding sentence was also greatly toned down; it read originally, "Those who live in poverty have the right to obtain from the possessions of others what they need for themselves and their families."

A keen debate developed in the commission over the theological concept of ownership. Ancel, Moralejo, McGrath, Henriquez, Doumith, Fernández, Butler, Poma, and Spanedda demanded a return to the previous text. The teaching of Thomas was summarized in detail: God intends the human race to have earthly goods in common. The institution of private ownership is the juridical organization of this fundamental reference of property, an organization needed precisely for the sake of the dignity and responsibility of the human being. It does not, however, remove the fundamental social responsibilities connected with ownership. Only on this basis can either liberal capitalism or communism be subjected to an adequate critique. After a thorough discussion it was decided to return to the former text; small changes were introduced, as was a reference to the teaching of Thomas Aquinas on earthly possessions. The long-term importance of this decision can hardly be overestimated.

F. The Purposes of Marriage and Birth Control

The discussions in the hall had shown that the majority and the minority had not drawn any closer on the subjects of the purposes or ends of marriage and their relation to each other and on the subject of birth control. Cardinal Browne had defended the strict subordination of marital life to the procreation of children. In contrast, Cardinal Léger, also a member of the mixed commission, had emphasized the personal character of modern marriage and had, no less decidedly, rejected the subordination of this goal of marriage to the procreation and rearing of children. The positions taken on birth control were also at odds.

Since the Pope had reserved the decision on birth control to himself and had established a special commission to resolve the problem, it was decided to leave the revision of the text to the pertinent subcommission and *some* members of the papal commission.[60] When Dearden, chairman of the subcommission on marriage, presented the revised text, he said that the subcommission had tried to follow a "middle way".[61] On the one hand, it did not want to anticipate the results of the papal commission, while, on the other, it did want to take into account the arguments and desired amendments sought by both groups. If we follow the intense debate in the mixed commission as recorded by Tromp, we are struck by the fact that the supporters of the traditional teaching on the subordination of marital love to the procreation of children defended their position with great keenness and clarity and wanted to see it embedded in the text. True enough, talk of the primary and secondary ends of marriage was avoided, but the point at issue was clearly formulated.[62] Léger raised objections but was unable to prevail. At his request only one sentence was added, saying that "the married couple themselves and no one else were ultimately responsible before God" for the judgment on how many children to have. The twelve members of the mixed commission who voted against that addition were clearly aware of the possibility that a denial of this parental authority might have dire consequences: civil or international institutions could issue laws regulating population growth.

The basic tendency of the text thus remained unchanged, even though many details were made clearer. On the subject of birth control explicit criteria were invoked by which couples were to be guided. The section

[60] The subcommission was made up of Bishops Dearden, Colombo, van Dodewaard, Petit, Morris, Castellano, Heuschen, and Scherer; the experts were Heylen, Lambruschini, Géraud, Delhaye, Prignon, Schillebeeckx, Van Leeuwen, and lay auditors Minoli, Work, Adjakpley, and Mr. and Mrs. Alvarez. The added members from the papal commission were Visser, secretary of that commission, along with Fuchs, Zalba, and Ford. See the list in Wenger, IV, 187.

[61] *RT*, 51.

[62] See no. 54.

ended with an admonition to "the children of the Church not to engage in forms of birth control that are not approved by the magisterium."[63] Because of differing judgments on the main questions, this text too would lead to considerable complications when it was presented again.

In this whole regard, it is striking how little the fathers and the commission came to grips with the reality of the relationship of the sexes in modern societies and with questions of the civil regulation of marriage, family, and the relationship of the sexes. We are not given the impression that at the meetings of the mixed commission the remarks of the laity on the spirituality of marriage and on the spiritual dimensions of conjugal and familial life met with any great receptivity. The interests of the members of the commission were focused on the two problems mentioned above.

G. War and Peace and the International Community of Nations

The problem of war and peace and the tasks of an international community of nations had been discussed by the Council fathers immediately after the Pope's journey to New York and his address to the United Nations. Central problems were deterrence and the condemnation of modern war and scientific weapons, on the one hand, and the claim to a right of self-defense, on the other. Also discussed were the problems of armaments, the production of weapons of mass destruction, and the question of the rights of national sovereignty, all of these being connected with the right of self-defense. The creation of international institutions for the safeguarding of peace in the world was also discussed. Finally, there was discussion of the refusal of military service for reasons of conscience. Remarkable about the discussion in the Council hall was the fact that bishops of the United States took hardly any part in the discussion, even though the policy of deterrence and the strategy of the Cold War were essentially the responsibility of the United States.

As a result of the discussion the subcommission under Schröffer presented an almost completely reformulated text. When presenting it later on the hall, Hengsbach insisted that the commission had tried to preserve the substance of the teaching in the previous text but had fundamentally changed the organization of the text and its expression. In addition, it had kept in mind the countless victims of a possible new world war, as well

---

[63] See no. 55.

as the moral conflicts faced by political and military leaders, who had to combine the duty of defending the rights of their people with the duty of avoiding a universal fratricide. Against this background the commission had endeavored to offer clear and powerful arguments on the substance but also to be circumspect in presenting the subject and not to succumb to casuistry or argument on a purely emotional level.[64] The new organization of the text was the work primarily of the mixed commission, since the subcommission had kept mostly to the old schema XIII. As a result of the rearrangements of the text by the mixed commission, the modern problems of war and the position taken on them by the Council were considerably clarified.

The Introduction and no. 82 on the nature of peace were extensively rewritten. While not excluding the forms of legitimate defense, the Introduction mentioned explicitly those who in view of the present situation renounce violence in the spirit of Christ. These remarks were followed by a first, somewhat lengthy section dealing with the avoidance of war. In this section the present situation was described and modern scientific weapons were mentioned, as were secret wars and the use of terrorism. On the other hand, the international principles of the natural law and of international law were invoked, and genocide in particular was strictly condemned. Attempts to contain war and the importance of international treaties were singled out; there was a call for a mentality focused on peace and for legal requirements regulating the refusal of military service, especially when those refusing performed other services for the public good.

Since the danger of war was not exorcized by the means thus far mentioned, the possibility was left open to leaders of states and responsible authorities to plan the legitimate defense of their people. But in the following section total war was sharply and solemnly condemned. By "total war" was meant every military action that led to the destruction of whole cities and their inhabitants. This judgment extended all the more to the destruction of entire regions.

The next section (no. 85) spoke of the arms race and the illusion that a peaceful order can be built on mutual deterrence. Finally, there was a lengthy, completely new section on the prohibition against waging war and on international measures for avoiding war. At this point the text develops the vision, originally presented in an authoritative way by Ancel, of an outlawing of war and an international supervision

---

[64] See Wenger, IV, 275.

of this ban by an international institution such as the United Nations. A present-day look back at history shows that this politics of peace, expanded by a policy of measures calculated to build up trust, was effective, at least initially. But a look back from today also shows how strongly the dominant powers are tempted to ignore such policies at any one time.

No. 87, the first article on the building up of the international community, contained an important and newly formulated contribution on the causes from which repeated military conflicts usually arose in the modern period. The text also described the indissoluble connection between a policy of peace and a policy of development, between the safeguarding of peace and work for an integral human community.

After the lengthy discussions in the mixed commission, the editorial commission worked on a text that could be presented to the fathers, still under the old title, "Pastoral Constitution." Working closely with the presidents of the subcommissions, the editorial commission completed the first chapters of the schema in the early days of November. On November 8 the editing of the first part was complete, and on November 9 that of the second part. The Vatican publishing house worked so quickly that it was possible for the text to be distributed to the fathers in the Council hall on November 12 and 13. Tromp reported that the night of November 9 the small editorial commission, consisting of Haubtmann, Moeller, Tucci, and Hirschmann, worked till five in the morning. As was to be expected, the printed text contained a series of typographical errors; Tromp remarked, "It's a moral miracle that these were relatively few."[65]

H. The *Textus Recognitus* and the Votes (November 15–17)

Even before the pamphlet containing the revised text was distributed, a struggle over this text began behind the scenes. Immediately after the conclusion of the work of the mixed commission, Father E. Lio, a Franciscan theologian working in Rome and one of the experts belonging to that commission, sent Cardinal Ottaviani a statement concerning what was said about marriage and the family. He claimed that essential elements of the Church's teaching had been deliberately concealed and that the text "was composed in a perspective that is opposed to that of the

---

[65] *RT* (14 Sept – Dec. 1965), 86.

Church."[66] For proof of his claim, Lio appealed to the Council of Florence,[67] the Catechism of the Council of Trent, the Code of Canon Law, the encyclical *Casti connubii*, a declaration of the Holy Office in 1944, the address of Pius XII to midwives in 1951, and the Roman synod held under John XXIII.[68] He denounced a second fact as well, that is, that the commission had deliberately said nothing about the intrinsic evil of marital onanism on the grounds that marital love, an equally essential purpose of marriage, could legitimize this onanism. Lio ended his remarks with the assertion that these statements in their present form could not be approved by the Council and that in the worst case there must be a subsequent explanation that the teaching of the Church on the primary purpose of marriage and on the intrinsic evil of marital onanism remained unchanged, despite what the Council said.

A second initiative came from another consultant of the mixed commission, the Dominican Gagnebet. He criticized schema XIII in its entirety because of the haste with which it had to be drafted; he suggested, as the only escape, accepting Paul VI's address to the United Nations as a conciliar text, linking it with some extracts from the first part of the schema, and letting either later commissions or episcopal synods work on the remainder of the schema.

On November 4 Ottaviani sent both of these texts to Paul VI, along with a letter of his own. He began his letter by saying that these men were consultors of the Holy Office and professors in theological schools of Rome. He added, "Because these reservations seem to me to echo so many other criticisms of this schema by bishops and experts, I regard it as my duty to make them known to Your Holiness, for I think it would be pointless to share them with the other members of the mixed commission, given the mentality of the majority of the fathers who make up that commission."[69] Father John Ford, S.J., made a similar move against the chapter on marriage.

While these initiatives were occurring in the background, the business of the Council continued. The revised text was presented on November 15 and 16. At the beginning of the voting on the individual numbers of schema XIII a supplementary pamphlet was distributed containing Garrone's general report on the revised text, McGrath's report on the Introduction, and Hengsbach's report on the second part of the schema.

---

[66] See Medina papers, II. 4.
[67] See DH 1327.
[68] See DH 3700–24; 3838; Art. 493.
[69] Medina papers, II. 4.

Very much to the surprise of the minority, all parts of schema XIII were approved by more than two-thirds of the votes. The largest blocks of negative votes were cast against Part I, chapter IV, nos. 40–42 (113 no votes) and 43–45 (112 no votes). In Part II, there were 140 no votes on chapter I, nos. 54–56; in chapter V nos. 81–86 received 144 negative votes.

Taken as a whole, Part I and chapter I received 453 *placet iuxta modum*; 467 *modi* concerned chapter III. In Part II, chapter I received 484 *placet iuxta modum*; chapter III, 469 *modi*; and chapter V, 523. The rules for voting provided that on individual numbers there could only be yes or no votes, whereas on whole chapters there could also be a *placet iuxta modum*. The total number of votes cast varied in the separate ballotings between 2,113 (minimum) and 2,260 (maximum). Careful analysis of the negative votes shows that seventy-four fathers rejected nos. 19–22, which dealt with atheism. Nos. 40–42 and 43–45, which saw over 100 negative votes cast, dealt generally with the role of the Church in the world and with what the Church receives from the world, a perspective unfamiliar and confusing to conservative circles. Nos. 51–53, which received 91 negative votes, dealt with marriage and family in the contemporary world, the holiness of these institutions, and marital love. Nos. 54–56, which received 140 negative votes, dealt with marital fertility. Nos. 81–86, which dealt with questions of peace and war, received 144 negative votes.

Once again, the commissions were faced with pressing work. The *modi*, which had to be submitted in writing, filled 220 mimeographed pages and had to be evaluated by November 29. It was agreed that the mixed commission would deal only with those that were accepted by the competent subcommissions. On the other hand, each bishop on the mixed commission had the right to return to any particular *modus* during the discussion, if he thought this necessary. As a result, the questions most extensively discussed were, once again, atheism, marriage, and war and peace. Each of these three questions again gave rise to serious complications.

I. A Violation of the Rules of Procedure?

On November 1, 1965, that is, before the debate in the full Council, the periodical *Concretezza* published a letter addressed to the General Secretariat of the Council and calling for an explicit condemnation of communism. Rumor had it that Bishop Carli had initiated the effort, that 450 fathers had signed the letter, and that the editorial subcommission had not taken it into account. In fact, the letter carried only 332 signatures. On December 4, *La Civiltà cattolica* published the list of the twenty-five original signers, the other bishops having signed later; neither Carli nor Lefebvre were among the twenty-five. The statement was sent in good time to the General Secretariat and passed on by the latter to the secretariat of the mixed commission, Msgr. Glorieux, who did not send the text any farther. Was this intentional? Glorieux later claimed it was an oversight caused by overwork.

On November 15 and 16, the two days when the revised text was presented, the signers of the letter distributed a text containing a strong condemnation of communism. Its key sentence was "Communism must be condemned not only because it is corrupted by atheism but also because the magisterium of the Church has declared it to be intrinsically warped by the serious errors with which it is indissolubly connected."[70] The new text carried 200 signatures.

How did the commission deal with this contribution? In presenting the *expensio modorum* in December, Garrone would explain that the commission was not prepared to accept this *modus*, but at the place in the text in which atheism was explicitly condemned, a reference to earlier condemnations had been introduced. In fact, the revised text of December 2 referred to the encyclical *Divini redemptoris* (March 19, 1937) of Pius XI, the encyclical *Ad apostolorum principis* (June 29, 1958) of Pius XII, the encyclical *Mater et magistra* (May 15, 1961) of John XXIII, and the encyclical *Ecclesiam suam* (August 6, 1964) of Paul VI.

Here is how the violation of the conciliar regulations was handled. Carli had turned to the Council of Presidents, described the facts of the case and asked whether the conciliar regulations had been violated and whether communism would be expressly condemned in schema XIII? Cardinal Tisserant, the acting president of the Council, did absolutely nothing about it. Finally, on November 26, Paul VI summoned Tisserant and Cicognani, as well as Garrone, Dell'Acqua, and Felici. Felici was asked to report on the case and its solution. He admitted the de facto violation of the conciliar regulations but said that it had not been done in order to cause mischief. He suggested that the request be explicitly taken up in the *expensio modorum*. He remarked that the matter was the business of the Council of Presidents. Tisserant explained that he had not convoked the Council of Presidents because Cardinal Wyszynski belonged to it, and he was very attached to his own ideas on communism.

---

[70] Cited from Wenger, IV, 165.

The Pope approved the course taken by the mixed commission and agreed that there would be no new express condemnation of communism. There was no desire to enter into this question once again and stir up political interpretations. On the other hand, it was permissible to mention the earlier encyclicals in a footnote. Only on November 26 — that is, after the meeting with the Pope — did Tisserant write to inform the other members of the Council of Presidents and send them a copy of Carli's letter.[71] In all this the Council was being manipulated.

J. The Marriage Question and the Papal Modi

When it came to the review of the *modi* on the questions of marriage and the family, it was decided that the competent subcommission and some members of the papal commission should undertake the work together.[72] This participation by the papal commission did not change anything in the overall orientation of the subcommission, since only the two bishops on the subcommission had the right to vote, and Bishop Reuss favored the majority. The work of the group was completed on November 20.

During this phase of the work, Msgr. Colombo, the Pope's theologian, called an extraconciliar meeting of the two commissions in order to discuss the following questions: "How is the pastoral problem of conjugal morality in the area of birth control to be resolved? What is a person charged with the care of souls to say in the immediate future? What advice is to be given in the confessional?"[73] Colombo asked these questions in order to stimulate a radical discussion on how the drafted text was to be handled in the Church. Ford and Visser thought it better not to publish the text in its present form on the grounds that it could only cause confusion, unless the text were accompanied by an address of the Holy Father or by a commentary that would guarantee the continuity of the teaching on marriage. The majority opposed this idea and pointed out the open questions that were still to be dealt with by the papal commission. Between November 21 and 24 Ford had a talk with Paul VI in which he

---

[71] See *AS* V/3, 609/610.

[72] Those involved were Bishops Binz and Reuss and theologians Fuchs, Visser, Ford, Zalba, de Locht, Auer, de Lestapis, Perico, Anciaux, and de Riedmatten (secretary). Due to illness Anciaux did not take part in the work.

[73] Cited from Jan Grootaers, "Le tre letture dello 'schema XIII,' con particolare riferimento al capitolo sul matrimonio," *Quesitalia* 9 (1966), 32.

warned that the Council's silence on birth control would lead to a situation in which people would regard the preceding teaching of the popes as open to free discussion.[74]

On November 21, at the Belgian College, the subcommission on marriage and the theologians of the Pope's commission on marriage questions held a joint meeting. The account of this meeting showed that there was a genuine spirit of compromise.[75] Binz, Petit, and Lambruschini thought it better to withdraw the text because its silence would cause confusion and allow divergent conclusions to be drawn about the traditional teaching. In contrast, the great majority thought that a withdrawal of the document would cause great disappointment, since the hopes of the faithful were so high. While wanting to keep the text, the majority did acknowledge some weakness in it. The Alvarezes, husband and wife, strongly emphasized the positive elements of the schema.

During this meeting de Locht suggested, for the time being, *dubitante ecclesia* [while the Church was in doubt], a brief schema with five sections. Visser and Ford thought that if the document were published, it would have to be accompanied by an address of the Pope that would eliminate all confusion and bring out the continuity in the teaching of the magisterium. The result of the discussions was that "the members of both commissions unanimously supported the conciliar text."[76] Despite this unanimity, however, the realists knew that the game was not yet won. Before the discussion in the mixed commission on November 24, van Dodewaard confided to Dupont that he "expected difficulties. Colombo had brought these up in the subcommission... but the others disregarded them despite his opposition."[77]

Meanwhile, behind the curtains the scenario for the following days was being prepared. On November 22 Colombo had a conversation with Ford, who handed him his own *modi* on marriage. According to the first *modus*, the use of contraceptives should be explicitly mentioned, accompanied by a reference to *Casti connubii*. A second *modus* explained the inviolability of human life; a third wanted an explicit reference made to *Casti connubii* in dealing with questions of birth control. In a letter to Paul VI,

---

[74] See ibid., 33.

[75] See the report, composed by de Riedmatten and sent to the Secretariat of State without showing it to Heylen (Tucci papers, XIX, 5). Heylen's report says that the meeting was held on November 21, while de Riedmatten mistakenly assigns it to November 22. Among Prignon's papers there are also notes made by Delhaye during the meeting.

[76] Heylen's report (typewritten and manuscript copy).

[77] *JDupont*, November 11, 1965, 215.

Colombo stressed his agreement with Ford that these *modi* "would be necessary," unconditionally necessary, especially the second.[78]

On that same day or the next, Colombo received Lio's observations, along with four *modi* that Lio wanted to introduce into the schema.[79] The first *modus* wanted a more balanced presentation of the good that is conjugal love and the good that children represent. Lio thought it unnecessary to use the technical terms "primary end" and "secondary end" in a pastoral document. He urged that, without getting into a discussion of the hierarchy in the ends of marriage, there be a clearer emphasis on children as the "most excellent goal of marriage." As for the second *modus*, Lio thought it necessary to bring out more clearly that the interpretations of the moral law that the magisterium had solemnly and constantly set forth on the subject of marital chastity were still in effect. The purpose of the third *modus* was to present marital chastity as the means of overcoming the unavoidable difficulties of marriage. Finally, Lio thought it opportune to explain in a footnote that the Council had no intention of resolving all the problems connected with birth control. For that purpose a special commission had been established.

In his memorandum for the Pope, Colombo took very seriously "the very weighty points made by Father Lio," which "are not entirely unfounded; they deserve serious consideration, given the importance of the subject."[80] The Milanese theologian thought that the schema gave the impression of a disproportion between the good of marital love and the parents' obligation to reproduce, to the disadvantage of the latter. This led to the conclusion that the Council was not truly following the constant teaching of the magisterium and intended to give it up. On the other hand, Colombo believed that in a pastoral document, addressed equally to all people of good will, it was not necessary to reaffirm the ends of marriage. He did judge it useful, however, in order not to anticipate the solution of the problems, that the report on the *modi* should make it clear that the conciliar text had no intention of changing the teaching on this point or of resolving the disputed question.

More serious, in Colombo's view, were the possible moral conclusions that might be drawn from the assertion of the equal importance

---

[78] Tucci papers, XIX, 5. The letter was also accompanied by Colombo's own *modi*, although we know only those of Ford.

[79] Lio's observations, which were delivered to Ottaviani and passed on by the latter to the Pope on November 4, were further circulated. We find them, under the date of November 22 or 23, in the papers of Medina, Tucci, Heylen, and others. In addition, on November 23 Colombo sent Tucci an altered text (four changes) (Tucci papers, XIX, 9).

[80] Tucci papers, XIX, 7. Colombo's two-page memorandum was dated November 22.

of the two ends of marriage (the good of the married couple and pro-creation). The resistance of the subcommission to following in this matter the clear line set down by the encyclical *Casti connubii* was most regrettable. The difficulty in this area was due to the fact that the papal commission had made the teaching a subject of discussion, a discussion bolstered by the opinion that a revision of the teaching was not impossible. For his part, Colombo thought that in this respect the goal must be the "greatest possible clarity of expression." It needed to be said plainly that the teaching on marital chastity proposed by *Casti connubii* and Pius XII remained in effect and was binding on the faithful.

From Monday, November 22, to Saturday, November 27, the mixed commission held meetings morning and afternoon, thirteen of them in all. During this period the work of the general congregations was sus-pended, and a number of important cardinals, König, Šeper, Florit, and Léger, were not present. The absence of these cardinals, who had played such important roles in the debates, shows the climate of exhaustion that became widespread toward the end of the Council.

It was in the course of this feverish work as the Council neared its end that the last great incident took place. During this week the atmosphere was tense to the point of breaking, and the nerves of the members of the commission were laid bare. On Wednesday afternoon, November 24, Bishop Dearden of Detroit, president of the subcommission on marriage, called Bishop Heuschen and handed over a letter that had been delivered to him; at the end of the meeting of the mixed commission the members were told of the arrival of papal *modi*. The result was a general despon-dency, "a feeling of depression throughout the room." According to Moeller and de Locht, "during the break after the meeting de Riedmatten and Colombo got into a very awkward conversation. De Riedmatten, red as a rooster and very agitated; Colombo white as a sheet and with an attitude of complete rejection of what de Riedmatten was saying."[81]

The papal *modi* were made known in a letter from Cicognani to Otta-viani. This letter was written in an apodictic style: "Some points in the text must be improved." The decisive passage read:

> Above all, reference must be made to the body of teaching that has been set forth, down to the present day, by the supreme magisterium of the Church, especially and with clarity by Pius XI in the encyclical that begins with the

---

[81] See *JPrignon*, November 24, 1965 (Prignon papers, 1618, 5).

words *Casti connubii* and by Pius XII in his address to the midwives; especially to be kept in view is that the content of this teaching is to be considered to be still in force. This matter is all the more serious and dangerous because at the present time the opinion is being adopted by some that the pronouncements of the popes are already outdated and are therefore to be ignored. Second, it is really necessary to reject openly the methods and means by which conception is prevented, that is, the methods of birth control discussed in the encyclical *Casti connubii*. For once doubts on this subject are admitted, or silence is kept about them, or opinions creep in about the need to allow them, they can be the cause of very serious dangers in the minds of people generally.

Cicognani's letter also demanded a treatment of conjugal chastity that befits human dignity in the use of marriage. Finally, it said that the four *modi* here presented must be introduced into the text.[82]

The four changes in the text were contained in an attachment. The first *modus* said that the divinely established meaning of marriage is obscured "by birth control methods and other distortions." It is in this context that a reference to Pius XI's encyclical *Casti connubii* was demanded. The second *modus* had to do with the controversy over the ends of marriage. The word "also" was to be removed in the sentence of the revised text that read that "true conjugal love... *also* means that the couple... are ready to cooperate with the love of the creator and redeemer, who through them daily enlarges and enriches his family." The third *modus* decreed that "the children of the Church may not, in regulating births, use methods that are forbidden or will be forbidden by the magisterium." Here again, the Pope demanded that reference be made to the encyclical *Casti connubii* and to the address of Pius XII to the midwives. The fourth *modus* called for the introduction of a passage on the need of marital chastity in overcoming difficulties.[83]

---

[82] Medina papers, II, 84; *AS* V/3, 604–5.

[83] For *modus* 1, see Caput I, p. 5, ln. 22: "Artes Anticonceptionales debent habere mentionem simul cum referentia ad Casti connubii. ita ut textus jam legatur: siquidem polygamia, divortii lue, amore sic dicto libero artibus anticonceptionalibus, aliisve deformationibus obscurantur." Cfr. Pius XII, Litt. Encycl. 'Casti connubii,' AAS 22 (1930), 559–60; Denz 2239–40 (3716–17).

For *modus* 2, see p. 2, ln. 11: "Omittatur verbum 'etiam,' atque brevis haec enuntiatio in extremum periodum addatur, ad lin. 13: 'Filii sunt praestantissimum matrimonii donum et ad ipsorum parentum (bonum) maxime conferunt.'"

For *modus* 3, see p. 9, ln. 28–29: "Haec dicantur: 'Quibus principiis innixi (docemus) filiis Ecclesiae in procreatione regulanda vias inire non licere, quae a Magisterio improbatae sunt vel improbentur,' vel: 'Quibus principiis innixis, filiis Ecclesiae in procreatione regulanda vias inire non licet, quae a Magisterio improbatae sunt vel improbentur.' Praeterea in adnotatione de duobus praestantissimis de hac materia documentis mentio fiat

That evening a number of cardinals began preparing statements for the next day. Suenens met with Heylen, Prignon, and Delhaye in order to work out counterproposals to the papal *modi*.[84] That same day (November 24), Prignon wrote: "We must expect very strong reactions in the Church, so strong that we, the experts, believe that it would be better to have no text at all than a text in that form." Helder Câmara was alerted; there were telephone conversations with Garrone, Ancel, and McGrath, with McGrath informing König, J. Butler (Mombasa), and Fernandes (New Delhi), so that they might take a position in the debate on the following day. Contact was also made with Léger and his working group.

Prignon was outraged by the incident, as was Léger. If the Pope had removed this question from the competency of the Council and reserved it to himself, he could not now impose his solution on the Council. In addition, Prignon was seriously convinced that if the *modi* as presented had to be accepted, the conciliar text "would face difficulty in being accepted by Christians." This being the case, it would be better to vote no.[85] Above all the Belgian group wanted to leave the door open for possible further developments. Since research into the problem was still going on, the Council should not canonize controverted directives that many regarded as outdated. They did not want the Pope later to be in a position to say that he could not go against the views of the Council and thus be able to reject any change whatsoever.

The meeting of the mixed commission that began around 9:30 a.m. on November 25 was one of the most dramatic in its history. The position of Cento and Browne and that of Léger, Charue, and Heuschen collided. The former regarded the Pope's intervention as an order, but the majority were of the view that the Pope was simply offering suggestions for improvement and that consequently his *modi* should be treated as were the other *modi* of the Council fathers. Further practical problems were caused by the fact that the papal *modi* dealt with a subject that the Pope had removed from consideration by the Council. Furthermore, that suggestions of such importance were being made now, at the end of the third

---

scilicet: de Encyclicis Litteris 'Casti connubii,'" AAS 22 (1930); cfr. locos in Denz. Schön 3716–18; ac de oratione a Pio XII ad obstetrices habita: AAS 43 (1951).

For *modus* 4, see p. 9, ln. 15: "Haec addantur: '... non posse, sed ad difficultates superandas omnino requiri ut conjuges castitatem conjugalem sincero animo colant.'" Cited from Grootaers, "Le treletture dello 'schema XIII,'" 35f.

[84] See *JPrignon*, November 24, 1965 (Prignon papers, 1618, 2).

[85] Ibid., 3.

reading of the text, was hardly in harmony with normal conciliar procedure. Colombo asked that the discussion be continued among the bishops alone, without the advisers. A different atmosphere was needed.[86]

On the afternoon of the same day Léger sent the Pope a statement. There was also a petition from the ten lay auditors and a paper by de Riedmatten. The latter said that with this step taken by the Pope the further work of the papal commission was invalidated.

In the record that Felici kept of the subsequent conversation of Paul VI with Tisserant, Cicognani, Garrone, Dell'Acqua, and Felici himself regarding the violation of the conciliar regulations, there are notations that reflect the agitated character of the discussion and the impassioned position taken by the Pope:[87]

> When the Pope then went on to speak of the suggestions he had made on the question of marriage, he voiced his disappointment at the reaction in the commission; he would accept other formulations, provided only that they reflected his thoughts: If the others had their consciences, he had his and had to follow it in order not to compromise the authentic teaching of the Church, which throughout this schema was not always expressed with the necessary clarity. And finally, what is the point of this talk of love, love, love, without saying that the primary end of marriage is the *bonum prolis*, the blessing of children? If you condemn abortion and the killing of children, why do you not also denounce sterilizing and contraceptives?

On the morning of November 26 the mixed commission already had a second letter from the Cardinal Secretary of State. This letter corrected the first. The *modi* that had been communicated were to be regarded as "counsels [*consigli*] from the Supreme Pontiff" and for this reason need not be taken over word for word; they did not have a definitive character. The majority of the mixed commission therefore decided to take the Pope's *modi* as a request that they could deal with freely. On November 27 Ottaviani informed the Pope of the results of the discussion in a letter whose tone was rather one of resignation: "the better part unfortunately remained in the minority."[88] Instead of speaking of birth control

---

[86] "Msgr. Colombo was dissatisfied. He suggested suspending the discussion and continuing it on the following morning at a meeting in which only the fathers (bishops) would take part" (*JCharue*, November 25, 1965, 45). His irritation was not surprising, since among the papal *modi* was one that was word for word the same as the one that Colombo had presented to the subcommission on Sunday and that had not been accepted (see *JPrignon*, November 24, 1965 [Prignon papers, 1618, 4]).

[87] *AS* V/3, 610.

[88] Cited from Medina papers, II, 4.

methods, the text now said that "conjugal love is often sullied by ego-ism, hedonism *and other illegitimate practices to prevent conception.*" At the same time, the place of this insert was changed by a few lines. The requested reference to *Casti connubii* was rejected for reasons of consistency and was put off to no. 55.

The second *modus* had asked for the removal of the word "also." The mixed commission explained that the word was intended to call attention to the fact that the procreation of children is not the sole end of marriage; there had been no intention of deciding the question of the hierarchy of the ends of marriage. The commission therefore decided to strike the word "also" and to add, instead, "without neglecting the other ends of marriage." This expressed the thought more clearly.

In regard to the Pope's third *modus,* Ottaviani again reported an impor-tant change of wording: the commission refused to take over the formula that referred to both the past and the future. Its text read: "The children of the Church... are not permitted to follow paths that have been con-demned by the magisterium in its interpretation of the divine law." To the requested references to *Casti connubii* and the address of Pius XII to the midwives were added the address of Paul VI to the cardinals (*AAS* 56 [1964], 581–89) and its statement that these questions called for a more thorough investigation. The address in question was on the occa-sion of the establishment of the papal commission on questions of pop-ulation and family. The text added that the Council did not have it in mind directly to suggest concrete solutions, since the Pope had reserved judgment to himself.

Finally, the commission wanted to avoid giving the impression that conjugal chastity was the only possible means of birth control. For this reason the reference to conjugal chastity that the Pope had requested in his fourth *modus* was introduced at a different place than the one he called for.

The outcome showed that the majority on the mixed commission wanted to leave open both the question of the hierarchy of the ends of marriage and the question of a new assessment of birth control.

On November 28, Paul VI took Ottaviani's letter reporting on the work of the mixed commission and wrote on it that he accepted the changes in the form given them by the commission.

No one denies that this intervention of the Pope elicited an extensive response in public opinion and among the Council fathers and also sowed a good deal of mistrust of the Pope's authority. The clearest expression of the view of the majority may be found in the letter that Maximos IV addressed to Paul VI on November 29. Regarding the most recent doctrinal tradition he observed that the encyclical *Casti connubii* contained arguments that "as formulated have been outdated by scientific discoveries." As for the address of Pius XII to the midwives, he wrote that "this was not an important document." It seemed to him that to stress the teaching of the two documents was "dangerous for the future at a time when the majority of the experts on your papal commission have expressed their opinion that these documents are not irreformable."[89]

After the commission had completed the text, Léger wrote again to Paul VI. He expressed his respect for the Pope but then spoke openly of the anxiety of a large number of the Council fathers and of pastors and Christians who were honestly trying the difficult task of keeping together fidelity to the Church and the demands of family life in the modern world. The Council, despite its authority, could not decide a question that it had never examined. Such a procedure threatened to cause "a serious loss of trust in the magisterium of the Church." Could the Council fathers "decide in good conscience so decisive an issue in the life of many faithful?" If they did so, they would close off "the way for any radical investigation of this question and would cause immeasurable disquiet in the world and a great distress in the Church."

On November 29 Canon Dondeyne shared with the Pope his reflections on the November 27 meeting of the mixed commission, and that same morning Heuschen gave a copy of it to Colombo.[90] Dondeyne rejected the procedure chosen and emphasized in particular the ambiguity that resulted regarding the implications of the text. The majority had agreed with this text while presupposing that the question was not decided and that other developments were possible in the future. The minority believed that the incorporation of citations of *Casti connubii* allowed the Church simply to stand by the teaching of Pius XI. On December 2 Colombo communicated his "observations" on the reflections of Professor Dondeyne. After December 3, Dell'Acqua saw to it that Dondeyne's reflections reached Suenens.[91]

---

[89] Medina papers, II, 4.

[90] See Suenens papers, 2661, 5. Suenens sent the letter to Léger on December 16 with the comments of Colombo (see Suenens papers, 2668; and Léger papers, 1565).

[91] Suenens papers, 2662, 2663 (the handwritten date was introduced by Paul VI). A French version of Colombo's remarks is given in Suenens papers, 2666. On December 3, de Lubac wrote in his diary: "This morning Father Martelet gave Colombo a copy of the answer to the difficulties which Ch. Dondeyne (of Louvain) had given him" (*Jde Lubac*, 676). Consequently, it is not improbable that Colombo's observations were inspired by Martelet. Moreover (according to Heuschen after a conversation with Colombo), Colombo gave the impression "that he is very concerned about the discipline of the Church

Colombo's remarks, which Paul VI had doubtless read, are of great interest. They throw light on the history of the sending of the *modi* and on the interpretation of the conciliar text. From them it emerges that the sending of the *modi* had its origin in the pastoral concern of Paul VI and those around him.[92] Papal circles became convinced that even if the Pope were to reaffirm that until some new directive were issued the teaching in *Casti connubii* was to be regarded as the binding teaching of the Church, the opinion would become ever more widespread that this teaching was not immutable. As a result, a climate of uncertainty would be created in the Church. *Lex dubia non obligat* (a law that is in doubt does not bind).[93]

In addition, besides fear of a drift into a situation of doctrinal confusion, there was also fear that "after a period of alleviation," it would be impossible in practice to return to this [traditional] teaching if, after examination, the magisterium should conclude that the teaching on conjugal chastity presented in *Casti connubii* must be preserved unchanged. It was therefore better to put a stop to any uncertainty that could arise out of a prolonged "situation of doctrinal confusion," so that this situation might not prove later on to be a serious tragedy.

Colombo made himself very clear on the interpretation of the text: No one thinks that by its incorporation into the conciliar text "the teaching of *Casti connubii* will acquire infallibility, since the Council has no intention of presenting any infallible teaching." Colombo also reaffirmed that this decision did not determine the work of the papal commission, as this was described in the address of Paul VI on June 23, 1964: The problem is not definitively resolved, at least not in all its aspects; although there is an obligation to be prudent, theologians are not forbidden to continue

---

and fears a subjectivist interpretation" (*JPrignon*, December 12, 1965 [Prignon papers, 1626, 2]).

[92] This is also the conclusion Congar drew after a conversation with Colombo. The latter had told him: "The intention (of the *modi*) was not didactic but pastoral. It was necessary to leave the papal commission completely free, without bringing any pressure to bear on it. Now *to say nothing* about the question of the means of birth control was to give the impression that the position taken by Pius XI and Pius XII was being changed. *It had to be said that nothing was being changed.* (I must confess that this neither pleases me nor greatly upsets me.)" (*JCongar*, November 28, 1965; II, 495).

[93] Heylen thought that the book of United States theologian John Noonan, which was widely known in Rome, had contributed to hastening the crisis and alarming Colombo's group. In the book's final chapters Noonan wrote that the silence of the Council was important for the development of this teaching, since if the Council had wanted to confirm the teaching of *Casti connubii*, it would have done so. See *JPrignon,* December 2, 1965 (Prignon papers, 1623, 1).

their studies and investigations, as is the case in all other questions that have been the subject of the authentic but non-infallible magisterium.

While the Council seemed to be reaching the end of this nerve-racking affair, preparation for the future was taking place behind the scenes. As many suspected, difficult times were looming. Married couples and priests were speaking out. On December 2 Suenens received a telegram from 150 Belgian intellectuals, asking him to do everything he could to keep the Council from deciding this question.[94] But these public reactions did not lead to renewed discussion in Rome, where people had rather the certainty that the conciliar text did not resolve the question.[95] On the other hand, preparation was already being made for the postconciliar period. Father de Locht worked up a statement on the present validity of *Casti connubii* and another entitled "Pastoral Care of Families after the Conciliar Decree on Marriage."[96]

But those arguing for a position of openness were not the only ones preparing for the future. On December 3, Ford continued his lobbying of the Pope. In a letter to Msgr. Macchi, Ford called the attention of the Pope to the interpretation given of the new text by the press and by those who claimed that the Council did not intend to decide this question.[97] Newspapers for December 1 and 2 had reported that the *modi* had simply not been accepted and that the revised text left the situation open. Ford was doubtless not the only one who reacted as he did. Garrone was summoned to the Secretariat of State, where "they gave him, for study and possible correction of the text, a new proposition from a very lofty personage."[98] This new *modus* asserted that the procreation of children was the primary end of marriage.[99] Heuschen and Garrone wrote an answer to this renewed attempt on behalf of a *modus* and by 2:30 p.m. brought to Dell'Acqua the document rejecting the change.

Garrone's report to the Council on December 2 underscored not only the meaning given to the new text but also contained a statement about

---

[94]   See *JPrignon*, December 2, 1965 (Prignon papers, 1623, 2).

[95]   This was the view of Suenens and Lercaro, among many others. See ibid.

[96]   Both were dated December 2. Suenens said that he found many good things in them, "but it is not yet possible to present them to the Holy Father." The moment was "poorly chosen," and "it was to be feared they would elicit a reaction from the people on the other side" (*JPrignon*, December 2, 1965 [Prignon papers, 1623, 2f.]).

[97]   Ford's letter to Macchi (Tucci papers, IXX, 4).

[98]   *JPrignon,* December 3, 1965 (Prignon papers, 1624, 2). The personage was a member of the Curia, not the Pope himself.

[99]   The formula in the text — "without slighting the other ends of marriage — would be changed to "without neglecting the other ends of marriage."

continuity in the teaching of the magisterium; at the end he explained that the Council did not want to decide the question of birth control.[100] On Saturday, December 4, the disputed chapter was accepted by 2,047 votes out of 2,209; there were 155 no votes and seven ballots were invalid. Surely even some in the majority saw themselves obliged in conscience to vote no. Next to the chapter on war and peace, this chapter on marriage was the one that received the most negative votes. On December 6, at the last general congregation of the Council, the vote was taken on the schema *Gaudium et spes* as a whole.

K. OUTLAWING WAR ONCE AGAIN

On Thursday, December 2, the first part of schema XIII, in its revised form, was distributed, while the second part was given to the fathers on the following day. At the same time a statement against the chapter on the outlawing of war and the preservation of peace was circulated.[101] It was signed by Cardinal Spellman, Archbishop of New York, Cardinal Shehan, Archbishop of Baltimore, as well as by Philip Hannan, Archbishop of New Orleans and the leader in this area, and by a number of bishops of other countries. The statement asked that chapter V be rejected for several reasons. In nos. 80 and 81 of the schema the possession of nuclear weapons was condemned as immoral. This ignored the fact that the possession of scientific weapons had preserved freedom in a large part of the world; the defense of a great part of the world against aggression was not a crime but a major service. The cause of wars is the quarrels and tensions between peoples, which in turn are caused by injustice and not by the possession of scientific weapons. Such statement did harm to the cause of freedom in the world. In addition, they contradict what is said in no. 79 of the schema as well as in the address of Paul VI to the United Nations in September 1965, where the right of nations to defend themselves is confirmed. Today, the great nations cannot defend themselves without scientific weapons. In no. 80 it is claimed that recent popes have already categorically condemned total war. No references are given for the claim. Finally, the Council cannot come to a decision in a matter on which no consensus exists among theological specialists.

[100] See *AS* IV/7, 464–69, especially 465.
[101] Prignon papers, 1323.

This attempt of some cardinals and bishops caused the fear to spread that schema XIII would not receive the needed majority in the final round of votes. It was supposed that this statement, supported as it was by two famous United States cardinals would awaken a considerable echo among other bishops. Given that there were other groups not friendly to the schema because of what was said of atheism; the failure formally to condemn communism; the question of marriage; and the refusal of military service, the chances seemed slim that the document would be adopted.

In this situation Bishop Schröffer, chairman of the commission addressing questions of war and peace, decided to distribute a statement, signed by himself and Garrone, that refuted the arguments of the United States cardinals. Schröffer pointed out that nowhere in nos. 80 and 81 was the mere possession of nuclear weapons condemned as immoral. The text said rather that a "danger exists," "an occasion offers, as it were," and so on, and that, on the other hand, the arms race is "not a sure way of preserving peace." Finally, nowhere was it said that scientific weapons are the causes of war, but instead, that "the arms race threatens to increase the causes of war." Moreover, nowhere is there any challenge to the right nations have of warding off unjust attacks; in fact, footnote 2 of this chapter refers to papal documents, and in particular to what Pius XII said on September 30, 1954, a text directly quoted in the note. Finally, Schröffer pointed out that in regard to the mass destruction described, a consensus was emerging among Catholic theologians.[102]

The statement obviously was effective. Spellman and Shehan recommended a positive vote in the definitive balloting. It was rumored that even the Pope made known his approval of the text.[103]

On December 4 the existing and improved text of the pastoral constitution was submitted for a series of twelve votes; at this point one could vote only yes or no. The number of voters fluctuated between 2,174 and 2,238. The highest number of no votes was cast on nos. 11–22 (131 no votes); nos. 46–52 (155 no votes); nos. 73–76 (121 no votes); nos. 77–80 (483 no votes); nos 91–93 of the Conclusion (128 no votes). The vote on the title showed 293 no votes. Nos. 11–22 dealt with the question of condemning communism and atheism. Nos. 46–55 contained teaching on marriage, the ends of marriage, and birth control. Nos. 73–76 were on political life; here the question of strikes and of support for political activity in the form of parties had led to discussion. Nos. 77–90 dealt with the

---

[102] See Medina papers, II, 4.
[103] See Wenger, IV, 280.

question of war and peace. The Conclusion (nos. 91–93) elicited a fairly large number of no votes, probably because of the overall orientation of the section toward dialogue with the world and because of the references to the Church as undergoing development. As for the title of the schema, the reporter, Garrone, had pointed out that only a small group of fathers had submitted suggestions for changing "Pastoral Constitution." In order to make clear the meaning of these words, a short explanation in the form of a footnote had been included in the draft of the text; it brought out the primarily doctrinal character of the first part and the more pastoral character of the second, although pastoral elements were to be found in the first part as well and doctrinal elements in the second part.

On December 6, during the 168th and final meeting of the Council, the vote was taken on the schema as a whole. Of the 2,373 voters 2,111 voted yes, 251 voted no, and 11 ballots were invalid. On December 7 the schema was definitively and solemnly approved by the Council fathers. This time there were only 75 no votes, 7 ballots were invalid, and 2,309 fathers voted yes.

Even in its final form as approved by the Council, *Gaudium et spes*, the Pastoral Constitution on the Church in the Modern World, which had at last come into being along such difficult paths, bore all the signs of the beginning of a dialogue between the Church and the world. The importance of *Gaudium et spes* and the wealth of perspectives it opened up can be seen not least in the fact that almost all the intra-ecclesial contentious issues of the postconciliar period involved *Gaudium et spes* and the letter and the spirit of this conciliar document. One may think, for example, of the controversy over the Church's moral teaching on marriage and sexuality or over Latin American liberation theology.

The fruitfulness of the approach taken in *Gaudium et spes* can be seen particularly in the area of the problems of war and peace. When faced with the difficulty posed in the abstract by the right of peoples to defend themselves, on the one hand, and the "impossibility" of using modern weapons of mass destruction, on the other, the document did not attempt to produce an abstract, theoretical balance. That would have been impossible. Instead, the text began with the dynamics of the gospel in order to promote institutional arrangements and set political processes in motion that would help to avoid wars. Here the dynamics of Christian faith and the existence of the Church in time became the point of departure for the development of perspectives and measures that make peace possible under the conditions of the time.

This was something different from an abstract, natural-law approach, such as was customary in earlier social doctrine. It became possible because the Church was here seen as existing in history and thereby asserted itself as a factor that releases energies and reveals perspectives. On the other hand — and this is the limitation, as it were, that *Gaudium et spes* carried with it — this point of view was not maintained in any consistent way either in part 1 or in part 2 of the document. Not without justification did Edmund Schlink, an observer at the Second Vatican Council, speak of the "strange atemporality"[104] in which the Church seems to exist in many passages of *Gaudium et spes*, despite the programmatic introduction to the document.[105] A critical acknowledgment of such limitations in no way diminishes the immense merits that those bishops and theologians, and also Paul VI, won for themselves by promoting and persevering in this project.

L. A System of Open Relations: The Church in the Modern World

An overall assessment of *Gaudium et spes*, is not a simple task. This document was developed within the Council itself and is very much indebted to the innovative concern of John XXIII, which was to bring about a renewal of the Christian message, an "updating" of the Church through a new openness to the world. The result was to open up a far-reaching horizon. The Council fathers, who at the beginning of the first period had addressed a message to humanity, which had already anticipated the opening words of the pastoral constitution, gave evidence that they were fundamentally inspired by the same profound concern as were the two popes of the Council. This agreement showed a profound longing to break through all the incrustations and enter into a new dialogue with the human race. Dialogue with the people of this age, with the "world," was also the chief concern of Paul VI.

It was an uncommonly arduous task to give suitable expression in a conciliar document to this longing, which sprang from the gospel-based participation of Christians, their communities, and their Church in the joys and distresses of humanity. A document had to be drafted for which there was no prior model. Unlike previous treatises on ecclesiology, this

---

[104] Edmund Schlink, *Nach dem Konzil* (Munich, 1966), 162.

[105] For an assessment of *Gaudium et spes,* especially for an uncovering of the basic theological lines of the document, see Peter Hünermann, "Die Frage nach Gott und der Gerechtigkeit: Eine kritische dogmatische Reflexion auf die Pastoralkonstitution," in *Visionen des Konzils: 30 Jahre Pastoralkonstitution "Die Kirche in der Welt von heute"*, ed. Gotthard Fuchs and Andreas Lienkamp (Münster, 1997), 123–44.

document was to deal not with hierarchical structures and the prerogatives characteristic of the Church, but rather with the relationship of the Church to the people of the present age. This meant travelling over hitherto untrodden terrain, since the customary social doctrine of the Church had never discussed this subject. The wearisome labors of the various commissions attested to the difficulties of grasping this new vision of the Church in the world. It is characteristic that the work received key impulses from exchanges with theologians in the ecumenical movement; at the time the World Council of Churches in Geneva was faced with essentially the same challenges. What emerged in the end was a document that was highly significant and dealt with essential matters, but that, in the view of the reporter and in the judgment of Paul VI, also needed further work; it was only a first attempt.

Two aspects, only seemingly contradictory, of the history of the document's influence show how central *Gaudium et spes* was for the entire Council. So deeply did Catholic Christendom identify with the document that its key words came to describe the entire conciliar message. David Seeber made this point: "In any case, from the very outset the influence of *Gaudium et spes* merged to such an extent with the history of the influence of the Council as a whole that the two are now hardly distinguishable."[106]

Another aspect underscores the importance of the pastoral constitution. In the postconciliar period there has been almost no great ecclesial controversy that has not been closely connected with what is said in *Gaudium et spes,* beginning with the controversies that surrounded *Humanae vitae* and lasting down to the issue of advising about unwanted pregnancy; the intense controversies over liberation theology and, as a result, the numerous quarrels over theology as practiced in the context of diverse cultures and traditions; and finally, the clashes that broke out in the postconciliar period about the hierarchy in the Church. All these questions were occasioned by and had roots in *Gaudium et spes.* This is obvious in the case of the first two subjects just mentioned. But we may also point to *Gaudium et spes* for the third issue as well, for it is no accident that in the first and foundational chapters on the Church in the world the term *church* does not occur very often. Instead, such expressions as "the disciples of Christ" or "the community of human beings... who are united in Christ" were chosen (no. 1). This emphasis in speaking of the Church

---

[106] David Seeber, "30 Jahre Pastoralkonstitution: Über *Gaudium et spes* hinaus," in Fuchs and Lienkamp, *Visionen des Konzils,* 14.

reflects the addressees of this conciliar document, *Gaudium et spes* is the first conciliar text in the history of the Church that is addressed to all human beings.

The purpose of the document is reflected in its structure. It begins with a detailed analysis of the situation of modern humanity; in its conciseness and complexity this analysis still has no equal. It speaks of the profound and rapid changes, the quickly growing power at the disposal of human beings, and the far-reaching processes of marginalization and the troubles and suffering that are connected with these changes. The analysis of old, traditional ways of life marks the discussion of new social forms and of the immense devastation that goes hand in hand with them. The document speaks of the psychological, moral, and religious changes, of the growth in knowledge and the confusions arising therefrom. It addresses the deeper levels of modern problems, and the psychological, moral, and religious changes that today's humanity must face.

This analysis of the situation is followed by a concise description of a Christian anthropology that, under the heading "The Human Being as God's Image," deals with the dignity of the human person, and with the human community and human creativity. If one compares this with previous theological anthropologies, one is struck by the impressive advance made here in the picture given of the human being. It had previously been customary to develop an anthropology on the basis of theological and philosophical principles, but here principles and empirical aspects of the person are combined in a new unity. As a result, theology acquires an entirely new depth. The relationship of the Church to reality, which John XXIII had in mind, is here given its first expression. The reading of this first part makes it clear that there is no opposition in principle between the modern world and the faith, although from the Christian viewpoint there is indeed a great deal in the modern world that must be seriously resisted because it contradicts God's saving will and human dignity.

The reciprocal interconnection of the Church and the world — without any leveling down and conformity — is brought out especially in the final chapter of the first part.[107] In this section the Council fathers took it for granted that the Christian community profits in many ways from the cultural, social, and economic developments of the human race, and even

---

[107] The fourth chapter is titled "Role of the Church in the Modern World" and has these subdivisions: "Mutual Relationship of Church and World," "What the Church Offers to Individuals," "What the Church Offers to Society," "What the Church Offers to Human Activity through Its Members," "What the Church Receives from the Modern World," and "Christ Alpha and Omega."

that in relation to the gospel itself, it has, as a result of cultural, scientific, and social advances, gained a deeper understanding of its own message and its own gifts. These are new accents, never heard before. Due to this very fact, the Council wins credibility for the other statements in which it speaks of the contribution made by Christians and the Church to a world worthy of human beings.

The second part of *Gaudium et spes* is devoted to particular important questions: (1) advancement of the dignity of marriage and family; (2) the proper promotion of cultural progress; (3) economic life; and (4) the life of the political community and the promotion of peace and of the building of the community of peoples. In connection with all these major, complex subjects the Council fathers contributed pioneering impulses, perspectives, and innovations. In regard to marriage and the family they set a personalist understanding of these two over against the hitherto largely dominant utilitarian and end-oriented definition of marriage and family that was derived from Stoicism and emphasized the procreation and rearing of children.

In the section on the place of culture in the modern world the fathers discovered a new theme for the Church and theology. In this section, although the word *globalization* is never used, we find an accurate anticipatory sketch of the tensions and polarizations arising between traditional ways of life and the ways of life resulting from scientific-technological and economic changes. Principles are developed, with human beings in mind, for passing judgment on this powerful cultural impulse. Perspectives are developed for a cultural ethos that Christians know is binding on them.

The chapter on economic life speaks clearly of the domination that economic thought is beginning to have on the present age and on the lives of peoples. The fathers address in a global way the major international problems of the economic order and the regulation of markets that even today are the subject of clashes. The text urges the development of international regulations in order that human beings on all continents may be able to earn a living.

If we bear in mind that the Council was held during the Cold War, we will be amazed at the clarity and prophetic vision with which the Council fathers support the free and active participation of all "in the establishment of the juridical foundations of the political community, in the administration of public affairs, in determining the aims and the terms of reference of public bodies, and in the election of public leaders" (no. 75). They derive all this from the dignity and social nature of the human person, as well as from the historical developments which social life has undergone in the modern age.

Finally, the chapter on the promotion of peace and the building of the community of nations deserves special recognition. Against the arms race, "one of the greatest curses on the human race" (no. 81), and against "total war" (no. 80), the fathers open up perspectives for a policy of detente that are to be focused on and made a reality through the formation of international institutions. This means the surrender of an abstract teaching on war, a teaching based on natural law, as well as of a pacifism that is likewise abstract and made a matter of principle but that leads to complete defenselessness against any aggressor. That teaching is replaced by a politics of peace that is energetic and characterized by moral imperatives and a Christian spirit. One of the great accomplishments of the Council was that such a conception could be developed despite considerable opposition from the United States episcopate and despite strong partisan positions taken against communism and its political representatives.

It is no accident that the most important postconciliar statements of bishops and the Pope on questions of culture, the economy, political development, and a peaceful order have followed paths sketched out by *Gaudium et spes,* for example, the pastoral letter of the United States bishops on the economy and the pastoral letter of the German episcopal conference on armaments and problems of peace.

The significance of the pastoral constitution and the fundamental importance of the positions taken in this document are not canceled out by the limitations of the individual chapters and the problems still remaining. The Council was clearly aware that its effort to define relations between the Church and the world was only a beginning. That is not surprising after an almost four-hundred-year long history of alienation. The objection was rightly raised, later on, that insufficient attention was given to the theology of the cross, the world's challenge to faith, and the breakdown and fragility of all human works. All that must be admitted. Even more serious are the theological objections that the Council did not keep to the line taken in *Lumen gentium,* but over lengthy stretches fell back into thinking based on natural law. These limitations, too, must be admitted. Nevertheless, the vision set down in this document and the overall direction it gave the Church seem more important.

In the Conclusion this vision is conjured up in an impressive way. The document speaks here of the task of individual faithful and of the local Churches, namely, to take what the Council set down in general terms and to concretize it and develop it further in particular cultures and situations, in order thereby truly to help all human beings, "whether they believe in God or whether they do not explicitly acknowledge him" (no. 91).

The Church is challenged to cultivate within itself "mutual esteem, reverence and harmony, and acknowledge all legitimate diversity"; "in this way all who constitute the one people of God will be able to engage in ever more fruitful dialogue. For the ties which unite the faithful together are stronger than those which separate them: let there be unity in what is necessary, freedom in what is doubtful, and charity in everything" (no. 92).

Finally, and movingly, the document addresses ecumenical unity: "At the same time our thoughts go out to those brothers and communities not yet living in full communion with us, with whom, nonetheless, we are united by our worship of the Father, the Son, and the Holy Spirit and the bonds of love" (no. 92). In closing, the document then speaks of the necessary dialogue with the various religions and of the common effort to obtain the true goods of humanity through the cooperation of all.

It is this spirit that came to characteristic wide areas of the Church after the Council, and it is this spirit that gives the document its full significance and power.

IV. EVANGELIZATION OF THE WORLD OR "PROPAGANDA FIDE"?

The discussion of the revised text on the Church's missionary activity began on October 7. The new schema, essentially the work of Congar with the energetic support of Ratzinger and Neuner, had easily won the approval of the Coordinating Commission and was sent to the fathers in the middle of June 1965. Döpfner reported later that even a man "as critical as Father Rahner" had accepted the text with enthusiasm.[108] The text, of course, did not please everyone, particularly because of its call for a fundamental reform of the Roman Congregation for the Propagation of the Faith. Since its establishment by Gregory XV in 1622, this Roman congregation had operated in an unchanging manner. An adaptation to the situation in modern missions, serious consideration of the young Churches, and a corresponding change in the Roman authorities seemed called for. Father Schütte, chairman of the subcommission that had done the work of revision, gave a series of public lectures on behalf of a reorganization that would change an administrative machine to a source of dynamic guidance for the Church's missions. The pertinent passage in the text that had been sent to the bishops read: "This congregation is made up of members chosen from all those who collaborate in the task

---

[108] See Wiltgen, 254.

of the missions, namely, cardinals, patriarchs, and bishops from around the world, no matter what their rite, along with the heads of the institutes and the papal works. All of them are to be called together at fixed times and, working collegially under the authority of the Pope, shall exercise supreme leadership of all missionary work."[109]

Behind the scenes Cardinal Roberti intervened firmly with regard to this section of the new schema on the grounds that, since the proposal had to do with a curial institution, it, like all such questions, was not the Council's business to decide but a matter solely for the papal commission for the reform of the Curia. In accordance with Roberti's wishes the text was altered, and Schütte communicated it to the fathers as an amendment suggested by the commission for the members. It now read: "Called to be participants in this congregation shall be representatives chosen from among all those who collaborate in the work of the missions: bishops from around the world, whatever their rite, and the heads of the institutes and the papal works. All these, who are to be called together at fixed times, share in the supreme leadership of the work of the missions."[110]

From the tension between these two texts, as from a focal point, there emerges the problem that faced the Council in dealing with missions. Should the missions continue along their previous track, with improvements introduced here or there, or does the changed situation call for a new kind of mission? The question was an urgent one. The fathers had discussed a new basic understanding of the Church and had analyzed the local Churches as well as episcopal collegiality. They had reflected on the Church in today's world and had approved of the ecumenical movement and dialogue with the religions. Did not all that have to be made concrete in a new form of missionary work? After all, what does *mission* mean in the modern world? What are its dimensions? How is it to be carried out and organized?

These questions were very dependent on the theological foundation given for missions. Among Protestant missiologists there was widespread discussion of the *missio Dei*, the sending for our salvation of the Son and the Spirit, as the true mission.[111] By the beginning of the 1960s this theological foundation was quite often connected with the idea of secularization: God effects salvation in the realm of the profane as well as in the

---

[109] *AS* IV/3, 682.

[110] Ibid., 707.

[111] D. G. Vicedom, *Missio Dei* (Munich, 1958); G. H. Anderson, *The Theology of Christian Mission* (New York, 1961); J. L. Newbigin, *Trinitarian Faith and Today's Mission* (Richmond, 1964).

realm of the holy. Missions, it began to be said, had as their goal historic work in the building of society and in the perfecting of humanity.[112] By comparison, the missionary command of Christ, proclamation, and Church, as well as conversion, fade into the background. Dialogue with the religions and cultures becomes central. Mission no longer means the *planting of the Church*.[113]

These questions, which arose first in Protestant mission theology, were very quickly taken over by Catholic theology. The demand, voiced from many sides in the hall, that the "theology of mission" be incorporated into the schema logically brought with it the demand also that some response be made to the tendencies just described. Thus the question of the organization of Propaganda Fide seemed like the final link in a whole chain of questions that built upon one another and were, all of them, conditioned by the final link.

An adequate historical evaluation of the schema as well as of the discussion in the hall and the final text has to begin with such questions and the norms implied in them. In this context we shall first describe the schema presented and, in a second step, the discussion it elicited in the hall.

A. The Schema of the Decree on the Missionary Activity of the Church

Framed by a Preface and a Conclusion,[114] the schema had five chapters: "Doctrinal Principles"; "Missionary Work"; "Missionaries"; "The Organization of Missionary Activities"; and "Cooperation." The divisions and the titles do not, as such, point to any innovation. After the doctrinal *principles*, the schema speaks of *missionary work*; the agents of this work are the *missionaries*; their *activities* are described in the fourth chapter, and the fifth deals with the *coordination* of these activities. One could imagine this division in a missionary manual of the preconciliar period or in a Neo-Scholastic textbook. But appearances can be deceiving. What lay behind these titles?

---

[112] See A. T. van Leeuwen, *Christianity and World History* (New York, 1964).

[113] In these tendencies there may also be seen an effort to save the missions of the future from the accusation of colonialism, the Europeanization of cultures, and a general striving for power.

[114] See *AS* IV/3, 663–92.

1. The Introduction

The first sentence cites *Lumen gentium*. The Church, "the universal sacrament of salvation," is sent to the nations in order to bring them the gospel. But the general movement characteristic of *Lumen gentium* is already abandoned when this sending is said to be entrusted to the apostles and that it is "the duty of their successors to carry on this work." Here a hierarchical understanding of the Church can be discerned. The next section of the Introduction points to the new situation in which the Church must be the salt of the earth and must gather human beings into a single family and single people of God. The third section speaks of the task: the people of God, following the way of Christ, must spread the kingdom of Christ everywhere and prepare the way for his return. From this polarity, which surfaces even in the Introduction, it can be said that the commission had not completely adopted the new vision of the Church.

2. Chapter 1: Doctrinal Principles

The Church is described as being by its nature missionary, since it derives its being from the mission, or sending, of the Son and the Spirit. From the "fountain-like love" of the Father flows the plan of salvation for humanity, a plan that is carried out through the sending of the Son and the Spirit. The sending of the Lord and the sending of the Spirit lead directly to the sending of the apostles and their successors. "The Lord Jesus, before freely giving his life for the world, established the apostolic ministry and promised the sending of the Holy Spirit, so that both [apostolic ministry and Spirit] are associated in the work of Christ that is to be carried on everywhere and always."[115] In what follows, the text speaks of the descent of the Spirit on the apostles at Pentecost but not of the Spirit's descent on the disciples! The missionary command of the Risen Christ is cited (Mt 28:19–20), and the text expressly says that the order of bishops has "inherited" this task "together with the successor of Peter, the visible head of the Church."[116] It is also said of the people of God that the entire Church must cooperate in carrying out this task.

The formulation just described takes over the most recent theological development, namely, the grounding of the Church's mission in the

---

[115] Ibid., 665.
[116] Ibid., 666.

doctrine of the triune God. Emphasis is placed on the hierarchy in the carrying out of Christ's missionary command, and the text does not adequately bring out that the sending of the Church as a whole is founded on Christ's command and that the ministry of bishops is the ministry of leading the Church in the accomplishment of its mission. This formula — that the mission is entrusted to the order of bishops and their head, the successor of Peter — is expressly repeated.[117]

After describing this trinitarian foundation, the first chapter sketches the conditions under which missionary activity takes place at the present time. The text first describes the various stages in the building up of a Church, beginning with the original planting, the emergence of young Churches, and the firm establishment of local Churches; it also notes the different circumstances possible in social processes. The text then turns to the planting of the Church, which is described as "mission" by a special title. (The text thus resists the kinds of one-sidedness that could be seen in the trend, described above, in *missio Dei* theology.) The missionary activity of planting a Church usually occurs in "certain territories" assigned "by the Holy See."[118] A distinction is made between this missionary activity in the strictest sense and the usual pastoral activity for the faithful.

The chapter seeks to explain the meaning and necessity of missionary activity directed toward pagans and peoples whom the gospel has not yet reached. Two reasons are given for the necessity of missionary activity directed to pagans. The first has to do with the salvation of individual human beings, and the second with their unification to form the people of God. The first argument is not very well formulated. It begins with the doctrine of God's universal saving will: "The Church holds that God can lead human beings to faith by ways known to him alone." At the same time, however, the Church knows that "through knowledge of Christ and his gospel human beings are enlightened in an unparalleled way and given spiritual gifts."[119]

The doctrine of God's universal saving will is here presented in so abstract and ahistorical a way that the definitive character of Christian revelation is obscured and the real necessity of mission is no longer made clear. The text overlooks the fact that the mystery of Jesus Christ, no matter how hidden, is awaited by humanity and was promised by the prophets. It does not say that the gospel brings the fulfillment of this

[117] Ibid.
[118] *AS* IV/3, 667.
[119] Ibid., 668.

desire and promise and at the same time passes judgment on the many ways in which human beings relate to God. As a result, all that remains in the text is the reference to the will of God, who wants "human beings to be saved by faith, called through the preaching of the Church, and justified for salvation through the Christian sacraments."

The commission itself evidently felt the weakness of this first argument and therefore laid special emphasis on the second: "But the primary reason for the missionary activity of the Church is derived from God's decree... that all who make up the human race should form one people of God, grow together into one body of Christ, and be built into a temple of the Holy Spirit." This argument, though certainly convincing theologically, can easily be distorted as if the only point being made here is the worldwide spread of a religion whose effect, the salvation of human beings, can as such also be attained by a plurality of religions. The weakness of this section makes it very clear that the new vision of God's universal plan of salvation and the problem of dialogue with the other religions and the status of the latter in salvation history have not been thought through and appropriated theologically.

The two short concluding sections of this first chapter deal with missionary activity in the life and history of humanity, but they hardly give an adequate description of the modern situation of missions; they only refer in a general way to sinners' need of redemption. Only in the final section, on the eschatological character of missionary activity, is it said that preaching the gospel initiates a process of transformation in the cultures of peoples as well as the hearts of individuals; as a result of this process good and evil are differentiated and men and women are set on the way to their fulfillment.

3. Chapter 2: Missionary Work

Of all the chapters, this one seems the most modern and the most realistic. A first section, on the preconditions for evangelization, speaks of preparing the ground, a preparation without which evangelization cannot occur: In order that Christians "may be able bear a fruitful witness to Christ, they must be united in esteem and love with those they want to evangelize, think of themselves as members of the society of those among whom they live, and take part in its cultural and social life."[120] Explicit

---

[120] Ibid., 670.

reference is made to the need for familiarity with national traditions, religions, and so on. A broader aspect of pre-evangelization is the *presence by charity*, the involvement of Christians in the troubles of the individuals and the societies in which they are living.

The actual preaching of the gospel and the gathering of the people of God are distinguished from this pre-evangelization. The freedom to bear witness to the gospel and the freedom to confess the Christian faith are expressly mentioned. The stages of the catechumenate and of Christian initiation, as well as the relevant liturgical celebrations of this process, are described. Reference is made to the irreplaceable role of communities both in the catechumenate and in Christian initiation.

The next section goes on to deal with the building up of Christian communities, the promotion of the charisms and of calls to the various ministries, and finally, the task of forming a local clergy and catechists. The remarks on the formation of the clergy and catechists include a call for a familiarity with one's own cultural milieu, with the religions practiced in it, and so on. In the section on catechists we note the concern for their adequate upkeep. The final section speaks of the task of fostering vocations to religious life. To this section is added a lengthy passage on the particular Church. This takes into account the actual development, namely, that almost everywhere dioceses have been erected, with the result that independent young Churches have come into being.

4. Chapter 3: Missionaries

This chapter contrasts strangely with chapter 2. The several sections deal with the missionary vocation, missionary spirituality, spiritual and moral formation, theological formation, and finally, missionary institutes. *Missionaries* are understood as individuals with a special vocation who are equipped with the relevant gifts and abilities and devote their entire lives to the missionary task and who as a rule do the work of missions in missionary institutes under legitimate ecclesiastical authority. No attention is paid in this third chapter to the various situations in which missionary work is done or to the forms this work takes. No mention is made of catechists and lay people, missionary physicians of both sexes, or the directors and teachers in mission schools. In the concluding thoughts missionary institutes are praised for their difficult work. Frequently the Holy See entrusts to them for evangelization extensive territories "in which they have gathered a new people for God, a local Church now dependent on its own pastors."

In this chapters missionaries and missionary institutes are seen as the agents who manage to do the entire work of mission, to the point of creating local Churches with their own hierarchies. This is a rather odd conception when one considers the many "independent accomplishments" of the recipients of mission, from the first converts all the way to the establishment of a local Church. The reader therefore looks ahead eagerly to how chapter 4, on the organization of missionary activities, and chapter 5, on collaboration, will be handled.

5. Chapter 4: The Organization of Missionary Activity

Since all Christians, according to the charisms and gifts of each, are obliged to contribute to the missionary activity of the Church, there must be an overall organization of this activity. Since the task of proclamation belongs to the college of bishops, this organization is "looked after by the central commission of the Pope." The commission in question, that is, Propaganda Fide, is to be appropriately formed so that it is a dynamic body of leaders, one that uses scientific methods and practical means that are appropriate to contemporary conditions. At this point there follows the already cited statement about the composition of this congregation or of its supreme organ of leadership.

At the local level the bishop is at the center of the diocesan apostolate. It is for him to preside over and coordinate the missionary activities of the diocese. He is urged to establish a pastoral council for this purpose. Regional coordination is in the hands of the episcopal conference, which is to act on those questions for which individual dioceses cannot provide answers. In this context the text addresses, in particular, the subject of supra-diocesan places of training for the clergy, pastoral centers, and the use of mass media.

When the text speaks of missionary institutes, it places the emphasis on the authority of the local ordinaries to control missionary work in their dioceses. It recommends that arrangements and agreements be made between the bishops and the institutes or between the episcopal conferences and the institutes with regard to the forms their collaboration is to take. These arrangements and agreements are then to be approved by the Holy See. One can see, from this relatively vague and loose language, the real difficulties present in the background. Finally, the institutes themselves are urged to enter into agreements among themselves, if they are working in the same missionary territory, in order that their work may be as effective as possible. In this context mention is made of their relations

with the episcopal conferences. As part of this cooperation, special attention is given to the establishment and support, by the missionary institutes,
of scientific organizations that will make use of missiology, ethnology,
history, the religious disciplines, and sociology.

6. Chapter 5: Collaboration

This chapter again specifies, in a longer list, the special tasks incumbent on various groups in the Church with regard to missions. It speaks
of the missionary task of the entire people of God, which is called upon
to "cooperate" or work together. Christian communities are exhorted to
cultivate a missionary spirit. The bishops are reminded to see to it that in
their dioceses there is a living missionary spirit and corresponding missionary activities, to support efforts and initiatives coming from below,
and also to free diocesan priests for these missionary tasks. The episcopal conferences are to support diocesan efforts.

A sketch is given of the missionary duties of priests. The tasks of the
religious institutes, the contemplative as well as the active, are described,
as are the contributions of the laity. In this concluding section of chapter
5 the entire range of missionary activities is envisaged. Mention is made
of the necessary groundwork to be done in regions already Christianized,
in order that the missions may have the necessary support. The text speaks
of native lay people and others coming from ancient Christian Churches
who work in mission countries — teaching in schools; carrying out temporal tasks; and cooperating in the work of the parish and diocese, in the
economic and social sector, in the work of development and of education.
The conclusion thanks those who work in the missions and calls upon all
not to close themselves to the urging of the Spirit.

If we look at this schema as a whole, we receive the impression that
both new departures and the great problems of the missions are illumined,
but that no useful solutions to these great questions are as yet being
offered.

B. The Discussion in the Hall

The discussion in the hall lasted until October 13 and was carried on
at a very high level. Since about one-third of the bishops present came
from mission regions where they were faced with enormous difficulties
and hoped for the strengthening and encouragement of missionary work,
it was not surprising that their contributions were marked, for the most

part, by great openness and a deep awareness of problems. The questions having to do with the restructuring of Propaganda Fide were addressed in cautious but nonetheless clear contributions. The bishops of mission countries and developing regions chose spokesmen in advance to articulate their concern and vision.

An attempt to summarize the discussion in the hall makes clear the following focal issues: (1) the present-day reality of missions and the Church's missionary activities; (2) the reason or grounds for the Church's missionary activities; (3) the essence, in our day, of the Church's missionary activities; (4) those who bear responsibility for directing the missionary activities of the Church and those who bear the main burden of the work; and (5) the coordination of missionary activities being carried on at any particular time and overall leadership in the missionary activities of the Church.

1. Present-day Reality

In drafting *Gaudium et spes*, the writers began with an analysis of the present situation. The draft on the missions did not contain a parallel introductory chapter that would analyze the situation of the missions. Individual characteristics of the present-day mission situation were indeed addressed, but there was no general picture. A whole series of Council fathers referred to this in their remarks, but they did not ask for a special chapter on the subject.

The contemporary reality found its clearest expression in the address of Arrupe, general of the Jesuits. He pointed out, to begin with, that a new perception of missionary work was needed, because ideas were widespread that presented a distorted picture of the reality of missions. To this end it was necessary to see the real state of today's world with its problems and its processes of change. Missions belong not only in underdeveloped countries but in highly developed industrial countries such as Japan, where only eight out of every thousand people are illiterate. This shows the enormous complexity of missionary activities.

Arrupe spoke of the difficulty of cooperating in the conversion of individuals. He mentioned explicitly the problems that exist in bringing peoples and cultures under the rule of God on earth. In light of this he castigated the infantilism, the sentimentality, the sense of superiority, the shortsightedness, and the superficiality often found in the Church's images and concepts of missions. These shortcomings result in wrong criteria for the selection of missionaries and missionaries suffering from a false image of themselves. The missions are regarded as supplicants or even as begging institutions. On the basis of this description of the situation Arrupe called for a radical reform in the Church's formation of consciousness; a different assessment of the various cultures, peoples, and races; and missionary efforts to match this new assessment.[121]

The complexity of present-day missionary challenges to the Church was also a theme of König's intervention, which spoke of modern society as characterized by the presence of a plurality of different religions.[122] A fairly large group of Latin American bishops pointed out, through their spokesman, the special kind of missionary work they must carry on. Numerous Indians in their dioceses had been baptized but had never experienced a real evangelization. Here, then, was a kind of formal Christianity without content, the facade of a Church without the reality.

Africans such as Michael Ntuyahaga, Bishop of Bujumbura, insisted strongly on the fact that young Churches had sprung up everywhere, yet the reality of these young Churches was not adequately grasped. "We live in a new missionary age, and this age is very important. Our time is, as it were, a turning point in which we are passing from a period of missions in the proper sense to a period of young Churches, which are autonomous and exist in their own right." He therefore called for a fundamentally new definition of relations between the old Churches and the new Churches, for new kinds of cooperation between missionary institutes and the new Churches, and finally, for a corresponding restructuring of Propaganda Fide.[123]

Archbishop D'Souza was even clearer. In his remarks, which for lack of time he submitted in writing, he asked that the Asiatic Churches in particular, which were working in countries with ancient cultures, be given the freedom to apply the fundamental principles that had been approved in the schema on the liturgy. In East Asia, he said, missionary activity took the form not of an "implantation" but of a "transplantation." The Church had not had to develop there like a mustard seed but had been put in place like a "prefabricated organization." As a result, "the heart of Christian life had not been directed to our culture," although that culture was the necessary means of expressing and spreading the gospel. But this approach, which was necessary for the sake of the gospel, was not brought out in the schema.[124]

---

[121] See AS IV/4, 208–12.
[122] Ibid., 137.
[123] Ibid., 196–98.
[124] Ibid., 184–87.

2. *The Grounds for the Church's Missionary Activity*

Many of the Council fathers addressed the question of the basis for the missionary activity of the Church. In almost every case missionary activity was seen as derived from the mission of the Son and the Holy Spirit. But the more proximate grounding of missionary activity was felt to be inadequate. Meouchi, the Maronite Patriarch of Antioch, complained that nothing at all was said about the faith as bringing salvation.[125] Frings asked for a more positive statement that the Church's mission contributes to the salvation both of individuals and of the human race, which cannot attain to definitive salvation without the Church's missionary activity.[126]

Joseph Cordeiro, Archbishop of Karachi, Pakistan, posed with clarity two fundamental questions that were not sufficiently treated in the text: If God with his universal will to salvation can bring human beings to salvation in varying ways, why should there be missions?[127] If non-Catholic Churches, and even the other religions, can contribute to the attainment of salvation, why should there be Catholic missions? His own answer, based on the Bible, was that in the preaching of the faith and in all missionary activity the primary goal is the glorification of God. Christ devoted his entire life to glorification of the Father; the same holds for missions. The salvation of human beings is linked to this glorification of God.

Numerous interventions stressed, though in differing language, the connection between God's saving will and the missionary activities of the Church; the intrinsic orientation of the Church's mission to the hearts of people; and the proclamation of the gospel as the center of all missionary activities. Finally, the role of the religions in the economy of salvation was described in varying ways. Their very plurality and their individual peculiarities pointed to the need for the Church and its missionary efforts. The ecumenical aspect was taken up occasionally in connection with the essential mission of the Church to humanity.

In connection with this question of the justification of missionary activity, even the derivation of missionary activity from the mission of the Son and the Holy Spirit was frequently discussed and criticized. The reason for the criticism was that, unlike *Lumen gentium*, the schema did not speak first of the mission of the entire people of God and only then that

---

[125] See *AS* IV/3, 708.
[126] Ibid., 739.
[127] *AS* IV/4, 150–53.

of the bishops and others having an official ministry. Alfrink castigated the schema because it spoke as though the mission of the Church "were entrusted almost solely to the hierarchical Church, while the other followers of Christ were capable only of cooperation with the bishops in this area." The Cardinal referred not only to *Lumen gentium* but also and especially to the schema on the lay apostolate, which spoke of the work of evangelization as the fundamental task of the people of God.[128]

Bishop McGrath of Panama likewise criticized this ecclesiological deficiency: the entire schema gave the impression that missionary activity was to be directed by the bishop and the activity itself was to be entrusted only to priests and religious. Only "incidentally" was anything said of the laity, and, when it was, lay people were not seen in the context of their families, their lay associations, and so on, with the result that the community of the Church, which is the sign of love, was not discussed at all. Also as a result of this hierarchical concept of mission, the sacramental dimension of mission was not seen, that is, that the Lord himself is present in his Church and in its officials and is working through his Spirit. McGrath also emphasized the need, resulting from the recently asserted teaching on collegiality, to emphasize and speak more fully of the responsibility of all the bishops, together with the successor of Peter, for the missions.[129]

No less impressive, in this same context, were the frequent references to persecution and the cross in the missions — the participation of the Church in the Lord's Way of the Cross.[130] These passages brought out in a concrete way the sacramental character of missionary activity. It became clear that the missions involve essentially a wrestling with the "powers of darkness" and conversion to the living God.

3. The Essence of the Church's Missionary Activity

The third issue was closely connected with the described situation of modern missions. Numerous interventions brought out the importance of the laity and their work in the missions. This importance is due to the witness to faith and love that is given by communities and families, no less than to specifically catechetical activities and to other professional activities applied to the building up and fostering of the Church in mission

---

[128] *AS* IV/3, 740–42.
[129] *AS* IV/4, 154f.
[130] See ibid., 746, 750.

countries. Many of the Council fathers devoted special attention to questions of education in the missions, from lower schools to universities. Some spoke of medical and charitable ministries. Along with this broad and colorful variety of missionary activities, special heed was given to preaching and catechesis, the appropriate celebration of the liturgy, and the administration of the sacraments. The stages mentioned in the schema — from pre-evangelization, proclamation proper, and the formation of communities, to independent young Churches — were given a positive evaluation, although a few speakers pointed out that these missionary activities proceeded to some extent side by side although crisscrossing to some degree.

4. Directing the Church's Missionary Activity

One of the most important questions discussed was that of responsibility for the direction of missionary efforts. The emphasis was placed sometimes on the responsibility of the episcopate as a whole in collegial union with the pope, and at other times on the responsibility of individual bishops in the young Churches. From the interventions there emerged with clarity the far-reaching problems that had arisen in connection with the formation of independent hierarchies in the young Churches of Africa, Asia, and Oceania. Previously, Rome had assigned and handed over missionary regions to missionary institutes, but with the establishment of hierarchies that were already made up to a high degree of native clergy, a new situation had arisen: the bishops of the young Churches had naturally claimed the same leadership authority as the bishops in the old Churches. But earlier structures were, in part, still operative, and this meant that the locals were treated as minors. The difficulties attending the transition in leadership were immense. In addition, there was the extensive financial dependence of the young Churches, a theme barely voiced but audible in the interventions.

The draft provided that agreements were to be made at various levels between the bishops and the missionary institutes and then to be approved by Rome. Important issues in this context were help in staffing the young Churches and the leadership authority of the bishops in the matter of pastoral emphases. Another issue was that of financial support. The missionary institutes had extensive ties to their homelands and home dioceses, and material aid had come from there for the work of the missions, but this was not automatically continued after the transition to a native hierarchy. It is noticeable that in the discussions these problems were touched on, but trouble areas were not sharply and clearly brought out. Evidently, there was a certain reluctance to describe the situation bluntly.[131]

The question of collaboration was addressed in this context. It was striking how strong an emphasis the missionary bishops placed in the collaboration of the native laity and their families and communities but also on lay people from abroad who commit themselves to the missions and on the newly emerged secular institutes and others. Great importance was also attributed to diocesan priests who were permitted to work, either temporarily or permanently, in the young Churches. Interestingly, almost no notice was taken of the fact that most of the missionary institutes of the traditional kind were groups of priests who were not properly to be counted as religious because they took no vows. Here is evidence that these groups of missionaries were largely included among the congregations and orders, even though they had an entirely different origin and a different interior image of themselves.

As regards the preparation of collaborators in missionary work, the main emphasis was somewhat different in the discussion than it was in the schema itself. Familiarity with the cultural, religious, and social setting of their new sphere of operation and development of communication skills were strongly emphasized alongside spiritual and theological formation.

5. The Role of the Congregation for the Propagation of the Faith

Finally, an especially delicate subject that was closely connected with the preceding set of issues was the position of the fathers on the organization of Propaganda Fide. A new name for it was suggested: Secretariat for the Evangelization of Peoples. The reason? The name Propaganda Fide carried too much baggage; the missions did not have to do solely with the spread of the faith; and the gospel includes more than the name Propaganda Fide conveys. At the same time, reference was made to the

---

[131] For insight into the concrete difficulties of missionary work, see Eugen Nunnenmacher, *Missionarisches Selbstverständnis nach dem Konzilsdekret "Ad Gentes" und nach persönlichen Äusserungen von Afrikamissionaren*, Studia Instituti Missiologici Societatis Verbi Divini 33 (Nettetal, 1984). The study was based on polls taken at the beginning of the 1970s. They made clear the difficulties that arose in many cases from changed political situations and from the flight from the land; borderline experiences in the formation of the clergy were discussed, and the dangers of superficial evangelization were emphasized.

possible offensiveness of the name to non-Christians.[132] Nonetheless, pro-posals were made for a fundamental reorganization of the congregation.

Bishop Martin from Rwanda-Burundi made a strong plea for including bishops from the young Churches as members of the congregation with full rights; in support of the plea he appealed to the Decree on the Pastoral Office of Bishops. He obviously had in mind a collegial governing committee, under the pope, in which the young Churches would share responsibility with representatives of the old Churches.[133] A further problem, which he mentioned very often, was the deployment of available forces, both of personnel and of finances; in these respects there needed to be greater fairness.[134] On the whole, the new Roman body had to be so structured that the great missionary task could be carried out in a comprehensive and dynamic way, with an eye on current problems. These ran from the problem of fostering prayer and penance for the mission fields and of the tasks of missionaries all the way to problems of matériel. The need was for a radically restructuring of this congregation.[135]

Mauritius Quéguiner, superior general of the Mission Étrangère de Paris, warned explicitly against excessive centralization, such as happens when the congregation's area of responsibility is expanded and reshaped. In addition, he regarded as urgently needed a closer collaboration among the missionary institutes both in formation and in work with the home-land bishops of priests and missionaries as well as with the bishops in the young Churches. He proposed that the training of future missionaries be done first in places of theological formation in their native lands and that only the special training of missionaries be done in places of formation belonging to the institutes. He suggested greater flexibility in the matter of incardination, both in the home dioceses and in the new Churches. We can sense, from such remarks, that new ways of collaboration, even at the organizational level, were taking shape here.[136]

A central theme running through many interventions was ecumenism; division among Christians was repeatedly denounced as a considerable obstacle to missionary work. The speakers spoke of ecumenical collaboration as necessary but also having its difficulties, especially due to the rapid spread of Free Church communities.

---

[132] See AS IV/4, 218.
[133] See ibid., 193.
[134] Ibid., 194.
[135] Ibid., 193.
[136] See ibid., 139–43.

C. The Revision of the Schema and the Final Votes

As early as October 12 the General Secretary called for a vote on the existing schema as "a basis for further revision." Of the 2,085 fathers present, 2,070 voted yes, 15 no. Although the end of the list of speakers had been reached, ten Council fathers spoke on October 13 in the name of large groups of bishops. E. Adjakpley, the Togolese regional secretary of the World Association of Catholic Youth, was the last bishop to speak. Father Schütte, the vice-president of the commission and the reporter on the schema, was given the final word. He thanked the fathers for their interventions and the commitment these showed, as well as for approving the schema in principle. In his view the most important point to be examined in the revision was whether the order of the chapters should be changed. At this point in his address considerable reserve could be felt. Regarding the ecclesiological question of whether the understanding of mission should start with the people of God or with the hierarchical structure of the Church, he thought both conceptions were possible. The commission, however, wanted to strive for greater balance, It also wanted to emphasize the ecumenical aspects of mission as strongly as possible and to stress the importance of the laity and their varied ministries. Among other particular points he mentioned the definition of the goal and necessity of missions and the definition of mission itself. He also mentioned as particular points the formation of missionaries, the different aspects of the process of evangelization and of dialogue with non-Christians, the importance of the Holy Spirit in the conversion of peoples, and the more administrative questions concerning the competence of bishops and of the papal missionary works.[137]

As early as October 15 the commission met and instructed the subcommissions, under the leadership of Schütte, to deal with the over 190 petitions, which totaled more than 500 pages. In great part these petitions were signed by entire groups of bishops. The subcommissions worked on the schema from October 19 to October 26. On October 27 the revised schema was unanimously approved by the commission.

The examination of the petitions showed that over 300 Council fathers opposed the correction Roberti had made with regard to the constitution of Propaganda Fide. For this reason the commission decided to replace the offensive text. It did not give the name of "members" to the representatives to be appointed from the young Churches and other groups, but

---

[137] Ibid., 330–32.

it did stress that they were to play "an active and crucial part in the guidance" of the curial authorities "under the authority of the pope."[138]

When Schütte presented the revised text to the Council on November 10, he pointed out an important external change. From chapter 2, on missionary work, the commission had removed the relatively brief statements about the young Churches and turned them into a separate chapter entitled "The Particular Churches." Thus even in the structure of the schema the commission took into account the significantly changed situation in the mission countries. But revisions on individual points were no less radical.

The first point the reporter mentioned was the rewording of statements on the motives and necessity of the Church's missionary activities. He insisted explicitly that the commission had here taken its guidance from *Lumen gentium*; it had also cited Christ's missionary command according to Matthew and according to Mark. With regard, however, to ecclesiological criticisms he remarked: "Although it is true that the necessity of promoting missionary work obliges the people of God as such, the commission nonetheless believed it ought to emphasize that the commission of Christ was directed first of all to the apostles and their successors."[139]

An effort had also been made to present the young Churches as subjects and not objects of missionary activity. The commission therefore explicitly defined the term *missionary* more closely to include priests and laity, religious men and women, natives and foreigners, who proclaim the gospel to those do not yet know it. As a result of the interventions, the commission also introduced a separate section on the laity. Finally, the reality of divided Christendom and the challenges and difficulties of ecumenical collaboration were presented in detail.[140]

On November 10–12, without further discussion, twenty votes were taken on the individual sections of the new schema. The no votes varied from 6 to 13, but among the yes votes there was a sizable number of *iuxta modum* votes. The fifth chapter received the most such votes, 712 of them, enough that the two-thirds majority needed for acceptance failed by 8 votes. Most of the *modi* had to do with the reorganization of Propaganda Fide. The rest had to do mostly with passages of the text that had been the main subjects of attention in the preceding discussion.[141]

---

[138] *AS* IV/6, 248f.

[139] *AS* IV/4, 262.

[140] See *AS* IV/6, 261–63.

[141] On chapter 1 there were 309 *iuxta modum* votes; on chapter 2, 7; on chapter 3, 3; on chapter 4, 2; on chapter 5, 712; on chapter 6, 153 (see ibid., 339f.).

When the *modi* were examined, it turned out that hundreds of the requests for change consisted of mimeographed pages, so that the work was greatly simplified. On November 30 a vote was taken on the newly revised text. The revised test was accompanied by an appendix giving the position of the commission on each of the suggested changes.

In his oral report to the assembly Schütte naturally dealt first of all with the great number of petitions relating to the organization of Propaganda Fide. There were suggestions from 461 fathers that the juridical phrase "with active voice" be included in order to show that the bishops really had a share in the government of this Roman congregation. They also suggested that the members of this governing committee be proposed by the episcopal conferences. They proposed, in addition, that the appointments be "for a limited period." The commission had agreed with the first request and added the words "deliberative voice." The right of the episcopal conferences to present the names of members was rejected, because there was no question here of a synod. In addition, the pope's freedom in making appointments was not to be limited. Where the right of presentation existed, the result was often stagnation or even immobility. The final suggestion was likewise rejected, because it seemed to enter too much into detail. It was the pope's prerogative here to make regulations for details.

The vote on the amended text showed 2,162 positive votes against 18 negative votes. In keeping with procedure the text was next presented to Paul VI, who in turn presented it for a final vote at the public session on December 7. There the Decree on the Missionary Activity of the Church was accepted by 2,394 fathers; there were 5 votes against it. This was the highest number of yes votes cast during the Second Vatican Council.

If we survey the uncommonly turbulent history of this document, we may well be struck by the stubbornness and determination of many Council fathers about rethinking and strengthening the missionary activity of the Church as an expression of its nature and mission in changed social, political, and even ecclesial conditions. At the beginning, the whole enterprise seemed a routine task in which the issue was a few organizational improvements. The crisis over its acceptance during the third period, despite the personal involvement of Paul VI, then led to a radical revision. There was great theological competence among the bishops and theologians to whom the work of drafting was entrusted, but the contribution of the Council fathers themselves was unusually extensive at both the theological and the pastoral levels.

In view of the crisis that Catholic and Protestant missions alike were undergoing at the beginning of the 1960s, the schema produced an important reappraisal of the foundations of the missions. The change from the traditional missions to the missionary activity of young local Churches was approved. Basic guidelines were sketched out for new kinds of collaboration among foreign missionaries, native clergy, and committed lay people in the work of building up the Church. Even after an interval of about forty years it is surprising to see the extent to which the Council fathers imagined and fostered perspectives that would have a future but were just emerging then.

Two theological limitations of this decree must be mentioned. First, despite all the theological efforts made to present in an adequate way the basis of missions, the critical and judgmental aspect of the gospel, which is so clearly attested in the New Testament, was hardly made clear. The sentence "Whoever believes and is baptized will be saved; whoever does not believe, will be condemned" (Mk 16:15) was cited, but its significance was not developed. The gospel is not clearly seen as the word of God that confronts the human person with a decision. This question is obviously connected with the evaluation of the non-Christian religions. The second limitation is one already mentioned: the heavily hierarchical concept of the Church that prevails in this document. A look at the composition of the commission responsible for the editing makes this fact seem even harder to understand.[142]

It is worth noting Lukas Vischer's appraisal of the decree in his report to the Central Committee of the World Council of Churches:

> The decree discussed in relative detail the necessity of collaboration with other Churches. While most of the other texts contain only a brief reference to the decree on ecumenism, this document repeats the content of that decree and emphasizes the close connection between the missionary task and the ecumenical movement.... These references can be very important for the collaboration of the Churches. For an ecumenical community will become a reality only when the Churches are in a position to bear a common witness. We are far from such a situation.... But the decree undoubtedly does broaden the foundations for a common witness, and the fact that it is the decree on the missions that has done the broadening is a sign that the common task of proclamation is shown to be an impulse for the ecumenical

---

[142] The subcommission consisted of Lokuang, Zoa, Lecuona, Riobé, and Schütte, superior general of the Society of the Divine Word. The experts were Congar, Ratzinger, Seumois, Neuner, Glazik, Moya, Beuys, Greco, Grasso, and Eldarov; the secretary was R. B. Peeters.

movement, even in the relationship between the Roman Catholic Church and the other Churches.[143]

D. Mission and Faith Go Together: An Appraisal of Ad gentes

The fathers of Vatican II faced a tremendous task when they had to compose a decree on missions. For 500 years Christian missions had been very closely bound up with the establishment of colonial empires by the peoples of Europe. Theology, including the theology of mission, had a Eurocentric bias until the period immediately before the Second Vatican Council.[144] This was true of both Catholic and Protestant missionary communities. It was not surprising, then, that the concept of Christian missions entered into a period of deep crisis due to the rise of independent Churches and hierarchies in formerly colonial areas new to political independence and the achievement of cultural autonomy and to new access to the non-Christian religions. The crisis was further deepened by a new emphasis on God's universal saving will. Were the religions with their rich cultural developments not among the real ways by which God saves?

Against this background the decree of Vatican II on the missions represented an exceptional achievement, one that provided an accompaniment and security in the difficult transition by which many mission areas became independent local Churches. The decree initiated and promoted new thinking about the mission of the Church. If it was clear, however, that the fundamental questions had not been fully answered, decisive forces were set in motion and perspectives for solutions were provided.

The entire decree in its definitive form contains six chapters framed by a short introduction and a conclusion. The first chapter, which gives the theological foundations, is the most important chapter both in size and in degree of elaboration. The sacred scriptures are mined in rich measure. The Fathers of the Church are cited extensively. Not only the important papal doctrinal documents on the missions but also the Constitution on the Church and the Decree on Ecumenism are cited. Except for Thomas Aquinas, none of the theologians of the Middle Ages or of early modern times is quoted. In establishing the foundations of mission, then, the Council fathers hark back essentially to the first millennium, that is, to a

---

[143] Lukas Vischer, "Le Concile de Vatican II," *Verbum Caro* 20 (1966), 29f.

[144] See the survey of the controversies in the theology of the missions by A. Freitag, *Mission und Missionswissenschaft* (Steyl-Kaldenkirchen, 1962), 21–67.

time when the Church did not carry out its mission principally in harmony with colonial endeavors. The important first chapter goes far beyond the title of the decree: *On the Missionary Activity of the Church.*

What basic lines of the theology of mission are sketched here? First comes the principle: the Church is by its nature missionary (no. 2), for the people of God originates in the love due to which the Son and the Spirit proceed from the Father, creation is brought forth, and the redemption of history is effected through the Old Testament and New Testament economy of salvation. The Fathers of the Church speak with great objectivity about the non-Christian religions through which God leads humanity in many ways toward salvation; but they did not see this as derogating from the eschatological character of the revelation of God in Jesus Christ: the religions stand in need of "enlightenment and correction" (no. 3). In order to exercise its mission at all, the Church has received the Holy Spirit, who enables it to gather the nations together, to speak in all tongues, and to overcome the dispersal at Babel through love (no. 4).

When, in the following two numbers (nos. 5 and 6), missionary activity is distinguished from the general mission of the Church and the proper agent of mission is defined, we see the narrowing of perspective that radically marked Catholic theology in the second millennium. This narrowing was first uncovered by Protestant exegesis beginning in the middle of the nineteenth century but was then picked up by Catholic exegesis. The Council fathers took no notice of that development. What did the bishops think they were dealing with? In no. 5 the missionary program of the Church is traced back to Jesus, who at the beginning of his public activity appointed the Twelve and thereby made them "the beginning of the sacred hierarchy." Subsequently, the mission of the risen Lord (John 21:21 is cited) is handed over to the apostles and is later extended to the pope and the college of bishops.

In contrast to the Council fathers, Rudolph Schnackenburg writes about the cited passage: "John's interest is in the handing on of the authority and commission of Jesus; the community of disciples is to make him present in the world and to continue his saving work. No limitation to the disciples there present can be seen and was hardly intended; John nowhere calls these disciples 'apostles' in the strict sense. In his eyes they represent the entire community of faith."[145] The different exegetical

---

[145] Rudolph Schnackenburg, *Das Johannesevangelium* (Freiburg, 1982⁴), IV/3, 385.

explanation given by the Council[146] leads in no. 6 to the odd conclusion that "this task, which must be carried out by the order of bishops, under the leadership of Peter's successor and with the prayers and cooperation of the whole Church, is one and the same everywhere and in all situations, although, because of circumstances, it may not always be exercised in the same way."

In the definition of mission the two different starting points for a theology of mission (the emphasis on the preaching of the gospel by the Münster school, and the idea of the implantation of the Church, maintained by Louvain and curial-canonical authors) are combined: "The special undertakings in which preachers of the gospel, sent by the Church, and going into the whole world, carry out the work of preaching the Gospel and implanting the Church among people who do not yet believe in Christ, are generally called 'missions.'"

The first chapter concludes with further summary thoughts on the plan of salvation of God, who is indeed at work in all human beings and in the religions and cultures but who has ordered everything to Christ; it also reflects on the meaning of missionary activity for human nature and human striving. The concluding section (no. 9) shows the incorporation of mission in the history of salvation, inasmuch as it belongs essentially to the time after the first coming of Christ and is directed to his second coming.

The chapters that follow deal with missionary work (II), the particular Churches (III), missionaries (IV), the management of missionary activities (V), and the collaboration of the worldwide Church in its mission (VI). Especially noteworthy in the description of missionary work in the proper sense (II) is the first section, which deals with the need that the Church, aided by believing Christians, has to become familiar with men and women, their cultural and historical heritage, their ways of life, and their problems and difficulties. Without this participation — this collaboration in the great cultural, social, and other challenges — missionary work has no ground under its feet. Only after gaining this familiarity can the proclamation of the gospel and the gathering of God's people begin. These activities lead finally to the building of Christian communities, the development of the various ministries, and to the kindling of the vocations that young Christian communities need. It can justly be said that in this second chapter the theological vision presented in the first chapter is translated into practical steps.

---

[146] These remarks apply also to the interpretation of Matthew 28:19f. and Mark 16:15f.

Only in the final stage of revision was the third chapter, on the particular Churches, promoted to the status of a separate chapter. It reflects the widespread situation in Asia and Africa and in most regions where young Churches had arisen. The chapter takes up explicitly the many tasks incumbent on the individual ministries in these young Churches, on bishops, priests, deacons, religious, and men and women catechists; it adds a lengthy reflection on lay people and their activities in the young Churches. There is an explicit call for the formation of an independent theology and of communal and private ways of life that are shaped by the Spirit and yet preserve the cultural traditions of the peoples.

In chapter IV the dominant Eurocentric conception still plays a decisive role in the very concept of a missionary. Although the entire people of God is called to mission, the Lord in a special way calls missionaries, men and women who possess the most varied charisms and are entrusted with the most varied ministries. It is expressly said that these vocations arise also, and especially, in the young Churches and that "mission" is not a concern only of the "old" Churches. Evidently, each different group of missionaries requires its own distinctive training. One is struck by the emphasis placed on lay missionaries who take part in the development of each people.

The fifth chapter speaks of the formation of an episcopal council that, together with the pope, is to direct the entire missionary activity of the Church. According to the decree, Propaganda Fide is considered the location of this work of the pope and the Synod of Bishops. We can read between the lines a hostile criticism of that Roman institution when the text says: "Although the Holy Spirit arouses a missionary spirit in the Church in many ways, and indeed often anticipates the work of those whose task it is to guide the life of the Church, nevertheless, this congregation should itself promote missionary vocations and spirituality, as also zeal and prayer for the missions, and it should furnish genuine and adequate information about them" (no. 29). The chapter speaks finally of the cooperation needed and not only of the various missionary works. Reference is made to the leadership role of the bishop in his own diocese, even in regard to missions. The task of the episcopal conferences is to coordinate, and missionary institutes are urged to collaborate. Specific mention is made of the promotion of scientific institutions that will serve missionary work and missionaries.

The sixth chapter speaks of cooperation in the framework of the world-wide Church. At the beginning, mention is made of the consciousness of responsibility on the part of all, both dioceses and communities. Then the duties of the bishops are named more concretely; these apply not only to their own dioceses but also to mission work. The active and contemplative congregations and religious institutes are urged to be cooperative. Finally, the document speaks in broad terms of lay people and their activities on behalf of the missions.

The entire document is doubtless an important milestone in the history of the theology of missions. In addition, it played an essential role in the stabilization and communication of a new and solid direction for Catholic missions at the end of the twentieth century.

V. *DIGNITATIS HUMANAE*: A CREATIVE SOLUTION

The document on religious freedom, *Dignitatis humanae*, which was the subject of heated controversy into the fourth period and was then accepted by an overwhelming majority, is one of the most important conciliar documents and, at the same time, a decisive document in the history of humanity. Its broadly humane, philosophical, and theological line of argument defines in a balanced way the relationship of believing men and women and of the Church, as well as of other religious communities, to the modern state and to society; in addition, the principles developed in this document provide structural bases for ecumenical relationships and the coexistence of the religions. The principles established in the document are at the same time very closely connected with the ecclesiology of the Council. They provide maxims for the exercise of ecclesial authority in the Church itself, and a juridical organization of areas of freedom within the Church. These last-mentioned aspects are not, however, developed in the document; they are conclusions that follow from the principles elaborated and the conceptual clarifications given in the document.

If the title of the present section speaks of "a creative solution," it is because the hitherto seemingly insoluble oppositions among the freedom of conscience of individuals and groups, the duty of the state to enact laws affecting questions of morality, and the efforts of religions and ideological groups to engage in missionary activity are creatively brought together in a framework that does not flatten these various elements, but rather preserves their special character while also integrating them into a rational correlation marked by freedom.

A chapter in the preparatory schema on the Church had set down, once again, the claim made by the Church since late antiquity that, because God is the author of civil society, society has a duty to worship him. In the present order of salvation, the worship established by God is that given by the Christian Church. It is this worship of God that civil society and its authorities must make their own.[147] This principle, which leads to an established or state Church, obliges once the Christian faith has spread in a society or public community, since the faith cannot be imposed by force. A civil system of laws marked by freedom and a corresponding public organization of the realm of freedom of conscience are, however, not reconcilable with this principled argument.

It was no accident that the renunciation of this line of argument, which had been accepted for about 1500 years, took place in the Secretariat for Christian Unity. Questions of religious freedom had been raised since the beginnings of the ecumenical movement. At Oxford in 1937, in connection with the Barmen Declaration, questions about the relationship between the Church and the modern state were debated. What freedoms must the Church claim from the state? During the assembly at which the World Council of Churches was established in Amsterdam in 1948, and again in New Delhi in 1961, questions of religious freedom and international coexistence were discussed, as were questions about the peaceful coexistence of the separated Churches. A distinction was made between proselytism and freedom to bear witness.

Theologians under the leadership of Cardinal Bea took into consideration the insights and reflections that had been developed in this area, as well as the public discussions that had arisen in connection with the Universal Declaration of Human Rights by the United Nations in 1948. The extent to which conflicts marked the discussions of religious freedom at that time was illustrated by the exclusion of neutral Spain from the Marshall Plan of the United States and the accompanying moral ostracism of Spain as a Catholic state where religious freedom was guaranteed by the constitution and in practice, but public propaganda by "non-Catholic religious communities" was prohibited. Italy, too, according to the Lateran

---

[147] See *Schema constitutionis de ecclesia*, 42: "God is the author of civil society and the source of all the good things that flow through this society to its members. Civil society ought, therefore, to honor and worship God. But in the present economy of salvation the manner is which God is to be worshiped can only be the manner of worship which he himself determined should be offered to him in the true Church of Christ. The state must therefore associate itself with the public worship offered by the Church, and do so not only in the persons of its citizens but also in the persons of those who have authority and represent the civil society" (*AS*, I/4, 67).

Concordats, was recognized as a Catholic state, but at the same time freedom of religion was accepted; the constitutional reality and practice were less strict than in Spain.[148]

To this line of thought in the area of ecumenism was added the public controversy over religious freedom as carried on especially in relation to the totalitarian states. Also to be taken into account was the intellectual climate of the Cold War in the preconciliar period and during the discussions at the Council.

What, then, was the heart of the solution and at the same time the innovative element in this document? The document does not take as its starting point either the freedom of conscience of the individual or the necessity that the state should issue legal regulations touching on questions of morality or religion. Nor does it start from the claim of the religions or the Church to proclaim the truth and the will of God. Instead, the fathers chose as the point of departure of their arguments the dignity of the human person as something that must be respected in principle by all institutions. But part of the very core of the dignity of the person is the religious relationship with God.

The first two words of the document, *Dignitatis humanae*, describe the content of the document. The text avoids an individualistic interpretation of freedom of conscience; it does not allow for public life a purely private conception of religion that is rooted in an agnostic theory of tolerance and puts all religions on the same level; it does not grant the state tutelage over religion, but neither can the religions or the Churches use state-sponsored coercion to preserve their public status. On the other hand, by starting with the dignity of the human person, there are numerous possible ways of relating the various factors so as to preserve freedom and respect for law and public morality.

The introduction starts from the growing awareness of the dignity of the human person, the demand for a responsible practice of freedom, and the corresponding call for a legal limitation of public power, most notably in dealing with "man's spiritual values, and especially with what concerns the free practice of religion in society" (no. 1). Set over against this demand and call is the profession of faith in the revelation of God in Jesus Christ and in the resultant mission. Explicit mention is made of the binding character of truth, "especially in what concerns God and his

---

[148] On the problem of religious freedom in Spain, see the excellent survey by Teodoro I. Jiménez Urresti, "Religious Freedom in a Catholic Country: The Case of Spain," *Concilium* 18 (1966), 91–108, with numerous bibliographical references.

Church, and [the obligation] to embrace it and hold on to it as [people] come to know it" (no. 1). The Council sees these two positions as connected by the fact that truth always and solely "in virtue of its own truth" penetrates the human intellect and binds consciences. From these two propositions it follows that religious freedom "has to do with freedom from coercion in civil society" (ibid.). This teaching "leaves intact the traditional Catholic teaching on the moral duty of individuals and societies towards the true religion and the one Church of Christ" (ibid.).

The basic position thus stated is discussed in two rather lengthy sections. The first section (chapter I) discusses the general foundation of religious freedom; the argument is based on the philosophy of law. Only in the second section (chapter II), which is titled "Religious Freedom in the Light of Revelation," does the argument become theological. The concluding section (no. 15) directs the reader's attention once more to the present historical situation and speaks of peaceful relations among people, relations that cannot exist without freedom of religion.

At the beginning of the general justification, religious freedom is defined as freedom from coercion in religious matters, a freedom grounded in the dignity of the human person. This human right to freedom can be known through reason as well as through revelation and must be anchored in the juridical order of society. The basing of religious freedom in the essence of the human person is based in turn on the orientation of the human being to truth and on the obligation to seek it. This fundamental exercise of what it is to be human "cannot be interfered with as long as the just requirements of public order are observed" (no. 2). But the search for truth must itself be in keeping with the dignity of the human person and its social nature. At this point the various forms of communication that are unconditionally necessary are named. Religious freedom extends to interior and exterior acts of a religious kind, whether private (or individual) or communal. The power of the state and the public order must serve human beings: "Therefore the civil authority... must recognize and look with favor on the religious life of the citizens" (no. 3).

In what follows, specific aspects of freedom are mentioned that are to be granted to religious communities: the right to the public profession of their faith, to a suitable celebration of worship, to establishments for instruction, to choose their own officials, and so on. In the eyes of the Council all these rights exist with the proviso that "the just requirements of public order are not violated" (no. 4). Special mention is made of the rights of families to order their domestic life and the rearing of their children in accordance with their religious convictions, which implies the acceptance of parents' choices in the schooling of their children. Because of its importance, the protection and advancement of religious freedom are the responsibility of citizens and social groups as well as of those who exercise authority in the state. Even when "in the circumstances of a particular people special civil recognition is given to one religious community in the constitutional organization of a State, the right of all citizens and religious communities to religious freedom must be recognized and respected by all" (no. 6).

To this general commitment to religious freedom and to its preservation and promotion there corresponds an obligation: "its use is subject to certain regulatory norms" (no. 7). Basic limits are set by the rights of others and by the common good. For this reason civil society has the right "to protect itself against possible abuses committed in the name of religious freedom" (no. 7); particular mention is made of inappropriate proselytism. In ending this first part of the decree, the fathers urge the protection of freedom against "a variety of pressures" but also insist that persons not evade legitimate authority under pretext of freedom but instead fulfill "the duty of obedience" (no. 8). Religious education will also contribute to proper understanding (no. 8).

The second, somewhat briefer, theological section of the document (chapter II) aims at persuading people within the Church, a task whose importance becomes clear when we recall the continuous opposition to the document by a minority initially rather considerable but melted down to a rather small circle at the end. At the beginning of this section, in no. 9, the text expressly admits that "revelation does not affirm in so many words the right to immunity from external coercion in religious matters." But at the same time it emphatically states that revelation "shows forth the dignity of the human person in all its fullness." From this it can been seen that there is a harmony between the doctrine of religious freedom and the Christian faith.

The argument begins with the constant tradition that human beings must, through faith, respond freely to the revelation of God. On this point the text contains references to sources from Lactantius down to the doctrinal utterances of Pius XII. The remarks that follow show how in his preaching and activity Jesus Christ respected human freedom and avoided any kind of coercion. On the cross he put the seal on this attitude: "He bore witness to the truth.... His kingdom does not make its claims by blows, but is established by bearing witness to and hearing the truth and grows by the love with which Christ, lifted up on the cross, draws men to himself" (no. 11). The apostles manifested the same outlook: "The Church, therefore, faithful to the truth of the Gospel, is following the path of Christ and the apostles when she recognizes the principle that religious liberty is in keeping with the dignity of man and divine revelation and gives it her support" (no. 12). In the course of time the spirit of the gospel "has contributed greatly" to making human beings aware of the dignity of their persons and coming to an understanding of the right of religious freedom.

It is only when religious freedom is practiced in civil society that "the Church enjoy[s] in law and in fact those stable conditions which give her the independence necessary for fulfilling her divine mission. Ecclesiastical authorities have been insistent in claiming this independence in society" (no. 13). Thus to stand up for religious freedom is not to weaken the Church and its place in history but rather to strengthen them.

The conclusion of the document takes the form of an exhortation that the members of the Church and those responsibile for the formation of their consciences should keep before their eyes the "sacred and certain teaching of the Church," bear witness to the truth of Jesus Christ, and approach "with love, prudence, and patience" those who do not know this truth (no. 14). The Council fathers then turn once again to the historical situation. They gratefully admit that freedom of religion has become a reality in many countries, but they do not remain silent about the deplorable fact that this is not true of all peoples. Yet in a world that is becoming ever more one reality, the effective defense of the right of religious freedom is an imperative requirement for the sake of peace and the peaceful co-existence of human beings.

The teaching in *Dignitatis humanae* is consonant with the theology of *Dei Verbum*, *Lumen gentium*, and *Gaudium et spes*. This harmony can be seen chiefly in the fact that the starting point for the theological line of argument in *Dei Verbum* and *Lumen gentium* is in each case God the Creator and Redeemer, who determines the unity and vocation of the human race. But this plan of salvation, which is attested and carried out by Jesus Christ, is at work in all human beings and is present in history and in the various circumstances of human life, as *Gaudium et spes* shows. Thus viewed, *Dignitatis humanae* is an essential expression of the theology of the Council.

In *Dignitatis humanae* the Council fathers substantially deepened and continued the teaching of John XXIII in *Pacem in terris*, the 1963 encyclical on human rights. In *Pacem in terris* an important place had already been given to human dignity as a point of reference; there, however, religious freedom had not been founded and developed by a detailed series of arguments but had simply been taught as a fact. By their profound examination of the doctrine of religious freedom, the fathers of the Council gave a theological dimension to the Universal Declaration of Human

Rights. From this point of view, *Dignitatis humanae* has doubtless played an important role in the process of evangelizing modern culture.

At the same time *Dignitatis humanae* unintentionally clarified the presuppositions for the dialogue among the religions of the modern world. Such dialogue urgently requires a public and legally validated freedom of religion that will allow it to proceed. By their religious justification of religious freedom, the Council fathers provided the other religions with a model of how they too, in light of their own roots, can approach the idea and conception of religious freedom without surrendering their own identity and mission.

There is one consequence that the Council fathers did not have in mind. The strict distinction between, on the one hand, the legal level with its element of compulsion, and on the other, the religious level, the freedom of faith, also has consequences for defining the relationship and distinction between institutional and juridical regulations within the Church, on the one hand, and questions of faith and the duty of believing, on the other. The history of the postconciliar period bears painful witness to the continued existence of this blind spot.

VI. A Half-hearted Reform: The Decree on the Ministry and Life of Priests

The Decree on the Ministry and Life of Priests was one of the Council's stepchildren. The history of its genesis permits us to understand the problems that showed up in the document. From the time the work on it began in the preconciliar commissions, the idea was always to deal with the discipline of the clergy and the Christian people without getting into the question of an appropriate theological description of the ministry of priests. Changing instructions on how to do the work were of little use in that kind of foundational thinking. During the third period, in October 1964, the schema that had been prepared was rejected by 1,199 negative votes against 930 positive ones.

When the new text was finally discussed during the final period, in October 1965, it drew numerous and far-reaching criticisms. Over 10,000 suggestions for changes were submitted. It is a minor miracle that a revision was done at all, and it is not surprising that the result was fragmentary from a theological point of view. The 2,390 yes votes, against 4 no votes, at the solemn final vote should not blind us to the unresolved problems in this text. While the text does offer an abundance of positive approaches and aspects, these are not thought through in depth and are offset by a lot of other statements that set a traditional sacerdotal image of the priest over against a theologically up-to-date understanding of ministry.

In order to reach a balanced judgment on this decree, we shall first present its overall flow, then explain its fundamental problems, sketch the ambivalent response given by the decree and its positive and negative statements, and, finally, deal with the perspectives that were opened up in the decree and that substantially predetermined postconciliar development.

A. An Overall Description of the Decree

Questions arise immediately about the directions implicit in the headings of the chapters. The first chapter is titled "The Priesthood in the Mission of the Church." This title implies that the chapter provides a theological foundation. The question arises, however, whether and to what extent the new emphases in ecclesiology are applied to the ministry of priests and made concrete there.

Under the heading "The Ministry of Priests," the second chapter brings together three different areas. The first part discusses the offices of priests, making use of the threefold distinction already used in *Lumen gentium*: preaching of the word, sanctifying, and shepherding. A second section, "Priests as Related to Others," discusses priests' relations with their bishops, their relations with other priests, their membership in the presbyterium, and finally, their relationship to the faithful. The third section concerns their distribution around the world, their being dispatched to other dioceses, and the promotion of vocations. The inner logic of the second chapter is not especially rigorous.

The third chapter bears the title "The Life of Priests." In a first section it speaks of the call of priests to perfection. The second section, "Special Spiritual Needs of the Priestly Life," has three numbers: the first speaks of hierarchical communion with the bishop and the obedience owed to him, the next discusses celibacy, and the third speaks of the use of possessions and the spirit of poverty. This whole second section proves to be, to some extent, a concrete application of the first section, which speaks of priests being called to perfection because through their ordination they are brought into a relationship with Christ. Their way to holiness consists in "exercising their functions sincerely and tirelessly in the Spirit of Christ" (no. 13). The conclusion speaks of the search for the will of God.

The third chapter, "The Menas of Support for Priestly Life," refers again to prayer, recommends the knowledge priests should cultivate, and affirms priests' right to a just remuneration and the establishment of diocesan institutions to provide for priests and to ensure that they receive appropriate social support. But after all this, one wonders how the bishops could harbor such an abstract and spiritualistic picture of the life of priests.

B. The Basic Problem

Ministry or office *(ministerium* or *munus)* signifies a relation. A relation requires at least two terms. Distinct from these is the foundation of the relation. The ministry of priests is the relation; *priests,* on the one side, and the *people of God,* on the other, are the terms; and the foundation is Jesus Christ, in whom the special ministry of priests has its basis. Now, when the Council dealt with the people of God, it undertook a series of definitions that play a part in the determination of the relation that is ministry. For one thing, the Council fathers discussed the situation of the Church in modern society, as *Gaudium et spes* eloquently testifies. For another, the Council fathers corrected the rejection of a universal priesthood for the people of God and the faithful that had been customary in Counter-Reformation theology; *Lumen gentium* speaks explicitly of this priesthood, as does *Sacrosanctum concilium,* the Constitution on the Sacred Liturgy. For a third thing, the Council fathers surmounted the conception of priestly ministry that had prevailed since the Middle Ages.

From the Middle Ages on, priestly ministry was seen as consisting essentially in the ability to consecrate the eucharistic body of the Lord. Because priests have this competence — that is, because priestly ministry was essentially ordered to the eucharistic sacrament as the other term of the relation — medieval theologians saw priests as having also a "power over the mystical body of Christ," that is, the body which is the Church. The Council's new definition of the people of God as the other term of the relation that is priestly ministry is connected fundamentally with a broader vision of priestly ministry as a whole: preaching and pastoral activity are now the primary tasks. These are connected directly with the people of God and not with the Eucharist. Only in this pastoral context is the sanctifying task of the priest determined. This new definition is expressed in both *Lumen gentium* and *Sacrosanctum concilium.* In *Lumen gentium,* however, it is applied primarily to bishops.

One would suppose that the Council fathers, conscious of the new emphases that they had approved in the earlier documents of Vatican II, where they took theological research as their guide, would give a corresponding picture in their presentation of the theological essence of the priestly ministry, and that from these new emphases they would draw conclusions for their conception of the priestly office. Such a supposition would be mistaken. Instead, the answer that the fathers gave to the various problems was ambivalent.

C. THE AMBIVALENT ANSWERS

The Introduction refers explicitly to the difficulty faced in working for the renewal of Church as intended by the Council. In that renewal priests had a very important role. There is also an explicit reference to "the vastly changed circumstances" that make the task of priests additionally difficult. The Council fathers thus seem to be aware of the problem. How then do they answer, in the first chapter, the question of the relationship of the priesthood to the mission of the Church? No. 2 speaks of the universal priesthood of the faithful and then — without reference to that priesthood — it singles out "official ministers" who hold "the sacred power of Order, that of offering sacrifice and forgiving sins, and [are] to exercise the priestly office publicly on behalf of men in the name of Christ."

In this context the offering of the sacrifice, as well as the forgiveness of sins, is the function of the priest. But the fact that (and the manner in which) this sacrifice, along with the forgiveness of sins, is also the business of the Church and of the people of God is not brought up here. In this context the point is made that priests "are able to act in the person of Christ the head" (no. 2). It is not said that they are at the same time representatives of the Church. How tangled up the different approaches seem to be — medieval-Counter-Reformational, patristic, and, at the same time, modern! Note the following sentences, in which the subject is the sacrifice that the people of God offers *and* the subject is the sacrifice of the sole mediator, Christ, which priests offer in an unbloody and sacramental form; note also the identity of these two realities. The text reads: "Through the ministry of priests the spiritual sacrifice of the faithful is completed in union with the sacrifice of Christ the only mediator, which in the Eucharist is offered through the priests' hands in the name of the whole Church in an unbloody and sacramental manner until the Lord himself comes" (no. 2).

This sentence gives the impression that the spiritual sacrifice that the faithful offer is something separate from the sacrifice of Christ. But the sacrifice of Jesus Christ is offered by priests in a sacramental manner and is thus the place where the spiritual sacrifice of the faithful acquires its full effectiveness and meaning. If, however, the sentence is thus interpreted, then one asks again what it means to say that priests celebrate the Eucharist "in the name of the whole Church."

There is a curious passage in no. 3. An allusion to Hebrews 5:1 describes the Old Testament priesthood, but, even though this priesthood was radically transcended by Christ, the statement is applied directly to priests and then to Jesus Christ as well. This passage shows how strongly an Old Testament, sacerdotal idea of the priest was still imprinted on the minds of the Council fathers. They could have reasoned differently than they did in order to stress the fact that priests must live among the people for whom they are responsible and must be familiar with the circumstances of their lives.

When the offices of priests are described in the second chapter (on the ministry of priests), the preaching of the word is given first place. Thereby, just as in *Lumen gentium,* the Constitution on the Sacred Liturgy, and the Decree on the Missionary Activity of the Church, the turn away from the medieval conception of ministry in the Church is completed. It is noticeable, however, that both in the remarks on the preaching of the word and in the discussion of the ministry of sanctification and the pastoral task, the priest alone appears as the subject of the action; there is no discussion of the active, mature involvement of the people of God. Thus it is said in connection with the pastoral ministry that the faithful are to be educated to a responsible maturity (no. 6); there is no acknowledgment that the priest may be dealing with mature and responsible Christians.

This one-sided attribution of all activity to the priests and the reduction of the laity to passive recipients are especially striking in the section on sanctification. "By Baptism priests introduce men into the People of God; by the sacrament of Penance they reconcile sinners with God and the Church; by the Anointing of the Sick they relieve those who are ill; and especially by the celebration of Mass they offer Christ's sacrifice sacramentally" (no. 5).

It is not surprising, therefore, that in the second section of the second chapter the hierarchical relation of the priests with the bishops comes first, then the relation of priests with other priests and the collegiality among them (no. 7). Only then is the relationship with the faithful addressed. This sequence presupposes an image of the priest as one who, through participation in the authority of the bishop, has the function of communicating the blessings of salvation to other human beings and, consequently, faces the essentially receptive people of God as the active giver of graces. Such a conception has no place for the idea that in modern society congregations and communities of believers might be able to nominate men for the priestly ministry and suggest them for ordination, and to do this with an awareness of their own responsibility for the kingdom of God and for the faith. It is not by chance that at the beginning of the relevant section the priests of the new covenant are called fathers and teachers of the people of God "by reason of the sacrament of Order" (no. 9).

The third section of this second chapter, which deals with the distribution of priests and priestly vocations, reflects the same underlying conception. Priests are responsible in their own way, along with the bishops, for the spread of the gospel throughout the world. They share in the mission of salvation "to the ends of the earth" (Acts 1:8). It is from this vantage point that the possibilities are tested for also sending priests to regions and local Churches that suffer from a lack of priests. As a result, the document does not ask the question of how the various local Churches are to assume responsibility for themselves and how they may be supported once they have grasped their responsibility for the spread and strengthening of the faith.

In just the same way priests are also made responsible for recruiting new priests. No. 11 reads: "The Shepherd and Bishop of our souls set up his Church in such a way that the people whom he chose and acquired with his blood should always and until the end of the world have its own priests, for fear Christians would ever be like sheep that have no shepherd." The duty of providing recruits is part of the priestly mission. The Church, the people of God, on the other hand, "ought to be made aware that it is their duty to cooperate in their various ways."

The third chapter, on the life of priests, deals in its first section with the call of priests to perfection. Ordination is seen as grounding this call. True enough, all Christians are called to perfection by their baptism, "but presbyters are bound by a special reason to acquire this perfection." The reason: "Since every presbyter in his own way assumes the person of Christ he is endowed with a special grace. By this grace, through his service of the people committed to his care and all the People of God, he is better able to pursue the perfection of Christ, whose place he takes" (no. 12).

The way to perfection is through the exercise of the functions entrusted to priests. In this context the offering of the eucharistic sacrifice is described as "their principal function." They ought to offer this sacramental sacrifice even if none of the faithful takes part in it. The old Code of Canon Law had prescribed that a priest ought not celebrate unless at least one other person was present to give the corresponding answers of the people; that precept is here removed. Erased at the same time, so to speak, is the institutional remembrance of the fact that the eucharistic sacrifice is fundamentally an act of the ecclesial community in which the priest presides.

In view of the multiplicity of their functions and the hectic pace of modern life, priests are advised to seek to unify their lives by aligning them with the will of God, just as Jesus Christ carried out the will of his Father. From this attitude priests will derive the strength to give their lives as the Good Shepherd did for his followers. "This pastoral charity flows especially from the eucharistic sacrifice. This sacrifice is therefore the center and root of the whole life of the presbyter, so that his priestly soul strives to make its own what is enacted on the altar of sacrifice" (no. 14).

If we look back over these explanations, we are struck both by their unity and by their restrictive character. They derive their unity from the fact that ordination fundamentally makes the priest a representative of Jesus Christ in a more powerful way than baptism makes Christians generally. From this it follows that the exercise of the duties of his office is at the same time his way to perfection and holiness. On the other hand, unless the priest involves himself in people's lives and interprets their conditions of life under the influence of the Spirit and by means of the discernment of spirits, how can he become aware of the duties of his office and find the way to a fulfilled life for himself? The remarks of the text on the call to perfection doubtless are inspired by a certain tendency to a Christomonism, which then finds expression in a narrow liturgico-sacramental spirituality.

In the second section, on the special spiritual requirements of priests, the same tendency appears. The first section spoke in general terms of the attitude of obedience of the priest, who must seek the will of the Father in all things. Here a positive note is struck: this attitude of obedience in no longer, as it was often in the past, to be identified simply with the execution of instructions from the pope, the priest's own bishop, and other superiors. The text speaks rather of "responsible and willing obedience" (no. 15).

In connection with continence for the sake of the kingdom of heaven, which Christ recommended, the point is made explicitly at the outset that celibacy is not required by the *essence* of priesthood. The tradition of the eastern Churches is expressly mentioned, and it is said that there are "excellent married priests"; in the Latin Church, however, celibacy is to be maintained. The reason:

> The whole mission of the priest is dedicated to the service of the new
> humanity which, Christ, the victor over death, raises up in the world through
> his Spirit and which is born "not of blood nor of the will of the flesh nor
> of the will of man, but of God" (Jn 1:13). By preserving virginity or
> celibacy for the sake of the kingdom of heaven presbyters are consecrated
> in a new and excellent way to Christ. They more readily cling to him with
> undivided heart and dedicate themselves more freely in him and through
> him to the service of God and of men (no. 16).

The Church is confident that if it prays fervently for such gifts, God
will grant, in sufficient measure, this call to celibacy. The whole Church
is exhorted, more urgently than in any other conciliar document, to pray
for "this precious gift of priestly celibacy." It is noteworthy that nothing
is said about the presuppositions of a celibate life, about its specific dangers, and the care to be taken for suitable forms of common life; neither
is anything said either about possible mistaken choices or failure or about
how the Church is to deal with such matters.

The next section is devoted to temporal goods. Priests are to use the
things of the world as though they used them not. Priests are encouraged to practice voluntary poverty, by which "they become more
clearly conformed to Christ and more ready to devote themselves to
their sacred ministry. For Christ being rich became poor for our sakes,
that through his poverty we might be rich" (no. 17). These remarks, like
the thoughts on the call of the priest to perfection, show how much a
traditional ascetical ideal remained determinative, one that largely overlooks the social dimension of the priest's ministry. The struggle for justice in modern society and the marginalization of broad sectors of the
population are overlooked, as are the corresponding virtues of solidarity, fraternal sharing, and participation in the sorrows and joys of
humanity.

The first part of the third section, which addresses aids for the priestly
life, warmly recommends various exercises of devotion: reading of scripture and celebration of the Eucharist, sacramental penance and examination of conscience, devotion to Mary, interior prayer, and eucharistic ado-
ration. It is odd that the Prayer of the Hours (the Breviary) is not
mentioned, nor is the Rosary. The next passage speaks of the further education needed in theology and the sciences, as well as in pastoral effectiveness. Finally, the last section of chapter III takes up the problem of
remuneration of the clergy. The establishment of suitable funds at the
diocesan or interdiocesan level is recommended, and the text speaks of
the need to develop social security provisions.

Only in the concluding exhortation is a very brief reference made to contemporary economic and social conditions and the changed habits of people. "Hence it is that the Church's ministers, and even sometimes the faithful, in the midst of this world feel themselves estranged from it and are anxiously seeking suitable methods and words by which they may be able to communicate with it. The new obstacles opposing the faith, the apparent fruitlessness of the work done, the bitter loneliness they experience — these can bring for priests the danger of a feeling of frustration" (no. 22). With an eye to these real difficulties the decree ends with words of comfort and encouragement.

D. The Perspectives of *Presbyterorum ordinis*

Because of its intrinsic limitations, the Decree on the Ministry and Life of Priests has not promoted a new and distinctive image of this important ministry in the Church. So it is not really surprising that immediately after the Council the question of the proper description of the presbyteral ministry was placed on the agenda once again and that there were considerable debates among the clergy. Polls conducted at the time showed a sizable gulf between the older clergy and the younger clergy; the two groups had very different conceptions of the presbyteral ministry. Against this background, the decree must be viewed as an attempt by the Council to give priests stability and to establish the traditional image of the priests, supplemented by a few new emphases.

VII. The Solemn Ceremonies at the Close of the Council

On November 9, 1965, Paul VI wrote a letter to Cardinal Tisserant, the first among the presidents of the Council, in order to let him know the dates for the closing solemnities. In the letter's opening sentence Paul VI emphasized that the presidents of the Council had kept him informed about the work of the Council as it approached completion and had asked him "to decide on the day and the solemn rites for the ending of the ecumenical Council."[149] Referring back to Vatican Council I, which had opened on December 8, 1869, Paul VI decided on the Feast of the Immaculate Conception of Mary as the final day of Vatican Council II.

---

[149] *AS* IV/6, 190.

By doing so, he emphasized once again (as John XXIII had done by having the opening solemnities of the Council take place on the Feast of the
Maternity of Mary in 1962) that the Council had been commended to the
special protection of Mary. At the same time, Paul VI let it be known that
the last public session of the Council would be held on December 7; on
that day solemn final approval would be given to the schemas still being
revised.

This solemn conclusion was enriched by a series of other gestures.
On December 4 there was an ecumenical liturgy of the Word, celebrated
with the observers at the Council in the Basilica of St. Paul's Outside the
Walls. On December 6 the participants in the Council received as a
memento a gold ring that the Pope had had made. The participants were
given a certificate for their attendance at the Council, and the mayor of
the city of Rome had a silver commemorative coin struck for them. Also
on December 6 the decree on the reorganization of the Curia was given
to the bishops. Then, on December 7, as Paul VI had planned, the final
solemn votes were cast and the documents on religious freedom, the missions, the ministry and life of priests, and on the Church in the modern
world were promulgated. Before the closing mass, which the Pope con-
celebrated with twenty-four Council fathers, the Roman Catholic Church
and the Orthodox Church of Constantinople mutually lifted the excommunications of 1054. And last, on December 8, the great closing liturgy
was celebrated in St. Peter's Square.

This entire solemn conclusion of the Council was not only of historical but also of theological interest. These gestures and rites, addresses
and homilies, showed what the Council, convoked under the call for
aggiornamento, had already changed in the Church. But they also showed
what limits it had not transcended and what divergent tendencies it had
left alive in the Church.

A. THE ECUMENICAL LITURGY OF THE WORD, DECEMBER 4, 1965

The liturgy of the Word in the spacious hall of the Basilica of St. Paul's
Outside the Walls was marked by a special atmosphere. While the observers
from the other Churches, whose number was 103 at the end of the Council, had indeed attended the Council's masses and prayers in St. Peter's,
they now played an immediate role in the celebration of this liturgy of the
Word. Paul VI presided, and the carefully chosen lessons were read by a
French Catholic, an American Methodist, and a Greek Orthodox Christian.

The celebration began with Psalm 27: A distressed petitioner, who relies on the Lord as his light, cries: "One thing alone I ask of the Lord, for this I long: To dwell in the house of the Lord all the days of my life." And the concluding verses read: "Lord, show me your way, lead me on level ground, in spite of my foes!... Wait for the Lord and be strong, take courage and wait for the Lord." The first reading, from 1 Chronicles 29:10–18, contains David's great prayer of thanksgiving for the numerous gifts made for the building of the Temple in Jerusalem. The second reading, from Romans 15:1–6, contains the exhortation to Christians that they not live for themselves but rather "take heed for your neighbors in order to do good for them and build them up." Christ, after all, did not live for himself. The text ends with the prayer for that "harmony" that befits those in Christ Jesus, "so that together you may with one voice glorify the God and Father of our Lord Jesus Christ." Finally, the reading from the gospel was the beginning of the Sermon on the Mount according to Matthew, that is, the Beatitudes.

The opening words of Paul VI's homily spoke of the atmosphere that permeated this praying community:

> Gentlemen, dear observers, or let me rather address you by the name that has taken on a vitality during these four years of the ecumenical Council: Brothers! Brothers and friends in Christ! The Council is ending and we will be saying good-bye to one another. At this moment of farewell we would like to make ourselves the interpreter of the reverend fathers of the Council who surround us here this evening in order that we may pray with you and say our farewells to you. Each of you will begin his journey back home, and we shall be alone. Allow me to confide my inner feeling: Your departure creates a *solitudo* around us that we did not know before the Council and that now saddens us. We would like to see you with us always![150]

The Pope was speaking of an experience that he, like most of the Council fathers as well as most of the observers, had had for the first time. Through the work done in common, the personal meetings, and the liturgies celebrated together there had arisen a closeness, an awareness, that had not existed before the Council.

After introductory thanks to the observers and guests, Paul VI gave a short appraisal of the four-year-long work. He noted the deeper understanding of the problems of ecumenism and of the task of working for unity but also the promising impulses given to an attainment of unity. He spoke of the discovery of the Christian treasures existing in the various

---

[150] *AS* IV/7, 624; for an English translation, see *Council Daybook, Session 4* (Washington, 1966), 353–54.

communities of the world and referred to doctrinal structures, mentalities, and forms of devotion. He referred to the admission of faults and short-comings and the request for forgiveness, the rejection of polemics and prejudices. He mentioned the great abundance of meetings that had taken place, for the first time in hundreds of years, and in particular the meeting with Patriarch Athanegoras.

Finally, he described the Council itself as a movement in the direction of still divided brothers and sisters, a movement not only marked by respect and spiritual joy over the community achieved but one that had found expression in doctrinal and disciplinary formulations. In this connection Paul VI begged the observers once again not to accuse the Catholic Church of pride or insensitivity because it held so zealously to the legacy of faith: "And do not accuse us of having betrayed or deformed this trust if, during the course of its age-old, scrupulous and loving meditation, the Church has uncovered treasures of truth and life which it would be a breach of faith to renounce." At the end of his address the Pope told a story about Russian philosopher Vladimir Soloviev. After litany-like petitions and the Our Father recited together, the Pope gave a blessing and the liturgy ended with the communal singing of the Magnificat.

Moving though the service was for its participants, it must be realized that it was not in the formal sense an ecumenical liturgy of the Word. The Pope did not preside over it with anyone else. Only in the readings did two members of other Churches play a part. It is striking that in his address Paul VI did not say a word about the texts read from the Old and New Testaments and apply them to the present situation. While in the official texts the address was described as a homily, it had nothing to do with that genre. The fact that the Church stands under the word of God, as was taught in *Dei Verbum*, did not emerge at all in this liturgy with the representatives of other Churches. The future work to be done was described thus: "There must be a thorough study of the great problem of the reincorporation into the unity of the visible Church of all who have the happiness and the responsibility of calling themselves Christians." This was a statement that certainly looked to the future but at the same time clearly signaled the obstacles in the way of conversion and a return to unity.

At the concluding reception in the Benedictine Monastery of St. Paul's, the Pope had Cardinal Bea present each of the observers to him; to each he gave a small bronze clock as a memento of the Council, along with a certificate of the person's participation in the Council. At the reception the spokesman for the delegates, observers, and guests expressed their experience in a way as positive as the Pope's had been:

> Never once in the four years have we felt any resentment at our presence. On the contrary, we have always been led to suppose that our presence has, in more ways than one, contributed to the success of the Council in the great task of reform to which it has set its hand. We believe that the days of mutual fear, rigid exclusiveness, and arrogant self-sufficiency on either side are passing away.... I would like you, dear Holy Father, to think of us as your friends — and indeed as your messengers — as we go our respective ways.[151]

B. THE LAST GENERAL CONGREGATION, DECEMBER 6, 1965

When the fathers of the Council came together on December 6 for the last general congregation, a farewell gift from Paul VI awaited them. But before the gold rings and the certificates were distributed, Secretary General Felici first made known the results of the vote on the pastoral constitution. Now that the preceding votes on the sections of the document had in every case yielded the necessary majorities, the vote on the document in its entirety was undertaken.

After this vote the texts were distributed for the concelebration at the public meeting of the Council on December 7, as were the already approved Constitution on Revelation, the Decree on the Apostolate of the Laity, and the text of the Decree on the Ministry and Life of Priests, which still had to be approved on December 7.

Then, with a witty reference to the feast of St. Nicholas, Felici read the certificate that Paul VI had composed for the distribution of the gold rings to the Council participants. According to this text, the rings were an expression of "the greatest good will" for the bishops who, together with the Pope, had discussed "how the luster and zeal of the Church of Christ" could be renewed. Along with these gifts the Pope also gave the bishops the apostolic blessing and asked that "the instructions and exhortations" of the Council "be carried out and observed" by the bishops and "your faithful."[152]

After the certificate the General Secretary promulgated Paul VI's Bull *Mirificus eventus,* announcing a Jubilee.[153] The Pope gave as the

---

[151] Cited from Wiltgen, 282–83.
[152] *AS* IV/7, 634.
[153] Ibid., 635–40; for an English translation, see *Council Daybook, Session 4*, 357–59.

purpose of this Jubilee, with its announcement of a plenary indulgence, that the entire Church might give thanks to God for the gifts of the Council, might help the Council to bear fruit, and might give the faithful the opportunity for a "renewal... in the lives of individuals, and in domestic, public, and social" life. With the help of such jubilees human beings turn away "from earthly and transient things to those that are eternal."

The bull made very clear how Paul VI conceived of the reception of the Council: the stress was entirely on personal conversions and the deepening of religious life through the following of Christ, not on structural reforms. This understanding of the reception flowed, in the view of Paul VI, from the conciliar event itself. The Council (he thought) was a council on the Church. The Church "had looked into itself," meditated on its own mystery, and thereby taught itself and called upon itself to grasp more fully the doctrine on its own origin, its own nature, and its own mission, even though all this was previously known. In this context Paul VI cited a sentence from his first encyclical, *Ecclesiam suam*.[154] Because of this ecclesial theme of the Council, the Pope set down as conditions for a Jubilee indulgence that during the period from January 1 to May 21, 1966, in addition to penance and the reception of the Eucharist, recipients must hear at least three instructions, or sermons in the style of a popular mission, on the Church. The faithful should gather around their bishops in the cathedrals in order to learn from them the directives developed by the Council.

It is noteworthy that nothing was said in this bull about John XXIII's intention to contribute to a renewal and *aggiornamento* of the Church; for example, the need to hold synods in order to carry out the intentions of the Council regarding the renewal of the Church.

Following upon the reading of the bull of Jubilee, Secretary Felici said farewell with a short Latin poem. The commemorative medals struck by the City of Rome had already been distributed.

After some announcements regarding the farewell reception of the Pope for the parish priests who had been invited to the Council, for the auditors, the Council fathers' drivers in Rome, and the experts, Cardinal Suenens spoke in the name of the moderators to express their thanks for the successful end of the Council. In addition to thanking God and the Pope, he expressly mentioned the members of the Council of Presidents, the

---

[154] *AAS* 56 (1964), 611.

General Secretariat, the Council fathers, the speakers and members of the commissions, and the advisers. Special thanks went to the observers and to the auditors as representatives of the people of God. With no less heartfelt gratitude he mentioned the many collaborators whose work had made the Council possible, from the ushers and the singers who had helped to structure the liturgy, to the printers at the Vatican press, and finally to the writers of the daily reports about the Council that were given to the public. The last general congregation ended with applause for the moderators.

Likewise on December 6 *L'Osservatore Romano* published the Motu Proprio *Integrae servandae* of Paul VI, on the start of the reform of the Curia.[155] The first step in the reform was the issuing of new norms for the Holy Office. The Pope began with a history of the Holy Office and its preeminence among the curial institutions. The name was changed to Congregation for the Doctrine of the Faith. The congregation's function was to "protect the teaching on faith and morals throughout the entire Catholic world." The pope would be the head of this congregation, which would be directed by a cardinal secretary.

The congregation's most important task would be "to investigate new teachings and new opinions... and to promote studies of these matters and congresses of scholars." The congregation was to reject new doctrines opposed to the principles of the faith, and to do so "after hearing the bishops of the region in question, if they had interest in the matter." As for the condemnation of books, it was explicitly established that authors should be given the opportunity to defend themselves, even in writing, and that the competent local bishop be informed in advance. Regarding offenses against the faith, it was expressly determined that the norms governing legal trials were to be followed. In addition, the congregation was to remain in close contact with the Pontifical Biblical Commission. Further, an advisory committee was established, to be made up of university professors.

Governing the individual provisions was the principle, "Since love casts out fear (1 Jn 4:18), the faith that is to be protected will be better served by an institution for the promotion of doctrine, one from which preachers of the gospel will draw new energies, while errors will be corrected and those in error will gently be called back to reason."[156] The document, especially its intention, sounded promising.

---

[155] See *AAS* 57 (1965), 952–55; for an English translation, see *Council Daybook, Session 4*, 354–55.
[156] Ibid., 953.

C. The Public Session, December 7, 1965

The public session on December 7 began around 9:00 a.m. with the lengthy procession of the Pope, the cardinals, and the twenty-four concelebrants. All sang the antiphon "You are Peter, and on this rock I will build my Church," and the choir intoned Psalm 131 (132). After the Pope solemnly enthroned the book of the gospels, the gesture of obedience was made by two representatives from each of the various groups making up the hierarchy; this was accompanied by the solemn chant of the choir, "This is my commandment, that you love one another." The conciliar prayer, "Adsumus, Domine," was recited for the last time, and the hymn to the Holy Spirit, "Come, Creator Spirit," was sung alternately by congregation and choir.

General Secretary Felici then read the opening words of the following four conciliar documents: the Declarations on Religious Freedom, the Decrees on the Missionary Activity of the Church and on the Ministry and Life of Priests; and the Pastoral Constitution on the Church in the Modern World. A vote was taken for the final time on all these documents. While the Council fathers were filling out their ballots, the Sistine Choir sang. The vote on the pastoral constitution was the last (the 544th) of the Council.

After this, Felici, speaking on behalf of the fathers, thanked the Pope for his gift of the gold rings which the General Secretary took as a sign that the Council had been nothing else than "a great manifestation of love." The prolonged applause of the Council fathers confirmed this expression of gratitude.

Next, Bishop Willebrands, secretary of the Secretariat for Christian Unity, went to the ambo to read the Joint Declaration of Paul VI and Patriarch Athenagoras. This was one of the most far-reaching events in the four-year history of the Council.[157] In the opening sentences Paul VI and Athenagoras recalled their meeting in Jerusalem and their reciprocal commitment to seek unity. One of the most important obstacles raised was the excommunication, in 1054, of Patriarch Michael Cerularius by Cardinal Humbert, the envoy of the Bishop of Rome, and the excommunication of this delegate and his entourage by the Patriarch. It was emphasized that those excommunications were directed at particular persons

---

[157] Down to the last days it was uncertain whether the declaration would materialize. Only on November 21, 1965, did the Roman and Constantinopolitan commission of experts begin to work on the text in Constantinople. Just before the proclamation a Roman emissary, Father Duprey, was again sent to Constantinople to seek clarification. For the details, see Caprile, 5:506–9; for an English translation, see *Council Daybook, Session 4*, 286.

and not against the Churches, that they did not aim at a break in ecclesial communion, and that they were marked "by excesses."

Paul VI and Athenagoras jointly declared that they "regret the wounding words, the unjustified accusations, and the reprehensible behavior which marked and accompanied the sad events of that period"; that they "regret the sentences of excommunication" and "lift the sentences, remove them from the midst of the Church, and consign them to oblivion." Finally, both men lamented "the distressing incidents that preceded or followed upon the excommunications and that, under the influence of various factors, among them chiefly mutual misunderstanding and mistrust, led ultimately to a complete break of ecclesial communion."[158] Paul VI and Athenagoras explained that this act of theirs did not automatically do away with "the old and new conflicts." But in the spirit of mutual trust, respect, and love the dialogue ought to continue and lead ultimately to a full communion in faith, "fraternal harmony, and the sacraments."

After the reading of this text Bishop Willebrands and Meliton, Metropolitan of Heliopolis, exchanged the kiss of peace. At about the same time and during the Liturgy of St. John Chrysostom in the patriarchal basilica of Constantinople, the same text was read in the presence of Patriarch Athenagoras I and seven delegates of the Pope, led by Cardinal Shehan, Archbishop of Baltimore. When the tumultuous cheering in St. Peter's Basilica had died down, Paul VI began the celebration of mass. After the solemn proclamation of the gospel by one of the concelebrating cardinals, the Pope gave a more than half-hour-long address on the question, What has been the religious significance of our Council? This carefully organized address, which was delivered with great earnestness, deserves closer analysis and reflection.[159]

Paul VI took as his starting point the experience of this great, busy Council, which had left behind many open questions, not because of exhaustion but in order that the Pope and the bishops might work on them in the future with full energy. He spoke of the experience of the bishops, who throughout those four years had been guided by the same faith and the same love. He spoke of their communion in prayer, their discipline, their joyous time together. The Council, he said, had clarified many elements in the legacy of belief that Christ had entrusted to the Church; it had "set forth" that legacy "in its integrity and in an orderly way."[160]

---

[158] *AS* IV/7, 653.
[159] For an English translation, see *Council Daybook, Session 4*, 359–62.
[160] *AS* IV, 655.

But Paul VI did not want to speak about what the Council had been and what it had achieved, for at this solemn time of farewell he could not adequately praise the merits of that great event. He preferred to concentrate on the *religious meaning* "of our Council." By "religious meaning" he understood the union with God for the sake of which the Church exists and which makes intelligible its faith, hope, and love and what it is and does.

His remarks were structured by the question, "Are we able to declare that we have given praise to God, sought the knowledge and love of him, made progress in the effort to contemplate him, in zeal to celebrate him, and in the art of proclaiming him to humanity that looks to us as shepherds and teachers of the ways of God?"[161] Two objections attach to the answering of this question and seem to oppose a positive answer. First, he said, "some may say that the Council spent its time less in dealing with questions about God than, above all, in a consideration of the Church, its nature, its structure, its ecumenical task, and its apostolic and missionary works." And, second, did not the Council concern itself, above all else, with "exploring the world of our time"?

The longest part of the address was devoted to answering the second question. The main line of thought was summed up in a thesis: "It must be truthfully asserted that the Catholic religion and human life are connected in a friendly alliance and that both strive for the human good. For the Catholic Church exists for the human race; it is as it were the life of the human race." In this context Paul VI cited a saying of St. Catherine of Siena: "In your nature, eternal God, I recognize my nature."[162] The Council thus opened to contemporary humanity the way leading upward to "liberation and consolation."[163]

The first question, about whether God was praised and honored by the Council and its works, gave Paul VI an opportunity to describe the age in which the Council took place. It was, in his view, an age of turning away from God and turning to mastery of the world; in this phenomenon, forgetfulness of God became habitual and human beings claimed for themselves a freedom no longer subject to any law that transcended human circumstances. Paul VI went on to speak of secularism as the principle that gave present-day society its order. The harshest verdict was passed on human reason: "It is also an age in which human reason

---

[161] Ibid.
[162] Ibid., 661.
[163] Ibid., 662.

reached the point of maintaining what is utterly absurd and robs men of every hope."[164] Finally, Paul VI blamed this age because it had thrown the religions of the peoples into confusion.

In contrast, the Council had set forth a theocentric and theological conception of human nature and the world and had thereby called people to turn to what the spirit of the age regarded as alien and strange, or even absurd, so that they might finally realize that "God is truthful; he really exists, he lives; he is a person, he is provident, he is filled with infinite goodness, not only in himself but also, in a supreme fashion, toward us. He is our creator, our truth, our happiness."[165] How did Paul VI answer the objection that the Council fathers occupied themselves not primarily with God and questions about God but with the Church? If the Church turned to her inmost self, it was not, he said, for the sake of self-knowledge but in order better to understand the word of Christ, which is at work within it through the Holy Spirit and to enter into this mystery more deeply. This was especially true of the conciliar documents on divine revelation, the liturgy, the Church, priests, religious, and the laity.

But what of the fact that the Church busied itself so extensively with "the world of our age"? The answer was that the Church "in previous times, in the past, and, above all, in the present century was absent and cut off from human culture."[166] The Council had effectively regained for the Church the inner attitude of learning about the human society to which it goes out, of rightly appraising it, and of serving it through the preaching of the gospel. Its turning to the world was not, therefore, a concession to the spirit of the age at the cost of fidelity to the gospel handed down; rather, this openness to the world and this turning to humanity were the result of the commission from Jesus Christ and of the words of the apostles.

In this context the Pope once against described contemporary man, this time as a Janus-like figure, who is to be viewed, on the one hand, with a holy reserve "because of the innocence of his childhood and the mystery of his poverty... and, on the other hand, as a human being burdened with atrocious acts."[167] The Council, which had thus turned to the world and the human beings of our time, was characterized as a great encounter, the encounter of two religions: "the religion, that is, the worship of the

---

[164] Ibid., 656.
[165] Ibid.
[166] Ibid., 657.
[167] Ibid., 658.

God, who willed to become man, and the religion — for that is what it must be regarded as being — that is, the worship of man, who wants to become God."[168] But the two religions did not come into conflict, for the Council took as its norm the story of the Good Samaritan. The synod turned to humanity with great love; it looked into the good face of humankind rather than into its evil face; it rejected errors and provided the means of salvation. At the same time, the Council strengthened and accepted what is good. The Pope also referred to the language of the liturgy and the incorporation into the Church of things dear to contemporary humanity, the latter perhaps an allusion to freedom of religion.

In concluding, the Pope defended the fact that at this Council the Church had not exercised its teaching office through dogmatic definitions but had directly addressed contemporary humanity and, though exercising doctrinal authority, had chosen the easy, friendly manner of speech proper to pastoral love, "for it wanted to be heard and understood by men." The whole intention of the fathers' work had been to show the Church as "the servant of the human race." The Church acted out of pastoral zeal and was not led astray by the spirit of the age.

With this defense against criticism from within the Church, the Pope combined an invitation to all human beings to acknowledge this turning of the Church to them: Christian faith and Christian love belong together. The Pope ended his address with a question: "In the last analysis, has not the Council taught us, in a simple, new, and solemn manner, to love human beings in order that we may love God? We say 'love human beings' not as a means to an end, but rather as the first goal, so to speak, through which we attain to the final goal, which transcends all things human." In this sense the Council had to do entirely with God and his glorification, with love of God.

This overview and interpretation of the Council was impressive. The Council was described as a service to God (a *liturgy*) that took the form of a new openness to the world and the service of humanity. It is striking that Paul VI did not mention any historical guilt of the Church; the word *conversion* did not occur. Nor was anything said about institutional changes in the Church or about an evolution of doctrine. The Church and the Council fathers were presented as those who stood in the light of God and turned to the wounded world and to a humanity entangled in sin, weakness, and many forms of darkness.

---

[168] Ibid.

The description of the Council as a dialogue with present-day men and women and with present-day situations seems rather naive when we reflect more closely on the manner in which the Council and its commissions did their work. It is also noteworthy that this concluding address said not a word about the ecumenical dialogue and the dialogue with the Old Testament people of God and the other religions. In this address, the saying that the community of believers is *in* the world but not *of* this world seems to have been turned into another saying: the Church stands *over and against* the world, is *turned to* the world.

After the Pope's address the profession of faith was sung by all. At the Preparation of the Gifts the Sistine Choir sang again. After the Eucharistic Prayer and the Our Father recited by all, the Pope gave communion to the lay auditors. This final celebration of the Eucharist in the Council hall ended with the solemn blessing.

After the mass-vestments had been set aside, Cardinal Bea, as president of the Secretariat for Christian Unity, exchanged the greeting of peace with Metropolitan Meliton, the delegate of Patriarch Athenagoras. General Secretary Felici announced the results of the final votes on the four conciliar documents,[169] and Paul VI gave his approval and solemnly proclaimed them. Then the Apostolic Letter *Ambulate in dilectione* was read; this was the document in which Paul VI lifted the excommunication of 1054. In its formulation this document made extensive use of the language of the declaration that had been composed jointly by Rome and Constantinople. After the reading of this letter the Pope and the Metropolitan embraced, and again there was loud applause.

The meeting ended with the prayer for the forgiveness of those sins that had been committed during the celebration of this Council. After the Our Father had been recited by all, Paul VI spoke the words of absolution, and all exchanged the kiss of peace. The Pope then intoned the *Te Deum*, the Book of the Gospels that had been enthroned at the beginning of the meeting was put away, and the great exodus began.

Father Semmelroth wrote: "The entire meeting today was a very splendid final conciliar celebration. At the end came the absolution of the

---

[169] The results were as follows: Declaration on Religious Freedom: 2,386 votes, 2,308 yes votes, 70 no votes, 8 invalid; Decree on the Missionary Activity of the Church: 2,399 votes, 2,394 yes votes, 5 no votes; Decree on the Ministry and Life of Priests: 2,394 votes, 2,390 yes votes, 4 no votes; Pastoral Constitution on the Church in the Modern World: 2,391 votes, 2,309 yes votes, 75 no votes, 7 invalid.

Council; one almost wished that this was indeed the ending. But tomorrow there is to be a concluding celebration in St. Peter's Square; costly stands and the papal throne have been set up."[170]

D. THE CONCLUDING CELEBRATION IN ST. PETER'S SQUARE, DECEMBER 8, 1965

On this chilly but cheerful December morning St. Peter's Square quickly filled with hundreds of thousands of the faithful. Beginning at 9:00 a.m., the bishops streamed into St. Peter's Basilica in order to don their vestments. The cardinals assembled in the Chapel of the Trinity and awaited the Pope there. When Paul VI entered the basilica, shortly before 10:30 a.m., the Council fathers began their lengthy procession through the main door into St. Peter's Square, to the main steps of the basilica. On both sides were the stands for the bishops; in the middle stood the massive altar and the papal throne. The bells of Rome rang out as the Pope was carried on the *sedia gestatoria* across the square to the altar. The Sistine Choir sang *Tu es Petrus* and, alternately with all the faithful, the hymn *Ave, Maris Stella* in honor of Mary, whose Immaculate Conception was being celebrated.

After a short pause for recollection, the Pope began with the prayers at the foot of the altar. None of the moderators or members of the Council of Presidents stood beside him. The Pope was accompanied instead by his almoner and the prefect of the sacristy, both members of the Curia. The epistle and the gospel were also read by Roman members of the Curia: an auditor of the Rota and a Vatican master of ceremonies. Thus a solemn papal mass, without concelebration by the Council fathers, marked the end of the Council.

After the gospel the Pope greeted those present, those following the celebration on radio or television, and finally all of humanity. He explained that he would restrict himself to this greeting because at the end of this mass messages were to be read that the ecumenical Council was addressing to groups of persons who represented, as it were, the manifold character of human life. After that, the decree ending the Council would be read.

The Pope's greeting, which, given its character, would have been expected at the beginning of the mass rather than after the gospel, was

---

[170] *TSemmelroth*, December 7, 1965.

marked by a sense of intense urgency. In this greeting the Pope endeavored to express the openness and movement of the Church to humanity and the solidarity of the Church with all, even those who do not understand the Church and regard it as alien to them:

> As the sound of bells leaps through the air and reaches each and every person with waves of sound, so our greeting reaches out to each and all at this moment — to those who accept the greeting and to those who do not. It penetrates the ear of every human being. From this center of Catholicism in Rome no one is unreachable in principle. In principle all human beings can and must be reached from here. In the eyes of the Catholic Church no one is a stranger, no one is excluded, no one is far away. Every person to whom our greeting is addressed is called and invited, is even, in a certain sense, present. The loving heart can say: "Every beloved is present!" And we, especially at this moment, and in virtue of our universal pastoral and apostolic commission, we love all, all![171]

Paul VI then greeted those of the faithful who were participating in the celebration from afar. He sent his greeting to the suffering and especially to those bishops who were prevented from taking part in the Council; he had in mind the silent and humiliated Church. Finally, he spoke explicitly once again of those "who do not know us. You who do not understand us. You who do not believe that we are useful and necessary to you, that we are your friends. And you also who, perhaps in good faith, fight against us, to all of you I send sincere, respectful, and hopeful greetings, greetings which — believe me! — are full of esteem and love this day!"[172]

Paul VI then interpreted these greetings. They are greetings "not of farewell which separates, but of friendship which remains and which... wishes to be born." They are greetings that call upon the invisible Lord himself to be present, so that "a spark of divine charity" may rise and "enkindle the principles, doctrines and proposals which the Council has organized and which, thus inflamed by charity, may really produce in the Church and in the world that renewal of thoughts, activities, conduct, moral force and hope and joy which was the very scope of the Council." Is this greeting a dream, mere poetry, the Pope asked. "No," he replied," this greeting is ideal, but not unreal." And, as proof, the Pope turned his gaze to Mary, the Mother of Christ: "Can our Council and our farewell greetings end without our turning our gaze to this humble woman who is our sister and at the same time our heavenly Mother and Queen, a clear

---

[171] AS IV/7, 869; for an English translation, see Council Daybook, Session 4, 362–63.
[172] Ibid.

and holy mirror of infinite beauty? In her the drama of humanity, the conflict between an ideal conception of life and reality as it is has found its resolution. Is not the beauty of this immaculate virgin an inspiring model? A source of encouragement and hope?"[173]

This short address was followed by the petitions in Latin and Greek and then in a series of modern languages. At the preparation of the gifts Cardinal Tisserant announced that on the occasion of the closing of the Council Paul VI was donating money for the completion of a hospital in Bethlehem, for the work of the Little Brothers of Jesus (founded by Charles de Foucauld) in Buenos Aires, for a catechetical project, and for an agricultural school in southern India; money was available, in addition, for a foundation of Caritas in Pakistan and Cambodia. After the Eucharistic Prayer and the Our Father, the Pope gave communion to some children from various continents. The mass ended with a solemn blessing.

This eucharistic celebration was followed by some important actions. The Pope blessed the cornerstone of a church titled Mary, Mother of the Church; this was to remind Rome of the Council. In this context we must remind the reader that in connection with the discussion of the constitution *Lumen gentium* on the Church, the majority of the Council fathers had voted against including this title in the text, because it blurred the place of Jesus Christ as sole mediator of salvation. A somewhat large group of bishops, especially from Spain and Poland, had spoken in favor of the title. Then, in his address at the final session of the third period of the Council, Paul VI had proclaimed this title. This was evidently an effort to accommodate the minority that had been defeated. That at this final solemn meeting he returned once again to this controversy and dedicated the cornerstone of the church caused a lot of people to shake their heads.

The formal ending of the celebration in St. Peter's Square consisted of the reading of messages to those in government, scientists, artists, women, workers, the poor, the sick and all the suffering, and the young. These messages were introduced by Paul VI himself, and they claimed to speak in the name of the Council. In his prefatory remarks Paul VI said: "Before it breaks up, the Council desires to exercise its prophetic function and to express its 'good news' for the world in short messages and in language easily understood by all." The first message, addressed to rulers, began with the words, "In this solemn moment, we, the fathers of the twenty-first ecumenical council of the Catholic Church, address...."[174]

---

[173] Ibid., 871.
[174] Ibid.; for an English translation, see *Council Daybook, Session 4*, 363–66.

These messages were neither composed nor approved by the Council. The Pope and his collaborators were responsible for them. It was obvious that Jacques Maritain had collaborated at least in the message to the representatives of science and perhaps in others. Only the day before had the texts been given to the cardinals who were to read the messages. The claim that the Council was speaking in them was a pretense.

Despite all the legitimate emphasis that was in keeping with the concluding celebration of the Council, both the introduction of Paul VI and the language of the messages themselves occasionally made an unpleasant and embarrassing impression. Why did the language have this effect? In these messages Paul VI addressed all in each case: all rulers, whether Christians or atheists, Muslims or Buddhists. He addressed all the scientists of the world, all the artists, workers, women, and the young. He placed each one in this very heterogeneous group of addressees in direct relationship to Jesus Christ and asked for recognition of Christ and of his message. Addressing rulers he said: "It is incumbent on you to promote order and peace among men here on earth. But do not forget: It is God, the living and true God, who is the father of humankind. And it is Jesus Christ, his eternal Son, who came to tell and teach us that we are all brothers and sisters. He is the great restorer of order and peace on earth, for it is he who guides the human race."[175]

One instinctively asks what such statements would say to a Muslim head of state or a communist dictator. Respect was not shown here for the rules for persuading others of the faith as set forth in the Decree on the Missionary Activity of the Church, or even the rules for dialogue with our contemporaries, as discernible in, for example, schema XIII.

The message to the scientists was essentially that they should devote themselves with all their energies to the search for truth and then to unite through faith with the Church as the seeker of truth; in very much the same way, artists were called to an alliance with the Church. The message to workers spoke of the Church and its connection with the working class. Paul VI stressed the point that the Church is a friend of the working class and that the hour had now struck for a reconciliation between the two. One instinctively asks how such language makes sense in light of what is said about the people of God in the *Lumen gentium*.

The message to the poor, the sick, and the suffering struck a more realistic tone, inasmuch as it spoke of the Council fathers rather than of an abstract Church: "Dear brothers and sisters, as fathers and pastors we

---

[175] Ibid.

sympathize deeply with your groans and we echo your laments." The message to women idealized a pre-modern image of woman and spoke of how proud the Church was "to have lifted women up and freed them" and in the course of the centuries to have illumined their fundamental equality with men "despite the difference in their personalities."[176] The message to the young was the one most in keeping with the addressees. The Church was concerned (it said) that the society which the young were building should "respect dignity, freedom, and the rights of the person."[177] The Church was concerned about the development of the faith in contemporary society and especially in the case of the young, being desirous of helping them not to succumb to the temptations of "philosophies of selfishness or pleasure and those of hopelessness and nihilism."

Father Semmelroth wrote in his diary that he had to translate the messages and the decree on the conclusion of the Council for German television. It had been a very difficult task, because the text had been distributed so late and only in French. Of the entire celebration he remarked: "It was very long and not as substantive as one really would have wished."[178] An important opportunity was lost with these messages, which differed considerably in tone and content from the message that the Council fathers had issued to the world after the opening of the Council.

The entire solemnity concluded with the reading of the apostolic letter *In Spiritu Sancto*, in which Paul VI declared the Council closed. This document speaks of the Council as one of the greatest events in the Church, not only because of the number of participating fathers from around the world but also because of the range of subjects dealt with in the four lengthy series of meetings and because of the results. Here reference was made in particular to the effort of the Council "to touch such believers in Christ as are still cut off from union with the Apostolic See and, beyond them, to touch the entire human family in the spirit of brotherhood."[179] This single mention of the Council's ecumenical concern in the entire closing solemnity — to say nothing of the failure to greet the other Churches — reflects the language and attitude of Pius XII rather than that of the Council and John XXIII.

It is difficult to reconcile, on the one hand, Paul VI's appearance before the United Nations, the fraternal kiss exchanged with the envoy of the

---

[176] Ibid., 879.
[177] Ibid., 884; for an English translation, see *Council Daybook, Session 4*, 285.
[178] *TSemmelroth*, 149.
[179] *AS* IV/7, 885.

Patriarch of Constantinople, and the moving words in St. Paul's Outside the Walls with this concluding papal celebration of the Council. They are the two faces of the Pope. They are the two faces of a Church in transition.

CHAPTER VI

THE COUNCIL AS AN EVENT IN THE ECUMENICAL
MOVEMENT

LUKAS VISCHER

I. THE NEW ATMOSPHERE

During the last days of the Council, thoughts often went back to the beginning. What had been accomplished? What had become of the expectations of that time? Non-Roman Catholic Christians were in agreement that quite a distance had been travelled. When the Council opened, hardly anyone would have dared to hope that such wide-ranging changes would come about; now, as the Council was coming to an end, there could be no doubt that the Roman Catholic Church had opened itself to dialogue with the other Christian Churches. Its earlier reserve toward the ecumenical movement had now been overcome. A new climate had come into being. The Roman Catholic Church had become a partner.

The very announcement of the Council had served as a signal. The fact that the relationship with the other Churches was to be so central a theme of the Council gave rise to great, sometimes unrealistic hopes. From the outset the word *ecumenism* was in every mouth, while during the periods of the Council the ideas of encounter, exchange, and dialogue became increasingly taken for granted. An atmosphere arose in which new relationships and collaboration among the Churches could grow. Walls began to fall. A Roman Catholic hierarchy that had previously avoided ecumenical contacts now began deliberately to seek them. Ever new encounters, handshakes, and fraternal kisses took place, celebrated by the press as "historic." Impulses and suggestions came from all sides for deepening this reciprocal understanding. Non-Catholic speakers were invited to address Catholic audiences, and Roman Catholic newspapers and periodicals gave generous space to their views.

Joy over this newly gained communion was dominant at the conclusion of the Council. Numerous non-Catholic Christians took part, openly or incognito, in the solemnities of the final days. A series of symbolic events underscored the Council's ecumenical character. At the plenary session on December 4, that is, four days before the end of the Council,

the observers had an opportunity to address a message to the Council.[1]
That afternoon the Pope invited the observers to join in prayer in the
Basilica of St. Paul's Outside the Walls. In his address there he gave
heartfelt praise for the role played by the observers during the Council:

> Your departure leaves us in a solitude which we did not experience before
> the Council and which now saddens us; we would like to see you with us
> always!... We have come to know you a little better, and not only as rep-
> resentatives of your respective confessions. Through you we have come into
> contact with Christian communities that live, pray, and act in the name of
> Christ, and with doctrinal systems and religious mentalities; and — let us
> not be afraid to say it — with Christian treasures of great value.[2]

Three days later came the dramatic announcement that the Holy See
and the Ecumenical Patriarchate had agreed "to erase from memory" the
reciprocal excommunications of 1054.

The question now was how this new readiness was to take effect. Could
it be taken for granted that communion would grow step by step? Or did
the conclusion of the Council signify at the same time the solidification
of the achieved results? Or had the Council given rise to a new style:
a readiness to meet, in mutual exchanges, the ever new challenges of the
age? Were the constitutions and decrees definitive utterances about which
there would be no more doubt? Or had the Roman Catholic Church
become a community "on the way"? In particular, what form were relations among the Churches to take? Would the intense exchanges that had
taken place during the Council continue? Had a model for future procedures been created? Could it be taken for granted that in the future the
Roman Catholic Church would continue to listen to voices from outside?

---

[1] It was originally planned that Lukas Vischer, observer from the World Council of
Churches (WCC), would deliver the message in the hall. At the last moment, however, it
was decided that it should be read by the Secretary of the Council. The message was
not included in the *Acta Synodalia*. See S. Schmidt, *Augustin Bea, The Cardinal of Unity*,
trans L. Wearne (New Rochelle, N.Y.: New City Press, 1992), 489.

[2] The text of this address is in *Observateurs-délégués et hotes de Sécrétariat pour
L'unité des chrétiens au Deuxième concile Oecuménique du Vatican* (Vatican City: Typis
Polyglottis Vaticanis, 1965), 59-64; for an English translation, see *Council Daybook, Session 4*, 353-54. At the end of his address the Pope spoke a parable that allowed for varying interpretations. Soloviev, the philosopher, said the Pope, was a guest in a monastery.
After a conversation at a late hour in the evening he wanted to retire to his cell but in the
darkness could not find the door. As a result, he walked up and down the corridor throughout the entire night. When day broke, everything became clearly visible. The Pope continued: "The truth is close at hand. Beloved brothers, may this ray of the divine light
enable us all to recognize the blessed door!" What did the Pope mean? Was this an invitation to dialogue about truth or a gentle request that all recognize the *true* door as being
the Roman Catholic Church?

At the end of the Decree on Ecumenism, the Council explicitly stated its urgent desire that "the initiatives of the sons of the Catholic Church, joined with those of the separated brethren, will go forward, without obstructing the ways of divine Providence, and without prejudging the future inspirations of the Holy Spirit" (no. 24).[3] Had the Council really initiated a period of dialogue?

Among the non-Catholic Christians there were, of course, some who were skeptical and critical. Many of them assumed that the ecumenical enthusiasm set off by the Council was nothing more than a passing fancy that would quickly wither. In their opinion the Council had brought no real opening to others but only an internal renewal of the Roman Catholic Church; that is, the Catholic Church had only found a new expression of its own catholicity.[4] *Plus ça change plus cela reste la même chose.* In their eyes narrow limits had been set beforehand to any dialogue. In fact, much was uncertain at the end of the Council. While many new perspectives had been opened, the Council had reaffirmed, in its essentials, the tradition of the Roman Catholic Church. What did this circumstance signify for the future? The opening to dialogue could indeed not be reversed, but at the end of the Council it had not been determined how much freedom of movement had really been created. An Orthodox theologian wrote: "Only the future will show whether the Second Vatican Council really took a significant step toward the restoration of a communion in the truth."[5]

Among the temporarily undecided questions were subjects of great practical importance, such as the new form of the law governing mixed marriages. Ever since the beginning of the Council, hopes had been expressed, both in the Roman Catholic Church and in other Churches, that the Council would lead to a new and more open practice. For many, in fact, especially members of congregations, a reassessment of the law governing mixed marriages was the decisive concern. The number of mixed marriages had been constantly increasing since World War II, especially in Western countries. The prevailing practice of the Roman Catholic

---

[3] The quoted sentence can be traced back to the suggestion of some observers. They had asked of the Secretariat for Promoting Christian Unity (SPCU) to what extent future dialogue could lead beyond the stage of discussion that had been reached at the Council.

[4] See Vittorio Subilia, *La nuova cattolicità del cattolicesimo: Una valutazione protestante del concilio vaticano II* (Turin, 1967).

[5] This was the judgment of John Meyendorff at the end of an article on the problem of the papacy ("Papacy, An Issue the Vatican Council Skirted. An Orthodox View," *Christianity Today* 10/66 [1965], 6-9).

Church was increasingly less accepted.[6] Was it really possible to speak
of ecumenical openness and dialogue when spouses belonging to different confessions could not meet as partners in the full sense of the term?

On November 19, 1964, at almost the end of the third period, the
Council was presented with a text on marriage that contained a series of
suggestions for a revision of the law. The discussion proved so difficult,
however, that the Council decided to leave the decision to the Pope, and
the fourth period ended without any decision being reached. In order to
underscore the urgency of the question, twenty-two observers from different confessional backgrounds joined in a common petition (October 1,
1965). A few months after the end of the Council, on March 18, 1966,
only four days before the visit of the Archbishop of Canterbury to Rome,
the Sacred Congregation for the Doctrine of Faith published an instruction that elicited widespread disappointment.[7] On the other hand, the fact
that the revision was intended to be experimental left room for hope that
in the foreseeable future a more satisfying solution might be found. The
debate continued at all levels.[8] The intensity of the controversy undoubtedly contributed in an important way to the fact that the Pope's Motu
Proprio of March 31, 1970, went beyond the existing rules in more than
one respect.[9]

As meetings between Roman Catholic Christians and followers of other
confessions increased in number, the question of the extent to which
ecclesial life could be shared also arose. Was baptism the sign of a fundamental unity that joined all together? Could the practice of conditional
baptism be henceforth relinquished? Did the Council also bring an end

---

[6] Bernhard Häring, for example, had written as early as 1962 that exclusion from the
sacrament is "a way of acting that used to induce fear in a closed society; in a pluralistic
society, however, it has the opposite effect" (*Lexikon für Theologie und Kirche* 7, 2d ed.
[1962], 444). Heinrich Böll's satirical tale *The Clown* (1963) contained an especially effective criticism.

[7] Cardinal Bea was greatly concerned that the instruction would poison the festive
atmosphere of the visit (see Schmidt, *Augustin Bea*, 621-23).

[8] A conference, organized by the WCC and held at Crêt Bérard, Lausanne, June 20-
24, 1966, made an attempt to place the question in a broader context ("Marriage and the
Division of the Churches," *Study Encounter* III/1 [1967], 21-35). The Joint Working Group
of the Roman Catholic Church and the WCC also dealt with the question (see Lukas Vischer, *Die eine ökumenische Bewegung* [Zurich, 1969], 98). When dialogues were held at
the national level, this question was usually given priority.

[9] There is a good survey of developments during and after the Council in Joachim Lell,
Mischehen: Die Ehe im evangelisch-lutherischen Spannungsfeld (Munich-Hamburg,
1967); and in Ursula Beykirch, *Von der konfessionsverschiedenen zur konfes-
sionsverbindenden Ehe?* (Forschungen zur Kirchenrechtswissenschaft 2; Würzburg, 1987),
155-219.

to proselytism? Was a common celebration of the Eucharist possible from now on? To what extent could instruction in the faith be done jointly by the Churches? All these questions were raised by the opening up of the Roman Catholic Church and called for answers.[10]

II. REGIONAL DIFFERENCES

The new climate in relations among the Churches did not appear in the same degree in all regions. The most extensive movement took place in the countries of western Europe and North America. The major initiatives at the Council came essentially from the bishops and theologians of those countries. There, too, the ecumenical aspect of the Council roused the greatest interest. Even before the Council there had been interconfessional contacts. Due chiefly to the spiritual witness of Abbé Paul Couturier in Lyons, the week of prayer for Christian unity (January 18-25) had acquired a new orientation and had created the framework for numerous unofficial contacts. Ever since the Second World War mixed groups gathered for conversation and prayer had increased in number. For example, in Germany, the Ecumenical Working Group of Catholic and Evangelical Theologians (also known as the Jaeger-Stählin Group, after its founders), had been established; it made efforts to move beyond controversial topics by finding new way of posing the issues. Thus the ecumenical soil had already been tilled in Europe; the work thus done secretly now emerged from concealment.

The media played an important role. Hundreds of journalists and television teams had streamed into Rome, mainly from the Western countries; the Second Vatican Council also became a subject of abiding interest in the secular press. As a rule, journalists were interested in the opening to ecumenism. Especially in confessionally divided countries such as Germany, the Netherlands, Switzerland, the United States, and

---

[10] A further unanswered question had to do with indulgences. To the surprise of all, a short debate on this symbolically important question occurred during the fourth period. In order to gain clarity on how the matter of indulgences was to be regulated in the future, the Pope took a poll of the episcopal conferences. Explanations were read for two days in the Council hall, and critical voices predominated. The topic caused such surprise that it was removed from the agenda, but the brief discussion left behind in the Roman Catholic world the unpleasant feeling that it would continue to be necessary in the future to deal with a subject people had thought had been forgotten.

Canada, the media contributed greatly to the cultivation of a special interest in the ecumenical aspect of the Council and made it a subject of public discussion. *Le Monde* in France,[11] the *Frankfurter Allgemeine Zeitung*
in Germany, *Trouw* in the Netherlands,[12] and other similar newspapers,
to say nothing of the ecclesiastical press, were spokesmen for the ecumenical movement and contributed to the development of the new climate
among the Churches.

The situation was different in the countries of eastern Europe. At the
governmental level the Council was indeed followed with great interest,
and its ecumenical implications were discussed in detail. The renewal of
the Roman Catholic Church would have far-reaching political consequences. Of special interest was the attitude the Council would take
toward communism. Would there be a condemnation? Or would the
Council choose a pragmatic approach and leave open the possibility of a
modus vivendi with the communist regimes? In any case, ecumenical
contacts within their own countries were not in the interests of the communist regimes; on the contrary, their goal was to limit the influence of
the Churches. The starting position of these regimes was thus not favorable to the ecumenical movement; there could be no public discussion.
In any case, the Churches themselves, forced onto the defensive by external circumstances, were inclined to be conservative in attitude. For these
reasons the impulses to both internal renewal and ecumenical openness
were only hesitatingly received.[13]

Different again was the situation in the Southern hemisphere. The
opening to ecumenism was everywhere noted with very great interest,
but the debates at the Council were not followed with an eye primarily
on confessional agreement. Attention was focused much more on the
question of the extent to which the Council would succeed in creating the
basis for a common identity of the Church itself in the modern world. The
debates on the independence of the local Churches, dialogue with other
religions, and the inculturation of the gospel were their main interests. For

---

[11] See Henri Fesquet, *The Drama of Vatican II* (New York: Random House, 1967).

[12] The especially intense public discussion in the Netherlands was to be explained in
large measure by the fact that the media there were organized by confessions. An ecumenical debate was preprogrammed by institutional structures.

[13] Among the unofficial visitors who appeared at the close of the Council in Rome
was Joseph Hromadka, professor on the Comenius Faculty in Prague and also president
of the Christian Peace Conference. His aim was to form his own image of the Council and
to establish the connection with bishops that had been described in the discussion of the
constitution *Gaudium et spes*. Among other things, he had an informal conversation with
Father V. Miano, a leading figure in the Secretariat for Nonbelievers.

example, the East Asian Christian Conference, which was the merger of the evangelical Churches in Asia, at its plenary assembly in Bangkok in February 1964, approved a declaration on relations with the Roman Catholic Church, in which the hope was expressed that an agreement on encounter with other religions might be found.[14]

In Latin America it was chiefly the political and socio-ethical aspects of the Council that drew attention. The responsibility of the Church in the face of poverty became a subject of discussion. During the Council, Dom Helder Câmara, Bishop of Recife, had already become an emblematic representative of renewal in that direction. Quite naturally, this aspect of the Council became the chief focus of the slowly developing ecumenical contacts.

At the end of the Council, then, the climate was marked by a lack of uniformity. In some parts of the world the foundation seemed to have been laid for a new era in the ecumenical movement; in other areas little had changed. For some, dialogue was linked chiefly with the hope of communion; others were guided by the perspective of a common witness.

III. THE ROLE OF THE OBSERVERS

The role of the observers became increasingly important from period to period. Their role had not been limited to keeping the Churches to which they belonged informed about the Council. In an increasing measure they took part in the events of the Council, and their voices were heard. The SPCU took pains to ask for their opinions and to make their positions known to the pertinent commissions and other offices. Every Thursday afternoon meetings were held in a room in a palazzo on the Piazza Navona, under a vault containing baroque paintings in honor of the arts; the purpose was to give an opportunity for remarks on the texts being debated. Oral and written ideas from the observers were willingly accepted. Even more important were personal meetings with Council fathers; conversations with observers inspired many Council father to speak up.

The number of observers increased from period to period, from fifty-four during the first period to over one hundred during the final period. They could be divided into two groups: representatives of the Churches

---

[14] East Asia Christian Conference, *The Christian Community within the Human Community: Statements from the Bangkok Assembly* (February-March 1964), 84.

of the Reformation, and representatives of the Orthodox Churches of the East. Almost all the observers were from the Northern continents. During the first period only the Anglican Communion and the World Methodist Council had representatives from Asia (Archdeacon Harold de Soysa) and Latin America (José Miguez-Bonino). Later a few more representatives came from the South, mainly in the delegation from the WCC.

The result was that it was the problematics of the Northern regions that prevailed, even among the observers. Attention was concentrated on those documents that raised the main controverted theological questions of previous centuries. Revelation, the Church, ecumenism — these elicited far more lively discussion than the problem of witnessing in the modern world. Only the WCC, sensitized by its worldwide membership, regarded the composition of the pastoral constitution *Gaudium et spes* as a key issue right from the first period.

Not all the observers participated in the debates with the same degree of involvement. Some made participation in the Council their priority; others stayed in Rome for only short periods. Some tried to influence the event through conversations, lectures, and well-directed suggestions; others were content with a more ceremonial presence. An especially important role was played by those observers who participated in the Council continuously over several periods and were therefore familiar with the procedures.

From the outset there was the question of relations among the observers. Agreement among them was by no means to be taken for granted, since each of the represented Churches judged the Council in the light of its theological and ecclesiological presuppositions and therefore could not automatically accept the judgment of other observers. On the other hand, most of the Churches represented by observers belonged to the WCC. Many of the observers had participated in ecumenical meetings and conferences; some, such as Vitaly Borovoy, Douglas Horton, José Miguez-Bonino, Albert Outler, Karekin Sarkissian, Edmund Schlink, and Krister Skydsgaard, had played leading roles in the WCC. Moreover, the WCC had had an important mediating function during the period of preparation for the Council. Ought it not be possible to make this communion among the Churches visible also in contacts with the Council?

Complete coordination was obviously out of the question, since the differences among the Churches were too great and the degree of the identification of the individual Churches with the WCC varied too widely. Nonetheless, a degree of coordination did arise. Beginning in the first period, the observers met for common prayer early every Monday morning in the Methodist church on the Tiber. They came to an agreement as to who was to speak in their name on official occasions. Observers repeatedly met in small groups in order to exchange information and to discuss further action. On certain questions coalitions repeatedly formed that crossed confessional boundaries. The already mentioned joint petition (October 1, 1965) on the problem of mixed marriages was a good example. On the question of indulgences, too, the observers acted with unanimity.

Among the observers the two representatives of the Taizé community had a special place. Brothers Roger Schutz and Max Thurian were interested mainly in contacts with the bishops. "We wanted first of all to be a presence of prayer and so accomplish the special vocation of the Taizé community, which is to work for the unity of all in one Church."[15] A small group of the Taizé brothers lived as a community in Rome. A large number of bishops participated in their prayers and regularly visited the community. Taizé cultivated contacts especially with the Latin American bishops. Solidarity with the poor was a priority of the community.

IV. Effects on the Already Existing Ecumenical Community

It became clear very early that the Council would have consequences for the character of the ecumenical movement. During the first session, Dr. W. A. Visser 't Hooft, at that time the general secretary of the WCC, already recognized the importance of the Council. *Nostra res agitur!* (This is our business!). Non-Catholics could not keep their distance from what happened at the Council. Anyone who accepted the fundamental concept of the ecumenical movement had to admit that the communion thus far achieved was partial. The participation of the Roman Catholic Church was essential for the integrity of the ecumenical movement. At the same time, there could be no doubt but that this broadening of the movement would bring radical disruptions with it. The joy at the broadening of the ecumenical movement was mingled with concern over the next steps. Visser 't Hooft gave eloquent expression to this conflict by citing Friedrich Nietzsche: "For good or for ill, the warm spring wind is blowing!"

Six challenges come to mind. First of all, the participation of the Roman Catholic Church meant that the line-up of partners would change

[15] Roger Schutz, *The Tablet,* March 2, 1963.

at the international level and especially at the national level. The previous network of relations would have to be revised. In many countries membership in the WCC had not brought any far-reaching changes with it, because the most important partner in the country, the Roman Catholic Church, did not belong to the WCC. Such Churches met Churches of other confessions at international conferences but were untouched by the ecumenical movement in their immediate surroundings. Now a new situation had arisen: the ecumenical movement was becoming almost everywhere an existential challenge. An Orthodox theologian explained: "Whereas the ecumenical movement was hitherto simply an interesting object, now I feel challenged 'viscerally.'"

Second, the opening up of the Roman Catholic Church forced the rethinking of established opinions and feelings. For generations the ecumenically involved Churches had distinguished themselves from one another. Only now, when a new relationship became possible, did the Churches become aware of how strongly their teaching and, above all, their spirituality was marked by their differentiation from the Roman Catholic Church. The remembrance of persecutions and confessional strife made every rapprochement seem a betrayal. It was now necessary to jump over their own shadow; there had to be an inner turn-around. Instead of emphasizing an identity defined negatively, through opposition to the Roman Catholic Church, new ways had to be found to represent their own tradition in dialogue. What had already taken place, at least initially, within the member Churches of the WCC now had to be extended to the Roman Catholic Church.

Third, the consensus reached in the ecumenical movement so far proved to be too narrow. The debates at the Council made it foreseeable that theological positions and perspectives not previously taken into account would in the future have to become part of theological conversation. A first experiment along such lines was a conference at the Ecumenical Institute in Bossey in March 1963. In order to carry out the preparation for the World Conference on Faith and Order (Montreal, July 1963) on the broadest possible basis, a group of Roman Catholic theologians was invited to present views on the planned themes. For the first time in the history of the WCC such themes as the nature of the Church, revelation, scripture and tradition, office and officials, and liturgy became the subjects of a joint theological discussion. The exchange left no doubt that a new situation for dialogue had arisen. The theological agenda of the ecumenical movement had changed radically.

Fourth, the new start represented by the Council led to new departures in the ecumenical movement, which, while at first sight having nothing to do with the Council, were, if not made possible, at least reinforced by the new situation. The fact that walls hitherto regarded as so solid in relation to the Roman Catholic Church had fallen showed that new initiatives could now be taken up within the other Churches themselves. Immediately before the beginning of the Council, the Lutheran, Reformed, and United Churches in Europe had decided on a new round of theological conversations; from the start it became clear that in comparison with previous contacts there was now a new atmosphere. This time the conversations were sustained by a will to action and led later on to the declaration of full communion between the two traditions.[16] A similar breakthrough began to emerge in relations between the Eastern Orthodox and the Oriental Orthodox Churches. During the Council completely unexpected contacts led to conversations between the WCC and the Seventh-day Adventists; on the Adventist side this move was promoted by an unofficial visitor to the Council, Bert Beverley Beach.[17]

Fifth, at the same time the individual Churches were forced to ask how they would react to the Council. Now that the Council had questioned so many things, the Churches had to make clear the extent to which they could maintain their previous attitude. A new self-consciousness was unavoidable. The Council provided the Churches with an example of a process of renewal. Would the Churches be satisfied to judge the Council and comment on it? Or were they ready to place something of value alongside it? In the Orthodox Churches the announcement of the Council led to a revival of old plans to hold a Pan-Orthodox Council. Kurt Schmidt-Clausen, general secretary of the Lutheran World Federation, stated that the Lutheran Churches ought to hold a Council like Vatican II, and Krister Skydsgaard opined, somewhat more realistically, that the Lutheran Churches ought at least to be involved in preparing for such a Council.[18]

---

[16] The declaration was called the "Leuenberger Agreement" after the place where it was made (see Elisabeth Schieffer, *Von Schauenburg nach Leuenberg: Entstehung und Bedeutung der Konkordie reformatorischer Kirchen in Europa* [Paderborn, 1983]).

[17] Beach several times spent lengthy periods in Rome as an unofficial observer from the Seventh-day Adventists and also published a book about the Council: *Vatican II: Bridging the Abyss* (Washington, D.C., 1968). In his report on the conversations held in two series from 1965 to 1971 we read: "Strange as it may seem, these yearly consultations are an indirect by-product of Vatican II" (see WCC, *So Much in Common* [Geneva: WCC, 1973], 98).

[18] On this point see Vilmos Vajta, "Interpretation of the Second Vatican Council," *Lutheran World* 13 (1966), 424.

Sixth, the opening of the Roman Catholic Church to ecumenism was a challenge especially to the WCC. What attitude would the Roman Catholic Church adopt toward the WCC? Would it allow the communion existing in the WCC to be extended to include itself? Or would new forms of collaboration have to be found? Could the familiar structures in the areas of mission, social witness, and inter-ecclesial aid continue unchanged? Discussion of the question had already begun after the first period of the Council. Lord Fisher of Lambeth, formerly one of the presidents of the WCC, suggested in an article that the WCC be reorganized. He said that a new situation had arisen, and it would be a shortsighted solution simply to build bridges between the WCC and the Roman Catholic Church: "The total dissimilarity between the Council [the WCC] and the Church of Rome would be a permanent embarrassment for both sides and would vitiate all attempts at cooperation."[19] Hermann Sasse, a Lutheran theologian who had played an important role in the Faith and Order movement, defended this suggestion:

> A strong federation of Christian Churches built on the Nicene Creed, limiting its functions to what separated Churches can do together without interfering in their inner life: this would cover the whole range of practical matters from welfare work to the common representation before the world. It would cover also the work of Faith and Order as a true dialogue between the churches.

On this basis, said Sasse, a new departure would be possible in the direction of a communion of Churches that would be catholic in the true sense.[20]

V. REFLECTIONS AND INITIATIVES OF THE WORLD COUNCIL OF CHURCHES

Long before the Council was coming to its end, the Christian communities that had sent observers to it had raised the question of the form that future relations should take. Their participation in the WCC had long habituated them to the deliberate planning of the ecumenical movement. Within the WCC the opinion quickly prevailed that action must be taken as soon as possible. The fact that the Roman Catholic Church

[19] See *Church Times*, February 8, 1963. The article gave rise to a lively discussion in the WCC (see the minutes of the Executive Committee, Geneva, February 11-15, 1962, p. 5 [mimeographed]).

[20] Hermann Sasse, "The Ecumenical Challenge of the Second Vatican Council," *Lutheran World* 13 (1965), 107-19.

had decided on active participation in the ecumenical movement gave rise to the hope that dialogue could be given an institutional basis. The question whether the ecumenical enthusiasm would continue made it seem advisable to give what had been achieved an institutional form as soon as possible and thereby also make further developments possible. The SPCU likewise had a public interest in being able to present tangible results as quickly as possible. The opening signaled by the Decree on Ecumenism could most effectively be confirmed by irreversible actions.

In the WCC, thinking on this subject had already begun quite early. Immediately after the first period, on January 24, 1963, an internal memorandum on the shaping of relations with the Roman Catholic Church was sent to a number of theologians and Church leaders with a request for their views. Among the recipients of the memorandum were Henrikus Berkhof, Eugene C. Blake, Franklin C. Fry, José Miguez-Bonino, Ernest Payne, Edmund Schlink, and Krister Skydsgaard. The main question in this inquiry was how the concept of a communion of Churches could stand its ground over and against the claims of the Roman Catholic Church. How was the danger of the ecumenical movement splitting into two camps to be avoided? For the first time, the idea emerged of establishing a joint working group of the WCC and the Roman Catholic Church. By and large the answers to the memorandum emphasized the need to introduce the foundational concept behind the WCC into the discussions of the Council. Since Msgr. Jan Willebrands, secretary of the SPCU, had expressly asked for suggestions and proposals for the work of the Council, the essential concerns of the WCC in regard to ecumenism were brought together in a lengthy letter to the SPCU.[21]

During the first session it became clear that the Council would draw up a text on the Church in the modern world. In an address that caused a sensation, Cardinal Suenens had introduced a distinction between texts *ad intra* and texts *ad extra* and urged that the Council take a position on the world's great problems. The intention of engaging in such a project caused people in the WCC to take notice. A description by the Council of the witness required in today's world could be of the greatest importance for ecumenical cooperation. It was therefore decided to make advances toward Bishop Emilio Guano of Livorno, president of the relevant commission; inquiries made of Willebrands had shown that such

---

[21] Letter of January 18, 1963, in the Archive of the WCC 994.3.50.1.

an expression of interest would be welcome. In mid-April a wide-ranging and detailed memorandum was sent to Bishop Guano. Several members of the commission later let the WCC know that the text had been received and attentively read and that it had had some effect on the debates.[22]

In August 1963 the Central Committee of the WCC met in Rochester, New York. This meeting had been preceded by the Fourth World Conference on Faith and Order, which was held July 12-26 in Montreal, Canada. Roman Catholic observers had taken part in the conference, and a common liturgy, in which Cardinal Émile Léger took part, had clearly shown something of the new atmosphere. The debates had shown that dialogue was taking place in a new situation.[23] In Rochester the Central Committee of the WCC was faced, for the first time, with the task of defining a position. According to the report of Lukas Vischer, the sole observer there, a lively discussion arose. The question of the very conception represented by the WCC was again the focus of attention.[24] How were people to be led to understand that the ecumenical movement had to be a *joint* undertaking of all the Churches if it was to lead to lasting results? "It is for this kind of dialogue with the Roman Catholic Church that we long, for we have begun to taste its fruitfulness within our own fellowship."

Work on the Decree *De oecumenismo* continued during the second period. The involvement of the Roman Catholic Church in the ecumenical movement was becoming ever clearer. For that very reason it was important in the eyes of the WCC that the best possible premises for

[22] See Charles Moeller, "Introduction to the Pastoral Constitution," in *Commentary*, 5:20 "It was Lukas Vischer's letter which made the then editiorial committee realize the need to speak about Christ's lordship and to make it a central idea." Otto Hermann Pesch gave a detailed report of this letter and its effect in his book *Das Zweite Vatikanische Konzil: Vorgeschichte, Verlauf, Ergebnisse und Nachgeschichte* (Würzburg, 1993); on one point, however, his presentation was not entirely accurate. He believed that the letter was "a bit of impudence, from the viewpoint of protocol," because the writer "bypassed all the proper channels" (210, 323f.). As a matter of fact, there had been preliminary conversations with both Willebrands and Guano. This is confirmed by a memorandum in the archives of the WCC.

[23] P. C. Rodger and L. Vischer, eds., *The Fourth World Conference on Faith and Order: The Report from Montreal 1963* (London: SCM Press, 1964). On the very day when the conference began, Roger Mehl of Strasbourg said: "In the presence of our brethren from the Roman Catholic Church who are here as observers… we should like to say that the churches belonging to the WCC do not regard the Vatican Council as an event which does not concern them, but as an event which affects them all because it really concerns the history of the true universal Church" (10-11).

[24] WCC, *Minutes and Reports of the Seventeenth Meeting of the Central Committee, Rochester, NY, August 26-September 2, 1963*, 32-34.

future collaboration be established in the decree. At the invitation of the Russian Orthodox Church the executive committee met in Odessa in February 1964. Careful preparations were made for the meeting. A memorandum was prepared that contained a detailed critique and concrete suggestions for the writing of the decree. A motion was made that with the blessing of the executive commission this memorandum should be presented to the SPCU.

After Nikos Nissiotis had given a report on the second period,[25] the executive committee occupied itself with the drafted memorandum. The committee decided to publish a shorter public statement under the title of "Christian Unity — The Present Stage."[26] The complete text was presented to Willebrands. The public statement gave a short description of the WCC, stressing the importance of the basis (§7) and of the solidarity of the member Churches among themselves. Although they were divided from one another, they were ready for a dialogue on equal terms. "It is a conversation in which all are expected to listen as well as to speak, and in which existing differences and tensions are frankly faced" (§9). They already form a communion and "recognize their solidarity with one another, render assistance to each other in case of need, and support one another in their witness to Christ and in their evangelistic and missionary task, and wherever it is possible to do so, take common action and render common witness on the basis of consultation and agreement with one another" (§10).

The detailed memorandum was written in a more direct and deliberate style. First of all, it subjected the current text of the Decree on Ecumenism to a detailed criticism. Before all else, it asked that the text recognize more fully the identity and individuality of the non-Roman Churches. The claim of the Roman Catholic Church to be the true Church was not being challenged here, but it should not determine in advance the shape of the dialogue. The memorandum then proposed a series of suggestions. It proposed, above all else, that the decree be preceded by an introduction in which the ecumenical movement was recognized as being a gift of the Spirit to *all* the Churches. In the further drafting of the decree the suggestions given in the memorandum were accepted over long stretches of the text.[27]

---

[25] See *Minutes of the Meeting of the Executive Committee*, February 10-14, 1964, Appendix 1 (mimeographed).

[26] "Christian Unity – The Present Stage," *Ecumenical Review* 16 (April 1964), 323-28.

[27] Above all, the suggestion of adding a preface to the decree was accepted. In it the Council expressed the thought that the ecumenical movement included all Churches. In the

As a result of constant exchanges with the SPCU, the question of how to structure future relations became topical once again. At the suggestion of Willebrands, an unofficial meeting was set up for April 15, 1964, in order to bring clarity to the subject. Cardinal Bea, Willebrands, Jérôme Hamer, and Pierre Duprey took part in it, all from the secretariat, while the WCC was represented by Visser 't Hooft, Vischer, and Nissiotis. The conversation took place in the greatest secrecy at the house of the Suore di Maria Bambina in Milan. The questions that the WCC had raised in its preceding statements were tackled in a very direct manner.

Hamer had prepared a paper for discussion. In it the different concepts in use were presented in a realistic way; the obstacles hindering the membership of the Roman Catholic Church in the WCC were listed. But at the same time the speaker asked: "Is not the energetic development of contacts, dialogue, and collaboration in all directions and by all those concerned the best cure for the fear of a monopoly by the Catholic Church?" Suggestions for the future envisaged this kind of response. Three groups were to be formed: (1) a group to study the principles and kinds of collaborations; (2) a theological group that included Faith and Order; and (3) a study group to deal with practical matters. Both sides stressed that these plans could be implemented only after the promulgation of the Decree on Ecumenism.

After the meeting in Milan both sides faced the task of obtaining the agreement of the competent authorities to the plan they had worked out together. In earlier days Bea had looked at the WCC with a degree of skepticism. As late as 1956 he had written in a letter: "The WCC thinks nowadays not so much of an assembly based on doctrine but of a coming world Church, and this in conscious contrast with the worldwide Roman Catholic Church and its claims."[28] His attitude changed, however, after he took over the leadership of the SPCU. It became ever clearer that the Roman Catholic Church had to depend on the WCC for its ecumenical contacts, especially with the Churches of the Reformation. Bea's contacts with Visser 't Hooft, set up by Willebrands, revealed to him the spiritual and theological dimension of the WCC. During the Council he cultivated connections with the WCC and urged the Vatican authorities to permit closer collaboration. He had a high opinion of the importance

new draft itself this thought was emphasized in particular by the fact that the text spoke no longer of "Principles of Roman Catholic Ecumenism," but of "Catholic Principles of Ecumenism."

[28] Schmidt, *Augustin Bea*, 244.

of the Milan meeting. "Along with further consultations that took place in Rome during the third period of the Council, that meeting would lead to very important decisions during the year that followed on the promulgation of the Decree on Ecumenism."[29]

The next regular meeting of the executive committee of the WCC was held on July 27-31, 1964, in Tutzing (Bavaria). In preparation for the discussion it was decided first to have a conference at which the leading personages from the member Churches, some observers from the WCC, and members of the executive committee could exchange views. This conference was held on July 24-27 in Rummelsberg, Bavaria. The main paper was delivered by Professor Edmund Schlink.

One point in particular gave rise to a lively discussion. The observers from the WCC expressed the view that under present circumstances the membership of the Roman Catholic Church in the WCC could not be counted on. From a different side and especially from Bishop Lesslie Newbigin (at that time the head of the WCC's Commission for World Mission), it was said, in contrast, that the WCC was in principle open to the membership of the Roman Catholic Church. Any Church that could agree with the fundamentals of the WCC could become a member. Simple collaboration was at best a temporary solution.

The discussion continued at the meeting of the executive committee in Tutzing. Lukas Vischer had written a detailed memorandum summarizing the resolutions and discussions in Milan and in Rummelsberg.[30] After a thorough discussion the executive committee gave the secretary general the authority for further dealings with the SPCU on the basis of some guidelines formulated during the meeting. The executive committee attached great importance to a list of the subjects that the planned joint working group would be competent to take up:

> A clear distinction must be made between the subjects which can properly be discussed between the WCC and the Roman Catholic Church and those which can and must be discussed in bilateral conversations between the individual member churches (or confessional bodies) and the Roman Catholic Church. Among the subjects which belong to the first category we would mention especially: a) practical collaboration in the field of philanthropy, social and international affairs; b) theological study programs which have a specific bearing on ecumenical relations (Faith and Order); c) problems which cause tensions between the churches (e.g. mixed marriages, religious

[29] Ibid., 473-74.
[30] "Bases of Cooperation," minutes of the meeting of the executive committee of the WCC, Tutzing, Germany, July 27-31, 1964, Appendix 3.

liberty, proselytism); d) common concerns with regard to the life and mission of the church (laity, Missions, etc.)[31]

A first opportunity to implement this program came even before the
beginning of the third period. On September 4, Willebrands visited the
WCC. The suggestions made in Milan were largely confirmed, and two
further points were made. Visser 't Hooft said that the multiplicity of the
member Churches of the WCC would have to be adequately represented
in the joint groups; as a result, the number of the WCC representatives
would have to be larger than that of the representatives of the Catholic
Church. Willebrands made the point that collaboration with the WCC
ought not to interfere with conversations with the individual confessional traditions. But it was also expressly stated that the Roman
Catholic Church would share responsibility for the internal coherence of
the WCC.

Conversations continued during the third period. It became increasingly clear that the first need was for the formation of a *single* joint working group whose mandate would be to clarify the bases of collaboration;
this would exclude the formation of further working groups as needed.
On November 14 (during the third period) Vischer had an opportunity,
during an audience, to present the plan for collaboration to the Pope.

With the proclamation of the Decree on Ecumenism the way was
opened up to implement the plan. But the changes that the Pope introduced at the last minute in the Constitution on the Church and the Decree
on Ecumenism gave rise again to doubts in the WCC. Visser 't Hooft
expressed the reactions of many when he spoke in an interview of a dark
day at the Council. But people quickly decided that this incident did not
detract from the ecumenical thrust of the Council and that all the arguments in favor of close collaboration remained unchanged.

The central committee of the WCC met in Enugu, Nigeria, on January 12-21, 1965. The Pope had approved the formation of a joint, or
mixed, working group. The approval of the central committee was given
after a detailed discussion. Vischer reported on the third period, and the
secretary general presented the suggestions for future collaboration.[32]

A solemn sequel came about almost by accident. The local assembly
of the Churches of Geneva, the so-called "Rassemblement oecuménique

---

[31] Ibid.
[32] Central Committee of the World Council of Churches, *Minutes and Reports of the
Eighteenth Meeting in Enugu, Nigeria* (Geneva, 1965), 36-39, 91-102; *Ecumenical Review*
17 (1965), 171-73.

des églises de Genève," invited Bea and Pastor Marc Boegner to deliver lectures there during the Week of Prayer for Unity. Bea agreed, being under the impression that he was dealing with the WCC. Instead of canceling the event, the planners changed it to a ceremony at which the formation of the joint working group would be officially announced. At the headquarters of the WCC Bea said: "I do not doubt that this step which corresponds so well to the letter and the spirit of the Decree on Ecumenism will have excellent results both in the field of mutual collaboration for the solution of the great problems of our day and also in that of dialogue properly so-called."[33] Following the ceremony, people were invited to a public gathering in Reformation Hall in Geneva. The hall was packed. The new beginning was celebrated in a festive mood.

Visser 't Hooft ended his address with the words "Now the work can begin." The program quickly took shape. As early as the spring of 1965, two conferences were held on subjects that were on the agenda of the fourth period. The first conference, which met March 28-31 in Geneva, took up the pastoral constitution *Gaudium et spes*. After a debate on the theological foundations of ecclesial witness in society, there was a detailed discussion of the task of developing "mutually acceptable criteria for social thought and action." In the WCC the planning of a world conference on Church and society was in high gear. The conference urged the Roman Catholic side to participate, and the hope was expressed that schema XIII, as the pastoral constitution was still called at that time, would provide the basis for close collaboration. The formation of a joint commission on questions of Church and society was urged to promote this collaboration.[34]

A few days later, April 5-10, a group met in Crêt Bérard, near Lausanne, for an exchange of views on collaboration in mission. It formulated a lengthy list of suggestions. Point 2 reads: "There are places where our mutual rivalries and hostilities are [a] stumbling block placed before men whom we wish to draw to Christ.... It is imperative that such scandals be eliminated as far as possible." Point 4: "There is need to provide channels of information reciprocally about the development of contacts at the regional, national and local levels." Point 6: "We draw attention to the importance of common planning for Christian witness in the life of secular universities and colleges." Point 10: "We believe that there are

---

[33] See *Ecumenical Review* 17 (1965), 133.
[34] "Consultation on Church and Society," report and minutes (duplicated) in the archives of the WCC.

situations in which a considerable amount of joint survey and planning of missionary action could be envisaged."[35]

Comprehensive collaboration quickly developed in other areas too. Within the WCC the dominant view was that contacts should be wide-ranging; as many areas as possible of the Churches' life should be incorporated into the ecumenical movement. Thus, in January 1964 a first meeting took place at Glion, Switzerland, that sought to clarify the question of the place of the laity in the Church; this was organized by the department for the laity in the WCC and COPECIAL (Standing Committee for International Congresses on the Apostolate of the Laity). A second meeting followed in September 1965 in Gazzada-Varese.[36] Both meetings laid the foundation for the strongly ecumenical direction taken at the congress of the laity that was held in Rome in 1967. On October 22-29, 1965, during the fourth period of the Council, a group of women met in Vicarello-Bracciano near Rome. The meeting was occasioned by the fact that Roman-Catholic women had been invited to the Council as "listeners." The WCC committee on the collaboration of men and women and the SPCU took the step of setting up a meeting between the "listeners" and leading women of the WCC.[37]

The newly appointed joint working group gathered for its first meeting on May 22-24 at the Ecumenical Institute in Bossey. The participants were Willebrands and Visser't Hooft as chairmen; Msgrs. Carlo Bayer and William Baum; Father Pierre Duprey; Bishop Thomas Holland; Archpriest Vitaly Borovoy; R. H. Edwin Espy; Nikos Nissiotis; Edmund Schlink; and Father Paul Verghese. Jérôme Hamer and Lukas Vischer were appointed secretaries of the group, which had to deal with a sizable agenda. The first task was to reach agreement on the foundations of the collaboration. Not by accident, the question of the nature of true dialogue was raised, a concept that had been become the focus of attention due to the encyclical *Ecclesiam suam*.[38] A lengthy discussion developed over

---

[35] Report on an "Informal Meeting on Mission" (duplicated), in the archives of the WCC.

[36] Proceedings of the Ecumenical Consultation on "Laity Formation," Gazzada, September 7-10, 1965; Rome, 1966.

[37] "Report," in the archives of the WCC 42.01.52.

[38] A small committee, made up of Yves Congar, Nikos Nissiotis, and Edmund Schlink, among others, was appointed to compose a paper on the subject. It was published in 1967 in the name of the working group (*Ecumenical Review* 19/4 [1967], 469ff.). Studies composed for the committee were likewise made available: Yves Congar, "Vorschläge für den Dialog"; N. A. Nissiotis, "Formen und Probleme des ökumenischen Dialogs"; Edmund Schlink, "Die Methode des ökumenischen Dialogs": all in *Kerygma und Dogma* 12/3 (1966), 181ff.

how, in the future, officially appointed observers were to be distinguished from advisers.

Above all else, however, the joint working group drew up a list of areas in which collaboration was to be sought. Central theological themes were to be clarified by a joint committee in collaboration with the Commission on Faith and Order. The reports on the two conferences in Geneva and Crêt-Bérard were largely approved. In the area of mission special emphasis was placed on holding a conference on proselytism. A broad spectrum of questions was addressed: from joint declarations on international events, to mutual aid between the Churches, to the establishment of a common date for Easter.

In order to provide the broadest possible support for the common work, a draft of a confidential report was presented for approval to the responsible authorities on both sides. The first step was the meeting of the executive committee of the WCC in the summer of 1965. It approved the broad lines of the text and suggested only a few changes.[39] The SPCU likewise declared its agreement. Encouraged by these statements, the joint working group was able to continue its work in specific areas when it held its second meeting at Ariccia, near Rome, November 17-20, 1963, during the second period of the Council. The members agreed on a short text entitled "Prayer and Worship at Ecumenical Events." A model was developed at two meetings of a small circle during the fourth period.[40]

By the end of the Council, therefore, common work had already advanced a good deal. Suggestions for wide-ranging plans existed in draft form. Agreement on the publication of a first report was as good as certain. In February 1966, the central committee of the WCC met in Geneva, where Vischer presented a concluding report on the Council.[41] The report of the joint working group was accepted without changes and released for publication.[42] The basis was thus laid for close collaboration. This developed with special rapidity within the Commission on Faith and Order and in the area of social witness. In fact, as

[39] Minutes of the Executive Committee, Geneva, July 11-15, 1965 (duplicated), 15.

[40] The meetings took place on October 16 and November 8 in Rome (see Vischer, *Die eine ökumenische Bewegung,* 76-82).

[41] World Council of Churches, "Minutes and Reports of the Nineteenth Meeting of the Central Committee, in Geneva" (Geneva, 1966); the reports of Vischer and Nissiotis on the fourth period were published in *Ecumenical Review* 18 (1966), 150-89, 190-206.

[42] "First Report of the Joint Working Group, 1966," *Ecumenical Review* 18 (1966), 561-67; see also Vischer, *Die eine ökumenische Bewegung,* 64-82.

early as a few weeks after the publication of the report a second conference was held in preparation for the World Conference on Church and Society in 1966.

As yet, however, nothing official was said about the Roman Catholic Church becoming a member of the WCC. Was the joint working group to be the definitive form of collaboration? Or was it possible and even necessary to count on further developments? As early as a year later the second report of the joint working group had this to say:

> Without at present bringing in other considerations, the members of the joint working group are of the opinion that at the present time the common goal of Christian unity would not be advanced by the entrance of the Roman Catholic Church into the WCC. This does not mean, however, that the group regards the present form of collaboration as final. It is conscious that the task of the joint working group must be given a new formulation in the near future and that the composition of the group must be changed. In this changed framework the group must pursue its study of the foundations, the unity, and the concrete achievements of the ecumenical movement. This quest will make known the next step.[43]

The part played by the WCC in the drafting of the Declaration on Religious Freedom deserves special mention. It is not an exaggeration to say that the WCC even had a part in the choice of this subject. Shortly after the establishment of the SPCU (June 5, 1960), Bea suggested that he and Visser 't Hooft meet for a discussion; the latter agreed. In a confidential letter to the presidents and vice-presidents of the central committee Visser 't Hooft wrote: "It seems to me important to find out what his plans are and that I can call his attention to some of our concerns (religious liberty et al.)." The conversation took place on September 22 in Milan. It was agreed that before the opening of the Council a discussion should be organized on the subject of "Religious Freedom as an Interecclesial Problem."[44]

This problem had been a central concern of the WCC ever since its foundation in Amsterdam. Representatives of the WCC had worked at the United Nations to have an appropriate consideration of the principle of religious freedom included in the Declaration on Human Rights. In the eyes of the WCC the acknowledgment of religious freedom was a presupposition of any dialogue and collaboration among the Churches.

---

[43] "Second Report of the Joint Working Group 1967," *Ecumenical Review* 18 (1967), 461-67; Vischer, *Die eine ökumenische Bewegung*, 86-87.

[44] It would be organized in the following year by the Conférence catholique pour les questions oecuméniques and the WCC and held May 1-12, 1961.

A special secretariat, headed by A. F. Carrillo de Albornoz of Spain, dealt exclusively with this subject. Bea recognized the importance of the question and throughout the years of the Council worked for a declaration on religious freedom. The WCC, for its part, consistently pushed for such a declaration.

Immediately before the opening of the Council, an article in the *Ecumenical Review* pointed out how important it was that the Roman Catholic Church take a clear position on the subject: "Issues of religious liberty are vital to the individual Christian and to the Christian Church in the modern world." The writer voiced his hope that a consensus would be reached on "the nature and the requirements of religious liberty" and thus enable the Churches to speak to the world with a new clarity.[45] The observers at the Council followed the debates on religious freedom with especially keen attention. The fact that the vote on the declaration was put off from the third to the fourth period deeply disturbed many of them, and the eventual approval of the declaration gave special satisfaction to the WCC.

In an article by A. F. Carrillo de Albornoz that appeared immediately after the close of the Council, we read: "The Declaration means, above all, a new Christian unanimity in matters of religious liberty.... For the first time for many, many centuries, all Christian churches proclaim the universality and inviolability of religious liberty for all men and all confessions, so that throughout the world this fundamental right should be provided with effective legal safeguards. This is completely new, and opens world-wide hopes and perspectives."[46]

There is a final important aspect that must be mentioned here: the regional and national Churches or Councils of Christians. At the time of the Council these were an essential structural element in the ecumenical movement. Like the WCC on the international level, these Churches or Councils sought to promote unity and a common witness of the Church at the regional, national, and often even local levels.[47] There was, of course, close collaboration between the WCC and the Church councils.

---

[45] Alford Carleton, "The Vatican Council and Issues of Religious Liberty," *Ecumenical Review* 14/4 (July 1962), 459.

[46] A. F. Carrillo de Albornoz, "The Ecumenical and World Significance of the Vatican Declaration on Religious Freedom," *Ecumenical Review* 18/1 (January 1966), 81.

[47] See Frank Short, "National Councils of Churches," in *History of the Ecumenical Movement*, ed. Harold E. Fey, vol. 2, *1948-1968*, 3d ed. (Geneva: WCC, 1993), 93-113. The declaration of the East Asia Christian Conference, held in February, 1964, clearly reflects this close connection; see "The Christian Community within the Human Community. Bangkok Assembly," Minutes, Part 2, 81-84.

Most of the regional and national Church councils were also connected structurally with the WCC. The question now was: What attitude would the Roman Catholic Church adopt? Would it deal only with the individual Churches or enter the multilateral community of Church councils?

It soon became clear that these councils remained an indispensable tool of the ecumenical movement even in the new situation. As early as March 10, 1965, and therefore before the end of the Council, the episcopal conference of the United States appointed a special commission to carry on conversations with the National Council of Churches in the United States.[48] In the summer of 1965 the WCC began a correspondence with selected Church councils in order to get a clearer picture of developments.[49] The joint working group took up the question. The WCC stressed the importance of multilateral collaboration.[50]

VI. DEVELOPMENTS IN THE WORLDWIDE CONFESSIONAL FAMILIES

The Council gave new importance to the worldwide confessional federations. Previously these federations had remained in the background of the ecumenical movement, its greater or lesser importance depending on its ecclesiological foundations. Because of its regular Lambeth Conferences, the Anglican Churches around the world felt more closely bound together than did the Lutheran, Reformed, Methodist, and Baptist Churches. Their links on the international level were too loose to permit them to represent their member Churches. With good reason, therefore, the WCC had been founded as a community not of world federations but of territorial Churches. But the Council brought about a change in presuppositions, since observers were sent only by world federations,[51] and it seemed natural, once the Decree on Ecumenism had been accepted, that the SPCU should engage in bilateral dialogues at the world level. This decision evidently represented a challenge for the WCC that was

---

[48] Letter from William Baum, March 25, 1965, in the archives of the WCC 42.01.52.

[49] On July 9, 1965, the Church councils of Kenya, Japan, India, the Sudan, and Sri Lanka were asked to send information.

[50] "Second Report of the Joint Working Group III, 5, c" (*Ecumenical Review* 18 [1967]).

[51] Visser 't Hooft and Bea had raised the question of sending observers during their first conversation in Milan (September 22, 1960). They agreed at that time that the WCC should establish the contacts with the world federations. Representatives of the world federations met with Willebrands the following year.

not immediately recognized by all its partners. What would be the relationship between the work of the joint working group and the bilateral confessional conversations?

A. Lutheran World Federation

For the Lutheran Churches, perhaps more than for other Churches, the Roman Catholic Church was their real ecumenical counterpart. As guardians of the Reformation heritage, they felt that the new situation challenged them with special intensity. They were also better equipped for dialogue with Rome than were the other Churches. In 1960, Krister Skydsgaard, in close collaboration with the Lutheran World Federation (LWF), had founded a center for interconfessional research in Copenhagen. Under its supervision, a publication, representative of the Lutheran world, on Lutheranism's relationship to Rome, appeared in German and in English even before the Council began.[52] The plenary assembly of the Lutheran World Federation in Helsinki (1963) gave its approval for the erection of a foundation for interconfessional study; in 1965 the institute in Strasbourg was established as a result.[53] Other, later publications took up questions raised by the Council.[54] All this intense work prepared the soil for dialogue with Rome.

Contacts between the Lutheran World Federation and Rome were limited at first to an exchange of courtesies. A planned visit of General Secretary Kurt Schmidt-Clausen to Rome during the second period had to be cancelled due to illness. In the spring of 1964, George A. Lindbeck, one of the Lutheran observers at the Council, spent several weeks in Rome in order to make contacts with numerous personages there. He wrote a memorandum, based on his impressions, for the attention of the executive committee of the Lutheran World Federation. In it, he reported especially on conversations with Willebrands; these talks made it clear to him

---

[52] Krister E. Skydsgaard, ed., *Konzil und Evangelium* (Göttingen: Vandenhoeck & Ruprecht, 1962); *The Papal Council and the Gospel* (Minneapolis: Augsburg Publishing House, 1962).

[53] See Jens Holger Schjorring, Prasanna Kumari, and Norman A. Hjelm, *From Federation to Communion: The History of the Lutheran World Federation* (Minneapolis: Fortress Press, 1997), 255f.

[54] Friedrich Wilhelm Kantzenbach and Vilmos Vajta, ed., *Wir sind gefragt: Antworten evangelischer Konzilsbeobachter* (Göttingen, 1966); Warren A. Quanbeck, ed., *Challenge and Response: A Protestant Perspective of the Vatican Council* (Minneapolis: Augsburg Publishing House, 1966).

that the SPCU was interested in continuing, after the Council, the contacts made during it.

Ideas about the form these would take were still vague. There was talk of an exchange of appointed "ambassadors," but also of joint commissions. "The present attitude of the Secretariat seems to be that the Roman Catholic Church should enter vigorously *both* into multilateral discussions as are represented, for example, by Faith and Order, *and* into bilateral conversations with other churches and confessions." Lindbeck was aware of the dangers connected with bilateral conversations: "Many people are legitimately concerned.... They fear that if the churches of a given confessional or denominational family increasingly act together in ecumenical matters, this will lead to an unfortunate fragmentation of the ecumenical movement, a decrease in the role of the WCC, and a tendency for the dialogue to polarize around Rome. These are real dangers." He nonetheless declared himself in favor of the acceptance of bilateral relationships.[55]

Lindbeck's memorandum was discussed in detail at a closed meeting of the executive committee in Reykjavik in August-September. The view taken of bilateral relationships was unanimous: "This is a legitimate and ecumenical activity of the Lutheran World Federation." The general secretary was commissioned to establish contacts with the SPCU. He was given a group of advisers consisting of Krister Skydsgaard, Vilmos Vajta. Hermann Dietzfelbinger, and Gerald Brauer.[56]

Kurt Schmidt-Clausen carried out his commission during the third period. At the beginning of November 1964, during the third period, he, together with two of the Lutheran observers, had a wide-ranging conversation with the SPCU. In a letter to Willebrands, dated November 23, he looked back at that event and stated:

> When the executive committee of the LWF met in Reykjavik at the beginning of September of the present year, it decided to authorize liaison and contacts with the Roman Catholic Church, provided the latter is interested in such contacts. The committee also expressed the view that the WCC and the other world federations should be consulted about these contacts. In our conversation the other evening we agreed that such an interest existed on both sides; that we would try to establish this liaison and these contacts by first forming a provisional joint committee (each side appointing up to five

---

[55] For the text of the memorandum, see the minutes of the executive committee of the Lutheran World Federation (which met in Reykjavik in August-September 1963), in the archives of the Lutheran World Federation.

[56] Ibid.

members who would, as far as possible, not come from the same continent); and that this joint committee would have as its task to explore the subjects, scope, and method of such conversational contacts.[57]

At the meeting of the officers of the executive committee in January 1965, Schmidt-Clausen reported on the contacts he had made. He described the task of these initial conversations as "to confront the Roman Catholics with the real meaning and true intentions of the Lutheran Reformation." The officers approved the plan for a provisional committee; the WCC was to be urged to send an observer. In order to give the plan the broadest possible support, in February 1965, the general secretary sent a confidential letter to all the member Churches and the national committees of the Lutheran World Federation, asking them for an opinion on the proposal. Encouraged by the affirmative answers, those responsible began to plan further contacts.

In May a small staffing group met in Rome to work out a program for the first meeting. On three successive days the following subjects were to be taken up: "(a) Content, shape, and scope of further liaison contact in study and action between the Lutheran World Federation and the Roman Catholic Church: retrospection and hopes; (b) Central theological issues for future dialogue; and (c) Recommendations." The regular meeting of the executive committee in Arusha, Tanzania, in June 1965, provided an opportunity for further discussion of the undertaking. The following were appointed members of the provisional committee: Hermann Dietzfelbinger (chairman), Gerald Brauer, Warren Quanbeck, Krister Skydsgaard, Vilmos Vajta, Kurt Schmidt-Clausen, and Carl Mau.

The first joint meeting took place at the end of August, immediately before the fourth period of the Council. The Roman Catholic delegation was led by Bishop Hermann Volk and included Yves Congar. Since it proved impossible to reach conclusive results right away, the group met a second time on April 13-15, 1966.

The report on the joint meeting suggested the formation of two commissions.[58] The first would devote itself to the question of "Gospel and Church," the second to the thorny pastoral problems of confessionally mixed marriages. The report was favorably received by both sides. Thus only a few months after the close of the Council the first bilateral dialogue at the world level had begun.

---

[57] See the correspondence in the archives of the Lutheran World Federation, GS.VI.2.
[58] "Report on the Conversation of the Roman Catholic/Evangelical-Lutheran Group," *Lutherische Rundschau* 16/4 (1966), 560ff.

The initiative of the Lutheran World Federation would not have been possible without the readiness of some national Lutheran Churches to enter into dialogue with the Catholic Church. This led, in turn, to new national initiatives and dialogues. The confidential circular letter from the general secretary in February 1965 strengthened the national committee of the Lutheran World Federation in North America in its decision to begin a dialogue with the episcopal conference of the North American bishops. The United Evangelical Lutheran Church in Germany, in an official text titled "Advice for Interconfessional Encounters," expressed its desire for a comprehensive dialogue with the Roman Catholic Church.

So extensive, from the very outset, was the interaction between international and national dialogues that a certain tension soon emerged. The prerequisites for a Lutheran-Catholic dialogue were not the same in all parts of the world. An agreement within Lutheranism about dialogue with the Catholic Church was seen from the outset as an urgent task. In his memorandum Lindbeck had already spoken of this problem: "Church-to-church encounters with Rome require a confession to act unitedly. Separate, regionally limited churches are at a disadvantage when it comes to participating in either bilateral or multilateral conversations, given the vast international bulk of the Roman Church.... Is it really possible to make the Lutheran World Federation an agency through which its member churches can effectively cooperate in dialogue? Yet, without it, they will, *qua* churches, remain relatively silent in the conversation with Rome." Thus viewed, the decision to enter into dialogue was a challenge to any Church that so decided.

B. The Christcatholic Church (Old Catholics)

Even though the Christcatholic *(Christkatholische)* Church had relatively few members, special attention was paid to developments within it.[59] Characterized as it was by its opposition to Vatican Council I, how would it respond to the debates in the present Council over the relationship between pope and bishops? To what extent could the bitter conflict that had broken out less than a hundred years before be overcome by the new perspectives developed at the new Council? In more than one

---

[59] The Christcatholic Church broke with Rome at the time of the First Vatican Council; it is sometimes referred to as the Old Catholic Church.

respect, the answer of the Christcatholic Church was a test of the ecumenical opening of the Roman Catholic Church.

At the Council the Christcatholic Church was represented by Dutch Canon Petrus Johannes Maan; during two periods Professor Werner Küppers, a German, was present as a second observer.

A first exchange between the two Churches had already taken place in 1963 in the Netherlands. A mixed or joint commission tackled the question of how the causes of the split were to be assessed. In the conviction that the time for a real dialogue had arrived, the Holy See was asked to set aside the conditions hitherto in effect for the acccptance of a dialogue.[60] But a new atmosphere soon came into existence not only in the Netherlands but on the international level as well. At the Nineteenth International Congress of Old Catholics in Vienna on September 22-27, 1965, the relationship with the Roman Catholic Church was in the forefront.[61] For the first time official Roman Catholic observers were present. Petrus Johannes Maan gave a report on the Council. One of the Roman Catholic observers, Professor Victor Conzemius, took the opportunity to present "Plea for a Dialogue among Catholics."[62] In a closing expression of wishes Old Catholic theologian Hans Frei stated that the presence of the observers made us "feel that with an open-minded and, at the same time, benevolently critical attitude of mind, the concerns of the Old Catholics might be taken into consideration within the bosom of the Roman Catholic Church and be re-evaluated."[63]

After the close of the Council, Urs Küry, Old Catholic Bishop of Switzerland, published "some first words of orientation." He said: "Our question can only be this: what progress has the Council made toward the goal of a greater and more resolute *Christocentric* Catholicism?" In his view decisive steps had been taken in this direction but further progress was needed. Küry mentioned as an example his reservations about the Roman Catholic understanding of the ecumenical movement: "Like our forbears, who after Vatican I called for a universal council, we must work for an ecumenical world in which Rome is not the sole center," but rather

---

[60] J. A. G. Tans and Marinus Kok, *Rome-Utrecht. Over de historische oorzaken van de breuk tussen de rooms-katholieke en de oud-katholieke kerken en de huidige beoordeling van de oorzaken* (Hilversum/Antwerp, 1966). The conditions in question were the acceptance of the formulary of Alexander VII and the constitution *Unigenitus* of Pope Clement XI.

[61] *Bericht über den 19. Internationalen Altkatholiken-Kongress, 22.-27. September 1965 in Wien* (Allschwil, 1965).

[62] Both lectures were published in *Internationale Kirchliche Zeitschrift* (*IKZ*) 55 (1965), 216-31, 254- 71.

[63] Ibid., 84f.

an ecumenical world in which initiative and decision are the work of the various traditions acting together. Küry challenged his Church not to evade dialogue, for this can "become an occasion for bearing witness to the Roman Catholic representatives about our special mission as a Church."[64] On January 6, 1966, in Germany, a group of twenty-one Old Catholic priests asked the newly consecrated bishop of Germany to take the initiative in seeking dialogue.[65]

The Roman Catholic response to the request from the Netherlands came after the end of the Council. In a letter to Cardinal Alfrink (March 14, 1966) Bea stated: "Although at an earlier time when the modern conception and method of dialogue were not yet in use... this condition was in force, I can now tell you officially that it will not be upheld by the Roman Catholic Church."[66] The conversations in the Netherlands could now be carried on as an official activity.[67] In other countries, too, joint commissions were set up (Switzerland, 1966; Germany, 1968).[68]

An international conference in Zurich that brought together representatives from Germany, Switzerland, and Austria (March 10-12, 1969) produced the so-called Zurich Note, a short text in which relations between the Old Catholic Church and the Roman Catholic Church were regulated. The central section of the text reads: "Catholics are authorized to ask Old Catholic priests for the sacraments of penance, the Eucharist, and the anointing of the sick, whenever there is a serious need or a truly spiritual advantage so advises and provided that access to a Catholic priest is physically or morally impossible. Under the same conditions, Old Catholics can be admitted to the sacraments."[69]

---

[64] Urs Küry, *Nach dem Abschluss des Zweiten Vatikanischen Konzils: Hirtenbrief auf die Fastenzeit 1966* (Allschwil, 1966). Küry spoke similarly in a later publication: *Unser Verhältnis zur römisch- katholischen Kirche 1870-1970: Hirtenbrief auf die Osterzeit 1970* (Allschwil, 1970).

[65] The new bishop was asked "to do all in his power to bring about a new unity among all those who realize that they have a duty to renew the Church that is founded on Peter and the apostles" (January 6, 1966) (see *IKZ* 74 [1984/2], 91).

[66] *IKZ* 56 (1966), 234ff.

[67] Ibid.

[68] See Walter Stählin, "Der offizielle Dialog zwischen der christkatholischen und der römisch-katholischen Kirche der Schweiz," *IKZ* 72 (1982), 103-6; Peter Bläser, "Das altkatholisch-römisch-katholische Gespräch," *IKZ* 60 (1970), 347-60; Werner Küppers, "Zwischen Rom und Utrecht: Zur neueren Entwicklung der Beziehungen zwischen Altkatholischer und Römisch-katholischer Kirche," in *Begegnung: Beiträge zur Hermeneutik des theologischen Gesprächs*, ed. Max Seckler (Graz, 1971); Werner Pelz, "Der Dialog zwischen den Altkatholischen und der Römisch-katholischen Kirche in Deutschland in den Jahren 1968-1973," *IKZ* 74 (1984), 85-128.

[69] *IKZ* 74/2 (1984), 122-23.

C. The Anglican Communion

The attitude of the Anglican Churches to the Council differed from that of the other Churches. The idea of dialogue was not new to Anglicans, and conversations with representatives of the Roman Catholic Church had already taken place. Admittedly, the Malines conversations in the 1920s had to be broken off without any concrete results, yet deep in the consciousness of the Anglican Church the hope remained alive that the hour of a breakthrough would come sooner or later. The relationship between the Roman Catholic Church and the Anglican Church in England was an ambiguous one. On the Catholic side, the dominant attitude was that England must be "won back" for the Roman Catholic Church, and yet repeated contacts were made between Roman Catholic and High Church Anglican circles and, in many cases, led to extensive agreement.

In 1949, Geoffrey Fisher, Archbishop of Canterbury, sent an emissary to Rome to find out whether a dialogue with Rome was feasible. It was therefore not surprising that the announcement of the Council gave birth to high expectations. Even though it soon became clear that the adjective *ecumenical* did not mean "interconfessional," the Church of England had from the outset a positive attitude toward the Council. In November, Archbishop Fisher announced that he would visit Pope John XXIII "to convey to the world that our two communions can speak to one another in charity, in happiness and in mutual confidence.... This is the great thing which I hope from this visit, that the capacity to speak without being suspect will be restored once more to Christendom." In a sermon delivered in the Anglican church in Rome he even spoke of his hope for a commonwealth of Churches.[70]

Fisher's visit had been announced as a courtesy visit, and that is how Rome ranked it. It served as a sign, however, all the more so because after the visit the Archbishop appointed a personal representative in Rome. From that point on, Canon Bernard Pawley followed the preparation for the Council, made numerous contacts with representatives of the Curia, and through his humorous, direct, and at the same time prudent manner won the sympathy of many.

The observers from the Anglican Church, especially Bishop John Moorman, likewise worked in the conviction that the Anglican Church

---

[70] Owen Chadwick, "The Church of England and the Church of Rome from the Beginning of the Nineteenth Century to the Present Day," in *Anglican Initiatives in Christian Unity*, ed. E. G. W. Bill (London: SPCK, 1967), 100-104.

had a special contribution to make, and they took care that it not be taken over by other confessional traditions.[71] From time to time, however, some were heard to call for a greater solidarity with other traditions, especially with the WCC.[72] During the first period the Anglican observers held back. In the summer of 1963 Bishop Moorman, in a letter to London, spoke in self-criticism of his regret that the Anglicans had not sufficiently responded to Bea's invitation to send their observations and suggestions on the subjects of the Council to the SPCU.[73] During the third and fourth periods the Anglican observers submitted memoranda on the question of birth control and on their understanding of mission.[74]

Between the second and third periods the Anglicans were thinking carefully about future relations between the two Churches. The numerous contacts between Catholics and Anglicans in many countries encouraged them to take new steps. At the end of 1963 the Archbishop and his collaborators asked themselves whether it would be useful to establish a permanent presence in Rome. It was decided to wait until the results of the Council had taken clearer form. In May 1964, Pawley was received by the Pope and was able to report to London that Paul VI "showed considerable interest in a visit from the Archbishop of Canterbury" and hoped it might occur before the end of the Council. The Pope would like, on that occasion, to talk about the form of a future dialogue. In his characteristically cautious manner Paul VI said that he could not match the Archbishop's visit with a visit of his own to England, but he was ready to look for the Archbishop wherever he might be staying in Rome.[75] The plan matured in the following year.

[71] Thus Moorman stated emphatically that it was important "that the Anglicans make their own contribution rather than allow the Methodists, Congregationalists and others to speak on behalf of them." He reported that he "already had to correct Dr. Horton who had affirmed that Canterbury was much nearer to Geneva" (internal memo, in the archives of the Council for Foreign Relations, Lambeth Palace, Rc Files 37/1).

[72] Within the Church the question was discussed of the extent to which the Anglican Communion was a "confessional family," similar to the Lutherans, Methodists, and Reformed, or must be regarded as a communion *sui generis*. In a letter to John Satterthwaite, the Archbishop's closest collaborator, David Paton insisted that the special position of the Anglican Communion should not be over-emphasized; good relations with other non-Roman traditions should not be neglected (September 10, 1964) (in Rc Files 42/4).

[73] In a letter dated July 23, 1963, Moorman wrote: "So far we have not taken any advantage of Cardinal Bea's invitation"; he said that he was working on a letter to the secretariat (see Rc Files 42/4).

[74] Memorandum of November 11, 1964, on the Decree on the Missionary Activity of the Church (RC Files 41/4); this was followed in the next year by two comments on birth control and a new one on collaboration in the mission of the Church (October 14, 1965).

[75] Report of Canon Pawley on his conversation of June 5, 1964 (RC Files 41/2).

At the beginning of 1965 Pawley was succeeded by the Rev. John Findlow.[76] At meetings with the Pope and the staff of the SPCU constant subjects were the visit of the Archbishop and the coming dialogue.[77] On November 13, during the fourth period, the Pope received the Anglican observers as a body. The latter were able to let the Pope know that the Archbishop intended to pay him an official visit in the spring and on that occasion would like to talk about the possibility of a dialogue between the Roman Catholic Church and the Anglican Communion. The Pope replied that this "could be arranged in all simplicity." The observers, however, noted with some concern that the Pope had only a vague grasp of the difference between the Church of England and the Anglican Communion. He asked, for example, whether the commission might include representatives of the Old Catholic and the Methodist Churches.[78]

The two roles of the Archbishop of Canterbury as the head of the Church of England and the first bishop of the Anglican Communion could not always be clearly separated. On the one hand, the Archbishop was active in his capacity as head of the Church of England; on the other, it was his responsibility to see that the universal character of the Anglican Communion was recognized by the Roman Catholic Church. The British representative at the Holy See also stressed this. Therefore, the ambassador asked the Archbishop to send to the coronation of Paul VI not only an Englishman but at least also an American and, if possible, someone "with a dusky skin."[79]

In any case, it would have to be made clear that a future dialogue would be carried on not with the Church of England but with the Anglican Communion. Both the Archbishop and the observers feared that Cardinal Heenan, an Englishman, would prefer to dialogue only with the Anglican Church in England. Thus Moorman wrote to Lambeth on September 6, 1965: "There is a real danger when the Council is over of

[76] Findlow brought extensive experience to his new post. From 1949 to 1956 he had been chaplain in Rome and from 1960 to 1964 chaplain at the British embassy in Athens, and he spoke fluent Italian. After his arrival in Rome at the beginning of 1965 conversations were begun about building an Anglican center in Rome. During the fourth period plans for the project took concrete form.

[77] Details are given in William Purdy, *The Search for Unity: Relations between the Anglican and Roman Catholic Churches from the 1950s to the 1970s* (London: Chapman, 1996), 91ff.

[78] See the report of John R. Satterthwaite to the Archbishop on November 13, 1965, and the diary of John Lawrence, an Anglican observer during the fourth period (Rc Files 44/3).

[79] Letter of Peter Scarlett, ambassador to the Holy See, to the Archbishop, June 10, 1963 (RC Files 39/1).

slipping back, and possibly the English hierarchy trying to clamp down on dialogue outside this country. Heenan, we know, is anxious to prevent us from having contacts on the continent.... We must therefore try to get around this."[80] The Archbishop was at that time seeking contacts with Roman Catholic leaders in France, Belgium, and the Netherlands. Mistrust of the Roman Catholic hierarchy in England was also the reason why Heenan was not kept informed of the planned visit of the Archbishop and of the dialogue. When news of these reached him, he was put out, and some diplomacy by the SPCU was required in order to calm the turmoil.[81]

At the beginning of December the Archbishop told the Pope he was planning a visit; with a promptness unusual at the Vatican, on December 9, one day after the close of the Council, the Pope expressed his joy at this visit. The meeting took place on March 22-24, 1966, in a festive atmosphere. Protests were isolated and came primarily from Ian Paisley and other Protestants of Northern Ireland. A liturgical service in the Sistine Chapel was followed by a lengthy conversation. The visit ended with common prayer at St. Paul's Outside the Walls.[82] On that occasion the joint declaration was read, on which the Pope and the Archbishop had agreed. The beginning of a serious dialogue between the Roman Catholic Church and the Anglican Communion was announced. It would take up not only "theological matters such as Scripture, Tradition and Liturgy but also matters of practical difficulty felt on either side."[83]

On the occasion of a visit of Willebrands to Lambeth in May, agreement was sought on the appointment of a joint preparatory commission. This presented its first report after three meetings in January 1967, September 1967, and January 1968.[84] It soon became clear that a long road lay ahead, longer than many had anticipated at the end of the Council. The meeting of Paul VI and Archbishop Ramsey had been warm and sincere, but this had not altered basic presuppositions. Anglican orders were still

---

[80] Letter of John Moorman, September 6, 1965, to John R. Satterthwaite (RC Files 44/1).

[81] Details in Purdy, *The Search for Unity*, 92-93. Purdy cites a letter from Cardinal Heenan to Msgr. Willebrands that culminates with the sentence: "Our great fear is that the Secretariat will continue to come between us and our Anglican fellow-countrymen."

[82] The meeting is described in detail in Owen Chadwick, *Michael Ramsey: A Life* (Oxford: Oxford University Press, 1991), 316-23.

[83] The full text of the declaration is published in Alan C. Clark and Colin Davey, *Anglican/Roman Catholic Dialogue: The Work of the Preparatory Commission* (Oxford: Oxford University Press, 1974), 1-4.

[84] On the course of the dialogue, see ibid.

regarded as invalid by the Roman Catholic Church. Paul VI had agreed only that the question could and should be studied anew.[85]

D. World Methodist Council

Although Methodist Churches today form a worldwide communion of churches, their origin is in the Anglo-Saxon world, their two centers being in Great Britain and the United States. The group of Methodist observers at the Council consisted chiefly of representatives of these two countries.[86] As a result, they naturally had special access to the English-speaking bishops and experts.

Among these observers three merit special mention: Professor Albert Outler of the Perkins School of Theology in Dallas, Texas; Bishop Fred Pierce Corson, at that time president of the World Methodist Council, and Harold Roberts of Richmond College in London. Outler (1910-89) was a brilliant, eloquent, and sometimes sarcastic theologian. He viewed the Council skeptically at the beginning but soon became convinced of the relevance of the event and took part with his special verve in the numerous debates. His analysis of the texts and, above all, his awareness of the Council as a spiritual event opened many doors to him.[87] At the end of the fourth period and at the invitation of the Paulist Fathers he delivered a lecture at the Grand Hotel before the assembled hierarchy of the United States. The peroration of the lecture was characteristic of him:

> There will be no more meetings of this sort again in our life-time. Our ways from here lie in a thousand directions — all in God's keeping, thank God! The splendours of Vatican II — this strange interlude when we have been so strangely one — will fade and be filed in the archives of our memories.

---

[85] In his biography of Ramsey, Chadwick summarized the situation as follows: "The meeting with the pope did not resolve Ramsey's difficulties. The pope conceded that the gulf over Anglican orders might be less unbridgeable than was supposed. But this was more important to Ramsey as a sign of charity than as a real concession; for Archbishops of Canterbury were contemptuous of any doctrine that a gulf about Anglican orders needed to be bridged.... That in his extreme old age Leo XIII had acted unwisely and erroneously [reference to the Bull *Apostolicae curae*, 1896, declaring Anglican orders invalid] made a problem for the Church of Rome, not for the Church of England" (Chadwick, *Michael Ramsey*, 321).

[86] The only exceptions were the already mentioned José Miguez-Bonino from Argentina and Emerito Nacpil from the Philippines.

[87] However, the exaggerations in which his biographer indulges have nothing to do with reality (Bob Parrott, *Albert C. Outler: Biography: The Gifted Dilettante* [Anderson, Ind.: Bristol Books, 1999).

But a new advent of the Holy Spirit has happened in our world in our time
— a new epiphany of love that has stirred men's hearts wherever they have
glimpsed it incarnated.... What must not fade is the clear conviction set
down in *De ecumenismo* that "there can be no ecumenism worthy of the
name nor any effective outreach to the world without an interior conversion,
a change of heart and holiness of life." The way to Christian unity is long
and arduous — and the end is not in sight. But on such a way, as on all providential journeys, the pilgrim people of God walk by faith and not by sight.[88]

While Outler had the ability to create an atmosphere of understanding,
Bishop Corson saw himself as a strategist. He took part in the sessions for
only a short time, but on each occasion he was able by his appearance to lend
a certain gravity to his coming. He sought after audiences with the Pope
and cultivated contacts with the cardinals and bishops of the United States.

During the Council, Corson and the leaders of the SPCU discussed the
formation of a joint commission. The executive committee of the World
Methodist Council at its meeting in Stockholm on August 26-31, 1965,
gave him and his closest advisers authority to conduct these conversations
and to work out a proposal.[89] During the fourth period an agreement with
the SPCU was sought. In the summer of 1966, the five-year assembly of
the World Methodist Council was held in London.[90] The acceptance of
official conversations was solemnly approved on that occasion. The
World Methodist Council established a Commission for Ecumenical Relations and charged it with this new task.[91] Three Roman Catholic observers
were invited, and the SPCU was represented at the conference by Father
Thomas Stransky. An address of Archbishop Cardinale, nuncio in Great
Britain, was greeted with enthusiastic applause.

The Methodist members of the new joint commission were Bishop
Corson, Dr. W. R. Cannon, Bishop F. G. Ensley, Dr. Bolaji Idowu, Professor Gordon Rupp, Dr. Eric Baker, and Dr. Harold Roberts, with Professor Outler as consultant.

---

[88] The address was published in *Perkins Perspective* 7/2 (January 1966).

[89] For a report on the meeting of the executive committee in Stockholm, see *World Parish* 5/2 (November 1965).

[90] The World Methodist Council is led by a number of committees. The council, which has about 500 members, meets every five years. It met in 1961, before the Vatican Coun-
cil, and again in 1966. It chooses an executive committee with 150 members, which as a rule meets twice between the meetings of the council. Current business is handled by the officers, a group of about twenty members. Simultaneously with the five-year meeting of the council a conference is held in which an undetermined number of participants may take part.

[91] See Lee F. Tuttle and Max W. Woodward, eds., *Proceedings of the Eleventh World Methodist Conference* (London and New York, 1967), 72.

What expectations attended on this new initiative? Opinions were divided. The responsibility that the decision implied was something new for the World Methodist Council; the new task gave it additional importance. For some, the new situation represented progress, but others voiced their skepticism. In his report to the council Dr. Lee F. Tuttle wrote, "There was, and continues to be, a justifiable sense of pride that both the WCC and the Secretariat on Unity of the Vatican Council selected the World Confessional Organization as the one instrument through which this important work could best be accomplished."[92] A different emphasis, however, was heard from Harold Roberts in his address to the assembly:

> Of course, we may expect dialogue at high levels. It is inevitable of course that you should have what are sometimes called these high-powered commissions. I think there are too many of them myself, and it is not always clear how much they achieve. While they are necessary — sometimes I think a regrettable necessity — it is in the local parishes and churches that the battle for unity will be lost or won. And how good a thing it is to hear that all over this country in local councils and elsewhere you have representatives of the Roman Catholic Church and there is joint social witness, joint prayer and joint witness within existing disciplines.[93]

The tension expressed by these two passages continued in the years that followed. The dialogue advanced quickly and contributed a great deal to the creation of a new feeling between Methodism and the Roman Catholic Church.[94] At the same time, however, it remained unclear to what extent the Methodist delegation could represent the rest of the Church in a binding way.[95]

Among the striking traits of Methodist–Roman Catholic relations was the heavy emphasis on spirituality. Vatican II was perceived as primarily a spiritual event, and its significance was rated highly. The challenge of the Council to the Methodist Churches was understood, more so than in other Churches, as an invitation to a new joint departure. In the course of the Council the open letter that John Wesley wrote to "a Roman

---

[92] Ibid., 80.

[93] Ibid., 178.

[94] Geoffrey Wainwright, *Methodists in Dialogue* (Nashville, Tenn.: Abingdon Press, 1995), 37-107.

[95] It was certainly no accident that at two meetings in the summer of 1965 (Lake Janulaska and Stockholm) one of the explicit subjects was the question of how the Methodist Churches could become a truly worldwide communion. One speaker said: "The proposal for an international Methodist Church might provide wholesome strength in the future discussions with the Roman Catholic Church" (see *World Parish* 5/1 [October 1965] and 5/2 [November 1965]).

Catholic" on July 28, 1749, acquired new importance. In that letter, starting from the common ground binding together the two traditions, Wesley sought to open the way for a new approach to each other. Shared convictions were enough "to provoke one another to love and good works, endeavoring to help each other on in whatever we are agreed leads to the Kingdom."[96] At the urging of the Methodist observers, in 1963 the World Methodist Council sent 700 copies of this letter to English-speaking Council fathers. "There resulted a literal stream of letters of appreciation from all over the world to the office for several months; at least two of these persons have spoken of John Wesley in terms of sainthood."[97]

Another striking trait of the Methodist witness at the Council was its heavy emphasis on the missionary involvement of the Church. Listen once more to Harold Roberts: "Let us remember that we need to witness together to Christ in the world.... If we work together and bear witness together to Christ in the secular world as his servants, while our difficulties will not disappear, we shall see them in a new light and approach them as things to be overcome."[98]

E. WORLD ALLIANCE OF REFORMED CHURCHES

In comparison with other confessional families, the World Alliance of Reformed Churches initially held back from dialogue. It, too, had indeed agreed to send observers to the Council; but when it became clear that the Council could lead to new relations with the Roman Catholic Church, the relevant authorities hesitated. Their caution was based not only on the fact that many Reformed Churches were, to an especially high degree, shaped by opposition to the Roman Catholic Church. As late as the 1950s, Reformed minorities in such countries as Spain, Portugal, and Colombia were in a difficult position in comparison with the Roman Catholic majority. The reaction of the World Alliance of Reformed Churches was also influenced by the fact that, far more than other confessional families, it had identified with the WCC. When preparation was being made after the World War II for the establishment of the WCC, the World Alliance decided to deploy all its resources in the building of this comprehensive

---

[96] Wainwright, *Methodists in Dialogue*, 38.
[97] Tuttle and Woodward, *Proceedings of the Eleventh World Methodist Conference*, 82.
[98] Ibid., 178.

ecumenical community and to limit its own activities to areas which could be perceived as within a confessional setting.[99] Thus when the possibility of bilateral dialogue appeared, it was logical that it chose first of all to place itself behind the WCC and to support the work of the newly formed joint working group.

The first opportunity for an exchange of views came at the general assembly of the World Alliance of Reformed Churches in Frankfurt (August 3-14, 1964). Signs of openness were not lacking; thus Roman Catholic observers were invited for the first time.[100] The debate did not, however, lead to any new initiatives at the level of the World Alliance. Typically enough, the general secretary, Pastor Marcel Pradervand, thought it necessary to defend sending observers in his report to the assembly: "In some quarters, we have been criticized for accepting the invitation of the Secretariat for Promoting Christian Unity.... In spite of these criticisms the Executive Committee's [decision] appears to us to have been wholly justified. We have no right whatever to refuse to enter into dialogue with other Christians, however difficult this dialogue may prove." At the same time, he assured the assembly "that in no sense [do] we wish to return to Rome. We are ready, in a spirit of obedience, to let ourselves be led by Christ to a unity which we do not yet see clearly but that He can give to His Church in the measure that it proves to be more obedient and faithful."[101]

In a special resolution the general assembly expressly welcomed the new developments in the Roman Catholic Church. The resolution noted that previous borders were shifting; new light had been shed on many controversies. Dialogue had become possible, and the challenge was felt as overwhelming. "Do we know and can we communicate that for which we stand? Have we the will to engage in fruitful discussion? Have we the firmness to maintain the truth we have already received while being receptive to new understanding?"[102] Yet a direct dialogue between the World Alliance and the Roman Catholic Church was not considered.

---

[99] The decisive move came shortly after World War II. The secretariat of the World Federation was moved at that time from Edinburgh to Geneva. The leading personalities of the World Federation were emphatic in their support for the establishment of the WCC (see *Proceedings of the Sixteenth General Council, Geneva, August 11-17, 1948* (Edinburgh, 1949), 91ff.

[100] The observers were Father Frans Thijssen and Father James Quinn, S.J.

[101] *Frankfurt 1964: Proceedings of the Nineteenth General Council of the Alliance of the Reformed Churches throughout the World Holding the Presbyterian Order, August 3-13, 1964* (Geneva: World Alliance of Reformed Churches, 1964), 65.

[102] Ibid., 242-46.

The resolution was satisfied with simply supporting the initiatives of the WCC. The role of the World Alliance was seen as providing help to the member Churches of the WCC in their dialogue with their Roman Catholic partners. In a second resolution the general assembly emphasized the urgent need of a new solution to the practice of mixed marriage and expressed the hope that the Council would speak out clearly on religious freedom.[103]

At the meeting of the executive committee in Baguio (Philippines) during the following year the question was discussed anew. In several countries contacts had been made between member Churches of the World Alliance and the Catholic Church. Was it appropriate now to extend these contacts to the international level? Professor James I. McCord held that it was, but Marcel Pradervand was against the proposal. The executive committee followed its general secretary and decided "to initiate no separate theological dialogue or theological discussions with the Vatican at this time but ... we support the discussions between the WCC that have begun and ... we make inquiries into the possibility and feasibility of some participation with the Lutherans in Roman Catholic discussions."[104]

A year later there had been no substantial change in the situation, but it was becoming clear that the reserve practiced hitherto could not be maintained for long. At its meeting in Strasbourg, the executive committee confirmed the decision made in Baguio, but at the same time it charged a small committee with reflecting further on the attitude of the World Alliance toward the Roman Catholic Church. The question was raised once again whether Methodists should carry on the dialogue jointly with the Lutheran World Federation.[105]

The suggestion to enter into a joint dialogue proved to be unrealistic. The Lutheran–Roman Catholic dialogue was already too far advanced to be altered in this way. Only in order to deal with the questions of mixed marriages was a joint commission formed; its first meeting was held in 1970.[106]

---

[103] Ibid., 48-49. A further resolution had to do with a common, fixed date for Easter. In an appendix to the Constitution on the Sacred Liturgy, the Council had come out in favor of a fixed date; the World Alliance of Reformed Churches made this suggestion its own (ibid., 42-43).

[104] "Minutes of the Executive Committee Meeting in Baguio City, Philippines, June 24-29, 1965," 6-7 (duplicated).

[105] "Minutes of the Executive Committee Meeting in Strasbourg, August 1966," 8.

[106] From the very outset the subject of mixed marriages was seen as one of the topics for the Lutheran–Roman Catholic dialogue. In 1969 André Appel, general secretary of the Lutheran World Federation, suggested that it handle the question jointly with the World

Meanwhile, the World Alliance of Reformed Churches had decided on its own to enter into a bilateral dialogue.[107]

Dialogues very quickly came into being in certain regions and countries. As early as 1965 a first meeting was held between the American Bishops' Committee for Ecumenical and Interreligious Affairs and the North American Area Council of the World Alliance of Reformed Churches at Krisheim (Philadelphia). Thus a dialogue was begun that over the ensuing years would have considerable results. In September 1975 the Swiss episcopal conference agreed to the formation of a joint commission for dialogue with the Swiss Federation of Evangelical Churches. Further Reformed–Roman Catholic commissions were added in the following years.[108]

F. Other Confessional Traditions

All the families of Churches mentioned thus far were already actively involved during the Council in establishing a new relationship with the Roman Catholic Church. In other Churches, however, the impulse given by the Council had no immediate structural consequences. Even in these Churches, however, the new openness of the Roman Catholic Church caused a new atmosphere to emerge. There, too, the possibilities of dialogue and of cooperation were grasped. But there was not, at least not immediately, any grappling with the new situation at the level of decision-making bodies.

At all the sessions of Vatican II the International Congregationalist Council was represented by a considerable number of qualified observers. Through their reports they contributed substantially, chiefly in the United States, to a positive assessment of the Council. A dialogue with the Roman Catholic Church, however, was not contemplated. The main reason for this was probably the fact that at that time negotiations for a union with the World Alliance of Reformed Churches were going on, and a

---

Alliance of Reformed Churches (see Harding Meyer and Lukas Vischer, eds., *Growth in Agreement: Reports and Agreed Statements of Ecumenical Conversations on a World Level*, Ecumenical Documents II [New York: Paulist Press; Geneva: World Council of Churches, 1984], 277-306).

[107] Ibid., 433-64.

[108] For details on national dialogues, see Lukas Vischer and Andreas Karrer, eds., *Reformed and Catholics in Dialogue*, Studies from the World Alliance of Reformed Churches 10 (Geneva: World Alliance of Reformed Churches, 1988).

dialogue with Rome was possible only through arrangement with the World Alliance. The reserve of the World Alliance, for its part, was probably due to, among other things, the same situation: its attention was focused entirely on the union with the Congregationalists. This union became a fact a few years later (1970) at the general assembly in Nairobi.

As an international confessional family, the Disciples of Christ (Churches of Christ) were represented at the Council. In fact, however, the main presence of the Disciples was in the United States, and their observers were exclusively Americans. After the Council there was a lively debate among the Disciples in the United States. In the summer of 1966 an entire issue of their periodical, *Midstream*, was devoted to an evaluation of the Council.[109] In February 1967, the Disciples' International Council on Christian Unity passed a resolution welcoming the new situation and urging the national Churches "to seize every possibility for creating a better understanding of the contemporary Roman Catholic Church by our people and for interpreting to the Roman Catholics the Christian Churches (Disciples of Christ)." Subsequently, a dialogue was begun at the national level in the United States; dialogue at the international level came only much later.

G. ORTHODOXY

From the outset Rome paid special attention to its relations with the Churches of the East. No effort was spared to move the Orthodox Churches to send observers. Visits, gestures, and symbolic actions followed upon one another in order to create new psychological conditions and a new atmosphere. By the end of the Council that purpose seemed to have been achieved. On December 7, the penultimate day of the Council, it was announced that the Pope and the Patriarch had agreed to "regret and remove from memory and from the midst of the Church the sentences of excommunication... the remembrance of which acts right up to our own times as an obstacle to our mutual approach in charity, and they condemn these to oblivion."[110] Bishop Willebrands read the statement to the assembled Council fathers, while

---

[109] "Estimates of Vatican II," *Midstream* 5/4 (1966).

[110] *Towards the Healing of Schism: The Sees of Rome and Constantinople: Public Statements and Correspondence between the Holy See and the Ecumenical Patriarchate 1958-1984*, ed. and trans. E. J. Stormon, S.J., Ecumenical Documents III (New York: Paulist Press, 1987), 127.

at the same moment the Secretary of the Holy Synod read it in the cathedral of the Phanar. The statement represented an important act of reconciliation.

On the evening of that same day all of those directly involved in the event were invited to a dinner at the Hotel Raffaelo. Even Metropolitan Nikodim was a member of the party; director of the foreign office of the Russian Orthodox Church, he had come to Rome to be present at the close of the Council. Benedictine Dom Emmanuel Lanne remembered that "on that evening hearts were rejoicing at the event of the morning and how the same thanksgiving was offered by the representatives of the first, second, and third Romes, who were present as brothers at the same feast."[111]

Peace seemed to have been achieved, especially in the eyes of Western media, between the Roman Catholic Church and Orthodoxy. Both sides, however, cautioned that the importance of the step taken should not be exaggerated. The joint declaration involved only the Ecumenical Patriarchate and not the whole of Orthodoxy. The text itself states realistically that "this gesture, expressive of justice and mutual forgiveness, cannot be sufficient to put an end to the subjects of difference, ancient and more recent, which still exist between the Roman Catholic Church and the Orthodox Church."[112] There was, nonetheless, a widespread expectation that dialogue could begin immediately and lead quickly to tangible results. The image was deceptive; the reality was more complex.

The Council had given rise to a new atmosphere between the Roman Catholic Church and Orthodoxy. The most important result was that lively relations had been established. Cardinal Bea wrote: "The time of silence has ended: a silence made up of a lack of contacts, separate lives, and separate developments on each side — a silence without love." Reserved though many Orthodox were in their assessment of the Council, they were nonetheless by and large in agreement that through the Council the Roman Catholic Church "had given evidence that it was no longer a Church in self-satisfied isolation, as it appeared to be after Vatican Council I."[113] The Roman Catholic Church had taken cognizance of the reality of other Churches; in the Decree on Ecumenism it acknowledged and

[111] E. Lanne, "La perception en Occident de la participation du Patriarche de Moscou à Vatican II," in *Vatican II in Moscow (1959-1965)*, ed. A. Melloni (Leuven: Peeters, 1997), 128.

[112] Stormon, *Towards the Healing of Schism*, 128.

[113] Maria Brun, *Orthodoxe Stimmen zum II. Vatikanum* (Fribourg, 1988), 222. The book contains many statements by the Orthodox on the Council in general and on particular subjects.

emphasized its close relationship with the Orthodox Church. It had prepared the ground so that the two traditions could understand each other to be sister Churches and could form their relationship correspondingly.

But the special closeness of the two traditions was at the same time a reason why large groups viewed the rapprochement with a certain distrust. The Orthodox Churches recognized in principle that the Roman See was first among the patriarchates.[114] As long as no living relationships existed, this recognition did not present an existential challenge. Now the question had to be faced. The Orthodox Churches had to enter into a debate with the Roman Catholic Church on how to understand "the Church." In Orthodox statements about the Council, critical observations on the ecclesiological presuppositions accepted by the Council predominated. From the very beginning the critique was repeatedly made that the Vatican Council had to be viewed not as an ecumenical council but as a synod of the Western Church. An ecumenical council would have to be supported by the Orthodox Churches and indeed by all Churches. From this point of view the sections of *Lumen gentium* that dealt with the position of the pope and the bishops were seen as an abiding obstacle.[115]

Even by the end of the Council the Orthodox Churches had still not found their way to a common position in face of the Roman Catholic Church. At the time of the Council all the Orthodox Churches were represented in the WCC, but even during the fourth period the number of Churches that sent observers to the Council was limited. The Patriarchate of Moscow was represented from the beginning, and, from the second period on, so was the Church of Georgia. Beginning in the third period the Ecumenical Patriarchate and the Patriarchate of Alexandria were also

---

[114] John Meyendorff et al., *La Primauté de Pierre dans l'Eglise orthodoxe* (Neuchâtel: Delachaux & Niestlé, 1960); in English, *The Primacy of Peter [in the Orthodox Church]* (London: Faith Press, 1963).

[115] See Father Iohannes Karmiris, "Die orthodoxe katholische Kirche über das II. Vatikanum und die auf ihm entwickelten Aspekte und Tendenzen hinsichtlich der christlichen Einheit," *Kyrios* 4 (1964), 247: "It is thus utterly clear that the Council does not have the essential traits of the ecumenical synods of antiquity, inasmuch as it has been convoked by the Patriarch of Rome alone, without the knowledge and prior agreement and approval of the other patriarchs, Church leaders, and their synods; nor does it deal with universal dogmatic and other questions that occupy the entire Church of Christ." Later on Karmiris judged that what was said in *De ecclesia* about infallibility is "predestined to become a source of difference." He also blamed the Council for tending to speak "with a view to a positive and well-disposed judgment of it by the Protestants" (*Ekklesia*, May 1, 1966). An extreme but typical sentence was that of Igor Troyanoff, the observer from the Russian Church in Exile: "The whole tragedy for Catholicism lies in that the Orthodox conception cannot be accepted in parts but only as a whole, as is whole and united the Orthodox Church itself" (see Council for Foreign Relations, Rc Files 44/7).

represented. In addition, observers from the Churches of Serbia and Bulgaria also came. The Patriarchates of Antioch and Jerusalem, and the Churches of Rumania, Cyprus, Greece, Poland, and Czechoslovakia kept their distance from the Council. More important, considerable differences existed between the Patriarchates of Constantinople and Moscow, "the second and third Romes." During the Council tensions repeatedly arose that made a unified attitude difficult.

Among the major figures who influenced events during the Council was undoubtedly the Ecumenical Patriarch Athenagoras I (1886-1972). After first being the head of the Greek Orthodox diaspora in North and South America, he was elected patriarch in 1949. His primary goal was the unity of the Orthodox Churches and, beyond that, of Christendom as a whole. He played an active role in the formation and life of the WCC. In the very first utterances of John XXIII he saw signs of a new era.[116] The announcement of the Council strengthened him in his conviction that everything must be done to solidify the union of the Orthodox Churches among themselves. In 1961, the First Pan-Orthodox synod brought together representatives of all the Orthodox Churches (September 25 to October 1). The hope behind the synod was to reach agreement on preparation for a Pan-Orthodox prosynod.

When, somewhat later, the question arose of sending observers to the Council, it meant a great deal to the Ecumenical Patriarch that there should be a common decision. Because of this outlook, a strangely conflictive situation arose as the Council was beginning; while Constantinople did not send any observers because of signals received from other Orthodox Churches, Moscow, thinking that Constantinople would send observers, sent representatives. Rome took all possible steps to avoid the resulting dead end; Father Pierre Duprey went to Constantinople twice as an emissary of the SPCU, in order to inform the Patriarch of developments at the Council. The Second Pan-Orthodox Conference in Rhodes (September 26-30, 1963) took up the question of relations with the Roman Catholic Church. With regard to the sending of observers it was decided that each Orthodox Church should be free to act according to its own judgment. At the same time, the Roman Catholic Church was offered a dialogue, but a dialogue of equals. Once again, Constantinople did not send observers to the second session, although Archimandrite André Scrima was present in Rome as the personal representative of the Patriarch.

---

[116] Message of Patriarch Athenagoras (January 15, 1959) in response to John XXIII's call for unity in his Christmas message (in Stormon, *Towards the Healing of Schism*, 30-31).

However, an entirely different kind of breakthrough occurred in a manner entirely unexpected. On December 4, 1963, toward the end of the second period, the Pope told the Council that he intended to undertake a pilgrimage to Jerusalem. Two days later Athenagoras responded to this announcement with the spontaneous suggestion that on the occasion of this pilgrimage "all the heads of the holy Churches of Christ, of the East and the West, of the three confessional groupings, were to meet one another in the holy city of Sion" in order to "open up, in the spirit of unity, a new and blessed road."[117] The journey of the Ecumenical Patriarch led to a new image of ecumenical contact: two Church leaders meeting as equals. In the words of the Pope, "Athenagoras, the Ecumenical Patriarch of Constantinople, along with eleven metropolitans, came to meet me and wished to embrace me as one embraces a brother, to take my hand and to lead me by the hand into the room where we were to exchange a few words, as if to say: we must, we must understand each other, we must make peace to show the world that we have become brothers again."[118] Even though the Church of Greece, in particular, did not approve the action of Athenagoras I, the influence of the event was considerable.

From that point on, relations between Rome and Constantinople developed rapidly. The Easter greeting that Athenagoras sent to the Pope was not only answered, but the Pope took the Patriarch's action as an occasion for reviving the ancient tradition of Easter greetings and extending it to other Churches.[119] In April a papal delegation visited the Phanar.[120] A further gesture, directed primarily to the Church of Greece, came a few months later, when, in the summer of 1964, the Pope decided to return a precious relic, the head of Andrew the apostle, to the cathedral of Patmos; in 1462 it had been given for safekeeping to Aeneas Silvius Piccolomini, then the pope. In September 1964, during the third period, the relic was first venerated by the Council fathers and afterward taken to Greece, where a great many of the people welcomed it.[121]

---

[117] Stormon, *Towards the Healing of Schism*, 55.

[118] Schmidt, *Augustin Bea*, 469-70.

[119] Ibid.,

[120] The delegation consisted of Archbishop Joseph Marie Martin of Rouen, Willebrands, and Duprey (see Stormon, *Towards the Healing of Schism*, 71-74).

[121] The next year saw two other similarly symbolic actions: the head of Titus was given back to Crete; and in October 1965 the bones of St. Sabas, one of the most important Fathers of Eastern monasticism, were returned to his monastery in the Jordan Valley. While the Holy See discovered the effective language of symbols in its dealings with Orthodoxy, contacts with the Western Churches were far more sober. Some observers suggested that a symbolic act of the greatest significance would be the opening of the secret archives of

During that summer the Pope once again invited all the Orthodox Churches to send observers. The Patriarchates of Constantinople and Alexandria complied with the invitation. The Third Pan-Orthodox Conference met during the third period (November 1-15) in Rhodes; the Pope sent it a message.[122] The conference remained reserved as to a dialogue with the Roman Catholic Church. It decided to continue the dialogue with the Old Catholic Church and the Anglican Communion. It did indeed approve once again of a dialogue with the Catholic Church, but at the same time it said that "before a fruitful beginning of a true theological dialogue, an indispensable preparation and the creation of suitable conditions are necessary."[123] The papal message received an answer when in February of the following year Metropolitan Meliton reported to the Pope in person the results of the conference.

To this initiative Bea responded in April 1965 with a visit to Constantinople. In his address the Cardinal urged further steps:

> The dialogue of charity ... is not restricted to an exchange of visits and the kiss of peace. Its first and most definite and practical effect is the decision we have taken together to make preparations in the midst of our respective Churches for all that unity involves.... The dialogue of charity is already beginning to bring about unity, and is at the same time the best preparation for the search for unity in the matters that still divide us, particularly certain points of doctrine.[124]

"There is a lot to be made good," the Cardinal said in that address. Before his departure he paid a visit to Hagia Sophia and had pointed out to him the spot on which in 1054 Rome's excommunication was leveled against the ecumenical patriarch. At that time the idea was probably already around that a way had to be found of transcending that event and its serious consequences. In fact, the idea of a joint declaration matured during the following months. During the fourth period the actual negotiations began amid the greatest secrecy. In a letter to the Patriarch on October 18, 1965, Bea suggested that a joint commission be established. Archimandrite Andre Scrima, one of Constantinople's observers at the Council, was asked to bring this message to Athenagoras and explain it.

---

the Inquisition. This was not possible at that time; see Cardinal Augustin Bea, *Ökumenismus im Konzil: Öffentliche Etappen eines überraschenden Weges* (Freiburg, 1969), 180-84, 217-37.

[122] Stormon, *Towards the Healing of Schism*, 80.

[123] Schmidt, *Augustin Bea*, 477.

[124] Stormon, *Towards the Healing of Schism*, 93.

Negotiations began in November. Meanwhile, in October some initial information had already leaked out in Rome. Metropolitan Emilianos, another observer from Constantinople, spoke openly of the plan. By means of uncompromising denials, both publicly and in private conversations, Willebrands succeeded in leading astray the press and other interested parties.[125] In this case, since the Patriarchate considered this to be its own business, the other Orthodox Churches were not consulted.[126] At the beginning of the joint commission's meeting, Metropolitan Meliton sketched the main lines of the plan. The other members accepted his thoughts in good measure. An important aspect of the matter for the Orthodox side was the hope of making "a contribution to the general cause of Christian unity"; the step to be taken, said Meliton, could serve as an example to other Christian Churches.[127] The joint text was approved on November 23, thus opening the way for the solemn ceremony at the end of the Council. After the ceremony Metropolitan Meliton went to London in order to explain the matter to the Archbishop of Canterbury.[128]

Relations between Rome and Constantinople were strengthened in the years that followed. In 1967 the Pope visited the Ecumenical Patriarchate, and a short time later Athenagoras repaid the visit. From then on reciprocal visits on the patronal feasts of both sees became an institution. Yet the planned dialogue could not immediately become a reality. In order to understand why this was so, we must take a quick look at the Russian Orthodox Church and its relationship with the ecumenical movement.

The foreign relations of the Russian Orthodox Church were largely determined during those years by the conflictive situation that had arisen with the regime of Nikita Khrushchev. Khrushchev pursued a double goal in relation to the Church. On the one hand, he used it in his dealings abroad in order to give the appearance of credibility to his policy of the

[125] John Lawrence, generally a well-informed observer, became convinced that Metropolitan Emilianos had made up the story. In his diary for October 13 he wrote: "Emilianos told the Pope that it would be a good thing to revoke the anathema of 1054 and then told the press that this was what the Pope was going to do. Roman rumours!" (Rc Files 44/3).

[126] In his report to the Archbishop of Canterbury, Metropolitan Meliton was emphatic "that this action had been taken by the Church of Constantinople in its own name, not in the name of all Orthodoxy." It is likely that Metropolitan Nikodim of Leningrad knew nothing of the imminent event when he decided to travel to Rome for the close of the Council. Archbishop Chrysostomos of Athens published a statement distancing himself from the gesture.

[127] Stormon, *Towards the Healing of Schism*, 121.

[128] See the memorandum in the archives of Lambeth Palace. In his conversation with the Archbishop, Meliton stressed the limited significance of the action (RC Files 44/7).

peaceful coexistence of the various political systems. On the other hand, on the domestic scene he used drastic measures in order to reduce the influence of the Churches on the populace. This is the only possible way to explain the fact that the acceptance of relations with the outside was accompanied by persecution of the Churches within the country. From a report, dated August 18, 1960, of the acting president of the (civil) council for the Russian Orthodox Church, we learn: "The council watches over the external activity of the Church and orientates activity in the interests of the foreign policy of the Soviet State, uses it in the peace campaign and in unmasking anti-soviet propaganda carried out in capitalistic countries, in favour of the explanation of Soviet legislation on cults and on religious conditions in the USSR."[129] That goal made it understandable that the Russian Orthodox Church was able to enter the WCC in 1961. It was also the background of the gradual opening to the Roman Catholic Church.

This does not mean that Church leaders were simply agents of the civil authorities. In their policies they were guided by ecclesial motives and interests. Metropolitan Nikodim, who had been the leader of the (ecclesial) department for foreign affairs since 1960, hoped that through international relations the situation of the Russian Orthodox Church could be improved. It was he who pushed for entrance into the WCC. Finally, backed by Father Vitaly Borovoy, who understood how, by intelligent analysis of situations, to use any relative advantages for the good of the Church,[130] Nikodim managed to win approval for an opening to the Roman Catholic Church. Nikodim was, in addition, an admirer of the Roman Catholics and of John XXIII in particular.[131]

It was important to ensure that the Russian Orthodox Church would be able to play an independent role in the WCC. Here civil and ecclesial interests converged. For the civil authorities the important thing was to neutralize the anti-Soviet attitude of the West. Work had to be done to prevent anticommunist forces from gaining a foothold either in the WCC or at the Second Vatican Council. This meant, as far as the Council was

---

[129] A. Roccucci, "Russian Observers at Vatican II," in Melloni, *Vatican II in Moscow*, 85. The memorandum says further that the Patriarchate of Moscow must strengthen its connection with other Orthodox Churches "in order to oppose the attempts of the Patriarch of Constantinople to unify the Orthodox Eastern Churches around himself, using them in the interests of the Vatican and of American foreign policy in these countries."

[130] A good example of Borovoy's working method is given in ibid., 66-67.

[131] Metropolitan Nikodim wrote a book entitled *Johannes XXIII: Ein unbequemer Optimist* (Zurich: Benziger, 1978), with a preface by Franz Cardinal König.

concerned, preventing a renewed condemnation of communism. For the ecclesiastical authorities the aim was to strengthen the position of the Church. The claim to a degree of autonomy in relation to Constantinople reflected deep-rooted convictions. The Russian Orthodox wanted to be an important voice within Orthodoxy.

The presence of Russian Orthodox observers caused a sensation. It also led the Holy See to pay special attention to relations with the Patriarchate of Moscow. After the first period Father Borovoy conveyed to the competent authorities the Pope's wish that Metropolitan Slipyi be released from prison and receive permission to take part in the Council. On February 10, Slipyi arrived in Rome. A few weeks later Pope John XXIII gave a private audience to Alexi Adjubei, Khrushchev's son-in-law, and his wife. The encyclical *Pacem in terris*, published in April 1963, was very favorably received in Moscow, thereby strengthening the impression that the Vatican was on its way to adopting a new attitude toward communist regimes. In July 1963 a Roman Catholic delegation took part in the celebration of the fifty-year jubilee of the episcopal consecration of Patriarch Alexei I: a first sign that the new Pope intended to continue relations with the Patriarchate of Moscow. Finally, the encyclical *Ecclesiam suam* (August 1964) committed the Church to dialogue.

The *Ostpolitik* of Pope Paul VI was aimed at easing the role of the observers and thereby of the Russian Orthodox Church itself. It was a way of telling the political authorities that the period of Pius XII was now past. The fact that during the final period of the Council the efforts of conservative circles failed to obtain the inclusion of a clear condemnation of communism in *Gaudium et spes* could be interpreted as a success for the Soviet Union.[132] On the other hand, the adoption of the Declaration on Religious Freedom was of the highest importance for the Russian Orthodox Church. "For us it was a source of great hope. No one else in the world had as great a need of this religious freedom as we did. For us the issue was a very concrete matter of daily life."[133]

The unification of the Orthodox Churches in a common approach to the Church of Rome was not something to be taken for granted, given the divergent interests of those involved. Even at the fourth Pan-Orthodox Conference, held at Chambésy in July 1968, no dialogue in the name of

---

[132] See *Gaudium et spes*, nos. 20-21.
[133] V. Borovoy, "Il significato del Concilio Vaticano II per la Chiesa ortodossa russa," in Melloni, *Vatican II in Moscow*, 85.

Orthodoxy as a whole was offered. Instead, there was to be a joint commission on the question of dialogue.

The Oriental Orthodox Churches deserve at least a reference here. All of them had observers at the Council, mostly beginning in the first period. As early as 1948 these Churches, with the exception of the Armenian Orthodox, had accepted the invitation to membership in the WCC; their delegates were present at the assembly in which the WCC was founded. Abuna Theophilos, Archbishop of the Ethiopian Orthodox Church, invited these delegates to a dinner. Looking back to that occasion, Father K. M. Simon of the Syrian Orthodox Church wrote: "At that meeting we realized to our great surprise that we knew almost nothing of one another or even of our common heritage, despite the fact that we formed a single faith-community and held the same doctrine."

The lack of unity and collaboration at that time was overcome to some extent in the years that followed.[134] Relations between the individual Oriental Orthodox Churches grew closer year by year. In particular, bonds were formed between the Ethiopian and the Syrian Orthodox Churches in India. The years of the Council saw the coming of the first conversations with theologians of the Eastern Orthodox tradition. A 1964 meeting in Aarhus, organized within the WCC, led to a theological agreement between the two families of Churches.[135] The decision to undertake these conversations was substantially facilitated by contacts among observers at the Council.

The meeting in Aarhus had unexpected consequences. Trusting in the agreement reached there, Emperor Haile Selassie of Ethiopia invited the Churches of the two traditions to a meeting in Addis Ababa. The suggestion proved unrealistic; nevertheless, in January 1965 the highest representatives of the Oriental Orthodox Churches met in the Ethiopian capital and resolved from then on to collaborate more closely in theological formation, the spread of the faith, and the shaping of relations with other Churches. The assembled representatives also established a standing committee. In gratitude for his action in behalf of unity they bestowed on the emperor the title Defender of the Faith.[136]

On the basis of further theological conversations, which were likewise made possible by the Faith and Order Commission of the WCC, a formal dialogue between the Eastern and the Oriental Orthodox Churches

---

[134] Fey, *History of the Ecumenical Movement*, 2:290-91.

[135] The agreements reached in those conversations were published in Paulus Gregorios, William H. Lazareth, and Nikos A. Nissiotis, eds., *Does Chalcedon Divide or Unite?* (Geneva: WCC, 1981).

[136] Fey, *History of the Ecumenical Movement*, 2:292.

began. But a joint dialogue with the Roman Catholic Church did not come about. In contrast, there were close contacts between Rome and individual Eastern Churches. Meetings came to be increasingly taken for granted. For example, when the Pope took part in the eucharistic congress in Bombay in 1964, he had a meeting with the representative of the Syrian Orthodox Church. Meetings in Rome followed. In May 1967, the first head of an Eastern Church, Khoren I, Katholikos of the Armenian Church in Cilicia, paid an official visit to the Pope.

H. United Bible Societies

An important area of collaboration was opened up by the Council's decision to use the national languages in the liturgy. This reform made the translation of the sacred scriptures an urgent task. On the evangelical side this was a task that had long since been taken up by the Bible Societies. The first national Bible Society came into being in 1804. The British and Foreign Bible Society became a model for many other such establishments. In 1946 it joined a world federation, the United Bible Societies. At the time of the Council thirty-five national Bible Societies belonged to this organization. The Bible Societies had had impressive achievements: the Bible had been translated into over 600 languages, and another 500 were in progress. Did it not seem reasonable to make use of this treasure in the imminent reform of the liturgy?

The way to the Council's decision had been prepared for by the liturgical and biblical movements within the Roman Catholic Church. Olivier Béguin, general secretary of the United Bible Society, had been attentively following those developments.[137] When the decision of the Council began to take shape, he was immediately informed of this by the observer from the WCC, and he began to make direct contacts. As early as February 1963 the president and general secretary of the United Bible Society sent a letter to Cardinal Bea in which they asked whether collaboration in translation, publication, and distribution could be the subject of a conversation. The Cardinal thought it advisable to wait a while.

In May 1963 the United Bible Society met in Hakone, Japan, where Olivier Béguin presented a detailed report on developments in the Roman

---

[137] As early as 1958 Béguin had composed a report on activities in the Catholic Church for the attention of the WCC.

Catholic Church.[138] The board agreed that the matter should be followed up in close contact with the national Bible Society. In June 1964 a meeting of Church leaders and translators in Driebergen, Holland, provided an occasion for a further exchange, and on November 10-13, with Bea's agreement, a mixed group of specialists met in order to agree informally on possible guidelines for collaboration. The group formulated a set of guiding principles.

Shortly thereafter, the Council approved the *Dogmatic Constitution on Divine Revelation (Dei Verbum)* (November 18, 1965), which contains the following explicit instruction:

> Access to sacred Scripture ought to be open wide to the Christian faithful.... But since the Word of God must be readily available at all times, the Church, with motherly concern, sees to it that suitable and correct translations are made into various languages, especially from the original texts of the sacred books. If it should happen that, when the opportunity presents itself and the authorities of the Church agree, these translations are made in a joint effort with the separated brethren, they may be used by all Christians (no. 22).

With this statement the foundation was finally laid for close collaboration. The urgency of this collaboration was also emphasized by the joint working group formed by the Roman Catholic Church and the WCC.[139] At its meeting on May 16-21 in Buck Hill Falls, the council of the United Bible Societies expressed its delight at this opening and stated that everything must be done to publish bibles that can be used by all the Churches: "It is important to avoid the publication of competitive Bibles." Even the disputed question of the place of the Old Testament apocrypha should not stand in the way of that goal.

In Rome, meanwhile, and within the SPCU, a special secretariat for bible translations was established. On April 4, 1966, the Pope agreed to a visit from Bea on this subject. Father Walter Abbott, S.J., was given the task of establishing coordination with the United Bible Societies. He was invited to Buck Hill Falls and given the opportunity to develop his ideas about this collaboration.

From that point on, it was possible to plan jointly and act jointly. The guidelines established at Crêt-Bérard were further expanded in the following year and finally published jointly as *Guiding Principles for*

---

[138] In addition, Béguin published a book entitled *Roman Catholicism and the Bible* (New York: Association Press, 1963).

[139] First Report of Joint Working Group, 16; second report, II, 6.

Interconfessional Cooperation in Translating the Bible.[140] Within a relatively short time, numerous interconfessional translations appeared
either of the entire Bible or of parts of it; by 1985 there were 160 of
them.[141]

VII. A TRANSITIONAL COUNCIL?

The ecumenical dimension of the Second Vatican Council was not limited to the presence and participation of observers. As period succeeded
period, the Churches themselves that had sent observers were increasingly involved; although the Council had been convoked and carried
through by the Roman Catholic Church, it was an event that affected the
other Churches. Since the beginning of the twentieth century, these other
Churches had drawn ever closer. As a result, the great *aggiornamento* to
which Pope John XXIII urged his Church took place within the context
of an already existing ecumenical community. The unexpected opening
of the Roman Catholic Church set a challenge both for that community
and for the individual Churches that belonged to it. Conversely, the
Roman Catholic Church was influenced and shaped by the non-Roman
Catholic Churches. Without them, and especially without the existing
ecumenical community, the Second Vatican Council would not have
become what it did become. The non–Roman Catholic Churches were
not mere spectators; they became participants in the conciliar event. They
took initiatives that started or at least hastened developments.

By the end of the Council the outlines of a new and broader ecumenical community had become visible. Would these outlines be filled in?
Or would they fade away once more? Only by a combined effort of all
the Churches could any real advance be made. Was it perhaps possible
to look beyond Vatican II and work for a truly ecumenical council? This
idea had already been voiced during the years of preparation. When it

---

[140] Edward H. Robertson, *Taking the Word to the World: Fifty Years of the United
Bible Societies* (Nashville, Tenn.: Thomas Nelson, 1996), 103-22; Walter M. Abbott, "The
Shape of the Common Bible," *CivCatt* (June 2, 1968); idem, "Easy Access to Sacred
Scripture for All," *Catholic Biblical Quarterly* 30/1 (January 1968); United Bible Societies, *The Bible Societies and the Roman Catholic Church* (London, 1969), with contributions from Walter M. Abbott, Laton E. Holmgren, Olivier Béguin, Wesley J. Culshaw,
and Otto Knoch; United Bible Societies, "Interconfessional Cooperation: Roman Catholics
and the Bible Societies," Background Paper XX (June 1969).
[141] Schmidt, *Augustin Bea*, 629-33.

became clear that the council convoked by John XXIII would be a gathering of Roman Catholic bishops, discussion immediately began about the presuppositions that needed to be verified so that there could be talk of a truly ecumenical council. A new interest had been awakened even in Churches in which the idea of a council had previously played hardly any role.[142]

The suggestion that the Churches work toward an ecumenical council offered perspectives that were at once critical and constructive. The Orthodox side, in particular, pointed out the limitations affecting the Second Vatican Council: "There is a sincere and welcome effort on the part of the Second Vatican Council to come into contact with the other churches and to share in their dialogue. But this ecumenism, we believe, has to become really ecumenical."[143] In the eyes of the Orthodox, Vatican Council II could at best act as a transition to a truly ecumenical council. In the WCC, too, voices pointing in this direction were increasingly heard as the Council continued.[144] A year after the Council, the Faith and Order Commission undertook a study of the significance of the early Church councils for the Church of today.[145] Most important, however, was the fact that, as our description has shown, in almost all the Churches a new debate arose over how the communion of Churches could find credible expression at the universal level. The discussion has continued down to our time.

---

[142] Hans Jochen Margull, ed., *Die ökumenischen Konzile der Christenheit* (Stuttgart, 1961); Lukas Vischer, "The World Council of Churches and the Vatican Council," *Ecumenical Review* 14 (1962), 281-95.

[143] Nikos A. Nissiotis, "Is the Vatican Council Really Ecumenical?" *Ecumenical Review* 16/4 (1964), 377.

[144] E.g., Lukas Vischer in a lecture given in Vienna in March 1965: "Ein ökumenisches Konzil?" in *Überlegungen nach dem Vatikanischen Konzil* (Zurich, 1966).

[145] WCC, *Councils and the Ecumenical Movement*, World Council Studies 5 (Geneva: WCC, 1968).

CHAPTER VII

THE CONCLUSION OF THE COUNCIL AND THE INITIAL
RECEPTION

GIUSEPPE ALBERIGO

The fourth and final phase of the Council, from the last weeks of work
in 1964 to the solemn closing ceremony on December 8, 1965, was
marked by frenetic activity; solemn approval was given to two constitutions, six decrees, and three declarations, that is, eleven of the sixteen
texts approved by Vatican II! The assembly did almost nothing but vote.
The commissions, now without any outside control, worked hard at organizing the texts. The Pope intervened repeatedly in almost all the texts
while also dissuading the fathers from a conciliar canonization of
John XXIII; these interventions humiliated the majority and weakened the
scope of some crucial texts. The undeniable importance of winning unanimous agreements led to the acceptance of changes that weakened the
perspectives perceived by the Council.

There was a blatant contrast between the innovative importance of
some texts that secured definitive approval during this period *(Nostra
aetate, Dignitatis humanae, Ad gentes, Gaudium et spes)*, even though
they were marked by serious internal discontinuities, and, on the other
hand, a considerable and widespread collapse within the Council of the
pursuit of the ideal. More than a few fathers were afraid that the energetic
striving for renewal that had driven the assembly to the difficult but exciting search for *aggiornamento* and unity had been irremediably weakened.
The uncertainty with which the Council formulated its rejection of the
"balance of terror" and a corresponding banning of atomic weapons was
a symptom of this situation.[1]

The decisions of Paul VI to arrogate to himself both the establishment
of a collegial body at the level of the universal Church (the Synod of
Bishops) and the treatment of some especially pressing problems (birth

---

[1] During these final weeks there was renewed pressure for a conciliar condemnation
of communism. Those who were renewing this old demand perhaps were hoping to find
a more receptive hearing in an atmosphere of less concern for the "rejection of condemnations" of which Pope John had spoken.

control and clerical celibacy), even though these were problems keenly felt not only within the assembly but throughout the whole of contemporary society, showed beyond a doubt that the conciliar stage was now left behind. This was confirmed by the placing, for the first time, of an elevated throne behind the table of the Council of presidents, a throne reserved for the pope.

I. The Wearying Task of Ending and the "Revenge" of the Preparatory Period

Almost all the fathers felt the struggle between an impatient desire to end their long stay in Rome and the conviction that they could not end the Council without approving the schemas on religious freedom and on the Church in the modern world. Despite some uncertainty, even attentive observers were asking whether "this fourth session will be the last of Vatican II. True enough, there are several signs suggesting that the desires of the pope and of the vast majority of the fathers tend in that direction.... But in this area any overly categorical prediction runs the risk of being proved wrong by facts, for while the pope proposes, it is the bishops who dispose."[2]

The demanding course leading to the end of the Council was further complicated by unexpected breakdowns and confusing regroupings of the majority. Several groups of fathers with different attitudes had seemed to have consolidated after the breaking-in period in 1962, but now, especially in connection with the debates on schema XIII, differences appeared among leaders of the majority; the disagreement between the French and the Germans on the approach to be taken in the schema may be taken as representative. A concomitant cause of the uncertainties can be seen in the lack of a unanimously recognized leader who would direct the development of so complex a schema, especially after illness had removed both Msgr. Guano and Professor Philips from the work.[3] On the other hand, the very use of the inductive method with its sociological

---

[2] R. Brouillet, report of September 21, 1965, cited in A. Melloni, *L'altra Roma: Politica e S. Sede durante il concilio Vaticano II (1959–1965)* (Bologna: Il Mulino, 2000), 349 n. 54.

[3] Philips was forced to leave Rome due to serious exhaustion; Guano was prevented by illness from finishing the preparation of schema XIII; and Lercaro was stricken by illness during the last weeks of work.

emphases underscored and heightened the differences between the concrete situations to which each bishop and group would naturally refer. In addition, debates and votes on entirely different subjects succeeded one another rapidly and often overlapped and crisscrossed during one and the same meeting. This caused weariness and even alienation, as numerous diaries bear witness.[4]

The "soft" approach of John XXIII was now a thing of the past, as was the fruitful guiding role taken by some leaders (Bea, Suenens, Léger) during the periods of work in 1963 and 1964. In 1965, however, a sense of emptiness seemed to be spreading due to weariness and to the difficulty of preserving a relationship of complete trust and harmony with Paul VI. Meanwhile, the aggressiveness and combativeness of the minority, which found its center in the *Coetus Internationalis Patrum* and some important representatives of the Curia (Cicognani, Felici), seemed now much more effective. Even the method of participation in the work was gradually altered. Alongside the quest for consensus in the conciliar assembly, there were more and more appeals to the Pope and pressures brought to bear on him, and he seemed moved by both.

Despite the drastic pruning to which the preparatory schemes were subjected in the autumn of 1962, much of the material readied during the preparatory period was still on the Council's table. The many conciliar commissions (which were based on the preparatory commissions) had taken steps to keep that material at hand; now, on the eve of the ending, it was a burden. It seems clear that if the fourth period had focused solely on the problems of the non-Christian religions, religious freedom, the word of God, a missionary renewal, and the state of the Church in the modern world (the latter being the only conciliar document without a direct precedent in the preparatory period), the work would have been done in a much more linear and fruitful way.

II. Characteristic Features of the Assembly: Method and New Subjects

During this final period the composition of the assembly, though marked by considerable continuity, felt the absence of bishops who had shared the experience of the early phases; it also felt the effects of the

---

[4] See *Volti di fine Concilio: Studi di storia e teologia sulla conclusione del Vaticano II*, ed. A. Melloni and J. Doré (Bologna: Il Mulino, 2000).

fact that 146 "new" bishops were participating in the Council for the first time; although not representing a high percentage of the total, this fact still had an impact.

The work was also affected by media attention that was far greater than in the past. That in this decisive phase the Council was tackling such subjects as religious freedom, the Catholic attitude to the Jews, and the Church's relationship with contemporary society gave rise to extraordinary interest on the part of the news media, even where, as in the United States of America, theological subjects had drawn little attention. Calm, objective labors were not always served by being uninterruptedly under the gaze of public opinion, especially because by now there was no such thing as secrecy. Nor can we underestimate the influence, almost nonexistent until 1965, of great international organizations and some centers of political power, in connection, for example, with the attitude of the Church to the Jewish people or the legitimacy of atomic weapons.[5]

The debates on the declaration on religious freedom and, still more, on the Church in the modern world brought the great majority of the fathers up against subjects entirely unfamiliar to them. Some of them saw the inadequacy of the Church's views or at least an embarrassing contradiction between the traditional Catholic position and the demands made by contemporary societies as well as by many of the faithful. The view that religious freedom was incompatible with the "rights of the truth" was still regularly taught in ecclesiastical institutes, as was the incompatibility of the Church and modern society, as taught in the *Syllabus* of Pius IX.

The schemas submitted to the Council were problematic in their inspiration and profoundly different among themselves. Some of the fathers expressed feelings that ranged from uneasiness to rejection. Others, however, were convinced that the Council was called upon to bring Catholicism out of the blind alley into which it had been led by outmoded positions by establishing fresh contact with the gospel sources of the Christian faith and by facing modern culture in a new spirit. As a result, the distance between these two different choices was especially strong, not only doctrinally but also psychologically.[6]

There was a profound difference between the inductive method and the usual deductive method. With his call to read the "signs of the times," John XXIII had hoped that the Council in tackling problems would start

---

[5] See Melloni, *L'altra Roma*, 234–44, 269–72.
[6] See J. Komonchak, "Le valutazioni sulla Gaudium et spes: Chenu, Dossetti, Ratzinger," in *Volti di fine Concilio*, 115–53.

not from eternal principles but from the consciousness that contemporary humanity had of its problems. John's approach was exemplified in the encyclicals *Mater et magistra* and, above all, *Pacem in terris*. These documents, perhaps precisely because of their approach, had won universal hearing and agreement. Nonetheless, it was hard for many fathers to accept a cultural "conversion" that they perceived as difficult and dangerous, whereas the familiar deductive method of Scholasticism seemed easy and safe.

This novel method was often followed using cultural tools that were still relatively unrefined in their application to the subjects the Council was facing. Some fathers were made uneasy not only by the use of the inductive method but also by some "sociological" views that had slipped in. While this allowed many non-European bishops to feel more at ease than ever before, it gave rise to uneasiness, disappointment, and even disaffection in fathers who had played a decisive role during the preceding periods.[7] It was not easy for the latter no longer to have a leading role, and the Council found it difficult to be deprived of them. The use of the inductive method was an exceptionally important change for Catholicism and also an expression of the difficulty in moving beyond the Eurocentrism in the shadow of which Vatican II had begun.

Gaudium et spes, more than anything else, triggered a synergistic and no longer polemical confrontation with modernity in the area of the presentation of the faith. On this point Vatican II attempted the kind of fruitful encounter with cultures that had taken place repeatedly in antiquity and the Middle Ages but had been interrupted after the Renaissance. There were many who held that an encounter and sympathetic relationship with "modern civilization" were utterly impossible and therefore could not even be suggested. The demonization of "the modern world" had become a security blanket for a large sector of Catholicism, although for some time now, and despite being greeted by distrust and hostility, there had been pastoral experiments and doctrinal developments that were inspired by a calmer vision of the Church's relationship with humanity. Vatican II drew inspiration for its own decisions from an awareness that the phase known as Christendom was now past, that is, the time when Christianity and, above all, Catholicism, in the West was lived as a social system that was self-sufficient

---

[7] See G. Ruggieri, "Delusioni alla fine del concilio: Qualche atteggiamento nell'ambiente cattolico francese," in *Volti di fine Concilio*, 193–224.

inasmuch as it embodied the faith and was ruled by the Church and its secular arm.[8]

III. THE BURDEN OF VOTING AND THE MATURING OF THE EPISCOPAL CONFERENCES

Between September 20 and December 6, 1965, a total of 256 votes were taken in the hall (votes no. 284 to no. 540) – 47 percent of all the votes taken during the entire Council. Almost all the fathers experienced this aspect of the fourth period as an increasingly intolerable burden. It became difficult to concentrate on problems, and disaffection spread. It was frustrating to have to stay in Rome, with its understandable inconveniences and expenses,[9] in order to take part in bursts of voting.[10] Whereas in the preceding periods involvement and participation had grown, the opposite feelings were now on the rise.

In fact, the entire organized course of the Council's work was deeply affected.[11] Many of the schemas still to be approved had already been discussed and now required mainly the work of the commissions and frequent votes. "New" schemas, on the other hand, and schema XIII in particular, required both thorough discussion in the hall and polishing by the commissions. As a result, it repeatedly became necessary to defer general congregations for several days at a time so that the commissions could work both morning and afternoon. Thus, on October 1 it was announced that there would be no general congregations from October 17 to October 24 and again from October 30 to November 8 and even that the fathers would be able to leave Rome. Referring to meetings of the representatives of the various episcopates, Etchegaray told Congar: "The

---

[8] Many bishops were able to accept this perspective because they knew the *Humanisme intégral* of Jacques Maritain.

[9] Congar wrote: "I spoke with Cardinal Richaud about the finances of the Council: How much was it costing? He had no idea, even though he is a member of the financial commission. This commission had met only twice and for less than an hour. There is a blackout on the subject of finances! It seems to have been thought initially of holding the Council *in a tent* erected on the courtyard of St. Damasus. That shows that at the beginning no one had any idea of what the Council could become: neither its duration nor the program of work nor the technical requirements.... John XXIII said, in fact, during the first period: When it comes to councils, we are all novices" (*JCongar*, November 7, 1965; II, 464).

[10] Only 1,521 bishops took part in the voting on *De presbyterorum ordine*.

[11] On September 21 the Council took a straw vote on religious freedom; later, requests for similar straw votes were turned down, with the result that the uneasiness of the assembly was further increased.

bishops are asking what they are to do. They want to work. During the 'empty week' of October 17–24 they were asked to think about only *one* subject: the discipline of penance (fasting, abstinence).... They have a feeling of a *void*."[12] The governing bodies of the Council were unable to prevent these inconveniences; the assembly seemed to be once more without a head. In fact, after the Council had voted on the importance of collegiality, the pace of work in the assembly slowed down.

Due perhaps in part to the lack of work in the full assembly, the territorial conferences acquired greater visibility during this period.[13] The main impulse to this came from the meetings of their secretaries, which Etchegaray promoted with intelligent perseverance; another impulse came from the decision to fill up the time when the general congregations were suspended with discussions among the presidents of the conferences; another, finally, came from the desire to confront the postconciliar period in advance.

Two initiatives were of special note. One was taken by the English-speaking bishops. On September 19, this group, which was especially large and came from all the continents, started the St. Paul's Conference, which was backed by Cardinal Heenan. From September 24 to November 26, it held a series of meetings for the main purpose of refining the idea of a postconciliar organization that would unite the 690 English-speaking bishops (the superior of the Mill Hill Missionaries joined the initiative).[14] It seems, however, that the postconciliar dispersion of the bishops put an end to the promising proposals exchanged in Rome, which might have given rise to an organization parallel to the Anglican Lambeth Conference.

During these weeks, at the subcontinental rather than cultural and linguistic level, the Latin American episcopate completed an "Overall Pastoral Plan" for the years 1966 to 1970.[15] The Latin American bishops had for some time belonged to CELAM, but the Council was obviously an opportunity for strengthening that relationship by drawing up a joint pastoral plan for the reception of Vatican II.

---

[12] *JCongar*, October 9, 1965; II, 428.

[13] See J. Famerée, "'Responsibilisation' des Conférences épiscopales et concession de 'facultés' aux évêques: signes de décentralisation?" in *Volti di fine Concilio*, 27–52.

[14] I thank R. Burigana for bringing the mimeographed minutes of these meetings to my attention. There is a copy in the Vatican II Archive of the ISR in Bologna.

[15] L. C. Marques, "Plan d'ensemble pour la réception de Vatican II au Brésil," in *Vatican II au Canada: Enracinement et réception*, ed. G. Routhier (Saint-Laurent: Fides, 2001), 481–500.

More generally, the national episcopal conferences were committed to clarifying and implementing the various aspects of the liturgical renewal, beginning with the translation of the various liturgies into their respective languages. In the countries of the Latin American continent and of Africa the renewal also implied a series of efforts at indigenization; the prototype of these was the Zairean rite for mass, which Cardinal Malula supported.

IV. CHARLES JOURNET AND JACQUES MARITAIN

These months saw two individuals who were in the forefront of French-speaking Catholicism intervening for the first time, though in quite different ways. The two had long been close to Montini and were especially esteemed by him when he became pope. Journet, a Swiss theologian, had been made a cardinal on February 22, 1965, and thus was able to intervene during the final session with the authority both of his scholarly reputation and of the confidence placed in him by the Pope. His interventions in favor of the declarations on non-Christian religions and religious freedom carried considerable weight.[16]

Maritain, a layman, could not intervene directly in the Council, but at the end of 1964 Paul VI asked him for his views on subjects that were to be discussed during the fourth period; Maritain drafted his views in the spring of 1965.[17] The French philosopher's main suggestion was the publication of an encyclical on truth, "the meaning [of which] is today obscured and threatened"; he also offered some "thoughts on the needs

---

[16] See J.-P. Torrell, "Présence de Journet à Vatican II," in *Charles Journet (1891–1975): Un théologien et son siècle*, ed. Ph. Chenaux, 41–68 (Fribourg: Éditions universitaires, 1992); idem, *Montini, Journet, Maritain: une famille d'esprit* (Brescia: Istituto Paolo VI, 2000).

[17] J. and R. Maritain, *Oeuvres complètes* 16 (Fribourg, 1999): "Quatre memorandums," sent in March 1965, on a series of problems submitted to him by Paul VI at the end of December 1964: I. *Sur la vérité* (1085); II. *La liberté religieuse* (1086–91); III. *L'apostolat des laïcs* (1092–1103); IV. *Prière commune et prière privée* (1104–30). Finally, in November 1965, Maritain sent the Pope a short note on *"Amour" et "Pouvoir"* (1131–35). See Ph. Chenaux, *Paul VI et Maritain: Les rapports du "montinianisme" et du "maritainisme"* (Brescia, 1994), 83–85, 111–14; also R. Mougel, "Maritain, Paul VI et l'Église du concile," *Notiziario dell'Istituto Paolo VI* 39 (2000), 82–100. According to a diary note, Maritain had feared (and perhaps hoped) being called to the Council as an "observer" (ibid., 85). Paul VI received Maritain at Castel Gandolfo on September 11, 1965, for the purpose of entrusting one of the final messages to him. Maritain wrote to the Pope about this on November 3, attaching the above-mentioned *"Amour" et "Pouvoir"* to his letter.

of the faithful in relation to truth."[18] The second memorandum had to do with religious freedom from the viewpoint of civil society, while the third was devoted to the apostolate of the laity; here Maritain emphasized the autonomous responsibility of the laity, for whom he did not use the expression "people of God" but rather "the faithful people."

The last and longest memorandum gave voice to a poorly concealed distrust of the liturgical reform approved by *Sacrosanctum concilium*, although the memorandum said that the writer accepted it.[19] After a couple of pages on the importance of private prayer, the central section deals with the use of the vernacular for the sacred books; the author gives a concise criticism of the French translations of the texts of the mass and of the gospels. The note ends with a few pages on some requirements for ecclesiastical studies.

While it is not easy to assess the influence of these notes on Paul VI,[20] they are another sign of the Pope's tendency to have recourse even to advisers completely removed from conciliar circles.[21]

V. The Results of the Fourth Period and the Final Messages

As had the earlier periods, the fourth concluded with a solemn closing session on December 7; but this was preceded by two other solemn sessions on October 28 and November 18. In October three decrees were given definitive approval *(Christus Dominus*; *Perfectae caritatis*; *Optatam totius)* along with two declarations *(Gravissimum educationis* and *Nostra aetate)*. These texts differed greatly from one another in the problems with which they dealt, in the complexity of their histories, and in their foreseeable impact on the Church.

Christus Dominus dealt with the pastoral activity of bishops and their relations with one another and with the Roman Curia; the text repeated,

---

[18] The beginning of the preparation of *Mysterium fidei*? This encyclical was published on September 3, 1965.

[19] Perhaps Maritain was already thinking along the lines that led him, shortly after the end of Vatican II, to write and publish his *The Peasant of the Garonne*.

[20] An important intervention of Maritain addressed to Paul VI had to do with the controversy over the section on the Jews in the declaration on the non-Christian religions. Appealing to his own long struggle against Catholic anti-Semitism, he asked that the text be strengthened (Mougel, "Maritain, Paul VI et l'Église du concile," 88 n.5).

[21] It is not clear that he did the same in regard to another important individual who became part of the Council only during this final brief time: Michele Pellegrino, the new Archbishop of Turin. Paul VI was a man influenced by ancient cultural harmonies.

in a softer voice, the third chapter of *Lumen gentium*. The decrees on the renewal of religious life and on priestly training were poor and destined to be forgotten. The two declarations had for their subjects Christian education and the attitude of the Church to the non-Christian religions. The latter was the one most eagerly awaited, because it inaugurated the movement beyond an age-long and tenacious Catholic anti-Semitism and beyond hostility to other religions.

At the public session in November, a dogmatic constitution *(Dei Verbum)* and a decree *(Apostolicam actuositatem)* reached safe harbor. The first, the development of which took all four years of the Council, took a position on the crucial question of the place of the word of God in Christian life. The second decree, which repeated the fourth chapter of *Lumen gentium* without any important novelties, dealt with the apostolate of the laity. The period of the "advancement of the laity" belonged rather to the tumultuous preconciliar years.

Finally, at the the last solemn session of the entire Council, approval was given to a declaration *(Dignitatis humanae)*, two decrees *(Ad gentes* and *Presbyterorum ordinis)*, and a pastoral constitution *(Gaudium et spes)*. The document on religious freedom (and no longer mere "tolerance") was another of the documents that caused the Council fathers very great difficulty and that were the most eagerly awaited by the public. Personal conscience was at last acknowledged in a solemn and unequivocal way; this made possible the interventions of John Paul II on behalf of human rights. Equally high expectations were roused by the *Pastoral Constitution on the Church in the Modern World,* which was to have an extraordinarily broad and profound echo in the postconciliar period. The Decree on the Ministry and Life of Priests, which had to do solely with the clergy, roused little interest, whereas the Decree on the Missionary Activity of the Church (coinciding in time, as it did, with the rapid progress of decolonization) was to receive considerable attention, especially in the non-European continents.

Connected with the decree on bishops was the decision of Paul VI to establish a synod of bishops,[22] as a consultative, not deliberative, body that would not have a permanent existence but would only meet periodically. This action, though formally a papal act, is to be included among

---

[22] He did so in *Apostolica sollicitudo*, September 15, 1965. See the draft on *De coetu seu consilio centrali,* which was drawn up in the fall of 1964 by the group representing the episcopal conferences; there is a report on it in P. C. Noël, "Le travail post-conciliaire: Les attentes du groupe de la *Domus Mariae* et l'organisation de l'après-concile," in *Volti di fine Concilio,* 267–308.

the results of the final stage of the Council. The call for a central collegial body that would regularly assist the Bishop of Rome in the exercise
of the *plenitudo potestatis* [full authority] over the universal Church had
looked for more solid results. Only later experience would confirm or not
confirm those who complained that the Pope's act was reductionistic in
its intention. In any case, the Synod was a complete novelty, having only
a distant analogue in the consistory of the eleventh to the fourteenth centuries. It does not seem rash to claim that Paul VI's decision would have
been unthinkable outside the atmosphere and context of the Council.

The disparity among the various documents approved during the fourth
period is obvious. The subjects with which they dealt were on very different levels and had very different impacts; the degree of development
that they showed and the degree of their correspondence to the basic
thrust of Vatican II were manifestly unequal. Despite considerable efforts
made, most of them did not depart from the orientation and themes given
them in the preparatory phase under the influence of the *vota* and of the
Curia's control of the commissions. After the collapse of the Döpfner
Plan, which would have reduced the length of the so-called minor
schemas, the conciliar machinery and the lobbies kept them alive until
they received final approval, despite the fact that they were somewhat
repetitious and insufficiently developed. One may ask whether, had the
Council acted differently with regard to these texts, it might have devoted
more attention and energy to producing a more satisfactory text for the
pastoral constitution, whose redaction was controlled instead by the race
against time.

These considerations seem, at least at first sight, to contradict the
results of the final votes. In fact, in dealing with all the texts submitted
to them for final approval, the fathers unhesitatingly gave unanimous consent, even though they felt interiorly a considerable dissatisfaction, especially with some documents. Many of the dissatisfied voiced their criticisms until the very end but then voted yes in a kind of self-censorship;
they were afraid that a negative vote would shatter the "atmosphere" of
the Council and would be turned against them when it came to the
approval of documents that they held dear. Weariness and a desire to
reach the end played an important part, helped (at least in some cases) by
lobbies within the Council itself. As is widely known, the influence of the
group of bishops from the religious orders and from the missions was
strong. Perhaps these were signs of a gradual waning of the conciliar
spirit that had nourished the commitment of so many bishops during the
earlier periods.

Paul VI's plan to solemnize the ending of the Council with a special liturgy on December 8, 1965, included the proclamation of seven "messages" from the Council, even though the Council had neither drafted nor approved them.[23] The intended addressees were seven categories of people: rulers; intellectuals and scientists; artists; women; workers; the poor, sick, and suffering; and youth. A comparison with the conciliar "Message to Humanity" of October 20, 1962, suggests some thoughts. In 1965 the fathers preferred, after a brief and general preface, to address not humanity but "categories" (to use the typical language of the Church's social teaching). The dominant concern, that is, was to identify partners in dialogue with the Church, but its identification of the other was substantially alien to the pastoral constitution that had been approved only the day before. The prophetic inspiration of 1962 also seemed now to have been diluted; the "event" was now over.

On the same occasion the announcement was made of the reciprocal withdrawal of the excommunications that had separated the Churches of Rome and Constantinople since 1054; the Churches were sisters once again. Despite its ceremonial character as a retrospective action, the symbolic weight of the withdrawal was profound; the aim was to approve of intended ecumenical commitments that would be in keeping with the original pronouncement of John XXIII, with the decree *Unitatis redintegratio* and with the important participation in the Council of observers from the non-Roman Churches. In this case, again, the action matured within the climate of the Council and would have been unimaginable only a few years before. It was difficult, however, to gauge whether it would remain a "historical" action, an end in itself, or be the door leading to further progress toward the restoration of full communion between the two Churches.

VI. Toward the Postconciliar Period

Even while it was meeting, Vatican II had raised the question of its self-interpretation in view of its reception in the postconciliar period.[24]

---

[23] *DC* 63 (1966), cols. 51–60. See C. Soetens, "Les messages finaux du Concile," in *Volti di fine Concilio*, 99–112.

[24] G. Routhier wrote some interesting pages on the attention that Vatican II paid to its own reception: "Reception in the Current Theological Debate," in *Reception and Communion among Churches*, ed. H. Legrand, J. Manzanares, and A. García y García (Washington, D.C.: Catholic University of America, 1997), 17–52. Noël takes a more analytic approach in "Le travail post-conciliaire," 267–308.

More than a few people were already paying watchful and increasing attention to the postconciliar period, trying by various means to determine the path of the future process of reception or at least to give it direction. Thus the question of reception had already been raised with clarity beginning in the early days of December 1962, on the eve of the first adjournment of the assembly's work. This was a time when the fathers were concerned about continuity between the atmosphere created during the first eight weeks and the atmosphere that would mark the renewal of their work; this was planned for several months later and — probably — under a different pope.

On December 8, 1962, in his homily marking the end of the Council's first period, John XXIII spoke of the "salutary fruits of the Council," fruits that would accrue not only to Catholics but to all "our brothers who call themselves Christians," and indeed to all human beings. "The diligent implementation of the decrees of the Council ... will truly be the new Pentecost that will cause the Church to flourish.... It will be a new leap forward for the kingdom of Christ."[25] It is noteworthy that in describing the postconciliar period the Pope used the same images he had used for the Council — "new Pentecost," "leap forward" — and that he viewed the postconciliar period in the universalist perspective of humanity as a whole.[26]

Two primary concerns about the postconciliar period emerged with special clarity during the debate on liturgical reform: first, the need for a central ad hoc body, distinct from the curial Congregation of Rites, to implement the reform; second, the primary competence of the episcopal conference in everything except the most general principles. The result

[25] General Secretariat of the Council, *Sacrosanctum Oecumenicum Concilium Vaticanum II: Constitutiones Decreta Declarationes: Editio typica* (Vatican City: Polyglot Press, 1966), 889–91.

[26] When John XXIII announced a council on January 25, 1959, he also announced a revision of canon law as a result of the future decrees of the council. In fact, the Council did not impose on the Church a program of revision in the form of clear, distinct, and binding norms. This explains the desperate character of the attempt to translate the conciliar decrees into a new Code of Canon Law, which was destined by definition to be an inadequate reflection. See E. Corecco, "Aspects of the Reception of Vatican II in the Code of Canon Law," in *The Reception of Vatican II*, ed. G. Alberigo, J.-P. Jossua, and J.A. Komonchak (Washington: CUA Press, 1987) 249-96. Significantly, this inadequacy was officially acknowledged in the document of 1983, *Sacrae disciplinae leges*, which accompanied the publication of the new code: "If ... it is impossible to translate perfectly into *canonical* language the conciliar image of the Church, nevertheless the Code must always be referred to this image as the primary pattern whose outline the Code ought to express insofar as it can by its very nature" (*Code of Canon Law*, Latin-English edition [Washington, D.C., 1983], xiv).

was the creation in 1964 of the Consilium for the Implementation of the Constitution on the Sacred Liturgy (the Consilium),[27] which was to be a prototype of other central bodies set up in the postconciliar period. The hermeneutical point was being made unequivocally: for the results of the Council to be assimilated, there was a need of new and appropriate institutional tools.

Similarly, during the development of the various conciliar decrees there was a concern to set down the premises that would guide reception. This was true of the documents on the means of social communication,[28] the apostolate of the laity,[29] problems of justice and peace,[30] and even for the reform of the Roman Curia.[31]

There was an even greater interest in the central problem of ecumenism, with the fathers concerned that the Secretariat for Christian Unity, which John XXIII had created, should be able to continue its special work after the conclusion of the Council[32] and might be able, above all, to compose an ecumenical directory. The Secretariat for Non-Christians and the Secretariat for Nonbelievers also continued in existence after the Council.

Even during the preparatory period and later during the debates on the Church, many Council fathers wanted the establishment of a episcopal body that would collaborate and share responsibility with the Bishop of Rome in making major decisions about the universal Church. Traces of this outlook remained both in the decree *Christus Dominus* and in the

---

[27] On October 10, 1963, the need of a transitional law governing the liturgical reform was affirmed (*History* 3:55–56, 234–35), and on January 3, 1964, A. Bugnini was appointed secretary of the commission for implementing the liturgical constitution (ibid., 241–48). A commission was established on January 26 of that same year. September 26, 1964, brought the publication of the instruction *Ad executionem Constitutionis de sacra Liturgia recte ordinandum*, which was signed by Lercaro, president of the Consilium, but also by Larraona, prefect of the Congregation of Rites. Many more provisions regarding the implementation of the reform would be published later.

[28] *Inter mirifica*, no. 19; Secretariat for the Communications media.

[29] *Apostolicam actuositatem*, no. 26; Secretariat for the Laity.

[30] *Gaudium et spes*, no. 90; Secretariat for Justice and Peace.

[31] *Christus Dominus*, no. 9. The decree provided for the composition of directories for the care of souls (no. 44). On August 6, 1966, a complex Motu Proprio, *Ecclesiae sanctae*, was published, in which *Normae ad quaedam exsequenda ss. Concilii Vaticani II Decreta statuuntur*; these norms dealt with *Christus Dominus, Presbyterorum ordinis, Perfectae caritatis*, and *Ad gentes*. In *Catholicam Christi ecclesiam* of January 6, 1967, norms were set down for implementing the Decree on the Lay Apostolate and the constitution *Gaudium et spes*.

[32] See M. Velati, "Paolo VI e l'ecumenismo," a paper read at the Brescia Colloquium of 1998 (in press).

Decree on the Missionary Activity of the Church. The desire was that after the Council the increasingly emphasized rule of the papacy might be balanced by a collegial body that would regularly assist the pope. We know that such desires were absorbed in Paul VI's decision to establish the synod of bishops.

A different case of hermeneutical "mortgaging" occurred in the fall of 1964, during the Black Week, when Paul VI decided to add a *Nota explicativa praevia* to the report of the Council's Doctrinal Commission on the final changes to be made in chapter III of the Constitution on the Church. As the very title shows, the organizers of the note were trying to establish a principle of interpretation in advance, even before the Council approved *Lumen gentium*.[33]

Finally, on November 18, 1965, in the homily that he delivered at the solemn session on November 18, 1965, Paul VI devoted a lengthy section to the "implementation of the Council" and to the "outlook to be adopted in the postconciliar period."[34] At that time the Pope chose to emphasize the great difference between the atmosphere during the Council ("a time of plowing that turns over the soil") and in the postconciliar period ("a time of organized and positive cultivation"). "Plowing" and "cultivation" do effectively characterize the two periods, but the striking thing is the distance and, potentially, the contradiction between the two activities: turning over the soil and cultivation. This way of reading the texts was formulated when Vatican II was still going on. Did the phrases echo the alarmed concern expressed by Msgr. Montini back in 1959[35] and the intentions of Pope Paul VI to normalize things?

It is true that later in the homily the Pope expressed his commitment to the creation of bodies that would oversee the implementation of the Council's decisions, with special attention to the episcopal conferences and with an intense desire that there be an atmosphere of communion in the work of implementing Vatican II. In the Pope's view, the Council

---

[33] *History* 4:388–452.

[34] General Secretariat of the Council, *Sacrosanctum Oecumenicum Concilium Vaticanum II: Editio typica*, 1044–57; English translation in *Council Daybook* (Washington, D.C.: NCWC, 1965), 235–37. Paul VI had earlier referred to the "implementation of the Council" and had said that implementation of the decrees would require a set of postconciliar commissions. On November 16 the Domus Mariae Group had sent a letter to Paul VI on the advantages of postconciliar commissions (see Noël, "Le travail post-conciliaire," 267–308).

[35] *History* 1:19.

had elicited three different reactions. "The first was enthusiasm ... a quasi-messianic dream.... A second phase followed: that of the actual working out of the Council ... a working out that raised problems." Finally, Paul VI saw the coming of "the third phase: discussion ends, understanding begins."

Conspicuously absent from the papal address was any idea of synodality; even *aggiornamento* was to mean "from now on, a wise fathoming of the spirit of the Council and a faithful application of its norms."[36] At first sight the question of active reception by the Church seems to be missing, even though the Pope's statement did not of itself deny an active reception by the faithful. The Council had sent messages and opened channels of dialogue; the papacy, rather than the people of God, would gather these up and manage them.

A few days earlier Yves Congar had noted in his diary, with considerable naiveté, that "people are talking about the Council and the postconciliar period, about which many are worried. How will things go? What structures will there be, what commissions will be at work? How will the spirit of the Council be preserved at the top and also in the episcopates?" The French Dominican's view was very clear; according to him "the Council has yielded its fruit due in large measure to the contribution of the theologians. The postconciliar period will preserve the spirit of the Council only if it makes its own the work of the theologians."[37]

On January 3, 1966, less than a month after the end of the Council, the Motu Proprio *Finis concilio* created a postconciliar structure parallel to that of several of the conciliar commissions. Specifically, five postconciliar commissions were established: bishops, religious, missions, education, and laity; these were made up of the members of the corresponding conciliar commissions. So too, the new central commission "for coordinating postconciliar work and interpreting the decrees of the Council" comprised the members of Vatican II's Council of Presidents and Coordinating Commission.[38] But no postconciliar commission was established that corresponded to the Doctrinal Commission of Vatican II. Doctrinal problems fell again directly under the jealously preserved competence of the Holy Office.

The significance of the facts that have been listed is inescapable. All the steps taken were inspired by the concern to determine in advance

---

[36] *AS* IV/6, 689–95.
[37] *JCongar*, November 7, 1965; II, 465.
[38] *AAS* 58 (1966), 37–40; see *Annuario pontificio 1966*, 1108–22.

the criteria and institutions that would direct the interpretation and application of the conciliar decrees. They were signs of the will of the conciliar assembly and of the Apostolic See that those decisions should be followed up, although perhaps hardly anyone had clear ideas in this area. At the same time they were evidence of a Roman option for an implementation that would proceed from the center. The implicit hermeneutical choice was transparently clear: first, Vatican II was reduced wholly and solely to the body of its decisions; second, these decisions were to be followed up to the extent that they could be located within the existing framework of Catholicism and, above all, of its Roman center.

The decade that followed the end of Vatican II was controlled by a mechanical understanding of reception, comparable to that which had marked the post-Tridentine period: knowledge of and commentaries on the texts of the Council's final decisions. The volumes containing such commentaries (which began to be published in all the major languages even while the Council was still at work) form a respectable library.[39] In the majority of instances the commentaries were by the theologians who had had a direct part in drafting the conciliar texts, so that the commentaries are primarily an interpretation from the viewpoint of the drafters.[40]

A first phase of the postconciliar period was devoted to the simple reading of the documents, that is, to an identification of their various contexts by a very objective and quasi-literal study of them, still without attempts at a systematic interpretation. A second phase was devoted to a more systematic reading that attempted to pick out the main lines of force running through the entire set of documents.[41] It was difficult, however, to initiate a new phase in which an effort might be made not only to grasp the key lines of thought and the instructions for application contained in the conciliar event and its decrees, but also to derive from them a global direction on the basis of a historical approach to the Council. In other words, it was not easy to move

[39] The most authoritative examples are the two volumes on *Lumen gentium* and *Gaudium et spes* that G. Baraúna edited; the three volumes that the *Lexikon für Theologie und Kirche* devoted to the decrees of Vatican II (English translation in *Commentary*); and finally, the volumes, one for each document, that Congar published in the Unam Sanctam series.

[40] To this category belongs, first and foremost, the commentary of G. Philips: *Lumen gentium: L'Église et son mystère au deuxième concile du Vatican: Histoire, texte et commentaire de la Constitution "Lumen gentium"*, 2 vols. (Paris, 1967).

[41] See the three volumes edited by R. Latourelle, *Vatican II: Assessment and Perspectives Twenty-five Years After (162–1987)* (New York, 1988).

beyond the individual documents and beyond an analytic study of them in order to see them within a comprehensive vision that combined all of them.

At the concrete level, even while the Council was still going on, and all the more so immediately after its conclusion, some people expressed an impatient desire for reception of the Council and others an attitude of worry and uneasiness about the consequences of the Council. It was not until the beginning of the seventies that a radical rejection of Vatican II found a voice.[42]

Even while the Council was continuing in Rome, the Brazilian conference had drawn up a five-year "General Pastoral Plan" to "establish the means and conditions needed if the Brazilian Church is to conform, as soon as possible and as fully as possible, to Vatican II's image of the Church."[43] Many other episcopates announced their programs for reception, in varied forms. In France the bishops of regions or individual dioceses focused on a variety of subjects: "The Hour of the Laity," "Priestly Dress," "The Postconciliar Period of Souls," "Where Is the Council Taking Us?"[44] The Spanish episcopate, while still in Rome, addressed a collective pastoral letter to clergy and faithful calling for "an implementation of the conciliar decrees" without immobilism and without an excessive thirst for novelty.[45] The Central African episcopate emphasized the need of lay commitment to development, to the formation of Christian communities, and to the spread of the gospel.[46] The bishops of South Africa stressed in their collective letter the importance of *Gaudium et spes* for the elimination of apartheid and every kind of discrimination.[47] The German episcopate at its 1966 annual meeting in Fulda likewise subscribed to a collective letter asking for a progressive assimilation of the Council in the perspective of the renewal of the Church.[48]

---

[42] See D. Menozzi, "Opposition to the Council (1966–1984)," in *The Reception of Vatican II*, 325-48.

[43] On October 12, 1965, these bishops thought of drafting a "Manifesto at the End of the Council"; the various parts of the pastoral plan echoed the various conciliar documents (see Marques, "Plan d'ensemble," and O. Beozzo, "Igreja no Brasil – o Planejamento pastoral em Questão," *REB* 42 [1982], 465–505).

[44] *DC* 63 (1966), 653–56.

[45] Ibid., 701–9.

[46] "Le laïcat africain au lendemain du Concile," in *DC* 63 (1966), 1603–10.

[47] "Lettre des évêques d'Afrique du Sud sur l'apartheid" (July 26, 1966), in *DC* 63 (1966), 1609–16.

[48] "Les évêques allemands et l'après-Concile" (September 30, 1966), in *DC* 63 (1966), 2049–53.

At the beginning of 1966 Paul VI, for his part, thought it opportune to urge the Roman Curia to overcome its reservations regarding the directions taken by the Council;[49] he also urged the Italian episcopate to adopt a positive attitude to the conciliar decrees.[50]

VII. From Vatican II to the Postconciliar Period: Context and Conditions for Reception

Did the fathers who left Rome at the end of 1965 find a different world from that of October 1962? Had the context of the Christian life and of the Church's activity been changed?

Not a long time had passed, less than forty months, and the majority of those who had been present at the opening of Vatican II were still on the scene. Life had gone on, however. Leading personalities of the stature of John XXIII in Rome and Kennedy in Washington had died, and Khrushchev was no longer in Moscow. The human conquest of space had developed by leaps and bounds; for the first time, probes had been sent to the moon, while others had set out for Mars, and astronauts had walked in space. The Cold War seemed to be hardening and spreading throughout the world. In the East the Chinese People's Republic had exploded its first atomic bond, breaking the monopoly of the West and the Soviets. In China, too, the Cultural Revolution had begun and appeared at the time to mark the summit of subversive power; in southeast Asia, meanwhile, the conflict in Vietnam was intensifying as the military involvement of the United States of America became ever greater. It gave rise to a growing wave of reactions from the young; the demonstrations at the large North American universities soon moved beyond protest against the intervention of their own country and initiated a time of radical protests that would spread throughout the entire West.

In Asia, war had broken out between India and Pakistan; the age of Gandhi was over. The state of Israel was now solidly established in Palestine, but it was generating a growing restlessness among the Palestinians. While the entire African continent was continuing to emerge from the colonial age, in Algeria a coup d'état against Ben Bella introduced a long and tragic period of terrorism in a key Islamic area. In Latin America,

---

[49] Paul VI at St. John Lateran on April 23, 1966, in *DC* 63 (1966), 865–70.
[50] See G. Alberigo, "La chiesa italiana tra Vaticano II e nuovo millennio," in *Il Vaticano II nella chiesa italiana: memoria e profezia* (Assisi, 1985), 43–67.

finally, a period of dictatorial or military regimes began that were more or less directly supported by dictatorships that had survived in Spain and Portugal.[51]

The unaligned countries, that is, countries outside the ideological blocs led by the United States and the USSR, were living in an atmosphere of "Third-Worldism" and "underdevelopment" and would later be identified as the "World of the South." The strong economic recovery now going on in the Atlantic countries only increased drastically the difference between the North and the South.

The *Ostpolitik* with which the Vatican, the center of Catholicism, was reversing its traditional attitude of intransigent opposition to the Soviet world had already begun but had not yet come to the attention of public opinion. John XXIII's distinction between ideologies and large historical movements was beginning to bear fruit. The initiative he had originally entrusted to the nuntio Msgr. Lardone continued with Msgr. Casaroli.

It will always be difficult to determine how aware of these very profound changes the bishops were as they returned to their dioceses. What is certain is that the world they had left behind in 1962 as they began the adventure of the Council had changed radically, and this confronted all of them with unexpected problems and challenges and threatened to make the conciliar decrees outdated, products of a cultural and social context that was rapidly changing.

The experience of implementation/reception of those decrees began in the open Council as a result of the approval and promulgation of the liturgical constitution at the end of the second period. That constitution had been an exceptionally interesting test, one that brought to light many of the problems that would trouble the postconciliar period.[52] A few months after the establishment of the Consilium, the Pope thought it appropriate to specify that he had established it to study the implementation of the liturgical reform according to appropriate norms, which were those of the Holy See. The Instruction *Ad exsecutionem Constitutionis de sacra liturgia*,[53] which was signed by Lercaro but also by Larraona, made clear the Pope's intention to follow a mixed norm, that is, to entrust the coordination of the implementation of the liturgical renewal to a postconciliar

---

[51] Reliable observers maintained that important groups in the United States of America also supported that kind of political regression.

[52] See *History* 3, 234–49.

[53] Instruction *Inter Oecumenici* on the orderly carrying out of the Constitution on the Liturgy (September 24, 1964), in *Documents on the Liturgy 1963–1979: Conciliar, Papal, and Curial Texts* (Collegeville, Minn.: Liturgical Press, 1982), 88–110.

commission, but one that would be accompanied by the pre-existing curial congregation.

While this could have been a fruitful approach, suggested by the desire to combine the conciliar thrust with preceding experience, it led in fact to an uninterrupted conflict that continued the tensions within the conciliar commission that had caused obstacles in drafting the constitution. The conflict would be ended by Paul VI when the postconciliar Consilium was absorbed into the curial congregation shortly after the end of Vatican II.

While this knotty situation in Rome would be a stumbling block on the path of liturgical reform, it was beyond doubt that the epicenter of renewal was not in Rome but on the "periphery," in the people of God assembled in local communities. The conciliar constitution had entrusted the greatest responsibility for the reform to the episcopal conferences, and the faithful were committing themselves to take the reform into their own hands in the name of *active participation*, which was the central theme of the entire constitution. Both in areas in which the liturgical movement had paved the way for the renewal and in those that had remained on the fringes, *Sacrosanctum concilium* gave rise to great popular interest and suggested a myriad of local initiatives.[54]

This dynamic activity, which was at least partially unexpected, bore witness to the depth of the expectations attendant on the conciliar decrees whenever these offered the possibility of real renewal and of active involvement by ordinary Christians. Desires long cultivated but always disappointed were now fulfilled. At least in some cases, that long wait explains why the reception found expression in spontaneous but disorderly ways, thereby causing some alarm and giving some enemies of the renewal the chance to voice fears and to denounce a supposed subversion of tradition.

The experience of the liturgical reform showed how the reception of Vatican II would differ depending on particular preconciliar situations and on the variety of conditions at the time when the Council ended.[55] In the Netherlands, to take one example, where ecumenical energies and impatience with preconciliar stagnancy were especially widespread, the impulse given by the Council was received profoundly and thoroughly.

[54] See *History* 3, 471–90.
[55] See *Convegno delle Commissioni nazionali di liturgia 1984* (Padua, 1985); P. Marini published an important series of articles in *Ephemerides liturgicae* (1999) on the first steps taken in the liturgical reform.

In quite different and distant areas, Latin America, for example, the conciliar message came as a novel stimulus that would find an adequate response only some years later, in 1968, when the episcopate held its general assembly at Medellín.

Just as Vatican II had been a synthesis of very different contributions, so now it roused varied echoes in the Churches called upon to assimilate it. The supposition that there would be an organized and uniform implementation directed by Rome, such as the one attempted in the sixteenth century after Trent, was not even on the horizon, although it continued to be cherished in Rome. From this point of view the conciliar desire for the creation of postconciliar bodies was ambiguous. Things would have been different if the adaptation of the Roman Curia to the spirit and impulses of the Council had been pursued. There would have had to be a reform of the Curia, which the Pope removed from the competence of the Council and was then dictated by Paul VI himself (and later by John Paul II) without perceptible structural changes.[56] If, on the other hand, people imagined that postconciliar central structures could direct the reception, they were not only deluding themselves but were adopting an ecclesiological viewpoint that was neo-centralist and therefore inconsistent with Vatican II. The beginning of the liturgical reform showed the impracticality of such a course.

This experience already bore witness that Vatican II, in accordance with the mark left on it by John XXIII, was read and interpreted as a most authoritative directive given to the Christian people to engage in an *aggiornamento* that would take place through a comparison of the teachings of the gospel with the demands of the social setting; an *aggiornamento* carried out in a *pastoral* way and therefore by looking for elements in common rather than those that divide, and in respect for freedom; an *aggiornamento* with *koinonia* and witness as its goals. The worldwide aspect of things, which Vatican II had increasingly kept before it, implied a reception allowing for various rhythms, styles, and impacts. A coordination of the reception could have hoped only to promote an exchange of information and experiences that would point out the excesses threatening communion and patiently highlight the gradual formation of the mosaic, the "symphony," created by the postconciliar Church.

---

[56] See G. Alberigo, "Fedeltà e creatività nella ricezione del concilio Vatican II: Criteri ermeneutici," *CrSt* 21 (2000), 383–402.

The Church of the postconciliar period was also to find itself tackling subjects on which the Council had agreed to say nothing, from the question of the ends of marriage and of responsible parenthood to priestly celibacy. Cardinal Léger, moved by apostolic anxiety, bore witness to the situation in a letter to Msgr. C. Colombo. After emphasizing his own loyalty to the Holy Father, the Canadian cardinal wrote:

> You know that the world expects from the Church a reply to this problem which torments so many consciences. Since a special commission was set up to study this question, we placed our trust in the decisions coming from this body. It is obvious that the Holy Father always has the right to intervene in the course of a council and that his teaching must be received with respect. But ... the manner of transmission, in the sometimes unintelligible style of the Roman Curia, was not such as to facilitate dialogue.... This commission ought to have had the freedom which the Secretariat for Unity had in drafting the schemas on ecumenism and religious freedom.... History teaches us that some doctrines which were vigorously imposed for centuries have received different interpretations now because of sociological changes that have occurred....
>
> The entire problem of birth control ought to be very carefully studied in the light of history. And I hope that some day the Church, while remaining faithful to the Church's tradition in the interpretation of natural law, will be able also to assuage the consciences of thousands of Christians whom a sometimes rigid teaching turns away from the practice of their religion, and that thousands of families will be able to continue to live their faith with trust in the mercy of God....
>
> It is clear that we must forbid what is contrary to the dignity of the sacrament of marriage, but we must emphasize, above all, the need of a lengthy education for engaged couples and Christian spouses, lest we cast them into the "clutches of Satan," as St. Paul puts it, by imposing on them methods that can easily lead to the breakup of the home, the temptation of adultery, and, above all, the death of the vital principle in every marriage, namely, mutual love.[57]

The trauma felt throughout the Christian world at the publication of the encyclical *Humanae vitae* in 1968 emphasizes how clear was Léger's foresight.

The reception of Vatican II nourished a climate of responsible freedom in very many bishops and in very numerous communities, but it did not produce a nucleus of leaders, a "conciliar party." Nor was the theological journal *Concilium* able to stimulate a consistent penetration of what the Council had said, for it very quickly took the line of looking beyond Vatican II instead of assimilating the impulses given by it.

---

[57] Naud papers, 119. I owe knowledge of this document to the kindness of G. Routhier.

VIII. Ecumenical Attitudes as the Council Concluded

Through their observers the non-Roman Churches and communities had paid careful attention during Vatican II.[58] So too they followed with great interest the ticklish transition to the postconciliar period. As Lukas Vischer observes at the end of his chapter in the present volume, "in almost all the Churches a new debate arose over how the communion of Churches could find credible expression at the universal level."

A few weeks after the end of Vatican II, Metropolitan Nikodim of Leningrad gave an interview in which he took a positive view of the Council, adding his conviction that in the future an atmosphere of cooperation between Rome and the other Churches could be expected.[59] The Old Catholics, for their part, devoted a pastoral letter to the Council that had just ended.[60] Of even greater interest was the lengthy report of L. Vischer to the central committee of the World Council of Churches.[61] In Vischer's view, considerable interest attached to the directory on ecumenism that the Secretariat for Christian Unity had composed; it was inspired by a desire to stimulate the spontaneous development of the ecumenical drive while avoiding overly rigid directives.

On the same occasion, however, Vischer also expressed a concern about the unequal assimilation of that drive within Catholicism, about the possible predominance of internal *aggiornamento* over ecumenical commitment, and about the danger that the conciliar Decree on Ecumenism might be taken as a point of arrival instead of as a point of departure. The report concluded with the statement that "Vatican II was an event that put to shame the overly narrow expectations" that followed upon the first announcement of the Council; rather, the Council was an unequivocal recognition of the prophetic importance of John XXIII's undertaking.

The Greek Orthodox theologian N. Nissiotis composed a parallel report on the same occasion.[62] In his view, the Council, which was a gift of God to the Church, had evoked different responses in the Western Churches and in the Eastern Churches (where it had less impact). In any case, the

---

[58] See A. Birmelé, "Le Concile Vatican II vu par les Observateurs des autres traditions chrétiennes," in Melloni, *Volti di fine Concilio*, 225–64.

[59] Interview of January 5, 1966, in *SOEPI*, 3/1966, 10.

[60] Ibid., 10/1966, 8.

[61] *DC* 63 (1966), cols. 529–60; summary in *Service oecuménique de presse et d'information (SOEPI)*, 5/1966, 12–14.

[62] *SOEPI*, 5/1966, 15–17.

more important contribution of Vatican II was to show the value of the conciliar system for the renewal of all the Christian Churches.

In other words, a new stage of the entire ecumenical movement had begun. The positive attitude of Roman Catholicism was the greatest novelty, one that compelled all others to rethink their attitudes and their ecumenical strategy. But even more important was the impulse that Vatican II gave to the quest for the union of Christians by pressing all to abandon a kind of passive acquiescence to the present situation.

IX. PERSPECTIVES FOR INTERPRETING THE COUNCIL

Vatican II was also a normative act at the highest level of authority. Its constitutions, decrees, and declarations had been solemnly accepted by the plenary assembly and promulgated by the Roman Pontiff, who had been one with the Council and who, finally, had assigned a *vacatio legis*, the point at which each text became binding.

After the two preceding councils, Trent and Vatican I, problems had arisen regarding the interpretation of the conciliar decisions. When the implementation of the decisions of the Council of Trent caused tensions, it was thought necessary to make the interpretation the work of a Roman ad hoc body, which took the name Congregation of the Council. Some centuries later, however, when the conclusions reached by Pius IX's council had given rise to insinuating interpretations of the primacy, it was not the pope but an entire episcopate, the German, that corrected the forced interpretations of the Prussian chancery. The Pope thought it right to intervene in his turn by accepting and confirming the interpretation given by the German bishops.

In what sense did the interpretation of Vatican II raise problems? The unusual nature of the Council's decisions, inspired as they were by a pastoral outlook and aimed at an *aggiornamento*, and therefore avoiding rigid and absolute prescriptions or condemnations, meant that it was not possible to fall back on older models of interpretation.[63] But on July 11, 1967, Paul VI established a Roman commission for the interpretation of the decrees.[64]

[63] Historian H. Jedin has emphasized the difference between the Council of Trent, which issued condemnatory canons, and Vatican II, which stressed that which unites, although there was no contradiction between the two councils (see *Vatikanum II und Tridentinum: Tradition und Fortschritt in der Kirchengeschichte* [Cologne, 1968]).

[64] See V. Carbone, *De Commissione decretis Concilii Vaticani II interpretandis* (Naples, 1969). From 1969 on, this commission's competence was limited to decisions of the Holy See regarding the implementation of the conciliar decrees. After 1984, this

Very quickly, "abusive interpretations" of the Council began to circulate. As early as 1965, Paul VI intervened in the Thirty-first General
Congregation of the Jesuits in order to draw the latter back from the dangers of an excessive worldliness. In July 1966, Cardinal Ottaviani, who
headed the Congregation for the Doctrine of the Faith, wrote a letter to
the bishops listing ten areas in which abusive interpretations had arisen.[65]
A few weeks later the Motu Proprio *Ecclesiae sanctae* issued universal
norms for the implementation of the decrees on bishops, priests, religious,
and missions.[66]

In 1959, John XXIII had also announced the future revision of the
Code of Canon Law. The end of the Council made this announcement
especially relevant and demanded a commitment to a codification that
would be respectful of Vatican II and in harmony with it — an undertaking that was neither easily nor quickly carried out.

Was the problem the interpretation of the decisions or the Church's
reception of the call to *aggiornamento* — an *aggiornamento* that could
be foreseen as necessarily different in different areas characterized by
different spiritual, cultural, and social situations? Even the pastoral
approach could not but accentuate different things in different situations.
This was, in a nutshell, the heart of the matter in the postconciliar period.

X. The Conclusion of the Council

Emotions, and evaluations, perspectives abounded among the lead
players at the Council, the bishops, among the experts and the observers,
and among all who had followed the course of the Council with their
own expecations.[67] Even amid satisfaction of having returned home for
good, there existed a nostalgia for the conciliar experience, which, independently of the part played by each individual, was seen as an event of
great importance in which they had had the opportunity to participate.

The definitive end of the Council's work produced a sense of satisfaction, but some fathers feared their decisions might have a negative

---

commission was absorbed by the Commission for the Interpretation of the Code of Canon
Law.

[65] *AAS* 58 (1966), 659–61.

[66] Ibid., 757–87.

[67] No estimate has been made of the expenses that the average bishop had to meet if
he attended all four periods of the Council. It is probable, however, that for many they were
a considerable burden that was added to the inconveniences of living for several months
outside their usual setting.

impact, while others worried about the weakness and incompleteness of the approved texts;[68] still others, finally, hoped that after four years during which the Church had lived in "a state of council," it might now return to a normal, calmer rhythm. Different from the period after other councils, no "council party" was formed, not even when an "anticonciliar party" formed when Msgr. Marcel Lefebvre rejected the decrees of the Council.

At the moment when the Council fathers left Rome, it seemed that the whole of Vatican II was condensed into the texts of its decisions, which were quickly collected into a corpus and published in various languages and widely circulated.[69]

The experts, some of whom had carried an exceptionally heavy burden, especially in the hectic atmosphere of this final period, felt relief at the end of their obligations.[70] A group of central European scholars finished preparations for the journal *Concilium*, which began publication in various languages in the year the Council ended, 1965.

Most of the press evaluations, while not of a piece, were substantially positive; criticisms from the conservative press were limited to some areas. Thus, according to R. La Valle in *L'Avvenire d'Italia*, the Council "put into practice an exceptional conjunction of the human and the divine, one that was more obvious, more exciting, and more convincing than so many others that we always have before our eyes but which are less promising, less enthralling. Rarely has it been given to the Church to become so adaptable and transparent an instrument of the Father's plan of salvation and of the fruits of the Paschal Mystery of Christ." On the same occasion this authoritative commentator added that

---

[68] As early as October 21, A. Nicora wrote in her diary (Bologna) that "the Council is thus ending rather sadly, without having the energy to perform the one act that would make it henceforth a vital seed for the life of the world: the canonization of John [XXIII]. The bishops are voting like so many sheep and voting again on schemes on which they have already voted."

[69] General Secretariat of the Council, *Sacrosanctum Oecumenicum Concilium Vaticanum II: Constitutiones Decreta Declarationes: Editio Typica;* S. Scatena, "La filologia delle decisioni conciliari," in *Volti di fine Concilio*, 53–97, brought out the weaknesses of this *editio typica*. Sometimes there were oversights, sometimes interventions that came after definitive votes or even after the dissolution of the Council. They were frequently due to the hectic pace of the final weeks, but sometimes they show a determination to alter what the Council had said. See also U. Betti, "A proposito degli *Acta Synodalia Sacrosancti Concilii Oecumenici Vaticani II*," *Antonianum* 96 (1981), 3–42.

[70] At the end of his diary Semmelroth observed: "The Council is ending but the impulses it gives will determine the life of the Church. I am happy that the work is over. But I am deeply grateful to God for having been involved in it. I derived a great deal from it" (*TSemmelroth*, December 8, 1965).

the Church continues, however, to live in history and, even after such a flood of graces, cannot utter its *Nunc dimittis, Domine* ... but on the contrary is called to a radical *regeneration*, in the measure in which the Greek *metanoia* and the Latin *reformatio* signify a new birth. In this sense and only in this sense is it legitimate and right to speak of a postconciliar period, that is, a period in which the entire Church makes a great communal effort to assimilate and apply the grace, that is, the revelation, that came to light in the Council. If talk about the Church in the postconciliar period were to signify only a fidelity of Christians to a historical event, great indeed and solemn but now past and ended, this would be only a senile illusion and an unforgivable fetishism. What is truly demanded is rather the "vocation" which the Lord has bestowed on his entire Church in and through the Council. A commitment, therefore, that has to do with the future above all, because it feeds not on the past but on a unparalleled present event: the paschal mystery of Jesus. Around him all the baptized are called for a specific and actual moment in which the supernatural destiny of our generations is at stake. The Council set some problems on the way to a solution; others it has only warned of; above all, it set in motion a series of reflections, the riches of which for the Church's life are truly unforeseeable, since they depend on the grace of the Spirit and on the ability of human beings to entrust themselves seriously and perseveringly to that grace.

Previously, when commenting on the conclusion of the Council's work, La Valle had voiced his conviction that

the Council is now part of history; we too become part of that history, but only in the degree that the Council is given a continuation, an implementation, a confirmation in the life of the Church as a whole. The reason for saying this is that in the minds of future generations the Council cannot be separated from the fruits it shall have produced, from the real novelties it shall have introduced, and from the development of Christian life it shall have fostered throughout the world.
Is it an unknown history, then? An unknown, yes. But not all the elements of it are unknown. We know now the premises that were sat in place during those years. Without indulging in the triumphalism of a renewed Church, in elusive optimism, in bombastic celebration that puts all the conciliar texts on the same level, we can say that the Council has revealed great riches to the Church, it has excavated treasures, it has removed the obstructions that blocked the springs of living water.... The Council thus kept many of its promises. Above all, however, it pointed out a way and, as though offering us the first fruits, showed how fruitful this way can be. Tomorrow's task is to travel this way, with serene faith, without fear and laziness, to wherever the Lord wants to lead his Church.[71]

The correspondent for *Le Monde*, Henri Fesquet, also attempted to take stock of the Council[72]:

---

[71] R. La Valle, *Il concilio nelle nostre mani* (Brescia, 1966), IX, XX, 642, and 645.
[72] H. Fesquet, *The Drama of Vatican II* (New York: Random House, 1967), 809–16.

there is little place for nostalgia now at this year's end of 1965, which will go down in history as the transitional date between two very distinct eras of Christianity. The more time passes, the better we will see this paradoxical truth the Council lived: a discontinuity in the continuity of the Church. With Vatican II Rome finally entered the twentieth century, which is indicative of both the Church's belatedness and her efforts toward aggiornamento. This Council abolished the notion that the Catholic Church, however widespread throughout the world, is a sect — a Western religion, bound in practice to Greco-Latin civilization, a religion of wealthy countries, a stranger to the great currents of history and contemporary thought as well as to the major preoccupations of modern man. The Council, so to speak, broke down the walls of the "Catholic" citadel and let some "fresh air" in from outside, to use John XXIII's image. At the same time the outside world saw something of the spiritual treasure of a Church that is not only an institution and a hierarchy but a foyer of faith, hope, and charity. The Church of Vatican II was undeniably more concerned with seeking new truths and new ways of serving men than with jealously protecting her rights and privileges. In a word, the Roman Church is now more imbued with the spirit of the Gospels, much to the surprise of anticlerics.

But this keen observer immediately added: "Is this to say that the Council was a total success, that on every point it achieved the much-needed pastoral and doctrinal *aggiornamento?* Far from it. To be honest, an assessment must take the negative into account as well as the positive." Fesquet distinguishes some "temporary failures":

> The Council came up short against four problems, at least two of which directly concern interpersonal relations between man and woman. Should this surprise us in a Church that is run by celibates who have so long regarded woman as a suspect and dangerous creature? 1) The first of these problems is birth control.... 2) Vatican II was enlightened enough to institute a married diaconate.... 3) Vatican II did not face up to the problem, which is so serious and so painful for a great many of the faithful, especially after the last two wars: the possibility that an innocent partner who has been deserted might remarry, as is possible in the Orthodox Church.... 4) The Council's desires concerning mixed marriages have remained without issue.

According to Fesquet, Vatican II also left other gaps, for example, the lack of "a *collective* gesture renouncing the external signs of wealth"[73] and the failure to change "the method of appointing bishops, of which the

---

[73] Speaking of insertions into the conciliar texts of propositions on poverty, Congar wrote: "I proposed (in conscience) two rather lengthy additions which Msgr. Mercier would like to see introduced regarding poverty. In my view, what is already there is sufficient, but Mercier, like Father Gauthier, would like to see it put everywhere. Many fathers are sick of it. It was not admitted" (*JCongar*, October 27; II, 455).

least that can be said is that it in no way corresponds to the legitimate aspirations of the 'people of God.'"

But, Fesquet went on, "without repudiating the most authentic contents of its tradition, the Roman Church has stopped considering herself as having a monopoly on truth.... In less than four years Rome entered the front ranks of the ecumenical movement, from which she had been tragically absent." Finally, in the area of doctrine the Council "ended the period of conceptualist, notional theology in the scholastic manner"; as a result, "truth is no longer considered as something inanimate which we possess; rather it is the mystery of a living person.... Individualism has given way to a communitarian vision of human reality, ... and a new anthropology is being elaborated." In addition, "the concept of evolution has been exorcized; ... the idea of tradition has been purged of its dross; ... theology is being penetrated by history and is turning its attention to the future." Citations could be multiplied, but the tone of them all is substantially the same.

Diplomatic delegations, too, submitted very positive assessments of the Council to their governments.[74] In the area under Soviet rule the fact that the Council did not issue new condemnations of the communist ideology was greeted with satisfaction and permitted further development of the Vatican's *Ostpolitik*.[75]

Almost everyone was wondering about the postconciliar period. Vatican II had put the bishops in the limelight. Would their return to their dioceses be an easy one or would their problems be made more difficult due to the renewed self-consciousness which the Council itself had urged upon Christians? What consequences would the spirit of the Council and the Council's decrees have?

On the whole the assessments made in these weeks seems largely positive, not only quantitatively but qualitatively as well. Some major themes that had accompanied the Council from the outset and were crucial for the external image of the Church were brought to completion, giving the lie to all the fears and pessimistic forecasts. More than ever, the conclusions reached by the Council on the word of God, religious freedom, relations with the Jewish people and the other religions, and relations with

---

[74] See Melloni, *L'altra Roma*, 380–86.
[75] Congar wrote: "I was told this morning that the Pope has rejected the idea of a formal condemnation of communism. Instead, there has been an announcement that he will visit Poland on May 2. The Pope has chosen a softening of relations in order to permit and even improve the life of the Church wherever it living in fact under communist rule" (*JCongar*, October 27, 1965; II, 454).

contemporary society were entrusted to the Churches and to the people of God. But the features of the Church had already been profoundly renewed and brought into a new balance.

The satisfaction and enthusiasm of the final days had perhaps hidden from the majority the difficulties that would quickly arise in translating the impulses given by the Council into the concrete life of the Church. But as in every life-giving action, it was perhaps necessary to underestimate the problems that would arise later and so avoid the danger of paralysis. Perhaps even more than in its earlier phases, Vatican II, faithful to the impulse from which it drew its very existence, looked forward with courage and optimism, without letting itself be influenced by understandable dangers.

CHAPTER VIII

TRANSITION TO A NEW AGE

GIUSEPPE ALBERIGO

The celebration of Vatican II ended seven years after the announcement of the Council. Almost four years had been devoted to its preparation and a little less to its labors. The conciliar assembly met for 168 general congregations and for eleven solemn sessions, at five of which it approved sixteen documents: four constitutions, nine decrees, and three declarations. It was thus the longest in conciliar history; a lengthy council such as Trent had prolonged periods of time between the actual working sessions. No less substantial was the mass of Vatican II's final documents, which make up more than a quarter of the entire body of decrees issued by the other twenty ecumenical or general councils from Nicea to Vatican I. In all, 3,058 fathers intervened in the work, almost all of them bishops, with the addition of a few superiors of religious orders and apostolic vicars from the missions.[1] More important was the provenance of the Council fathers; geographically and culturally, they covered the entire planet, their provenance limited only by the serious ideological barriers set up by the Soviet governments.[2] The episcopal monopoly on the Council seems more disconcerting now than it did in the 1960s. The presence of a few parish priests, religious sisters, and laymen and laywomen was largely decorative and hardly affected this monopoly.[3]

What was the importance, the significance, of Vatican II? As we end this complex historical revisitation of the Council, we cannot avoid this

---

[1] Those having a right to take part in the Council were 2,904 in 1962 but 3,093 in 1965. The percentage of those intervening dropped from 84 percent to 80 percent (see General Secretariat of the Council, ed., *I padri presenti al concilio ecumenico Vaticano II* (Vatican City, 1966). We still lack an investigation into the motives of those who absented themselves from the Council.

[2] Of the total number of participants, 1,060 fathers came from Europe, 408 from Asia, 351 from Africa, 1,036 from the Americas (including 347 from Canada and the United States), and 74 from Oceania. As usual, the most numerous national group was the Italian, but, with less than one-fifth of the assembly, it was a much less imposing percentage than at previous councils (see R. Caporale, *Vatican II: Last of the Councils* [Baltimore: Helicon, 1964]).

[3] For this aspect, see G. Alberigo, "Facteurs de 'laïcité' au Concile Vatican II," in *"Anthropos Laïkos": Mélanges A. Faivre* (Fribourg, 2000), 13–31.

question, even though the *history* of the conciliar event is one thing and
an assessment of what it means (and may mean) is another. While a reconstruction of what happened between January 25, 1959, and December 8,
1965, is an indispensable prerequisite for any reflection on the Council that
will not be arbitrary, it does not imply any necessary conclusions.

As compared with Trent and Vatican I, the atmosphere in which the
Council ended its work was incomparably more tranquil both among the
bishops, who had reached almost complete unanimity, and among the
faithful, who were called upon to stop being passive and to play an active
part in the assimilation of the Council's decisions. Moreover, there was
tranquility in relations among the various "separated" Christian Churches.
But Vatican II urged Catholicism to renew itself through a sincere confrontation of the gospel, a confrontation effected in the light of faith and
under the influence of the signs of the times. The postconciliar period
inaugurated the long season of reception by the Churches.[4]

Both Paul VI and John Paul II repeatedly described the Council as the
major Christian event of the twentieth century, but these were occasional
statements that do not amount to a definitive judgment.

I. Too Soon or Too Late?

It is well-known that the announcement of a new council took almost
everyone by surprise; only a few isolated individuals had dared dream of
the possibility. In time, and especially after the end of the Council in
1965, some began to ask a more demanding question: Did Vatican II
come too soon or too late?[5] According to French theologian Yves Congar in 1960:

> From the viewpoint of theology and of union [of the Churches] it seemed
> that the Council was coming twenty years too soon. In fact, too few years
> have passed since things began to budge. Some ideas have already changed.
> But in twenty years we would have an episcopate of men who had grown
> up with ideas rooted in the Bible and tradition, with a realistic missionary
> and pastoral consciousness. We were not yet at that point. On the other
> hand, a good many ideas had already made an impact, and the very
> announcement of the Council, with its goal of union, and in the more human

---

[4] See *Nachkonziliare Dokumentation* (Trier, 1967ff.), a series of short works published
by Paulinusverlag.

[5] On the eve of the Council's work, H. Küng had already raised the question (see "Le
Concile vient-il trop tôt?" *ICI* 168 [1962]).

and more Christian climate of the pontificate of John XXIII, could itself accelerate some processes. Undoubtedly, many bishops who had hitherto been closed to the idea of ecumenism would now open themselves to it because Rome was in favor of it. Some "good ideas" might make their way in two years more than in twenty years of barely tolerated work.[6]

The *vota* sent to Rome by the episcopate in 1960 seemed to legitimate Congar's concern. But was not the crisis that appeared after the Council, and especially in 1968, already latent in the Catholicism of the 1950s? Did not the encyclical *Humani generis* bear witness to a deep-rooted and uncontrolled uneasiness? Was not Catholicism in ever greater danger of not adequately reflecting the note or mark of catholicity, even to the point of looking like a sect? With things in that state, would not a council deferred for twenty more years have been held in a situation so compromised as to make renewal impossible?

An interesting exercise would be to imagine what would have happened if the initial preparations begun under Pius XII in 1948 had been followed up.[7] Admittedly, ten years earlier a council might have been the occasion for avoiding or at least reducing the deterioration of the Catholic ecclesiastical world; on the other hand, it is difficult to underestimate the danger that an assembly held at that time would have been overwhelmed by theological conflict. It is only too easy to imagine that if an assembly completely different from Vatican II had met, it would probably have reached conclusions analogous to those desired by Cardinal Ruffini as late as 1960: "The coming Council will be able to give their [recent popes'] principal teachings a definitive value that will set them above and beyond all discussion."[8]

Objectively speaking, the collapse of the initiative taken in 1948 was due to the immaturity of Catholicism and of the papacy, as well as to the international context, rather than to the age of Pope Pacelli, who at the time was younger than Roncalli was in 1959, or to worries about the influence the strong presence of the Communist Party in Italy might have had on the freedom of a council. It seems, therefore, that before Vatican II was convoked by John XXIII, the celebration of a council that would be free and open to renewal was neither plausible nor feasible.

---

[6] *JCongar*, end of July 1960; I, 4–5.

[7] See G. Caprile, "Pio XII e un nuovo progetto di concilio ecumenico," *CivCatt* 117/3 (1966), 209–27; and F. C. Uginet, "Les projets de concile général sous Pie XI et Pie XII," in *Deuxième*, 65–78.

[8] *Divinitas* 1/1960, 15, cited by Fouilloux in *History*, 1:138; see also Komonchak, *History*, 1:274–85.

Pope John's insight came at a propitious moment not only in the life of Catholicism and the whole of Christianity but also in the world; after the end of the Second World War, as the world made its transition to the second half of the twentieth century, it expressed in various contexts its inclination toward renewal and its need of it. Kennedy's presidency in the United States, the beginning of the USSR's emergence from the dark period of Stalinism, the attempts to put human beings in space, and the start of decolonization — all these pointed in that direction.

At the time of the Council of Trent the question was raised of whether it had been celebrated too late. In that case, however, people had called for a council for decades, and the actual convocation took place only after a decade, at the end of 1545, when complicated political conflicts and the inertia of the papacy were at last overcome.

All the worries and alarms that had accompanied the announcement of Pope John's council proved groundless. Not only did the episcopate willingly accept it and, despite inevitable inconveniences, take a full part in it, but the faithful too and, on a broader scale, public opinion followed the celebration of the Council with unusual interest. The opposition between ideological blocs did indeed limit the participation of some episcopates, but it did not prevent or hamper the Council. In fact, the settlement of the Cuban crisis in the fall of 1962 left a sense that the Council would have a calming influence. Finally, the death of John XXIII before the conclusion of the work not only did not impede its resumption but was the best guarantee of it.

II. A COUNCIL FOR THE SAKE OF *AGGIORNAMENTO*

The principal identifying mark of Vatican II was *aggiornamento*. John XXIII had described it as a "council of *aggiornamento*." An enthusiastic reference to this aspect was already to be found in the address of January 25, 1959, when he announced the convocation of a council. Among the guiding norms he placed "a very clear and well defined correspondence with the spiritual needs of the present hour." John XXIII saw the Council not as "a gathering for speculation" that would be in a way disengaged from historical events, but as "a living, vibrant body that sees and embraces the entire world in the light and love of Christ" (June 1960). This perspective was later given full expression in the bull announcing the Council, in which the Pope distanced himself from "distrustful souls [who] see only darkness burdening the face of the earth," whereas the real need was to follow the recommendation of Jesus and to know how to distinguish "the signs of the times."

Beginning in 1958, on the occasion of his election, Roncalli repeatedly cited the passage of the New Testament in which John the Baptist committed himself to making the ways level and straight so that the people of God might be able to see the Lord. Finding expression in the term *aggiornamento*, a word typical of John XXIII's vocabulary,[9] this commitment took on a universal meaning, so much so that it entered, untranslated, into various languages. In using this word the Pope was saying that Christians and the entire Church had to accept the need to face up to a new era in the life of humankind and therefore to the understanding of the gospel in the setting of humanity and the Church today.

Underlying this call was a different way of viewing the Church. No longer seeing the Church as an unalterable reality, as though it were the heavenly Jerusalem already descended on earth, John XXIII liked to compare the Church to a living garden that needs to be constantly tended rather than to a museum of precious but dead things. If the Church was not to be alien from or deaf to the life of people, it was absolutely necessary that it devote itself to recognizing the "signs of the times" and to understanding their meaning so that it might realize at what point in history it now existed and adapt its witness to and its proclamation of the eternal gospel accordingly.[10]

---

[9] In Roncalli's vocabulary the term acquires its full meaning only after 1953, when at the age of 70 he committed himself to pastoral service as Patriarch of Venice. The occasion for it came at the provincial council of the Veneto, the purpose of which was "the updating (*aggiornamento*) of some points of discipline" (A. G. Roncalli, *Scritti e discorsi 1953–1958*, 4 vols. [Rome, 1959–62], I:12, IV:163, 164). In 1957, when he was opening the Synod of Venice, he said: "Do you hear the word *aggiornamento* repeated so often? See in it our holy Church which is always young and ready to follow the various twists of life's circumstances, in order that it may adapt, correct, improve, and stir up its enthusiasm" (ibid., 3:264). Here we see emerging the deeper meaning of the word, a more inclusive one than it had had up to that point in such expressions as "a course for bringing students up to date" or "updating the code of canon law" (Roncalli used these as well), where it had a technical and functional meaning.

[10] On June 28, 1961, the Pope spoke of "work on the condition of the Church and on its *aggiornamento* after twenty centuries of life" as the main task of Vatican II (see *DMC*, 3:574). A year later, on August 1, 1962, he explained that the Council was "intended as a council of *aggiornamento*, chiefly in the area of a deeper knowledge and love of revealed truth" (*DMC*, 4:448). Finally, in February of 1963 he stated, referring to the Council, that "the pastoral aspect of the *aggiornamento* of structures, namely, the good of souls, continues to be our keenest concern" (*DMC*, 5:128). He also knew *aggiornamento* could be misunderstood; for example, on September 9, 1962, he rejected "a mistaken understanding of *aggiornamento* that looks solely to making life sweeter or flattering nature too much" (*DMC*, 4:515).

The elderly pontiff was thus urging the Church to adopt the attitude of a seeker and to move beyond the assumption of certainty that had become habitual in modern and contemporary Catholicism in reaction to the traumas inflicted first by the Protestant Reformation and then by the French Revolution. In this way the Church would regain the sense of pilgrimage traditional in the people of God.

Aggiornamento has been hastily understood by some as a synonym of *reform,* by others as a way to avoid that heated and controverted term,[11] and by still others, as an invitation to a pursuit of modernity. But thorough analysis of the overall teaching of John XXIII allows us to conclude that by *aggiornamento* he meant a readiness and disposition to seek a renewed inculturation of the Christian message in new cultures. The Council was thus placed in the perspective of a Christian reply to the calls for the renewal of humanity.

Aggiornamento was, then, a summary pointer in the direction in which the Council was to open the way for the Church — neither disciplinary reforms nor doctrinal modifications, but a complete immersion in tradition for the purpose of rejuvenating Christian life and the Church. The formula intended to combine fidelity to tradition and prophetic renewal; the reading of the "signs of the times" was to become part of a reciprocal synergy along with the testimony of the gospel proclaimed. *Aggiornamento* called for a new attitude, which was described with crystalline clarity in the allocution *Gaudet Mater Ecclesia*: "Nowadays, however, the Spouse of Christ prefers to make use of the medicine of mercy rather than severity. She considers that she meets the needs of the present day by demonstrating the validity of her teaching rather than by condemnations."

The conciliar assembly immediately showed its spontaneous approval of this approach, but it took a great deal of effort to appropriate it culturally.[12] Vatican II dealt expressly with *aggiornamento* in the writing of two of its most important documents: the constitution *Lumen gentium* and the decree *Unitatis redintegratio*. After calling to mind the truth that the Spirit "by the power of the Gospel... permits the Church to keep the freshness of youth.... [and] constantly... renews her" (*LG*, 4), *Lumen gentium* acknowledges that "the Church includes sinners within it; it is holy and at the same time is in need of purification; therefore it devotes

---

[11] See G. Alberigo, "L'amore alla Chiesa: dalla riforma all'aggiornamento," in *"Con tutte le tue forze": I nodi della fede cristiana oggi: Omaggio a Giuseppe Dossetti,* ed. A. and G. Alberigo (Genoa, 1993), 169–94.

[12] In the decrees of Vatican II the word *aggiornamento* does not occur except in equivalent Latin expressions, such as *accommodatio, renovatio accommodata,* and so on.

itself to penance and renewal." The same constitution returns to the theme in chapter II: "Through the action of the Holy Spirit [the Church] ceaselessly renews itself" (9); "The Holy Spirit... makes the faithful able and ready to assume responsibilities and offices that are useful for the renewal and further building up of the Church" (12). The constitution *Gaudium et spes* repeats the commitment of the Church "to constant self-renewal and self-purification," and connects this with its response to contemporary atheism (*GS*, 21). The decrees *Optatam totius* and *Presbyterorum ordinis* confirm that the Council desired renewal of the entire Church, that its "pastoral goals" were the "internal renewal of the Church" (PO 12; see OT, preface).

It is, however, *Unitatis redintegratio* that contains even fuller and more telling formulations. It recalls the obligation all Christians have of "examining their fidelity to Christ's will for the Church and ... of energetically undertaking the work of renewal and reform" (*UR*, 4). A little further on an entire section devoted to the renewal of the Church says that "the Church on its pilgrimage is called by Christ to the constant reform that it always needs as a human and earthly institution; so that if anything, whether in behavior or in ecclesiastical discipline or even in the way teaching is formulated (a formulation that must be carefully distinguished from the deposit of faith), has been, due to circumstances, less carefully observed, it will at the right moment be rectified and properly ordered" (*UR*, 6).

But the results of this analysis of the conciliar documents are insufficient for grasping the overall significance of the work of Vatican II in relation to the renewal of the contemporary Church. In fact, the Council, first and foremost as an event and then also through its collection of decrees, made a much more important contribution to the restoration of a unitary vision of the Christian message. To look in isolation at those passages of the decrees that are devoted to *aggiornamento* would do injury to the global meaning of the Council's teaching. The mind of Vatican II was that the *aggiornamento* should permeate the entire life of the Church. It was in this perspective that the Council took over John XXIII's directive that no new definitions should be formulated. This was not simply a matter of circumspection in dealing with the other Christian Churches; not only did the Council not introduce new dogmas, for its own teachings it chose an indicative and hortatory form, avoiding condemnations and the preceptive approach that had marked, for example, the documents of Trent.

According to Chenu, "*Aggiornamento* does not mean a few verbal changes in a stereotypical language, plus the addition of some decorative images; it has to do rather with the permanent and authentic substance of the faith, an interior invention of concepts, categories, and symbols that will be in harmony with the mentality, culture, language, and esthetics of people today."[13] Chenu had a clear grasp of the significance of John XXIII's key word; he insisted that "*aggiornamento* means to refashion the Church, its manner of speaking, and its structure, into a Church that, within the unchanging truth received from Christ and safeguarded in it, seeks and finds the means of making this truth intelligible and communicable through dialogue." According to the French Dominican, "The specific way of bringing about the *aggiornamento* of the Church is to watch for the 'signs of the times,' these being so many reminders of the gospel and so many indicators, written in the hearts of human beings, of their capacity for receiving the grace of Christ."[14]

By and large the perspective of an *aggiornamento* was accepted by the conciliar assembly with conviction and commitment, although there were some discontinuities. Indeed, it is impossible to ignore the drive toward rejuvenation that inspired the approach and contents of the conciliar constitutions and some of the decrees and declarations. Other conciliar documents, however, obeyed calls for the preservation of the status quo, as, for example, the decree on the Oriental Churches and the declaration on Christian Education. Only gradually did the Council fathers realize that *aggiornamento* could not remain a simple aspiration but would have to be translated into specific, even if embryonic, proposals that would show the Churches the direction in which to move rather than give them a detailed program. Every time the Council agreed to adopt an attitude of searching[15] and committed itself to move beyond earlier, but now obsolete spiritual and cultural phases, it made *aggiornamento* its own.

III. A Pastoral Council

John XXIII also assigned the attribute *pastoral* to the Council. Some of the more alert participants immediately asked themselves what the

---

[13] M.-D. Chenu, "Un pontificat entré dans l'histoire," *Témoignage chrétien* (June 7, 1963), also in *La Parole de Dieu*, vol. 2, *L'Évangile dans le temps* (Paris, 1964), 190–91.

[14] M.-D. Chenu, "Dans la coulée de *Pacem in terris:* Idéologies et mouvements de l'histoire," in *Peuple de Dieu dans le monde* (Paris, 1966), 57.

[15] This approach was severely criticized by M. Maccarrone; in his view councils should exercise a judicial and therefore decisive function.

correct meaning of the Pope's directive was.[16] The Pope's pastoral intuition would create uneasiness not only among the conciliar minority, who
feared that the doctrinal dimension would be played down, but also
among the majority. While sincerely agreeing with the Pope and glimps-
ing the epochal importance of his directives, the majority would experience not a few difficulties in translating it into practice. What does a *pastoral* presentation of the gospel mean? Or an *aggiornamento* of the
formulations of the faith and of the Church? The shift implied in these
perspectives also necessitated modifications for which there was no established model.

This description ("pastoral") was very quickly perceived as an
unequivocal sign that this would be a "new" council. From the very
beginning of the work, the great majority of the bishops who intervened
at Vatican II committed themselves to making this pastoral approach their
own.[17] The widespread criticisms and rejection of the preparatory drafts
were based precisely on their abstract, doctrinaire, and polemical trend,
in contrast to the pastoral approach suggested by the Pope and insistently
called for by the bishops. Almost inadvertently, the call for a pastoral
council acquired within the assembly a meaning that differentiated innovative from traditionalist trends. As early as December 1962 it was clear
to Chenu that "the word 'pastoral' is becoming, if not a sign of contradiction, then at least a word of agreement or of confrontation.... The pastoral aspect has become the primary criterion used in formulating and
proposing the truth and not simply the motive for practical decisions to
be adopted. 'Pastoral,' therefore, describes a theology, a way of thinking
theology and teaching the faith, or, better, a vision of the economy of
salvation."[18]

In 1965 Chenu was already claiming that

> this entire council is pastoral, in the sense that in it the Church is becoming
> aware of its mission. This entire council is doctrinal, because its aim is to

---

[16] See Chenu, "Un concile 'pastoral'" *Parole et mission* 21 (April, 1963), 182–202;
also in *La Parole de Dieu* 2:655–72. Chenu rejected the idea that *doctrine* meant principles and *pastoral* the conclusions drawn.

[17] It is enough to recall the written observations on the first group of preparatory
schemas, which were sent to Rome in the summer of 1962, and the conciliar debate on
scripture and tradition that took place in October and November of that year (see G. Ruggieri, "L'impatto della allocuzione *Gaudet mater ecclesia* sui lavori conciliari," in *Vatican II commence,* 315–28).

[18] Chenu, "Un concile pastorale"; see also G. Ruggieri, "Appunti per una teologia in
papa Roncalli," in *Papa Giovanni*, ed. G. Alberigo (Bari-Rome, 1987), 248–59.

make the presence of the gospel real through and in the Church. How sen-
sationally original! a council which, without ignoring the errors, the mis-
deeds, and the darknesses of the present time, is not tensed up and hostile
to them, but recognizes in this age's hopes and values so many implicit
appeals to the gospel; in them it finds material for and a legitimation of a
dialogue.[19]

What was involved here, then, was a new attitude of the Roman Church
and the possibility of making Vatican II a new kind of council, both
Church and Council being characterized by a global, unified, and faithful vision of what it is to proclaim and bear witness to the faith. Could
this pastoral dimension become an adequate response to new needs?
Or would it be condemned to remain a general term that was nothing
more than a manifestation of good will?

Like *aggiornamento*, the pastoral orientation of John XXIII was
received with enthusiasm, but the Council found itself unprepared for this
unexpected task and had serious difficulties in translating it into concrete
perspectives. But that the Council moved, even if imperfectly and amid
opposition, beyond the conception of Christianity as a sum of "doctrine"
and "discipline" (the two often simply juxtaposed), was an important
development, for it led to a substantial rethinking of ecclesiastical reform
and of ecclesiology itself. This movement was marked by the emphasis
on the pastoral and *aggiornamento*, on the basis of a global, unified vision
of Christianity controlled by the idea of communion between the one
Shepherd, Christ, and the faithful.

The combination of the pastoral principle with the method of *aggiornamento* challenged how Church decline and reform were thought about
in medieval and modern times. The Council left that way of thinking
behind both in its dialectic of abuses and reforms (a dialectic often running
itself into the ground in the interplay of denunciations, plans, and insufficient or inefficient reforms) and even in its theoretical statement, which
was largely responsible for the recent over-development of ecclesiology.

For all their verboseness and a certain discontinuity among them (both
of these defects due to the bringing together of diverse orientations in
so large an assembly), the documents of Vatican II avoided not only
definitions but also the formulation of penalties.[20] The description "pastoral" was used both in the title of the decree *The Pastoral Office of*

---

[19] M.-D. Chenu, "Una constituzione pastorale della Chiesa," in *DO-C*, no. 205 (1966),
reprinted in *Peuple de Dieu*, 11–34, quotation at 17.

[20] This was officially made clear on March 6, 1964, and again on November 16 of that
year in connection with the theological "note" to be assigned to the Council's documents.

Bishops and in the title *Pastoral Constitution on the Church in the Modern World.* Other documents, however, were described differently: *Dogmatic Constitution on the Church, Dogmatic Constitution on Divine Revelation.*[21]

Due to the vast amount of the preparatory material, which had been worked up in a qualitatively different perspective, the Council traveled many roads: from the apostolate of the laity to the training and ministry of priests, from religious life to Christian education and the means of social communication. As a result, the assembly moved back and forth between the formulation of a summa of social doctrine and that of a summary of canonical norms, thereby incurring the danger of coming to a standstill. But, driven as it was by urgent expectations, it succeeded in large measure in avoiding that danger. Above all, it was in a position to point out dynamic perspectives for an *aggiornamento* of Church life in areas evangelized long ago and in areas only recently evangelized *(Christus Dominus* and *Ad gentes).* For its part, the *Pastoral Constitution on the Church in the Modern World* fulfilled, at least in embryonic form, the commitment the Council had made in the Message to Humanity of October 1962, namely, "to inquire how we ought to renew ourselves, so that we may be found increasingly faithful to the gospel of Christ ... [and] to present to the men of this age God's truth in its integrity and purity."[22]

In this setting the Council substantially reduced the dominance of the institutional system over Christian life which had reached its culmination with Vatican I's dogmas of the primacy and infallible teaching office of the Bishop of Rome (1870) and with the introduction of a universal Code of Canon Law in 1917. In fact, through the application to the Church of the New Testament idea of service,[23] the premise was placed for a subordination of all institutional functions to the life of faith and to the dynamic that establishes the "communion of saints." This is the proper and full meaning of assertions such as that the "office ... which the Lord committed to the pastors of his people, is, in the strict sense of the term, a service, which is called very expressively in sacred

---

[21] C. Theobald, "Le Concile de Vatican II et la 'forme pastorale' de la doctrine," in *La parole de salut,* ed. B. Sesboüé and C. Theobald, Histoire des dogmes IV (Paris, 1996), 471–510.

[22] See A. Grillmeier, "Die Reformidee des II. Vatikanischen Konzils und ihre Forderung an uns," in *Wahrheit und Verkündigung: Für M. Schmaus* (Munich, 1967), 2:1467–88.

[23] The Latin word *servitium* occurs eighty times in the body of the texts of Vatican II, especially in the constitutions on the Church and on the Church in the modern world.

scripture a *diakonia*" (*LG*, 28) and that Christians are called upon to "pattern ourselves daily more and more after the spirit of the Gospel and work together in a spirit of brotherhood to serve the human family" (*GS*, 92).

The rediscovery of the importance of *diakonia* not only for the personal life of Christians but also for the attitude of the community is rich in implications.[24] In relation both to the internal structuring of the Church and to the Church's relations with human societies, the idea of *diakonia* requires a rethinking of attitudes and, equally, of the very meaning of ecclesial institutions. At the same time, therefore, the room that institutions take up in the ecclesial community must be controlled, as must also the models to which such institutions have conformed themselves.

The pastoral principle and *aggiornamento*, taken together, laid the premises for moving beyond the hegemony of *theology,* understood as an isolating of the doctrinal dimension of the faith and as its abstract conceptualization, and also beyond the domination of *juridicism,* insofar as this meant freezing the dynamics of Christian experience into juridical formulas.

It follows from all this that the pastoral character of the Council and the summary description of the Council's purpose as an *aggiornamento* explain, balance, and enrich each other. Clumsy attempts have proposed to interpret the pastorality of Vatican II as a sign of weakness in order to reduce the authority of its documents. But, forty years after the end of Vatican II, the insight of John XXIII, which the great majority at the Council made their own and which was supported by Paul VI, is one of the most important contributions of Vatican II; it is a direction that deserves to be more deeply explored and is capable of fruitful developments.[25] The Council's pastoral character, finally, raises questions about "doctrinal" ecumenism and calls for a global approach to the search for unity. It is the very conception of unity that finds in the pastoral vision of Christianity an impulse to describing unity in concrete and flexible terms.

[24] Some ideas, in a rudimentary stage, were suggested by M. Löhrer, "La gerarchia al servizio del popolo cristiano," in *La Chiesa del Vaticano II*, ed. L. Baraúna (Florence, 1965), 699–712.

[25] A. Scola also sees in the *pastoral dimension* one of the characteristic marks of the Council ("*Gaudium et spes*: dialogo e discernimento nella testimonianza della verità," in *Il concilio Vatican II: Recezione e attualità alla luce del Giubileo*, ed. R. Fisichella, 103–14 (Milan: Cinisella Balsamo, 2000).

IV. A COUNCIL OF UNION

The official press release about the papal allocution of January 25, 1959, said that "in the thinking of the Holy Father the celebration of the ecumenical council not only looks to the building up of the Christian people, but is also intended as an invitation to the separated Communities to engage in the search for truth, for which so many souls all over the world are longing today."[26] Along with the Council's "eminently pastoral" purpose, the Pope stressed with special enthusiasm that the Council was intended as a "a renewed invitation to the faithful of the separated Churches to participate with us in this banquet of grace and brotherhood."[27] More than any other aspect, the ecumenical dimension elicited surprise, public interest, and some very lively apprehensions.

The Pope's intentions were further clarified when, during a meeting at the end of April, he sketched a series of ecumenical steps: "In the East, first a rapprochement, then a drawing together, and the complete union of so many separated brothers with their ancient common Mother; and in the West the generous pastoral collaboration of the two clergies."[28] That it should be the Pope who took the first step toward the unity of the Christian Churches and who presented this process, not in terms of a simple "return," but in terms of a "working together to become a single flock,"[29] was so unexpected and almost improbable that it elicited a variety of reactions and called for a rethinking of the entire ecumenical strategy.

Accepting a suggestion of Bea and of Jaeger, the Bishop of Paderborn, John XXIII decided that the preconciliar and conciliar commissions would be flanked by a Secretariat for Christian Unity and that it would be the

---

[26] *OssRom*, January 26–27, 1959. In the first unofficial commentary on the announcement, *OssRom* wrote that the Council would not be a "council of fear" but rather a "council of unity" (February 1, 1959). On May 23, during an audience, Maximos IV, Patriarch of the Maronites, presented John XXIII with a memorandum that suggested the creation, at Rome, of "a new congregation or a special Roman commission" on relations with the non-Roman Christian Churches (*Le Lien* 33 [1968], 65).

[27] A few days later, on January 29, when addressing the parish priests of Rome, the Pope emphasized the ecumenical aspect of the Council. According to one press service, he said that "there was no hiding the difficulties in the way of carrying out this program, if only because it will be extremely difficult to restore harmony and reconciliation among the various Churches which have been too long separated and are often rent by internal dissensions." The Pope meant "to tell them to put an end to their discords and get back together, without a detailed historical investigation to determine who was right and who was wrong; there may have been responsibility on all sides"; see Gian Franco Svidercoschi, *Storia del Concilio* (Milan, 1967) 39.

[28] *DMC* 1:903.

[29] *ADA* I, 16, 28.

intermediary for inviting observers delegated by the other Christian Churches. The invitation met with a widespread and growing welcome, unlike the rejection that Pius IX received when he convoked Vatican I. But in what did the participation of the observers and other invited guests at Vatican II consist? These outsiders were excluded from the meetings of the commissions but were present at the general congregations; at a weekly meeting they and the representatives of the secretariat debated the subjects being discussed at the Council; finally, they had a network of close relations with bishops and theologians.

Were they therefore in large measure members, even if *sui generis*, of the Council?[30] We have a variety of authoritative testimonies to the real impact their viewpoints had on the directions taken by the Council and therefore on the body of its documents.[31] Nor may we ignore the observers' participation in the liturgical part of the general congregations; on these occasions the spiritual communion and the sharing in the word of God had a continuity, a solemnity, and an intensity entirely out of the ordinary.[32] On December 4, 1965, at St. Paul's Outside the Walls this communion was confirmed at a liturgy in which both Paul VI and the observers took part, so that there was a *communicatio in sacris* (shared worship), however imperfect. While this was not the intended purpose of the decisions to invite and to send observers, in fact a communion was formed, the authenticity of which was all the greater because it was a spontaneous fruit.

Another fact worth considering is that the involvement of the non-Catholics was not limited to a few of the subjects taken up at Vatican II (ecumenism, religious freedom) but extended to all the subjects discussed. In fact, the main object of their involvement was a sharing in the very purpose of the Council, namely, the quest for a renewed fidelity to the gospel on the part of Christians and, first of all, of the Roman Catholic Church.

---

[30] See G. Alberigo, *Ecclesiologia in devenire: A proposito di "concilio pastorale" e di Osservatori a-cattolici al Vaticano II* (Bologna, 1990); also published as "Ekklesiologie im Werden: Bemerkungen zum 'Pastoralkonzil' und zu den Beobachtern des II. Vatikanums," *Ökumenische Rundschau* 40 (1991), 109–28.

[31] See A. Birmelé, "Le Vatican II vu par les observateurs," in *Volti di fine concilio*, 225–64. After the close of the Council, Orthodox observer Evdokimov noted how "the impressions of the observers were unanimous: when they found themselves acting not as spectators but taken into the midst of the work itself and invited to take part in it, as well as expressing their views with complete freedom in private groups or in the commissions, they had the impression that they were witnesses to a real historical event." Reformed observer Roux likewise concluded that during the Council a real "togetherness" had come about; this was as unexpected as it was meaningful and fruitful.

[32] See K. E. Skydsgaard, "Last Intention of the Council," *Ecumenical Studies* 3 (1966), 151–54.

The initial hypothesis was that the observers were to have only the function of getting information back to their Churches and bearing witness to the Council; but their role developed beyond what was foreseen and surpassed any limitations dictated by prudence.

To the extent that there is reason to maintain that a habitual communion developed between the non-Catholic observers and the members of Vatican II, how can we deny that the observers were in some manner true and proper members of the Council? They were informal members, certainly, such as had been seen on other occasions in the conciliar tradition. As a result, there emerged at Vatican II, even if only in filigree, a pastoral-sacramental conception of Christianity and of the Church that tended to replace a preceding doctrinal-disciplinary conception. In this connection the primacy of the pastoral dimension was combined, in a reciprocal fruitfulness, with the full involvement of the observers in Vatican II. In a council inspired by a strictly doctrinal conception of a council and therefore geared to be a tribunal for "judging" the truth, the participation of non-Catholic Christians could only have been *affective* and therefore, in the final analysis, decorative.

While Vatican II did not draft a text on either *aggiornamento* or on the pastoral, it did approve the *Decree on Ecumenism,* with the significant opening words *"Unitatis redintegratio."* We may wonder whether writing a separate decree was the most suitable way to deal with the question of Christian unity or whether, on the contrary, having a decree specifically devoted to the question did not involuntarily prevent a greater presence of the theme throughout the entire work of the Council? But then we must realize that, prior to the Council, the Roman attitude toward the ecumenical question was so attached to the demand for a "return" that a formal correction was indispensable.

Whatever one thinks of that question, it is undeniable that among the major contributions of Vatican II was the powerful relaunching of the ecumenical thrust which culminated in the meeting of Paul VI and Athenagoras in Jerusalem and in the withdrawal of the excommunications issued by Rome and Constantinople against each other. The comparison with the preconciliar situation calls for attention. Not only did *Unitatis redintegratio* introduce the problem of unity into Catholicism, while sweeping away the problem of the "return" of "heretics" and "schismatics" to the Church of Rome, but it also gave explicit form to a true and proper Catholic ecumenism.[33] This represented a real reversal,

---

[33] A few years earlier the encyclical letter *Humani generis* of Pius XII had excluded any and every contamination of Catholicism by the ecumenical movement. The misfortunes

which initially left more than a few council fathers incredulous and dis-
mayed; they may even have been more numerous than those who welcomed it with relief and delight.[34] Could the Council have pressed on
further in this direction? The fact is that the Secretariat for Christian
Unity found itself involved to the limits of its powers in the development
of all the principal schemas. This made it possible to achieve texts that
were attentive to ecumenical problems, even when they were not directly
of ecumenical importance.

V. THE SHAPE OF THE CHURCH AND DIALOGUE WITH THE WORLD

The decision of Paul VI to continue and see to its end the Council that
had been conceived, convoked, and opened by his predecessor had been
an act of loyalty to John XXIII and to the episcopate;[35] and, given the
obvious complexity involved in beginning a pontificate under the gaze of
a general council and of the public attention it was drawing, it was also
a display of courage. While the decision evidently implied Pope Montini's
acceptance of the Council as it had been defining itself ever since the
announcement in 1959, it also opened a new phase. Between 1963 and
the end of Vatican II there came to light, due to the authority of Montini
as pope, directions and characteristics of the conciliar event that Archbishop Montini had had occasion to speak of earlier or that he had come
to envisage during his experience as a member of the assembly.

Aggiornamento, the pastoral principle, and commitment to unity
remained essential elements in the identity of the Council, but they could
not but be influenced by the meaning Paul VI gave to them. In addition,
Paul VI added some other characteristics: commitment to dialogue with

---

of Yves Congar suffice to document ecclesiastical hostility toward any ecumenical initiative; Roncalli himself experienced that hostility the hard way. For Congar's dramatic ups
and down during the decade 1946–1956, see Y. Congar, *Journal d'un théologien
1946–1956*, ed. É. Fouilloux (Paris, 2000).

[34] This reversal later led Paul VI to make his own the description "sister Churches"
for the Churches separated from Rome.

[35] In Milan, when remembering the just deceased pope, Montini explicitly pledged to
continue John's legacy, saying: "Can we really abandon a path traced out in so masterful
a way, even for the future, by John XXIII? There is reason for thinking that we cannot."
Confirmation of the direction to be taken by Paul VI came on the occasion of his first message, when he said, "The most important part of this pontificate will be spent in continuing ecumenical council Vatican II, toward which the eyes of all people of good will are
turned."

the world, the search for the greatest possible consensus among the Council fathers, and the priority given to a deepening of the theology of the Church. While John XXIII had put the emphasis chiefly on the Council as an opportunity for change, Paul VI, in charge of a now ongoing council, combined the original approach with directives for its content.

When Paul VI opened the second period of work on September 29, 1963, he mentioned among the purposes of the Council an exposition of the theology of the Church and dialogue with the contemporary world. A year later, on September 14, 1964, the Pope in his address reasserted the duty of the Church to define itself and the need to express the whole of the teaching that Vatican I, with its focus on papal prerogatives, had formulated incompletely. Finally, in the summer of 1965, shortly before the final period of the Council, Paul VI emphasized as a goal of the Council that it should take a position "in a more tranquil and fraternal harmony" on all the subjects still open.

The importance and relevance of an attitude of dialogue was to be a main focus of Montini's pontificate.[36] Paul VI referred to the dialogue of the Church with humanity both in the allocution delivered at the opening of the first conciliar period of his pontificate and in the address that ended the work on December 7, 1965. It is well-known that the importance of an attitude of dialogue was fundamentally alien to the teaching of Pius XII, which was focused on giving authoritative teaching to all. It does not seem rash to claim that Montini, while greatly venerating Pius XII, saw the need for a less intransigent and more receptive attitude. A demand for this had been voiced in various Catholic circles and found a place for itself in the new climate created by the pontificate of John.

On the basis of new pastoral experiments going on in the Church of France, M.-D. Chenu had repeatedly urged the need for dialogue.[37] The idea found a place in the fathers' "Message to Humanity," which had begun the Council's work, in the pastoral constitution *Gaudium et spes*, and in the declaration *Nostra aetate*. Paul VI made dialogue a central attitude of the Church, especially in dealing with contemporaries.

---

[36] See *Paolo VI e il rapporto Chiesa-Mondo al Concilio* (Brescia: Istituto Paolo VI, 1991).

[37] In 1963 the Dominican theologian called for giving *dialogue* its full signification, that is, "giving it its whole wealth of meaning: recognition of the other as other, loving others as they are and not as people to be won over, accepting that they are different from me, without trying to encroach on their consciences and on their searching, without asserting my reservations before I give my trust." See G. Alberigo, "Un Concile à la dimension du monde: Marie-Dominique Chenu à Vatican II d'après son Journal," in *Marie-Dominique Chenu: Moyen-âge et modernité* (Paris, 1997), 155–72.

In his address at the closing session on December 7, 1965, Paul VI
reminded his listeners that "the teaching authority of the Church ...
descended, so to speak, in order to dialogue with humanity; and, while
always retaining its own proper authority and powers, it has made its own
the easy and friendly language of pastoral charity; its desire is to be heard
and understood by all.... It has endeavored to use today's ordinary conversational style." This readiness for dialogue was based on the "study
of the modern world," as the Pope said on that same occasion.[38] But
while Paul VI's appraisal of the contemporary world was sympathetic, it
was primarily critical. Consequently, the dialogue represented an attitude
of openness but not necessarily of agreement or brotherliness.

The central place of ecclesiology had been solemnly set forth by the
Pope in his first encyclical letter, *Ecclesiam suam*, which was published
in the summer of 1964 but was regarded by Montini as a document for
the opening of the phase of the Council that followed upon his election.[39]
Back in 1959 Pope John's announcement had suggested a council that
would complete the teaching on the Church that had been approved by
the First Vatican Council before its interruption in 1870; in fact, the
preparatory work for that council had extended to a vast range of subjects.
But John XXIII had not made his own the concentration of the previous
council on ecclesiology; he had even named the new council Vatican II,
thereby giving it an identity distinct from that of the never completed
council of Pius IX.

The emphasis given by Paul VI, which repeated the viewpoint
expressed in 1962 to the secretary of state, displayed the well-grounded
and widespread conviction that the papal prerogatives confirmed in 1870
needed a completion from the viewpoint of the episcopate.[40] Paul VI
sought to emphasize that, as he saw it, John XXIII had "picked up the
broken thread of Vatican Council I and had cut through the mistrust
wrongly derived from that council, as though the supreme powers granted
to the Roman pontiff were enough for him to govern the Church without

[38] See *Council Daybook, Session 4*, 361.

[39] He referred to this in his allocution of September 29, 1963 (see G. Colombo, "Genesi, storia e significato dell'enciclica *Ecclesiam suam*," in *"Ecclesiam suam": Première
lettre encyclique de Paul VI* [Brescia, 1982], 131).

[40] The thought is repeated several times: the Council is "the natural continuation and
completion of the first Vatican council" (allocution of December 4, 1963; *Council Daybook, Sessions 1 and 2*, 331-35); "the teaching which ecumenical council Vatican I set out
to affirm needs completion" (allocution of September 14, 1964; *Council Daybook, Session 3*, 6-10); again in the allocution of November 21, 1964, after the definitive approval
of the constitution on the Church (*Council Daybook, Session 3*, 303-307).

the help of ecumenical councils." This purpose and, above all, giving an organized form to the hierarchical structure were to be the heart of Vatican II: "The hour has sounded in history when the Church... must say of herself what Christ intended and willed her to be.... The Church must give a definition of herself."[41]

The deep-rooted conviction that the Council must focus on "the nature of the Church, which is both monarchical and hierarchical,"[42] led Paul VI to bring into play, much more directly and frequently than his predecessor had, the way of thinking about the Church that had been assimilated chiefly from the encyclical *Mystici Corporis*. Thus Pope Paul emphasized the "hierarchical constitution" to the point of introducing the possibility of a "hierarchical communion."[43] This made it difficult for him to be fully attuned to the ecclesiology of the conciliar majority, which had preferred not to repeat the description of the Church as a *mystical* body; the difficulty led finally to the *Nota explicativa praevia* for chapter III of *Lumen gentium*.

Finally, the fact that he presided over the later phases of the Council's work and then over its conclusion led the Pope to stress the need for the greatest possible agreement within the assembly. As Pope John had the responsibility for arousing commitment and a sense of responsibility in the fathers, Pope Paul, driven by deep conviction, made an effort to obtain unanimous votes for the definitive approval of the conciliar texts. In a variety of circumstances this eager desire of the Pope called for great patience, readiness to listen (even to excessive demands), and tenacity.

The conciliar assembly, for its part, shared Paul VI's longing for dialogue and mentions this in many of its texts. The impression is sometimes given, however, that the word is being used casually and superficially. While the attitude toward dialogue represented a real advance over the sour attitude of superiority of the preceding ecclesiastical magisterium, at times an overly facile and, in the end, trite use of the word can be seen.

The search for a consensus, too, was broadly and positively received by the fathers, even though it exacted its price in the clarity and coherence of the approved texts. The demand pushed by the Pope awakened deep resonances in the minds of the bishops, leading them, when nothing else was possible, even to sacrifice abstract doctrinal consistency.

[41] Allocution of September 14, 1964.

[42] Allocution of November 21, 1964.

[43] Allocution of September 14, 1964. It is of interest that Paul VI habitually described the Church as "mystical body" (see the allocutions of September 29, 1963 (*Council Daybook, Session 1 and 2*, 143-50); December 4, 1963; November 21, 1964; and October 28, 1965 (*Council Daybook, Session 4*, 164-66).

On the other hand, the Pope's preference for a concentration on ecclesiology had to deal with the extensive list of subjects that crystalized during the first period of work and with the fact that the Council had opened with a discussion of liturgical reform and not with a study of the schema on the Church. In other words, Paul VI was faced with the unfolding of a council that reflected a wide range of subjects, and he also could not ignore the expectations that had grown up among the fathers with regard to a variety of problems.[44]

VI. VATICAN II AND TRADITION

John XXIII, whose education and culture were deeply traditional, had had no hesitation in describing the Council in a completely traditional way: a council of bishops (even with representatives of the non-Catholic Churches present) that is free and responsible and therefore deliberates effectively — "an echo of ancient forms."[45] The Pope had given a positive value to the conciliar tradition: "a form which the history of the Church has taught to us and which has always yielded fruitful results." It would be, therefore, not a council of Christendom, such as Lateran IV was, but also not a council of union, like the Council of Florence. Much less did John XXIII want a council based on a conflict, as Trent had been, or a council bent on resistance and opposition to modern society, like Vatican I. John XXIII was clearly convinced that questions of doctrinal change ought not be raised. He said as much in his opening address: "The salient point of this Council is not … a discussion of one article or another of the fundamental doctrine of the Church…. For this a Council was not necessary."[46] Paul VI, in his turn, showed himself especially aware of safeguarding tradition.

In fact, the problem was posed during the Council in the terms already used by Roncalli when he reminded his hearers that "the substance of

[44] In his allocution on December 4, 1963, at the end of the second period of work, Paul VI expressed a wish that it would be possible, when work resumed, "to produce schemas that would be shorter and so set up that it would not be difficult for the Council to pass judgment on some basic propositions, while leaving their illustrative expansion and operative development to postconciliar commissions." As all know, this possibility, which was translated into the unsuccessful Döpfner Plan, had no sequel.

[45] See G. Alberigo, "Die Rezeption der grossen christlichen Überlieferung durch das Zweite Vatikanische Konzil," in *Dogmengeschichte und katholische Theologie*, ed. W. Löser, K. Lehmann, and M. Lutz-Bachmann (Würzburg, 1985), 303–20.

[46] We may ask whether this last statement was an indirect allusion to the prerogatives of primacy and infallibility that were confirmed in 1870.

the ancient doctrine of the deposit of faith is one thing, and the way in which it is presented is another. And it is the latter that must be taken into great consideration with patience if necessary, everything being measured in the forms and proportions of a magisterium that is predominantly pastoral in character." In dealing with the various subjects it faced, the Council devoted itself to developing formulations that were ever more faithful to revelation and more suited to the understanding of educated contemporaries.

A comparison of the texts of the preparatory schemas with the documents finally accepted helps us measure the substantial continuity with Christian tradition as understood in Catholicism, but also the discontinuity with the Catholicism of the medieval Christian centuries and the post-Tridentine period. No substantial novelties emerged, but an effort was made (even if not always satisfactory) to restate the ancient faith in language intelligible to contemporary humanity and freed of the more or less parasitical encrustations that had hardened in place over the centuries.

A significant factor in the Council's fidelity to tradition was its liturgical experience. The spiritual and doctrinal importance of the daily enthronement of the gospel and of the celebration of the liturgy in the various rites (both practices decided by John XXIII) was considerable, as is attested by many notes in the diaries of the fathers.[47] But was not the Council committed, before all else, to promoting an *aggiornamento* of liturgical life? And, in fact, the constitution *Sacrosanctum concilium* was inspired by the great ancient liturgical tradition that had been revived and mediated by decades of experience of the liturgical movement. The notion people sometimes have that Vatican II set out in a radically new direction springs from a hasty and superficial reading that mistakes the return to ancient liturgical practices for subversive innovation. Reviving the active participation of the faithful instead of reducing liturgies to dry and remote ritualism was anything but an innovation!

---

[47] See H. Raguer, "La celebración de la eucaristía en las congregaciones del concilio Vaticano II," in *Fovenda sacra liturgia: Miscelánea en honor del doctor Pere Farnés* (Barcelona, 2000), 97–104. Ch. Theobald's chapter above quotes de Lubac's observation that "the enthronement of the gospel, a beautiful symbol ... was set before all each morning of the Council: it was not always fully understood. Many thought it simply the homage which the Church of Vatican II wished to pay to the Bible. Without being entirely mistaken, this interpretation was very incomplete (as was, at times, that of the Constitution itself, as we saw earlier). It does not capture the real meaning of the rite. After being carried in procession, the book of gospels was not placed on a lectern but really installed on a throne, because it represented Christ himself."

Moreover, the Council composed a constitution that was devoted to tradition in the deepest meaning of the word: tradition is the transmission of Christian revelation itself. It is significant that *Dei Verbum* was one of its major and most telling documents, and the only one the composition of which lasted through the entire duration of the assembly, from 1962 to 1965.

On the whole, Vatican II made a significant contribution to the restoration of a unified vision of the Christian message. Moving beyond a division into sectors (dogma, moral theology, discipline, and so on), which was the fruit of the "university" stage of Christian thought, the Council also began the movement beyond the reduction of the gospel message to a moral code, one of the major effects of that division. Without yielding to integralist or fundamentalist temptations, the effort was made to get back to the unity and the complexity of the gospel message. In this context the norms set down in the *Decree on Ecumenism* for formulating and explaining the faith, as well as the acknowledgment of a "hierarchy of truths" (*UR*, 11), can be read not only as an admission that particular aspects of revelation do not bring us equally close to Christ, but also, and above all, as a directive to seek expressions of the faith that are less conditioned by the stage of the faith's inculturation in Western culture and are open to the new ways of perception and thought of contemporary humanity.

The proposal for renewal offered by Vatican II can be grasped in its fullness and innovative scope if we appreciate the conciliar assembly's witness to communion and if we properly appraise the connection and reciprocal interaction of its major documents. From the active participation of the faithful in worship and in the Church's life, from the conception of the Church as a "mystery" and distinct from the reign of God, from the rediscovery of the "people of God" and the "communion" among the Churches and their bishops, to the broadening of the perspective of communion so as to embrace all the Christian traditions, and to the appreciation of the pilgrim condition of the Christian community in the world, the Council established the basis for transcending ecclesiocentrism and therefore for relativizing ecclesiology itself. Seen against this background the recognition of the sovereignty of God's word *(Dei Verbum)* and of the inalienability of conscience *(Dignitatis humanae)* began the refocusing of Christian thought on the constitutive elements of the human condition as seen in the light of gospel revelation.

Many bishops were convinced that their participation in the Council had had an authentic spiritual significance. This participation had an impact on the personalities of many of them and fostered a certain number of quite surprising "conversions," although an assessment of them is very difficult.[48] P. Parente was one of the highest representatives of the Holy Office; consequently, his switch of sides on the subject of episcopal collegiality caused a sensation. We may also mention the cases of Léger, a Canadian, and of Italians Lercaro and Motolese. Each of them, in his own way, experienced the Council as a spiritual event that demanded a radical change in the way he served as bishop. In April 1966, Léger wrote, "Each can say that the Council meant nothing to him if it did not convert him, if it did not change his life, if it did not make him aware of responsibilities hitherto unsuspected or too often neglected." A year later he went to Africa to share the lot of the lepers there.[49] Lercaro devoted himself to a thorough reform of the Diocese of Bologna and became a radical witness to peace;[50] Motolese experienced a doctrinal "conversion" in which he cast off the conservative attitude he had had during the Council.[51] Conversion was also spoken of in connection with Helder Câmara.[52] It is still impossible to know how many bishops followed a similar course.

VII. THE PARALLELOGRAM OF FORCES: EPISCOPATE — POPE — CURIA — PUBLIC OPINION

Yet it was precisely in the cause of defending tradition that the conciliar minority carried on its opposition, a defense that the combative Marcel Lefebvre would carry to the point of breaking communion. This fact leads us to go more deeply into the parallelogram of forces within the large conciliar assembly. While the final votes on the documents consistently and disconcertingly showed majorities close to unanamity, there were considerable swings of mood and direction. Approximately 1,500 fathers took part in all the periods of work; the other 700 to

---

[48] See Caporale, Vatican II, 120–21.

[49] See D. Robillard, P.-É. Léger: Évolution de sa pensée 1950–1967 (Quebec, 1993); and R. Burigana and G. Routhier, "La conversion œcuménique d'un évêque et d'une église," Science et Esprit 52/2 (2000), 171–91.

[50] See A. Alberigo, ed., Giacomo Lercaro: Vescovo della Chiesa di Dio (1891–1976) (Genoa, 1991).

[51] M. Bergonzini, Bishop of Volterra, wrote on September 30, 1964, in his diary, in connection with the reports on the De revelatione, that "the report of the majority was given by Msgr. Florit, who can be called the second convert, after Msgr. Parente, to the dominant thinking at the Council. The Lord be thanked for it" (129) (diary edited by A. Leonelli [Modena, 1993], 129).

[52] See Dom Helder Câmara, The Conversions of a Bishop: An Interview with José de Broucker (London: Collins, 1979).

800 fathers came and went and thus altered the overall picture, even from the viewpoint of their composition by continent and age.[53]

The passage of time, with its "periods of adjustment," then the habituation it produced, the inevitable weariness,[54] and above all, the succession of subjects being discussed, as well as the change of leaders — all these had great impact. In the overall picture of the assembly some constants can be seen, such as the distrust of many Italian and Spanish fathers at the prospect of feared "innovations" (the introduction of the mother tongues into the liturgy, the recognition of religious freedom, the assertion of the central place of the Bible in the Church); the apathy of many bishops from the United States except when the discussion was of religious freedom or relations with the world; and the marginalization of many fathers from Asia, who were uncomfortable in a cultural climate unfamiliar to them.

Gradually and spontaneously the Council took shape. The national or continental conferences played an almost institutional role, beginning with those that had existed for some time (for example, the German and the Latin American[55]). Then there were also smaller groups, similar to parliamentary lobbies, such as the one that formed to discuss problems of poverty or the one that Etchegaray, with the strong support of Helder Câmara, fostered among the secretaries of the episcopal conferences and that met at the Domus Mariae. A unique experiment was the group known as the *Coetus Internationalis Patrum*, which, despite the warnings of Paul VI against the formation of groups within the Council, organized conservative bishops, whatever their place of origin. Finally, there

---

[53] The deceased, the newly named, the arrival of men not present in preceding periods, and, finally, the absence of bishops who had earlier been present all contributed to the changed picture.

[54] Prignon observed on September 25: "The thing that is most worrying is the growing weariness of the fathers. I was struck yesterday morning, Friday, by the number of fathers who were walking the corridors an hour after the session began. I ask myself what is to be done with the bishops once the debates in the hall are over. There is a real need of a solution" (Prignon papers, 1591). A few days later he observed: "For the last three or four days the debate in the assembly has become quite dull. One can sense that the bishops are incredibly weary. Many walk the corridors as early as 10 a.m. Today, even while Msgr. Garrone was presenting his final report after the close of the debate on schema XIII, the hum of the conversations in the side naves of St. Peter's drowned out the speaker's voice. It is time for the debates in the assembly to be concluded, because the situation is really getting worse." Bishop Jauffrès likewise wrote on October 13: "We remain at our places somewhat under constraint and perforce, solely because of the votes, about ten of them, that follow inexorably at intervals too close to allow the members time to go to the bar and return."

[55] These had a remote similarity to the "nations" that had a true and proper structural function in the late medieval councils.

emerged spontaneously on the periphery of the Council places for meeting and exchange of views; these often played a role in the formation of opinion. This was true of the Belgian College, the residence of Cardinal Suenens and theologian G. Philips, but also of the *DO-C*, the Dutch news center, where dozens of crowded lectures were given on the major problems being discussed in St. Peter's.[56]

The basic division into the commissions that drew up and then amended the texts prevented the assembly from taking on a structure. Even after the barrier of secrecy was broken, each commission pursued its demanding goal of reworking a particular schema, but without having a panoramic vision of the progress of the Council. This deficiency had a special influence during the long months between each period of work and the next, when only the commissions were active. The repeated failure of mixed commissions showed the jealousy that controlled almost all the commissions.

In addition to the internal dynamic of the conciliar assembly, and intertwined with it, the Council had complicated relations and contacts with the Pope, with the Roman Curia, and with public opinion. The decision of John XXIII not to take part personally in the conciliar sessions was continued by Paul VI. But both popes had roles of extensive and decisive importance in the life of Vatican II. During the preparation and the four periods of activity, the Pope gradually became the decisive point of reference for the assembly. From the rejection of the elections of commission members to the crucial confirmation of the vote of November 1962, and on to the creation of the Coordinating Commission, Pope John intervened repeatedly in the life of the Council.[57]

Pope Paul VI, in his turn, had numerous occasions to intervene during the next three periods, from altering the *Ordo Concilii* to the revision of the formula of promulgation, from the "reservation" to himself of some important matters (celibacy, marriage, the synod) to the series of improvements suggested for almost all the schemas, with bewildering instructions and frequently in support of the positions of the minority.[58] On the

---

[56] The texts of these lectures were published in various languages; a list drawn up by Luigia Caponi contained at least 230 between 1963 and 1965.

[57] In his diary for January 28, 1963, John XXIII noted, with regard to Vatican II: "I confess that my conscience was bothered by the fact that, *contrary* to what went on during the first two months, from October 11 to December 8 the Pope took his position, to be exercised with discretion, as the true president by the greatest right, that is, as head of the Catholic Church."

[58] Jan Grootaers, "Le crayon rouge de Paul VI," in *Commissions,* 316–51.

other hand, throughout history there has been a recurrent dialectical relationship between pope and council, and it can be recognized that at Vatican II this relationship did not involve basic oppositions but was
restricted to conflicts that, if they were sometimes sharp, were on the
whole limited.

The two popes who presided over the Council were not only very different in personality and character but also played quite distinct roles.
Roncalli "created" the Council, gradually worked out its shape, got it
going with his inaugural address, and guided it during the first uncertain
months and the first intersession with its problems. The imprint he left
upon it survived after his death, and Vatican II still felt its effects during
the second period of work.

Only gradually did Paul VI take over the papal role in the Council,
after having first gained its trust by quickly and faithfully reconvoking it.
Objectively as well as in appearance, his perspective on the Council was
opposed, although complementary, to that of Roncalli. Montini's task
was, in fact, to carry through and conclude the Council. His style was
obviously different from that of his predecessor, and this difference was
due in part to the advanced phase in which the assembly's work was
being done. The time was no longer one of basic choices but rather of the
successful elaboration of texts, the building of consensus, and the transition to the postconciliar period. Paul VI's chosen method was a constant
trickle of interventions in the texts, perhaps under the naive belief that
such interventions could be taken as simply the corrections of any Council father.[59] In reality, on each occasion there was an "incident" and a

---

[59] In this context what the Pope wrote of the schema on revelation on October 17,
1965, is interesting: "We want to make known to you immediately that it is our intention
to invite the conciliar commission *De doctrina fidei et morum* to be willing to consider the
suitableness of completing some points in the schema on revelation, for we think it our
duty to seek a doctrinal security that will allow us to join our approval to that of the Council fathers. We think, moreover, that our intervention in the conciliar commission is completely in keeping with the regulations, because it is our task not only to ratify or reject
the text in question, but also, like any Council father, to work for its improvement by suitable suggestions. The truth of this emerges also, and above all, from the fact that on September 24 of this year the secretary general of the ecumenical Council made our remarks
known to the commission. This seems to be the clearest and most respectful way of making known to the commission everything useful in the work assigned to it. Let us therefore be permitted to say emphatically that there has been no injury to the authority of the
Council, as you suspect, but rather that a needed contribution has been made to the exercise of its functions. As for respect for the freedom of the Council and for the established
regulations, nothing can give me greater pleasure than to remind you of principles that are
no less dear to Romans than to Anglo-Saxons. the Council has respected them in the most
complete way" (Paul VI papers, A3/37b and B3/27b and c).

resulting trauma. The interventions were so many occasions for the minority to voice again its own points of view and to slip them into the cracks
thus opened up.

There was this difference from other councils: a conflict emerged
between the Council and the Roman Curia,[60] an obvious sign of the institutional importance that the Curia had assumed. Perhaps its historical
memory had already warned the Curia of the problems that the celebration of a council raised for the central bureaucracy. On the other hand,
whereas the Holy Office had been given responsibility for the attempt at
a council that had been made under Pius XII,[61] John XXIII disappointed
the expectations such a precedent had created by entrusting the preparation for Vatican II to the secretary of state. We know that first Cardinal
Tardini and later A. Cicognani guided the various phases of the Council
with great diligence, while also involving all parts of the Curia.
This avoided the danger of having a Curia hostile "from outside," but it
also put Roman ecclesiastical circles in charge of both the antepreparatory and the preparatory phases.[62]

Given this background, the fact that the conciliar commissions were
also directed by the heads of the corresponding branches of the Curia and
that the Secretary of State presided over the Coordinating Commission
turned the Curia (which was distrustful first of John XXIII for convoking the Council and then of Paul VI because of old hostility to Montini)
into one of the principal players in the entire life of Vatican II. It was a
player with a long history, one that existed before the Council and would
survive it. Furthermore, it was a player that had its own vision of the
Church, to which it clung jealously in the ancient and deep-rooted conviction that the people "from across the Alps" were untrustworthy and
hostile toward the papacy and Rome. There can be no denying the tenacity with which representatives of the Curia claimed that the preparatory
schemas were "covered" by the authority of the Pope and therefore could
not be rejected!

The presence within the Curia itself of views that were loyal to the
Council did not change the structural fact of an authoritative and powerful ecclesiastical player that pursued goals different from those of the
conciliar majority. Such personages as Cardinal Ottaviani, head of the

[60] H. Jedin, *Memorie della mia vita* (Brescia, 1987), 310.
[61] See G. Alberigo, "Passaggi cruciali della fase antepreparatoria (1959–1960)," in
Verso il Concilio, 15–42.
[62] See A. Indelicato, *Difendere la dottrina o annunciare l'Evangelo: Il dibattito nella
Commissione centrale preparatoria del Vaticano II* (Genoa, 1992).

Holy Office and president of the Council's central Doctrinal Commission, or Msgr. P. Felici, general secretary of the Council, along with the two secretaries of state in office during those years, had an impressive influence on the Council, either directly or by working on the Pope. In contrast, German Cardinal Frings and Canadian Cardinal Léger, to give but two important examples, were forced repeatedly to defend the autonomy and freedom of the Council.

The greatest impact of the Curia's work was to be seen in the importance that the preparatory schemas retained to the very end of the Council's work. Despite the drastic pruning of the texts in the fall of 1962, the material clung to life very tenaciously.[63] More than a few of the preparatory schemas ended up as conciliar decrees, and parts of schemas rejected by the assembly were retrieved for new schemas. Thus the constitution *Lumen gentium* is disconcerting because of the mosaic of propositions from the preparatory draft and of others, very different in origin, that were developed during the Council.[64]

Felici, for his part, while exercising the duties of general secretary with persevering shrewdness, systematically defended the interests of the Curia and gained an influence on the Council's work that was far greater than the objective value of those interests and the degree of consensus that they enjoyed within the assembly. Finally, Cicognani ably led the Coordinating Commission, even to the point of applying to the Council political criteria proper to the Secretariat of State.[65]

From the very outset John XXIII saw the danger of curial "control" of the Council, and he persistently emphasized the need of a clear and firm separation of the two.[66] The modest results he achieved were proof of the "institutional solitude" that marked his pontificate. Paul VI, in his turn, perhaps influenced by an uneasy relationship with the curial structure within which he had passed almost his entire life, took care to give explicit assurances to the Curia, guaranteeing that the Council would have nothing to say about curial reform.

---

[63] A survival that lasted beyond the Council, since even in recent years some Roman documents have closely followed positions and even formulations from that time, despite their having been formally disregarded by the Council.

[64] G. Alberigo and F. Magistretti, eds., *Constitutionis dogmaticae Lumen gentium Synopsis historica* (Bologna, 1975).

[65] A crystal-clear instance was the obstacles Cicognani placed in the way of the conciliar declaration on the non-Christian religions, in particular, the section on the Jewish people.

[66] See G. Alberigo, "Giovanni XXIII e il concilio," in *Dalla laguna al Tevere: Angelo Giuseppe Roncalli da San Marco a San Pietro* (Bologna, 2000), 191–230.

Despite this, curial pressure on the Council did not lessen; indeed, on the occasion of the creation of the first postconciliar organization (the one in charge of liturgical reform), the Curia unleashed a real offensive and won, first of all, humiliating conditions and, shortly after, the absorption of that body into the Congregation of Rites. A similar fate awaited the conciliar and postconciliar body that was most unrelated to the Curia: the Secretariat for Christian Unity. This was gradually subordinated to and finally absorbed by the Sacred Congregation for the Doctrine of Faith, which thus gained final competence in the area of inter-Christian relations, a competence it had earlier had until the creation of the secretariat and the ecumenical "turning point"!

Finally, the Council had important relations with public opinion by way of the major print media and the television networks, which kept people informed about the Council's work, and of communities of the faithful — laity and priests — who followed the debates and were able to talk about them with their bishops during the intersessions. During the preparation and until the close of the first period of the Council, the obligation of "secrecy" had hindered or at least restricted timely news of what was happening at the Council. Beginning in 1963, however, the pressure of public opinion and a less timid attitude on the part of the bishops broke down the strange pretense that the desire for information about the work of an assembly in which over 3,000 persons were taking part could be satisfied with laconic and vague communiqués that concealed even the names of those who spoke during the discussions.

Day by day the media kept not only the public at large but even many members of the Council informed; they compensated for the difficulty many had in understanding the debates (always conducted in Latin) and often provided a key for interpreting the significance of each session, something that often escaped many of the same fathers. In some circumstances the timeliness and effectiveness of television broadcasts had unforeseen effects even on the course of the work.[67]

It is much more difficult to measure the influence of the contacts that the bishops had with their Churches during the intersessions. It is not unreasonable, however, to maintain that at times the hopes and wishes that cropped up in every region of the Catholic world brought pressure to bear on the bishops.

---

[67] See *History*, 2:221–32.

In summary, Vatican II, like other councils before it, seemed to be a place of freedom, not only in the sense that each participant felt free to make known his personal convictions without fear, but also, and above all, because, while the Council was in session, Catholics, not only in the Council hall but outside it as well, were living in an uncommon climate of freedom. In that atmosphere it was possible to raise all problems, even if they were limited in dealing with them and solving them. The peaceful climate created by John's pontificate and continued by Paul VI contributed to the movement beyond the "triumphalist" style that had frequently infected the official utterances of the Catholic Church. The attitude, shared also by some in the episcopate, that, sometimes arrogantly, claimed for the Church of Rome a superiority over everyone else, could vanish unregretted; this was due in part to the presence, unobtrusive indeed and respectful, of the observers.

The climate of openness that marked the celebration of Vatican II allowed an intense and uninterrupted interaction between its main components: a lively assembly that was in fruitful contact with the world outside it. But it was also an assembly whose representative character was lessened because it was composed almost exclusively of clerics and because the world of women was largely absent from it.[68]

VIII. THEOLOGY AT THE COUNCIL

A hundred or so theologians, both diocesan and members of the religious orders, played a part in Vatican II, either as experts or in some informal way. Some had a modest role, but many others had a very considerable influence on the work. Setting aside some paradoxical exaggerations, such as the claim that Vatican II was a council of theologians, we may ask what contribution Catholic theology, as well as Christian theologians present as observers, made to the work of the Council.[69]

Vatican II was an occasion for testing the ecclesial fruitfulness of the rich and complex activity that had been going on in theology since the 1930s. Once the overwhelming world war had ended in 1918 and the

---

[68] See C. McEnroy, *Guests in Their Own House: The Women of Vatican II* (New York, 1996).

[69] For an assessment, see *Acta congressus internationalis de Theologia Concilii Vaticani II* (Vatican City, 1968).

anti-modernist storm had passed, theology, especially in Central Europe, entered a period of extraordinary fruitfulness that found vigorous expression at the Council, where it played a dominant part.[70] The interaction of apostolic movements that arose in the developed societies shaken by the crisis of 1929 (Chenu, Thils, Philips), the close encounter with Protestant theological thought, the Russian emigrants, the demands of ecumenism (Beauduin, Congar), and the impulses given by some currents of philosophical thought (K. Rahner, E. Schillebeeckx, J. Daniélou) all contributed to a renewal of doctrinal thinking. The same can be said of the renewal of biblical exegesis (Cerfaux), the rediscovery of the original Christian sources (de Lubac), the knowledge gained of the conciliar tradition (Jedin), and the perception of procedural problems (Dossetti).[71]

The seeds sown during the painful and dark years of anti-modernism showed an unexpected vitality. While the dominance of the ideologies and their violent clash and the accelerated secularization of society did indeed create obstacles and problems for Christians and the Churches, they did not hinder — and even seem to have unintentionally fostered — an upswing of creativity.

Very few had expected a new council, but when John XXIII announced it, after surprise and some bewilderment, theologians competed in making themselves available and ready to contribute. As a result, Vatican II became a great melting-pot for the developments of the preceding decades, which had often been marginalized by hierarchical concerns or by the monopolistic warnings of the "Roman" theologians. Nevertheless, the best representatives of the Roman schools were in their turn involved in collaborating at the Council. From Jesuit S. Tromp, the backbone of the theological commission, to Dominican M.-R. Gagnebet, drafter of the preparatory schema on *De ecclesia*, to Franciscan U. Betti, a close and strong fellow-worker with Msgr. Florit — these and so many others made loyal contributions as they accepted an encounter with an "ultramontane" theology foreign to them.

The Council was also the occasion for bringing into the limelight a younger generation of theologians, who often made a fresher contribution

---

[70] See G. Alberigo, "Vatican II et la réflexion théologique," *Lumière et Vie* 29 (1990), 7–15.

[71] On German theology, see P. Hünermann, "Deutsche Theologie auf dem Zweiten Vatikanum," in *Kirche sein: Nachkonziliare Theologie im Dienst der Kirchenreform: Für H. J. Pottmeyer*, ed. W. Geerlings and M. Seckler, 141–62 (Freiburg, 1994); and H. Wolf and C. Arnold, eds., *Die deutschsprachigen Länder und das II. Vatikanum* (Paderborn, 2000). On theology at Louvain, see *Vatican II et la Belgique*.

to the discussions: H. Küng, J. Ratzinger, E. Lanne, P. Duprey, and J.-M. Tillard, to name a few.[72] A unique role as mediator among the diverse trends fell to Carlo Colombo of Milan, especially once Cardinal Montini became Paul VI. Among the observers, too, some high-ranking theologians stood out, for example, K. E. Skydsgaard, O. Cullmann, and A. Scrima.

The universal trauma inflicted by the Second World War, the incipient technological revolution, and the decisive confrontation of the two great ideological blocs were the prelude to a new and more complex historical turning point, foreseen by Pope John, that formed the setting for the Council and its task. Faced with such an enormous challenge, the theology brought into operation by the Council, despite gaps and inadequacies, made the constructive contribution of beginning to reverse the situation that during the final years of Pacelli's pontificate had displayed very worrying signs of turning in upon itself. But we may add that the lack of a suitable place in which the theologians could have gone more deeply into the subjects progressively tackled (such as theologians had at Trent) may have made the work of the general congregations more difficult.

In light of all this, we can evaluate both the scope and the limits of what was gained at the Council. Even from the viewpoint of its doctrinal accomplishments Vatican II seems to have been chiefly a point of departure rather than a point of arrival. The conciliar assembly itself offered a model of a dynamic hermeneutic that takes into account the progressive expansion of its decisions. It is, in fact, perfectly clear that only the acquisition of an ecclesiology of communion, first in the constitution *Sacrosanctum concilium* and then in the Constitution *Lumen gentium*, made further developments possible. The decree *Unitatis redintegratio* and the declaration *Dignitatis humanae*, but also the decree *Ad gentes* and finally, the constitution *Dei Verbum* contain propositions that presuppose the development already acquired by the Council. This hermeneutical criterion, even if it was not always followed consistently, nevertheless constitutes a point of reference that cannot be ignored in postconciliar interpretation.

IX. A Turning Point?

What kind of council did Pope John want? Or were his statements so vague that this question cannot be asked? In his naiveté did he move

---

[72] Among the "absentees" I must mention at least H. U. von Balthasar.

back and forth between an impossible council for union and a reform council such as Trent, the effectiveness and authoritativeness of which he had learned and experienced during his entire ecclesiastical formation? Or, on the contrary, was a precise and well-defined intention at work in the convocation of the Council, although its object resists being classified according to pre-existing models and therefore poses some ticklish problems? Did John XXIII intend to sketch out a new species within the traditional genre of council, one that would be adequate for enabling the Church to respond to the renewed demands of evangelization?

In fact, John XXIII did not hesitate to describe the Council in a completely traditional way; it was to be an assembly of bishops. But this does not contradict the fact that he wanted a council that would effect an epochal transition, that is, would cause the Church to leave behind the post-Tridentine era and, to some extent, the centuries-long Constantinian stage, and enter a new phase of witness and proclamation. This would be made possible by a recovery of powerful and permanent elements of the tradition judged suitable for nourishing and guaranteeing fidelity to the gospel during so difficult a transition. Seen in this perspective, the Council acquired special importance, once again more as an event than as a place for developing and producing norms.

The Council was intended to be the "flash of light from above" of which Pope John spoke several times and which, as the Council approached, he began to speak of as a "new Pentecost." The image of a new Pentecost was thenceforth regularly connected with the Council, to the point of receiving its confirmation in the papal prayer for the Council which asked the Spirit to renew "his wonders in our time as though on a new Pentecost." Roncalli was aware of the theological and historical significance of Pentecost, and the fact that he called for a repetition of it was a carefully thought out way of emphasizing, by the use of typically Christian language, the exceptional character of this historical juncture and the extraordinary prospects that it opened up. It was therefore necessary that the Church should face this juncture and these prospects with a very profound renewal, so that it might be able to show itself to the world and teach humanity the evangelical message with the same power and urgency that marked the original Pentecost. In addition, the appeal to Pentecost gave first place to the action of the Spirit and not that of the pope or of the Church and its doctrinal universe.

A comprehensive evaluation of the results of the Council requires a complex analysis that applies at different levels. One plausible approach might be to compare the climate during the preparation for the Council

(January 1959–October 1962) and the climate that prevailed at its end in December 1965.[73] Despite the secularism rampant at least in the West, John XXIII's announcement triggered an explosion of attention and interest among the public. Nevertheless, the announcement was as disruptive as it was laconic, and it therefore gave rise to many questions about the future council.

As early as 1959 three memoranda were circulating from authoritative individuals and groups: Swiss theologian Otto Karrer, Jesuit Augustin Bea, and the steering committee of the Catholic Conference on Ecumenical Questions. The three documents expressed cautious ecumenical expectations while warning against possible conciliar actions that could contradict these expectations (doctrinal definitions, condemnations) and hoping for actions that would ease the road to unity (emphasis on communion rather than on the juridical aspect of things, lessening of centralization, recognition of the central place of sacred scripture).

Next came the lengthy preparation, controlled by the *vota* of the bishops and extending from the creation of the complex machinery of the preparatory commissions to the production of over seventy schemas to be submitted to the Council. But in its "episcopal" phase, both out on the periphery and at the center, the fathers refrained from or did not have the energy for drawing up a plan for the future assembly. The supposition behind the schemas prepared in advance for the Council was that these schemas would almost always confirm recent papal teaching. John XXIII, for his part, used a pedagogy that was progressive and charismatic, concerned almost solely with providing all with directives that were solid and suited to the epochal conjuncture, trusting as he did in the ecclesial body's instinct of faith and in the creative abilities of the episcopal assembly.

Only beginning in 1962, and in the light of the preparatory work done and the disappointing schemas, did some important individuals submit directly to the Pope plans intended as alternatives to the approach taken in the preparatory work. First, Cardinal Suenens, the young Archbishop of Malines, and then Canadian Cardinal Léger presented the Pope with a *Plan* as well as some remarks in which they distanced themselves from the preparatory material; they stressed the point that this material was muddled and distant from or even contradictory to the original approach set forth by the Pope. John XXIII paid special attention to Suenens's suggestions; he made them known to a group of cardinals and took them into

---

[73] See G. Alberigo, "Il Vaticano II dalle attese ai risultati: una 'svolta'?" in Melloni, *Volti di fine Concilio*, 395–415.

account in his important radio message *Lumen Christi* of September 11, 1962. The Church was urged to realize that it was faced with a new world in which it had a duty to represent the values of equality, poverty, justice, peace, and Christian unity. The Council, therefore, would be, as it were, "an encounter with the face of the risen Christ."[74] But even now Pope John XXIII did not dictate the agenda for the Council's work; he did, however, vigorously offer an exceptionally wide-ranging perspective.

The opening address, *Gaudet Mater Ecclesia*, allows us, far more than any casual address could, to know the spirit, goals, and limits of the Council. The duty of Vatican II would be "not only to guard this precious treasure, as if we were concerned only with antiquity, but to dedicate ourselves with an earnest will and without fear to that work which our era demands of us." In light of the epochal conjuncture, the salient point of the Council was that "from the renewed, serene, and tranquil adherence to all the teaching of the Church... the Christian, Catholic, and apostolic spirit of the whole world, expects a step forward toward a doctrinal penetration and a formation of consciousness." An indication of the method to be used was also given: it would be necessary to distinguish between "the substance of the ancient doctrine... and the way in which it is presented." The Pope's concern was with something both more and less than a program of work; the important thing was the attitude he proposed for the Council fathers, one that left them the freedom to be the protagonists at the Council.

Only a few days later, when Cardinal Bea had grasped the full significance of the address, did he present an actual *Program for the Council* in which he repeated point by point the directives given in the allocution and argued for a reduction of the doctrinal schemas and their reformulation consistent with the intentions enunciated by the Pope. A couple of days after that, Cardinal Montini too addressed a lengthy and demanding letter to Secretary of State Cicognani about "the lack of an organized plan for the Council." The Cardinal of Milan, referring to Suenens's *Plan*, which focused on the Church *ad intra* and *ad extra*, was looking for a way

---

[74] On two crucial points the papal radio message closely followed the Suenens plan: first of all, when it took as its inspiration the passage from Matthew (28:19–20): "Go ... and baptize": "The raison d'être of the Council was," therefore, "the most energetic renewal of the response of the entire world, the modern world, to the testament of the Lord." Second, the message devoted special attention to the proclamation to the poor: "Another obvious point: in the underdeveloped countries the Church must show itself as what it is and intends to be: the Church of all, and especially the Church of the poor." The text of this speech can be found in *Council Daybook, Sessions 1 and 2*, 18- 21.

to soften the blow represented by the shipwreck of the preparatory schemas.

While these several proposals were still unknown to the majority of fathers, the conciliar assembly approved a message to humanity that expressed the determination of the bishops to become ever more faithful witnesses to the gospel of Christ by truly renewing the Church. Their purpose: "that the light of faith will shine more clearly and vigorously," even as the fathers "carry in our hearts the hardships, the bodily and mental distress, the sorrows, longings, and hopes of all the peoples." The intention was to give utterance to the sympathy of the Church *ad extra* and, in addition, to oppose the schemas that had been prepared without any attention to the world.

If a program, in the true and proper sense, had not been formulated for Vatican II, some important directives did emerge: first and foremost, the feasibility of an ecumenical perspective, with its corollary, a rejection of condemnations; then the need to rethink the theology of the Church, going beyond simply "completing" Vatican I. In addition, the problem of the relationship of the bishops with the Roman Curia and the reform of the latter was also raised. In another area, under the heading of the Church *ad extra*, there was a growing awareness of the need for the Council to tackle the relationship of the Church with the contemporary world in a perspective less narrow than that envisaged in concordats or in social doctrine, but rather one in accordance with the commitment the bishops took on in the message sent out at the beginning.

Vatican II, then, was to proceed in keeping with a compromise between the great themes that *Gaudet Mater Ecclesia* brought to the awareness of the episcopate and the series of "minor" problems that had taken up so much space in the *vota* of the bishops and led to dozens of schemas.

The wager that John XXIII made in having a council that would act on its own and not be "guided" from above (or by the curial bureaucracy) yielded considerable results, although the Council also paid a price for this. As we now reread the Council's work and the texts the assembly produced, we can see some leaps forward toward a deeper doctrinal penetration into the deposit of faith, as well as a formulation of it more suited to pastoral needs; we also see discontinuities and resounding omissions. The biggest of these has to do with commitment to the poor and with the poverty of the Church.[75] The repeated wishes for the reform of

---

[75] After Paul VI's renunciation of the tiara in November 1964, shortly before the conclusion of the Council's work, several hundred bishops who were moved by the importance of the subject and disappointed by its meager reception in the documents of

the Curia likewise had no effect. Even problems of major importance, such as racism, which was still producing seriously discriminatory policies, or the traditional religions, which had extensive followings in Africa, did not figure in the agenda of Vatican II.

But a global consideration of the results of Vatican II cannot pass over some methodological gains, which, though not expressed in specific formulations, played a very important role in the conciliar debates and supported many of the Council's conclusions. The fact that the traditional deductive method was set aside, even if incompletely, is undeniable. The advances already won in preconciliar theological study had an influence in this, but we must not forget that they met with a suspicion of heterodoxy. The repeated reliance of the Council on the new method signified a turning point that was sometimes opposed but proved to be irreversible. The contrast with the "secular" sciences and, not least, with theological thinking of a Protestant kind had exerted pressure on Catholic theology, but in vain, for the papal magisterium had kept Catholic theology bound up with an obsolete methodological outlook. The courageous and far-sighted innovation introduced by Thomas Aquinas in the Middle Ages, when he accepted Aristotelianism, seemed, paradoxically, to be definitive and to have become immovable. The danger of a gradual "essentialization" of doctrinal statements and therefore a tragic impoverishment of the Christian message was ignored in the name of neo-Scholasticism. Here again, the climate created by the Council permitted the beginning of an *aggiornamento* that could restore breadth and depth to Catholic thought.

With this recourse to the inductive method was connected the acceptance of history. The pressing need of a radical critical revision of the attitude of Catholicism to history had already found an as yet undeveloped expression in the teaching of Pius XII, in the form of a desire that the Church should learn to read history.[76] With Pacelli's successor this new

---

the Council signed a series of thirteen proposals having to do with their personal commitment to make up for the deficiencies in their "life of poverty according to the gospel" (see M.-D. Chenu, "Vatican II and the Church of the Poor," *Concilium* 104 [1977], 56–61). No one has even yet attempted an assessment of the concrete impact of those solemn commitments. There was also talk at the time of establishing a Vatican secretariat on poverty (see *Service Oecuménique de presse et d'information*, 31 [1966], 2–3).

[76] In an address to new cardinals on February 20, 1946, Pius XII denied that the Church could become petrified "in one phase of history and close itself against any further development." He even asserted that the Church "as it moves on, follows, without stopping and without being pushed, the providential path traced by times and circumstances" (see *Discorsi e radiomessaggi di SS Pio XII* 7 [Vatican City, 1946], 391). A number of years later, in his Easter homily of 1957, the same Pope spoke of "the signs of a coming dawn" (ibid., 19 [1958], 94).

outlook was realized much more rapidly than anyone had expected. In the bull announcing the Council Pope John XXIII emphasized the permanent relationship of Christ with history, a relationship that becomes even closer at critical moments when the Church must be more intensely involved. After reminding his readers of this basic principle, John XXIII applied it to "today." He said that there is "now a crisis in society," that "humanity is at the turning point that leads to a new era," that it is passing through an especially full and significant phase. These were very clear-cut assessments, in which the Pope expressed his convictions, intended less as a technical and political statement than as a judgment about an epochal shift.[77]

This means that John XXIII chose the deeper level, where long-term trends are found that affect the destiny of humanity as a whole. In other words, history, understood both as the past and as the present life of humanity, is the context of the divine plan of salvation, within which, and not despite which, the Christian reality unfolds. It is there that Christians live the course of their pilgrimage, as the decree *Ad gentes* reminds us: "God decided to enter into the history of mankind in a new and definitive manner, by sending his own Son" (*AG*, 3).[78] As far as the relationship between the Church and history is concerned, Vatican II as a whole constituted a change of direction from the orientation prevalent in Catholicism for at least four centuries.

The perspective that the Council was urging the Church to adopt was only sketched in its basic elements rather than worked out in a complete and organized way. The most decisive signs appear to be those contained in the constitutions on the liturgy, the Church, and the word of God, inasmuch as these show in a concrete way the relevance of the historical condition of Christianity. The insufficiency and marginal status of pneumatology in the overall shape of the Council have been repeatedly noted. The effects of these defects are felt with special keenness in the area of the relationship to history, an area in which it was not enough simply to mention the role of the Spirit; the topic should have been more thoroughly discussed and articulated. Without an adequate development of this aspect, the Council's statements lent themselves to simplistic readings that do not capture either the real historical density of events or the important implications they contain, which cannot be perceived without moving to a different level of understanding.

---

[77] For the full text of the Bull of Convocation, see *Council Daybook, Sessions 1 and 2*, 6-9.

[78] See G. Alberigo, "Cristianesimo, storia, teologia," in Associazione Teologia Italiana, *Teologia e istanze del sapere oggi in Italia* (Padua: Edizioni Messaggero, 1991), 103–27.

It is no accident that Christian history displays a wealth of ambiguities, both in the sense of deafness and blindness to the major twists of history and in the sense of misinterpretations of the messianic meanings of history itself. In fact, at the concrete level, the Council showed in more than one case that it was applying criteria that it had itself formulated in keeping with a *lectio facilior*. This happened both in dealing with the problems of the influence of the media in modern societies and in the facile historical optimism of a "Western" kind that runs through so much of the constitution *Gaudium et spes*, as well as in the tentativeness with which the same document reads the gospel background of the cry of the peoples for peace.

In any case, Vatican II did legitimize the possibility of reading Christianity not only in the perspective of salvation and the providential plan that is at work in it, but also at a positive level through the rigorous application of the historico-critical method.

A concise evaluation must emphasize rather the elements of continuity between the expectations sketched out in a purely intellectual way before the Council and the results achieved. Despite a large correspondence between many of those expectations and the conclusions, it seems that Vatican II, even though burdened by a number of decrees of preconciliar inspiration, did on the whole go beyond the expectations and bring about a deeper and more organic "turnabout" than the petitions voiced on the eve of the Council had the farsightedness and courage to desire.

The great majority of the fathers agreed with the new perspectives pointed out by John XXIII on October 11, 1962; his "wager" on the fruitfulness of a council placed in the hands of the bishops had a positive result, even amid uncertainties and inconsistencies. A "new" council was born, that is, different from those of earlier traditions, to the extent that its course was not defined by responses to heretical deviations (like the councils of antiquity) or by a need to organize Christianity (like the Lateran councils) or by emergencies (Constance, Basel, and Trent) or, finally, by a predetermined plan (Vatican I). Vatican II showed itself to be a council pledged to respond in a positive way, that is, by proposing once again to present-day humanity the essential contents of the gospel in accordance with the criteria of set by the pastoral principle and by *aggiornamento*. It would be incorrect to claim that these criteria were always applied consistently in the work and documents of the assembly. The limits of available time made the task a very difficult one, especially since the criteria had been too long unfamiliar and even alien to Catholicism and there had been no recent application and no conceptual penetration of them.

The conciliar assembly also found the courage and conviction to move beyond the Eurocentric thinking that marked it at the beginning. The episcopates of the Third World gradually found room in which to move, and they exerted a growing influence on the Council's work and documents. This "de-Europeanization" was to be confirmed, above all, by the impact that the Council had on the continents of the "periphery." The culture and the experience that these episcopates brought to bear also strengthened in a decisive way the calls for moving beyond the juridical approach that the conception of the Church had absorbed in the West. From this there came, in turn, Vatican II's push to subordinate the institutional aspect of the Church to the sacramental.

The unparalleled makeup of the assembly, which was so numerous and so diverse in its membership, helps explain the difficulty of setting a program in advance for Vatican II; it also clarifies the leap in quality that can be seen when comparing the preparatory formulations with the final texts and, even more, when comparing the climate of Christianity in the 1950s with that prevailing at the end of the Council. When a new council was announced, almost no one could have imagined the kind of "guiding" instead of "preceptive" decisions that would characterize the body of documents from Vatican II. At most, people were led to hope for a refusal to issue condemnations.

The movement beyond the stage of ecclesiocentrism implied not only the decline of the dominance of ecclesiology but also, and above all, the rediscovery of other dimensions of Christian life and faith. That is, the expectation was that there would be a reversal of priorities, an abandonment of the reference to ecclesiastical institutions and their authority and effectiveness as the center and measure of the faith and the Church. Instead, it was faith, communion, and readiness to serve that form the Church, that were to be the guiding values by which the evangelical adequacy of the structure and behavior of the institutions was to be measured. The rethinking and reversal of priorities also implied a recognition of the value of the *sensus fidei* and the signs of the times as ecclesial norms, instead of following the internal logic proper to institutions, which was too often guided by power and not by *exousia*, authority.

If we adopt this point of view, it is easy to see why the reception of Vatican II, and perhaps even the very understanding of the Council, are still uncertain and undeveloped. On the one hand, the sovereignty of the word of God, the central place of the liturgy and the Eucharist, and the

commitment to communion (from the base level of parochial communities to communion among diocesan communities to a communion among
the different Christian traditions) appear only on and off, and then inadequately, as the center of the Church's life. Very frequently the faithful
find themselves faced with a pervasive ecclesiastical (and secular) bureau-
cratization that has been produced by a misunderstood *aggiornamento*
but is in fact an assimilation to secular institutions. Alongside innovations that are important for communion, such as the election of a Slavic
bishop as successor to Peter or the pastoral journeys of the Bishop of
Rome, there are others, such as the synod of bishops, that are obviously
impotent; still others, such as pastoral and presbyteral councils, especially in Europe, seem to have been exhausted after only a few years of
experiment.

The episcopal conferences that contributed in an important way to the
vitality of Vatican II appear nowadays to be ambushed by bureaucrati-
zation and centralism, both of which cut off their capacity to become
effective signs of communion among the Churches.[79] The diligence with
which venerable institutions such as synods and catechisms have been
revived carries the risk that these will simply be repetitions without an
effective influence on ecclesial life due to the lack of a sufficient effort
at rethinking both synods and catechisms in the spirit of courageous
aggiornamento. Finally, never before has there been such a succession of
urgent provisions for the reform of the Roman Curia as there has been in
recent decades, but these have been marginal in their importance, that is,
they have been far from introducing an effective *aggiornamento* to the
new conditions affecting the faith and ecclesial communion.

Could the Council have done more? Seen from the viewpoint of the
history of Vatican II the question is embarrassing and the answer uncertain. The prospects opened up by John XXIII by the very act of convoking another council after that of 1870 and, much more, those sketched in
the opening address appear to have been as promising as they were
demanding. As we have seen, many Council fathers had much more limited outlooks. A suggestion such as that presented by Lercaro at the
beginning of December 1962 — that the Council focus on poverty in all
its dimensions, spiritual, cultural, and institutional — fell into a void
despite the interest it roused in the episcopates of the Third World.
The same fate befell the request put forward by Patriarch Maximos IV and

---

[79] See F. Guillemette, *Théologie des Conférences épiscopales: Une herméneutique de
Vatican II* (Montreal, 1994).

repeated by many others, that the Council devise a plan for a central episcopal body that would be regularly assigned to collaborate with the pope
in major decisions affecting the universal Church.

And yet Vatican II left a Catholic Church quite different from that
within whose bosom it opened. The state of Christendom, which was still
dominant in Europe and in worldwide Catholicism, appeared on December 8, 1965, to be a thing of the past. Fragments of it survive, sometimes
tenaciously unwilling to admit the historical change that has occurred,
but these fragments seem to be only nostalgic tremors. In the long run the
emergence from the Counter-Reformation period and from the Constantinian era marks the revolution begun at the Council, a revolution that is
necessarily complex and gradual and for which the Council laid down the
basis and marked the onset.

X. The "Secret" or Hidden Council

One of the shrewdest of the observers, K. Skydsgaard, a Lutheran,
urgently desired to seek out the "secret council" that lay behind the institutional one; that is, he wanted to shed light on the Council as an event
in search of the gospel.[80] This suggestion is valuable in helping to avoid
thinking of the celebration of the Council as simply an episode, a pause
in the ecclesiastical routine. In fact, the pastoral nature of Vatican II and
its goal of *aggiornamento* gave the participation of the bishops, theologians, and observers critical importance and led them to discover therein
a deep shared experience which transcended the often narrow and formal
limits of relations among ecclesiastics. Hundreds of individuals who had
no knowledge of one another, were sometimes distrustful of one another,
and were of different generations, with different experiences, languages,
and profoundly different and distant cultures, found themselves starting
a common undertaking whose implications went far beyond the carrying
out of an institutional task, even the essential one of elaborating and
approving documents.

Here again it is necessary to take into account the situation preceding
Vatican II. After the Vatican Council of 1870, Prussian Chancellor von
Bismarck had maintained that from then on the Catholic bishops were
simply local representatives of the pope; only the pope had effective

---

[80] K. E. Skydsgaard, "Last Intention of the Council," *Ecumenical Studies* 3 (1966),
151–54.

power and authority over the Catholic Church. Even though Pius IX denied this thesis, the bishops until the end of the pontificate of Pius XII appeared increasingly to be subordinate to the pope and the Roman Curia, which the reform of Pius X had strengthened and which had the Holy Office as the supreme congregation. A large part of theology and canon law had provided a doctrinal basis for this attitude. The social philosophy of the modern centralized state also provided an "analogue" that was very influential and was adopted by the Church.

Pius XII's *Mystici corporis* made up for the fateful omission of Vatican Council I by solemnly affirming the dignity of bishops as successors of the apostles and heads of the particular Churches, but it also repeated that "they are not entirely independent, because they are subject to the rightful authority of the Roman pontiff, even while they enjoy the ordinary power of jurisdiction, which is communicated directly to them by the same Supreme Pontiff." Thus, despite a certain progress in respect to the constitution *Pastor aeternus*, the debate about the origin of the governing authority of the bishops was closed. In fact, according to the encyclical every bishop received his authority "directly from the pope," that is, along with his appointment and not on the occasion of his consecration and in virtue of it. Thus the subordination of every bishop to the pope was strengthened.

Again, on the occasion of the definition of Mary's Assumption in 1950, the involvement of the episcopate was essentially just an element in the spectacle. A short time later French Bishop Guerry wrote: "A bishop, at least in the Latin West, is increasingly distant from souls; he is taken up with administrative tasks and resembles, externally, an ecclesiastical 'prefect.' Even though he alone wears the ring of a husband married to his Church, he is ordinarily more easily moved from one diocese to another than some parish priests."[81] The formation of episcopal conferences was slow and difficult, and individual bishops were isolated in facing their own responsibilities and the authoritative curial congregations and were often intimidated by the nuncio.

It is not surprising, then, that almost all the bishops came to the Council with a timid attitude. The reasons for this varied: they had a poor knowledge of the city of Rome; in the hall they were seated beside bishops whom they did not know (seating followed the order of appointment); they had a poor knowledge of Latin; their familiarity with the

---

[81] E. M. Guerry, *L'évêque* (Paris, 1954), 10. Msgr. Guerry's book had a large part in opening things up before Vatican II.

subjects discussed was modest and often outdated;[82] soon they had the impression that the debate was boringly repetitive, all the more so because it was not easy to distinguish among various points of view. Finally, almost no one knew the plan of the Council or even the length of time they would have to remain away from home, at considerable inconvenience and expense. Many diaries attest, especially at the beginning, to a passive "schoolboy" attitude. They were participating in a solemn and meaningful event, but they had no clear grasp of its plan.

The place where each bishop carried out his responsibility to the Council was, first and foremost, the assembly, that is, the general congregations in the morning. But these were wearisome occasions, since, for all practical purposes, the bishops only listened; the vast majority of the bishops never spoke during the almost 200 general congregations held between October 13, 1962, and December 7, 1965. Several hundred bishops, however, were assigned to the commissions, where opportunities for being active were much more frequent. In addition, there were meetings of the episcopal conferences, at which they did not have to make the tiring effort to understand Latin or other unknown languages. Nor can we pass over the important relationship of the bishops with the theologians; this was one of the key bonds created by Vatican II, even though on several occasions the theologians, even if unwillingly, relieved some bishops of their responsibility, so that the latter had the impression of being excluded from the most important phases of the Council's work.

In any case, Vatican Council II was the masterpiece of the Catholic episcopate and, behind the scenes, of the Spirit.[83] It is, in fact, undeniable that only a radical development within the bishops themselves made possible the change, the "reversal," from an inert and timid passivity in the replies sent to Rome in 1960 by so many hundreds of bishops to the body of decrees approved by the Council. It is right and proper to be aware of the limitations and discontinuities in the documents produced by the

---

[82] According to de Lubac, on the subject of the complex debate on revelation, "some supporters of the 'two sources' view tried once again to introduce some formulas representing their side; it seems to me that they do not correctly understand the problem, and that many of those who reject their views do not understand it any better. One of the drawbacks of the procedure followed in this council is that neither general congregations nor the commissions ever provide, before discussion of a schema begins, an extensive report on the subject by a competent and impartial individual" (*Jde Lubac*, October 11, 1965).

[83] In December 1962 Cardinal Siri noted in his diary: "The influence of the Holy Spirit is ordinarily exerted not only *salva libertate*, but in such a way as not to be directly perceived by the psychological consciousness of the subject" (in B. Lai, *Il papa non eletto: Giuseppe Siri cardinale di Santa Romana Chiesa* [Rome, 1993], 383).

Council, but it is impossible not to see the qualitative leap taken from the *vota* with which the bishops responded to the invitation of John XXIII and the image of Christianity and the Church that Vatican II created, precisely in virtue of the consensus of almost the entire body of the same bishops.[84] It is undeniable that the vast majority of the Council fathers were spontaneously and almost instinctively aligned with the position of the Bishop of Rome. But there is also no doubt that these bishops rapidly developed a considerable awareness of their own inalienable responsibility and gave voice to it beginning in the fall of 1962 in votes of great importance and significance.

After 1959 there developed, slowly and almost unnoticed, a widespread climate that predisposed a large number of bishops, especially from the countries of the Atlantic world, but also elsewhere, to see Vatican II as a unique opportunity for a renewal of the Church along the lines of the demands formulated in more recent decades by the liturgical, biblical, and ecumenical movements, along with the movement back to the sources, and under the pressure of the secularization of society. When, in the summer of 1962, it became possible for the bishops to acquaint themselves with the first parcel of schemas sent out, the reactions sent to Rome were, in the great majority of instances, ones of dissatisfaction, except for the schema on liturgical renewal. This dissatisfaction was certainly not stirred up by a comparison of the schemas with the views formulated two years before; on the contrary, it was the first manifestation of a new way of seeing the Council.

The enthusiasm created in Rome by the prolonged presence of over two thousand bishops, of as many experts (theologians, canonists, historians), and of a great number of journalists, played an increasingly significant role in keeping the bishops informed and aware. This was the soil that fed the experience of responsibility in so many of the fathers by profoundly altering their convictions. As a result, we can understand the constant presence of a very large majority which showed itself in all the key votes,[85] from those on the sacramental nature of episcopal consecration and on collegiality to those on the ecumenical attitude to be adopted by

---

[84] See G. Alberigo, "L'expérience de la responsabilité épiscopale faite par les évêques à Vatican II," in *Le ministère des évêques au Concile Vatican II et depuis*, ed. H. Legrand and C. Theobald (Paris: du Cerf, 2001) 22-47.

[85] According to Prignon, "it became increasingly difficult for the representatives of the majority to have the bishops say anything against the texts presented; they were ready to vote in the schemas submitted to the assembly without any reaction.... The assembly explicitly wants to finish the work" (*JPrignon*, October 4, 1965 [Prignon papers, 1598]).

Catholicism, from those on the central place of the Bible to those on friendly relations with humanity, and on to those on religious freedom and relations with the Jewish people.

Vatican II was thus much more than a completion of the ecclesiological documents of Vatican I; it also set forth a picture of a bishop that was profoundly different from that which had taken fixed form in more recent centuries, especially in areas of the world long Christian. It was a picture that in large measure was based on the experience of the *episkopoi* of the first Christian centuries, but it was traced with an anxious determination to respond to the cultural demands of contemporary societies and of the Christian communities living in these societies. The images of the prince bishop, the lord bishop, or the episcopal official, so widespread for centuries, were completely alien and outdated, as was that of the episcopal politician or the bishop who was an "important person" in society. The criteria followed in forming the new image were the pastoral principle and *aggiornamento* lived in a spirit of service and fraternal sharing.

There were several ways of being in the minority at the Council: the Armenians were an ethnic minority;[86] Uniates were a minority among Catholics;[87] many Spaniards and Italians were among the minority in the assembly;[88] bishops from the periphery, that is, non-Europeans,[89] in particular, the Africans[90] and the Asians, were a statistical minority. All of this undoubtedly was an obstacle to their full and tranquil participation in the work, especially on the occasion of certain debates (relations with the Orthodox Churches; declaration on the Jews; religious freedom). Moreover, their situation demanded a keener awareness of their special role and a greater consciousness of their own responsibility.

A new experience, which caught many bishops off balance, was that of conflict. Too many of them were accustomed to a calm, dull vision of Christianity and of the Church; for quite a few, differences in points of

---

[86] See the diary of Msgr. C. Zohrabian, *Un vescovo armeno al Vaticano II: Le memorie di Mons. C. Z.*, ed. F. Santi Cucinotta (Caltanisetta, 1978).

[87] See the diary of Melkite Bishop N. Edelby, *Il Vaticano II nel diario di un vescovo arabo*, ed. R. Cannelli (Cinisello B., 1996).

[88] See the diary of Cardinal G. Siri, Archbishop of Genoa, which is often dramatic (see Lai, *Il papa non eletto*); a similar attitude marked the diary of Msgr. L. C. Borromeo, Bishop of Pesaro, in *Rivista di Storia della Chiesa in Italia* 52, ed. N. Buonasorte (1998), 111–69.

[89] See the diary of Msgr. V. Zazpe, Bishop of Rafaela in Argentina (unpublished ms at the ISR).

[90] See the notes of J. Malula, auxiliary bishop of Leopoldville, in *Oeuvres complètes*, ed. L. Saint Moulin (Kinshasa, 1997).

views and the conflicts they caused were even a defect typical of lay societies. In any case, they imagined the Council would be an orderly and quick-acting assembly, as, indeed, Roman curial circles had led them to think. But from the very first general congregation on October 13, 1962, Vatican II proved to be much less "calm"; all bets were off, and each bishop was called upon to have a personal opinion.

The work of the assembly, as it gradually got to the heart of the most complex problems, was complicated not only from the organizational and procedural points of view but even from a doctrinal viewpoint. All the fathers were caught up in harrowing and prolonged tensions, like that of October 1963 in the matter of straw votes on chapter III of the *De ecclesia*, or that of the Black Week in November 1964 in connection with religious freedom, the declaration on the Jews, and ecumenism. Even before votes were taken, no one was able to avoid taking a position in the lively discussions that developed almost everywhere in the Council. These were the occasion of a perhaps rough initiation — disagreeable for some, traumatic for others — into a less static and more dynamic vision of their own faith. They were compelled to acknowledge that many subjects that had seemed satisfactorily settled in the far-off days of seminary formation were instead open and debated, with solutions sometimes diametrically opposed being put forth.

When the subjects tackled were the situation of the Church in society and the recognition of the value of religious freedom, the trauma was just as great. Many were forced to recognize that the system of concordats for regulating relations with the states was obsolete and that freedom of conscience was an authentic gospel value. The Church could not be only a *magistra* (teacher); it had also to agree to learn from others and to share the joys, hopes, griefs, and anxieties of humanity.

According to the diaries, the experience of participation in Vatican II was lived with powerful effects and feelings: joy, interest, pride, and apprehension.[91] Day after day a "conciliar" consciousness developed in the minds of the great majority;[92] that is, a consciousness that the Council and the hopes roused by it were in the hands of the bishops; that they,

---

[91] In his letter to his diocese on December 2, 1962, Montini emphasized the point that "this spiritual experience will certainly remain an indelible one in those who have had the good fortune to take part in the Council: a pleasant experience most of the time, deeply poignant at other times, sometimes dramatic, and at given moments thought-provoking and distressing" (G.B. Montini, *Discorsi et scritti sul Concilio (1959-1962)* (Brescia, 1983) 198.

[92] Even a bishop such as Siri, who had little liking for the Council, acknowledged as much in November 1964: "One has the impression that a greater awareness of things is

along with the pope, were really responsible for the proclamation of the gospel at this point in history; that each of them had a role of unimagined, extraordinary importance.

XI. COUNCIL AND SOCIETY

Just as almost all the Christian councils have been influenced by the social context in which they were held, so too they desired to find an echo in their various societies. While Trent sought to win the backing of the public authorities in the struggle against Protestantism and Vatican I chose an attitude of opposition to the societies of its time, Vatican II adopted an outlook of friendship with contemporary humanity.

European Catholicism had emerged from the Second World War with an attitude very much like the one it had during the centuries when Western Catholic society had lived as a self-sufficient social system that was based on the faith and was ruled concordantly by the Church and its secular arm, the political authorities. The spread of Christian political parties, which reached its high point in the 1950s, tended to filter out and control, at least seemingly, the consequences of the secularization that was spreading throughout the continent in the wake of reconstruction and the resultant prosperity. On the other hand, societies were caught up in an ideological conflict that was potentially worldwide. In the West this conflict took the form of anticommunism. The Soviet regimes, by persecuting Christians contained within their borders, had produced the conviction that communism was subversive to Christianity, social order, and freedom. A close-knit Catholic Church marked by a strong Marian piety, seemed to be an agency specially suited to withstand this subversion.

But this was not all there was to Catholicism. At least in Europe, the decades from the 1920s to the 1940s had been exceptionally rich in ideas that crisscrossed and enriched each other and that prepared the soil for moving beyond the juridico-institutional stage of Catholic ecclesiology, which by then had been reduced to a baroque "hierarchology." Even when political and cultural circles in Europe were aware of this ferment of ideas, they often remained diffident toward them or shortsighted in

ever more widespread among the bishops and that they are developing a sense of responsibility" (in Lai, *Il papa non eletto*, 399).

interpreting them. Some regarded these ideas as forms of dangerous restlessness inasmuch as they might break down and weaken solidarity against communism. Others thought of them as pathetic tremors of a Christianity that had succumbed to the secularization of culture and history and was trying, in vain, to escape its own decline.[93] In this difficult situation many of the leading circles in the West did not seem much more enlightened than Josip Stalin, who during those same years was asking how many divisions the pope had at his disposal.

It would be very difficult, and perhaps out of place, to identify specific echoes of European culture in the unfolding of Vatican II. To begin with, there can be no denying a leading role to the Central European episcopates. German, Belgian, Dutch, and French theologians and bishops were the leading players during the difficult beginning of the assembly. Only in a second phase did a solid and fruitful dialectical exchange take place with Europeans from the countries of the Soviet bloc and with Africans, Latin Americans, and Asians. The result was a broadening of geographic and cultural horizons, an appreciation of intercultural pluralism, and a recognition of the need to go beyond one's usual boundaries and to share the problems and perspectives of the "other."

The possibility arose of not reading Christianity solely in the perspective of salvation and of the providential plan that presides over it, but also on a positive level through the rigorous use of the historico-critical method. Nostalgia and flights to a misconceived "providence" were disregarded. What had happened? How are we to explain these conclusions that seem so far removed both from the situation prevailing in preconciliar Catholicism and from the general cultural climate? This was a climate in which attention was focused mainly on the ideological conflict between the major political blocs as symbolized by the divisions between the "two" Germanys and regularly echoed within the individual societies on every continent, a situation in which postwar reconstruction followed the criteria of conserving or restoring the former social conditions. It was also a situation in which resounding political contradictions were current in Europe: the survival of Francoism and Salazarism in the Iberian Peninsula, Great Britain's wearying effort to reorganize after the disappearance of the empire

---

[93] See G. Alberigo, "I movimenti cristiani e la teologia della secolarizzazione nell'Europa occidentale," *Il pensiero politico* 21 (1988), 149–85; and V. G. Kiernan, "La secolarizzazione dell'Europa," in *Storia d'Europa* 5: *L'età contemporanea, secc. XIX-XX* (Turin, 1996), 591–636.

and the weakening of the Commonwealth, and the restlessness that was spreading in the Baltic and Danubian countries behind the Iron Curtain.

Within the Council the division between the bishops of the German Federal Republic and those of the Democratic Republic of Pankow was overcome; the Spanish bishops distanced themselves, with difficulty, from the climate created by the Franco dictatorship; the Italians left behind the "autarchic" mentality produced by twenty years of fascism and came into contact with the ideas and experiences of a universe much larger and richer than their own little world. At the global level the Council offered everyone the possibility of looking beyond the usual European horizon and discovering the riches of the "new" Latin American, African, and Asian Churches they were now meeting as equals. The result was the activation of a dynamism which the Cold War had frozen; there was once again the possibility of "thinking big."

The unlimited affirmation of religious freedom was like an explosion for contemporary societies.[94] The strongest impulse in this direction came from the North American bishops, but it would be impossible to ignore the importance of this demand in European culture, especially because this freedom was being systematically denied in the countries behind the Iron Curtain. The Declaration on Religious Freedom was all the more striking because Vatican II did not limit itself to reaffirming the "freedom of the Church" over against the political authorities but was able also to recognize the importance of personal conscience, even in the face of ecclesiastical authority.[95]

A great deal of interest was also aroused by the turnabout effected in *Gaudium et spes* when it ceased demonizing economic prosperity (this had been typical of the social teaching of the Church) and accepted the desirability of the welfare state, two cornerstones of modern culture. But despite major pressures brought to bear on the fathers throughout their entire work, the Council was unable to devote adequate and privileged attention to the poor. Was this perhaps because poverty was considered a problem for other continents? Or perhaps because of the impenetrability of the optimistic anthropology then prevalent in European culture?

[94] See *Dignitatis humanae; Nostra aetate; Ad gentes,* 3, 9, 11, 15, 18; *Gaudium et spes,* 19, 28, 29, 92; and M. Ruokanen, *The Catholic Doctrine of Non-Christian Religions according to the Second Vatican Council* (Leiden, 1992).

[95] See J. A. Komonchak, "Vatican II and the Encounter between Catholicism and Liberalism," in *Catholicism and Liberalism: Contributions to American Public Philosophy* (Cambridge, 1994), 76–99.

Beginning in 1965, history accelerated. Innovations and problems accumulated. A postmodern feeling, perhaps even a culture, developed, a postmodernity that was discontinuous and uneven to the extent that "de-Europeanization" advanced, although with contradictory effects. In the post-ideological societies consumerism spread as a common denominator, while radical cultural differences remained and economic differences deepened. Once ideological oppositions were removed, tendencies to unification faded away while stress was placed on pluralistic demands, which tended to degenerate into particularisms.

In this setting Christianity, on all the continents and in every type of society, found itself facing a critical challenge: effect a reinculturation of the gospel message or be left in the past. Inculturation into the classical world, brought about by the first Christian generations and then gradually modified through two millennia, showed its obsolescence even in its basic grammar. The anthropology borrowed from Greek culture, especially after the Constantinian revolution, appears to have been transcended today or even to have become unknown in the thinking of the new generations. The dualism of flesh-spirit, soul-body, that dominated Western Christianity is becoming every day more of a limitation than a vehicle for communicating the Christian faith. An anthropology of separation and contrast (man-woman, white-black, rich-poor) is being rejected as incompatible with the consciousness of equality.

Vatican II intuited the imminence of this challenge, even if only in a confused way and without having the time or energy to develop a complete response. The powerful core of its heritage consists in the conscious acceptance of this challenge, in the loyal and creative renewal of the Council's intuition, and in the bold effort to develop the scattered seeds.

In Latin America there has been an interesting echo of the Council's intuition in the spread of base communities and the formulation of liberation theology. On the African continent inculturation has appeared primarily at the liturgical level; *Sacrosanctum concilium* led to important experiments in African liturgies. In Asia, a peaceful confrontation with the great religious traditions of the East has become more coherent and more fruitful.

On the social level the thrust of the Council has contributed to the movement beyond the stage of ideologies. The thaw in Catholicism in relation to the communist world opened up a perspective that made possible the election of a Slavic bishop to the papacy in 1978 and then the fall of the Berlin Wall. The collapse of the Soviet system provided the context for the disappearance of Catholic or Christian political parties.

The main reason for their existence had faded: the conviction of Christians that they lived apart within hostile societies and had to join together in self-defense. Correspondingly, the attitude of "lay" cultures that regarded Christians as a body apart and socially unreliable began to fade.

In 1985, A. Casanova, a French Marxist, asked: "In face of the movement of peoples and the development of state-sponsored monopolistic capitalism in the sixties, what kind of political economy, for example, was supposed by the theology of the Council fathers? How did they think of relations between the Church and the history of societies? How did Vatican II, in its day, look at questions of peace and war?" His response was without reservation:

> The time, the reasons, and the consequences of its development placed it at the heart of the changes, the struggles, and the innovations that have made our century a period of crises in civilization and of revolutions whose radical novelty can only be measured against the background of the entire history of humanity. The debates held in Rome between 1962 and 1965, the nature of the principal orientations adopted, the tensions and developments during the Council and in the twenty years after it give the last council an importance unmatched by those of the past.[96]

Despite the lack of attention on the part of many governing groups, Vatican II made a contribution to detente at the international level as well as within individual societies.[97] The experience of the Catholic episcopate in achieving a free deliberative assembly of worldwide dimensions represents a sign of this.

XII. PROSPECTS

> It would be premature to try to determine at this time the place which — Vatican Council II will have in history. In the history of the Church the Council of Trent inaugurated a "Tridentine" period, due to the zeal with which the papacy completed it and executed its decrees. In order for *this* council to have the effect of beginning an era and determining for a long time the face of the Church, it will be necessary to see whether the deepened awareness which the Church acquired of itself, its internal renewal, and its new relationship with the "world" will succeed in proving real,

---

[96] A. Casanova, *Le concile vingt ans après: Essai d'approche marxiste* (Paris, 1985), 9, 16.

[97] Paradoxically, it would seem that the ruling group of the Soviet Union paid unusual attention to Vatican II (see A. Melloni, ed., *Vatican II in Moscow (1959–1965)* [Leuven: Peeters, 1997]).

whether the spirit and norms in its decrees will succeed in permeating the life of the Church.[98]

That is what H. Jedin wrote a few weeks after the end of Vatican II. This authoritative historian continued:

This will be possible only if, as happened after Trent, its decrees are accepted as binding norms and not as the starting point for a theological and ecclesiastical revolution that would lead to the self-destruction of the Church. It is, first and foremost, up to the bishops and episcopal conferences to use the powers and responsibilities given them by the Council and not to allow decentralization, which in itself is fruitful, to cause disorder and chaos.[99]

A few years later Jedin, who had collaborated as an expert at Vatican II, remarked: "It is now established that it [Vatican II] penetrated more deeply into the history of the Church than the First Vatican Council; in any event, its effects are comparable to those of Trent.... It can hardly be disputed that it represented a turning point in the history of the Church."[100]

Karl Rahner, an important theological contributor to Vatican II, said in 1979 that the Council "was not an arbitrary pile of episodes and decisions, but possessed an essential internal continuity throughout all its individual events" and it was "in germinal form the first official self-actuation of the Church *as a worldwide Church*." Therefore, since "from a theological point of view there have been three great epochs in the history of the Church," the third "has hardly begun and has manifested itself officially at Vatican II."[101] At Vatican II something new occurred that was "irreversible and lasting," said the same Rahner in an article that complemented the one just cited.[102] The novelty can be summed up in a turning to the world, a relationship with the world, a commitment to the reformulation of the role of theology, the introduction of an ecumenical mentality, and an optimism about universal salvation.

---

[98] H. Jedin, *Breve storia dei Concili* (Rome-Brescia, 1978), 284.

[99] Ibid. This appraisal was already present in the edition of 1966.

[100] H. Jedin, "The Second Vatican Council," in *The Church in the Modern Age,* vol. 10 in *History of the Church,* ed. H. Jedin, K. Repgen, and J. Dolan (New York, 1981), 146.

[101] Karl Rahner, "Basic Theological Interpretation of the Second Vatican Council," in his *Theological Investigations* 20 (New York, 1981), 77–89.

[102] Karl Rahner, "The Abiding Significance of the Second Vatican Council," ibid., 90–102. In his view the turnabout at Vatican II was comparable to that introduced by Paul when he shifted the epicenter of Christianity from Jerusalem to Rome. E. Klinger drew inspiration from Rahner in his essay, "Der Glaube des Konzils: Ein dogmatischer Fortschritt," in *Glaube im Prozess: Christsein nach dem II. Vatikanum: Für K. Rahner,* ed. E. Klinger and K. Wittstadt (Freiburg, 1984), 615–26.

According to French Dominican M.-D. Chenu, there were four cornerstones of the Council's theology: "the priority of mystery over institution; the recognition of the irreducible value of the human subject in the structure and dynamics of salvation; the Church's consciousness of its own existence in history; and the recognition of the value of earthly realities."[103]

Cardinal J. Bernardin, an influential North American prelate who was consecrated a bishop just after the end of Vatican II, said in 1985 that

> the Council has had a powerful impact on the Church and on society throughout the world. In the past twenty years we have become much more aware that the Catholic Church can no longer be dominated by the particular Churches of the North Atlantic community. The Church is truly universal. Its most exciting growth is taking place in Africa and India. There is also a great surge of renewal in Latin America, where, in many places, the Church is identifying itself more and more with the people, with the poor.[104]

At the center of the future agenda Bernardin saw that

> in a world that is increasingly independent and marked by the threat of nuclear destruction, the Church has come to realize that it has an important role to play. The Church recognizes that it must work to develop an interdependence that not only provides for the physical needs of all but also serves the moral and spiritual needs of the human family. Although this role is part of the Church's mission, and the Church is well equipped to play it on an international scale, the problem of accomplishing unity amid growing diversity remains primary on the Church's agenda. The Church must seek to reconcile the differences and to bridge the chasms between the Northern and the Southern hemispheres, between the rich and the poor of the world.[105]

The Cardinal of Chicago maintained that

> a second item on the Church's future agenda has its origin in two of the major teachings of the Council. In its documents the Council repeated the traditional doctrine about the hierarchical nature of the Church, but it also insisted that the Church is the entire People of God. Many of the present tensions in the Church can be attributed to that twofold approach of the Council. We need to work out more clearly how these two truths are interrelated — not just on the theoretical level, but on the practical level as well. In keeping with its affirmation of the imagery of the Church as the People of God, the Council made a major contribution in pointing out

---

[103] M.-D. Chenu, "Panorama della teologia post-conciliare," in *La chiesa post-conciliare* (Florence, 1969), 28–35.

[104] J. Bernardin, "Foreword," in *Vatican II by Those Who Were There,* ed. A. Stacpoole (London, 1986), XI-XV.

[105] Ibid.

the rightful place of the laity in the Church. It also began the process of enabling them to assume that position. At the same time, however, some confusion has resulted about the appropriate role of an ordained priesthood. How to make our own a vision of the Church that recognizes the distinctive charism of all believers as well as the unique and essentially different charism of presbyteral ministry is another item on our future agenda.[106]

O. H. Pesch gave the title "Third Age in the History of the Church" to the final chapter of his summary history of Vatican II. Following mainly the viewpoint of Rahner, he brought out the permanent significance of the Council.[107] Pesch distinguished between "permanent results" — liturgical reform, the Church as people of God, friendliness toward humanity, the dialogue with the religions — and "ambivalent results": the tensions between *communio* and hierarchical structure and between collegiality and papacy, the problems of the ecumenical journey and of the place of the Bible in the Church.

While one isolated Protestant's appraisal was that Vatican II's importance was limited and insufficient to alter the identity of Roman Catholicism,[108] many other Protestant commentaries voiced a radically different view.[109] E. Vilanova has given a summary overview of thirty years of interpretation.[110]

According to G. Dossetti, in the Council's documents

> there are, in certain formulas or in certain points dealing with institutions, mistakes, compromises, and ambiguities that need to be identified. This is a task that needs to be done because any lack of clarity of thought certainly does not serve the things of the Spirit. While it is indeed a fine thing and important to recognize the wonderful workings of the Spirit, it is not useless to know what the formulas composed by human beings are really trying to say. This prevents the danger of thinking that things were said that were not said or that problems still unsolved were solved. It is true that the Spirit works despite any mistake or any lack of human clarity, but it is no less true that we are bound to do everything we can to eliminate these obstacles.[111]

---

[106] Ibid.

[107] O. H. Pesch, *Das zweite Vatikanische Konzil (1962–1965): Vorgeschichte — Verlauf — Ergebnisse — Nachgeschichte* (Würzburg, 1993), 351–61.

[108] V. Subilia, *La nuova cattolicità del Cattolicesimo* (Turin, 1967).

[109] See H. Roux, *De la désunion vers la communion* (Paris, 1978), 215–304.

[110] E. Vilanova, *El concili Vaticà (1962–1965): trenta anys d'interpretaciôns* (Barcelona, 1995).

[111] G. Dossetti, "Per una valutazione globale del magistero del Vaticano II," in *Il Vaticano II: Frammenti di una riflessione*, ed. F. Margiotta Broglio (Bologna, 1966), 24–25, 101.

XIII. Historical Importance

It is easy to see that Vatican II was held at a point between the decline of the age of ideology and the beginning of the postmodern period.[112] A correct appraisal of this historical setting of the Council is decisive for bringing into focus its broad significance. To the extent that it was an event marking a transition to a new age, its significance was two-fold: it was a point of arrival marking the end of the postridentine period of controversialism and perhaps the end also of the long Constantinian centuries, and it anticipated and was the point of departure for a new historical cycle.

We may therefore ask whether Vatican II was not made obsolete by the very fact of its having been held. Was Vatican II not simply the delayed and redecorated conclusion of Vatican I? Can it have anything to say to the third millennium? Again, has not the acceleration of history, helped in part by the Council, introduced the world to a climate utterly different from that of the 1960s and has it not thereby made Vatican II and its message outdated?

We may ask whether the obsolescence of the conciliar decrees (or at least many parts of them) is not greater than that of the conciliar event and its significance. The present *History* has gradually provided evidence of the recurring compromises in the development of the texts. Indeed, compromise was required for obtaining a broad consensus bordering on unanimity; in some cases, however, compromise was the result of an inadequate preceding development (as in the case of chapter III of *Lumen gentium* and a good part of *Gaudium et spes*). Close attention ought to be paid to the importance of these compromises, which weakened the conceptual and programmatic force of some pages of Vatican II and, in the postconciliar period, provided the basis for recurring and barren debates. It was the very nature of this Council and its final texts that they limited the importance of the compromises. In fact, it was the Council as such, as a great source of communion, comparison, and exchange, that

---

[112] H. Jedin recalled in his *Storia della mia vita* (Brescia, 1987) that "Vatican II turned a new page in the history of the Church" and that "even when I was beginning my work on the history of the Council, I was convinced that 'the Tridentine age of the Church was now past' and that the Church had long since entered a new phase of its history; from the Church's present perspective the Council of Trent can be treated as and judged to be 'history.' Of course, it was only Vatican Council II that changed this intuition into a common intellectual realization" (271, 278). In the preface to the third volume of his *Storia del Concilio di Trento* (Brescia 1970), he remarked that "participation in this vital experience of a council [Vatican II] was an incomparable intuitive lesson for a historian of councils, just as, conversely, his knowledge of the history of the Councils redounded in favor of his participation in the new council" (7).

was the fundamental message that constituted the framework and core of reception.

It is in that light that the conciliar decrees are to be situated and interpreted.[113] They are tesserae in a complex and multicolored mosaic that can be read adequately only as a whole. The isolation of the tesserae under the influence and in function of a hermeneutic of details contradicts the deeper nature of Vatican II.[114]

On the doctrinal level, the crucial points in the contribution made by the Council have to do with the central place of the word of God; the importance of the trinitarian mystery; and the role of the Spirit, the conception of the Church, and the attitude of friendship and participation in human history. These contributions are not coextensive with any single final text of the Council, however important it may be. They are, instead, the combined result of a comprehensive reconsideration of the conciliar event.

First of all, there is the central place and sovereign role of the word of God. Turning to account a direction that had already merged timidly at the beginning, Vatican II repeatedly highlighted the mystery-dimension of the Christian message. *Mystery* is used here in the charged and biblical sense of the word,[115] that is, the totality of revelation, which as a whole is meta-rational and knowable only in parts by means of partial

---

[113] On November 15, 1965, a notification from the Secretary General of the Council confirmed that "inasmuch as everything set forth by the Council is the teaching of the supreme magisterium of the Church, each and every Christian should receive and embrace it as understood by the sacred council itself; this understanding is made known both by the subjects treated and by the way in which it is formulated, in light of the rules of theological interpretation" (*AS* IV/6,. 419). See J. Gehr, *Die rechtliche Qualifikation der Beschlüsse des Zweiten Vatikanischen Konzils* (St. Ottilien, 1997).

[114] According to G. Dossetti, "Rilettura della portata dottrinale della costituzione conciliare *De sacra Liturgia*," an unpublished paper from the end of December 1965 (Dossetti papers), the course of interpretation can be structured as follows: "When the Council has concluded, a first step should be simply a reading of the approved documents, that is, a simple discovery of what they say, in accordance with a very objective and almost literal examination of them, with no heed paid yet to a systematic assembly of them into a whole. This first reading will be a source of a series of pointers for a second reading, which ought to have a more systematic character and aim at extracting the main lines of force running through the entire set of documents. After this second phase, there will have to be a third, the most important, in which the aim will be not only to grasp the lines of force at work in the thought and the operative directives which the documents contain; rather, from this understanding there can also be derived a direction for a global spirituality, flowing from this comprehensive gift that has been bestowed on the Church and on humanity."

[115] The concordance compiled by Ph. Delhaye, M. Gueret, and P. Tombeur (*Concilium Vaticanum II: Concordance, Index, Listes de fréquence, Tables comparatives* [Louvain, 1974]), shows the term *mystery* occurring 125 times in the body of documents.

approximations that complement rather than exclude one another. Mystery, thus understood, runs through the entire celebration of Vatican II and the texts of its decrees, from the liturgical constitution to the constitution on the Church. Closely connected with this is the Council's decision, carried out laboriously but tenaciously, to accept the determining role of the word of God; this decision found expression in *Dei Verbum* but also in *Sacrosanctum concilium* and *Lumen gentium.*

From this centrality and sovereign role of the word of God flows a radical rethinking of a conceptual, abstract understanding of truth. The conception of Christianity as truth, consisting in an organized set of dogmatic propositions rather than as devotion to and following of the person of the Christ of God, was established centuries ago under the influence of contacts with Hellenistic culture. The dominance of the metaphysical approach and its development in the direction of essentialism gave ever greater importance to truth as an intellectual abstraction. Truth, instead of being identified with the person of Christ, was seen as an organized, abstract, and atemporal set of concepts. The biblical perspective, according to which Christian truth is the trinitarian mystery revealed in the person of Jesus Christ, an inexhaustible mystery from which every generation and every culture draws things old and things new, took second place. Truth as a system of univocal dogmatic formulations tended to become the definitive measure of faith and communion. Error in the formulation of doctrine involved exclusion from communion.

For a long time, then, Christianity, especially in the Latin-Germanic West, experienced and presented the gospel message according to conceptual modalities that entailed a fragmentation and "de-historicizing" of the message itself. The slide from Christ as "way, truth, and life" (Jn 14:6) toward a doctrinal and impersonal way of conceiving truth opened the way for theology as a scholastic elaboration, as a separate factor that dominated the life of the Church. Another result was a conception of the Church as a doctrinal and disciplinary institution, to which was assigned the safeguarding and defense of the truth. Following on the breakup of Christian unity, each Church laid down the boundaries of its own theological truth and committed itself to removing this truth from the influence of historical development by means of an essentialist solidification not only of doctrine but even of its formulations.

The end result was a narrowed vision of Christianity and of the Church itself. The Church emphasized doctrinal factors and the juridico-institutional order to the point of regarding these, at least implicitly, as coextensive with the faith and the Church. It thus became usual, especially in the Catholic tradition, to regard doctrinal formulations and uniformity of structures as central — to the point of making them the very being of the Church.

Vatican II moved away from this monolithic and one-dimensional understanding of Christian truth, for it realized that the criterion of authenticity for this truth is not an internal conceptual coherence but the person of Jesus the Christ in the full reality of his mystery. The faith and the Church are no longer seen as coextensive with doctrine; the latter is not even the most important dimension if it is true that the Church is a communion of living stones, a body in continuous development. The acceptance of doctrine and especially of a single formulation of it can no longer be the ultimate criterion in deciding membership in the *Una sancta.*

In this context the criteria given in the decree of Vatican II on ecumenism for formulating and expounding the faith are explicit. In this regard the initial statement of *Unitatis redintegratio* is central: "The manner and order in which Catholic belief is expressed should in no way become an obstacle to dialogue with our brethren" (*UR*, 11). It would be eccentric to think that the requirement stated in the same section — "At the same time, Catholic belief must be explained more profoundly and precisely, in such a way and in such terms that our separated brethren can also really understand it" — was understood as a bit of tinsel, lacking any value and meaning. Rather it urges an effort to rethink radically, in greater depth and with greater fairness, the modalities and formulations of the Catholic faith. No less discerning is the recognition of a "hierarchy of truths."[116] The radical thrust of this passage, and indeed of the entire decree *Unitatis redintegratio*, is in the direction of ways of expressing the faith less influenced by the dominance of Western culture and more open to contemporary humanity's ways of perceiving and thinking.

These conciliar tendencies reconnect Catholic Christianity with the most authentic wellsprings of its own tradition. They restore great freedom to spirituality as well as to theology and permit an ongoing rediscovery of the eschatological dimension. Moreover, the rediscovery of the dimension of mystery has given a push in the direction of a rapprochement with the great Oriental Christian traditions, just as the

---

[116] This criterion was already formulated, though without development, in the constitution *Dei Filius* of the First Vatican Council (chapter IV): "Reason, if it is enlightened by faith, does indeed when it seeks persistently, piously and soberly, achieve by God's gift some understanding, and that most profitable, of the mysteries ... from the connexion of these mysteries with one another and with the final end of humanity" (N. P. Tanner, ed., *Decrees of the Ecumenical Councils* [London/Washington, D.C., 1990], 2:808).

recognition of the critical importance of the word of God implies a new convergence with the Reformation tradition, beyond the inflexibilities of Trent and, above all, of the post-Tridentine and controversialist periods.

It is in this same perspective that the courageous break with anti-Semitism is to be seen. Vatican II consolidated the change made by John XXIII beginning in the very first days of his pontificate. Perhaps the resistance from tenacious minorities, along with Jewish entreaties that were not always prudent, hindered a more positive conquest of the age-old hostility of the Church toward the Jewish people. In any case, here again the Council marked a point of no return.

No less decisive and important was the reference to the trinitarian mystery as well as to the role of the Spirit. From its first announcement and throughout its entire course, the Council was motivated by reliance on the Holy Spirit. It is worth noting that with increasing frequency John XXIII emphasized "the need of a continuous outpouring of the Holy Spirit as if on a new Pentecost that will renew the face of the earth." The image of a new Pentecost was regularly associated with the Council, which "will be truly a new Pentecost that will cause the interior riches of the Church to blossom." The call for a revival of pneumatology is inherent in the Council's conception of the Church. This conception, which moved beyond the Christo-monistic limitations typical of *Mystici corporis*, was based precisely on a rediscovery of the role of the Spirit.

There is no denying that the preconciliar work in the area of pneumatology and the trinitarian dimension was fragmentary and inadequate. During the work of the Council no proposal was ever made for a treatment of these subjects, and yet they equally, and increasingly, formed the horizon against which the Council developed its subjects, inasmuch and to the extent that the great majority of fathers felt an urgent need to escape from an overly static doctrinal approach incapable of being assimilated by new cultures. It does not seem an exaggeration to claim that the action of the Spirit and the dynamism of the Trinity were a constant running through the Council itself and the body of its decrees. Perhaps as a result also of the witness given by the observers, especially in view of the dynamic action of the Spirit, the Council was not deaf but showed an impulse, weak as it may have been, to reintegrate the trinitarian and pneumatological dimensions in Catholic thought and devotion.[117]

---

[117] Considerations of this sort are absent in the contributions published as *Il Concilio Vaticano II: Ricezione e attualità alla luce del Giubileo* (Vatican City, 2000).

The third aspect that seems to have been of central importance was the conception of the Church. The point of reference at the outset was an explicit ecclesio-centrism tinged with triumphalism. The reason for this was a christo-monism that identified the Church with the mystical body of Christ and, in tendency, with the kingdom, that made the Church coextensive with the Roman Church, and exalted the Bishop of Rome as the apex of the ecclesial pyramid.

The Council, however, located the Church in the perspective of conciliarity. In this setting even the "reform of the Church," understood as a remedy for decadence (de-formatio) in relation to an organic, definitive order of the Church, was set aside. The combination of the pastoral principle with the method of aggiornamento led to a criticism of the medieval-modern theme of decadence and reform as applied to the Church. The Council moved beyond this idea both as regards the dialectic of abuses and reform (a dialectic often exhausting itself in the back and forth among denunciations, plans, and inadequate or ineffective reforms), and as regards even the enunciation of the theory, which was responsible in good measure for the over-concentration on ecclesiology. A Church thought of as a pilgrim people of God led by the sole Shepherd under the movement of the Spirit is always in aggiornamento when the criterion of service is used.

Moving beyond the stage of ecclesio-centrism implies not only the end of the dominance of ecclesiology but also, and above all, the rediscovery of the other dimensions of Christian life and of the faith. Vatican II acted in the perspective of a reversal of priorities, leading to the abandonment of the reference to ecclesiastical institutions — their authority and their effectiveness — as the center and measure of the faith and of the Church. Instead, it is faith, communion, and readiness for service that "make" the Church; these are the values by which the Church's adequacy in the service of the gospel are measured, and they are recognized as ecclesial criteria, not the internal logic of institutions but the sensus fidelium and the signs of the times.

An important element of novelty that is enunciated in the Constitution on the Sacred Liturgy (Sacrosanctum concilium) and then repeated in other conciliar decrees is the introduction of the perspective in which the Church is seen as a communion of different local communities rather than as a very large, unified, worldwide organization. In this perspective the structure of the Church can no longer be outlined as a pyramid in which life goes on around a vertical axis and with a lessening pace as it moves down. On the contrary, dominance attaches now to an essentially horizontal image (not an ascending one), which locates all the Churches and their bishops on a level of parity (sister Churches) although not of identity.

In its turn, the application to the Church of the biblical notion of a "people" and of a people that is on the way and seeking, transcends the gradual petrification of the conception of the Church that Bellarmine illustrated with an analogy between the Church and the kingdom of France. Dynamic factors are given their proper value alongside the static ones, for example, the common priesthood of the faithful, which was the basis for removing the centuries-old separation between clergy and laity, as well as the "essentialist" conception of the Church. The fact that *Lumen gentium* began with a chapter on the mystery of the Church barred the way to any further intensification of ecclesiology.

Vatican II opened up room for the *universitas fidelium* (*LG*, 12, 5: "the whole body of the faithful") to live the Christian experience with the freedom of the children of God and in obedience to the movements of the Spirit. It is an experience which Vatican II described as the active participation of all the faithful in the liturgy *(Sacrosanctum concilium)*, drawing nourishment from the word of God *(Dei Verbum)*, a commitment to evangelization *(Ad gentes)*, and friendship with human beings *(Gaudium et spes)*. The general demand that dominated in the announcement of the Council, namely, that there be an organized rethinking of the conception of the Church, found expression in the presence of ecclesiological statements in all the principal documents of Vatican II. These statements do not always seem coordinated and consistent among themselves, but this does not necessarily limit the extent to which the resulting image is one of a Church that is open and incomplete and therefore susceptible of further enrichments.

Expectations and fears at the beginning of the Council were focused on emphasizing episcopal responsibility and on relations between the pope and the bishops, especially in the area of leadership of the universal Church *(plenitudo potestatis/vocatio in partem sollicitudinis)*. This set of problems, when reconsidered against the background of the Council's work and of the fundamental harmony between episcopate and pope that was experienced during the Council, took on new dimensions. Nevertheless, it took up a great deal of room in the course of the Council and was consolidated in some major conclusions that dealt with the "state of the Church." From a general point of view, the decision that episcopal consecration is sacramental stands out the most. At the end of a lengthy debate the Council recognized the sacramentality of episcopal ordination, repeating the ancient fourth canon of the Council of Nicea. Therefore, in the act of ordination that incorporates him into the episcopal college, a bishop receives the offices of liturgical leader, guide, and judge, while he is also given a coresponsibility for the universal Church. This decision does not touch the prerogatives of the Bishop of Rome, as the Council repeated over and over.

At the same time, however, the figure of the bishop and, even more, the episcopal college (an expression bitterly debated) are given an importance that was for a long time undervalued, when not denied outright. At the territorial level (regional, national, continental) collegiality has found room for its exercise in the episcopal conferences, which during and after Vatican II have acquired a diffusion and importance hitherto unknown. At a universal level the tiring and unsatisfying experience of the synod of bishops represented something new, a periodic opportunity for comparison and exchanges, but, as was easily foreseen, it has not touched the personal practice of the pope in the exercise of his responsibilities.[118]

On a more modest level the Council revived the ancient figure of the permanent and even married deacon. This had an important and widespread impact, especially in areas where the shortage of clergy is acute. The most difficult problem connected with the positive picture of deacons seems to be that of their effective distinction from priests, a distinction that does not consist wholly in their being in a subordinate position.

The relativization of ecclesiology due to the restoration of the complexity of the faith experience and the attention given to history and to the social context make it possible to pay renewed attention to the importance of the eschatological perspective. The heavenly Jerusalem, seen as the prototype and destiny of the Church, emerges from the haze of mythology and regains its meaning as a goal. The Council fathers did not have the courage to take over Roncalli's evocative comparison of the Church to a garden, but the rich sixth paragraph of *Lumen gentium*, on the biblical images of the Church, makes a decisive contribution to restoring balance to preconciliar theology and offers the possibility of important developments.

Finally, friendship and sharing in human history complete the conciliar revolution. Even before *Gaudium et spes*, but also before the declarations on religious freedom and on the non-Christian religions, the

---

[118] Nor was there any follow up on the suggestions for changing the college of cardinals that were repeatedly made and were under consideration by Paul VI at the beginning of his pontificate.

announcement of the Council and then its celebration aroused vast expectations, and this far beyond the borders of Catholicism. Expectation arose of an attitude of sympathy for "those far off" and nonbelievers and of the abandonment of the sour attitude the Catholic Church had often adopted toward "modern civilization" and the other religions.

Beginning at least as far back as the French Revolution, the Catholic Church had adopted an attitude of rejection of modernity, which was seen as incurably hostile to Christianity.[119] The standard that prevailed was the exercise of papal authority as enunciated by Pope Gregory XVI in his programmatic encyclical *Mirari vos*, which was to mark the direction taken by the papacy for a century and a half. After recalling the dangers lurking due to the "wide-ranging conspiracy of the wicked" and having thanked God who had granted a "respite from terror," Gregory XVI did not hesitate to say, even if with great uneasiness, that he must discontinue his "indulgent kindness" and, in virtue of the divine authority he had received, "curb with the rod."[120] Repeatedly expressed wishes for a reconsideration of this outlook remained fruitless; in fact, more recent ideologies only hardened Roman intransigence.

Pope Roncalli quickly distanced himself from the prejudiced hostility between faith and modern history that had culminated in proposition LXXX of the *Syllabus* of Pius IX. Also included in his new outlook was a substantial retrieval of human history as a category connected with the Christian faith, not alien or contradictory to it, and a rejection of negative judgments on the present of the sort that had been deduced from a mistrust in principle and passively accepted from the past. The address with which he opened the Council was wholly permeated by a perception of the newness of the human condition and of the greater possibilities that this offers to the faith. John XXIII had also given a historical dimension to the thorny problems attached to the way in which doctrinal authority was exercised. In his view, "nowadays... the Spouse of Christ prefers to make use of the medicine of mercy rather than severity"; instead of launching new condemnations, the Church must show the soundness of its teaching.

Paul VI, for his part, gave theological legitimacy to the concept and practice of dialogue as he gathered up the demands formulated by various circles. The Council gladly accepted this outlook, which seemed to

---

[119] See F. X. Kaufmann, ed., *Vatikanum II und Modernisierung: Historische, theologische und soziologische Perspektiven* (Paderborn, 1996).

[120] *Acta Gregorii papae XVI* 1 (Rome, 1901), 169–74. See P. Hegy, *L'autorité dans le Catholicisme contemporain: Du Syllabus à Vatican II* (Paris, 1975).

confirm Roncalli's attitude of "brotherhood." Only subsequent developments in ecumenical relations would show clearly the qualitative distance between these two attitudes.

In this regard, the ideas offered by the constitution *Gaudium et spes* and, equally, by the conciliar *Declaration on Religious Freedom* make possible theological developments of great importance, especially in the areas of the signs of the times and freedom of conscience. By restoring the bond of friendship with human history, which was felicitously expressed by Gregory the Great,[121] the Council furthered the full reappropriation of the meaning of historical evolution. Almost all the texts approved by the Council contain references to the historical situation; while some of them are casual and of little importance, others are more deliberate and full of meaning.[122] The Council recognizes and legitimizes the organic connection between history and salvation both in speaking of single events and as a general methodical requirement for the life of Christians and of the Church. The liturgical constitution says that "zeal for the promotion and restoration of the sacred liturgy is rightly held to be a sign of the providential dispositions of God in our time" (*SC*, 43). Here the inductive method is applied in an exemplary manner.

The same thought is echoed in more general terms in the *Decree on Ecumenism*, in which the Council urges all Catholics "to recognize the signs of the times and to take an active and intelligent part in the work of ecumenism" (*UR*, 4). Similarly, the *Decree on the Ministry and Life of Priests* urges priests and laity "to recognize... the signs of the times" (*PO*, 9).

The problem of the signs of the times, an expression that Roncalli had already used in the bull of convocation, with explicit reference to Matthew 16:4, was taken up with special diligence during the writing of the *Pastoral Constitution on the Church in the Modern World*. In fact, the very title itself represented a further grasp of the close connection between faith and history.[123] This involvement of the Church is connected both with its mission of salvation (*GS*, 3) and with the need "to answer

---

[121] "You must realize that with the passage of time the knowledge of our spiritual fathers increased.... The closer the world is brought to its end, the wider the door of eternal knowledge is opened to us" (Gregory the Great, *Homiliae in Ezechielem* II/IV, 12, ed. M. Adriaen, CCSL 142 (Turnhout, 1971), 267–68.

[122] See G. Alberigo, "Cristianesimo e storia nel Vaticano II," *CrSt* 5 (1984), 577–92.

[123] See G. Turbanti, *Un concilio per il mondo moderno* (Bologna, 2000); and G. Ruggieri, *La teologia dei "segni dei tempi": acquisizioni e compiti* (Cinisello Balsamo, 2000).

the ever recurring questions which men ask about the meaning of this present life and of the life to come" (*GS* 4). The Church is urged to recognize in the life of humanity the more evident and significant events and tendencies and to interpret their evangelical meaning. There is present here, as in filigree, the inductive-deductive method in accordance with which the Church is, on the one hand, obliged to discern, on the basis of history itself, the meaningful junctures in the life of humanity, and on the other, is called to reveal the significance and values of these same historical junctures by reference to the gospel.

The problem is taken up again in the section that introduces the first part of the constitution, which is devoted to the Church and human vocation. Here the expression *signs of the times* is no longer used; the fathers, after moving beyond a provisional text according to which time is a sign and voice of the presence or absence of God, finally reached an interesting compact formulation. The people of God is here considered in light of two characteristics: it is guided by faith in the Spirit, and it shares with all humanity the condition of being in history. This people is obliged to discern in historical events the authentic signs of the presence of God and of God's plan of salvation (*GS,* 11). In this perspective it is the entire people of God that, to the extent that it is caught up in the human condition and its historical unfolding, is called upon to recognize signs of the Messiah in the moments of humanity's life as these occur.

Thus the dichotomy between secular history and sacred history is left behind, without, however, sacralizing history, which would be equally unacceptable. History is thus recognized as being a *locus theologicus*, that is, as a reality in which faith can and ought to nourish its own ceaseless quest for the kingdom, not in order jealously to take possession of history but to make of it the privileged place of friendship with people. At the same time, the ambiguity of history and its unfolding is not ignored or even resolved optimistically.

The overthrow of a centuries-long Catholic Eurocentrism was laborious and slow, especially because it required the abandonment of mental habits so deeply rooted as to have become unconscious. The cosmopolitan composition of the conciliar assembly contributed in some degree to this process, especially as, little by little, bishops born on the continents of the Third World and belonging to religious orders became members of the Council. Here again there was the beginning of a complex conversion, all the more so since Eurocentrism and Roman centralization were intertwined without being identical. This can be seen clearly in the debate on missionary activity. Moreover, Eurocentrism had begun to break up because of the *Ostpolitik* undertaken by John XXIII and then by Paul VI, which meant departing from the inflexible attitude of preceding pontificates toward the Soviet regimes.[124]

By means of a "programmed" and constant trickle of innovative actions (observers from Moscow at Vatican II, liberation of Msgr. Slypyi, participation of bishops from behind the Iron Curtain in the Council, the audience for Adjubeij, the decision not to repeat the condemnation of the communist ideology), Catholicism began to emerge from a suffocating identification with the Atlantic group (from the German Federal Republic to the United States).

Official Catholic parlance describes Vatican II as *ecumenical*.[125] Strictly speaking, the description errs through excess. The description can be extended only to those councils whose authority was recognized, at the time or later, by all the major Christian traditions. It was not by chance that in the manuscript of the document announcing the Council John XXIII used, instead, the adjective *general*. From the viewpoints of canon law and Christian tradition there can be no doubt: Vatican II was a council in the Roman Catholic tradition and therefore general. On the other hand, the reconstruction of its course, the shape it took on, and the impact it made on the Christian world show that in this case the description of it as general is inadequate by defect. From this point of view, it may be asserted that while Vatican II was canonically a general council, it adopted an ecumenical perspective, as is shown by the echo it roused in Christian areas other than the Roman.

After the end of the Council the prevailing multicultural climate has made it more difficult to claim that there is a single model for Catholic bishops. After the death of John XXIII the proposal was made that the Council should canonize him in order to provide the postconciliar Church with a model. As we know, the effort was blocked by the authorities.[126]

---

[124] See G. Tuninetti, *Mons. Francesco Lardone (1887–1980): Il nunzio apostolico precursore della Ostpolitik* (n.p., 1997); and A. Casaroli, *Il martirio della pazienza: La S. Sede e i paesi comunisti (1963–89)* (Turin, 2000).

[125] See Y. Congar, *Le concile de Vatican II* (Paris, 1984), 57–63; and H. J. Sieben, *Katholische Konzilsidee im 19. und 20. Jahrhundert* (Paderborn, 1993), 309–50.

[126] The period after the Council of Trent had an accepted model for bishops: Charles Borromeo. Despite Roman distrust, his example played an enormous role in all areas of Christendom as a model of a pastor devoted to the *salus animarum* (see G. Alberigo, "Carlo Borromeo come modello di vescovo nella Chiesa posttridentina," *Rivista Storica Italiana* 79 [1967], 1031–52; idem, "Carlo Borromeo between Two Models of Bishop," in *San Carlo Borromeo and Ecclesiastical Politics in the Second Half of the XVI Century*, ed. J. M. Headley and J. B. Tomaro, 250–63 [Washington, 1988]). Jedin had earlier remarked that "holy bishops are the necessary complement of Trent's work of reform.

The end of European hegemony makes richer, but also more complex, the process of reception of the Council itself. The Tridentine model, which was current in Catholicism for four centuries, appears inadequate precisely because of the universal dimension and the variety that the Church took on with Vatican II.[127] It was Jedin, as he ended his university teaching in July 1965, who said to his young listeners: "You have the good fortune of experiencing a great turning point in the history of the Church, a new beginning such as the Church has not known for centuries."[128]

Reception can come only over a lengthy period and with different modalities and meanings. The tenacious resistance of the forms Catholicism had taken on during the second millennium is not surprising. The importance of Vatican II will be measured by the capacity of the impulses and directives it contains to give form to and nourish a new stage of Catholicism. Rome's plans to apply the results of the Council in the form of a guided and controlled implementation have already shown their inadequacy.

No "council party" has arisen, that is, a movement committed to applying the conciliar directives. One reason for this is the repeated official declarations of fidelity to the Council from the Catholics at the top. On the other hand, the proposals for a "revision" of Vatican II are short-lived and have awakened no echo.[129] Only time will determine the extent to which the Council carried out its historical task. As of now, however, it is impossible to imagine a revival of pre-Vatican II Catholicism.

XIV. Locating Vatican II in History

Vatican II was open to the other Christian confessions and to a variety of cultural influences; it also wished to restore the Church's effective subordination to the word of God and its involvement in human history to the point of seeing in it meaningful signs of the gospel. In all these respects the Council can be seen as recapturing important thrusts — interrupted but

---

Without them the best thing would have been lacking: the spirit that gives life" ("Il concilio di Trento nella storia della chiesa," *Gregorianum* 26 [1945], 130).

[127] Even during the Council, Paul VI had urged the development of a *Lex Ecclesiae fundamentalis* that would give Catholicism as a whole some "constitutional" norms. Onclin's letters contain a proposal by Cardinal J. Döpfner, "Animadversiones ad Codicem Juris Canonici recognoscendum" (February 4, 1964), probably prepared for Paul VI.

[128] H. Jedin, "Tradition und Fortschritt in der Kirche," *Echo der Zeit*, August 15, 1965.

[129] See Cl. Barthe, *Quel avenir pour Vatican II? Sur quelques questions restées sans réponse* (Paris, 1999), 16.

not broken — of the Christian tradition that are brought together in the fullest sense of the word "catholic." As a result, the period of Christian history that is involved in the celebration of Vatican II goes back much farther than people are aware. This period includes not only Vatican I (1869–70), which preceded it historically, but even Trent (1545–62), a council that was strictly monoconfessional and monocultural.

Trent, which followed on the medieval councils of the West, experienced and sanctioned a drastic reduction, both qualitative and quantitative, of the Catholic world. Rarely had a great council seen so meager a representation of the episcopate, a situation made worse by the almost exclusively Latin and Mediterranean makeup of the assembly. This was the basis on which that Council effectively stopped the imminent dissolution of Catholicism and began its recovery. But it is not possible to ignore the costs of that undertaking; a drastic isolation of Christianity in the Roman tradition, which was separated and excluded, at least in its European epicenter, from exchanges with the other Christian traditions of both East and West; a posture of defense against modern culture; and finally, the *cordon sanitaire* that prevented its "contamination" by alien cultures. Never in Christian history had the *massa damnata* been given so broad a content; never had Christianity so intensified and heightened its own alienation from the events in which humanity was involved.

Catholicism thus moved in a direction that was new when compared with the age-old earlier tradition. During the sixteenth to the nineteenth centuries this trend gradually became radical, all the more so since the conflict first with the Protestant Reformation and then with modern culture was transformed from an active war to a war of holding a position and resisting everything else. Repeated attempts to break down this siege mentality by establishing open contacts with other cultures (in the Far East and in Latin America) were systematically cut short. A similar fate awaited the sorties attempted by those saints, from Philip Neri to Charles de Foucauld, whose inclination was to build bridges between the Christian condition and the common human condition.

This attitude of modern Catholicism was put to the test when the French Revolution swept away the still existing outward semblances of Christian society and triggered a "de-christianization." Over a century later the October Revolution seemed to be a historical personification of the devil, and a kind of a posteriori confirmation of the rightness of the choice made centuries before, as Catholicism moved toward a closed conception of the Church and a corresponding organization. In this setting Pius IX entrusted a "final council," Vatican I, with approving the attitude of the Church as a society in which authority descends from the top and the relationship among the members is mediated by the dependence of all on the sole authority of the Pope. The result was a quite novel ecclesiology, although not entirely unknown, both in its structure and in its domination of the Christian economy. Ecclesio-centrism reached new levels when compared with the entire previous tradition.

This was the background for the decision of John XXIII to hold a new kind of council. The idea was to call into council not only Catholicism but also, within the limits of such a compromised situation, the whole of Christianity. The goal was to emerge, by means of a common commitment and effort, from a long historical period that seemed now to be over, without a future. The crises that would become so public at the end of the 1960s (and for which some wanted to blame Vatican II) were already incubating, from the sacral persona of priests to the identification of penance with auricular confession. These were the symptoms of a profound and widespread malaise that even Pius XII had perceived to some extent but had diagnosed as a pathological condition to be suppressed and eliminated rather than as an uneasiness caused by an increasingly intolerable historical lag. In fact, there was no longer any question of simply correcting deviations and intolerable conditions; the post-Tridentine period was now in dispute and fidelity to the mainstream Christian tradition required a courageous effort to think things through again.

This epochal change was the cause and the purpose of Vatican II. Starting with the experience of the Jerusalem community, the holding of a council had always been a privileged moment in which the Church focused on and expressed its own deepest self-consciousness. And that is, above all else, what a council is: an experience of communion in inquiry, of sharing a journey through the human condition, and this with regard not only to a privileged few but to the Church as a whole. This is why the early Church venerated the first four councils as it venerated the four gospels; this is why the great councils are the heritage of all Christians, and every believer has the right and duty of defending their full and complete value against any kind of reductionism.

But reductionism is precisely the danger that one runs in claiming that there is no "before" and "after" in the history of the Church. A one-dimensional line may perhaps seem to be a sign of continuity, but it is, above all, a symptom of inertia and death, not life. Concretely, Vatican II showed a profound and intense awareness of the unsuitability of many preconciliar tendencies when it came to expressing the *sensus fidei*. This awareness led the Council — on some key points such as the concept of revelation, the mystery of the Church, the relationship between the people of God and the ecclesiastical hierarchy, *Romanità* as a mark of the Church, the acceptance of a Catholic ecumenism, and the vision of the Church *in* history — to restore ties with the most authentic and earliest tradition, beyond the ad hoc formulations and controversialist approaches of the more recent centuries.

And yet the most important novelty of Vatican II did not consist in its new formulations but rather in the very fact that it was convoked and held. From this point of view the Council represents a point of no return; the conciliar age has begun again and has found a very important place in the consciousness of the Church. It is impossible to imagine a politically more skillful and more effective "normalization" of the Council and of the impulse it has given to the Church than to deny its epochal significance. That would be a way of emptying out its meaning, which, while avoiding its brusk rejection by the traditionalists, would bury it in the normality of the post-Tridentine period.

The frequent emphasis here on the importance of Vatican II as a total event and not solely for its formal decisions may have led some readers to suspect the intention of playing down the documents approved by the Council. It would seem hardly necessary to remove such a suspicion. It is obvious, in fact, that Vatican II has entrusted to the Church the texts approved during it, with the different descriptions the assembly itself gave to them. But the very reconstruction of the course of the Council has clearly shown the importance of the conciliar experience for the correct and full use of the documents themselves. The interpretation of Vatican II would not be satisfactory if it were limited to an analysis of the text of the documents, with the possible additions of some excursuses on the work of composing them. On the contrary, it is the knowledge of the event in all its aspects that provides satisfactory interpretive criteria for grasping the full meaning of Vatican II and its documents.[130] It would be paradoxical to imagine or fear that recognition of the importance of Vatican II as a global event could reduce or lessen the importance of the Council's documents.

There can be no denying the great impact of the Council on the Christian Churches and the importance of the experience of conciliar life on those who participated in it. These two make up the necessary context of the decrees approved; to imagine the latter as unconnected with the former would lead to an unsound and one-eyed interpretation of them. This

---

[130] See the essays published in *Evento*.

is all the more true when we bear in mind that the documents of this council were directives, not rules. The understanding of them and, all the more, their reception are possible only in the light of their connection with the conciliar event.

Placing Vatican II in its historical context makes it possible to see that it has its own place in the conciliar tradition. The elements of continuity with that tradition are considerable, but the elements of novelty are also and perhaps more important. The historical characteristics of this council as reconstructed without preconceptions and on the basis of the sources contribute to a deeper knowledge of it.

EXCURSUS

THE SOURCES FOR THE SECOND VATICAN COUNCIL

Giuseppe Alberigo

During its preparation and celebration (1959–65), the Second Vatican Council produced an impressive amount of documentation. Even an approximate count of the number of written texts generated by the event is impossible, and this is to say nothing of the personal contacts or of the communications made through radio and television. As for other great assemblies held in the contemporary world, a crucial difficulty for a satisfactory historical reconstruction of Vatican II arises from the uncertainty of knowledge of the sources. Contrary to what was true of past councils, a history of Vatican II must take into account the difficulties in learning about, gathering, and controlling the immense mountain of written sources.

The most satisfying edition of the documentation of a great Christian assembly, the Council of Trent (1545–63), was sponsored by the Görres-Gesellschaft; it was based on diaries, especially those of Trent's secretary, Massarelli; on the acts of the general congregations; on letters, especially those exchanged between the prelates in Trent and Rome; and on the theological treatises written in service of the conciliar debates. This division of sources, which proved quite reasonable for the documentation on Trent, can also be used for Vatican II. The difference between the two councils is the quantity of the sources, since not only was Vatican II able to use printing much more easily than Trent could, but in addition the Vatican Printing Office played a special role that was not always simply instrumental, a subject that deserves special study. Moreover, the typewriter, the tape recorder, the mimeograph machine, and the photocopier made communication easier.

In seeking to make use of the sources listed above, it is proper to begin with the *Acta*, distinguishing the *antepreparatory* period (1959–60), the *preparatory* period (1961–62), and the *conciliar* period (1962–65), this last being divided in turn into a *first period* (1962), a *second period* (1963), a *third period* (1964), and a *fourth period* (1965). The official documentation for these years, that is, that which passed through the General Secretariat of the Council, was collected by the secretariat itself and then preserved, organized, and made accessible in the *Archivio del concilio Vaticano II* under the direction of V. Carbone and by order of

Paul VI.[1] Unfortunately, Paul VI's instruction did not also extend to the archive of the secretariat of state for the conciliar documentation kept there, which is very relevant, given the part played by the secretaries of state during the preparation (Tardini) and the course of the Council (Cicognani).

Independent of this latter archive, some rudimentary archives were spontaneously started,[2] while the greater part of the conciliar letters (without counting the many that were scattered) was kept in diocesan archives and with individuals (participants in the Council and their heirs). Only here can we count on finding diaries, letters, and treatises to complement the acts.

Toward the end of the 1980s, when plans were launched for preparing a history of Vatican II, it became clear that the most difficult problem was the availability of sources.[3] At that time the official acts of the antepreparatory period were available, that is, the documentation for the period immediately following the announcement by John XXIII. These were published in the fifteen folio volumes of the *Acta et Documenta Concilio oecumenico Vaticano II apparando: Series prima (antepraeparatoria)*,[4] which contain, above all, the *vota* submitted for the conciliar agenda.

The same secretariat later collected and published, in ten volumes, the acts of the preparatory period. The *Acta et documenta concilio oecumenico Vaticano II apparando. Series secunda (praeparatoria)* make it possible to follow the preparatory work done by the commissions and by the central commission, leading to the composition of over seventy schemas of decrees. At that time, however, in the late 1980s, this series was still incomplete.[5] During this preparatory period the General Secretariat and press service of the Pontifical Central Preparatory Commission for Vatican II published a twenty-seven issue *Notiziario* from June 1960 to June 23, 1962.

---

[1] See V. Carbone, "L'Archivio del Concilio Vaticano," *Archiva Ecclesiae* 34–35 (1991–92), 57–67.

[2] Léger's letters in the Fondation Léger in Montreal; the letters of Lercaro and Dossetti at the Istituto per le Scienze Religiose in Bologna.

[3] See A. Melloni, "Tipologia delle fonti per la storia del Vatican II," in *Per la storicizzazione del Vaticano II = CrSt* 13 (1992), 493–514.

[4] *ADA* I: Acts of Pope John XXIII; II/1-108: Proposals and summary; III: Proposals of the Roman Curia; IV/1–3: Proposals from Universities; an Index volume.

[5] *ADP* I: Acts of Pope John XXIII; II/1-4: Central Commission; III/1-2: Commissions and Secretariats; IV/1-3: Subcommissions of the Central Commission.

The publication of the sources dealing with the Council proper required a greater commitment (these sources included the general congregations, the commissions, the governing bodies, and the General Secretariat). The publication of this formidable documentation was the work of Msgr. Carbone, who produced thirty-four folio volumes of the *Acta Synodalia Sacrosancti Concilii Vaticani II*.[6] In the late 1980s, however, only the volumes for the general congregations were available, not those on the governing bodies and the General Secretariat. During the years of the Council, a press service published a *Notiziario* in several languages, but this was regarded as unsatisfactory. *L'Osservatore Romano* also published compressed summaries of events in the general congregations as well as some interventions on the subjects being discussed.

In addition, there existed by the late 1980s a small library of chronicles of the Council — volumes that brought together what the representatives of the major newspapers had published day after day. A place apart among these belongs to the weighty volumes of Jesuit G. Caprile, *Il concilio Vaticano II*; to the articles he had already published in *La Civiltà Cattolica* he added some important documents.[7] The volumes published by J. L. Martín Descalzo, H. Fesquet, H. Helbling, R. Laurentin, R. La Valle, R. Rouquette, X. Rynne, A. Wenger, and R. M. Wiltgen, to name only the best known, likewise constitute testimonies of considerable interest, because the articles collected therein were written while the news was still fresh and close in time to the facts reported. In fact, these articles often had some influence on council fathers who read them.

Also available were a limited number of testimonies by participants, who were often among the leading figures at the Council,[8] and the acts of the two popes, John XXIII and Paul VI. Finally, valuable information was contained in the numerous commentaries on the conciliar documents published in the years immediately following the end of the Council and

---

[6] *AS* I/1–4: First period; II/1–6: Second period; III/1-8: Third period; IV/1-7: Fourth period; V/1-3: General Secretariat; An index volume; Two volumes of appendices See V. Carbone, "Genesi e criteri della pubblicazione degli atti del Concilio Vaticano II," *Lateranum* 44 (1978), 579–94; and G. Lefeuvre, "Les Actes du Concile du Vatican," *Revue théologique de Louvain* 11 (1980), 186–200, 325–51.

[7] The conciliar documentation collected by Caprile extends beyond what he himself had published, and has been fruitful for our knowledge of various aspects of the conciliar event.

[8] J. Zimmermann, *Erlebtes Konzil: Briefe vom Zweiten Vatikanischen Konzil 1962–1965* (Augsburg, 1966); *Für die Menschen bestellt: Erinnerungen des Alterzbischofs von Köln J. Kard. Frings* (Cologne, 1973); W. A. Visser 't Hooft, *Memoirs* (London, 1973); A. Liénart, *Vatican II* (Lille, 1976); Lercaro, *Lettere;* H. Jedin, *Lebensbericht: Mit einem Dokumentenanhang*, ed. K. Repgen (Mainz, 1984).

in many cases composed by men who had taken part in the drafting the documents.[9]

This set of sources was the point of departure for the studies made in this history. While they served as an essential and irreplaceable basis, they were also insufficient. In addition, there is the Archivio del Vaticano II, which Paul VI wisely wanted kept separate from the Archivio segreto Vaticano so that it would not be subject to the misfortunes that marked the documentation on the Council of Trent or to the restrictions that limit consultation of the secret archive. The Archivio del Vaticano II contains documentation far more extensive than what has been published, especially regarding the basic work of the conciliar commissions and subcommissions. In fact, the assembly only approved documents on the basis of what had been composed by working groups. On this last activity, much more complex and less well organized than the activity of the general congregation, a vast documentation is preserved in the Archivio, unfortunately still completely unpublished and difficult to consult. On the other hand, the same archive had no interest in "private" documentation, except for an extensive but unexplored collection of articles on Vatican II from the press.

Given this state of affairs, it was necessary to add to the preparatory studies for this history a further activity of identifying, collecting, and studying complementary sources on an international scale.[10] This led to the establishment or expansion of centers for the collection, classification, and study of such documents: in Leuven, Louvain-la-Neuve, Bologna, São Paulo, and Paris. This activity made it possible to reach a sizable number of private sources that help to explain and to complete the official sources collected by the General Secretariat.[11] All this has made it possible to gain a more nuanced and realistic picture of the course of

---

[9] Among the best known are the two volumes of commentary on *Lumen gentium* and *Gaudium et spes*, edited by G. Baraúna and published in various languages; the three volumes that the *Lexikon für Theologie und Kirche* devoted to the decrees of Vatican II (translated and published in the five volumes of *Commentary*); and the volumes, one for each document, that Yves Congar included in the collection *Unam sanctam*. Also, G. Philips published *Lumen gentium: L'Église et son mystère au deuxième Concile du Vatican: Histoire, texte et commentaire de la Constitution "Lumen gentium,"* 2 vols. (Paris, 1967).

[10] See J. Grootaers and Cl. Soetens, eds., *Sources locales de Vatican II* (Leuven, 1990); J. Famerée, "Instruments et perspectives pour une histoire du Concile Vatican II: La 'carte' des sources privées (mise à jour)," in *A la veille*, 258–68.

[11] Contact was established with 745 participants in Vatican II, of whom 438 were fathers and 304 were experts and others. The complete list has been published in *Il concilio inedito: Fonti del Vaticano II,* ed. M. Faggioli e G. Turbanti (Bologna 2001); further additions will be made known at the website: www.fcire.it

Vatican II than the necessarily more impersonal official sources could produce.

In fact, almost seventy diaries that were kept by individuals during the course of the Council's work have been identified and analyzed. Some have been published, although rarely in accordance with critically satisfactory criteria;[12] many more are still unpublished or in process of publication.[13] Consultation of these diaries has yielded a decisive contribution to the reconstruction of the history of the Council and, in particular, to knowledge of the work of the commissions and of activity on the periphery of the assembly. The notes of Father S. Tromp on the meetings of the theological commission; the notes, which are especially full and documented, of Dominican Y. Congar; the diary of German theologian O. Semmelroth; and that of Jesuit R. Tucci, editor-in-chief of *La Civiltà Cattolica*, to mention only a few: these have been irreplaceable sources for bringing into focus an endless number of moments in the life of the Council and in the preparation of the documents. The best proof of this claim is the very large number of passages taken from these and other diaries and cited in this *History*.

Also fruitful has been knowledge of the *Letters* which some participants — even those of the first rank, from G. Lercaro to H. Câmara — sent daily from the Council to their correspondents.[14] Both of these

---

[12] E. Cavaterra, *Il prefetto del S. Offizio: Le opere e i giorni del card. Ottaviani* (Milan, 1990); *Carnets conciliaires de Mgr. A. Jauffrès* (Aubenas-sur-Ardèche, 1992); B. Lai, *Il papa non eletto: G. Siri* (Rome- Bari, 1993); M. Bergonzini, *Diario del Concilio*, ed. A. Leonelli (Modena, 1993); P. Raina, *Kardynal Wyszynski, Czasy Prymasowskie 1962–1963* (Warsaw, 1994); M.-D. Chenu, *Notes quotidiennes au concile*, ed. A. Melloni (Paris, 1995); N. Buonasorte, "Il concilio Vaticano II attraverso le pagine del diario di L. C. Borromeo," *Rivista di Storia della Chiesa in Italia* 52 (1998), 111–19; G. Militello, ed., *Un vescovo al concilio: mons. G. B. Parodi* (doctoral dissertation, Rome, Lateran University, 1988); U. Betti, "Pagine di Diario 11 ott. 1962–20 dic. 1965," in *La "Dei verbum" trent'anni dopo* (Rome, 1995), 299–373; idem, *Diario del Concilio: 11 ottobre 1962–Natale 1978* (Bologna 2003); N. Edelby, *Il Vaticano II nel Diario di un vescovo arabo*, ed. R. Cannelli (Cinisello B., 1996); M. Toschi, "Enrico Bartoletti e il suo diario al concilio," in *Cristianesimo nella Storia: Saggi in onore di Giuseppe Alberigo*, ed. A. Melloni et al. (Bologna, 1996), 407–35; F. Santi Cucinotta, ed., *Un vescovo al Vaticano II: mons. C. Zohrabian* (Caltanisetta, 1998).

[13] Still unpublished are the diaries of A.-M. Albareda/Olivar, C. Butler, A. M. Charue, H. de Lubac, J. Döpfner, J. Dupont, L. Dworschak, J. Fenton, E. Florit, J. H. Griffiths, J. C. Heenan, J. A. Jungmann, M. Labourdette, P. É. Léger, A. Nicora, G. Philips, J. Pont y Gol, A. G. Ramos, O. Semmelroth, R. Tucci, G. Urbani, V. Zazpe. Only vague information exists about others.

[14] A first volume of the letters Helder Câmara sent to Brazil every day has been published: Dom Helder Câmara, *Vaticano II: Correspondéncia conciliar: Circulares a família dio Sáo Joaquim*, ed. L. C. Marques (Recife 2004). An investigation also ought be made into the existence of letters addressed to members of the Council.

sources (diaries and letters) have made it possible to grasp the actual experience of participation in the assembly, of the constant contacts being made inside and outside the assembly, and of the sentiments generated by the conciliar experience.

Another kind of source that it has been possible to retrieve and use is the almost infinite number of alternative versions of the schemas discussed at the Council; these are much greater in number than the schemas studied at the general congregations and published in the *Acta Synodalia*.[15] The very structure of the assembly's work, which demanded rigid time tables and pre-established ways of doing things, stimulated a spontaneous composition of alternative formulations that shows the climate of freedom and zeal that existed in the Council.

In addition, in the course of the work fathers and experts produced a very large number of opinions, memoranda, and notes on subjects being discussed or on procedural aspects of the functioning of the assembly. This was true, above all, of the *De ecclesia* and of schemas that had not received much development in the preconciliar period — from religious freedom to the situation of the Church in the contemporary world. Perhaps the lack of an institutional body, like Trent's "congregations of theologians," assigned to the doctrinal examination of the subjects that the Council gradually took up helped to cause some overlapping of proposals, the knowledge of which is nevertheless indispensable for a correct reconstruction of the texts of the documents.

Fundamental for detailed knowledge of the course of the Council was not only the documentation on the work of the numerous commissions,[16] which were frequently divided into subcommissions, but also the documentation on the informal working groups, which often played a substantial role.[17]

---

[15] See, for example, the numerous drafts of *De ecclesia* published in G. Alberigo and F. Magistretti, eds., *Synopsis Historica Constitutionis Dogmaticae Lumen Gentium* (Bologna: Istituto per le Scienze Religiose, 1975).

[16] See G. Turbanti, "Quellenbericht über die Konzilskommissionen," in *Beitrag,* 251–58.

[17] For the Church of the Poor Group, see D. Pelletier, "Une marginalité engagée: le groupe 'Jésus, l'Église et les Pauvres,'" in *Commissions,* 63–89. For the meetings of the secretaries of the episcopal conferences, see J. Grootaers, "Une forme de concertation épiscopale au Concile Vatican II: La 'Conférence des Vingt-deux' (1962–1963)," *Revue d'Histoire Ecclésiastique* 91 (1996), 66–112; and P. Noël, "Gli incontri delle conferenze episcopali durante il concilio: Il 'gruppo della Domus Mariae,'" in *Evento,* 95–133. On the periodic meetings of religious journalists and on the CCCC there is a wealth of documentation in a special section of the Tucci archive; see also J. Grootaers, "Informelle Strukturen der Information am Vatikanum II," in *Biotope der Hoffnung: Zu Christentum*

A problem fraught with difficulties had to do with the sources for the three lengthy intersessions, on which official documentation is exceptionally scanty, despite the fact that conciliar activity during those months was often decisive for the shape of various texts of Vatican II. Here the diaries and letters, but also press leaks and debates in specialized periodicals, furnished valuable information.

Especially fruitful additions to the official sources came from surviving letters by leading men at the Council, whether fathers, such as Suenens, Döpfner, Lercaro, Léger, Bea, Carli, Ruffini, Liénart, Garrone, Guano, Hengsbach, and C. Colombo, or theologians, such as Tromp, Congar, Semmelroth, Rahner, Philips, Dupont, Haubtmann, Tucci, and Prignon. Unfortunately, despite repeated attempts, it has not been possible to consult the letters of other leading lights, such as Cicognani, Felici, Ottaviani, Parente, Ratzinger, and Tisserant. We have repeatedly mentioned the regrettable inaccessibility of the Council letters of Paul VI.

Changed historical conditions meant that the political authorities did not have representatives at the Council, as they did at Trent. But their interest in the Council was no less keen, and they did not limit themselves to attending the opening and closing solemnities. The embassies in Rome, whether to the Italian Republic or to the Vatican, closely followed the Council's work and, still more, the climate in the conciliar assembly, availing themselves in these areas of ecclesiastical advisers or even members of the Council. The information regularly sent to the respective governments is not without interest. The dispatches recently became available and have contributed to knowledge of the history of the Council.[18]

For one area of documentation on Vatican II there were no precedents: the participation of the observers and guests from the non-Roman Catholic Churches. This material, too, is scattered. The access generously given to the archives of the World Council of Churches in Geneva was invaluable, but a great deal more material remains with individual observers or their Churches. The documents here are reports to their home communities, notes on work, suggestions regarding the schemas being

---

und Kirche heute, ed. N. Klein, H. R. Schlette, and K. Weber (Olten, 1988), 268–81. On the numerous paraconciliar groups nothing matches the study conducted some years ago by Salvador Gómez de Arteche y Catalina, Grupos "extra aulam" en el II concilio Vaticano y su influencia (doctoral dissertation, Biblioteca de la Facultad de Derecho de la Universidad de Valladolid).

[18] See A. Melloni, L'altra Roma: Politica e S. Sede durante il concilio Vaticano II (1959–1965) (Bologna, 2000).

discussed, texts of lectures, and so on; these constituted the basis for bringing out the sometimes very important contribution of these unique participants, some of whom have published their diary notes or their memoirs.[19] A case apart was the semi-official meetings held every Tuesday afternoon by the observers and the Secretariat for Christian Unity. Documents having to do with the meetings are scattered, and it has been possible only by much labor to gain possession of reports or notes on the course of these meetings, which were of great interest.

Rome during the Council saw a multiplication of undertakings associated with Vatican II. Some of these had a special influence on the fathers, such as the hundreds of lectures sponsored by the Dutch Documentation Center (DO-C), which were well attended and then published in various languages. Equally influential were the bulletins published by several episcopal conferences.[20]

---

[19] For example, D. Horton, *Vatican Diary 1962–1965,* 4 vols. (Philadelphia: United Church Press, 1964–66).

[20] See Secrétariat conciliaire de l'Épiscopat Français, *Études et Documents*; and "Conferenza Episcopale Italiana," from the second period on. Some periodicals also proved to be interesting sources; for example, *Informations Catholiques Internationales* (Paris), *Herder Korrespondenz* (Freiburg), *La Documentation Catholique* (Paris), *De Maand* (Brussels), *The Tablet* (London), *Il Regno* (Bologna), *America* (New York), *Katholiek Archief* (Amsterdam), and *Orientierung* (Zurich). The same can be said for journals such as *Irénikon* (Chevetogne), *Istina* (Paris), *The Ecumenical Review* (Geneva), *Ökumenische Rundschau* (Stuttgart), *Unitas* (Rome), and *Catholica* (Münster). Useful information is also furnished by the bulletins of specialized press agencies: *Katholische Nachrichten-Agentur, NCWC News Service* (Washington, D.C.), and *Service Oecuménique de presse et d'information (SOEPI)*. See J. Grootaers, "L'information religieuse au début du Concile: instances officielles et réseaux informels," in *Vatican II commence*, 211–34.

INDEX OF NAMES

INDEX OF SUBJECTS